Readings in Comparative Politics

Political Challenges and
and
Changing Agendas

Mark Kesselman

Columbia University

Second Edition

WADSWORTH
CENGAGE Learning

Australia • Brazil • Japan • Korea • Mexico • Singapore • Spain • United Kingdom • United States

WADSWORTH
CENGAGE Learning™

Readings in Comparative Politics: Political Challenges and Changing Agendas, Second Edition

General Editor: Mark Kesselman

Executive Acquiring Sponsoring Editor: Carolyn Merrill

Acquiring Sponsoring Editor: Edwin Hill

Development Manager: Jeffrey Greene

Associate Editor: Katherine Hayes

Editorial Assistant: Matthew DiGangi

Media Editor: Laura Hildebrand

Senior Marketing Manager: Amy Whitaker

Marketing Coordinator: Josh Hendrick

Marketing Communications Manager: Heather Baxley

Content Project Manager: Aimee Chevrette Bear

Art Director: Linda Helcher

Print Buyer: Paula Vang

Senior Rights Acquisition Account Manager: Katie Huha

Senior Photo Editor: Jennifer Meyer Dare

Photo Researcher: Lisa Jelly Smith

Compositor: Pre-PressPMG

Typographical and punctuation errors in the original published versions of readings have been corrected in the versions excerpted here. Acknowledgements and authors' affiliations have been deleted, and in some sections footnotes have been abridged, deleted, and/or renumbered.

For product information and technology assistance, contact us at **Cengage Learning Academic Resource Center, 1-800-423-0563.**

For permission to use material from this text or product, submit all requests online at **www.cengage.com/permissions.** Further permissions questions can be emailed to **permissionrequest@cengage.com.**

Library of Congress Control Number: 2009923077

Student Edition:

ISBN-13: 978-0-547-21274-6

ISBN-10: 0-547-21274-7

Wadsworth Cengage Learning
20 Channel Center Street
Boston, MA 02210
USA

Cengage Learning products are represented in Canada by Nelson Education, Ltd.

For your course and learning solutions, visit **academic.cengage.com.**

Purchase any of our products at your local college store or at our preferred online store **www.ichapters.com.**

To the incomparable Judy, who was there from the start.

Printed in Canada
1 2 3 4 5 6 7 13 14 12 11 10

Contents

Preface   *vii*

Chapter 1
INTRODUCTION   1

1.1   FRANCIS FUKUYAMA
      The End of History?   10

1.2   SAMUEL P. HUNTINGTON
      The Third Wave: Democratization in the Late Twentieth Century   18

1.3   AZAR GAT
      The Return of Authoritarian Great Powers   29

1.4   SAMUEL P. HUNTINGTON
      The Clash of Civilizations?   37

1.5   JERRY Z. MULLER
      Us and Them   52

1.6   JAMES HABYARIMANA ET AL.
      Is Ethnic Conflict Inevitable? Parting Ways Over Nationalism
      and Separatism   59

Chapter 2
STATES AND REGIMES   72

2.1   ANTHONY W. MARX
      Making Race and Nation: A Comparison of the
      United States, South Africa, and Brazil   74

2.2   SUSAN STRANGE
      The Retreat of the State: The Diffusion of Power
      in the World Economy   81

2.3   SASKIA SASSEN
      The State and Globalization   89

2.4   STEVEN LEVITSKY AND LUCAN A. WAY
      The Rise of Competitive Authoritarianism   95

2.5   ROBERT I. ROTBERG
      Failed States in a World of Terror   105

2.6   JOHN RAPLEY
      The New Middle Ages   113

CHAPTER 3

GOVERNING THE ECONOMY   121

3.1   PETER GOUREVITCH
      Political Economy   123

3.2   DAVID COATES
      Models of Capitalism in the New World Order   129

3.3   PETER A. HALL AND DAVID SOSKICE
      An Introduction to Varieties of Capitalism   138

3.4   RICHARD F. DONER, BRYAN K. RITCHIE,
      AND DAN SLATER
      *Systemic Vulnerability and the Origins of Developmental
      States: Northeast and Southeast Asia in Comparative Perspective*   150

3.5   ROBERT J. S. ROSS AND ANITA CHAN
      From North-South to South-South   164

3.6   JOSEPH E. STIGLITZ
      Globalism's Discontents   170

CHAPTER 4

THE CHALLENGE OF DEMOCRACY   182

4.1   AMARTYA SEN
      Democracy as a Universal Value   184

4.2   ROBERT DAHL
      Polyarchy: Participation and Opposition   194

4.3   PHILIPPE C. SCHMITTER AND TERRY LYNN KARL
      What Democracy Is . . . and Is Not   201

4.4   JUAN J. LINZ AND ALFRED STEPAN
      Toward Consolidated Democracies   212

4.5   VALERIE BUNCE
      *Rethinking Democratization: Lessons from the
      Postcommunist Experience*   222

4.6   GUILLERMO O'DONNELL
      Illusions About Consolidation   232

4.7   THOMAS CAROTHERS
      The End of the Transition Paradigm   247

CHAPTER 5
COLLECTIVE IDENTITIES 257

5.1 PIPPA NORRIS AND RONALD INGLEHART
Cultural Obstacles to Equal Representation 258

5.2 SEYLA BENHABIB
The Claims of Culture 269

5.3 HOWARD WINANT
Race in the Twenty-First Century 276

5.4 HAROLD L. WILENSKY
*Migration and Politics: Explaining Variation Among
Rich Democracies in Recent Nativist Protest* 288

5.5 WALKER CONNOR
A Nation Is a Nation, Is a State, Is an Ethnic Group, Is a . . . 300

5.6 VALI NASR
Lessons from the Muslim World 310

CHAPTER 6
POLITICAL INSTITUTIONS 316

6.1 JUAN LINZ
The Perils of Presidentialism 318

6.2 EDWARD D. MANSFIELD AND JACK SNYDER
Democratic Transitions, Institutional Strength, and War 329

6.3 MICHAEL MCFAUL
Are New Democracies War-Prone? 338

6.4 HENRY E. HALE
*Divided We Stand: Institutional Sources of Ethnofederal
State Survival and Collapse* 345

6.5 BENJAMIN REILLY
Electoral Systems for Divided Societies 357

6.6 S. LAUREL WELDON
*Protest, Policy, and the Problem of Violence Against Women:
A Cross-National Comparison* 364

CHAPTER 7
POLITICAL CHALLENGES AND CHANGING AGENDAS   371

7.1   ADAM PRZEWORSKI AND MICHAEL WALLERSTEIN
       Democratic Capitalism at the Crossroads   372

7.2   SIDNEY TARROW
       A Movement Society?   379

7.3   ROBERT D. PUTNAM
       Bowling Alone: America's Declining Social Capital   392

7.4   BO ROTHSTEIN AND DIETLIND STOLLE
       *The State and Social Capital: An Institutional Theory
       of Generalized Trust*   403

7.5   FAREED ZAKARIA
       The Future of Freedom: Illiberal Democracy at Home and Abroad   412

7.6   BILL McKIBBEN
       An Alternative to Progress   421

7.7   JEFFREY D. SACHS
       Common Wealth: Economics for a Crowded Planet   429

PREFACE

What a period to be studying comparative politics! The Chinese proverb that expresses a hope for interesting times has been amply fulfilled in the current period—too much so, some might say. Never more than in this new millennium do students need to step back from the whirl of the daily headlines and nightly news and gain help in separating the wheat from the chaff. But what is wheat? What is chaff? That is, how can we determine which events are of more enduring significance and which will be forgotten by the time this book is published?

Readings in Comparative Politics (RCP) samples some of the most important work in the subdiscipline. Unlike international relations, for example, with its trinity of realism, liberal institutionalism, and constructivism, comparative politics is gloriously—or lamentably (depending on the observer)—catholic, eclectic, and sprawling. In my view, so much the better. I do not aim to provide a coherent picture of a field that I believe reflects the messiness of the political world. Nor do I claim to survey comprehensively the many methodological, theoretical, regional, or political perspectives to be found in comparative politics. My aim is to provide a rich array of readings to highlight important issues and contributions in this vitally important subdiscipline of political science.

Readings in Comparative Politics (RCP) provides articles with diverse perspectives on a substantial but not exhaustive range of issues within comparative politics. I do not assume that students have an extensive background in comparative politics or political science. Nor do I seek to impart professional training. My aim is to provide students with a wide range of influential, thoughtful, and clearly written articles that focus on key issues within comparative politics.

This Second Edition of RCP has been substantially revised from the First Edition. Over a dozen readings have been substituted for readings included in the first edition. In several cases, a selection is followed by a published reply in order to stimulate discussion. For the same reason, discussion questions have been included at the end of each chapter.

The book opens with an Introduction that describes the scope of the field. Although there is a brief discussion of its methods, RCP focuses on substantive, not methodological, issues. Following the Introduction, widely cited articles provide alternative frames for analyzing comparative politics. The next six chapters focus on major issues in the field. Each chapter opens with a brief introduction that identifies some important questions. Each article that follows is preceded by an introduction that helps students situate the article and identify its major arguments. As noted, discussion questions are provided at the end of each chapter.

Chapter 2 analyzes states and regimes. I have selected articles that suggest that state formation and survival are political processes, neither inevitable nor necessarily benign. The articles in Chapter 3 highlight the fact that economies, whether private (capitalist) or not, are governed; that is, political choices and institutions help to constitute and affect economic outcomes. Chapter 4 surveys aspects of democratic development. These articles stress that democracy is contingent, imperfect, and shaped by the context in which it is embedded. Chapter 5 stresses the rich, variable, and constructed nature of political identities. Chapter 6 suggests that institutions are shaped by political struggles, arenas in which such struggles occur, and influential in shaping political conflicts and outcomes. The book concludes, in Chapter 7, with articles that highlight some current challenges in comparative politics and invite reflection on proposals for change.

The revised edition of RCP builds on the splendid contributions of Joel Krieger, co-editor of the first edition of RCP and very dear friend. To my great regret, Professor Krieger decided to focus his energies on other projects and not participate in co-editing RCP. I am most grateful for his help in organizing the First Edition of the book, in selecting many readings, and in writing several introductions.

RCP is in part an outgrowth of Professor Krieger and my co-editorship (along with William Joseph) of *Introduction to Comparative Politics* (ICP), an introductory textbook, and a shorter, simpler version of ICP, *Introduction to Comparative Politics* (*Brief Edition*, ICP-Brief), both published by Wadsworth/Cengage. The four core themes of those books—a world of states, governing the economy, the democratic challenge, and political identities—have a counterpart in four chapters in RCP. Instructors may find it useful to assign RCP in a course in which ICP is the core text. The two books complement each other, in that RCP provides in-depth and comparative analyses of issues surveyed in more systematic fashion in the country chapters of ICP and ICP-Brief.

I am most grateful for the expert assistance of the Wadsworth/Cengage editorial and production team: Edwin Hill, acquiring sponsoring editor; Jeff Greene, development manager; and Matt DiGangi, editorial assistant. Leslie Kauffman, senior project manager, development, at LEAP Publishing Services, went above and beyond. For their thoughtful reviews of the first edition of RCP, that have been most helpful in preparing this revised edition, many thanks to the following colleagues:

Florin Fesnic, *University of Bucharest* and *University of Illinois*
Tracy Slagter, *University of Wisconsin—Oshkosh*
Stanley Spangler, *Bentley College*

Mark Kesselman

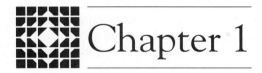 Chapter 1

INTRODUCTION

Brave New World

We borrow the title of Aldous Huxley's satirical novel, *Brave New World,* to describe developments in the twenty-first century. New it certainly is. No work of science fiction could have predicted some of the watershed political events in world politics as the twentieth century drew to a close and a new century began. Some of the most notable developments helped make the world more peaceful, just, and prosperous. Examples include the implosion of the Soviet Union, beginning with the fall of the Berlin Wall in 1989, followed by the end of the Cold War (the decades-long period of intense hostility between the Soviet Union and the United States that began after World War II); widening and deepening of democratic changes in many countries; technological advances that promote economic growth, health, and well-being; and robust growth in some countries, notably developing countries like China, India, and Brazil. However, these positive developments were offset by changes of a more disturbing character. At the end of the first decade of the twenty-first century, the United States experienced persistent economic stagnation, linked to financial instability and a housing crisis, which rippled through the entire world economy. Far worse was an upsurge of violence on a global scale beginning in the 1990s: ethnic cleansing, organized rape, and genocide in Rwanda and the former Yugoslavia; civil wars; interstate wars; and terrorist attacks inspired by religious, ethnic, economic, and political grievances. Early in the new century, there was a resurgence of tension between the United States and Russia that recalled the tense period of the Cold War. For example, in 2008 a bitter dispute between Russia and the former Soviet Republic of Georgia, now an independent country and a close U.S. ally, boiled over into military hostilities.

Although the twentieth century has been called the most violent in history, the twenty-first century may eventually claim that dubious title. This revised edition of *Readings in Comparative Politics* (RCP) includes a range of articles that aim to make sense of our present turbulent epoch.

In past years, the United States was often a major participant in the world's violent conflicts, but those conflicts were fought on foreign territory. The United States dispatched military forces to other regions of the world and exerted extensive political and economic influence abroad. U.S. soil, however, appeared to be a safe sanctuary fully protected from foreign incursion. This situation was virtually unique; almost all countries in the world have experienced armed conflict on their territory. The United States' good fortune in this respect ended with a crash, or rather four crashes, on September 11, 2001, when terrorists hijacked U.S. airplanes with several hundred civilian passengers aboard and used them as weapons. They crashed two planes into the twin towers of the World Trade Center in New York City, causing almost three thousand deaths and reducing the massive buildings to a mountain of smoking rubble. A third plane crashed into the Pentagon in Washington, D.C., the headquarters of the most formidable military in the world. Passengers on the fourth plane thwarted the hijackers' plan to crash into the Capitol building or the White House; the passengers attacked the hijackers, and the plane crashed in a Pennsylvania field. In one fateful hour, U.S. and world politics were changed for decades to come. In the most diverse spheres, from immigration to security, from criminal justice to popular culture, Americans live in the shadow of the September 11 attacks. Moreover, repercussions of September 11 rippled throughout the world. President George W. Bush ordered attacks on Afghanistan and Iraq, on the grounds that their regimes were linked to terrorism. The decision to invade Iraq provoked intense controversy in the United States and abroad.

Although one cannot attach precise dates to some other current transformative developments, they are no less influential. Cases in point include the AIDS pandemic, which has ravaged Africa and other regions; global warming, which threatens the stability and well-being of the global village in coming decades; and the deep economic crisis beginning in 2008 but with deep roots in previous years—to name just three.

Globalization and *the global era* are frequently applied as general catch terms to identify the growing depth, extent, and diversity of cross-border connections that are a key feature of the contemporary world. Discussions of globalization often begin with accounts of economic activities, including the reorganization of production and the global redistribution of the workforce (the "global factory") and the increased extent and intensity of international trade, finance, and foreign direct investment. Globalization involves the movement of peoples due to migration, employment, business, and educational opportunities.

The term *globalization* links a highly diverse set of changes. Consider the attacks in the United States on September 11. The hijackers were members of al-Qaida, a thoroughly transnational network with cells on many continents. The hijackers trained and lived in locations thousands of miles apart. They communicated by cell phone and courier and transferred funds through a sophisticated system linking international banks and traditional moneychangers based in bazaars.

Globalization includes other profound changes that are less visible but equally significant. For example, new applications of information technology (such as the

Internet and CNN) blur the traditional distinction between what is around the world and what is around the block, instantly transforming cultures and eroding the boundaries between the local and global. These technologies make instantaneous communication possible. They link producers and contractors, headquarters, branch plants, and suppliers in real time anywhere in the world. Employees may be rooted in time and place, but employers can shop for what will bring them the greatest advantages in a global labor market. Employees who have an apparently secure job today may be unemployed tomorrow as employers downsize or move their operations offshore. But job destruction in one region may be offset by job creation elsewhere.

The dilemma that globalization represents can be illustrated by the theme chosen by the American Political Science Association (the official organization of U.S. political scientists) for its 2008 annual meeting: "Categories and the Politics of Global Inequalities." The theme came hard on the heels of the program for the 2004 meeting, whose theme was "Global Inequalities."

The varied elements of globalization erode the ability of even the strongest countries to control their destinies. No state can fully guarantee economic and psychological security for its citizens. None can preserve pristine national models of economic governance or distinctly national cultures, values, understandings of the world, or narratives that define a people and forge their unity.

In the brave new world in which we live, countries face a host of challenges simultaneously from above and below. The capacities of states to control domestic outcomes and assert sovereignty are compromised by regional and global technological and market forces, as well as growing security concerns. Countries are assaulted by ethnic, nationalist, and religious challenges that often involve both internal and external components. The challenge of democratic self-government is heightened when many of the decisions that fundamentally affect citizens' lives are made by organizations located outside a country's borders. Some examples include international financial institutions (IFIs), governments of other countries, transnational corporations, and nongovernmental organizations (NGOs).

The hard and fast distinction between domestic and international politics has been blurred by the complex set of cross-border economic, cultural, technological, political, and security processes, institutions, and relations that constitute the contemporary global order. Because the subfield of comparative politics has been profoundly influenced by globalization and it studies some aspects of globalization, we have opened this Introduction by highlighting the brave new world of globalization. But comparative politics is not identical to globalization. It does not study all aspects of globalization, and it studies some topics not directly related to globalization. What, then, is comparative politics? What are its scope and methods? Where does it fit within the broader discipline of political science? What kinds of issues do specialists in comparative politics address?

What and How Comparative Politics Compares[1]

To compare is one of the most common human exercises, whether in the classroom study of literature or politics or animal behavior or in selecting dorm rooms or listing your favorite movies. In the observation of politics, the use of comparisons is very old, dating at least from Aristotle, the ancient Greek philosopher. Aristotle categorized Athenian city-states in the fifth century B.C. according to their form of political rule: rule by a single individual, rule by a few, or rule by all citizens. He added a normative dimension (a claim about how societies should be ruled), by comparing good and corrupt versions of each type. The modern study of comparative politics refines and systematizes the age-old practice of evaluating some feature of X by comparing it to the same feature of Y in order to learn more about it than isolated study would permit.

The term *comparative politics* refers to a subfield within the academic discipline of political science, as well as to a method or approach to the study of politics.[2] The subject matter of comparative politics is the domestic politics of countries or peoples. Within the discipline of political science, comparative politics is one area of specialization. In addition, most political science (or government) departments in U.S. colleges and universities include courses and academic specialists in three other subfields: political theory, international relations, and American politics. Political economy and methodology are also sometimes identified as subfields within political science.

More generally, the subfields of political science usefully highlight important clusters of concerns and encourage specialized study. But one should not regard the subfields as airtight compartments. Nor should the boundaries among subfields be erected into barriers to understanding. For example, because it is widely believed that students living in the United States should study American politics intensively and with special focus, the fields of American and comparative politics often remain separate. The pattern of distinguishing the study of politics at home

---

[1]Portions of this and other sections of the Introduction are drawn from "Introducing Comparative Politics," chap. 1 in *Introduction to Comparative Politics: Political Challenges and Changing Agendas,* fifth ed., edited by Mark Kesselman, Joel Krieger, and William A. Joseph (Boston: Houghton Mifflin, 2010). Wadsworth/Cengage.

[2]For analyses of the scope and methods of comparative politics, see Philippe Schmitter, "Comparative Politics," in *The Oxford Companion to Politics of the World*, second ed., edited by Joel Krieger (New York: Oxford University Press, 2001), 160–165; several essays in *Political Science: The State of the Discipline*, edited by Ira Katznelson and Helen V. Milner (New York: W.W. Norton & Company, and Washington, D.C., American Political Science Association, 2002); and Mark Irving Lichbach and Alan S. Zuckerman, eds., *Comparative Politics: Rationality, Culture, and Structure,* 2nd ed., (New York: Cambridge University Press, 2009). More general discussions of political analysis include Henry E. Brady and David Collier, *Rethinking Social Inquiry: Diverse Tools, Shared Standards* (Lanham, MD: Rowman & Littlefield, 2004).; and Janet M. Box-Steffensmeier, Henry E. Brady, and David Collier, *The Oxford Handbook of Political Methodology* (New York: Oxford University Press, 2008).

from politics abroad is also common elsewhere, so students in Canada may be expected to study Canadian politics as a distinct specialty, and Japanese students would likewise be expected to master Japanese politics.

Yet there is no logical reason why study of the United States should not be included within the field of comparative politics, and there is good reason to do so. (Indeed, the 2008 annual meeting of the American Political Science Association had a plenary session whose subtitle was: "Should the [Political Science] Discipline Eliminate the Subfield of American Politics?") We therefore include in RCP several readings that analyze American politics. (See readings by Marx, Coates, Hall and Soskice, and Putnam.) Indeed, many studies in comparative politics (and an increasing number of courses) have integrated the study of American politics with the study of politics in other countries. Comparative study can place U.S. politics in a much richer perspective and, at the same time, make it easier to recognize what is distinctive and most interesting about the United States and other countries.

Comparative politics—the study of what occurs within national borders—is typically distinguished from international relations, commonly defined as the study of interactions among states as well as the study of international institutions like the United Nations. Up to a point, this distinction makes sense. In order to study in depth, one must limit the scope of what is studied. But the distinction can also hinder understanding if carried too far. Important issues like immigration, nationalism, economic development, and the conduct and impact of war straddle the fence between comparative politics and international relations. This is especially true in the era of globalization, in which cross-border exchanges are dense and influential. (For examples, see the selections by Sassen, Stiglitz, Mansfield and Snyder, and Doner, Ritchie, and Slater.) Indeed, fuller understanding of these concerns can be gained by applying insights and tools from other disciplines, such as sociology, economics, and history. Yet, however useful interdisciplinary study may be, it requires building on the contributions developed in more specialized fields.

The comparative approach seeks to identify similarities and differences among countries, as well as political institutions, processes, and policies. As students of comparative politics (we call ourselves comparativists), we believe that the chances for making valid and reliable statements about most political observations are increased by comparing more than one case. We often hear statements such as "The United States has the best health care system in the world." Comparativists immediately wonder what kinds of health care systems exist in other countries, what they cost and how they are financed, who is covered by health insurance, and so on. Besides, what does *best* mean when it comes to health care systems? Is it the one that provides the widest access? The one that is most technologically advanced? The one that is most cost effective? The one that produces the healthiest population? We would not announce the best movie or the best car without considering other alternatives or deciding what specific factors enter into our judgment. (The selection by Linz [6.1], comparing presidential versus parliamentary systems, provides a fine example of this kind of comparison.)

Theory and Method in Comparative Politics

How do comparativists go about comparing? The comparativist looks at similarities and differences among countries, states, institutions, policies, and conflicts. An important approach within comparative politics tries to develop causal theories—hypotheses that can be expressed formally in a causal mode: "If X happens, then Y will be the result." Such theories include factors (the independent variables, symbolized by X) that are believed to influence some outcome, and the outcome (the dependent variable, symbolized by Y) to be explained. For example, it is commonly argued that if a country's economic pie shrinks, conflict among groups for resources will intensify. This hypothesis suggests what is called an inverse correlation between variables: as X varies in one direction, Y varies in the opposite direction. As the total national economic product (X) decreases, then political and social conflict over economic shares (Y) increases. Even when the explanation does not involve the explicit testing of hypotheses (and often it does not), comparativists try to identify similarities and differences among countries and to identify significant patterns.

Many comparativists do not believe in the possibility of developing causal theories based on general laws that explain specific events (what are called covering laws). They argue that there are many reasons why this is an impossible project. For example, it is likely that a group of particular events such as revolutions are the result of diverse causes. In one case, international intervention may be critical; in another case, it may be insignificant. Consequently, it is futile to seek a unified theory of revolutions.

Comparativists who reject the covering-law approach propose other ways of understanding politics. Some claim that the road to understanding lies in engaging in statistical analysis to identify patterns or correlations among different elements without claiming causal importance among these correlations. Other comparativists assert that maximum understanding can be gained by developing deductive models to understand how political participants engage in strategic decision making. Some comparativists seek to identify specific mechanisms that contribute to producing particular outcomes in specific settings. And yet other comparativists claim that the goal of comparative politics should be to interpret the motivations of political actors and capture the incredible richness and complexity of political activity. The debate among comparativists is wide open. We do not highlight this key methodological debate in RCP, although selections reflect many of the approaches that we have just identified. The major focus of RCP, however, is on substantive problems rather than theoretical or methodological debates.

We do wish to emphasize, however, the limits on just how scientific political science—and thus comparative politics—can be. Two important differences exist between the hard (or natural) sciences like physics and chemistry and the social sciences. First, social scientists study people who exercise free will. Because people have a margin for free choice, their choices, attitudes, and behavior cannot be fully explained by causal analysis. This does not mean that people choose in an arbitrary fashion. We choose within the context of material constraint, institutional dictates, and cultural prescriptions. Indeed, comparative politics analyzes how these and other factors orient political choices in systematic ways. But there will probably always be a wide gulf between the natural and social sciences because of their different objects of study.

A second difference between the natural and social sciences is that, in the natural sciences, experimental techniques can be applied to isolate the contribution of distinct factors to a particular outcome. Controlled experiments make it possible to change the value or magnitude of a factor—for example, the force applied to an object—and measure how the outcome has consequently changed. Like other social scientists, however, political scientists, including comparativists, rarely have the opportunity to apply such experimental techniques.

Some political scientists have tried to emulate the hard sciences by organizing controlled laboratory experiments. (Habyarimana and associates [1.6] report such an experiment.) The procedure is to measure the importance of a factor by varying its weight between a focus group and a control group. All else equal, it is hypothesized that the difference in the observed outcome between the two groups is due to the variation in the manipulated factor.

However, there is a large gulf between the artificial world of the laboratory and the real world of politics. In the real world, unlike in the laboratory, variables cannot easily be isolated or manipulated. Moreover, people's motivations differ in the laboratory setting and in their natural environment. (Paying volunteers a fee to participate does not guarantee that they will act the same as they would in a natural setting.)

Some political scientists employ statistical techniques, such as multivariate analysis, that attempt to identify the specific causal weight of a variable in explaining a political outcome. But it is difficult to measure precisely how, for example, a person's ethnicity, gender, or income influences choosing a candidate when casting a ballot. Nor can we ever know for sure what exact mix of factors—conflicts among elites, popular ideological appeals, the weakness of the state, or the discontent of the masses—induces an ethnic minority to revolt.

Under these circumstances, comparativists have developed more modest expectations. One response is to seek to develop what is called middle-level theory. Such a theory explains phenomena found in a limited range of cases, which in comparative politics means a specific set of countries with the same or similar characteristics, political institutions, or processes. If we study only individual countries without any comparative framework, then comparative politics would become merely the study of a series of isolated cases. It would be impossible to recognize what is most significant in the collage of political characteristics that we find in the world's many countries. As a result, the understanding of patterns of similarity and difference among countries would be lost, along with an important tool for evaluating what is and what is not unique about a country's political life.

If we go to the other extreme and try to make universal claims, we would have to ignore the interesting differences and patterns of variation. For the political world is incredibly complex, shaped by an extraordinary array of factors and an almost endless interplay of variables. Indeed, after a brief period in the 1950s and 1960s when many comparativists tried—and failed—to develop a grand theory that would apply to all countries, most comparativists have abandoned the attempt and turned to developing middle-level theories.

For example, comparativists have analyzed the efforts in many countries to replace (or attempt to replace) authoritarian forms of government, such as military dictatorships and one-party states, with more democratic regimes. In studying democratic transitions, comparativists do not treat each national case as unique or try to construct a universal pattern that ignores all differences. Applying middle-level theory, we identify the influence on the new regime's political stability of specific variables such as institutional legacies, political culture, levels of economic development, the nature of the regime before the transition, and the degree of ethnic conflict or homogeneity. Comparativists have been able to identify patterns in the emergence and consolidation of democratic regimes in southern Europe in the 1970s (Greece, Portugal, and Spain) and have compared them to developments in Latin America, Asia, and Africa since the 1980s, and in eastern and central Europe since the revolutions of 1989. (But see the selection by Bunce, highlighting the importance of differences among these settings, and the one by Carothers, who advocates abandoning the attempt to develop a theory of democratic transitions.)

Conclusion

The study of comparative politics has never been more timely, important, or fascinating. The brave new world of the twenty-first century cries out for disciplined analysis. RCP presents a diverse selection of articles and excerpts from books that take a step back from the often bewildering whirl of daily politics to analyze in depth a wide range of issues.

Following this Introduction and readings that provide overviews of the current shape of world politics, six chapters identify important issues within comparative politics: states and regimes, governing the economy, the challenge of democracy, collective identities, political institutions, and political challenges and changing agendas. For each, we provide an introduction and readings on important issues within the topic. The topics we have identified are key areas within comparative politics, and the readings among the best in the field. However, we do not claim that the organization of RCP represents the only way to organize the material. Moreover, many other excellent articles could be included. We have tried to choose readings that are accessible to students without an extensive background in political science, and we include a broad range of current approaches and claims. The analyses range from theoretical explorations of general issues to descriptions of specific events. Some selections reflect a detached perspective; others seek to combine scholarly rigor and political engagement. The diversity of topics, approaches, and positions reflects the current ferment in the field of comparative politics, the complexity of its subject matter, and the fast-changing state of politics in the world.

The turmoil of the brave new world of the twenty-first century suggests the need for humility on the part of students and scholars. A social scientist has remarked that it is easier to predict the past than the future! Our aim in this Introduction and throughout RCP is not to develop a blueprint for predicting (or creating) the future but to provide analyses of important issues within comparative politics. We hope that these readings stimulate you to think more deeply and develop your own position on the many important issues analyzed in *Readings in Comparative Politics*.

The End of History?

Francis Fukuyama

This influential article was written as the Soviet Union was disintegrating and the Cold War ending. Francis Fukuyama ventured a bold prediction: that the end of communism spelled the end of any alternative on the world stage that could compete with the dominant form of political and economic organization championed by the West: democratic capitalism. Critics (including authors of other selections in Chapter 1) have pointed out that, even in the relatively short time since the end of the Cold War, far from ending, history has changed in extensive and unpredictable fashion. As other readings in this chapter describe, the world has been intensely divided by conflicts over religion, ethnicity, and globalization, as well as rivalry among major states. In fairness, Fukuyama did not claim that the future would be conflict-free, only that no broad-based ideological vision comparable to democratic capitalism would exist that could command widespread support throughout the world. Is he correct that there are no ideological rivals to liberal democratic capitalism? Assuming that his argument is valid, does it matter so long as extensive conflicts persist in the world?

I n watching the flow of events over the past decade or so, it is hard to avoid the feeling that something very fundamental has happened in world history. The past year has seen a flood of articles commemorating the end of the Cold War, and the fact that "peace" seems to be breaking out in many regions of the world. Most of these analyses lack any larger conceptual framework for distinguishing between what is essential and what is contingent or accidental in world history, and are predictably superficial. . . .

And yet, all of these people sense dimly that there is some larger process at work, a process that gives coherence and order to the daily headlines. The twentieth century saw the developed world descend into a paroxysm of ideological violence, as liberalism contended first with the remnants of absolutism, then

Francis Fukuyama, "The End of History?" *National Interest* 16 (Summer 1989), reprinted in Foreign Affairs Agenda, *The New Shape of World Politics: Contending Paradigms in International Relations* (New York: W. W. Norton, 1997), 1–25. Reprinted by permission of the author.

bolshevism and fascism, and finally an updated Marxism that threatened to lead to the ultimate apocalypse of nuclear war. But the century that began full of self-confidence in the ultimate triumph of Western liberal democracy seems at its close to be returning full circle to where it started: not to an "end of ideology" or a convergence between capitalism and socialism, as earlier predicted, but to an unabashed victory of economic and political liberalism.

The triumph of the West, of the Western *idea*, is evident first of all in the total exhaustion of viable systematic alternatives to Western liberalism. In the past decade, there have been unmistakable changes in the intellectual climate of the world's two largest communist countries, and the beginnings of significant reform movements in both. But this phenomenon extends beyond high politics and it can be seen also in the ineluctable spread of consumerist Western culture in such diverse contexts as the peasants' markets and color television sets now omnipresent throughout China, the cooperative restaurants and clothing stores opened in the past year in Moscow, the Beethoven piped into Japanese department stores, and the rock music enjoyed alike in Prague, Rangoon, and Tehran.

What we may be witnessing is not just the end of the Cold War, or the passing of a particular period of postwar history, but the end of history as such: that is, the end point of mankind's ideological evolution and the universalization of Western liberal democracy as the final form of human government. This is not to say that there will no longer be events to fill the pages of *Foreign Affairs'* yearly summaries of international relations, for the victory of liberalism has occurred primarily in the realm of ideas or consciousness and is as yet incomplete in the real or material world. But there are powerful reasons for believing that it is the ideal that will govern the material world *in the long run.* . . .

III

Have we in fact reached the end of history? Are there, in other words, any fundamental "contradictions" in human life that cannot be resolved in the context of modern liberalism, that would be resolvable by an alternative political-economic structure? If we accept the idealist premises laid out above, we must seek an answer to this question in the realm of ideology and consciousness. Our task is not to answer exhaustively the challenges to liberalism promoted by every crackpot messiah around the world, but only those that are embodied in important social or political forces and movements, and which are therefore part of world history. For our purposes, it matters very little what strange thoughts occur to people in Albania or Burkina Faso, for we are interested in what one could in some sense call the common ideological heritage of mankind.

In the past century, there have been two major challenges to liberalism, those of fascism and of communism. The former[1] saw the political weakness, materialism, anomie, and lack of community of the West as fundamental contradictions in liberal societies that could only be resolved by a strong state that forged a new "people" on the basis of national exclusiveness. Fascism was destroyed as a living ideology by World War II. This was a defeat, of course, on a very material level, but it amounted to a defeat of the idea as well. What destroyed fascism as an idea was not universal moral revulsion against it, since plenty of people were willing to endorse the idea as long as it seemed the wave of the future, but its lack of success. After the war, it seemed to most people that German fascism as well as its other European and Asian variants were bound to self-destruct. There was no material reason why new fascist movements could not have sprung up again after the war in other locales, but for the fact that expansionist ultranationalism, with its promise of unending conflict leading to disastrous military defeat, had completely lost its appeal. The ruins of the Reich chancellory as well as the atomic bombs dropped on Hiroshima and Nagasaki killed this ideology on the level of consciousness as well as materially, and all of the proto-fascist movements spawned by the German and Japanese examples like the Peronist movement in Argentina or Subhas Chandra Bose's Indian National Army withered after the war.

The ideological challenge mounted by the other great alternative to liberalism, communism, was far more serious. Marx, speaking Hegel's language, asserted that liberal society contained a fundamental contradiction that could not be resolved within its context, that between capital and labor, and this contradiction has constituted the chief accusation against liberalism ever since. But surely, the class issue has actually been successfully resolved in the West. As Kojève (among others) noted, the egalitarianism of modern America represents the essential achievement of the classless society envisioned by Marx. This is not to say that there are not rich people and poor people in the United States, or that the gap between them has not grown in recent years. But the root causes of economic inequality do not have to do with the underlying legal and social structure of our society, which remains fundamentally egalitarian and moderately redistributionist, so much as with the cultural and social characteristics of the groups that make it up, which are in turn the historical legacy of premodern conditions. Thus black poverty in the United States is not the inherent product

---

[1] I am not using the term "fascism" here in its most precise sense, fully aware of the frequent misuse of this term to denounce anyone to the right of the user. "Fascism" here denotes any organized ultra-nationalist movement with universalistic pretensions—not universalistic with regard to its nationalism, of course, since the latter is exclusive by definition, but with regard to the movement's belief in its right to rule other people. Hence Imperial Japan would qualify as fascist while former strongman Stoessner's Paraguay or Pinochet's Chile would not. Obviously fascist ideologies cannot be universalistic in the sense of Marxism or liberalism, but the structure of the doctrine can be transferred from country to country.

of liberalism, but is rather the "legacy of slavery and racism" which persisted long after the formal abolition of slavery.

As a result of the receding of the class issue, the appeal of communism in the developed Western world, it is safe to say, is lower today than any time since the end of the First World War. This can be measured in any number of ways: in the declining membership and electoral pull of the major European communist parties, and their overtly revisionist programs; in the corresponding electoral success of conservative parties from Britain and Germany to the United States and Japan, which are unabashedly pro-market and antistatist; and in an intel-lectual climate whose most "advanced" members no longer believe that bour-geois society is something that ultimately needs to be overcome. This is not to say that the opinions of progressive intellectuals in Western countries are not deeply pathological in any number of ways. But those who believe that the future must inevitably be socialist tend to be very old, or very marginal to the real political discourse of their societies.

One may argue that the socialist alternative was never terribly plausible for the North Atlantic world, and was sustained for the last several decades primarily by its success outside of this region. But it is precisely in the non-European world that one is most struck by the occurrence of major ideological transformations. Surely the most remarkable changes have occurred in Asia. Due to the strength and adaptability of the indigenous cultures there, Asia became a battleground for a variety of imported Western ideologies early in this century. Liberalism in Asia was a very weak reed in the period after World War I; it is easy today to for-get how gloomy Asia's political future looked as recently as ten or fifteen years ago. It is easy to forget as well how momentous the outcome of Asian ideologi-cal struggles seemed for world political development as a whole.

The first Asian alternative to liberalism to be decisively defeated was the fascist one represented by Imperial Japan. Japanese fascism (like its German version) was defeated by the force of American arms in the Pacific war, and liberal democ-racy was imposed on Japan by a victorious United States. Western capitalism and political liberalism when transplanted to Japan were adapted and transformed by the Japanese in such a way as to be scarcely recognizable.[2] Many Americans are now aware that Japanese industrial organization is very different from that pre-vailing in the United States or Europe, and it is questionable what relationship the factional maneuvering that takes place with the governing Liberal Democra-tic Party bears to democracy. Nonetheless, the very fact that the essential ele-ments of economic and political liberalism have been so successfully grafted onto uniquely Japanese traditions and institutions guarantees their survival in the long

---

[2] I use the example of Japan with some caution, since Kojève late in his life came to conclude that Japan, with its culture based on purely formal arts, proved that the universal homogenous state was not victorious and that history had perhaps not ended. See the long note at the end of the second edition of *Introduction à la Lecture de Hegel,* 462–3.

run. More important is the contribution that Japan has made in turn to world history by following in the footsteps of the United States to create a truly universal consumer culture that has become both a symbol and an underpinning of the universal homogenous state. V. S. Naipaul traveling in Khomeini's Iran shortly after the revolution noted the omnipresent signs advertising the products of Sony, Hitachi, and JVC, whose appeal remained virtually irresistible and gave the lie to the regime's pretensions of restoring a state based on the rule of the *Shariah*. Desire for access to the consumer culture, created in large measure by Japan, has played a crucial role in fostering the spread of economic liberalism throughout Asia, and hence in promoting political liberalism as well.

The economic success of the other newly industrializing countries (NICs) in Asia following on the example of Japan is by now a familiar story. What is important from a Hegelian standpoint is that political liberalism has been following economic liberalism, more slowly than many had hoped but with seeming inevitability. Here again we see the victory of the idea of the universal homogenous state. South Korea had developed into a modern, urbanized society with an increasingly large and well-educated middle class that could not possibly be isolated from the larger democratic trends around them. Under these circumstances it seemed intolerable to a large part of this population that it should be ruled by an anachronistic military regime while Japan, only a decade or so ahead in economic terms, had parliamentary institutions for over forty years. Even the former socialist regime in Burma, which for so many decades existed in dismal isolation from the larger trends dominating Asia, was buffeted in the past year by pressures to liberalize both its economy and political system. It is said that unhappiness with strongman Ne Win began when a senior Burmese officer went to Singapore for medical treatment and broke down crying when he saw how far socialist Burma had been left behind by its ASEAN neighbors.

But the power of the liberal idea would seem much less impressive if it had not infected the largest and oldest culture in Asia, China. The simple existence of communist China created an alternative pole of ideological attraction, and as such constituted a threat to liberalism. But the past fifteen years have seen an almost total discrediting of Marxism-Leninism as an economic system. Beginning with the famous third plenum of the Tenth Central Committee in 1978, the Chinese Communist party set about decollectivizing agriculture for the 800 million Chinese who still lived in the countryside. The role of the state in agriculture was reduced to that of a tax collector, while production of consumer goods was sharply increased in order to give peasants a taste of the universal homogenous state and thereby an incentive to work. The reform doubled Chinese grain output in only five years, and in the process created for Deng Xiao-ping a solid political base from which he was able to extend the reform to other parts of the economy. Economic statistics do not begin to describe the dynamism, initiative, and openness evident in China since the reform began.

China could not now be described in any way as a liberal democracy. At present, no more than 20 percent of its economy has been marketized, and most importantly it continues to be ruled by a self-appointed Communist party which has given no hint of wanting to devolve power. Deng has made none of Gorbachev's promises regarding democratization of the political system and there is no Chinese equivalent of *glasnost*. The Chinese leadership has in fact been much more circumspect in criticizing Mao and Maoism than Gorbachev with respect to Brezhnev and Stalin, and the regime continues to pay lip service to Marxism-Leninism as its ideological underpinning. But anyone familiar with the outlook and behavior of the new technocratic elite now governing China knows that Marxism and ideological principle have become virtually irrelevant as guides to policy, and that bourgeois consumerism has a real meaning in that country for the first time since the revolution. The various slowdowns in the pace of reform, the campaigns against "spiritual pollution" and crackdowns on political dissent are more properly seen as tactical adjustments made in the process of managing what is an extraordinarily difficult political transition. By ducking the question of political reform while putting the economy on a new footing, Deng has managed to avoid the breakdown of authority that has accompanied Gorbachev's *perestroika*. Yet the pull of the liberal idea continues to be very strong as economic power devolves and the economy becomes more open to the outside world. There are currently over 20,000 Chinese students studying in the U.S. and other Western countries, almost all of them the children of the Chinese elite. It is hard to believe that when they return home to run the country they will be content for China to be the only country in Asia unaffected by the larger democratizing trend. The student demonstrations in Beijing that broke out first in December 1986 and recurred recently on the occasion of Hu Yao-bang's death were only the beginning of what will inevitably be mounting pressure for change in the political system as well.

What is important about China from the standpoint of world history is not the present state of the reform or even its future prospects. The central issue is the fact that the People's Republic of China can no longer act as a beacon for illiberal forces around the world, whether they be guerrillas in some Asian jungle or middle class students in Paris. Maoism, rather than being the pattern for Asia's future, became an anachronism, and it was the mainland Chinese who in fact were decisively influenced by the prosperity and dynamism of their overseas co-ethnics—the ironic ultimate victory of Taiwan. . . .

If we admit for the moment that the fascist and communist challenges to liberalism are dead, are there any other ideological competitors left? Or put another way, are there contradictions in liberal society beyond that of class that are not resolvable? Two possibilities suggest themselves, those of religion and nationalism.

The rise of religious fundamentalism in recent years within the Christian, Jewish, and Muslim traditions has been widely noted. One is inclined to say that the revival of religion in some way attests to a broad unhappiness with the impersonality and spiritual vacuity of liberal consumerist societies. Yet while the emptiness at the core of liberalism is most certainly a defect in the ideology—indeed, a flaw that one does not need the perspective of religion to recognize[3]—it is not at all clear that it is remediable through politics. Modern liberalism itself was historically a consequence of the weakness of religiously-based societies which, failing to agree on the nature of the good life, could not provide even the minimal preconditions of peace and stability. In the contemporary world only Islam has offered a theocratic state as a political alternative to both liberalism and communism. But the doctrine has little appeal for non-Muslims, and it is hard to believe that the movement will take on any universal significance. Other less organized religious impulses have been successfully satisfied within the sphere of personal life that is permitted in liberal societies.

The other major "contradiction" potentially unresolvable by liberalism is the one posed by nationalism and other forms of racial and ethnic consciousness. It is certainly true that a very large degree of conflict since the Battle of Jena has had its roots in nationalism. Two cataclysmic world wars in this century have been spawned by the nationalism of the developed world in various guises, and if those passions have been muted to a certain extent in postwar Europe, they are still extremely powerful in the Third World. Nationalism has been a threat to liberalism historically in Germany, and continues to be one in isolated parts of "post-historical" Europe like Northern Ireland.

But it is not clear that nationalism represents an irreconcilable contradiction in the heart of liberalism. In the first place, nationalism is not one single phenomenon but several, ranging from mild cultural nostalgia to the highly organized and elaborately articulated doctrine of National Socialism. Only systematic nationalisms of the latter sort can qualify as a formal ideology on the level of liberalism or communism. The vast majority of the world's nationalist movements do not have a political program beyond the negative desire of independence *from* some other group or people, and do not offer anything like a comprehensive agenda for socio-economic organization. As such, they are compatible with doctrines and ideologies that do offer such agendas. While they may constitute a source of conflict for liberal societies, this conflict does not arise from liberalism itself so much as from the fact that the liberalism in question is incomplete. Certainly a great deal of the world's ethnic and nationalist tension can be explained in terms of peoples who are forced to live in unrepresentative political systems that they have not chosen.

While it is impossible to rule out the sudden appearance of new ideologies or previously unrecognized contradictions in liberal societies, then, the present world seems to confirm that the fundamental principles of socio-political

---

[3] I am thinking particularly of Rousseau and the Western philosophical tradition that flows from him that was highly critical of Lockean or Hobbesian liberalism, though one could criticize liberalism from the standpoint of classical political philosophy as well.

organization have not advanced terribly far since 1806. Many of the wars and revolutions fought since that time have been undertaken in the name of ideologies which claimed to be more advanced than liberalism, but whose pretensions were ultimately unmasked by history. In the meantime, they have helped to spread the universal homogenous state to the point where it could have a significant effect on the overall character of international relations. . . .

V

The passing of Marxism-Leninism first from China and then from the Soviet Union will mean its death as a living ideology of world historical significance. For while there may be some isolated true believers left in places like Managua, Pyongyang, or Cambridge, Massachusetts, the fact that there is not a single large state in which it is a going concern undermines completely its pretensions to being in the vanguard of human history. And the death of this ideology means the growing "Common Marketization" of international relations, and the diminution of the likelihood of large-scale conflict between states.

This does not by any means imply the end of international conflict *per se*. For the world at that point would be divided between a part that was historical and a part that was post-historical. Conflict between states still in history, and between those states and those at the end of history, would still be possible. There would still be a high and perhaps rising level of ethnic and nationalist violence, since those are impulses incompletely played out, even in parts of the post-historical world. Palestinians and Kurds, Sikhs and Tamils, Irish Catholics and Walloons, Armenians and Azeris, will continue to have their unresolved grievances. This implies that terrorism and wars of national liberation will continue to be an important item on the international agenda. But large-scale conflict must involve large states still caught in the grip of history, and they are what appear to be passing from the scene.

The end of history will be a very sad time. The struggle for recognition, the willingness to risk one's life for a purely abstract goal, the worldwide ideological struggle that called forth daring, courage, imagination, and idealism, will be replaced by economic calculation, the endless solving of technical problems, environmental concerns, and the satisfaction of sophisticated consumer demands. In the post-historical period there will be neither art nor philosophy, just the perpetual caretaking of the museum of human history. I can feel in myself, and see in others around me, a powerful nostalgia for the time when history existed. Such nostalgia, in fact, will continue to fuel competition and conflict even in the post-historical world for some time to come. Even though I recognize its inevitability, I have the most ambivalent feelings for the civilization that has been created in Europe since 1945, with its north Atlantic and Asian offshoots. Perhaps this very prospect of centuries of boredom at the end of history will serve to get history started once again.

The Third Wave: Democratization in the Late Twentieth Century

Samuel P. Huntington

Like the selection by Fukuyama [1.1], Samuel Huntington's *The Third Wave* was written toward the end of the twentieth century, when many authoritarian and communist regimes were crumbling and being replaced by democratic regimes. Huntington designates the changes as the "third wave of democratization." He identifies two previous periods of democratization. In contrast to his "Clash of Civilizations?" [1.4], a somber analysis published two years later, *The Third Wave,* describes a kind of domino effect, in which authoritarian regimes are being replaced by democratic regimes following the end of communism.

Huntington suggests that previous democratic waves were succeeded by reversals, and he notes that several reversals of democracy have occurred within the third wave. Nonetheless, he is quite optimistic about the direction of world history. As other selections in this chapter suggest, with the hindsight of two decades since publication of *The Third Wave,* it is difficult to be as optimistic. Indeed, Huntington himself provided a gloomy assessment in his influential article, "The Clash of Civilizations?" [1.4], published only two years after publication of *The Third Wave.* The later article identifies a trend that apparently overshadows in importance the third wave of democracy. Confining attention to the prospects for democracy, assessments by O'Donnell [4.6] and Carothers [4.7] provide further reasons for skepticism.

What explains why waves of democratization, that is, democratic transitions, are concentrated in particular periods? Can you think of factors in the international arena, as well as domestic developments, that might explain such waves? How well does your analysis help explain reversals of democracy?

The Waves of Democratization

Political systems with democratic characteristics are not limited to modern times. In many areas of the world tribal chiefs were elected for centuries and

Samuel P. Huntington, *The Third Wave: Democratization in the Late Twentieth Century* (Norman: University of Oklahoma Press, 1991), 13–26.

in some places democratic political institutions long existed at the village level. In addition, the concept of democracy was, of course, familiar to the ancient world. The democracy of the Greeks and the Romans, however, excluded women, slaves, and often other categories of people, such as resident aliens, from participation in political life. The extent to which ruling bodies were, in practice, responsible to even this restricted public was also often limited.

Modern democracy is not simply democracy of the village, the tribe, or the city-state; it is democracy of the nation-state and its emergence is associated with the development of the nation-state. The initial push toward democracy in the West occurred in the first half of the seventeenth century. Democratic ideas and democratic movements were an important, although not a central, feature of the English Revolution. The Fundamental Orders of Connecticut, adopted by the citizens of Hartford and neighboring towns on January 14, 1638, were the "first written constitution of modern democracy."[1] By and large, however, the Puritan upheavals did not leave a legacy of democratic institutions in either England or America. For over a century after 1660 government in both places tended to become even more closed and less broadly representative of the people than it had been earlier. In a variety of ways, an aristocratic and oligarchic resurgence occurred. In 1750 no democratic institutions at the national level existed in the Western world. In 1900 such institutions existed in many countries. By the late twentieth century many more countries possessed democratic institutions. These institutions emerged in waves of democratization (see Figure 1.1).

A wave of democratization is a group of transitions from nondemocratic to democratic regimes that occur within a specified period of time and that significantly outnumber transitions in the opposite direction during that period of time. A wave also usually involves liberalization or partial democratization in political systems that do not become fully democratic. Three waves of democratization have occurred in the modern world. Each wave affected a relatively small number of countries, and during each wave some regime transitions occurred in a nondemocratic direction. In addition, not all transitions to democracy occurred during democratic waves. History is messy and political changes do not sort themselves into neat historical boxes. History is also not unidirectional. Each of the first two waves of democratization was followed by a reverse wave in which some but not all of the countries that had previously made the transition to democracy reverted to nondemocratic rule. It is often arbitrary to attempt to specify precisely when a regime transition occurs. It is also arbitrary to attempt to specify precisely the dates of democratization waves and

---

[1] G. P. Gooch, *English Democratic Ideas in the Seventeenth Century*, 2d ed. (New York: Harper, 1959), p. 71.

Category	Number of Countries	First Wave	First Reverse	Second Wave	Second Reverse	Third Wave	Third Reverse?
L	3						
K	12						
J	6						
I	1						
H	9						
G	10						
F	3						
E	4						
D	5						
C	10						
B	1						
A	10						
Democratic Countries		33 (Max)	11 (Min)	52 (Max)	30 (Min)	65 (Max)	61 (Min)
Net Change		+33	−22	+41	−22	+35	−4
Total Countries = 74							

■ Democratic or semidemocratic phases

▓ Nondemocratic phases of previously democratic countries

Figure 1.1 Democratization Waves and Reverse Waves.

reverse waves. It is, nonetheless, often useful to be arbitrary, and the dates of these waves of regime changes are more or less as follows:

First, long wave of democratization	1828–1926
First reverse wave	1922–42
Second, short wave of democratization	1943–62
Second reverse wave	1958–75
Third wave of democratization	1974–

The first wave of democratization. The first wave had its roots in the American and French revolutions. The actual emergence of national democratic institutions, however, is a nineteenth-century phenomenon. In most countries during that century democratic institutions developed gradually and it is, hence, difficult as well as arbitrary to specify a particular date after which a political system could be considered democratic. Jonathan Sunshine, however, sets forth two reasonable major criteria for when nineteenth-century political systems achieved minimal democratic qualifications in the context of that century: (1) 50 percent of adult males are eligible to vote; and (2) a responsible executive who either must maintain majority support in an elected parliament or is chosen in periodic popular elections. Adopting these criteria and applying them rather loosely, one can say that the United States began the first wave of democratization roughly about 1828. The abolition of property qualifications in the older states and the admission of new states with universal manhood suffrage boosted to well over 50 percent the proportion of white males actually voting in the 1828 presidential election. In the following decades other countries gradually expanded the suffrage, reduced plural voting, introduced the secret ballot, and established the responsibility of prime ministers and cabinets to parliaments. Switzerland, the overseas English dominions, France, Great Britain, and several smaller

---

Note: Classification of countries in Figure 1.1:
(A) Australia, Canada, Finland, Iceland, Ireland, New Zealand, Sweden, Switzerland, United Kingdom, United States
(B) Chile
(C) Austria, Belgium, Colombia, Denmark, France, West Germany, Italy, Japan, Netherlands, Norway
(D) Argentina, Czechoslovakia, Greece, Hungary, Uruguay
(E) East Germany, Poland, Portugal, Spain
(F) Estonia, Latvia, Lithuania
(G) Botswana, Costa Rica, Gambia, Israel, Jamaica, Malaysia, Malta, Sri Lanka, Trinidad and Tobago, Venezuela
(H) Bolivia, Brazil, Ecuador, India, South Korea, Pakistan, Peru, Philippines, Turkey
(I) Nigeria
(J) Burma, Fiji, Ghana, Guyana, Indonesia, Lebanon
(K) Bulgaria, Dominican Republic, El Salvador, Guatemala, Honduras, Mongolia, Namibia, Nicaragua, Panama, Papua New Guinea, Romania, Senegal
(L) Haiti, Sudan, Suriname

European countries made the transition to democracy before the turn of the century. Shortly before World War I, Italy and Argentina introduced more or less democratic regimes. Following that war the newly independent Ireland and Iceland were democratic and a mass movement toward democracy occurred in the successor states to the Romanov, Hapsburg, and Hohenzollern empires. In the very early 1930s, after the first wave had effectively ended, Spain and Chile moved into the democratic column. All in all, in the course of a hundred years over thirty countries established at least minimal national democratic institutions. In the 1830s Tocqueville predicted this trend as it began. In 1920 James Bryce reviewed its history and speculated as to whether the "trend toward democracy now widely visible, is a natural trend, due to a general law of social progress."[2]

The first reverse wave. Even as Bryce speculated about its future, however, the democracy trend was tapering off and reversing. The dominant political development of the 1920s and the 1930s was the shift away from democracy and either the return to traditional forms of authoritarian rule or the introduction of new mass-based, more brutal and pervasive forms of totalitarianism. The reversals occurred largely in those countries that had adopted democratic forms just before or after World War I, where not only democracy was new but also, in many cases, the nation was new. Only one country, Greece, of the dozen countries that introduced democratic institutions before 1910 suffered a reversal after 1920. Only four of the seventeen countries that adopted democratic institutions between 1910 and 1931 maintained them throughout the 1920s and 1930s.

The first reverse wave began in 1922 with the March on Rome and Mussolini's easy disposal of Italy's fragile and rather corrupt democracy. In little over a decade fledgling democratic institutions in Lithuania, Poland, Latvia, and Estonia were overthrown by military coups. Countries such as Yugoslavia and Bulgaria that had never known real democracy were subjected to new forms of harsher dictatorship. The conquest of power by Hitler in 1933 ended German democracy, ensured the end of Austrian democracy the following year, and eventually of course produced the end of Czech democracy in 1938. Greek democracy, which had been unsettled by the National Schism in 1915, was finally buried in 1936. Portugal succumbed to a military coup in 1926 that led to the long Salazar dictatorship Military takeovers occurred in Brazil and Argentina in 1930. Uruguay reverted to authoritarianism in 1933. A military coup in 1936 led to civil war and the death of the Spanish republic in 1939. The new and limited democracy introduced in Japan in the 1920s was supplanted by military rule in the early 1930s.

These regime changes reflected the rise of communist, fascist, and militaristic ideologies. In France, Britain, and other countries where democratic institutions remained in place, antidemocratic movements gained strength from the alienation of the 1920s and the depression of the 1930s. The war that had been

---

[2] James Bryce, *Modern Democracies*, vol. 1 (New York: Macmillan, 1921), p. 24.

fought to make the world safe for democracy had instead unleashed movements of both the Right and the Left that were intent on destroying it.

The second wave of democratization. Starting in World War II a second, short wave of democratization occurred. Allied occupation promoted inauguration of democratic institutions in West Germany, Italy, Austria, Japan, and Korea, while Soviet pressure snuffed out incipient democracy in Czechoslovakia and Hungary. In the late 1940s and early 1950s Turkey and Greece moved toward democracy. In Latin America Uruguay returned to democracy during the war and Brazil and Costa Rica shifted to democracy in the late 1940s. In four other Latin American countries—Argentina, Colombia, Peru, and Venezuela—elections in 1945 and 1946 ushered in popularly chosen governments. In all four countries, however, democratic practices did not last and dictatorships were in place by the early 1950s. In the later 1950s Argentina and Peru moved back toward limited democracy which was, however, highly unstable as a result of the conflict between the military and the populist Aprista and Peronista movements. Also in the late 1950s, in contrast, the elites in both Colombia and Venezuela negotiated arrangements to end the military dictatorships in those countries and to introduce democratic institutions that were to last.

Meanwhile, the beginning of the end of Western colonial rule produced a number of new states. In many no real effort was made to introduce democratic institutions. In some democracy was tenuous: in Pakistan, for instance, democratic institutions never really took hold and were formally abrogated in 1958. Malaysia became independent in 1957 and maintained its "quasi-democracy" except for a brief period, 1969–71, of emergency rule. Indonesia had a confused form of parliamentary democracy from 1950 to 1957. In a few new states—India, Sri Lanka, the Philippines, Israel—democratic institutions were sustained for a decade or more and in 1960 Africa's largest state, Nigeria, began life as a democracy.

The second reverse wave. By the early 1960s the second wave of democratization had exhausted itself. By the late 1950s political development and regime transitions were taking on a heavily authoritarian cast. The change was most dramatic in Latin America. The shift toward authoritarianism began in Peru in 1962 when the military intervened to alter the results of an election. The following year a civilian acceptable to the military was elected president, but he was displaced by a military coup in 1968. In 1964 military coups overthrew civilian governments in Brazil and Bolivia. Argentina followed suit in 1966 and Ecuador in 1972. In 1973 military regimes took over in Uruguay and Chile. The military governments of Brazil, Argentina, and, more debatably, Chile and Uruguay were examples, according to one theory, of a new type of political system, "bureaucratic authoritarianism."[3]

---

[3] See Guillermo A. O'Donnell, *Modernization and Bureaucratic-Authoritarianism: Studies in South American Politics* (Berkeley: University of California, Institute of International Studies, 1973), and David Collier, ed., *The New Authoritarianism in Latin America* (Princeton: Princeton University Press, 1979).

In Asia the military imposed a martial law regime in Pakistan in 1958. In the late 1950s Syngman Rhee began to undermine democratic procedures in Korea, and the democratic regime that succeeded him in 1960 was overthrown by a military coup in 1961. This new "semiauthoritarian" regime was legitimated by elections in 1963 but turned into a full-scale highly authoritarian system in 1973. In 1957 Sukarno replaced parliamentary democracy with guided democracy in Indonesia, and in 1965 the Indonesian military ended guided democracy and took over the government of their country. In 1972 President Ferdinand Marcos instituted a martial law regime in the Philippines, and in 1975 Indira Gandhi suspended democratic practices and declared emergency rule in India. On Taiwan the nondemocratic KMT regime had tolerated liberal dissenters in the 1950s, but these were suppresed in the "dark age" of the 1960s and "any sort of political discourse" was silenced."[4]

In the Mediterranean area, Greek democracy went down before a "royal" coup d'etat in 1965 and a military coup in 1967. The Turkish military overthrew the civilian government of that country in 1960, returned authority to an elected government in 1961, intervened again in a "half coup" in 1971, allowed a return to an elected government in 1973, and then carried out a full-scale military takeover in 1980.

During the 1960s several non-African British colonies became independent and instituted democratic regimes that lasted for significant periods of time. These included Jamaica and Trinidad and Tobago in 1962, Malta in 1964, Barbados in 1966, and Mauritius in 1968. The vast bulk of the new countries that became independent in the 1960s, however, were in Africa. The most important of these countries, Nigeria, started out as a democracy but succumbed to a military coup in 1966. The only African country consistently to maintain democratic practices was Botswana. Thirty-three other African countries that became independent between 1956 and 1970 became authoritarian with independence or very shortly after independence. The decolonization of Africa led to the largest multiplication of independent authoritarian governments in history.

The global swing away from democracy in the 1960s and early 1970s was impressive. In 1962, by one count, thirteen governments in the world were the product of coups d'etat; by 1975, thirty-eight were. By another estimate one-third of 32 working democracies in the world in 1958 had become authoritarian by the mid-1970s.[5] In 1960 nine of ten South American countries of Iberian heritage had democratically elected governments; by 1973, only two, Venezuela and Colombia, did. This wave of transitions away from democracy was even more striking because it involved several countries, such as Chile, Uruguay

---

[4] Tun-Jen Cheng, "Democratizing the Quasi-Leninist Regime in Taiwan," *World Politics* 41 (July 1989), pp. 479–80.

[5] S.E. Finer, *The Man on Horseback: The Role of the Military in Politics*, 2d ed. (Harmondsworth: Penguin Books, 1976), p. 223; Sidney Verba, "Problems of Democracy in the Developing Countries," Remarks, Harvard–MIT Joint Seminar on Political Development, October 6, 1976, p. 6.

("the Switzerland of South America"), India, and the Philippines, that had sustained democratic regimes for a quarter century or more. These regime transitions not only stimulated the theory of bureaucratic-authoritarianism to explain the Latin American changes. They also produced a much broader pessimism about the applicability of democracy in developing countries and they contributed to concern about the viability and workability of democracy among the developed countries where it had existed for years.[6]

The third wave of democratization. Once again, however, the dialectic of history upended the theories of social science. In the fifteen years following the end of the Portuguese dictatorship in 1974, democratic regimes replaced authoritarian ones in approximately thirty countries in Europe, Asia, and Latin America. In other countries, considerable liberalization occurred in authoritarian regimes. In still others, movements promoting democracy gained strength and legitimacy. Although obviously there were resistance and setbacks, as in China in 1989, the movement toward democracy seemed to take on the character of an almost irresistible global tide moving on from one triumph to the next.

This democratic tide manifested itself first in southern Europe. Three months after the Portuguese coup, the military regime that had governed Greece since 1967 collapsed and a civilian government took over under the leadership of Constantine Karamanlis. In November 1974, the Greek people gave Karamanlis and his party a decisive majority in a hotly contested election and the following month they overwhelmingly voted not to restore the monarchy. On November 20, 1975, just five days before Eanes's defeat of the Marxist-Leninists in Portugal, the death of Gen. Francisco Franco ended his thirty-six-year rule of Spain. During the following eighteen months, the new king, Juan Carlos, assisted by his prime minister, Adolfo Suárez, secured parliamentary and popular approval of a political reform law that led to the election of a new assembly. The assembly drafted a new constitution, which was ratified by a referendum in December 1978 and under which parliamentary elections occurred in March 1979.

In the late 1970s the democratic wave moved on to Latin America. In 1977 the military leaders in Ecuador announced their desire to withdraw from politics; a new constitution was drafted in 1978; and elections in 1979 produced a civilian government. A similar process of military withdrawal in Peru led to the

---

[6] The shift in political development literature from a focus on democracy to a focus on stability and the highlighting of developmental contradictions and crises is briefly described in Samuel P. Huntington, "The Goals of Development," in *Understanding Political Development*, ed. Myron Weiner and Samuel P. Huntington, (Boston: Little, Brown, 1987), pp. 3ff. The concern about Western democracy is reflected in Michel Crozier, Samuel P. Huntington, and Joji Watanuki, *The Crisis of Democracy* (New York: New York University Press, 1975), and Richard Rose and B. Guy Peters, *Can Government Go Bankrupt?* (New York: Basic Books, 1978).

On February 11, 1976, at the request of CIA leaders I delivered a talk to Agency analysts on "The Global Decline of Democracy." Needless to say, I had some very persuasive theories to explain the depth and seriousness of this phenomenon. The third democratization wave was then twenty-one months old.

election of a constituent assembly in 1978, a new constitution in 1979, and the election of a civilian president in 1980. In Bolivia, military withdrawal produced four confusing years of coups and aborted elections beginning in 1978, but the eventual election of a civilian president in 1982. That same year defeat in the war with Great Britain undermined the Argentine military government and produced the election in 1983 of a civilian president and government. Negotiations between military and political leaders in Uruguay led to the election of a civilian president in November 1984. Two months later, the long process of *abertura*, or opening, that had begun in Brazil in 1974 reached a decisive point with the selection of that country's first civilian president since 1964. Meanwhile, the military was also withdrawing from office in Central America. Honduras installed a civilian president in January 1982; Salvadoran voters chose José Napoleon Duarte as president in a hotly contested election in May 1984; and Guatemala elected a constituent assembly in 1984 and a civilian president in 1985.

The democratic movement also had its manifestations in Asia. Early in 1977, the premier democracy of the Third World, India, which for one and a half years had been under emergency rule, returned to the democratic path. In 1980 responding to violence and terrorism, the Turkish military for the third time took over the government of that country. In 1983, however, they withdrew and elections produced a civilian government. In the same year, the assassination of Benigno Aquino set in motion the train of events that led in February 1986 to the end of the Marcos dictatorship and the restoration of democracy in the Philippines. In 1987 the military government in Korea submitted its candidate for president to a highly contested electoral campaign and a relatively fair election, which he won. The following year the opposition secured control of the Korean parliament. In 1987 and 1988, the government on Taiwan significantly loosened the restrictions on political activity in that country and committed itself to the creation of a democratic political system. In 1988 military rule in Pakistan came to an end, and the opposition, led by a woman, won an electoral victory and took control of the government.

At the end of the decade, the democratic wave engulfed the communist world. In 1988 Hungary began the transition to a multiparty system. In 1989 elections for a national congress in the Soviet Union produced the defeat of several senior Communist party leaders and an increasingly assertive national parliament. In early 1990, multiparty systems were developing in the Baltic republics and the Communist Party of the Soviet Union (CPSU) abandoned its guiding role. In 1989, in Poland Solidarity swept the elections for a national parliament and a noncommunist government came into existence. In 1990 the leader of Solidarity, Lech Walesa, was elected president, replacing the Communist Gen. Wojciech Jaruzelski. In the last months of 1989, the communist regimes in East Germany, Czechoslovakia, and Romania collapsed, and competitive elections in these countries were held in 1990. In Bulgaria the communist regime also began to liberalize, and popular movements for democracy appeared in Mongolia. In 1990 what appear to be reasonably fair elections occurred in both these countries.

Meanwhile, back in the Western hemisphere, the Mexican ruling party, for the first time, only narrowly won a presidential election in 1988 and lost, for the first time, a state governorship in 1989. The Chilean public in 1988 voted in a referendum to end Gen. Augusto Pinochet's extended grip on power and the following year elected a civilian president. U.S. military intervention ended a Marxist-Leninist dictatorship in Grenada in 1983 and Gen. Manuel Noriega's military dictatorship in Panama in 1989. In February 1990 the Marxist-Leninist regime in Nicaragua went down to electoral defeat, and in December 1990 a democratic government was elected in Haiti.

The 1970s and early 1980s also witnessed the final phase of European decolonization. The end of the Portuguese empire produced five nondemocratic governments. In 1975, however, Papua New Guinea became independent with a democratic political system. The liquidation of the remnants, mostly islands, of the British empire produced a dozen minuscule new nations, almost all of which maintained democratic institutions, although in Grenada these institutions had to be restored by outside military intervention. In 1990 Namibia became independent with a government chosen in an internationally supervised election.

In Africa and the Middle East movement to democracy in the 1980s was limited Nigeria shifted back from military rule to a democratically elected government in 1979 but this in turn was overthrown by a military coup at the beginning of 1984. By 1990 some liberalization had occurred in Senegal, Tunisia, Algeria, Egypt, and Jordan. In 1978 the South African government began a slow process of reducing apartheid and expanding political participation for nonwhite minorities but not for the overwhelming black majority in that country. After a pause and then the election of F. W. de Klerk as president, the process was resumed in 1990 with negotiations between the government and the African National Congress. By 1990 democratic rumblings were occurring in Nepal, Albania, and other countries whose previous experience with democracy had been modest or nonexistent.

Overall, the movement toward democracy was a global one. In fifteen years the democratic wave moved across southern Europe, swept through Latin America, moved on to Asia, and decimated dictatorship in the Soviet bloc. In 1974 eight of ten South American countries had nondemocratic governments. In 1990 nine had democratically chosen governments. In 1973, according to Freedom House estimates, 32 percent of the world's population lived in free countries; in 1976, as a result of emergency rule in India, less than 20 percent of the world's population did. By 1990, in contrast, close to 39 percent of humankind lived in free societies

In one sense, the democratization waves and the reverse waves suggest a two-step-forward, one-step-backward pattern. To date each reverse wave has eliminated some but not all of the transitions to democracy of the previous democratization wave. The final column in Table 1.1, however, suggests a less optimistic prognosis for democracy. States come in many shapes and sizes, and in the post-World War II decades the number of independent states doubled. Yet

Table 1.1

Democratization in the Modern World

Year	Democratic States	Non-democratic States	Total States	Percentage Democratic of Total States
1922	29	35	64	45.3
1942	12	49	61	19.7
1962	36	75	111	32.4
1973	30	92	122	24.6
1990	59	71	130	45.4

Note: This estimate of regime numbers omits countries with a population of less than one million.

the proportions of democratic states in the world show a considerable regularity. At the troughs of the two reverse waves 19.7 percent and 24.6 percent of the countries in the world were democratic. At the peaks of the two democratization waves, 45.3 percent and 32.4 percent of the countries in the world were democratic. In 1990 roughly 45.4 percent of the independent countries of the world had democratic systems, the same percentage as in 1922. Obviously whether Grenada is democratic has less impact than whether China is democratic, and ratios of democratic to total states are not all that significant. In addition between 1973 and 1990 the absolute number of authoritarian states decreased for the first time yet as of 1990 the third wave of democratization still had not increased the proportion of democratic states in the world above its previous peak sixty-eight years earlier.

1.3

The Return of Authoritarian Great Powers

Azar Gat

Azar Gat questions analyses, such as those of Fukuyama [1.1] and Huntington [1.2], claiming that there is a worldwide movement toward democracy. He does not believe democratic countries have decisive advantages in competition with undemocratic regimes. He provides evidence from the history of the twentieth century to support his case. In particular, an accidental factor explains democracies' victory over fascism and communism: U.S. military, political, and economic superiority. Azar Gat considers this a contingent development, that is, there was no necessary reason why the United States, a large prosperous and powerful democracy, would emerge on the world stage.

Nor does the matter end there. The United States played a key role in persuading other countries to become democratic in the second half of the twentieth century. However, he suggests, the tide may have turned in the twenty-first century, with the growing importance of authoritarian China and the reversal of liberal tendencies in a resurgent Russia.

Azar Gat apparently accords little importance to the ideological appeals of liberal democracy that are so important for Fukuyama [1.1] and Huntington [1.2]. Is he correct to downplay the importance of ideology compared to the geopolitical factors that he analyzes?

The End of the End of History

Today's global liberal democratic order faces two challenges. The first is radical Islam—and it is the lesser of the two challenges. Although the proponents of radical Islam find liberal democracy repugnant, and the movement is often described as the new fascist threat, the societies from which it arises are generally poor and stagnant. They represent no viable alternative to modernity and pose no significant military threat to the developed world. It is mainly the potential

---

Azar Gat, "The Return of Authoritarian Great Powers," *Foreign Affairs* 86, no. 4 (July/August 2007): 59–69 (excerpts).

use of weapons of mass destruction—particularly by nonstate actors—that makes militant Islam a menace.

The second, and more significant, challenge emanates from the rise of nonde-mocratic great powers: the West's old Cold War rivals China and Russia, now operating under authoritarian capitalist, rather than communist, regimes. Au-thoritarian capitalist great powers played a leading role in the international system up until 1945. They have been absent since then. But today, they seem poised for a comeback.

Capitalism's ascendancy appears to be deeply entrenched, but the current pre-dominance of democracy could be far less secure. Capitalism has expanded relentlessly since early modernity, its lower-priced goods and superior economic power eroding and transforming all other socioeconomic regimes, a process most memorably described by Karl Marx in *The Communist Manifesto*. Contrary to Marx's expectations, capitalism had the same effect on communism, eventually "burying" it without the proverbial shot being fired. The triumph of the market, precipitating and reinforced by the industrial-technological revolution, led to the rise of the middle class, intensive urbanization, the spread of education, the emergence of mass society, and ever greater affluence. In the post-Cold War era (just as in the nineteenth century and the 1950s and 1960s), it is widely believed that liberal democracy naturally emerged from these developments, a view fa-mously espoused by Francis Fukuyama. Today, more than half of the world's states have elected governments, and close to half have sufficiently entrenched liberal rights to be considered fully free.

But the reasons for the triumph of democracy, especially over its nondemocra-tic capitalist rivals of the two world wars, Germany and Japan, were more con-tingent than is usually assumed. Authoritarian capitalist states, today exemplified by China and Russia, may represent a viable alternative path to modernity, which in turn suggests that there is nothing inevitable about liberal democracy's ulti-mate victory—or future dominance.

Chronicle of a Defeat not Foretold

The liberal democratic camp defeated its authoritarian, fascist, and communist rivals alike in all of the three major great-power struggles of the twentieth century—the two world wars and the Cold War. In trying to determine exactly what accounted for this decisive outcome, it is tempting to trace it to the special traits and intrinsic advantages of liberal democracy.

One possible advantage is democracies' international conduct. Perhaps they more than compensate for carrying a lighter stick abroad with a greater ability to elicit international cooperation through the bonds and discipline of the global market system. This explanation is probably correct for the Cold War, when a greatly expanded global economy was dominated by the democratic powers, but it does not apply to the two world wars. Nor is it true that liberal democracies succeed because they always cling together. Again, this was true, at least as a contributing factor, during the Cold War, when the democratic capitalist camp kept its unity, whereas growing antagonism between the Soviet Union and China pulled the communist bloc apart. During World War I, however, the ideological divide between the two sides was much less clear. The Anglo-French alliance was far from preordained; it was above all a function of balance-of-power calculations rather than liberal cooperation. At the close of the nineteenth century, power politics had brought the United Kingdom and France, bitterly-antagonistic countries, to the brink of war and prompted the United Kingdom to actively seek an alliance with Germany. Liberal Italy's break from the Triple Alliance and joining of the Entente, despite its rivalry with France, was a function of the Anglo-French alliance, as Italy's peninsular location made it hazardous for the country to be on a side opposed to the leading maritime power of the time, the United Kingdom. Similarly, during World War II, France was quickly defeated and taken out of the Allies' side (which was to include nondemocratic Soviet Russia), whereas the right-wing totalitarian powers fought on the same side. Studies of democracies' alliance behavior suggest that democratic regimes show no greater tendency to stick together than other types of regimes.

Nor did the totalitarian capitalist regimes lose World War II because their democratic opponents held a moral high ground that inspired greater exertion from their people, as the historian Richard Overy and others have claimed. During the 1930s and early 1940s, fascism and Nazism were exciting new ideologies that generated massive popular enthusiasm, whereas democracy stood on the ideological defensive, appearing old and dispirited. If anything, the fascist regimes proved more inspiring in wartime than their democratic adversaries, and the battlefield performance of their militaries is widely judged to have been superior.

Liberal democracy's supposedly inherent economic advantage is also far less clear than is often assumed. All of the belligerents in the twentieth century's great struggles proved highly effective in producing for war. During World War I, semiautocratic Germany committed its resources as effectively as its democratic rivals did. After early victories in World War II, Nazi Germany's economic mobilization and military production proved lax during the critical years 1940–42. Well positioned at the time to fundamentally alter the global balance of power by destroying the Soviet Union and straddling all of continental Europe, Germany failed because its armed forces were meagerly supplied for the task. The reasons for this deficiency remain a matter of historical debate, but one of the problems was the existence of competing centers of authority In the Nazi system, in which Hitler's "divide and rule" tactics and party functionaries' jealous guarding of their assigned domains had a chaotic effect. Furthermore, from the fall of France in June 1940 to the German setback before Moscow in December 1941, there was a widespread feeling in Germany that the war had practically been won. All the same, from 1942 onward (by which time is was too late), Germany greatly intensified its economic mobilization and caught up with and even surpassed the liberal democracies in terms of the share of GDP devoted to the war (although its production volume remained much lower than that of the massive U.S. economy). Likewise, levels of economic mobilization in imperial Japan and the Soviet Union exceeded those of the United States and the United Kingdom thanks to ruthless efforts.

Only during the Cold War did the Soviet command economy exhibit deepening structural weaknesses—weaknesses that were directly responsible for the Soviet Union's downfall. The Soviet system had successfully generated the early and intermediate stages of industrialization (albeit at a frightful human cost) and excelled at the regimentalized techniques of mass production during World War II. It also kept abreast militarily during the Cold War. But because of the system's rigidity and lack of incentives, it proved ill equipped to cope with the advanced stages of development and the demands of the information age and globalization.

There is no reason, however, to suppose that the totalitarian capitalist regimes of Nazi Germany and imperial Japan would have proved inferior economically to the democracies had they survived. The inefficiencies that favoritism and unaccountability typically create in such regimes might have been offset by higher levels of social discipline. Because of their more efficient capitalist economies, the right-wing totalitarian powers could have constituted a more viable challenge to the liberal democracies than the Soviet Union did; Nazi Germany was judged to be such a challenge by the Allied powers before and during World War II. The liberal democracies did not possess an inherent advantage over Germany in terms of economic and technological development, as they did in relation to their other great-power rivals.

So why did the democracies win the great struggles of the twentieth century? The reasons are different for each type of adversary. They defeated their nondemocratic capitalist adversaries, Germany and Japan, in war because Germany and Japan were medium-sized countries with limited resource bases and they came up against the far superior—but hardly preordained—economic and military coalition of the democratic powers and Russia or the Soviet Union. The defeat of communism, however, had much more to do with structural factors. The capitalist camp—which after 1945 expanded to include most of the developed world—possessed much greater economic power than the communist bloc, and the inherent inefficiency of the communist economies prevented them from fully exploiting their vast resources and catching up to the West. Together, the Soviet Union and China were larger and thus had the potential to be more powerful than the democratic capitalist camp. Ultimately, they failed because their economic systems limited them, whereas the nondemocratic capitalist powers, Germany and Japan, were defeated because they were too small. Contingency played a decisive role in tipping the balance against the nondemocratic capitalist powers and in favor of the democracies.

American Exception

The most decisive element of contingency was the United States. After all, it was little more than a chance of history that the scion of Anglo-Saxon liberalism would sprout on the other side of the Atlantic, institutionalize its heritage with independence, expand across one of the most habitable and thinly populated territories in the world, feed off of massive immigration from Europe, and so create on a continental scale what was—and still is—by far the world's largest concentration of economic and military might. A liberal regime and other structural traits had a lot to do with the United States' economic success, and even with its size, because of its attractiveness to immigrants. But the United States would scarcely have achieved such greatness had it not been located in a particularly advantageous and vast ecological-geographic niche, as the counterexamples of Canada, Australia, and New Zealand demonstrate. And location, of course, although crucial, was but one necessary condition among many for bringing about the giant and, indeed, *United* States as the paramount political fact of the twentieth century. Contingency was at least as responsible as liberalism for the United States' emergence in the New World and, hence, for its later ability to rescue the Old World.

Throughout the twentieth century, the United States' power consistently surpassed that of the next two strongest states combined, and this decisively tilted the global balance of power in favor of whichever side Washington was on. If any factor gave the liberal democracies their edge, it was above all the existence of the United States rather than any inherent advantage. In fact, had it not been for the United States, liberal democracy may well have lost the great struggles of the twentieth century. This is a sobering thought that is often overlooked in studies of the spread of democracy in the twentieth century, and it makes the world today appear much more contingent and tenuous than linear theories of development suggest. If it were not for the U.S. factor, the judgment of later generations on liberal democracy would probably have echoed the negative verdict on democracy's performance, issued by the fourth-century-BC Greeks, in the wake of Athens' defeat in the Peloponnesian War.

The New Second World

. . . Since 1945, the enormous gravitational pull exerted by the United States and the liberal hegemony has bent patterns of development worldwide.

Because the totalitarian capitalist great powers, Germany and Japan, were crushed in war, and these countries were subsequently threatened by Soviet power, they lent themselves to a sweeping restructuring and democratization. Consequently, smaller countries that chose capitalism over communism had no rival political and economic model to emulate and no powerful international players to turn to other than the liberal democratic camp. These small and medium-sized countries' eventual democratization probably had as much to do with the overwhelming influence of the Western liberal hegemony as with internal processes. Presently, Singapore is the only example of a country with a truly developed economy that still maintains a semiauthoritarian regime, and even it is likely to change under the influence of the liberal order within which it operates. But are Singapore-like great powers that prove resistant to the influence of this order possible?

The question is made relevant by the recent emergence of nondemocratic giants, above all formerly communist and booming authoritarian capitalist China. Russia, too, is retreating from its postcommunist liberalism and assuming an increasingly authoritarian character as its economic clout grows. Some believe that these countries could ultimately become liberal democracies through a combination of internal development, increasing affluence, and outside influence. Alternatively, they may have enough weight to create a new non-democratic but economically advanced Second World. They could establish a powerful authoritarian capitalist order that allies political elites, industrialists, and the military; that is nationalist in orientation; and that participates in the global economy on its own terms, as imperial Germany and imperial Japan did.

It is widely contended that economic and social development creates pressures for democratization that an authoritarian state structure cannot contain. There is also the view that "closed societies" may be able to excel in mass manufacturing but not in the advanced stages of the information economy. The jury on these issues is still out, because the data set is incomplete. Imperial and Nazi Germany stood at the forefront of the advanced scientific and manufacturing economies of their times, but some would argue that their success no longer applies because the information economy is much more diversified. Nondemocratic Singapore has a highly successful information economy, but Singapore is a city-state, not a big country. It will take a long time before China reaches the stage when the possibility of an authoritarian state with an advanced capitalist economy can be tested. All that can be said at the moment is that there is nothing in the historical record to suggest that a transition to democracy by today's authoritarian capitalist powers is inevitable, whereas there is a great deal to suggest that such powers have far greater economic and military potential than their communist predecessors did.

China and Russia represent a return of economically successful authoritarian capitalist powers, which have been absent since the defeat of Germany and Japan in 1945, but they are much larger than the latter two countries ever were. Although Germany was only a medium-sized country uncomfortably squeezed at the center of Europe, it twice nearly broke out of its confines to become a true world power on account of its economic and military might. In 1941, Japan was still behind the leading great powers in terms of economic development, but its growth rate since 1913 had been the highest in the world. Ultimately, however, both Germany and Japan were too small—in terms of population, resources, and potential—to take on the United States. Present-day China, on the other hand, is the largest player in the international system in terms of population and is experiencing spectacular economic growth. By shifting from communism to capitalism, China has switched to a far more efficient brand of authoritarianism. As China rapidly narrows the economic gap with the developed world, the possibility looms that it will become a true authoritarian superpower.

Even in its current bastions in the West, the liberal political and economic consensus is vulnerable to unforeseen developments, such as a crushing economic crisis that could disrupt the global trading system or a resurgence of ethnic strife in a Europe increasingly troubled by immigration and ethnic minorities. Were the West to be hit by such upheavals, support for liberal democracy in Asia, Latin America, and Africa—where adherence to that model is more recent, incomplete, and insecure—could be shaken. A successful nondemocratic Second World could then be regarded by many as an attractive alternative to liberal democracy.

Making the World Safe for Democracy

Although the rise of authoritarian capitalist great powers would not necessarily lead to a nondemocratic hegemony or a war, it might imply that the near-total dominance of liberal democracy since the Soviet Union's collapse will be short-lived and that a universal "democratic peace" is still far off. The new authoritarian capitalist powers could become as deeply integrated into the world economy as imperial Germany and imperial Japan were and not choose to pursue autarky, as Nazi Germany and the communist bloc did. A great-power China may also be less revisionist than the territorially confined Germany and Japan were (although Russia, which is still reeling from having lost an empire, is more likely to tend toward revisionism). Still, Beijing, Moscow, and their future followers might well be on antagonistic terms with the democratic countries, with all the potential for suspicion, insecurity, and conflict that this entails—while holding considerably more power than any of the democracies' past rivals ever did.

So does the greater power potential of authoritarian capitalism mean that the transformation of the former communist great powers may ultimately prove to have been a negative development for global democracy? It is too early to tell. Economically, the liberalization of the former communist countries has given the global economy a tremendous boosts, and there may be more in store. But the possibility of a move toward protectionism by them in the future also needs to be taken into account—and assiduously avoided. It was, after all, the prospect of growing protectionism in the world economy at the turn of the twentieth century and the protectionist bent of the 1930s that helped radicalize the nondemocratic capitalist powers of the time and precipitate both world wars.

On the positive side for the democracies, the collapse of the Soviet Union and its empire stripped Moscow of about half the resources it commanded during the Cold War, with eastern Europe absorbed by a greatly expanded democratic Europe. This is perhaps the most significant change in the global balance of power since the forced postwar democratic reorientation of Germany and Japan under U.S. tutelage. Moreover, China may still eventually democratize, and Russia could reverse its drift away from democracy. If China and Russia do not become democratic, it will be critical that India remain so, both because of its vital role in balancing China and because of the model that it represents for other developing countries.

But the most important factor remains the United States. For all the criticism leveled against it, the United States—and its alliance with Europe—stands as the single most important hope for the future of liberal democracy. Despite its problems and weaknesses, the United States still commands a global position of strength and is likely to retain it even as the authoritarian capitalist powers grow. Not only are its GDP and productivity growth rate the highest in the developed world, but as an immigrant country with about one-fourth the population density of both the European Union and China and one-tenth of that of Japan and India, the United States still has considerable potential to grow—both economically and in terms of population—whereas those others are all experiencing aging and, ultimately, shrinking populations. China's economic growth rate is among the highest in the world, and given the country's huge population and still low levels of development, such growth harbors the most radical potential for change in global power relations. But even if China's superior growth rate persists and its GDP surpasses that of the United States by the 2020s, as is often forecast, China will still have just over one-third of the United States' wealth per capita and, hence, considerably less economic and military power. Closing that far more challenging gap with the developed world would take several more decades. Furthermore, GDP alone is known to be a poor measure of a country's power, and evoking it to celebrate China's ascendency is highly misleading. As it was during the twentieth century, the U.S. factor remains the greatest guarantee that liberal democracy will not be thrown on the defensive and relegated to a vulnerable position on the periphery of the international system.

(handwritten annotations)

① what is fukuyama's proposal / thesis (pg. 10)?

② What is huntington's ↑ ? How does that relate?

③ What does Huntington mean when he talks about civ. civilizations?

④ What civilization?

⑤ when will civilization will crash?

Fukuyama → there will be no dominant rival to liberal democratic captalism, but there can still be conflict

H → there will be rivalry, that is culture-based.

![[symbol]] 1.4

The Clash of Civilizations?

Samuel P. Huntington

In *The Third Wave*, published in 1991, Samuel Huntington agreed with Francis Fukuyama [1.1] that the future would be relatively beneficent. (See 1.2, a selection from *The Third Wave*.) Not long after, however, he claimed in "The Clash of Civilizations?" that the future might be quite turbulent. In previous periods in world history, he asserts, major conflicts pitted states against each other. However, future conflicts will involve cultural differences, that is, clashes of civilizations. He predicts that the most important cleavage of all will be "the West versus the rest."

"The Clash of Civilizations?" was widely cited after the September 11, 2001, when the attacks on the Pentagon and New York's World Trade Center seemed to corroborate his argument. However, critics, such as Amartya Sen [4.1], have questioned Huntington's argument. For one thing, they claim, there is no necessary or inevitable clash of civilizations. All civilizations share certain core values, for example, those codified in the UN Universal Declaration of Human Rights. Further, most of the time in most places, people from different cultural and religious backgrounds coexist peacefully. Thirdly, cultures are not the homogeneous entities implied by "The Clash of Civilizations?"; they are complex, often internally divided, and changing. Moreover, many scholars argue that states remain central actors in world conflicts. How well does Huntington's thesis withstand these criticisms?

The Next Pattern of Conflict

World politics is entering a new phase, and intellectuals have not hesitated to proliferate visions of what it will be—the end of history, the return of traditional rivalries between nation states, and the decline of the nation state from the conflicting pulls of tribalism and globalism, among others. Each of these visions catches aspects of the emerging reality. Yet they all miss a crucial, indeed a central, aspect of what global politics is likely to be in the coming years.

It is my hypothesis that the fundamental source of conflict in this new world will not be primarily ideological or primarily economic. The great divisions among humankind and the dominating source of conflict will be cultural.

Nation states will remain the most powerful actors in world affairs, but the principal conflicts of global politics will occur between nations and groups of different civilizations. The clash of civilizations will dominate global politics. The fault lines between civilizations will be the battle lines of the future.

Conflict between civilizations will be the latest phase in the evolution of conflict in the modern world. For a century and a half after the emergence of the modern international system with the Peace of Westphalia, the conflicts of the Western world were largely among princes—emperors, absolute monarchs and constitutional monarchs attempting to expand their bureaucracies, their armies, their mercantilist economic strength and, most important, the territory they ruled. In the process they created nation states, and beginning with the French Revolution the principal lines of conflict were between nations rather than princes. In 1793, as R. R. Palmer put it, "The wars of kings were over; the wars of peoples had begun." This nineteenth-century pattern lasted until the end of World War 1. Then, as a result of the Russian Revolution and the reaction against it, the conflict of nations yielded to the conflict of ideologies, first among communism, fascism-Nazism and liberal democracy, and then between communism and liberal democracy. During the Cold War, this latter conflict became embodied in the struggle between the two superpowers, neither of which was a nation state in the classical European sense and each of which defined its identity in terms of its ideology. . . .

. . . With the end of the Cold War, international politics . . . becomes the interaction between the West and non-Western civilizations and among non-Western civilizations. In the politics of civilizations, the peoples and governments of non-Western civilizations no longer remain the objects of history as targets of Western colonialism but join the West as movers and shapers of history.

The Nature of Civilizations

During the cold war the world was divided into the First, Second and Third Worlds. Those divisions are no longer relevant. It is far more meaningful now to group countries not in terms of their political or economic systems or in terms of their level of economic development but rather in terms of their culture and civilization.

What do we mean when we talk of a civilization? A civilization is a cultural entity. Villages, regions, ethnic groups, nationalities, religious groups, all have distinct cultures at different levels of cultural heterogeneity. The culture of a village in southern Italy may be different from that of a village in northern Italy, but both will share in a common Italian culture that distinguishes them from German villages. European communities, in turn, will share cultural features that distinguish them from Arab or Chinese communities. Arabs, Chinese and Westerners, however, are not part of any broader cultural entity. They constitute civilizations. A civilization is thus the highest cultural grouping of people and the broadest level of cultural identity people have short of that which distinguishes

[handwritten: European Civilization / Chinese Civilization / Asian Civilization]

humans from other species. It is defined both by common objective elements, such as language, history, religion, customs, institutions, and by the subjective self-identification of people. People have levels of identity: a resident of Rome may define himself with varying degrees of intensity as a Roman, an Italian, a Catholic, a Christian, a European, a Westerner. The civilization to which he belongs is the broadest level of identification with which he intensely identifies. People can and do redefine their identities and, as a result, the composition and boundaries of civilizations change.

Civilizations may involve a large number of people, as with China ("a civilization pretending to be a state," as Lucian Pye put it), or a very small number of people, such as the Anglophone Caribbean. A civilization may include several nation states, as is the case with Western, Latin American and Arab civilizations, or only one, as is the case with Japanese civilization. Civilizations obviously blend and overlap, and may include subcivilizations. Western civilization has two major variants, European and North American, and Islam has its Arab, Turkic and Malay subdivisions. Civilizations are nonetheless meaningful entities, and while the lines between them are seldom sharp, they are real. Civilizations are dynamic; they rise and fall; they divide and merge. And, as any student of history knows, civilizations disappear and are buried in the sands of time.

Westerners tend to think of nation states as the principal actors in global affairs. They have been that, however, for only a few centuries. The broader reaches of human history have been the history of civilizations. In *A Study of History*, Arnold Toynbee identified 21 major civilizations; only six of them exist in the contemporary world.

[handwritten: EX. Western Civilization / Includes Europe & North America]

Why Civilizations Will Clash

Civilization identity will be increasingly important in the future, and the world will be shaped in large measure by the interactions among seven or eight major civilizations. These include Western, Confucian, Japanese, Islamic, Hindu, Slavic-Orthodox, Latin American and possibly African civilization. The most important conflicts of the future will occur along the cultural fault lines separating these civilizations from one another.

Why will this be the case?

First, differences among civilizations are not only real; they are basic. Civilizations are differentiated from each other by history, language, culture, tradition and, most important, religion. The people of different civilizations have different views on the relations between God and man, the individual and the group, the citizen and the state, parents and children, husband and wife, as well as differing views of the relative importance of rights and responsibilities, liberty and authority, equality and hierarchy. These differences are the product of centuries. They will not soon disappear. They are far more fundamental than differences among political ideologies and political regimes. Differences do not

[handwritten: Civilizations many differences → / Language, history, importance of rights, / authority, etc.]

necessarily mean conflict, and conflict does not necessarily mean violence. Over the centuries, however, differences among civilizations have generated the most prolonged and the most violent conflicts.

Second, the world is becoming a smaller place. The interactions between peoples of different civilizations are increasing; these increasing interactions intensify civilization consciousness and awareness of differences between civilizations and commonalities within civilizations. North African immigration to France generates hostility among Frenchmen and at the same time increased receptivity to immigration by "good" European Catholic Poles. Americans react far more negatively to Japanese investment than to larger investments from Canada and European countries. Similarly, as Donald Horowitz has pointed out, "An Ibo may be . . . an Owerri Ibo or an Onitsha Ibo in what was the Eastern region of Nigeria. In Lagos, he is simply an Ibo. In London, he is a Nigerian. In New York, he is an African." The interactions among peoples of different civilizations enhance the civilization-consciousness of people that, in turn, invigorates differences and animosities stretching or thought to stretch back deep into history.

Third, the processes of economic modernization and social change throughout the world are separating people from longstanding local identities. They also weaken the nation state as a source of identity. In much of the world religion has moved in to fill this gap, often in the form of movements that are labeled "fundamentalist." Such movements are found in Western Christianity, Judaism, Buddhism and Hinduism, as well as in Islam. In most countries and most religions the people active in fundamentalist movements are young, college-educated, middle-class technicians, professionals and business persons. The "unsecularization of the world," George Weigel has remarked, "is one of the dominant social facts of life in the late twentieth century." The revival of religion, "la revanche de Dieu," as Gilles Kepel labeled it, provides a basis for identity and commitment that transcends national boundaries and unites civilizations.

Fourth, the growth of civilization-consciousness is enhanced by the dual role of the West. On the one hand, the West is at a peak of power. At the same time, however, and perhaps as a result, a return to the roots phenomenon is occurring among non-Western civilizations. Increasingly one hears references to trends toward a turning inward and "Asianization" in Japan, the end of the Nehru legacy and the "Hinduization" of India, the failure of Western ideas of socialism and nationalism and hence "re-Islamization" of the Middle East, and now a debate over Westernization versus Russianization in Boris Yeltsin's country. A West at the peak of its power confronts non-Wests that increasingly have the desire, the will and the resources to shape the world in non-Western ways.

In the past, the elites of non-Western societies were usually the people who were most involved with the West, had been educated at Oxford, the Sorbonne or Sandhurst, and had absorbed Western attitudes and values. At the same time, the populace in non-Western countries often remained deeply imbued with the indigenous culture. Now, however, these relationships are being reversed. A de-Westernization and indigenization of elites is occurring in many non-Western countries at the same time that Western, usually American, cultures, styles and habits become more popular among the mass of the people.

Fifth, cultural characteristics and differences are less mutable and hence less easily compromised and resolved than political and economic ones. In the former Soviet Union, communists can become democrats, the rich can become poor and the poor rich, but Russians cannot become Estonians and Azeris cannot become Armenians. In class and ideological conflicts, the key question was "Which side are you on?" and people could and did choose sides and change sides. In conflicts between civilizations, the question is "What are you?" That is a given that cannot be changed. And as we know, from Bosnia to the Caucasus to the Sudan, the wrong answer to that question can mean a bullet in the head. Even more than ethnicity, religion discriminates sharply and exclusively among people. A person can be half-French and half-Arab and simultaneously even a citizen of two countries. It is more difficult to be half-Catholic and half-Muslim.

Finally, economic regionalism is increasing. The proportions of total trade that were intraregional rose between 1980 and 1989 from 51 percent to 59 percent in Europe, 33 percent to 37 percent in East Asia, and 32 percent to 36 percent in North America. The importance of regional economic blocs is likely to continue to increase in the future. On the one hand, successful economic regionalism will reinforce civilization-consciousness. On the other hand, economic regionalism may succeed only when it is rooted in a common civilization. The European Community rests on the shared foundation of European culture and Western Christianity. The success of the North American Free Trade Agreement depends on the convergence now underway of Mexican, Canadian and American cultures. Japan, in contrast, faces difficulties in creating a comparable economic entity in East Asia because Japan is a society and civilization unique to itself. However strong the trade and investment links Japan may develop with other East Asian countries, its cultural differences with those countries inhibit and perhaps preclude its promoting regional economic integration like that in Europe and North America.

Common culture, in contrast, is clearly facilitating the rapid expansion of the economic relations between the People's Republic of China and Hong Kong, Taiwan, Singapore and the overseas Chinese communities in other Asian countries. With the Cold War over, cultural commonalities increasingly overcome ideological differences, and mainland China and Taiwan move closer together. If cultural commonality is a prerequisite for economic integration, the principal East Asian economic bloc of the future is likely to be centered on China. This bloc is, in fact, already coming into existence. . . .

Culture and religion also form the basis of the Economic Cooperation Organization, which brings together ten non-Arab Muslim countries: Iran, Pakistan, Turkey, Azerbaijan, Kazakhstan, Kyrgyzstan, Turkmenistan, Tadjikistan, Uzbekistan and Afghanistan. One impetus to the revival and expansion of this organization, founded originally in the 1960s by Turkey, Pakistan and Iran, is the realization by the leaders of several of these countries that they had no chance of admission to the European Community. Similarly, Caricom, the Central American Common Market and Mercosur rest on common cultural foundations. Efforts to build a broader Caribbean-Central American economic entity bridging the Anglo-Latin divide, however, have to date failed.

As people define their identity in ethnic and religious terms, they are likely to see an "us" versus "them" relation existing between themselves and people of different ethnicity or religion. The end of ideologically defined states in Eastern Europe and the former Soviet Union permits traditional ethnic identities and animosities to come to the fore. Differences in culture and religion create differences over policy issues, ranging from human rights to immigration to trade and commerce to the environment. Geographical propinquity gives rise to conflicting territorial claims from Bosnia to Mindanao. Most important, the efforts of the West to promote its values of democracy and liberalism as universal values, to maintain its military predominance and to advance its economic interests engender countering responses from other civilizations. Decreasingly able to mobilize support and form coalitions on the basis of ideology, governments and groups will increasingly attempt to mobilize support by appealing to common religion and civilization identity.

The clash of civilizations thus occurs at two levels. At the micro-level, adjacent groups along the fault lines between civilizations struggle, often violently, over the control of territory and each other. At the macro-level, states from different civilizations compete for relative military and economic power, struggle over the control of international institutions and third parties, and competitively promote their particular political and religious values.

The Fault Lines between Civilizations

The fault lines between civilizations are replacing the political and ideological boundaries of the Cold War as the flash points for crisis and bloodshed. The Cold War began when the Iron Curtain divided Europe politically and ideologically. The Cold War ended with the end of the Iron Curtain. As the ideological division of Europe has disappeared, the cultural division of Europe between Western Christianity, on the one hand, and Orthodox Christianity and Islam, on the other, has reemerged. The most significant dividing line in Europe, as William Wallace has suggested, may well be the eastern boundary of Western Christianity in the year 1500. This line runs along what are now the boundaries between Finland and Russia and between the Baltic states and Russia, cuts through Belarus and Ukraine separating the more Catholic western Ukraine from Orthodox eastern Ukraine, swings westward separating Transylvania from the rest of Romania, and then goes through Yugoslavia almost exactly along the line now separating Croatia and Slovenia from the rest of Yugoslavia. In the Balkans this line, of course, coincides with the historic boundary between the

Hapsburg and Ottoman empires. The peoples to the north and west of this line are Protestant or Catholic; they shared the common experiences of European history—feudalism, the Renaissance, the Reformation, the Enlightenment, the French Revolution, the Industrial Revolution; they are generally economically better off than the peoples to the east; and they may now look forward to increasing involvement in a common European economy and to the consolidation of democratic political systems. The peoples to the east and south of this line are Orthodox or Muslim; they historically belonged to the Ottoman or Tsarist empires and were only lightly touched by the shaping events in the rest of Europe; they are generally less advanced economically; they seem much less likely to develop stable democratic political systems. The Velvet Curtain of culture has replaced the Iron Curtain of ideology as the most significant dividing line in Europe. As the events in Yugoslavia show, it is not only a line of difference; it is also at times a line of bloody conflict.

Conflict along the fault line between Western and Islamic civilizations has been going on for 1,300 years. After the founding of Islam, the Arab and Moorish surge west and north only ended at Tours in 732. From the eleventh to the thirteenth century the Crusaders attempted with temporary success to bring Christianity and Christian rule to the Holy Land. From the fourteenth to the seventeenth century, the Ottoman Turks reversed the balance, extended their sway over the Middle East and the Balkans, captured Constantinople, and twice laid siege to Vienna. In the nineteenth and early twentieth centuries as Ottoman power declined Britain, France, and Italy established Western control over most of North Africa and the Middle East.

After World War II, the West, in turn, began to retreat; the colonial empires disappeared; first Arab nationalism and then Islamic fundamentalism manifested themselves; the West became heavily dependent on the Persian Gulf countries for its energy; the oil-rich Muslim countries became money-rich and, when they wished to, weapons-rich. Several wars occurred between Arabs and Israel (created by the West). France fought a bloody and ruthless war in Algeria for most of the 1950s; British and French forces invaded Egypt in 1956; American forces went into Lebanon in 1958; subsequently American forces returned to Lebanon, attacked Libya, and engaged in various military encounters with Iran; Arab and Islamic terrorists, supported by at least three Middle Eastern governments, employed the weapon of the weak and bombed Western planes and installations and seized Western hostages. This warfare between Arabs and the West culminated in 1990, when the United States sent a massive army to the Persian Gulf to defend some Arab countries against aggression by another. In its aftermath NATO planning is increasingly directed to potential threats and instability along its "southern tier."

This centuries-old military interaction between the West and Islam is unlikely to decline. It could become more virulent. The Gulf War left some Arabs feeling proud that Saddam Hussein had attacked Israel and stood up to the West. It also left many feeling humiliated and resentful of the West's military presence in the Persian Gulf, the West's overwhelming military dominance, and their apparent inability to shape their own destiny. Many Arab countries, in addition to the oil exporters, are reaching levels of economic and social development where autocratic forms of government become inappropriate and efforts to introduce democracy become stronger. Some openings in Arab political systems have already occurred. The principal beneficiaries of these openings have been Islamist movements. In the Arab world, in short, Western democracy strengthens anti-Western political forces. This may be a passing phenomenon, but it surely complicates relations between Islamic countries and the West.

Those relations are also complicated by demography. The spectacular population growth in Arab countries, particularly in North Africa, has led to increased migration to Western Europe. The movement within Western Europe toward minimizing internal boundaries has sharpened political sensitivities with respect to this development. In Italy, France and Germany, racism is increasingly open, and political reactions and violence against Arab and Turkish migrants have become more intense and more widespread since 1990.

On both sides the interaction between Islam and the West is seen as a clash of civilizations. The West's "next confrontation," observes M. J. Akbar, an Indian Muslim author, "is definitely going to come from the Muslim world. It is in the sweep of the Islamic nations from the Maghreb to Pakistan that the struggle for a new world order will begin." Bernard Lewis comes to a similar conclusion:

> We are facing a mood and a movement far transcending the level of issues and policies and the governments that pursue them. This is no less than a clash of civilizations— the perhaps irrational but surely historic reaction of an ancient rival against our Judeo-Christian heritage, our secular present, and the worldwide expansion of both.[1]

Historically, the other great antagonistic interaction of Arab Islamic civilization has been with the pagan, animist, and now increasingly Christian black peoples to the south. In the past, this antagonism was epitomized in the image of Arab slave dealers and black slaves. It has been reflected in the ongoing civil war in the Sudan between Arabs and blacks, the fighting in Chad between Libyan-supported insurgents and the government, the tensions between Orthodox Christians and Muslims in the Horn of Africa, and the political conflicts, recurring riots and communal violence between Muslims and Christians in Nigeria. The modernization of Africa and the spread of Christianity are likely to enhance the probability of violence along this fault line. Symptomatic of the intensification of this conflict was the Pope John Paul II's speech in Khartoum in February 1993 attacking the actions of the Sudan's Islamist government against the Christian minority there.

On the northern border of Islam, conflict has increasingly erupted between Orthodox and Muslim peoples, including the carnage of Bosnia and Sarajevo, the simmering violence between Serb and Albanian, the tenuous relations between

---

[1] Bernard Lewis, "The Roots of Muslim Rage," *The Atlantic Monthly,* vol. 266, September 1990, p. 60; *Time,* June 15, 1992, pp. 24–28.

examples

Bulgarians and their Turkish minority, the violence between Ossetians and Ingush, the unremitting slaughter of each other by Armenians and Azeris, the tense relations between Russians and Muslims in Central Asia, and the deployment of Russian troops to protect Russian interests in the Caucasus and Central Asia. Religion reinforces the revital of ethnic identities and restimulates Russian fears about the security of their southern borders. This concern is well captured by Archie Roosevelt:

> Much of Russian history concerns the struggle between the Slavs and the Turkic peoples on their borders, which dates back to the foundation of the Russian state more than a thousand years ago. In the Slavs' millennium-long confrontation with their eastern neighbors lies the key to an understanding not only of Russian history, but Russian character. To understand Russian realities today one has to have a concept of the great Turkic ethnic group that has preoccupied Russians through the centuries.[2]

Russians vs. Turks (rivalry)

The conflict of civilizations is deeply rooted elsewhere in Asia. The historic clash between Muslim and Hindu in the subcontinent manifests itself now not only in the rivalry between Pakistan and India but also in intensifying religious strife within India between increasingly militant Hindu groups and India's substantial Muslim minority. The destruction of the Ayodhya mosque in December 1992 brought to the fore the issue of whether India will remain a secular democratic state or become a Hindu one. In East Asia, China has outstanding territorial disputes with most of its neighbors. It has pursued a ruthless policy toward the Buddhist people of Tibet, and it is pursuing an increasingly ruthless policy toward its Turkic-Muslim minority. With the Cold War over, the underlying differences between China and the United States have reasserted themselves in areas such as human rights, trade and weapons proliferation. These differences are unlikely to moderate. A "new cold war," Deng Xaioping reportedly asserted in 1991, is under way between China and America.

examples

The same phrase has been applied to the increasingly difficult relations between Japan and the United States. Here cultural difference exacerbates economic conflict. People on each side allege racism on the other, but at least on the American side the antipathies are not racial but cultural. The basic values, attitudes, behavioral patterns of the two societies could hardly be more different. The economic issues between the United States and Europe are no less serious than those between the United States and Japan, but they do not have the same political salience and emotional intensity because the differences between American culture and European culture are so much less than those between American civilization and Japanese civilization.

The interactions between civilizations vary greatly in the extent to which they are likely to be characterized by violence. Economic competition clearly predominates between the American and European subcivilizations of the West and between both of them and Japan. On the Eurasian continent, however, the

---

[2] Archie Roosevelt, *For Lust of Knowing,* Boston: Little, Brown, 1988, pp 332–333.

proliferation of ethnic conflict, epitomized at the extreme in "ethnic cleansing," has not been totally random. It has been most frequent and most violent between groups belonging to different civilizations. In Eurasia the great historic fault lines between civilizations are once more aflame. This is particularly true along the boundaries of the crescent-shaped Islamic bloc of nations from the bulge of Africa to central Asia. Violence also occurs between Muslims, on the one hand, and Orthodox Serbs in the Balkans, Jews in Israel, Hindus in India, Buddhists in Burma and Catholics in the Philippines. Islam has bloody borders. . . .

The West Versus the Rest

Identify the reasons why the western civilization is largely in conflict with most others.

The West is now at an extraordinary peak of power in relation to other civilizations. Its superpower opponent has disappeared from the map. Military conflict among Western states is unthinkable, and Western military power is unrivaled. Apart from Japan, the West faces no economic challenge. It dominates international political and security institutions and with Japan international economic institutions. Global political and security issues are effectively settled by a directorate of the United States, Britain and France, world economic issues by a directorate of the United States, Germany and Japan, all of which maintain extraordinarily close relations with each other to the exclusion of lesser and largely non-Western countries. Decisions made at the U.N. Security Council or in the International Monetary Fund that reflect the interests of the West are presented to the world as reflecting the desires of the world community. The very phrase "the world community" has become the euphemistic collective noun (replacing "the Free World") to give global legitimacy to actions reflecting the interests of the United States and other Western powers.[3] Through the IMF and other international economic institutions, the West promotes its economic interests and imposes on other nations the economic policies it thinks appropriate. In any poll of non-Western peoples, the IMF undoubtedly would win the support of finance ministers and a few others, but get an overwhelmingly unfavorable rating from just about everyone else, who would agree with Georgy Arbatov's characterization of IMF officials as "neo-Bolsheviks who love expropriating other people's money, imposing undemocratic and alien rules of economic and political conduct and stifling economic freedom."

Western domination of the U.N. Security Council and its decisions, tempered only by occasional abstention by China, produced U.N. legitimation of the

---

[3] Almost invariably Western leaders claim they are acting on behalf of "the world community." One minor lapse occurred during the run-up to the Gulf War. In an interview on "Good Morning America," Dec. 21, 1990, British Prime Minister John Major referred to the actions "the West" was taking against Saddam Hussein. He quickly corrected himself and subsequently referred to "the world community." He was, however, right when he erred.

West's use of force to drive Iraq out of Kuwait and its elimination of Iraq's sophisticated weapons and capacity to produce such weapons. It also produced the quite unprecedented action by the United States, Britain and France in getting the Security Council to demand that Libya hand over the Pan Am 103 bombing suspects and then to impose sanctions when Libya refused. After defeating the largest Arab army, the West did not hesitate to throw its weight around in the Arab world. The West in effect is using international institutions, military power and economic resources to run the world in ways that will maintain Western predominance, protect Western interests and promote Western political and economic values.

That at least is the way in which non-Westerners see the new world, and there is a significant element of truth in their view. Differences in power and struggles for military, economic and institutional power are thus one source of conflict between the West and other civilizations. Differences in culture, that is basic values and beliefs, are a second source of conflict. V. S. Naipaul has argued that Western civilization is the "universal civilization" that "fits all men." At a superficial level much of Western culture has indeed permeated the rest of the world. At a more basic level, however, Western concepts differ fundamentally from those prevalent in other civilizations. Western ideas of individualism, liberalism, constitutionalism, human rights, equality, liberty, the rule of law, democracy, free markets, the separation of church and state, often have little resonance in Islamic, Confucian, Japanese, Hindu, Buddhist or Orthodox cultures. Western efforts to propagate such ideas produce instead a reaction against "human rights imperialism" and a reaffirmation of indigenous values, as can be seen in the support for religious fundamentalism by the younger generation in non-Western cultures. The very notion that there could be a "universal civilization" is a Western idea, directly at odds with the particularism of most Asian societies and their emphasis on what distinguishes one people from another. Indeed, the author of a review of 100 comparative studies of values in different societies concluded that "the values that are most important in the West are least important worldwide."[4] In the political realm, of course, these differences are most manifest in the efforts of the United States and other Western powers to induce other peoples to adopt Western ideas concerning democracy and human rights. Modern democratic government originated in the West. When it has developed in non-Western societies it has usually been the product of Western colonialism or imposition.

The central axis of world politics in the future is likely to be, in Kishore Mahbubani's phrase, the conflict between "the West and the Rest" and the responses of non-Western civilizations to Western power and values.[5] Those responses generally take one or a combination of three forms. At one extreme,

---

[4] Harry C. Triandis, *The New York Times*, Dec. 25, 1990, p. 41, and "Cross-Cultural Studies of Individualism and Collectivism," Nebraska Symposium on Motivation, vol. 37, 1989, pp. 41–133.

[5] Kishore Mahbubani, "The West and the Rest," *The National Interest*, Summer 1992, pp. 3–13.

non-Western states can, like Burma and North Korea, attempt to pursue a course of isolation, to insulate their societies from penetration or "corruption" by the West, and, in effect, to opt out of participation in the Western-dominated global community. The costs of this course, however, are high, and few states have pursued it exclusively. A second alternative, the equivalent of "band-wagoning" in international relations theory, is to attempt to join the West and accept its values and institutions. The third alternative is to attempt to "balance" the West by developing economic and military power and cooperating with other non-Western societies against the West, while preserving indigenous values and institutions; in short, to modernize but not to Westernize. . . .

The Confucian-Islamic Connection → non-westerners formed
to create their own political/economic sphere of power seperate from the west.

The obstacles to non-Western countries joining the West vary considerably. They are least for Latin American and East European countries. They are greater for the Orthodox countries of the former Soviet Union. They are still greater for Muslim, Confucian, Hindu and Buddhist societies. Japan has established a unique position for itself as an associate member of the West: it is in the West in some respects but clearly not of the West in important dimensions. Those countries that for reason of culture and power do not wish to, or cannot, join the West compete with the West by developing their own economic, military and political power. They do this by promoting their internal development and by cooperating with other non-Western countries. The most prominent form of this cooperation is the Confucian-Islamic connection that has emerged to challenge Western interests, values and power.

Almost without exception, Western countries are reducing their military power; under Yeltsin's leadership so also is Russia. China, North Korea and several Middle Eastern states, however, are significantly expanding their military capabilities. They are doing this by the import of arms from Western and non-Western sources and by the development of indigenous arms industries. One result is the emergence of what Charles Krauthammer has called "Weapon States," and the Weapon States are not Western states. Another result is the redefinition of arms control, which is a Western concept and a Western goal. During the Cold War the primary purpose of arms control was to establish a stable military balance between the United States and its allies and the Soviet Union and its allies. In the post-Cold War world the primary objective of arms control is to prevent the development by non-Western societies of military capabilities that could threaten Western interests. The West attempts to do this through international agreements, economic pressure and controls on the transfer of arms and weapons technologies.

The conflict between the West and the Confucian-Islamic states focuses largely, although not exclusively, on nuclear, chemical and biological weapons, ballistic missiles and other sophisticated means for delivering them, and the guidance, intelligence and other electronic capabilities for achieving that goal.

The West promotes nonproliferation as a universal norm and nonproliferation treaties and inspections as means of realizing that norm. It also threatens a variety of sanctions against those who promote the spread of sophisticated weapons and proposes some benefits for those who do not. The attention of the West focuses, naturally, on nations that are actually or potentially hostile to the West.

The non-Western nations, on the other hand, assert their right to acquire and to deploy whatever weapons they think necessary for their security. They also have absorbed, to the full, the truth of the response of the Indian defense minister when asked what lesson he learned from the Gulf War: "Don't fight the United States unless you have nuclear weapons." Nuclear weapons, chemical weapons and missiles are viewed, probably erroneously, as the potential equalizer of superior Western conventional power. China, of course, already has nuclear weapons; Pakistan and India have the capability to deploy them. North Korea, Iran, Iraq, Libya and Algeria appear to be attempting to acquire them. A top Iranian official has declared that all Muslim states should acquire nuclear weapons, and in 1988 the president of Iran reportedly issued a directive calling for development of "offensive and defensive chemical, biological and radiological weapons."

Centrally important to the development of counter-West military capabilities is the sustained expansion of China's military power and its means to create military power. Buoyed by spectacular economic development, China is rapidly increasing its military spending and vigorously moving forward with the modernization of its armed forces. It is purchasing weapons from the former Soviet states; it is developing long-range missiles; in 1992 it tested a one-megaton nuclear device. It is developing power-projection capabilities, acquiring aerial refueling technology, and trying to purchase an aircraft carrier. Its military buildup and assertion of sovereignty over the South China Sea are provoking a multilateral regional arms race in East Asia. China is also a major exporter of arms and weapons technology. It has exported materials to Libya and Iraq that could be used to manufacture nuclear weapons and nerve gas. It has helped Algeria build a reactor suitable for nuclear weapons research and production. China has sold to Iran nuclear technology that American officials believe could only be used to create weapons and apparently has shipped components of 300-mile-range missiles to Pakistan. North Korea has had a nuclear weapons program under way for some while and has sold advanced missiles and missile technology to Syria and Iran. The flow of weapons and weapons technology is generally from East Asia to the Middle East. There is, however, some movement in the reverse direction; China has received Stinger missiles from Pakistan.

A Confucian-Islamic military connection has thus come into being, designed to promote acquisition by its members of the weapons and weapons technologies needed to counter the military power of the West. It may or may not last. At present, however, it is, as Dave McCurdy has said, "a renegades' mutual support pact, run by the proliferators and their backers." A new form of arms competition is thus occurring between Islamic-Confucian states and the West. In an old-fashioned arms race, each side developed its own arms to balance or to achieve superiority against the other side. In this new form of arms competition, one side is developing its arms and the other side is attempting not to balance but to limit and prevent that arms build-up while at the same time reducing its own military capabilities.

Implications for the West

This article does not argue that civilization identities will replace all other identities, that nation states will disappear, that each civilization will become a single coherent political entity, that groups within a civilization will not conflict with and even fight each other. This paper does set forth the hypotheses that differences between civilizations are real and important; civilization-consciousness is increasing; conflict between civilizations will supplant ideological and other forms of conflict as the dominant global form of conflict; international relations, historically a game played out within Western civilization, will increasingly be de-Westernized and become a game in which non-Western civilizations are actors and not simply objects; successful political, security and economic international institutions are more likely to develop within civilizations than across civilizations; conflicts between groups in different civilizations will be more frequent, more sustained and more violent than conflicts between groups in the same civilization; violent conflicts between groups in different civilizations are the most likely and most dangerous source of escalation that could lead to global wars; the paramount axis of world politics will be the relations between "the West and the Rest"; the elites in some torn non-Western countries will try to make their countries part of the West, but in most cases face major obstacles to accomplishing this; a central focus of conflict for the immediate future will be between the West and several Islamic-Confucian states.

This is not to advocate the desirability of conflicts between civilizations. It is to set forth descriptive hypotheses as to what the future may be like. If these are plausible hypotheses, however, it is necessary to consider their implications for Western policy. These implications should be divided between short-term advantage and long-term accommodation. In the short term it is clearly in the interest of the West to promote greater cooperation and unity within its own civilization, particularly between its European and North American components; to incorporate into the West societies in Eastern Europe and Latin America whose cultures are close to those of the West; to promote and maintain cooperative relations with Russia and Japan; to prevent escalation of local inter-civilization conflicts into major inter-civilization wars; to limit the expansion of the military strength of Confucian and Islamic states; to moderate the reduction of Western military capabilities and maintain military superiority in East and Southwest Asia; to exploit differences and conflicts among Confucian and Islamic states; to support in other civilizations groups sympathetic to Western values and interests; to strengthen international institutions that reflect and legitimate Western interests and values and to promote the involvement of non-Western states in those institutions.

In the longer term other measures would be called for. Western civilization is both Western and modern. Non-Western civilizations have attempted to become modern without becoming Western. To date only Japan has fully succeeded in this quest. Non-Western civilizations will continue to attempt to acquire the wealth, technology, skills, machines and weapons that are part of being modern. They will also attempt to reconcile this modernity with their traditional culture and values. Their economic and military strength relative to the West will increase. Hence the West will increasingly have to accommodate these non-Western modern civilizations whose power approaches that of the West but whose values and interests differ significantly from those of the West. This will require the West to maintain the economic and military power necessary to protect its interests in relation to these civilizations. It will also, however, require the West to develop a more profound understanding of the basic religious and philosophical assumptions underlying other civilizations and the ways in which people in those civilizations see their interests. It will require an effort to identify elements of commonality between Western and other civilizations. For the relevant future, there will be no universal civilization, but instead a world of different civilizations, each of which will have to learn to coexist with the others.

1.5

Us and Them

Jerry Z. Muller

Jerry Muller suggests that most Americans naively believe that ethnic harmony is the rule, ethnic conflict the exception. (As Walker Connor, a leading specialist on ethnicity, describes in selection 5.5, ethnicity is based on the belief that one shares kinship with others, that is, that members of a group are linked by common descent.) On the contrary, according to Muller, conflict among ethnic groups is extremely common in many settings. In extreme cases, in the phenomenon that comparativists describe as ethnonationalism, members of an ethnic group may demand their own ethnically homogenous state. This involves gaining control of a state in a particular territory and expelling members of other ethnic groups. (The misleadingly innocent term *ethnic cleansing* has become widely used to describe the violent expulsion or destruction of ethnic minorities.)

Ethnonationalism is one of the major causes of violence in the world today. In light of this disturbing situation, comparativists have devoted extensive efforts to understanding the sources of ethnonationalism and have proposed ways to minimize interethnic violence. (For some examples, see Hale [6.4] and Reilly [6.5].)

Muller is quite pessimistic about the prospects for reducing ethnic violence. He suggests that ethnonationalism is associated with modernization and therefore "is likely to gain ground in [modernizing] societies." He suggests that in some circumstances, "partition may be the most humane lasting solution to such intense communal conflicts."

Can you suggest some pros and cons of this possible solution to ethnic conflict? The next selection consists of responses to Muller's article by two sets of critics, as well as his reply.

The Enduring Power of Ethnic Nationalism

Projecting their own experience onto the rest of the world, Americans generally belittle the role of ethnic nationalism in politics. After all, in the United States people of varying ethnic origins live cheek by jowl in relative peace. Within two or three generations of immigration, their ethnic identities are attenuated

---

Jerry Z. Muller, "Us and Them," *Foreign Affairs* 87, no. 2 (March/April 2008): 18–35 (excerpts).

by cultural assimilation and intermarriage. Surely, things cannot be so different elsewhere.

Americans also find ethnonationalism discomfiting both intellectually and morally. Social scientists go to great lengths to demonstrate that it is a product not of nature but of culture, often deliberately constructed. And ethicists scorn value systems based on narrow group identities rather than cosmopolitanism.

But none of this will make ethnonationalism go away. Immigrants to the United States usually arrive with a willingness to fit into their new country and reshape their identities accordingly. But for those who remain behind in lands where their ancestors have lived for generations, if not centuries, political identities often take ethnic form, producing competing communal claims to political power. The creation of a peaceful regional order of nation-states has usually been the product of a violent process of ethnic separation. In areas where that separation has not yet occurred, politics is apt to remain ugly. . . .

The Politics of Identity

There are two major ways of thinking about national identity. One is that all people who live within a country's borders are part of the nation, regardless of their ethnic, racial, or religious origins. This liberal or civic nationalism is the conception with which contemporary Americans are most likely to identify. But the liberal view has competed with and often lost out to a different view, that of ethnonationalism. The core of the ethnonationalist idea is that nations are defined by a shared heritage, which usually includes a common language, a common faith, and a common ethnic ancestry.

The ethnonationalist view has traditionally dominated through much of Europe and has held its own even in the United States until recently. For substantial stretches of U.S. history, it was believed that only the people of English origin, or those who were Protestant, or white, or hailed from northern Europe were real Americans. It was only in 1965 that the reform of U.S. immigration law abolished the system of national-origin quotas that had been in place for several decades. This system had excluded Asians entirely and radically restricted immigration from southern and eastern Europe.

Ethnonationalism draws much of its emotive power from the notion that the members of a nation are part of an extended family, ultimately united by ties of blood. It is the subjective belief in the reality of a common "we" that counts. The markers that distinguish the in-group vary from case to case and time to time, and the subjective nature of the communal boundaries has led some to discount their practical significance. But as Walker Connor, an astute student of nationalism, has noted, "It is not what is, but what people believe is that has behavioral consequences." And the central tenets of ethnonationalist belief are that nations exist, that each nation ought to have its own state, and that each state should be made up of the members of a single nation. . . .

The Rise of Ethnonationalism

Today, people tend to take the nation-state for granted as the natural form of political association and regard empires as anomalies. But over the broad sweep of recorded history, the opposite is closer to the truth. Most people at most times have lived in empires, with the nation-state the exception rather than the rule. So what triggered the change?

The rise of ethnonationalism, as the sociologist Ernest Gellner has explained, was not some strange historical mistake; rather, it was propelled by some of the deepest currents of modernity. Military competition between states created a demand for expanded state resources and hence continual economic growth. Economic growth, in turn, depended on mass literacy and easy communication, spurring policies to promote education and a common language—which led directly to conflicts over language and communal opportunities.

Modern societies are premised on the egalitarian notion that in theory, at least, anyone can aspire to any economic position. But in practice, everyone does not have an equal likelihood of upward economic mobility, and not simply because individuals have different innate capabilities. For such advances depend in part on what economists call "cultural capital," the skills and behavioral patterns that help individuals and groups succeed. Groups with traditions of literacy and engagement in commerce tend to excel, for example, whereas those without such traditions tend to lag behind.

As they moved into cities and got more education during the nineteenth and early twentieth centuries, ethnic groups with largely peasant backgrounds, such as the Czechs, the Poles, the Slovaks, and the Ukrainians found that key positions in the government and the economy were already occupied—often by ethnic Armenians, Germans, Greeks, or Jews. Speakers of the same language came to share a sense that they belonged together and to define themselves in contrast to other communities. And eventually they came to demand a nation-state of their own, in which they would be the masters, dominating politics, staffing the civil service, and controlling commerce.

Ethnonationalism had a psychological basis as well as an economic one. By creating a new and direct relationship between individuals and the government, the rise of the modern state weakened individuals' traditional bonds to intermediate social units, such as the family, the clan, the guild, and the church. And by spurring social and geographic mobility and a self-help mentality, the rise of market-based economies did the same. The result was an emotional vacuum that was often filled by new forms of identification, often along ethnic lines.

Ethnonationalist ideology called for a congruence between the state and the ethnically defined nation, with explosive results. As Lord Acton recognized in 1862, "By making the state and the nation commensurate with each other in theory, [nationalism] reduces practically to a subject condition all other nationalities that may be within the boundary. . . . According, therefore, to the degree of humanity and civilization in that dominant body which claims all the rights of the community, the inferior races are exterminated, or reduced to servitude, or out-lawed, or put in a condition of dependence." And that is just what happened. . . .

The Balance Sheet

Analysts of ethnic disaggregation typically focus on its destructive effects, which is understandable given the direct human suffering it has often entailed. But such attitudes can yield a distorted perspective by overlooking the less obvious costs and also the important benefits that ethnic separation has brought.

Economists from Adam Smith onward, for example, have argued that the efficiencies of competitive markets tend to increase with the markets' size. The dissolution of the Austro-Hungarian Empire into smaller nation-states, each with its own barriers to trade, was thus economically irrational and contributed to the region's travails in the interwar period. Much of subsequent European history has involved attempts to overcome this and other economic fragmentation, culminating in the EU.

Ethnic disaggregation also seems to have deleterious effects on cultural vitality. Precisely because most of their citizens share a common cultural and linguistic heritage, the homogenized states of postwar Europe have tended to be more culturally insular than their demographically diverse predecessors. With few Jews in Europe and few Germans in Prague, that is, there are fewer Franz Kafkas.

Forced migrations generally penalize the expelling countries and reward the receiving ones. Expulsion is often driven by a majority group's resentment of a minority group's success, on the mistaken assumption that achievement is a zero-sum game. But countries that got rid of their Armenians, Germans, Greeks, Jews, and other successful minorities deprived themselves of some of their most talented citizens, who simply took their skills and knowledge elsewhere. And in many places, the triumph of ethnonational politics has meant the victory of tra-ditionally rural groups over more urbanized ones, which possess just those skills desirable in an advanced industrial economy.

But if ethnonationalism has frequently led to tension and conflict, it has also proved to be a source of cohesion and stability. When French textbooks began with "Our ancestors the Gauls" or when Churchill spoke to wartime audiences of "this island race," they appealed to ethno-nationalist sensibilities as a source of mutual trust and sacrifice. Liberal democracy and ethnic homogeneity are not only compatible; they can be complementary.

One could argue that Europe has been so harmonious since World War II not because of the failure of ethnic nationalism but because of its success, which re-moved some of the greatest sources of conflict both within and between coun-tries. The fact that ethnic and state boundaries now largely coincide has meant that there are fewer disputes over borders or expatriate communities, leading to the most stable territorial configuration in European history.

These ethnically homogeneous polities have displayed a great deal of internal solidarity, moreover, facilitating government programs, including domestic transfer payments, of various kinds. When the Swedish Social Democrats were developing plans for Europe's most extensive welfare state during the interwar period, the political scientist Sheri Berman has noted, they conceived of and sold them as the construction of a *folkhemmet*, or "people's home."

Several decades of life in consolidated, ethnically homogeneous states may even have worked to sap ethnonationalism's own emotional power. Many Europeans are now prepared, and even eager, to participate in transnational frameworks such as the EU, in part because their perceived need for collective self-determination has largely been satisfied.

New Ethnic Mixing

Along with the process of forced ethnic disaggregation over the last two centuries, there has also been a process of ethnic mixing brought about by voluntary emigration. The general pattern has been one of emigration from poor, stagnant areas to richer and more dynamic ones.

In Europe, this has meant primarily movement west and north, leading above all to France and the United Kingdom. This pattern has continued into the present: as a result of recent migration, for example, there are now half a million Poles in Great Britain and 200,000 in Ireland. Immigrants from one part of Europe who have moved to another and ended up staying there have tended to assimilate and, despite some grumbling about a supposed invasion of "Polish plumbers," have created few significant problems.

The most dramatic transformation of European ethnic balances in recent decades has come from the immigration of people of Asian, African, and Middle Eastern origin, and here the results have been mixed. Some of these groups have achieved remarkable success, such as the Indian Hindus who have come to the United Kingdom. But in Belgium, France, Germany, the Netherlands, Sweden, the United Kingdom, and elsewhere, on balance the educational and economic progress of Muslim immigrants has been more limited and their cultural alienation greater.

How much of the problem can be traced to discrimination, how much to the cultural patterns of the immigrants themselves, and how much to the policies of European governments is difficult to determine. But a number of factors, from official multiculturalism to generous welfare states to the ease of contact with ethnic homelands, seem to have made it possible to create ethnic islands where assimilation into the larger culture and economy is limited.

As a result, some of the traditional contours of European politics have been upended. The left, for example, has tended to embrace immigration in the name of egalitarianism and multiculturalism. But if there is indeed a link between ethnic homogeneity and a population's willingness to support generous income-redistribution programs, the encouragement of a more heterogeneous society may end up undermining the left's broader political agenda. And some of Europe's libertarian cultural propensities have already clashed with the cultural illiberalism of some of the new immigrant communities.

Should Muslim immigrants not assimilate and instead develop a strong communal identification along religious lines, one consequence might be a resurgence of traditional ethnonational identities in some states—or the development of a new European identity defined partly in contradistinction to Islam (with the widespread resistance to the extension of full EU membership to Turkey being a possible harbinger of such a shift).

Future Implications

Since ethnonationalism is a direct consequence of key elements of modernization, it is likely to gain ground in societies undergoing such a process. It is hardly surprising, therefore, that it remains among the most vital—and most disruptive—forces in many parts of the contemporary world.

More or less subtle forms of ethnonationalism, for example, are ubiquitous in immigration policy around the globe. Many countries—including Armenia, Bulgaria, Croatia, Finland, Germany, Hungary, Ireland, Israel, Serbia, and Turkey—provide automatic or rapid citizenship to the members of diasporas of their own dominant ethnic group, if desired. Chinese immigration law gives priority and benefits to overseas Chinese. Portugal and Spain have immigration policies that favor applicants from their former colonies in the New World. Still other states, such as Japan and Slovakia, provide official forms of identification to members of the dominant national ethnic group who are noncitizens that permit them to live and work in the country. Americans, accustomed by the U.S. government's official practices to regard differential treatment on the basis of ethnicity to be a violation of universalist norms, often consider such policies exceptional, if not abhorrent. Yet in a global context, it is the insistence on universalist criteria that seems provincial.

Increasing communal consciousness and shifting ethnic balances are bound to have a variety of consequences, both within and between states, in the years to come. As economic globalization brings more states into the global economy, for example, the first fruits of that process will often fall to those ethnic groups best positioned by history or culture to take advantage of the new opportunities for enrichment, deepening social cleavages rather than filling them in. Wealthier and higher-achieving regions might try to separate themselves from poorer and lower-achieving ones, and distinctive homogeneous areas might try to acquire sovereignty—courses of action that might provoke violent responses from defenders of the status quo.

Of course, there are multiethnic societies in which ethnic consciousness remains weak, and even a more strongly developed sense of ethnicity may lead to political claims short of sovereignty. Sometimes, demands for ethnic autonomy or self-determination can be met within an existing state. The claims of the Catalans in Spain, the Flemish in Belgium, and the Scots in the United Kingdom have been met in this manner, at least for now. But such arrangements remain precarious and are subject to recurrent renegotiation. In the developing world, accordingly, where states are more recent creations and where the borders often cut across ethnic boundaries, there is likely to be further ethnic disaggregation and communal conflict. And as scholars such as Chaim Kaufmann have noted, once ethnic antagonism has crossed a certain threshold of violence, maintaining the rival groups within a single polity becomes far more difficult.

This unfortunate reality creates dilemmas for advocates of humanitarian intervention in such conflicts, because making and keeping peace between groups that have come to hate and fear one another is likely to require costly ongoing military missions rather than relatively cheap temporary ones. When communal violence escalates to ethnic cleansing, moreover, the return of large numbers of refugees to their place of origin after a cease-fire has been reached is often impractical and even undesirable, for it merely sets the stage for a further round of conflict down the road.

Partition may thus be the most humane lasting solution to such intense communal conflicts. It inevitably creates new flows of refugees, but at least it deals with the problem at issue. The challenge for the international community in such cases is to separate communities in the most humane manner possible: by aiding in transport, assuring citizenship rights in the new homeland, and providing financial aid for resettlement and economic absorption. The bill for all of this will be huge, but it will rarely be greater than the material costs of interjecting and maintaining a foreign military presence large enough to pacify the rival ethnic combatants or the moral cost of doing nothing.

Contemporary social scientists who write about nationalism tend to stress the contingent elements of group identity—the extent to which national consciousness is culturally and politically manufactured by ideologists and politicians. They regularly invoke Benedict Anderson's concept of "imagined communities," as if demonstrating that nationalism is constructed will rob the concept of its power. It is true, of course, that ethnonational identity is never as natural or ineluctable as nationalists claim. Yet it would be a mistake to think that because nationalism is partly constructed it is therefore fragile or infinitely malleable. Ethnonationalism was not a chance detour in European history: it corresponds to some enduring propensities of the human spirit that are heightened by the process of modern state creation, it is a crucial source of both solidarity and enmity, and in one form or another, it will remain for many generations to come. One can only profit from facing it directly.

1.6

Is Ethnic Conflict Inevitable? Parting Ways Over Nationalism and Separatism

James Habyarimana, Macartan Humphreys,
Daniel Posner, Jeremy Weinstein
Richard Rosecrance, Arthur Stein, and Jerry Z. Muller

Muller's claim [1.5] about the prevalence of ethnic conflict provoked the responses included here. First, James Habyarimana and his coauthors deny that ethnic conflict is as pervasive as Muller claims. In the vast majority of cases throughout the world, they suggest, different ethnic groups live side by side without resorting to violence. Further, they report an experiment that they conducted with members of different ethnic groups in Uganda, Africa. In their view, it suggests that the roots of ethnic conflict and violence may have a rational basis. Understanding how and why can have important policy implications. For example, it may be possible to reduce the likelihood of ethnic conflict by designing political institutions with this goal in mind. (See the selections by Hale [6.4] and Reilly [6.5] for similar arguments.)

Richard Rosecrance and Arthur Stein criticize Muller for, in their view, defending the idea that "every separately defined cultural unit should have its own state." They claim that this solution is politically destabilizing and economically foolish. The future belongs to large multiethnic states, like India, China, and the United States, not to small, ethnically pure, states. In brief, "big is back."

Muller is not persuaded by his critics. Why not? Identify and evaluate the contending positions in this debate.

Better Institutions, Not Partition

James Habyarimana, Macartan Humphreys, Daniel Posner, and Jeremy Weinstein

Jerry Muller ("Us and Them," March/April 2008) tells a disconcerting story about the potential for ethnic diversity to generate violent conflict. He argues that ethnic nationalism—which stems from a deeply felt need for each people to have its own state—"will continue to shape the world in the twenty-first century." When state and ethnic-group boundaries do not coincide, "politics is apt to remain ugly."

James Habyarimana, Macartan Humphreys, Daniel Posner, Jeremy Weinstein as well as Richard Rosecrance, Arthur Stein, and Jerry Z. Muller, "Is Ethnic Conflict Inevitable? Parting Ways Over Nationalism and Separatism," *Foreign Affairs* 87, no. 4 (July/August 2008): 138–141 (excerpts).

Muller points to the peace and stability in Europe today as evidence of the triumph of "the ethnonationalist project": it is only because of a half century of violent separation of peoples through expulsions, the redrawing of state boundaries, and the outright destruction of communities too weak to claim territories of their own that Europe today enjoys relative peace. Elsewhere, the correspondence between states and nations is much less neat, and there Muller seems to agree with Winston Churchill that the "mixture of populations [will] . . . cause endless trouble." He advocates partition as the best solution to this difficult problem.

If correct, his conclusion has profound implications both for the likelihood of peace in the world and for what might be done to promote it. But is it correct? Do ethnic divisions inevitably generate violence? And why does ethnic diversity sometimes give rise to conflict?

In fact, ethnic differences are not inevitably, or even commonly, linked to violence on a grand scale. The assumption that because conflicts are often ethnic, ethnicity must breed conflict is an example of a classical error sometimes called "the base-rate fallacy." In the area of ethnic conflict and violence, this fallacy is common. To assess the extent to which Muller falls prey to it, one needs some sense of the "base."

How frequently does ethnic conflict occur, and how often does it occur in the context of volatile mismatches between ethnic groups and states? A few years ago, the political scientists James Fearon and David Laitin did the math. They used the best available data on ethnic demography for every country in Africa to calculate the "opportunities" for four types of communal conflict between independence and 1979: ethnic violence (which pits one group against another), irredentism (when one ethnic group attempts to secede to join co-ethnic communities in other states), rebellion (when one group takes action against another to control the political system), and civil war (when violent conflicts are aimed at creating a new ethnically based political system). Fearon and Laitin identified tens of thousands of pairs of ethnic groups that could have been in conflict. But they did not find thousands of conflicts (as might have been expected if ethnic differences consistently led to violence) or hundreds of new states (which partition would have created). Strikingly, for every one thousand such pairs of ethnic groups, they found fewer than three incidents of violent conflict. Moreover, with few exceptions, African state boundaries today look just as they did in 1960. Fearon and Laitin concluded that communal violence, although horrifying, is extremely rare.

The base-rate fallacy is particularly seductive when events are much more visible than nonevents. This is the case with ethnic conflict, and it may have led Muller astray in his account of the triumph of European nationalism. He emphasizes the role of violence in homogenizing European states but overlooks the peaceful consolidation that has resulted from the ability of diverse groups— the Alsatians, the Bretons, and the Provençals in France; the Finns and the Swedes in Finland; the Genoese, the Tuscans, and the Venetians in Italy—to live together. By failing to consider the conflicts that did not happen, Muller may have misunderstood the dynamics of those that did.

Of course, ethnic divisions do lead to violent conflict in some instances. Violence may even be so severe that partition is the only workable solution. Yet this extreme response has not been required in most cases in which ethnic divisions have existed. Making sense of when ethnic differences generate conflict—and knowing how best to attempt to prevent or respond to them when they do—requires a deeper understanding of how ethnicity works.

Muller offers one explanation for why ethnic identities figure so centrally in political conflict. Corresponding as it does to "enduring propensities of the human spirit," he argues, ethnonationalism "is a crucial source of both solidarity and enmity." This explanation echoes a fairly conventional account of ethnic conflict according to which people tend to prefer members of their own group and, in some cases, have active antipathy toward out-group members, making conflict the inevitable result. This is an appealing narrative. It helps outsiders make sense of the seemingly gratuitous violence of Africa's bloodiest conflicts. It resonates with the demonization of immigrants and the threats of ethnic domination that politicians around the world invoke in election campaigns. It appears consistent with demands for greater autonomy and self-government by ethnic enclaves in eastern Europe and the former Soviet Union. If ethnic diversity generates antipathies so deep that they cannot be realistically resolved, separation becomes the obvious and, perhaps, only feasible antidote, as Muller concludes. But positive feelings toward in-group members and antipathies for out-group members might not be the correct explanation for why political action is often organized along ethnic lines.

Indeed, recent research points to at least two alternative explanations. One argument suggests that members of the same group tend to work together to achieve collective ends not because of their discriminatory preferences but because of efficiency: they speak the same language, have access to the same types of information, and share social networks. In environments with scarce resources, they may even choose to work together against other groups, whether or not they care for or even like their peers. Thus, political coalitions form along ethnic lines not because people care more for their own but simply because it is easier to collaborate with their ethnic peers to achieve collective ends.

A second account emphasizes the norms that may develop within ethnic groups. Even when people see no efficiency gains from working with their co-ethnics and have no discriminatory preferences, they may still favor their own simply because they expect them to discriminate in their favor as well. Such reciprocity is most likely to develop in environments that are devoid of the institutions and practices—for example, enforceable contracts and impartial state institutions—that protect people from being taken advantage of by others. In such cases, reciprocity is a protection against being cheated.

Distinguishing these different theories is important because each one suggests a starkly different strategy for dealing with ethnic conflict. If the problem is tribal or national antipathies, there may well be some utility in separating groups. But if it stems from the technological advantages that accrue to members of the same ethnic group, then initiatives that break down barriers to cooperation (for example, Julius Nyerere's introduction of Swahili as a common language in Tanzania in the 1970s) are more likely to bear fruit. If instead discrimination in favor of one's ethnic peers is a coping strategy that individuals employ to compensate for the absence of functional and impartial state institutions, then the best response may be greater investment in formal institutions so that individuals are assured that cheating will be punished and that cooperation across ethnic lines will be reciprocated.

To discern these competing perspectives, we set out to study ethnicity and conflict using experimental games. We put people in strategic interactions with members of their own and other ethnic groups and examined the decisions they made. We carried out our research in Uganda, where differences between ethnic groups have been a basis for political organization and the source of persistent national political crisis and violent conflict since independence.

Remarkably, we found no evidence that people care more for the welfare of individuals from their own ethnic groups than for the welfare of those from other groups. Given the opportunity to make anonymous donations of cash to randomly selected partners, individuals were just as generous to out-group members as they were to their co-ethnics. One could easily tell a story that links Uganda's decades of ethnic conflict to tribal antipathies (and many have), but our research provided no evidence of such antipathies at work among a diverse sample of Ugandans.

We also found only weak evidence that impediments to cooperation across group lines explain the ethnic dynamics of Ugandan politics. In another set of experiments, we randomly matched participants with a partner and confronted the pairs with tasks that put a premium on successful communication and cooperation. We found no relation between the success in completing these tasks and the ethnic identities of the participants; success rates were just as high when individuals were paired with members of their own ethnic groups as when they were paired with people outside their ethnic groups. Hence, efficiency gains alone cannot easily account for the propensity of political coalitions to take on an ethnic character.

Instead, our studies suggested that patterns of favoritism and successful collective action within ethnic groups should be attributed to the practice of reciprocity, which ensures cooperation among group members. Our subjects showed no bias in favor of in-group members when given the opportunity to make cash donations anonymously, but their behavior changed dramatically when they knew that their partners could see who they were. When they knew that other players would know how they behaved, subjects discriminated strongly in favor of their co-ethnics. This shows, at least in our sample of Ugandans, that ethnic differences generate conflict not by triggering antipathy or impeding communication but by making salient a set of reciprocity norms that enable ethnic groups to cooperate for mutual gain.

Our experimental findings—from a setting quite different from the European context that Muller treats but in which ethnic divisions run equally deep—reveal that what might look from the outside like an intractable problem of discriminatory preferences may instead reflect norms of reciprocity that develop when individuals have few other institutions they can rely on to police the behavior of others.

Of course, ethnicity may not work in Uganda today the same way that it does in other parts of the world or that it did at other points in history. But our results do point out a need to consider seriously the possibility that the conventional view is at best an incomplete and at worst an incorrect explanation for why ethnic nationalism generates conflict when and where it does.

If ethnic hatreds are not at work, separating groups may not make much sense as a strategy for mitigating the corrosive effects of ethnic divisions. It might be far more important to invest in creating impartial and credible state institutions that facilitate cooperation across ethnic lines. With such institutions in place, citizens would no longer need to rely disproportionately on ethnic networks in the marketplace and in politics. In this respect, modernization may be the antidote to ethnic nationalism rather than its cause.

Separatism's Final Country

Richard Rosecrance and Arthur Stein

Muller argues that ethnonationalism is the wave of the future and will result in more and more independent states, but this is not likely. One of the most destabilizing ideas throughout human history has been that every separately defined cultural unit should have its own state. Endless disruption and political introversion would follow an attempt to realize such a goal. Woodrow Wilson gave an impetus to further state creation when he argued for "national self-determination" as a means of preventing more nationalist conflict, which he believed was a cause of World War I.

The hope was that if the nations of the Austrian, Ottoman, and Russian empires could become independent states, they would not have to bring the great powers into their conflicts. But Wilson and his counterparts did not concede to each nation its own state. They grouped minorities together in Hungary, Italy, and Yugoslavia, and the Soviet Union ultimately emerged as a veritable empire of nationalities. Economists rightly questioned whether tiny states with small labor forces and limited resources could become viable, particularly given the tariffs that their goods would face in international trade.

More important, the nationalist prospect was and remains hopelessly impractical. In the world today, there are 6,800 different dialects or languages that might gain political recognition as independent linguistic groups. Does anyone seriously suggest that the 200 or so existing states should each, on average, be cut into 34 pieces? The doctrine of national self-determination reaches its reductio ad absurdum at this point.

Furthermore, the one-nation, one-state principle is unlikely to prevail for four good reasons. First, governments today are more responsive to their ethnic minority communities than were the imperial agglomerations of yesteryear, and they also have more resources at their disposal than their predecessors did. Many provinces populated by discontented ethnic groups are located in territories adjacent to national capitals, not overseas. And many governments in this era of globalization have annual budgets equivalent to nearly 50 percent of their GDPs, much of which is spent on social services. They can—and do—accommodate the economic needs of their states' differentiated units. They also respond to those units' linguistic requests. Basques, Bretons, Punjabis, Québecois, and Scots live quite well inside the bonds of multinational sovereignty and in some cases better than residents of other provinces with no claims of being a distinct nation.

Second, the achievement of separate sovereignty today depends on external recognition and support. Prospective new states cannot gain independence without military assistance and economic aid from abroad. International recognition, in turn, requires the aspiring nationalist movement to avoid international terrorism as a means of gaining attention. If a separatist group uses terrorism, it tends to be reviled and sidelined. If an ethnic group does not have enough support to win independence by peaceful electoral means inside its country, its resorting to terrorism only calls into question the legitimacy of its quest for independence.

Recognizing this, the Québecois abandoned the terrorist methods of the Quebec Liberation Front. Most Basques castigate Basque Homeland and Freedom (known by its Basque acronym ETA). Enlightened Europeans have withdrawn their support for the Chechen rebels. And the continued terrorist shelling of Israeli cities from a Hamas-dominated Gaza might undermine the previous international consensus in favor of a two-state solution to the Palestinian problem, or at least warrant an exceptional approach to Gaza.

With the possible exception of the Palestinians, the notion that any of these peoples would be better off in smaller and weaker independent states in a hostile neighborhood is unrealistic. Occasionally, dissidents make the case that if they were to leave the state unit, they would be taken into the comforting embrace of the European Union or the North American Free Trade Agreement, thereby gaining access to a large market. But that would depend a great deal on outsider support for their cause. The United Kingdom might not wish to see Scotland in the EU and would be in a position to veto its membership. The United States and Canada might not agree to let an independent Quebec join NAFTA. The belief that when a tiny nation is born it falls automatically into the loving hands of international midwives is questionable. The truth varies from case to case.

Third, although globalization initially stimulated ethnic discontent by creating inequality, it also provides the means for quieting discontents down the road within the fold of the state political system. Distributed economic growth is a palliative for political discontent. Indonesia, Malaysia, Singapore, and Thailand contain different ethnic groups that have largely profited from the intense economic resurgence of their states stimulated by globalization. Northern and southern Vietnam are culturally different, but both have benefited from the country's economic growth. Cambodia has a diverse population, but it has gained greatly from China's move to externalize some of its production.

Fourth, a discontented population may react to ethnic discrimination, but it also responds to economic need, and whatever its concerns, it does not always have to seek independence to alleviate them. It has another safety valve: emigration to another country. The state of Monterrey has not sought independence from Mexico; rather, many of its inhabitants have moved, legally or illegally, to the United States. The huge emigration from the Maghreb to France and Italy reflects a similar attitude and outcome; the dissatisfied populations of North Africa can find greater welfare in Europe. And when Poles move to France or the United Kingdom, they do not secede from the mother country but demonstrate greater satisfaction with French or British rule. Emigration is the overwhelming alternative to secession when the home government does not sufficiently mitigate economic disparities. . . .

. . . The apostles of national self-determination would do well to consider a still more important trend: the return to bigness in the international system. This is happening not only because great powers such as China, India, and the United States are now taking on greater roles in world politics but also because international economics increasingly dwarfs politics. To keep up, states have to get bigger. The international market has always been larger than the domestic ones, but as long as international openness beckoned, even small powers could hope to prosper and attain some degree of economic influence. In the past decade, however, the tariff reductions proposed in the Doha Round of international trade negotiations have failed, industrial duties have not fallen, and agriculture has become even more highly protected than it was in the nineteenth century. Globalization has clearly distributed economic boons to smaller countries, but these states still require greater political scale to fully realize globalization's benefits. To generate scale, states have negotiated bilateral and multilateral trade preferences with other states regionally and internationally, thereby gaining access to larger markets. The EU has decided to make up in the enlargement of its membership and a bigger free-trade area what it lacks in internal economic growth. The 27 countries of the EU currently have a combined GDP of over $14 trillion, besting the United States' $13 trillion, and the union's expansion is not over yet. . . .

. . . In Asia, current tensions between China and Japan have not prevented proposals for a free-trade zone, a common currency, and an investment bank for the region. Chinese in Indonesia, Malaysia, the Philippines, Singapore, Taiwan, and Vietnam draw their adopted countries toward Beijing. China will not expand territorially (except titularly when Taiwan rejoins the mainland), but it will move to consolidate an economic network that will contain all the elements of production, except, perhaps, raw materials. Japan will adjust to China's primacy, and even South Korea will see the writing on the wall. . . .

. . . Under the present circumstances, secessionists will generally be better off remaining inside existing states, if only because the international system now advantages larger agglomerations of power. Economies of industrial scale are promoting economies of political size. In U.S. politics, the problem of outsourcing gets much political attention, but how is it possible to prevent that activity when national production and the national market are too small? Only larger political entities can keep production, research and development, and innovation within a single economic zone. Big is back.

Muller Replies

My essay is not agenda-driven or prescriptive. It is meant to suggest that the power of ethnic nationalism in the twentieth century has been greater than is generally recognized and that the probability of its ongoing global impact is greater than is generally appreciated. I argue that Americans often have a distorted sense of substantial areas of the world because they tend to generalize on the basis of their own national experience or, rather, a truncated and idealized version of that experience. Of course, ethnicity (and its conceptual cousin, race) has long played a role in American life and continues to do so, as reflected in everything from residential patterns to voting behavior.

But by and large, ethnic identification in the United States tends to erode across generations, and the notion that different ethnic groups ought to have their own political entities is marginal. (Voting districts drawn along racial lines echo conceptions of ethnic nationalism. And the Chicano vision of the reconstitution of Aztlán—a lost nation of indigenous Americans said to include Mexico and much of the American Southwest—would qualify as ethnonationalist but seems to have limited appeal.) Thus, Americans have a hard time imagining the intensity of the desire that many ethnic groups abroad have for a polity of their own or the determination of others to maintain the ethnic structure of existing polities. If Poles and Ukrainians get along tolerably well in Chicago, why not Sunni Arabs, Kurds, and Turkmen in Kirkuk?

I further argue that this misperception also occurs among educated western Europeans, who project the cooperative and pacific model of the EU onto the rest of the world while losing sight of the history of ethnic disaggregation that seems to have served as a precondition for the comity of contemporary Europe. The propensity to impose on the rest of the world one's own categories and idealized conceptions of one's historical and current experiences leads to a kind of misleading universality, apt to result in misunderstanding and miscalculation.

There are categories of self-definition that are unfamiliar or uncomfortable to some people's sensibilities—including ethnonational identity, caste (common in India), or tribe (common in much of Africa and the Muslim world). But the fact that some people may find these categories unreal (since they know that beneath the skin humans are ultimately the same: put them in a room together with a game to play, and see how little they differ) does not make them any less real to those who do believe in them.

The problem of taking seriously the diverse ways in which people in different parts of the world define themselves is exacerbated by the universalizing and scientistic pretensions of some streams of academic political science. "Scientism" refers to the endeavor to apply the methods and criteria of the natural sciences to all realms of human experience—although for some they are inappropriate. This includes the effort to explain all phenomena with simplified theories of human motivation and the attempt to replicate the hard sciences by using laboratory conditions to study political science. History provides a useful source of data with which to study the range and complexity of human behavior. It is a highly imperfect laboratory, where both the data and their interpretation are influenced by the methodological and ideological predispositions of the investigator. But it is often superior to the alternative: apparently scientific forms of explanation.

My claim is not that the violence of the European experience will repeat itself but a more modest one: that ethnic tensions are likely to be exacerbated, rather than eliminated, by the occurrence of similar processes of modernization in other parts of the world. Contrary to what James Habyarimana, Macartan Humphreys, Daniel Posner, and Jeremy Weinstein claim, nowhere do I argue that "ethnic divisions inevitably generate violence." And while I quoted Churchill, I did not endorse his views as a general policy prescription.

What I actually wrote, toward the end of my article, was this: "Sometimes, demands for ethnic autonomy or self-determination can be met within an existing state. . . . But such arrangements remain precarious and are subject to recurrent renegotiation. In the developing world, accordingly, where states are more recent creations and where the borders often cut across ethnic boundaries, there is likely to be further ethnic disaggregation and communal conflict. And as scholars such as Chaim Kaufmann have noted, once ethnic antagonism has crossed a certain threshold of violence, maintaining the rival groups within a single polity becomes far more difficult.

". . . When communal violence escalates to ethnic cleansing, moreover, the return of large numbers of refugees to their place of origin after a cease-fire has been reached is often impractical and even undesirable.

". . . Partition may thus be the most humane lasting solution to such intense communal conflicts."

Habyarimana, Humphreys, Posner, and Weinstein continue their misrepresentations by claiming that I attribute ethnic tension merely to "enduring propensities of the human spirit"; in fact, I attribute ethnic tension to "some enduring propensities of the human spirit that are heightened by the process of modern state creation." My explanation, drawn largely from the sociologist Ernest Gellner, is actually echoed by the four co-authors, albeit in a different vocabulary, when they write that members of the same ethnic group tend to come together because "they speak the same language, have access to the same types of information, and share social networks." As so often happens in the social sciences, here is an attempt at product differentiation through rebranding—recasting known insights in a new vocabulary.

More novel is the authors' belief that their quasi-scientific experiments in Uganda provide useful new avenues for public policy. They say that their game-playing experiments provide insights as to how the diverse ethnic actors would behave when freed of the social and political contexts in which their actions are known to others. Perhaps, but it is precisely the nature of the real world that this would never be the case.

Moreover, their conclusion that the problem lies in a weak institutional environment characterized by an "absence of functional and impartial state institutions" is both true and misleading, for it fails to consider that the very multiplicity of ethnicities is among the major sources of this institutional environment. A reading of Chinua Achebe's 1960 novel, No Longer at Ease—about the plight of an idealistic young civil servant who tries to embody the ethos of impartiality in a setting in which such norms are at odds with the understanding of his co-ethnics, who regard his bureaucratic position as a form of group property—would cast more light on the situation than hundreds of experimental games.

This is not the place for a full critique of the much-cited calculations of Fearon and Laitin on the incidence of interethnic violence in Africa from 1960 to 1979. If one lives in a neighborhood where three in a thousand interactions result in violence and one has three interactions per day, one is violently attacked only three times a year. But is that a safe neighborhood or a dangerous one? The assertion that "with few exceptions, African state boundaries today look just as they did in 1960" is also both true and misleading. It attests as much to the ability of the dominant ethnic coalitions to suppress attempts at rebellion as to the absence of ethnic conflict.

The Biafran War (1967–70) counts as only one incident of interethnic violence in Fearon and Laitin's data and resulted in no change of borders. The million or so lives lost do not register in their calculations. Had Fearon and Laitin repeated their computations for the years since 1979, the murder of some 800,000 Rwandans (mostly Tutsis) would also have appeared as a matter of small statistical consequence.

The claim by Richard Rosecrance and Arthur Stein that the ethnonationalist ideal of a separate state for each cultural unit has been a source of instability is true or, at least, a half-truth. That is what a good part of my article is about. But the fact that ethnonationalism is destabilizing has not diminished its appeal or impact. The other half-truth is that the fulfillment of the ethnonationalist ideal has had a stabilizing effect, at least for large groups.

However, as my article notes and as Rosecrance and Stein emphasize, not every ethnonational aspiration can be realized, and ethnonational aspirations for autonomy and self-determination can be realized within larger political units through federalism—the devolution of power and income to subnational units. As such, federalism represents a form of "semi-partition," as the political scientist Donald Horowitz has noted. It has the very real advantage of permitting participation in larger political and economic units. But, as Horowitz has also noted, "federalism is not cheap. It involves duplication of facilities, functions, personnel and infrastructure" and often entails jurisdictional disputes. Moreover, "states that could benefit from federalism typically come to that realization too late, usually after conflict has intensified."

Rosecrance and Stein may be right that a greater pool of income can alleviate ethnonational aspirations. But it is worth recalling that the governments in a position to distribute sums equivalent to 50 percent of their GDPs are in Europe, whereas the ethnic groups in potential conflict are in Africa, Asia, and Latin America, where there is less wealth and so less GDP available for redistribution. Moreover, massive government redistribution through taxation may itself inhibit economic growth or make capturing the state apparatus too enticing a prize compared with other pursuits.

Various claims by Rosecrance and Stein are questionable, if not clearly mistaken. The authors assert that mass emigration can serve as an "alternative to secession when the home government does not sufficiently mitigate economic disparities." First, this assumes that all discontents are ultimately expressions of individually conceived economic interest, a radical simplification of human motivation that ignores the desire of some people to share a common culture and their perception that protecting that culture requires political autonomy. For example, throughout much of the first half of the twentieth century, French Canadians emigrated from Canada to the United States, where over time they assimilated into the larger population. Québecois nationalism represents a rejection of that path.

Second, the authors' emigration-as-safety-valve strategy ignores the fact that in contrast to the earlier era of globalization (from the late nineteenth century through World War I), the current era of globalization is characterized by governments better able and more inclined to police their borders and, hence, by the comparatively limited mobility of people across national borders. Moreover, discontent in the relatively wealthy states of the West with some recent streams of immigration has already led to pressures for governments to exercise greater control over the movement of people from particular regions. It is far from clear that emigration from the Maghreb to France, for example, will be allowed to continue indefinitely.

Rosecrance and Stein's assertion that a new era of bigness in international economic affairs is here is truer than the implications they draw from it. The economic advantages of the division of labor do expand with the extent of the market, as Adam Smith explained over two centuries ago. But it is simply not true that "to keep up, states have to get bigger." States can negotiate treaties and other forms of association that allow for freer international trade. As the authors note in passing, smaller nations have opted for inclusion in transnational markets and have often prospered as a result. . . .

. . . Still, Rosecrance and Stein do raise an important issue that I did not explore in my article: the question of external recognition and support for potential new states. What ought to be the response by external countries, such as the United States, to ethnonationalist claims for independence? If one takes seriously the forces leading to the enduring power of ethnonationalism—rather than dismissing them as archaic, illusory, or subject to elimination by good governance conjured out of the blue—the implications for policy are by no means self-evident.

I leave aside the purely legal and philosophical issues, since the "right" to self-determination, like so many others, often conflicts with other purported rights. Representatives of existing states are strongly disposed against the redrawing of borders and the formation of new states. They see self-interest in maintaining the international status quo, which may or may not be justified by prudence. To recognize that national self-determination does provide satisfactions of its own and may well result in viable states is not to say that the endless creation of new states is either viable or desirable. Yet there are dangers both in supporting ethnonationalist claims and in denying them prematurely.

One danger of the international recognition of insurgent ethnonationalist claims to sovereignty is that it may lead to unilateral secession (as in the recent case of Kosovo) as opposed to mutually agreed separation. Secession without ethnic partition usually means that the new political entity will include a substantial minority of people whose co-ethnics dominate the state from which the new state has seceded. This provides a ready source for new ethnic tensions within the new state and international tensions between the new state and the old. Mutually agreed partition that separates the rival ethnic groups may be preferable in order to minimize the likelihood of future conflict. Another danger of a greater international willingness to recognize ethnonationalist movements is that it may create an incentive for the governments of existing countries to violently crush incipient ethnic political movements before they can organize.

There are perils, however, in a blanket refusal of the international community to recognize the claims of legitimate ethnonationalist movements. For having deemed secession an impossibility, governments may feel no incentive to respond to the desire of ethnic groups for greater power and self-determination within the confines of the current states. To recognize the enduring power of ethnic nationalism is not to support it or provide a ready recipe for action but to offer a more realistic appreciation of the dilemmas that will continue to arise in the twenty-first century.

Discussion Questions

1. The selections in this chapter emphasize different kinds of factors that shape political developments. Several articles highlight the influence of culture and ideology, others, the importance of geopolitical factors like state power. Compare how well scholars included in this section defend the importance of one factor or the other. Do you think one is more important? Or does it depend on particular situations? And if so, what are the conditions under which the two vary in importance?
2. What causes political conflict? Identify two or more factors described in selections in this chapter. Choose a political conflict that has been in the news recently and analyze what role, if any, was played by the causes of conflict you have identified.
3. Which selection in this chapter presents the most convincing evidence to support its major argument? Provide reasons for your choice.

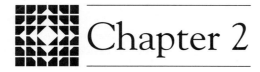 Chapter 2

STATES AND REGIMES

Within a given country, the state is almost always the most powerful cluster of institutions. But just what is the state? The way the term is used in comparative politics is probably unfamiliar to many students. In the United States, it usually refers to the states in the federal system—Texas, California, and so on. But in the study of comparative politics, *state* refers to the cluster of political institutions responsible for making, implementing, enforcing, and adjudicating important policies in a country. The most important state institutions are the national executive, notably, the president or prime minister and cabinet, along with the army, police, and administrative bureaucracy, as well as the legislature and courts.

The fact that states are the fundamental objects of analysis in comparative politics does not mean that all states are the same. States vary considerably in the degree of power that they wield in the international order. And they differ considerably in the extent to which they are able to maintain law and order within their borders. As the selection by Rotberg [2.5] makes clear, some states are no more powerful than rival forces within a territory.

States also vary in terms of their internal organization. The term *regime* highlights differences among the kinds of political institutions that make up the state. Perhaps the most important distinction is whether regimes are democratic or authoritarian.

The concepts of regime or system are also used to highlight different forms of democratic and authoritarian institutions. For example, within democracies, an important contrast is between presidential and parliamentary systems. (See the selection by Linz [6.1].)

States assert, usually with considerable success, the right to issue rules—notably, laws, administrative regulations, and court decisions—that are binding for people within the country. Even democratic regimes, in which top officials are chosen by elections in which all citizens can participate, can survive only if they can preserve enforcement (or coercive) powers both internally and with regard to other states. Many countries have highly undemocratic regimes, whose political survival depends on a heavy dose of repression. However, in the modern world, nearly all states claim to be democratic, even when, as the selections by Levitsky and Way [2.4] and O'Donnell [4.6] describe, a democratic facade may be erected to obscure authoritarian practices.

For several hundred years, states have been among the principal actors on the world stage. Yet the usual description of the world as neatly divided into independent states has always been misleading. Many regions, including most of Africa and Asia for much of the nineteenth and early twentieth centuries, were colonies of European powers. Furthermore, no state fully monopolizes power within its borders. This is true even for the most authoritarian states, such as Nazi Germany in the 1930s and 1940s, and the Soviet Union for the seventy years of its existence.

Recently, however, many scholars have asserted that globalization—defined as cross-border flows of people, capital, commodities, and ideas (culture)—has fundamentally undermined state supremacy. Publications with titles like *The Retreat of the State?* (an excerpt from which is included in this chapter), "The Eclipse of the State?", and *Challenging the State* have analyzed how economic and technological developments—for example, the Internet and transnational corporate activity—have weakened states' ability to control activities within their borders.[1] On the other hand, to adapt Mark Twain after newspapers mistakenly announced his death, reports of the death of the state may be greatly exaggerated![2] The relationship of states to globalization is one of the most controversial topics in comparative politics today. (See the selections in this chapter by Strange [2.2], Sassen [2.3], and Rotberg [2.5].)

When you read the articles in this chapter, think about why it matters that states vary in terms of their regimes and the extent of their autonomy. What impact do differences in states and regimes have for political and social life? States and regimes are so central to the study of comparative politics that many articles in other chapters of RCP will consider this issue.

---

[1] Susan Strange, *The Retreat of the State?: The Diffusion of Power in the World Economy* (New York: Cambridge University Press, 1996); Peter Evans, "The Eclipse of the State? Reflections on Stateness in an Era of Globalization," *World Politics* 50, No. 1 (October 1997): 62–87; and Merilee S. Grindle, *Challenging the State: Crisis and Innovation in Latin America and Africa* (New York: Cambridge University Press, 1996).

[2] Robert Wade alludes to Twain's wry remark in the title of his fine essay suggesting the limits of globalization. See "Globalization and Its Limits: Reports of the Death of the National Economy Are Greatly Exaggerated," in *National Diversity and Global Capitalism*, ed. Suzanne Berger and Ronald Dore (Ithaca, NY: Cornell University Press, 1996), chap. 2.

2.1

Making Race and Nation: A Comparison of the United States, South Africa, and Brazil

Anthony W. Marx

On the basis of a comparison of the United States, South Africa, and Brazil, Anthony Marx describes why states in the first two countries played "the race card," involving a white alliance to marginalize blacks, whereas the Brazilian state did not. Marx suggests that the reason for this difference is that there was more intense polarization between dominant white groups in South Africa and the United States than in Brazil during the period when the modern state was being constructed. By forging a compromise in South Africa and the United States that excluded black inhabitants from citizenship, whites were able to remain dominant. In Brazil, on the other hand, there was less polarization among competing white groups, which reduced the pressure to compromise on the basis of a racially exclusionary formula. Can you apply Marx's argument to other countries and other forms of exclusion? For example, does it help explain gender-based discrimination?

◆ ◆ ◆ States are compulsory and continuous associations claiming control of society within a territory. They differ over time and place in their capacity to rule, in their autonomous power, and in their particular forms. But all states seek to contain challenges or instability threatening order and growth. To do so, ruling elites structure relations between states and civil society, shaping norms and reinforcing social and political identities accordingly.[1] The central identity encouraged by states is that of the nation, defined as the popular loyalty of a population held together in being obliged to serve and be served by the state.[2] By encouraging allegiance to the nation, states enhance their claimed monopoly of legitimacy.[3] Accordingly, state elites and others have been inspired by the goal of the nation-state, a coincidence of institutional rule and allegiance to it that would diminish internal conflict. As John Stuart Mill argued, "the boundaries of governments should coincide in the main with those of nationalities" or "fellow-feelings."[4] . . .

Citizenship is a key institutional mechanism for establishing boundaries of inclusion or exclusion in the nation-state.[5] It selectively allocates distinct civil, political, and economic rights, reinforcing a sense of commonality and loyalty among those included.[6] But by specifying to whom citizenship applies, states also define those outside the community of citizens, who then live within the state as objects of domination. Even in formal democracies, some are not included nor have their interests served. Such imposed exclusion inadvertently may serve as a unifying issue, mobilizing the excluded group to seek inclusion in the polity as a central popular aspiration.[7] Gradual expansion of citizenship is then gained through protracted contestation.[8] The goal of gaining citizenship rights, which were not originally universal, thus has often served as a frame for mobilization.[9] Extending a provocative analogy, groups use their voice to overcome their enduring and forced exit from the polity.[10]

The process of defining the nation with rules of citizenship is of obvious relevance for how racial categories are established and reinforced. Coercive powers have been used to define citizenship according to race—states bind the nation they claim to represent by institutionalizing identities of racial inclusion and exclusion. The extension of citizenship rights has been blocked by constructing racial boundaries. Barbara Fields has suggested that such official racial domination began at a particular historical moment, when the modern nation-state emerged.[11]

States then play a central role in imposing the terms of official domination, with unintended consequences. Official exclusion, as by race, legitimates these categories as a form of social identity, building upon and reshaping historical and cultural solidarities. In the short run, such exclusion benefits those included and hurts others. But in the longer run, institutionalized exclusion may further consolidate subordinate identity and encourages self-interested mobilization and protest. State-sanctioned racial categories impose real costs on their subjects but also offer oppressed populations both legal grounds for redress and bases for political mobilization. The reverse reasoning would also hold. Where and when a state does not impose categorical exclusion, potential subordinates are not so directly disadvantaged. But in the longer run, the preferable absence of such exclusion also may deprive informally subordinated peoples of an unavoidable demarcation unifying them as a group. Ironically, the lack of official racial domination then becomes an obstacle to effective collective action forcing redress of real inequality. In either case, state rule and solidarity from below continually interact.

Arguing that states have the capacity to establish racial boundaries of citizenship, provoking resistance accordingly, does not explain why a state does or does not enforce a racial cleavage. Such an explanation must be cognizant that the state is itself not unitary, but reflects divisions of the society in which it is embedded, and is itself often torn by competing global, national, and local pressures. For instance, does the state construct and use race because of international pressures, to preserve itself, to ensure revenues, to meet specific interests, to avoid class conflict, or to reflect popular racist beliefs? To proceed further, it is useful to turn to comparative historical analysis, looking both inside the state and outside to its social context. How autonomous was the state? How consequential were different state structures? The analytic category of "the state," though suggestive, must be broken down to explain the motives for particular forms of nation-building and for specific official policies and outcomes.

Comparing and Excavating Historical Foundations

South Africa, the United States, and Brazil are the three most prominent cases in which European settlers dominated indigenous populations or slaves of African origin. In all three of these major regional powers, modern social and economic indicators demonstrate significant disparities between black and white. The legacies of slavery and of conquest established a common pattern of discrimination.[12] Indeed, there has been a rich tradition of comparison between two or three of these "big three" cases, the histories of which have often interacted.[13]

The common history of racial dynamics, so understood, makes the comparison of South Africa, the United States, and Brazil obvious. Their differences make comparison fruitful. Given earlier economic development in the United States and other significant variations of history, culture, state structures, and demography, the similarities in South African and U.S. rhetoric and practices of racial domination are striking, particularly in regard to segregation policies between the world wars.[14] There has also been remarkable comparability in the ideology and strategy of resistance challenging racial domination.[15] Yet a dichotomy of racial domination and conflict in South Africa and the United States, contrasted with Brazil's so-called racial democracy and relatively mild black protest, is too simple. Despite the commonality of early discrimination and maintained inequality, post-abolition state policies encoded differing racial orders, with varying results. South African apartheid was more centrally imposed and pervasive than was Jim Crow segregation and exclusion in the more decentralized post-Reconstruction United States. And if South African race relations bark most loudly and the United States a bit more softly, why was Brazil the dog that didn't bark? These divergent outcomes present a useful puzzle.

Including Brazil is pivotal, reminding us that legal racial domination was not inevitable. While South Africa and the United States used earlier discrimination as the base for constructing continued racial domination, the connection between past and present in Brazil is more problematic. There, early prejudice and large-scale slavery seem oddly inconsistent with the later absence of legal segregation. . . . Brazil's distinctiveness did not then rest upon less historical discrimination, but rather in the country's purposeful denial of that legacy. What accounts for this divergence? . . .

Was there something similar about transitional moments in South Africa and the United States, but different for Brazil, that can account for the pattern of outcomes? One possible answer stands out immediately. Abolition and/or state consolidation in South Africa and the United States emerged out of the bloodiest conflicts in the histories of those countries, while Brazil suffered nothing remotely comparable to the Boer War or Civil War.[16] This divergence fits the general pattern of outcomes. But why would imperial conquest or internal wars and their aftereffects have produced apartheid and Jim Crow? Indeed, just the opposite might seem logical. It was the more liberal abolitionist British and Northerners who won those wars, yet later policies toward blacks were closer to those advocated by the defeated Afrikaners and Southerners. Something more than who won was at work. Furthermore, why would the lack of major internal war result in the absence of official racial domination in Brazil? Again this result is counterintuitive. The more peaceful process of abolition and state consolidation in Brazil left the earlier racial order and social hierarchy relatively undisturbed, yet in Brazil earlier racial discrimination was not codified in later state institutions.

Looking just at pivotal moments cannot fully account for the divergence in racial orders. Outcomes even ran counter to the victors' possible advantage. If the British had aligned themselves with and protected black South Africans, they could have forged a majority coalition to outvote Afrikaners. With the hubris of victory, the U.S. North assumed they could indeed forge such a coalition with blacks and impose reforms under Reconstruction, but this project was abandoned. Instead, the British and the North sought a coalition with the Afrikaners and the white South, respectively, because those defeated whites had earned a reputation in the prior conflict as being capable of violent disruption. Afrikaners and Southerners posed a viable threat of continuing disruption after the Boer War and during Reconstruction. Liberal interest in blacks was overshadowed by the stronger imperative to unify whites within the nation-state, in part because blacks themselves, divided by ethnicity in South Africa and outnumbered in the United States, were not seen as a comparably violent threat.[17] Earlier images of racial inferiority, shared by whites across ethnic or regional lines, reinforced the idea that blacks were not capable of organized and united disruption, and so could and should be subordinated. The strategic and ideological imperatives for a white coalition then set the terms of official racial domination. During the "moments of madness"[18] capping cataclysmic and violent change, official policies established the trajectory of racial order for close to a century.

South African and U.S. nation-state consolidation followed a similar logic. "Liberal" and industrializing forces defeated agrarian powers tied to coercive labor practices, with the victors then facing the challenge of reconciling divided loyalties reinforced by conflict. Ethnic tensions and sectionalism had to be diminished, even if they could not be altogether vanquished.[19] Afrikaners and Southerners demanding that citizenship not be extended to blacks were appeased. Intrawhite conflict was diminished by projecting white racial unity and domination. Blacks were sacrificed on the altar of white unity. In this sense, in the aftermath of the Civil and Boer Wars, further open conflict was contained by inscribing inequalities on which whites generally agreed into social institutions.[20] As Stinchcombe concludes, "the tragedy of social life is that every extension of solidarity . . . to nation, presents also the opportunity of organizing hatred at a larger scale."[21] Institutionalizing common prejudice against blacks reinforced white nationalism.[22] Both countries followed a "golden law . . . that every white bargain must be sealed by an

African sacrifice."[23] The pragmatic goal of conflict resolution and nation-state building consistently eclipsed liberal calls for racial justice.

Why did intrawhite conflict trigger the particular use of racial cleavage for domination and nation building? In South Africa and the United States, issues of race and the treatment of Africans were embedded in emerging ethnic or regional conflict, reinforcing existent racist ideologies. Issues of race exacerbating intrawhite conflict were then turned into an instrument for encouraging unity. And as elites victorious in war were more concerned with winning over their white rivals than blacks, constructing a racial order of white supremacy could and did diminish intrawhite conflict. Racial domination was embraced or allowed because it was potentially powerful enough to gradually integrate white populations in violent conflict with each other. Continuing ethnic or section conflicts would have exacerbated disruption. Neither capital nor labor could be so excluded because prosperity required the inclusion of both business and workers. And national unity could not be built on the exclusion of foreigners, who were needed as immigrant labor. . . .

Brazilian nation-state making and race making followed an altogether different linked trajectory. There was no competing European fragment akin to the Afrikaners in South Africa, so that the Portuguese were unchallenged in establishing central colonial authority.[24] In general, slavery was countrywide, producing little regional conflict over abolition, nor the elaboration of a programmatic racist ideology to defend slavery against such challenges.[25] A relative lack of early conflict was further preserved by Brazil's slow economic growth, contrasted with faster development producing more class conflict earlier among whites in South Africa and the United States. Brazilian unity had been preserved by compromise, and the continued rule of Portugal and Portuguese-descendant emperors ensured the persistence of an established order and religious-social hierarchy, with slaves at its bottom.[26] Brazil then modernized and peacefully transformed itself from colony to empire and to republic, and from slaveholding to free.[27] A "prefabricated" central state was in place when the winds of modernity hit. Abolition did raise the question of whether and how to incorporate blacks, but in the relative absence of major intrawhite conflict, there was little impetus to unify whites through racial exclusion. Whites were already relatively united; the nation was already bound up, at least among elites.

Brazilian elites found that they could maintain their long-established social order of white privilege without enforcing racial domination. Having experienced larger slave revolts, the Brazilian ruling class was more fearful of blacks than their U.S. or South African counterparts. They were eager to submerge potential racial conflict. Policies were debated and discrimination was evident in preferences for European immigrants and bars on Africans entering the country.[28] Racial categories were even encoded, but Brazil did not use these categories as a basis for domination. Inherited and continued racial inequality was denied or explained as reflecting unavoidable but fluid class distinctions. Some Afro-Brazilians were able to advance themselves, encouraging accommodation. Further miscegenation was promoted to "whiten" and unite the population. Seeking "the best of both worlds," such racial democracy maintains the structure of white privilege and non-white subordination, [and] avoids the constitution of race into a principle of collective identity and political action."[29] That prejudice was not legally instantiated had significant consequences. With no official segregation requiring strong state intervention, the republic decentralized power with little conflict or dissent.[30]

This analysis suggests a schematic pattern. For all three countries, racial discrimination was historically embedded, distinguishing blacks as blacks. But elites sharing this prejudice acted differently in response to the particular conflicts they faced or feared. In the United States and South Africa, nineteenth-century builders of the nation-state faced the threat of a potential triadic tension between two white groups and blacks. A coalition among whites was encouraged by enforcing an ideology and practice of racial domination, shifting the conflict to a more manageable dyadic form of white over black. Intrawhite conflict required reconciliation, and racial domination was imposed to unify white nationalism and allow for state centralization. In Brazil, with no comparably violent ethnic and less regional conflict standing in the way of unity, no reconciliation by exclusion was pursued. A more inclusive nationalism developed in place of a biracial divide. The earlier consolidated Brazilian state required no dyadic racial crutch to preserve the polity even as the form of rule repeatedly shifted. Thus, racial domination was constructed selectively and strategically as a tool for pursuing the goal of the nation-state, a twentieth-century preoccupation.

Notes

1. See Theda Skocpol, "Bringing the State Back In," in Peter Evans, Dietrich Rueschemeyer, and Theda Skocpol, eds., *Bringing the State Back In* (Cambridge: Cambridge University Press, 1985), pp. 7, 14; Katznelson, *Liberalism's Crooked Circle* (Princeton University Press, 1996), pp. 125, 178.
2. See Charles Tilly, "Reflections on the History of European Statemaking," in Charles Tilly, ed., *The Formation of National States in Western Europe* (Princeton: Princeton University Press, 1975), pp. 1–83. Tilly notes that such nationalism was encouraged with selection of personnel, control of groups, education, and other policies.
3. Bertrand Badie and Pierre Birnbaum, *The Sociology of the State* (Chicago: University of Chicago Press, 1983), p. 37.
4. Katznelson, p. 119.
5. Frank Parkin, *Max Weber* (London: Travistock, 1982), p. 100; Frank Parkin, *Marxism and Class Theory: A Bourgeois Critique* (New York: Columbia University Press, 1979), p. 95.
6. T. H. Marshall, *Citizenship and Social Class* (London: Pluto, 1992); and as quoted in Katznelson, *Liberalism's Crooked Circle*, p. 119.
7. Judith N. Shklar, *American Citizenship: The Quest for Inclusion* (Cambridge, Mass.: Harvard University Press, 1991), p. 3; Sidney Tarrow, *Power in Movement* (Cambridge: Cambridge University Press, 1994), p. 62.
8. Tarrow, *Power in Movement*, p. 76; Shklar, *American Citizenship*, p. 28; Charles Tilly, *Popular Contention in Great Britain, 1758–1834* (Cambridge, Mass.: Harvard University Press, 1995); Michael Lipsky, "Protest as a Political Resource," *American Political Science Review* 62 (1968), pp. 1144–58; Craig Calhoun, *Social Theory and the Politics of Identity* (Cambridge: Blackwell, 1994), p. 25; Margaret R.

Somers, "Citizenship and the Place of the Public Sphere," *American Sociological Review* 58.5 (October 1993), p. 589.

9. Aldon Morris and Carol McLurg Mueller, eds., *Frontiers in Social Movement Theory* (New Haven: Yale University Press, 1992), p. 189.

10. Albert O. Hirschman, *Exit, Voice and Loyalty* (Cambridge, Mass.: Harvard University Press, 1970).

11. Barbara Fields, "Slavery, Race and Ideology in the United States of America," *New Left Review* 181 (1990), p. 101. For a related discussion of racism as a "pitfall of nationalism," see Frantz Fanon, *The Wretched of the Earth* (New York: Grove, 1968), pp. 125–31.

12. Herbert S. Klein, *African Slavery in Latin America and the Caribbean* (New York: Oxford University Press, 1986), p. 10. Europe, with its absence of major domestic slaveholding, and history of ethnic exclusion, is not included in this comparative study.

13. See, for example, Pierre Van den Berghe, *Race and Racism* (New York: Wiley, 1967); Stanley B. Greenberg, *Race and State in Capitalist Development* (New Haven: Yale University Press, 1980); George M. Fredrickson, *White Supremacy* (Oxford: Oxford University Press, 1981); John W. Cell, *The Highest Stage of White Supremacy* (Cambridge: Cambridge University Press, 1982); Carl N. Degler, *Neither Black nor White* (Madison: University of Wisconsin Press, 1971).

14. C. Vann Woodward, *The Strange Career of Jim Crow* (New York: Oxford University Press, 1957), p. 97; George Reid Andrews, "Comparing the Comparers: White Supremacy in the United States and South Africa," *Journal of Social History* 20 (1987), p. 588; George M. Fredrickson, "Black–White Relations Since Emancipation: The Search for a Comparative Perspective," in Kees Gispen, ed., *What Made the South Different?* (Jackson: University Press of Mississippi, 1990), p. 141.

15. George M. Fredrickson, *Black Liberation: A Comparative History of Black Ideologies in the United States and South Africa* (New York: Oxford University Press, 1995).

16. Donald Pierson, *Negroes in Brazil* (Chicago: University of Chicago Press, 1942), p. 335.

17. See Andrews, "Comparing the Comparers," p. 589; A. Leon Higginbotham, Jr., "Racism in American and South African Courts: Similarities and Differences," *New York University Law Review* 65.3 (June 1990), p. 491; Richard M. Valelly, "Party, Coercion, and Inclusion: The Two Reconstructions of the South's Electoral Politics," *Politics and Society* 21.1 (March 1993), pp. 37–67.

18. Aristide Zolberg, "Moments of Madness," *Politics and Society* 2 (1978).

19. See V. O. Key, Jr., *Southern Politics in State and Nation* (New York: Knopf, 1949), p. 15.

20. See Michel Foucault, *Power/Knowledge*, ed. Colin Gordon (New York: Pantheon, 1980), p. 90.

21. Arthur Stinchcombe, "Social Structure and Politics," in Nelson W. Polsby and Fred Greenstein, eds., *Handbook of Political Science* (Reading: Addison-Wesley, 1975), vol. 3.

22. Kimberlie Crenshaw, "Race, Reform and Retrenchment," *Harvard Law Review* 101.7 (May 1988), p. 1360; William Julius Wilson, *Power, Racism and Privilege* (New York: Free Press, 1973), p. 35; George M. Fredrickson, *The Black Image in the White Mind* (Middletown, Conn.: Wesleyan University Press), p. 151; Connor, *Ethnonationalism*, p. 94.

23. Donald Denoon, *A Grand Illusion* (London: Longman, 1973), p. 158.

24. See Louis Hartz, *The Founding of New Societies* (San Diego: Harcourt Brace Jovanovich, 1964).

25. Fredrickson, *Black Liberation*, pp. 5, 8.

26. See Carlos Hasenbalg, "Race Relations in Post-Abolition Brazil," Ph.D. dissertation, University of California at Berkeley, 1978, p. 258; Carlos Hasenbalg, "Desigualdades Raciais no Brasil," *Dados* 14 (1977), p. 7; Roberto Da Matta, *Carnivals, Rogues and Heroes* (Notre Dame, Ind.: University of Notre Dame Press, 1991), pp. 139–40; Florestan Fernandes, *The Negro in Brazilian Society* (New York: Columbia University Press, 1969), pp. 180–1.

27. Scott, "Defining the Boundaries of Freedom," p. 96; Gilberto Freyre, *Brazil: An Interpretation* (New York: Knopf, 1945), pp. 120–1. See also Hartz, *Founding of New Societies*, pp. 78, 124.

28. Célia Marinho de Azevedo, *Onda Negra, Medo Branco* (Rio de Janeiro: Paz e Terra, 1987).

29. Hasenbalg, "Race Relations in Post-Abolition Brazil," p. 260.

30. Brazil's informal racial order is an example of what Foucault describes as the "effects of power which don't pass directly via the state apparatus yet often sustain the state more effectively than its own institutions, enlarging and maximizing its effectiveness." See Foucault, *Power/Knowledge*, p. 73.

The Retreat of the State: The Diffusion of Power in the World Economy

Susan Strange

According to Susan Strange, a fundamental shift has occurred in the distribution of power within the world: "The impersonal forces of world markets . . . are now more powerful than the state to whom ultimate political authority over society and economy is supposed to belong." (Susan Strange, *The Retreat of the State: The Diffusion of Power in the World Economy* [Cambridge, UK: Cambridge University Press, 1996], p. 4.) In other words, forces outside the state, notably, technology and global finance, have undermined state power. The decline of state power is masked by several factors. First, states now raise and spend more money than ever before (fully half of the country's total gross domestic product [GDP] in some cases). Second, the state's presence in the daily lives of citizens is evident everywhere. And, third, many groups in the world today seek their own state. When their demands are rejected (the usual case), they may resort to violence in an attempt to achieve their aim. However, Strange notes, the fact that states continue to play a prominent role on the world's stage does not mean that they remain the dominant actors on that stage.

It seems apparent that states are less and less able to control what occurs across and within their physical and electronic borders, whether it is the flow of commerce and finance, people, communication, or ideas.

Are states, in Shakespeare's phrase, "full of sound and fury signifying nothing?" Or do they continue to remain the most powerful instrumentalities in the world? How would you go about analyzing this question? Some hints: it may be useful to disaggregate state power, that is, to distinguish among kinds of power, as well as to ask: Power for what purpose?

The Declining Authority of States

Today it seems that the heads of governments may be the last to recognise that they and their ministers have lost the authority over national societies and

---
Susan Strange, *The Retreat of the State: The Diffusion of Power in the World Economy* (Cambridge, UK: Cambridge University Press, 1996), 3–10, 12–14.

economies that they used to have. Their command over outcomes is not what it used to be. Politicians everywhere talk as though they have the answers to economic and social problems, as if they really are in charge of their country's destiny. People no longer believe them. Disillusion with national leaders brought down the leaders of the Soviet Union and the states of central Europe. But the disillusion is by no means confined to socialist systems. Popular contempt for ministers and for the head of state has grown in most of the capitalist countries—Italy, Britain, France and the United States are leading examples. Nor is the lack of confidence confined to those in office; opposition parties and their leaders are often no better thought of than those they wish to replace. In the last few years, the cartoonists and the tabloid press have been more bitter, less restrained critics of those in authority in government than at any other time this century. Although there are exceptions—mostly small countries—this seems to be a worldwide phenomenon, . . . more evident in some places than others, but palpable enough to suggest that some common causes lie behind it. . . .

. . . The argument put forward is that the impersonal forces of world markets, integrated over the postwar period more by private enterprise in finance, industry and trade than by the cooperative decisions of governments, are now more powerful than the states to whom ultimate political authority over society and economy is supposed to belong.

Where states were once the masters of markets, now it is the markets which, on many crucial issues, are the masters over the governments of states. And the declining authority of states is reflected in a growing diffusion of authority to other institutions and associations, and to local, and regional bodies, and in a growing asymmetry between the larger states with structural power and weaker ones without it.

There are, to be sure, some striking paradoxes about this reversal of the state-market balance of power. One, which disguises from many people the overall decline of state power, is that the *intervention* of state authority and of the agencies of the state in the daily lives of the citizen appears to be growing. Where once it was left to the individual to look for work, to buy goods or services with caution in case they were unsafe or not what they seemed to be, to build or to pull down houses, to manage family relationships and so on, now governments pass laws, set up inspectorates and planning authorities, provide employment services, enforce customer protection against unclean water, unsafe food, faulty buildings or transport systems. The impression is conveyed that less and less of daily life is immune from the activities and decisions of government bureaucracies.

That is not necessarily inconsistent with my contention that state *power* is declining. It is less effective on those basic matters that the market, left to itself, has never been able to provide—security against violence, stable money for trade and investment, a clear system of law and the means to enforce it, and a sufficiency of public goods like drains, water supplies, infrastructures for transport and communications. Little wonder that it is less respected and lacks its erstwhile legitimacy. The need for a political authority of some kind, legitimated either by coercive force or by popular consent, or more often by a combination of the two, is the fundamental reason for the state's existence. But many states are coming to be deficient in these fundamentals. Their deficiency is not made good by greater activity in marginal matters, matters that are optional for society, and which are not absolutely necessary for the functioning of the market and the maintenance of social order. Trivialising government does not make its authority more respected; often, the contrary is true.

The second paradox is that while the governments of established states, most notably in North America and western Europe, are suffering this progressive loss of real authority, the queue of societies that want to have their own state is lengthening. This is true not only of ethnic groups that were forcibly suppressed by the single-party government of the former Soviet Union. It is true of literally hundreds of minorities and aboriginal peoples in every part of the world—in Canada and Australia, in India and Africa, even in the old so-called nation-states of Europe. Many—perhaps the majority—are suppressed by force, like the Kurds or the Basques. Others—like the Scots or the Corsicans—are just not strong enough or angry enough to offer a serious challenge to the existing state. Still others such as the native Americans, the Aboriginals, the Samis or the Flemish are pacified by resource transfers or by half-measures that go some way to meet their perceived need for an independent identity. Only a few, such as the Greenlanders, the Slovaks or Slovenes or the unwanted, unviable Pacific island-states, have succeeded in getting what they wanted—statehood. But once achieved, it does not seem to give them any real control over the kind of society or the nature of their economy that they might have preferred. In short, the desire for ethnic or cultural autonomy is universal; the political means to satisfy that desire within an integrated world market economy is not. Many, perhaps most, societies have to be content with the mere appearance of autonomy, with a facade of statehood. The struggle for independence has often proved a pyrrhic victory.

The final paradox which can be brought as evidence against my basic contention about the hollowness of state authority at the end of this century is that this is a western, or even an Anglo-Saxon phenomenon, and is refuted by the Asian experience of the state. The Asian state, it is argued, has in fact been the means to achieve economic growth, industrialisation, a modernised infrastructure and rising living standards for the people. Singapore might be the prime example of a strong state achieving economic success. But Japan, Korea, Taiwan are all states which have had strong governments, governments which have successfully used the means to restrict and control foreign trade and foreign investment, and to allocate credit and to guide corporate development in the private sector. Is it not premature—just another instance of Eurocentrism therefore—to assume the declining authority of the state?

There are two answers to this third paradox. One is that all these Asian states were exceptionally fortunate. They profited in three ways from their geographical position on the western frontier of the United States during the Cold War.

Their strategic importance in the 1950s and after was such that they could count on generous military and economic aid from the Americans, aid which was combined with their exceptionally high domestic savings and low patterns of consumption. The combination gave a head start to rapid economic development. Secondly, and also for strategic reasons, they could be—almost had to be—exempted from the pressure to conform to the norms of the open liberal economy. They were allowed, first formally and then informally, to limit foreign imports and also to restrict the entry of the foreign firms that might have proved too strong competitors for their local enterprises. At the same time, they were given relatively open access first to the large, rich US market for manufactures, and later, under some protest, to the European one. And thirdly, the technology necessary to their industrialisation was available to be bought on the market, either in the form of patents, or in the person of technical advisors from Europe and America or through corporate alliances which brought them the technology without the loss of managerial control.

Now, I would argue, these special dispensations are on the way out, and not only because the Cold War is over. The Asian governments will be under increasing pressure from Washington to adopt more liberal non-discriminatory policies on trade and investment. And they will also be under pressure from within to liberalise and to allow more competition, including foreign competition, for the benefit of consumers and of other producers. In short, the exceptionalism of the Asian state during the Cold War has already been substantially eroded, and will continue to be so. As it has been at other times, and in other places, there will be contests for control over the institutions and agencies of government in most of the Asian countries. There will be contests between factions of political parties, between vested interests both in the private sectors and in the public sector. There will be power struggles between branches of the state bureaucracy. Both the unity and the authority of government is bound to suffer.

The Neglected Factor—Technology

The argument in the book depends a good deal on the accelerating pace of technological change as a prime cause of the shift in the state-market balance of power. Since social scientists are not, by definition, natural scientists, they have a strong tendency to overlook the importance of technology which rests, ultimately, on advances in physics, in chemistry and related sciences like nuclear physics or industrial chemistry In the last 100 years, there has been more rapid technological change than ever before in human history. On this the scientists themselves are generally agreed. It took hundreds—in some places, thousands—of years to domesticate animals so that horses could be used for transport and oxen (later heavy horses) could be used to replace manpower to plough and sow ground for the production of crops in agriculture. It has taken less than 100 years for the car and truck to replace the horse and for aircraft to partly take over from road and rail transport. The electric telegraph as a means of communication was invented in the 1840s and remained the dominant system in Europe until the 1920s. But in the next eighty years, the telegraph gave way to the telephone, the telephone gave way to radio, radio to television and cables to satellites and optic fibres linking computers to other computers. No one under the age of thirty or thirty-five today needs convincing that, just in their own lifetime, the pace of technological change has been getting faster and faster. The technically unsophisticated worlds of business, government and education of even the 1960s would be unrecognisable to them. No fax, no personal computers, no accessible copiers, no mobile phones, no video shops, no DNA tests, no cable TV, no satellite networks connecting distant markets, twenty-four hours a day. The world in which their grandparents grew up in the 1930 or 1940s is as alien to them as that of the Middle Ages. There is no reason to suppose that technological change in products and processes, driven by profit, will not continue to accelerate in future.

This simple, everyday, commonsense fact of modern life is important because it goes a long way to explaining both political and economic change. It illuminates the changes both in the power of states and in the power of markets. Its dynamism, in fact, is basic to my argument, because it is a continuing factor, not a once-for-all change.

For the sake of clarity, consider first the military aspects of technical change, and then the civilian aspects—although in reality each spills over into the other. In what are known as strategic studies circles, no one doubts that the development of the atom bomb in the middle of the twentieth century, and later of nuclear weapons carried by intercontinental missiles, has brought about a major change in the nature of warfare between states. Mutual assured destruction was a powerful reason for having nuclear weapons—but equally it was a good reason for not using them. After the paradoxical long peace of the Cold War, two things began to change. The expectation that, sooner or later, nuclear war would destroy life on the planet began to moderate. And confidence began to wane that the state could, by a defensive strategy, prevent this happening. Either it would or it wouldn't, and governments could do little to alter the probabilities. Thus, technology had undermined one of the primary reasons for the existence of the state—its capacity to repel attack by others, its responsibility for what Adam Smith called 'the defence of the realm'.

At the same time technology has had its effect on civilian life. Medical technology has made human life both longer and more comfortable. Electrical technology has liberated millions of women from the drudgery that imprisoned previous generations in the day-long labour of preparing food, keeping the family's clothes clean and mended, and houses clean and warm. As washing machines, vacuum cleaners, dishwashers, central heating and refrigerators and freezers spread down the income levels, more people had more to lose from inter-state conflict. Comfort bred conservatism in politics. Moreover, the new wealth was being acquired by the Germans and the Japanese who had actually been defeated in World War II. Acquiring territory was no longer seen as a means to increase wealth. Losing territory did not mean the state became poorer or weaker. Gaining market shares in the world outside the territorial borders of the state, however, did enable formerly poor countries like Japan, Taiwan or Hong Kong to earn the foreign exchange with which to buy capital goods, foreign technology and the necessary resources of energy and raw materials. As John Stopford and I have argued, competition for world market shares has replaced competition for territory, or for control over the natural resources of territory, as the 'name of the game' between states. In this new game, the search for allies among other states goes on, but not for their added military capabilities. It is for the added bargaining power conferred by a larger economic area.

Moreover, the search for allies is not confined to other states or intergovernmental organisations. It is supplemented by a search for allies among foreign-owned firms. These firms may be persuaded, in exchange for access to the national market, to raise the finance, apply their technology, provide the management and the access to export markets—in short, to take all the steps necessary to locate production of goods or services within the territory of the host state. In most developing or ex-socialist countries, the prospect of new jobs and extra export earnings brought by such investments have become powerful reasons for a change of attitude toward the so-called 'multinationals'.

The Second Neglect—Finance

Not the least of the TNC's attractions to host states is its ability to raise finance both for the investment itself and—even more important—for the development of new technology. . . . Besides the accelerating pace of technological change, there has been an escalation in the capital cost of most technological innovations—in agriculture, in manufacturing and the provision of services, and in new products and in new processes. In all of these, the input of capital has risen while the relative input of labour has fallen. It is this increased cost which has raised the stakes, as it were, in the game of staying up with the competition. This is so whether we look at competition from other firms who are also striving for larger market shares, or whether we look at governments trying to make sure that the economies for whose performance they are held responsible stay up with the competition in wealth-creation coming from other economies. Thus, to the extent that a government can benefit from a TNC's past and future investments without itself bearing the main cost of it, there are strong reasons for forging such alliances.

But the escalating costs of technological change are also important for a more fundamental reason, and not just because it explains the changing policies of host states to TNCs. It has to do with change in the world system. The cost of new technology in the production structure has added to the salience of money in the international political economy. . . . Briefly, the escalating capital costs of new technologies could not have been covered at all without, firstly, some very fundamental changes in the volume and nature of credit created by the capitalist market economy; and secondly, without the added mobility that in recent years has characterised that created credit. The *supply* of capital to finance technological innovation (and for other purposes) has been as important in the international political economy as the *demand* from the innovators for more money to produce ever more sophisticated products by ever more capital-intensive processes of production. . . .

Politics, Power and Legitimacy

There are three premises underlying the argument in this book. . . . The first premise is that politics is a common activity; it is not confined to politicians and their officials. The second is that power over outcomes is exercised impersonally by markets and often unintentionally by those who buy and sell and deal in markets. The third is that authority in society and over economic transactions is legitimately exercised by agents other than states, and has come to be freely acknowledged by those who are subject to it. . . .

[I also develop three propositions. The first] is that there is growing asymmetry among allegedly sovereign states in the authority they exercise in society and economy. In international relations, back to Thucydides, there has always been some recognition of a difference between small states and great powers, in the way each behaves to others and in the options available to them in their relations with other states. But there has been a tendency all along to assume a certain uniformity in the nature and effectiveness of the control which each state has over social and economic relations within their respective territorial boundaries. The attributes of domestic sovereignty, in other words, were assumed automatically to go with the regulation accorded each state by its peers. Now, I shall argue, that assumption can no longer be sustained. What was regarded as an exceptional anomaly when in 1945 the United States conceded two extra votes in the UN General Assembly for the Soviet Union—one for the 'sovereign' republic of the Ukraine and one for Byelorussia—now hardly attracts comment. The micro-states of Vanuatu and the Republic of San Marino are admitted to the select circle of member-states of the United Nations. But no one really believes that recognition of their 'sovereignty' is more than a courteous pretence. It is understood that there is only a difference of degree between these and many of the smaller and poorer members of the international society of states who are established occupants of seats in the UN.

The second proposition is that the authority of the governments of all states, large and small, strong and weak, has been weakened as a result of technological and financial change and of the accelerated integration of national economies into one single global market economy. Their failure to manage the national economy, to maintain employment and sustain economic growth, to avoid imbalances of payments with other states, to control the rate of interest and the exchange rate is not a matter of technical incompetence, nor moral turpitude nor political maladroitness. It is neither in any direct sense their fault, nor the fault of others. None of these failures can be blamed on other countries or on other governments. They are, simply, the victims of the market economy.

The third proposition complements the second. It is that some of the fundamental responsibilities of the state in a market economy—responsibilities first recognised, described and discussed at considerable length by Adam Smith over 200 years ago—are not now being adequately discharged by anyone. At the heart of the international political economy, there is a vacuum, a vacuum not adequately filled by inter-governmental institutions or by a hegemonic power exercising leadership in the common interest. The polarisation of states between those who retain some control over their destinies and those who are effectively incapable of exercising any such control does not add up to a zero-sum game. What some have lost, others have not gained. The diffusion of authority away from national governments has left a yawning hole of non-authority, ungovernance it might be called. . . .

The State and Globalization

Saskia Sassen

Contrary to claims that the state's role has declined as a result of globalization (for example, see Strange [2.2]), Saskia Sassen suggests that the state continues to be fundamentally important. She asserts that states have gained an important new role by promoting globalization. Rather than constituting the retreat of the state, pro-globalization interventions involve a vigorous assertion of power and often encounter determined local resistance. To pursue the new priorities, the state may sponsor legislative reforms, issue administrative regulations, and decide judicial disputes in a way that aims to dismantle the long-established distinction between the public treatment of foreign-based as opposed to domestic business firms and banks. This represents a fundamental change. Traditionally, tax laws, tariffs, procurement policies, and other government activities favored domestically owned firms over foreign firms. Sassen describes the new development as the "denationalization" of the state. It promotes a borderless world, at least in terms of economic exchanges, by making it easier for companies to operate across national borders.

Compare Sassen's analysis with that of Strange [2.2], who believes that states are far less important nowadays. Can both be correct?

One of the roles of the state vis-à-vis today's global economy has been to negotiate the intersection of national law and foreign actors—whether firms, markets, or supranational organizations. This raises a question as to whether there are particular conditions that make execution of this role in the current phase distinctive and unlike what it may have been in earlier phases of the world economy. We have, on the one hand, the existence of an enormously elaborate body of law developed mostly over the past hundred years, which secures the exclusive territorial authority of national states to an

---

Saskia Sassen, "The State and Globalization," in *The Emergence of Private Authority in Global Governance,* ed. Rodney Bruce Hall and Thomas J. Biersteker (Cambridge, UK: Cambridge University Press, 2002), chap. 5, 94–95, 103–106. © Rodney Bruce Hall and Thomas J. Biersteker 2002. Reprinted with the permission of Cambridge University Press.

extent not seen in earlier centuries, and, on the other, the considerable institu-tionalizing, especially in the 1990s, of the "rights" of non-national firms, the deregulation of crossborder transactions, and the growing influence/power of some of the supranational organizations. If securing these rights, options, and powers entailed an even partial relinquishing of components of state authority as constructed over the past century, then we can posit that this sets up the conditions for a necessary engagement by national states in the process of globalization.

We need to understand more about the nature of this engagement than is rep-resented by concepts such as deregulation. It is becoming clear that the role of the state in the process of deregulation involves the production of new types of regulations, legislative items, court decisions—in brief, the production of a whole series of new "legalities." The background condition here is that the state remains as the ultimate guarantor of the "rights" of global capital, i.e., the pro-tector of contracts and property rights, and, more generally, a major legitimator of claims. In this regard the state can be seen as incorporating the global project of its own shrinking role in regulating economic transactions and giving it oper-ational effectiveness and legitimacy. The state here can be conceived of as rep-resenting a technical administrative capacity which cannot be replicated at this time by any other institutional arrangement; although not in all cases, this is a capacity backed by military power, with global power in the case of some states. The objective for foreign firms and investors is to enjoy, transnationally, the protections traditionally exercised by the state in the national realm of the economy for national firms, notably guaranteeing property rights and contracts. How this gets done may involve a range of options. To some extent this work of guaranteeing is becoming privatized, as is signaled by the growth of interna-tional commercial arbitration, and by key elements of the new privatized insti-tutional order for governing the global economy.

It is in fact some states, particularly the United States and the UK, that are producing the design for these new legalities, i.e., items derived from Anglo-American commercial law and accounting standards, and are hence imposing these on other states given the interdependencies at the heart of the current phase of globalization. This creates and imposes a set of specific constraints on the other participating states. Legislative items, executive orders, adherence to new technical standards, and so on will have to be produced through the partic-ular institutional and political structures of each of these states. In terms of research and theorization, this is a vast uncharted terrain: it would mean exam-ining how that production takes place and gets legitimated in different countries. This signals the possibility of crossnational variations (which then would need to be established, measured, interpreted). The emergent, often imposed consensus in the community of states to further globalization is not merely a political decision: it entails specific types of work by a large number of distinct state institutions in each of these countries. Clearly, the role of the state will vary significantly depending on the power it may have both internally and internationally.

The US government as the hegemonic power of this period has led/forced other states to adopt these obligations toward global capital. And, in so doing, it has contributed to strengthening the forces that can challenge or destabilize what have historically been constructed as state powers.[1] In my reading this holds both for the United States and for other countries. One way in which this becomes evident is in the fact that, while the state continues to play a crucial, though no longer exclusive, role in the production of legality around new forms of economic activity, at least some of this production of legalities is increasingly feeding the power of a new emerging structure marked by denationalization or privatization of some of its components. . . .

In my reading, studies that emphasize deregulation and liberalization do not sufficiently recognize an important feature, one which matters for the analysis here: the global financial system has reached levels of complexity that require the existence of a crossborder network of financial centers to service the operations of global capital. Each actual financial center represents a massive and highly specialized concentration of resources and talent; and the network of these centers constitutes the operational architecture for the global capital market. . . .

Precisely because global processes need to be coordinated and serviced and because many of these functions materialize to a large extent in national territories, national states have had to become deeply involved in the implementation of the global economic system. In this process states have experienced transformations of various aspects of their institutional structure. This signals that the global economy and the national state are not mutually exclusive domains. Globalization leaves national territory basically unaltered but is having pronounced effects on the exclusive territoriality of the national state—that is, its effects are not on territory as such but on the institutional encasements of the geographic fact of national territory. But alongside and, in my reading, distinct from this diminished territorial authority of the state, there is the denationalizing of specific state agendas. The work of states in producing part of the technical and legal infrastructure for economic globalization has involved both a change in the exclusivity of state authority and in the composition of the work of states. Economic globalization entails a set of practices that destabilize another set of practices, i.e., some of the practices that came to constitute national state sovereignty.

Implementing today's global economic system in the context of national territorial sovereignty required multiple policy, analytic, and narrative negotiations. These negotiations have typically been summarized or coded as "deregulation." There is much more going on in these negotiations than the concept "deregulation" captures. The encounter of a global actor—firm or market—with one or another instantiation of the national state can be thought of as a new frontier. It is not merely a dividing line between the national economy and the global economy. It is a zone of politico-economic interactions that produce new institutional forms and alter some of the old ones. Nor is it just a matter of reducing regulations. For instance, in many countries, the necessity for autonomous central banks in the current global economic system has required a thickening of regulations in order to delink central banks from the influence of the executive branch of government and from deeply "national" political agendas.

Central banks illustrate this well. These are national institutions, concerned with national matters. Yet over the last decade they have become the institutional home within the national state for monetary policies that are necessary to further the development of a global capital market and indeed, more generally, a global economic system. The new conditionality of the global economic system—the requirements that need to be met for a country to become integrated into the global capital market—contains as one key element the autonomy of central banks. This facilitates the task of instituting a certain kind of monetary policy, e.g., one privileging low inflation over job growth even when a president may have preferred it the other way around, particularly at reelection time. While securing central bank autonomy has certainly eliminated a lot of corruption, it has also been the vehicle for one set of accommodations on the part of national states to the requirements of the global capital market. A parallel analysis can be made of ministries of finance (known as the Treasury in the United States and the UK) which have had to impose certain kinds of fiscal policies as part of the new conditionalities of economic globalization.

There is a set of strategic dynamics and institutional transformations at work here. They may incorporate a small number of state agencies and units within departments, a small number of legislative initiatives and of executive orders, and yet have the power to institute a new normativity at the heart of the state; this is especially so because these strategic sectors are operating in complex interactions with private, transnational, powerful actors. Much of the institutional apparatus of the state remains basically unchanged; the inertia of bureaucratic organizations, which creates its own version of path dependence, makes an enormous contribution to continuity. . . .

Further, the new types of crossborder collaborations among specialized government agencies concerned with a growing range of issues emerging from the globalization of capital markets and the new trade order are yet another aspect of this participation by the state in the implementation of a global economic system. A good example is the heightened interaction in the past three or four years among competition policy regulators from a large number of countries. This is a period of renewed concern about competition policy because economic globalization puts pressure on governments to work toward convergence given the crosscountry diversity of competition laws or enforcement practices. This convergence around specific competition policy issues can coexist with ongoing, often enormous differences among these countries when it comes to laws and regulations about those components of their economies that do not intersect with globalization. There are multiple other instances of this highly specialized type of convergence: regulatory issues concerning telecommunications, finance, the Internet, etc. It is, then, a very partial type of convergence among regulators of different countries who often begin to share more with each other than they do with colleagues in their home bureaucracies.

What is of particular concern here is that today we see a sharp increase in the work of establishing convergence.[2] We can clearly identify a new phase in the past ten years. In some of these sectors there has long been an often elementary convergence, or at least coordination, of standards. For instance, central bankers have long interacted with each other across borders, but today we see an intensification in these transactions, which becomes necessary in the effort to develop and extend a global capital market. The increase of crossborder trade has brought with it a sharpened need for convergence in standards, as is evident in the vast proliferation of International Organization for Standardization (ISO) items. Another example is the institutional and legal framework necessary for the operation of the crossborder commodity chains identified by Gereffi.[3]

One outcome of these various trends is the emergence of a strategic field of operations that represents a partial disembedding of specific state operations from the broader institutional world of the state that had been geared exclusively to national agendas. It is a field of crossborder transactions among government agencies and business sectors aimed at addressing the new conditions produced and demanded by economic globalization. In positing this I am rejecting the prevalent notion in much of the literature on globalization that the realm of the national and the realm of the global are two mutually exclusive zones. My argument is rather that globalization is partly endogenous to the national, and is in this regard produced through a dynamic of denationalizing what had been constructed as the national.[4]

It is also a field of particular types of transactions: they are strategic, cut across borders, and entail specific interactions with private actors. These transactions do not entail the state as such, as in international treaties, but rather consist of the operations and policies of specific subcomponents of the state—for instance, legislative initiatives, specialized technical regulatory agencies, or some of the agendas pursued by central banks. These are transactions that cut across borders in that they concern the standards and regulations imposed on firms and markets operating globally,[5] and hence produce a certain convergence at the level of national regulations and law in the creation of the requisite conditions for globalization. The result is a mix of new or strengthened forms of private authority and partly denationalized state authority, such as the instituting of private interests into state normativity.[6]

Notes

1. See, in this regard, Giovanni Arrighi, *The Long Twentieth Century: Money, Power, and the Origins of Our Times* (London: Verso, 1994); Diana E. Davis (ed.), "Chaos and Governance," *Political Power and Social Theory*, 13, Part IV: Scholarly Controversy (Stamford, Conn.: JAI Press, 1999).

2. I use the term convergence for expediency. In the larger project I posit that conceptualizing these outcomes as convergence is actually problematic and often incorrect. Rather than a dynamic whereby individual states wind up converging, what is at work is a global dynamic that gets filtered through the specifics of each "participating" state. Hence my central research concern is not so much the outcome, "convergence," but the work of producing this outcome.

3. Gary Gereffi,"Global Production Systems and Third World Development," in Barbara Stallings (ed.), *Global Change, Regional Response: The New International Context of Development* (New York: Cambridge University Press, 1995), pp. 100–42.

4. Further, insofar as it is partly embedded in national settings, e.g., global cities, the state has had to re-regulate specific aspects of its authority over national territory.

5. An important point, which is usually disregarded in much general commentary about the global economy, is that a firm can participate in the latter even if it operates inside a single country: the key is whether it participates in a market or a transaction that is part of the global "system." My concern in this regard has been to show that there is considerable institutional development of that which is called the global economy—it is not simply a matter of goods or money crossing borders. For a firm's operations to be part of the global economy, they need to be encased in this institutional framework. If they are not, they may constitute an informal crossborder transaction or part of the new transnational criminal economy. A simplified illustration of the point that the distinctiveness of participating in the global economy does not necessarily lie in the fact of crossing borders is, for example, a US-based firm (whether US or non-US) that invests in a non-US firm listed on the New York stock market. The point here is that there is a regime—a set of conditions and legalities—that governs the listing of foreign firms on a stock market that has been incorporated in the global system and that governs the conditions under which the investor can acquire stock in that firm. I see the key, determining issue to be whether the firms and investors involved are operating under the umbrella of this regime. This umbrella is partly constituted through national institutions and partly, perhaps increasingly so, through the new privatized institutional framework I discuss later. What comes together in this example in my reading are some of the specifications I summarize in the global city model and in the notion of denationalization. On the other hand, the following would not be an instance of firms operating in the global economic system, even though it entails actual physical crossing of borders: two individuals residing in different countries making a deal informally for one of them to bring items, also informally—without following regulations, including WTO regulations—for the second individual to sell in the second country, with both individuals using informal accounting and trust systems to guarantee enforcement of the conditions of the agreement. This is an extreme contrast; there are many cases that are more ambiguous than this.

6. As I indicated earlier, I conceptualize denationalization as multivalent. Thus, in the case of human rights, matters which had been considered the prerogative of states—security and protection of its citizens—are universalized and in that sense denationalized (see Sassen, *Denationalization: Economy and Polity in a Global Digital Age* [Princeton: Princeton University Press, forthcoming]).

The Rise of Competitive Authoritarianism

Steven Levitsky and Lucan A. Way

While most regimes throughout the world have been authoritarian, some analysts predicted that authoritarian regimes would eventually crumble in face of popular demands for democracy. (See Huntington [1.2] and selections in Chapter 4 for analyses of this issue.) On the contrary, Steven Levitsky and Lucan Way believe that new forms of authoritarian regimes have emerged. They display the trappings of democracy, especially by holding elections, and they proclaim their support for democracy. But they fail to practice what they preach. Although democratic trappings do matter—they provide opponents of the regime with some resources and protections—the appearance of democracy is far from the reality. Rather than regarding democracy as the wave of the future, then, Levitsky and Way believe that competitive authoritarian regimes are here to stay.

In reading their article, think about why authoritarian leaders might adopt the trappings of democracy. How might competitive authoritarianism be exploited by opposition groups?

The post–Cold War world has been marked by the proliferation of hybrid political regimes. In different ways, and to varying degrees, polities across much of Africa (Ghana, Kenya, Mozambique, Zambia, Zimbabwe), post-communist Eurasia (Albania, Croatia, Russia, Serbia, Ukraine), Asia (Malaysia, Taiwan), and Latin America (Haiti, Mexico, Paraguay, Peru) combined democratic rules with authoritarian governance during the 1990s. Scholars often treated these regimes as incomplete or transitional forms of democracy. Yet in many cases these expectations (or hopes) proved overly optimistic. Particularly in Africa and the former Soviet Union, many regimes have either remained hybrid or moved in an authoritarian direction. It may therefore be time to stop thinking of these cases in terms of transitions to democracy and to begin thinking about the specific types of regimes they actually are.

Steven Levitsky and Lucan A. Way, "The Rise of Competitive Authoritarianism," *Journal of Democracy* 13, no. 2 (April 2002): 51–65 (excerpts). © National Endowment for Democracy and The Johns Hopkins University Press. Reprinted with permission of The Johns Hopkins University Press.

In recent years, many scholars have pointed to the importance of hybrid regimes. Indeed, recent academic writings have produced a variety of labels for mixed cases, including not only "hybrid regime" but also "semidemocracy," "virtual democracy," "electoral democracy," "pseudodemocracy," "illiberal democracy," "semi-authoritarianism," "soft authoritarianism," "electoral authoritarianism," and Freedom House's "Partly Free."[1] . . .

Defining Competitive Authoritarianism

This article examines one particular type of "hybrid" regime: *competitive authoritarianism*. In competitive authoritarian regimes, formal democratic institutions are widely viewed as the principal means of obtaining and exercising political authority. Incumbents violate those rules so often and to such an extent, however, that the regime fails to meet conventional minimum standards for democracy. Examples include Croatia under Franjo Tudjman, Serbia under Slobodan Milošević, Russia under Vladimir Putin, Ukraine under Leonid Kravchuk and Leonid Kuchma, Peru under Alberto Fujimori, and post-1995 Haiti, as well as Albania, Armenia, Ghana, Kenya, Malaysia, Mexico, and Zambia through much of the 1990s. Although scholars have characterized many of these regimes as partial or "diminished" forms of democracy, we agree with Juan Linz that they may be better described as a (diminished) form of authoritarianism.[2]

Competitive authoritarianism must be distinguished from democracy on the one hand and full-scale authoritarianism on the other. Modern democratic regimes all meet four minimum criteria: 1) Executives and legislatures are chosen through elections that are open, free, and fair; 2) virtually all adults possess the right to vote; 3) political rights and civil liberties, including freedom of the press, freedom of association, and freedom to criticize the government without reprisal, are broadly protected; and 4) elected authorities possess real authority to govern, in that they are not subject to the tutelary control of military or clerical leaders.[3] Although even fully democratic regimes may at times violate one or more of these criteria, such violations are not broad or systematic enough to seriously impede democratic challenges to incumbent governments. In other words, they do not fundamentally alter the playing field between government and opposition.[4]

In competitive authoritarian regimes, by contrast, violations of these criteria are both frequent enough and serious enough to create an uneven playing field between government and opposition. Although elections are regularly held and are generally free of massive fraud, incumbents routinely abuse state resources, deny the opposition adequate media coverage, harass opposition candidates and their supporters, and in some cases manipulate electoral results. Journalists, opposition politicians, and other government critics may be spied on, threatened, harassed, or arrested. Members of the opposition may be jailed, exiled, or—less frequently—even assaulted or murdered. Regimes characterized by such abuses cannot be called democratic.

Competitive authoritarianism must therefore be distinguished from unstable, ineffective, or otherwise flawed types of regimes that nevertheless meet basic standards of democracy, and this includes what Guillermo O'Donnell has called "delegative democracies."[5] According to O'Donnell, delegative democracies are characterized by low levels of horizontal accountability (checks and balances) and therefore exhibit powerful, plebiscitarian, and occasionally abusive executives. Yet such regimes meet minimum standards for democracy. Delegative democracy thus applies to such cases as Argentina and Brazil in the early 1990s, but not to Peru after Fujimori's 1992 presidential self-coup.

Yet if competitive authoritarian regimes fall short of democracy, they also fall short of full-scale authoritarianism. Although incumbents in competitive authoritarian regimes may routinely manipulate formal democratic rules, they are unable to eliminate them or reduce them to a mere façade. Rather than openly violating democratic rules (for example, by banning or repressing the opposition and the media), incumbents are more likely to use bribery, co-optation, and more subtle forms of persecution, such as the use of tax authorities, compliant judiciaries, and other state agencies to "legally" harass, persecute, or extort co-operative behavior from critics. Yet even if the cards are stacked in favor of autocratic incumbents, the persistence of meaningful democratic institutions creates arenas through which opposition forces may—and frequently do—pose significant challenges. As a result, even though democratic institutions may be badly flawed, both authoritarian incumbents and their opponents must take them seriously.

In this sense, competitive authoritarianism is distinct from what might be called "façade" electoral regimes—that is, regimes in which electoral institutions exist but yield no meaningful contestation for power (such as Egypt, Singapore, and Uzbekistan in the 1990s). Such regimes have been called "pseudodemocracies," "virtual democracies," and "electoral authoritarian" regimes. In our view, they are cases of full-scale authoritarianism.[6] The line between this type of regime and competitive authoritarianism can be hard to draw, and noncompetitive electoral institutions may one day become competitive (as occurred in Mexico). It is essential, however, to distinguish regimes in which democratic institutions offer an important channel through which the opposition may seek power from those regimes in which democratic rules simply serve as to legitimate an existing autocratic leadership.

Finally, competitive authoritarianism must be distinguished from other types of hybrid regimes. Regimes may mix authoritarian and democratic features in a variety of ways, and competitive authoritarianism should not be viewed as encompassing all of these regime forms. Other hybrid regime types include "exclusive republics"[7] (regimes with strong democratic institutions but highly restrictive citizenship laws) and "tutelary" or "guided" democracies—competitive regimes in which nondemocratic actors such as military or religious authorities wield veto power.

Four Arenas of Democratic Contestation

Due to the persistence of meaningful democratic institutions in competitive authoritarian regimes, arenas of contestation exist through which opposition forces may periodically challenge, weaken, and occasionally even defeat autocratic incumbents. Four such arenas are of particular importance: 1) the electoral arena; 2) the legislature; 3) the judiciary; and 4) the media.

1) The electoral arena. The first and most important arena of contestation is the electoral arena. In authoritarian regimes, elections either do not exist or are not seriously contested. Electoral competition is eliminated either de jure, as in Cuba and China, or de facto, as in Kazakhstan and Uzbekistan. In the latter, opposition parties are routinely banned or disqualified from electoral competition, and opposition leaders are often jailed. In addition, independent or outside observers are prevented from verifying results via parallel vote counts, which creates widespread opportunities for vote stealing. As a result, opposition forces do not present a serious electoral threat to incumbents, and elections are, for all intents and purposes, noncompetitive. Thus Kazakhstani president Nursultan Nazarbayev was reelected in 1999 with 80 percent of the vote, and in Uzbekistan, President Islam Karimov was reelected in 2000 with 92 percent of the vote. (As a rule of thumb, regimes in which presidents are reelected with more than 70 percent of the vote can generally be considered noncompetitive.) In such cases, the death or violent overthrow of the president is often viewed as a more likely means of succession than his electoral defeat.

In competitive authoritarian regimes, by contrast, elections are often bitterly fought. Although the electoral process may be characterized by large-scale abuses of state power, biased media coverage, (often violent) harassment of opposition candidates and activists,[8] and an overall lack of transparency, elections are regularly held, competitive (in that major opposition parties and candidates usually participate), and generally free of massive fraud. In many cases, the presence of international observers or the existence of parallel vote-counting procedures limits the capacity of incumbents to engage in large-scale fraud. As a result, elections may generate considerable uncertainty, and autocratic incumbents must therefore take them seriously. . . .

Although incumbents may manipulate election results, this often costs them dearly and can even bring them down. In Peru, for example, Fujimori was able to gain reelection in 2000 but was forced to resign amid scandal months later. Similarly, efforts by Milošević to falsify Serbian election results in 2000 led to a regime crisis and the president's removal. Regime crises resulting from electoral fraud also occurred in Mexico in 1988 and Armenia in 1996.

2) The legislative arena. A second arena of contestation is the legislature. In most full-scale authoritarian regimes, legislatures either do not exist or are so thoroughly controlled by the ruling party that conflict between the legislature and the executive branch is virtually unthinkable. In competitive authoritarian regimes, legislatures tend to be relatively weak, but they occasionally become focal points of opposition activity. This is particularly likely in cases in which incumbents lack strong majority parties. In both Ukraine and Russia in the 1990s, for example, presidents were faced with recalcitrant parliaments dominated by former communist and other left-wing parties. The Ukrainian parliament repeatedly blocked or watered down economic reform legislation proposed by President Kuchma, and in 2000–2001, despite Kuchma's threats to take "appropriate" measures if it did not cooperate, parliament blocked the president's effort to call a referendum aimed at reducing the powers of the legislature. Although incumbents may attempt to circumvent or even shut down the legislature (as in Peru in 1992 and Russia in 1993), such actions tend to be costly, particularly in the international arena. Thus both Fujimori and Yeltsin held new legislative elections within three years of their "self-coups," and Yeltsin continued to face opposition from the post-1993-coup parliament.

Even where incumbent executives enjoy large legislative majorities, opposition forces may use the legislature as a place for meeting and organizing and (to the extent that an independent media exists) as a public platform from which to denounce the regime. In Peru, despite the fact that opposition parties exerted little influence over the legislative process between 1995 and 2000, anti-Fujimori legislators used congress (and media coverage of it) as a place to air their views. In Ukraine in November 2000, opposition deputy Aleksandr Moroz used parliament to accuse the president of murder and to distribute damaging tapes of the president to the press.

3) The judicial arena. A third arena of potential contestation is the judiciary. Governments in competitive authoritarian regimes routinely attempt to subordinate the judiciary, often via impeachment, or, more subtly, through bribery, extortion, and other mechanisms of co-optation. In Peru, for example, scores of judges—including several Supreme Court justices—were entwined in the web of patronage, corruption, and black-mail constructed by Fujimori's intelligence chief, Vladimiro Montesinos. In Russia, when the Constitutional Court declared Yeltsin's 1993 decree disbanding parliament to be unconstitutional, Yeltsin cut off the Court's phone lines and took away its guards. In some cases, governments resort to threats and violence. In Zimbabwe, after the Supreme Court ruled that occupations of white-owned farmland—part of the Mugabe government's land-redistribution policy—were illegal, independent justices received a wave of violent threats from pro-government "war veterans." Four justices, including Chief Justice Anthony Gubbay, opted for early retirement in 2001 and were replaced by justices with closer ties to the government.

Yet the combination of formal judicial independence and incomplete control by the executive can give maverick judges an opening. In Ukraine, for example, the Constitutional Court stipulated that President Kuchma's referendum to reduce the powers of the legislature was not binding. In Slovakia, the Constitutional Court prevented Vladimír Mečiar's government from denying the opposition seats in parliament in 1994, and in Serbia, the courts legitimized local opposition electoral victories in 1996. Courts have also protected media and opposition figures from state persecution. In Croatia, the courts acquitted an opposition weekly that had been charged with falsely accusing President Tudjman of being a devotee of Spain's Francisco Franco. Similarly, in Malaysia in 2001, a High Court judge released two dissidents who had been jailed under the regime's Internal Security Act and publicly questioned the need for such a draconian law.[9]

Although competitive authoritarian governments may subsequently punish judges who rule against them, such acts against formally independent judiciaries may generate important costs in terms of domestic and international legitimacy. In Peru, for example, the pro-Fujimori congress sacked three members of the Constitutional Tribunal in 1997 after they attempted to block Fujimori's constitutionally dubious bid for a third presidential term. The move generated sharp criticism both domestically and abroad, however, and the case remained a thorn in the regime's side for the rest of the decade.

4) The media. Finally, the media are often a central point of contention in competitive authoritarian regimes. In most full-blown autocracies, the media are entirely state-owned, heavily censored, or systematically repressed. Leading television and radio stations are controlled by the government (or its close - allies), and major independent newspapers and magazines are either prohibited by law (as in Cuba) or de facto eliminated (as in Uzbekistan and Turkmenistan). Journalists who provoke the ire of the government risk arrest, deportation, and even assassination. In competitive authoritarian regimes, by contrast, independent media outlets are not only legal but often quite influential, and journalists—though frequently threatened and periodically attacked—often emerge as important opposition figures. In Peru, for example, independent newspapers such as *La República* and *El Comercio* and weekly magazines such as *Sí* and *Caretas* operated freely throughout the 1990s. In Ukraine, newspapers such as *Zerkalo nedeli, Den,* and, more recently, *Vicherni visti* functioned as important sources of independent views on the Kuchma government.

Independent media outlets often play a critical watchdog role by investigating and exposing government malfeasance. The Peruvian media uncovered a range of government abuses, including the 1992 massacre of students at La Cantuta University and the forgery of the signatures needed for Fujimori's party to qualify for the 2000 elections. In Russia, Vladimir Gusinsky's Independent TV was an important source of criticism of the Yeltsin government, particularly with respect to its actions in Chechnya. In Zimbabwe, the *Daily News* played an important role in exposing the abuses of the Mugabe government. Media outlets may also serve as mouthpieces for opposition forces. In Serbia, the Belgrade radio station B-92 served as a key center of opposition to Milošević in the second half of the 1990s. Newspapers played an important role in supporting opposition forces in Panama and Nicaragua in the late 1980s.

Executives in competitive authoritarian regimes often actively seek to suppress the independent media, using more subtle mechanisms of repression than their counterparts in authoritarian regimes. These methods often include bribery, the selective allocation of state advertising, the manipulation of debts and taxes owed by media outlets, the fomentation of conflicts among stockholders, and restrictive press laws that facilitate the prosecution of independent and opposition journalists. In Russia, the government took advantage of Independent TV's debts to the main gas company, Gazprom, to engineer a takeover by government-friendly forces. In Peru, the Fujimori government gained de facto control over all of the country's privately owned television stations through a combination of bribery and legal shenanigans, such as the invalidation of Channel 2 owner Baruch Ivcher's citizenship. Governments also make extensive use of libel laws to harass or persecute independent newspapers "legally." In Ghana, for example, the Jerry Rawlings government used colonial-era libel statutes to imprison several newspaper editors and columnists in the 1990s, and in Croatia, the Open Society Institute reported in 1997 that major independent newspapers had been hit by more than 230 libel suits. Similarly, Armenia's government used libel suits to quiet press criticism after the country's controversial 1996 elections.[10]

Yet efforts to repress the media may be costly to incumbents in competitive authoritarian regimes. For example, when in 1996 the Tudjman government in Croatia tried to revoke the license of Radio 101, a popular independent station in the capital, the massive protests that broke out both galvanized the opposition and temporarily split the ruling party. In Ukraine in 2000, charges that President Kuchma had sought the killing of an opposition journalist led to large domestic protests and partial isolation from the West. In Peru, the persecution and exiling of Ivcher provoked substantial protest at home and became a focal point of criticism abroad.

Inherent Tensions

Authoritarian governments may coexist indefinitely with meaningful democratic institutions. As long as incumbents avoid egregious (and well-publicized) rights abuses and do not cancel or openly steal elections, the contradictions inherent in competitive authoritarianism may be manageable. Using bribery, co-optation, and various forms of "legal" persecution, governments may limit opposition challenges without provoking massive protest or international repudiation.

Yet the coexistence of democratic rules and autocratic methods aimed at keeping incumbents in power creates an inherent source of instability. The presence of elections, legislatures, courts, and an independent media creates periodic opportunities for challenges by opposition forces. Such challenges create a serious dilemma for autocratic incumbents. On the one hand, repressing them is costly, largely because the challenges tend to be both formally legal and widely perceived (domestically and internationally) as legitimate. On the other hand, incumbents could lose power if they let democratic challenges run their course.[11] Periods of serious democratic contestation thus bring out the contradictions inherent in competitive authoritarianism, forcing autocratic incumbents to choose between egregiously violating democratic rules, at the cost of international isolation and domestic conflict, and allowing the challenge to proceed, at the cost of possible defeat. The result is often some kind of regime crisis, as occurred in Mexico in 1988; Nicaragua in 1990; Zambia in 1991; Russia in 1993; Armenia in 1996; Albania in 1997; Ghana, Peru, Serbia, and Ukraine in 2000; and Zambia (again) in 2001. A similar crisis appears likely to emerge in Zimbabwe surrounding the March 2002 presidential election.

In some cases, such as those of Kenya, Malaysia, Russia, and Ukraine, autocratic incumbents weathered the storm. In several of these countries, the regime cracked down and dug in deeper. In other cases, such as Nicaragua in 1990, Zambia in 1991, and Ghana and Mexico in 2000, competitive authoritarian governments failed to crack down and lost power. In still other cases, including Peru and Serbia, autocrats attempted to crack down but, in doing so, were badly weakened and eventually fell.

But succession is not democratization. Although in many cases (Croatia, Nicaragua, Peru, Slovakia, Serbia) incumbent turnover resulted in democratic transitions, in other cases, including Albania, Zambia, Ukraine, and Belarus, newly elected leaders continued or even intensified many of the authoritarian practices of their predecessors. Hence, while the removal of autocratic elites creates an important *opportunity* for regime change and even democratization, it does not ensure such an outcome.

Although it is beyond the scope of this article to explain variations in the capacity of competitive authoritarian regimes to survive crises brought about by episodes of democratic contestation, one pattern is worth noting.[12] In regions with closer ties to the West, particularly Latin America and Central Europe, the removal of autocratic incumbents has generally resulted in democratization in the post–Cold War period. In Latin America, for example, four out of five competitive authoritarian regimes democratized after 1990 (the Dominican Republic, Mexico, Nicaragua, and Peru, but not Haiti). Similarly, during the same period four out of five competitive authoritarian regimes in Central Europe democratized (Croatia, Serbia, Slovakia, and Romania, but not Albania). By contrast, the record of competitive authoritarian regimes in Africa and the former Soviet Union is strikingly different. Among former Soviet republics, only one competitive authoritarian regime (Moldova) democratized in the 1990s.

This evidence suggests that proximity to the West may have been an important factor shaping the trajectory of competitive authoritarian regimes in the 1990s. Linkages to the West—in the form of cultural and media influence, elite networks, demonstration effects, and direct pressure from Western governments—appear to have raised the costs of authoritarian entrenchment, making the democratization of competitive authoritarian regimes more likely. Where Western linkages were weaker, or where alternative, nondemocratic hegemons (such as Russia or China) exerted substantial influence, competitive authoritarian regimes were more likely either to persist or to move in a more authoritarian direction. . . .

Conceptualizing Nondemocracies

We conclude by echoing Thomas Carothers' call to move beyond what he calls the "transition paradigm."[13] It is now clear that early hopes for democratization in much of the world were overly optimistic. Many authoritarian regimes have survived the "third wave" of democratization. In other cases, the collapse of one kind of authoritarianism yielded not democracy but a new form of nondemocratic rule. Indeed, a decade after the collapse of the Soviet Union, the majority of the world's independent states remained nondemocratic. Yet whereas an extensive literature has emerged concerning the causes and consequences of democratization, emerging types of democracy, and issues of democratic consolidation, remarkably little research has been undertaken on the emergence or persistence of nondemocratic regimes.

The post–Cold War Western liberal hegemony, global economic change, developments in media and communications technologies, and the growth of international networks aimed at promoting democracy and human rights all have contributed to reshaping the opportunities and constraints facing authoritarian elites. As a result, some forms of authoritarianism, such as totalitarianism and bureaucratic authoritarianism, have become more difficult to sustain. At the same time, however, several new (or partially new) nondemocratic regime types took on greater importance in the 1990s, including competitive authoritarianism. A range of other nondemocratic outcomes also gained in importance, including other types of hybrid regimes, postcommunist patrimonial dictatorships, and cases of sustained state collapse ("chaosocracy").[14] Research on these nondemocratic outcomes is critical to gaining a better understanding of the full (rather than hoped for) set of alternatives open to post–Cold War transitional regimes.

Notes

1. Terry Lynn Karl, "The Hybrid Regimes of Central America," *Journal of Democracy* 6 (July 1995): 72–87; William Case, "Can the 'Halfway House' Stand? Semidemocracy and Elite Theory in Three Southeast Asian Countries," *Comparative Politics* 28 (July 1996): 437–64; Richard A. Joseph, "Africa, 1990–1997: From *Abertura* to Closure," *Journal of Democracy* 9 (April 1998): 3–17; Larry Diamond, *Developing Democracy: Toward Consolidation* (Baltimore: Johns Hopkins University Press, 1999); Fareed Zakaria, "The Rise of Illiberal Democracy," *Foreign Affairs* 76 (November–December 1997): 22–41; Thomas Carothers, *Aiding Democracy Abroad: The Learning Curve* (Washington, D.C.: Carnegie

Endowment for International Peace, 1999); Gordon P. Means, "Soft Authoritarianism in Malaysia and Singapore," *Journal of Democracy* 7 (October 1996): 103–17; Andreas Schedler, "Mexico's Victory: The Democratic Revelation," *Journal of Democracy* 11 (October 2000): 5–19; and M. Steven Fish, "Authoritarianism Despite Elections: Russia in Light of Democratic Theory and Practice," paper prepared for delivery at the 2001 Annual Meeting of the American Political Science Association, San Francisco, 30 August–2 September 2001.

2. Juan J. Linz, *Totalitarian and Authoritarian Regimes* (Boulder, Colo.: Lynne Rienner, 2000), 34.

3. See Scott Mainwaring, Daniel Brinks, and Aníbal Pérez Linan, "Classifying Political Regimes in Latin America, 1945–1999," *Studies in Comparative International Development* 36 (Spring 2001). This definition is consistent with what Larry Diamond calls "mid-range" conceptions of democracy (Larry Diamond, *Developing Democracy*, 13–15).

4. Obviously, the exact point at which violations of civil and political rights begin to fundamentally alter the playing field is difficult to discern and will always be open to debate. However, the problem of scoring borderline cases is common to all regime conceptualizations.

5. Guillermo O'Donnell, "Delegative Democracy," *Journal of Democracy* 5 (January 1994): 55–69.

6. Larry Diamond, *Developing Democracy*, 15–16; Richard Joseph, "Africa, 1990–1997"; Jason Brownlee, "Double Edged Institutions: Electoral Authoritarianism in Egypt and Iran," paper presented at the 2001 Annual Meeting of the American Political Science Association, San Francisco, 30 August–2 September 2001.

7. Philip G. Roeder, "Varieties of Post-Soviet Authoritarian Regimes," *Post-Soviet Affairs* 10 (January–March 1994): 61–101.

8. In Kenya, government-backed death squads were responsible for large-scale violence, particularly in ethnic minority areas. See Joel Barkan and Njuguna Ng'ethe, "Kenya Tries Again," in Larry Diamond and Marc F. Plattner, eds., *Democratization in Africa* (Baltimore: Johns Hopkins University Press, 1999), 185. Substantial violence against opposition forces was also seen in Serbia and Zimbabwe in the 1990s.

9. *The Economist*, 14 July 2001, 37.

10. H. Kwasi Prempeh, "A New Jurisprudence for Africa," *Journal of Democracy* 10 (July 1999): 138; Nebojsa Bjelakovic and Sava Tatic, "Croatia: Another Year of Bleak Continuities," *Transitions-on-Line*, *http://archive.tol.cz/countries/croar97.html* (1997). Mikhail Diloyen, "Journalists Fall Through the Legal Cracks in Armenia," *Eurasia Insight* (June 2000).

11. These dilemmas are presented in an insightful way in Andreas Schedler, "The Nested Game of Democratization by Elections," *International Political Science Review* 23 (January 2002).

12. For a more developed explanation, see Steven Levitsky and Lucan A. Way, "Competitive Authoritarianism: Hybrid Regime Change in Peru and Ukraine in Comparative Perspective," Studies in Public Policy Working Paper No. 355 (Glasgow: University of Strathclyde Center for the Study of Public Policy, 2001).

13. Thomas Carothers, "The End of the Transition Paradigm," *Journal of Democracy* 13, no. 1 (January 2002): 5–21.

14. See Richard Snyder, "Does Lootable Wealth Breed Disorder? States, Regimes, and the Political Economy of Extraction," paper presented at the 2001 Annual Meeting of the American Political Science Association, San Francisco, 30 August–2 September 2001. See also Juan J. Linz, *Totalitarian and Authoritarian Regimes*, 37.

Failed States in a World of Terror

Robert I. Rotberg

Some states do not have the power and capacity to carry out the basic requirements of a state: maintaining law and order in their territory; ensuring their citizens
at least a minimum of food, shelter, and other material resources; and protecting
the country from military threats. Robert Rotberg describes such cases as failed
states. He warns that they pose a danger to their own citizens and to their neighbors by engaging in violent activities in an attempt to increase their control. They
may also provide a safe haven for terrorist groups to train and organize. In rare
cases, Rotberg notes, failed states may collapse altogether, producing anarchy
and chaos. Why does this happen? Why are failed states more likely to be found
in some regions? What are the pros and cons of the case for the international
community, for example, the United Nations, intervening when states fail?

The Road to Hell

In the wake of September 11, the threat of terrorism has given the problem of
failed nation-states an immediacy and importance that transcends its previous
humanitarian dimension. Since the early 1990s, wars in and among failed states
have killed about eight million people, most of them civilians, and displaced
another four million. The number of those impoverished, malnourished, and deprived of fundamental needs such as security, health care, and education has totaled
in the hundreds of millions.

Although the phenomenon of state failure is not new, it has become much
more relevant and worrying than ever before. In less interconnected eras, state
weakness could be isolated and kept distant. Failure had fewer implications for
peace and security. Now, these states pose dangers not only to themselves and
their neighbors but also to peoples around the globe. Preventing states from failing, and resuscitating those that do fail, are thus strategic and moral imperatives.

Robert I. Rotberg, "Failed States in a World of Terror," *Foreign Affairs* 81, no. 4 (July/August
2002). Reprinted by permission of *Foreign Affairs,* 81, no. 4, July–August 2002. Copyright 2002
by the Council on Foreign Relations, Inc.

But failed states are not homogeneous. The nature of state failure varies from place to place, sometimes dramatically. Failure and weakness can flow from a nation's geographical, physical, historical, and political circumstances, such as colonial errors and Cold War policy mistakes. More than structural or institutional weaknesses, human agency is also culpable, usually in a fatal way. Destructive decisions by individual leaders have almost always paved the way to state failure. President Mobutu Sese Seko's three-plus decades of kleptocratic rule sucked Zaire (now the Democratic Republic of Congo, or DRC) dry until he was deposed in 1997. In Sierra Leone, President Siaka Stevens (1967–85) systematically plundered his tiny country and instrumentalized disorder. President Mohamed Siad Barre (1969–91) did the same in Somalia. These rulers were personally greedy, but as predatory patrimonialists they also licensed and sponsored the avarice of others, thus preordaining the destruction of their states.

Today's failed states, such as Afghanistan, Sierra Leone, and Somalia, are incapable of projecting power and asserting authority within their own borders, leaving their territories governmentally empty. This outcome is troubling to world order, especially to an international system that demands—indeed, counts on—a state's capacity to govern its space. Failed states have come to be feared as "breeding grounds of instability, mass migration, and murder" (in the words of political scientist Stephen Walt), as well as reservoirs and exporters of terror. The existence of these kinds of countries, and the instability that they harbor, not only threatens the lives and livelihoods of their own peoples but endangers world peace.

Into the Abyss

The road to state failure is marked by several revealing signposts. On the economic side, living standards deteriorate rapidly as elites deliver financial rewards only to favored families, clans, or small groups. Foreign-exchange shortages provoke food and fuel scarcities and curtail government spending on essential services and political goods; accordingly, citizens see their medical, educational, and logistical entitlements melt away. Corruption flourishes as ruling cadres systematically skim the few resources available and stash their ill-gotten gains in hard-to-trace foreign bank accounts.

On the political side, leaders and their associates subvert prevailing democratic norms, coerce legislatures and bureaucracies into subservience, strangle judicial independence, block civil society, and gain control over security and defense forces. They usually patronize an ethnic group, clan, class, or kin. Other groups feel excluded or discriminated against, as was the case in Somalia and Sierra Leone in the 1970s and 1980s. Governments that once appeared to operate for the benefit of all the nation's citizens are perceived to have become partisan.

→ Civil Society?

As these two paths converge, the state provides fewer and fewer services. Overall, ordinary citizens become poorer as their rulers become visibly wealthier. People feel preyed upon by the regime and its agents—often underpaid civil servants, police officers, and soldiers fending for themselves. Security, the most important political good, vanishes. Citizens, especially those who have known more prosperous and democratic times, increasingly feel that they exist solely to satisfy the power lust and financial greed of those in power. Meanwhile, corrupt despots drive grandly down city boulevards in motorcades, commandeer commercial aircraft for foreign excursions, and put their faces prominently on the local currency and on oversize photographs in public places. President Robert Mugabe of Zimbabwe, for example, purchased 19 expensively armored limousines for his own motorcade before his reelection earlier this year.

In the last phase of failure, the state's legitimacy crumbles. Lacking meaningful or realistic democratic means of redress, protesters take to the streets or mobilize along ethnic, religious, or linguistic lines. Because small arms and even more formidable weapons are cheap and easy to find, because historical grievances are readily remembered or manufactured, and because the spoils of separation, autonomy, or a total takeover are attractive, the potential for violent conflict grows exponentially as the state's power and legitimacy recede.

If preventive diplomacy, conflict resolution, or external intervention cannot arrest this process of disaffection and mutual antagonism, the state at risk can collapse completely (Somalia), break down and be sundered (Angola, the DRC, and Sudan), or plunge into civil war (Afghanistan and Liberia). The state may also lapse and then be restored to various degrees of health by the UN (Bosnia and Cambodia), a regional or subregional organization (Sierra Leone and Liberia), or a well-intentioned or hegemonic outside power (Syria in Lebanon, Russia in Tajikistan). A former colonial territory such as East Timor can be brought back to life by the efforts and cash infusions of a UN-run transitional administration.

Law and Order

State failure threatens global stability because national governments have become the primary building blocks of order. International security relies on states to protect against chaos at home and limit the cancerous spread of anarchy beyond their borders and throughout the world. States exist to deliver political (i.e., public) goods to their inhabitants. When they function as they ideally should, they mediate between the constraints and challenges of the international arena and the dynamic forces of their own internal economic, political, and social realities.

The new concern over state failure notwithstanding, strong, effective states are more numerous now than before 1914. This shift occurred after the collapse of the Ottoman and Austro-Hungarian empires, continued with the demise of colonialism in Africa and Asia, and concluded with the implosion of the Soviet Union. In 1914, 55 polities could be considered members of the global system; in 1960, there were 90 such states. After the Cold War, that number climbed to 192. But given the explosion in the number of states—so many of which are small, resource-deprived, geographically disadvantaged, and poor—it is no wonder that numerous states are at risk of failure.

States are not created equal. Their sizes and shapes, their human endowments, their capacity for delivering services, and their leadership capabilities vary enormously. More is required of the modern state, too, than ever before. Each is expected to provide good governance; to make its people secure, prosperous, healthy, and literate; and to instill a sense of national pride. States also exist to deliver political goods—i.e., services and benefits that the private sector is usually less able to provide. Foremost is the provision of national and individual security and public order. That promise includes security of property and inviolable contracts (both of which are grounded in an enforceable code of laws), an independent judiciary, and other methods of accountability. A second but vital political good is the provision, organization, and regulation of logistical and communications infrastructures. A nation without well-maintained arteries of commerce and information serves its citizens poorly. Finally, a state helps provide basic medical care and education, social services, a social safety net, regulation and supply of water and energy, and environmental protection. When governments refuse to or cannot provide such services to all of their citizens, failure looms.

But not all of the states that fit this general profile fail. Some rush to the brink of failure, totter at the abyss, remain fragile, but survive. Weakness is endemic in many developing nations—the halfway house between strength and failure. Some weak states, such as Chad and Kyrgyzstan (and even once-mighty Russia), exhibit several of the defining characteristics of failed states and yet do not fail. Others, such as Zimbabwe, may slide rapidly from comparative strength to the very edge of failure. A few, such as Sri Lanka and Colombia, may suffer from vicious, enduring civil wars without ever failing, while remaining weak and susceptible to failure. Some, such as Tajikistan, have retrieved themselves from possible collapse (sometimes with outside help) and remain shaky and vulnerable, but they no longer can be termed "failed." Thus it is important to ask what separates strong from weak states, and weak states from failed states. What defines the phenomenon of failure?

The Essence of Failure

Strong states control their territories and deliver a high order of political goods to their citizens. They perform well according to standard indicators such as per capita GDP, the UN's Human Development Index, Transparency International's Corruption Perception Index, and Freedom House's Freedom in the

World report. Strong states offer high levels of security from political and criminal violence, ensure political freedom and civil liberties, and create environments conducive to the growth of economic opportunity. They are places of peace and order.

In contrast, failed states are tense, conflicted, and dangerous. They generally share the following characteristics: a rise in criminal and political violence; a loss of control over their borders; rising ethnic, religious, linguistic, and cultural hostilities; civil war; the use of terror against their own citizens; weak institutions; a deteriorated or insufficient infrastructure; an inability to collect taxes without undue coercion; high levels of corruption; a collapsed health system; rising levels of infant mortality and declining life expectancy; the end of regular schooling opportunities; declining levels of GDP per capita; escalating inflation; a widespread preference for non-national currencies; and basic food shortages, leading to starvation.

Failed states also face rising attacks on their fundamental legitimacy. As a state's capacity weakens and its rulers work exclusively for themselves, key interest groups show less and less loyalty to the state. The people's sense of political community vanishes and citizens feel disenfranchised and marginalized. The social contract that binds citizens and central structures is forfeit. Perhaps already divided by sectional differences and animosity, citizens transfer their allegiances to communal warlords. Domestic anarchy sets in. The rise of terrorist groups becomes more likely.

Seven failed states exist today: Afghanistan, Angola, Burundi, the DRC, Liberia, Sierra Leone, and Sudan. They each exhibit most, if not all, of the traits listed above. Internal hot wars are also a leading indicator of failure, but failure usually precedes the outbreak of war. Hence, the extent of internecine antagonisms and how they are handled are important predictors of failure. Likewise, the nature of the rulers' approach toward minorities, working classes, and other weak or marginalized peoples is indicative.

Among today's failed states, Angola and Sudan have oil wealth, and Angola, the DRC, and Sierra Leone boast diamonds and other mineral resources. But all four countries' governments, as well as those of Afghanistan, Burundi, and Liberia, share a common feature: they deliver security in limited quantities and across circumscribed areas. Moreover, their per capita GDP rates are very low, life expectancies are declining, and basic governmental services are lacking. In each case, the ruling regime projects little power. Each confronts ongoing civil strife, a proliferation of substate authorities, porous borders, high rates of civilian casualties, and a challenge to the regime's intrinsic legitimacy by competing internal forces. Utter collapse is possible in each case, as is dismemberment, outside tutelage, or an interim assumption of UN control. All remain on the humanitarian watch list as potent sources of displaced persons and refugees. (Sierra Leone, however, has recently established a rudimentary government and has quieted its civil war with the assistance of 17,000 British and UN soldiers. But it was a collapsed state from the late 1990s until 2000.)

Total Collapse

Truly collapsed states, a rare and extreme version of a failed state, are typified by an absence of authority. Indeed, a collapsed state is a shell of a polity. Somalia is the model of a collapsed state: a geographical expression only, with borders but with no effective way to exert authority within those borders. Substate actors have taken over. The central government has been divided up, replaced by a functioning, unrecognized state called Somaliland in the north and a less well defined, putative state called Punt in the northeast. In the rump of the old Somalia, a transitional national government has emerged thanks to outside support. But it has so far been unable to project its power even locally against the several warlords who control sections of Mogadishu and large swaths of the countryside. Private entrepreneurialism has displaced the central provision of political goods. Yet life somehow continues, even under conditions of unhealthy, dangerous chaos.

An example of a once-collapsed state is Lebanon, which had disintegrated before Syria's intervention in 1990 provided security and gave a sense of governmental legitimacy to the shell of the state. Lebanon today qualifies as a weak, rather than failed, polity because its government is credible, civil war is absent, and political goods are being provided in significant quantities and quality. Syria provides the security blanket, denies fractious warlords the freedom to aggrandize themselves, and mandates that the usually antagonistic Muslim and Christian communities cooperate. The fear of being attacked preemptively by rivals, or of losing control of critical resources, is alleviated by Syria's imposed hegemony. Within that framework of security, the Lebanese people's traditional entrepreneurial spirit has transformed a failed state into a much stronger one.

The Art of Prevention

Experience suggests that the prevention of state failure depends almost entirely on a scarce commodity: international political will. In part, prevention relies on outsiders' recognizing early that a state's internal turmoil has the potential to be fatally destructive. That recognition should be accompanied by subregional, regional, and UN overtures, followed, if required, by private remonstrations—that is, quiet diplomacy. If such entreaties have little effect, there will be a need for public criticism by donor countries, international agencies, the UN, and regional groupings such as the European Union (EU) or the Association of Southeast Asian Nations. These entities should also cease economic assistance, impose "smart sanctions," ban international travel by miscreant leaders, and freeze their overseas accounts—much as the EU and the United States did to Mugabe and his cohort in February. Furthermore, misbehaving nations should be suspended from international organizations. In retrospect, if the international

[handwritten marginal note: Somalia now once was Lebanon till Syria Intervention]

community had more effectively shunned Siad Barre, Mobutu, Idi Amin of Uganda, or Sani Abacha of Nigeria, it might have helped to minimize the destruction of their states. Ostracizing such strongmen and publicly criticizing their rogue states would also reduce the necessity for any subsequent UN peacekeeping and relief missions.

Zimbabwe is an instructive case. Two years ago, Mugabe began employing state-sponsored violence to harass opponents and intimidate voters during the runup to parliamentary elections. But South Africa and the other members of the Southern African Development Community (SADC) refrained from public criticism of Zimbabwe. The EU and the United States expressed displeasure at Mugabe's tactics of terror but likewise decided that constructive engagement would be more effective than an open rebuke. As brutally as Mugabe was acting, outsiders believed that Zimbabwe's despot could be persuaded to behave more responsibly.

Instead, Mugabe set about destroying the economic and political fabric of his country. Zimbabwe, once unquestionably secure, economically strong, socially advanced, and successfully modern, has plummeted rapidly toward failure—mimicking Afghanistan in the 1980s and 1990s, Burma from the 1960s onward, and the DRC, Liberia, Nigeria, and Sierra Leone in the 1990s. In the last several years, Zimbabwe's per capita GDP has fallen annually by 10 percent, while HIV infection rates have climbed to nearly 30 percent. Two thousand Zimbabweans die of AIDS each week. Life expectancy has dropped from 60 to 40 years, while annual inflation has increased from 40 to 116 percent. Corruption has become blatant. The central government no longer effectively provides fundamental political goods such as personal security, schooling, and medical facilities and treatment. Public order has broken down. This year many Zimbabweans may starve due to extremely serious food shortages, and fuel supplies are dwindling. Political institutions have ceased to function fully. Sizable sectional, ethnic, and linguistic fissures exist, and disaffection is everywhere. Even though the state remains intact, the government's legitimacy is now seriously challenged.

By the time of the presidential election in March, therefore, Mugabe had already driven his country to the very edge of failure. Observers, especially South Africa and its neighbors, focused on the election as a way to remove him, provided it were free and fair. But Mugabe persistently refused to play by the common rules of democratic contests. Ahead of the election, he escalated violence against his opponents and anyone who failed to obey him and his ruling party. He unleashed a wave of thugs against the opposition and white farmers. He bombed independent newspapers and tried to jail their editors. He packed the nation's supreme court and refused to carry out its rulings when it still failed to toe the line. Meanwhile, Zimbabwe's neighbors, its major overseas friends, and trading partners, and UN Secretary-General Kofi Annan continued to try to bring about change through quiet diplomacy. But Mugabe ignored New York, London, Washington, and Brussels. He thumbed his nose at President Thabo Mbeki of South Africa and President Olusegun Obasanjo of Nigeria, reneging on solemn promises about fair play, the rule of law, and respect for free speech and media freedom.

Very belatedly, on the eve of the election, the EU and the United States finally turned firm and imposed sanctions. But it was too late, well past the many opportunities for South Africa, the SADC, the United States, and the EU to isolate Mugabe. Ostracizing Mugabe and his close colleagues much earlier in 2001, through gradually escalating smart sanctions, might have led to freer and fairer elections in 2002 and helped to level the playing field. At the very least, international public criticism of Mugabe's tactics might have helped to encourage the growth of civil society in Zimbabwe. But Mbeki's trenchant criticisms were hesitant and muted. And South Africa, the regional superpower, did not threaten to cut off Zimbabwe's supplies of electric power and petroleum. No one in the West or in Africa effectively warned Mugabe that attacking one's own people, destroying a state, and stealing an election were impermissible.

2.6

The New Middle Ages

John Rapley

John Rapley suggests that when state control declines, the outcome may be quite different from the chaos depicted by Rotberg [2.5]. In the megacities of the global South, vast population concentrations, involving 10 million people or more, are crowded into shantytowns. These are areas where the state's representatives—police, tax collectors, social workers, to name a few—are unknown. In some cases, "private actors have assumed statelike functions." For example, private gangs may maintain law and order and provide some social services. They do so in order to profit from criminal activities such as extortion and drug dealing.

Rapley suggests that these situations can be described as the new Middle Ages or new medievalism. The new Middle Ages resemble the Middle Ages in Europe from the fifth to the sixteenth centuries in that authority resides in multiple sites rather than being concentrated in one institutional location—the state. Although the new medievalism is most evident in the megacities of poor countries, Rapley suggests that similar tendencies can be observed elsewhere in the world.

Suggest other places where one can find tendencies of the new medievalism in today's world. What about the United States? What explains the development of the new Middle Ages? Why might it exist in rich countries? Which other readings in this chapter help us understand the phenomenon and why it occurs? Rapley suggests that there may be positive aspects of this development. Which ones? Do you agree?

Gangsters Paradise

You enter the ghetto through a warren of decrepit alleys crowded with locals seeking refuge from the hot night air of their cramped homes. Suspicious stares alert you that you have entered Kingston's gangland. But if the local don—or "area leader," in the polite lexicon of official Jamaica—has granted you permission to enter, you are safe. Here, news travels like dye in water.

John Rapley, "The New Middle Ages," *Foreign Affairs* 85, no. 3 (May/June 2006): 95–103.

The local gang maintains its own system of law and order, complete with a holding cell fashioned from an old chicken coop and a street-corner court. It "taxes" local businesses in return for protecting them, punishing those who refuse to pay with attacks on property and people. It provides a rudimentary welfare safety net by helping locals with school fees, lunch money, and employment—a function that the Jamaican government used to perform. But over the last couple of decades, keen to reduce spending, it has scaled back many of its operations, leaving a vacuum. As one kind of authority has withdrawn, another has advanced.

Jamaica's gangs—each a fluid but cohesive organization with a clearly demarcated territory—fund their activities partly through their participation in one of the industries in the vanguard of globalization: the transshipment of illegal drugs. Although at first glance the gangs seem to be at odds with the government, the local police frequently cooperate with the dons, whose ruthlessly efficient rule can make the cops' jobs easier. The result is a tenuous quid pro quo: if the dons keep order, the police turn a blind eye to the drug trade. Besides, direct assaults on the gangs are often futile. Even when the police capture dons or their gunmen, convictions are next to impossible to obtain because potential witnesses remain silent out of loyalty or fear. Just as the rise of the modern state generated conventional symbols of loyalty—flags, anthems, national heroes—so does gangland culture reflect the new power structure. The dons patronize deejays who celebrate them in song, and huge crowds turn out for the gang leaders' funerals, waving flags that symbolize their rule.

Kingston's gang-controlled neighborhoods are just one result of a growing worldwide phenomenon: the rise of private "statelets" that coexist in a delicate, often symbiotic relationship with a larger state. Large sections of Colombia have gone this way, as have some of Mexico's borderlands and vast stretches of the Andes and the adjoining rain forest. Countries such as Afghanistan and Somalia are more or less governed by warlords, and Pakistan's borderlands submit to Islamabad only when the state's armed forces force them to. Private militias have carved up whole swaths of the Democratic Republic of the Congo and Papua New Guinea, and at one point militias ruled the Solomon Islands. And the list is growing.

Policy debates and the academic literature . . . have been preoccupied lately by discussions of so-called failed states. Not all cases in which private actors have assumed statelike functions, however, involve chaos or failure. The gang-controlled communities in Jamaica, for instance, are often among the safest in the country. The performance of traditional state functions in such communities may actually have improved as the official government has receded. Often what takes place is not so much collapse as reconfiguration—what some scholars have described as the emergence of a new Middle Ages. And close study suggests that the power of statelets and other new political actors will be less transitory, more significant, and more resistant to intervention than is usually assumed.

Rise and Fall

Historians invented the term "Middle Ages" to describe the period between the fall of the Roman Empire in the late fifth century and the rise of modern monarchies with their own new empires in the sixteenth. The era was considered an interregnum during which Europe's tribes developed ad hoc arrangements to manage the affairs of a suddenly anarchic world.

When the Pax Romana dissolved, roads and seaways grew more dangerous. Trade declined, cities emptied, and economic activity retreated to the countryside. In the provinces, nobles who had previously collected taxes for Rome found themselves adrift. Some disappeared from history. Others negotiated power-sharing arrangements with the leaders of nomadic tribes, collecting taxes for the new overlords in return for protection. Still others, commanding their own armed forces, simply created their own political domains. . . .

All this fragmentation yielded the medieval world's complex structure: highly localized economies, social systems founded on plural identities, and a political system composed of multiple and overlapping authorities, each drawing on an autonomous resource base. Complicating the picture further was the fact that the resource bases themselves overlapped: kings could tax trade, while both lords and bishops could tax production. Stability thus rested on constant cooperation and negotiation; when these failed, the result was conflict.

What killed off the European Middle Ages was capitalism. The modern state system dates from the Peace of Westphalia, in 1648, which recognized that governments were sovereign over their territories and that no institution within their borders was exempt from their rules. But medievalism was pushed aside for good only as national economies gradually developed and centralized governments supplanted the plethora of medieval authorities over the next couple of centuries. The growth of cities and the advent of overseas exploration boosted tax revenues from trade and enriched the urban middle classes. Because taxing trade was generally a royal prerogative, the coffers of royal treasuries filled; the nobility, which depended on revenues from agriculture, began an irreversible economic slide. At the same time, the rising business class began to eclipse the lords politically by filling the emergent states' bureaucracies, in which offices were often sold to the highest bidders.

New developments in warfare, including the mastery of gunpowder, favored standing military organizations over mercenary armies and forces raised from feudal estates. The need to protect sea-lanes for trade drove the expansion of centrally controlled navies, and "patriotic" armies appeared on land, filled with conscripts united around new anthems and flags and managed by large new bureaucracies. Financing these militaries required raising new revenues, which led to the rise of increasingly centralized governments. These governments in turn established secure borders and customs posts and sought greater control over their (taxable) citizens. To spur continued economic growth, these governments also ended up regulating commerce, policing cities, expanding education, improving public health, and building and standardizing domestic infrastructure such as roads, railways, and canals. And thus the foundations of the modern world were laid.

Back to the Future

In the last decades of the twentieth century, as capitalism began to operate on an increasingly global scale, the nation-state and the other structures and institutions of the modern era started to fray around the edges, leading scholars to talk of a new medievalism. The concept most often emerged in debates about European integration, as the growing influence of the European Union and its forerunners, the devolution of state powers to regional governments, and the rise of assertive municipalities led some to proclaim a return to Europe's medieval past, with its overlapping loyalties and coexisting local and transnational identities. On closer inspection, however, the concept applies less well to Europe than to the developing world, where the spread of modernity has often been curtailed before it has gone very far.

With the demise of European colonialism, the governments of many newly independent countries in the developing world tried to bring the fruits of modernity to—and thereby win the loyalty of—their people, who in some cases had not even heard of the countries in which they lived. (Even today, there are Indian villages whose inhabitants remain unaware of the existence of "India.") States tried to consolidate their sovereignty with a carrot-and-stick approach. They cracked down on ethnic and regional movements that contested the state's legitimacy, producing violent episodes such as the Biafra War in Nigeria and India's invasions of the princely states. Simultaneously, they sought to seduce their citizens by providing them with employment, patronage, education, and health care.

Although this model of the state as patronage provider worked for a while, it was expensive and ultimately unsustainable. From the 1970s onward, the globalization of capital markets forced all governments to compete internationally for investment, pressuring them to reduce their deficits, taxes, and expenditures. New theories of public management prodded rich and poor states alike to reduce their role in the economy by using private and semiprivate contractors to deliver many services. And in developing countries, change often came simply as a result of fiscal necessity: governments ran out of resources and had to adjust to leaner times through cutbacks in public services. Such retrenchment may have been efficient, but it was also highly visible and seen as regressive by these governments' populations—a perception compounded by their ubiquitous tendency to use sales taxes to shift the tax burden from highly mobile capital and skilled labor to less mobile taxpayers.

Wandering through many cities of the developing world today, one comes up against the limits of modernity. Vast metropolises, growing so quickly their precise populations are unknown, are dotted with shantytowns and squatter camps that lack running water, are crisscrossed by open gutters of raw sewage, and are powered by stolen electricity. Developing states are constantly struggling to catch up. In some places, they succeed, barely. In others, they are losing control of chunks of their territory.

Many of Rio de Janeiro's favelas, for example, are now so dangerous that politicians enter only with the local gang leader's permission. The gangs deliver votes in exchange for patronage. Beyond that, politicians and the state remain largely invisible and irrelevant. The gangs do not wish to secede from Brazil, but they can compel its government to negotiate the terms of its sovereignty. As a result, gang-controlled communities remain safe zones for the transshipment of drugs from the Andes to the world at large. The gangs demonstrate, almost celebrate, their independence and defiance of authority at raucous late-night dances patrolled by local cadres. Such warlordism would have been familiar to the western Europeans of a millennium ago.

Still, although the weakness of the state today is most pronounced in the developing world, the state's retreat is also a global phenomenon. The sovereignty of states was consolidated when they gained control over their territories and populations and secured the exclusive right to tax their output. As economic activity has become increasingly detached from particular local contexts, however, the state's ability to tax production has waned. And so the "barons" of the new global political economy are growing less and less constrained.

The shift toward knowledge-intensive products, reductions in the transport costs of both goods and labor, and the rapid acceleration of technological change have loosened the state's hold on its traditional resource base. At the end of the Middle Ages, states assumed the role of intermediaries between the local and world economies. But today's postmodern economy comprises not centralized national economies operating under state guidance, but small, fragmented, and increasingly autonomous economic units that are increasingly capable of evading state control. What is emerging is a global economy increasingly centered on what some theorists have called "global cities"—major urban centers that are connected less to their hinterlands and more to their counterparts elsewhere.

Because neoliberal policies have done more to free the movement of capital and goods and services than to reduce barriers to human migration, the balance of negotiating power has shifted in favor of the managers of multinational or even global firms. In many countries, this has skewed the distribution of income, leading to the emergence of pockets of vast wealth and areas of abject poverty. As the more prosperous players plug into a global economy and their production relies ever less on local labor, they retreat into secure enclaves protected by private security forces—a process former U.S. Secretary of Labor Robert Reich has called the "secession of the successful." Marginalized communities have essentially done the same thing, using a different kind of private security force—the gang—to maintain order in the global cities' multiplying and expanding ghettos.

Mind the Gap

There has long been a chasm between the planet's rich and poor. What is unusual about the income gap today is that it has widened just as dramatic improvements in communications technology have filtered down to even the most impoverished villages. The world's poorest citizens are thus more exposed than ever before to images of how the richest people live, creating an expectations gap between what states can offer and what their citizens demand. The gap has often been filled by private agents, who are more flexible than states and better positioned to exploit current opportunities. In the cities of the developing world, groups ranging from criminal gangs to Islamist civil-society networks have assumed many of the functions that states have abandoned, funding their operations through informal taxes as well as with proceeds from the drug trade, human trafficking, and money laundering.

Violence, too, has been increasingly privatized. The "peace dividend" from the end of the Cold War released millions of people from armed service but left in place much of the infrastructure of violence. Demobilized soldiers and fighters who once served in the proxy armies maintained by the superpowers during the Cold War (guerrilla forces, "national liberation movements," and the like) have gravitated toward mercenary armies, militias, and gangs and now provide security forces for the "new nobility," such as Kingston's dons and the residents of gated communities.

In the postmodern economy, the distinction between formal and informal sectors has blurred. Nonstate actors forge networks linking global cities so as to create a highly adaptive economy that exists largely beyond states' notice. The narcotics trade, for example, uses the lines of communication between the homelands of immigrants from Jamaica, Colombia, and elsewhere and the markets of their new, rich countries of residence. These paths are highly flexible, as demonstrated by the ability of drug gangs to redirect shipments along circuitous routes as soon as one course is blocked. And such paths are not only open to criminals. Resourceful Somali expatriates revived the ancient institution of hawala in order to send money to relatives back home, where the government had collapsed. Later, of course, al Qaeda adapted the system to fund its operations.

The new medievalism, it should be noted, is not always malignant or violent. In many sub-Saharan African countries, for example, the postcolonial state never succeeded in implanting itself deeply in the day-to-day lives of its citizens, let alone their consciousness. In such lands, the state's retreat has led to the reactivation of traditional political actors such as ethnic communities and religious brotherhoods. Islamist brotherhoods in Dakar, for example, collect voluntary contributions from large networks of overseas Senegalese, which they then use to support their clients in Dakar's poor quarters.

People everywhere, finally, are leaving behind national symbols and cultures and turning to local and global hybrids. In Dakar, French, the language of the elite, is being displaced by the local tongue of Wolof and hip-hop lingo from the United States. A similar trend is happening in Jamaica, where English is losing ground to the local patois, accompanied by language derived from dancehall reggae and rap. And so the coexistence of local and transnational identities that typified the European Middle Ages has reappeared.

Déjà vu?

Given the extent of U.S. primacy, it has become a commonplace to compare today's United States to the Roman Empire. The comparison might be telling in unexpected ways. After all, the Roman Empire did not fall to another empire; all of its "peer competitors" had long since been dispatched when it collapsed. Nor, historians are now concluding, did it fall as a result of internal decline, whether cultural, spiritual, or economic. Rather, the empire fell because barbarian tribes gnawed at its edges and eventually toppled its core. Its sheer wealth set it apart from the petty kingdoms on its frontiers, which, denied access to Rome's riches, grew resentful, envious, and finally obstreperous, bringing the mighty low through the death of a thousand cuts.

Today, pundits writing about the future of the U.S. empire tend to adopt an inward-looking approach similar to that of earlier generations of historians of the Roman Empire. For example, scholars debate topics such as whether the U.S. economy can bear the cost of maintaining so many overseas military and diplomatic operations. But they tend to neglect the vast portion of humanity kept at bay beyond the empire's borders, who regard it with the same mixture of awe, longing, and bitterness with which the barbarians once regarded the Eternal City.

As states recede and the new medievalism advances, the outside world is destined to move increasingly beyond the control—and even the understanding— of the new Rome. The globe's variegated informal and quasi-informal statelike activities will continue to expand, as will the power and reach of those who live by them. The new Romans, like the old, might not enjoy the consequences.

Discussion Questions

1. In what ways, if any, is the new medievalism described by Rapley [2.6] linked to what Strange [2.2] describes as the retreat of the state? More generally, what explains the new medievalism?
2. Various articles in this and other chapters describe great variations in forms of state. In light of these differences, is it even useful to use the same concept (state) for such different objects? What, if any, are core features that all states share?
3. Suggest a typology of states, that is, a way to make sense of variations among states. Provide an empirical example of each type of state in your typology. Suggest an actual state that does not exactly fit any category of your typology and tell why.

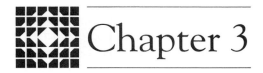 # Chapter 3

GOVERNING THE ECONOMY

As an intellectual discipline, political economy emerged in the eighteenth century as a broad inquiry into the character and best way of organizing economic life. The discipline, which straddles the divide between political science and economics, considers how the production, exchange, and distribution of goods shapes life opportunities and how governments could and should influence economic outcomes. Political economy analyzes how governments affect economic performance and how economic performance in turn affects a country's political processes. In this chapter of *Readings in Comparative Politics,* we include a set of contributions that address key questions and debates in comparative political economy.

How a country organizes production and intervenes to manage the economy is one of the key elements in its overall pattern of political as well as economic development. Whether in the developed or developing world, success in steering a national economy is an important goal. International economic competitiveness contributes to the political status of countries and influences their capacity to deliver the goods for their citizens. And, of course, all governments in the contemporary world are under intense pressure to achieve durable economic development—to design and implement successful strategies for governing the economy—or face the political consequences for failure.

The study of political economy is highly contested terrain. Some political economists emphasize the distributive impact of economic policy for the fate of broad collectivities, from regions of the world to nations, classes, genders, and ethnic groups. Others focus on individuals pursuing particular goals through the rational calculation of costs and benefits. Still others analyze how non-rational factors affect economic choices. In addition to these issues of methodology and theory, the field is rife with other debates. For several centuries, there was a fierce ideological and political conflict in the world between communism and capitalism. As the contribution by Fukuyama [1.1] describes, that debate apparently ended with the crumbling of the Soviet Union and the triumph of capitalism. (One of the ironies of our current era is that the People's Republic of China—self-proclaimed as communist—has been one of the world's major participants in the international capitalist economy, and perhaps the major victor in international economic competition!) However, the readings by Coates [3.2] and Hall and Soskice [3.3] make clear that the end of the Great Debate between communism and capitalism does not mean that convergence has occurred around one particular economic model. The debate now involves capitalism against capitalism, to borrow the title of a book that analyzes competing forms of capitalist states and economies.[1] Coates [3.2] identifies models of capitalism. And Hall and Soskice [3.3] describe varieties of capitalism. There are both analytical and normative issues involved in the debate. Analytically, scholars have questioned how to make sense of the different ways that the balance has been struck between states and markets. Normatively, the issue involves how that balance *should* be drawn. More concretely, although still at a quite abstract level, what is the most effective and desirable state economic orientation? One that aims to minimize state intervention and maximize the freedom of private actors and market forces? Or one that promotes more extensive and robust state intervention and regulation of private market forces, for example, by the state organizing vocational training programs, subsidizing research and development (R&D), or redistributing economic resources to promote equality? And just what are the criteria for judging effective or desirable state interventions in the economy? The financial crisis that erupted in 2008 put the state's role in promoting economic health on the front pages of newspapers and led nightly TV newscasts.

Another key question involves assessing how far cross-border economic transactions, multinational corporations, and the institutions of global economic governance (such as the World Trade Organization and the International Monetary Fund) have overtaken states as the key players that shape political-economic outcomes.

As the contributions in this chapter will make clear, political economy is a vital aspect of comparative politics, and an area of inquiry useful in analyzing some of the most critical challenges facing nation-states and transforming the global order today. As you read the contributions, think about where you stand on the issues analyzed in the readings.

---

[1] Michael Albert, *Capitalism vs.Capitalism: How America's Obsession with Individual Achievement and Short-Term Profit has Led it to the Brink of Collapse* (London: Whurr, 1993).

Political Economy

Peter Gourevitch

In this contribution, Peter Gourevitch traces the evolution of political economy, the academic discipline that encompasses the selections in this chapter of *Readings in Comparative Politics*. As Gourevitch explains, political economy began as a broad and unified economic, political, and moral inquiry before subdividing into two distinct branches. One approach emphasizes the interconnectedness of politics, culture, social organization, and economics. The other approach focuses on individual rationality as the driving force behind the preferences and means-ends calculations that are thought to determine economic (as well as other social and political) outcomes. Gourevitch concludes that both theoretical and policy debates in political economy today reveal the origins as well as the bifurcated evolution of this robust intellectual tradition.

The discipline termed political economy examines the relationship of individuals to society, the economy, and the state. Having begun as an integrated field of moral, economic, and political inquiry, it has subsequently fragmented into the study of the economy as an autonomous system, the application of rational individualist reasoning to all aspects of society, and the debate over policy problems with an economic dimension.

Origins of the Concept—A Unified Theory

Emerging in the eighteenth century, political economy drew on the individualism of Hobbes and Locke, the pragmatism of Machiavelli, and the empiricism of Bacon. Its theorists desanctified social discourse. They thought of governments and all human institutions as instruments, as devices formed by human beings to solve problems, as "efficient institutions," not as divine creations nor the accretion of tradition. Political and social institutions were akin to machines: if broken, they were to be fixed, using standards of empiricism, pragmatism, and utility.

Political economy stressed purposive action by goal-seeking individuals. Adam Smith and David Ricardo used it to theorize about the market economy and to attack mercantilist policies. James Mill and Jeremy Bentham used it to integrate representative government with the calculus of utilitarianism, equating good policy with the aggregation of individual preferences: "the greatest good for the greatest number." Political economists wrote about everything: morals, prisons, freedom, wealth, art, goodness, virtue, constitutions, leadership, war, and peace. Over time, however, the concept of political economy fragmented into discrete components so varied that contemporary users of the label do not necessarily communicate with or know anything about each other. Still, we may identify two large limbs on the tree of political economy, each stressing a different postulate of the founders: one branch focuses on the postulate of individual rationality, the other on the postulate of interconnectedness, or the interaction between economics and other forces.

The Postulate of Individual Rationality

Methodological individualism can be applied to any branch of human behavior (or nonhuman, for that matter). In this approach, social analysis requires a secure "micro" foundation on individuals having a coherent goal (the maximization of welfare) and the capacity for ends-means calculations in pursuit of that goal. Preference functions are taken as given and human nature is held constant. What varies are incentives. Variance in human behavior derives from the rewards or punishments induced by alternative institutional arrangements.

These assumptions have led to various branches of work. At its most abstract, modern economics behaves like mathematics, drawing out the implications of a few key axioms as a deductive body of thought without any particular real-world reference. The ideas are tested solely by their internal logic, valued for beauty, elegance, coherence. In the more applied form, propositions about the economy are derived from theory and confronted with data from actual economies. The empirical debates have to do with such topics as monetarism, Keynesianism, inflation, market structure, rational expectations, and efficient institutions.

By and large, contemporary economics has been self-contained. It has not been interested in examining the influence upon economic behavior of variables that lie outside its logic: values, culture, history, politics, ideology. Prestige in research has gone to theory and to econometrics. Expertise specific to countries, historical periods, companies, and policy has had low prestige, as evidenced by the Nobel Prizes or appointments at leading universities. In recent years, however, applied topics and noneconomic influences on economic behavior have gained new favor as objects of theoretical attention.

Economic reasoning, the presumption of optimizing behavior by individuals, has been applied to many topics in fields other than economics. Social choice, public choice, and rational choice are all labels used for these efforts. . . .

The Postulate of Interconnectedness

This approach rejects the autonomy and self-sufficiency of neoclassical economics. The economy is seen as a societal output. Economic performance derives from political choices, social organization, culture, circumstances, history. The economy is constructed, not somehow natural. Tocqueville, Marx, Saint-Simon, Comte, Durkheim, and Weber worked in this integrated manner in the nineteenth century, as did Talcott Parsons in the twentieth century.

Contemporary social science links positivist research techniques to these kinds of systemic questions in modern political economy. . . .

Policy Debates

These differing intellectual approaches to the relationship between politics and economics are reflected in policy debates:

a) The role of public policy in shaping market efficiency. The analytic separation of market and society entails a quarrel over the role of the state and public policy in producing growth and efficiency. The minimalist view sees least as best; the state need only be a "night watchman," keeping peace, preventing crime, allowing an autonomous economy to function. By contrast, the "developmental state view" sees the market as requiring substantial provision of public goods, that is, items whose diffuse benefits fail to elicit enough private rewards to be provided by the market. These include education, research, public health, physical infrastructure, and uniform standards. Advocates of industrial policy argue that state policy can contribute to efficiency in the strategic promotion of selected industries. Theorists of regulation explore policies concerning market and firm structure to consider efficient institutions.

The policy disputes involve both highly advanced industrial economies and those at early stages of development. They arise from disagreement over the past, as well as the present. The minimalists claim that economic growth occurs when prices are right, a condition best achieved with little state action, for which they offer British and U.S. growth as proof. State intervention leads to "rent-seeking," an extraction of wealth by officials who contribute nothing to efficiency, or to interest group distortion of policy, favoring efficient sectors over potentially efficient ones (urban residents, for example, using political control to keep down food prices, thereby preventing farmers from earning income through exports).

The state activists dispute this interpretation of the U.S. and British past, noting state promotion of canal and railroad building and other infrastructure, and cite Alexander Hamilton and Adam Smith as advocates of this approach. They cite Germany and Japan as examples of state "involved" growth, a model now being taken up by the East Asian newly industrializing economies (NIEs), particularly the Republic of Korea (South Korea), Taiwan, Hong Kong, and

Singapore. The minimalists dispute this interpretation of those countries. Economists would see this as an argument over the volume and quality of public goods the state needs to supply; political scientists would see this as an argument over the political circumstances that produce growth-promoting policies, be they activist or minimalist; sociologists would see this as an argument about the determination of collective goals and social structures needed to sustain growth. . . .

The Asian financial crisis of 1997 provoked a sharp debate, still continuing, about the capacity of developmental states to surmount "crony capitalism," the adequacy of orthodox models of financial adjustment, and the role of international agencies in domestic policy.

b) Foreign economic policy. How should a nation relate to the international economy? The neoclassical argument hinges on free trade: the optimal policy for a country is to have open borders. This view has been challenged since the nineteenth century by conservative nationalists as well as by political radicals. Nationalists sought self-sufficiency and political military strength, radicals social transformation; neither thought that these goals could be reached by free trade within a capitalist economy. In their view, the market would act to favor those already strong, the first industrializers.

The debate continues for developing countries. Critics of dominance by the advanced industrial countries argued that the free market traps developing countries in a subordinate role in the international division of labor. In the Latin American view, the solution to the problem lay in state-directed import substitution industrialization (ISI) strategies. A few countries in East Asia opted for export-oriented industrialization (ESI) strategies instead: state intervention was extensive, but oriented toward promoting industries that would produce goods for export rather than toward replacing imports. In the event, ESI countries have developed more rapidly than those that chose ISI.

There is still much discussion regarding the political economy of development. The United States and international advisers have pressed governments to privatize, deregulate, and open their borders. Japan and some European advisers have argued that states need to invest in education, encourage research, and subsidize key growth industries. In the meantime, intellectual barriers that isolated regions of the world within specialized subfields have been surmounted. Comparisons between Latin America and Asia are now common. Similarly, there is comparison of deregulation in statist economies and transition problems in the former communist countries. Economic development has been revived as a field of economics; comparative political economy flourishes.

The advanced countries, meanwhile, have witnessed a revival of long-standing political tensions over the proper response to growing international trade. Can countries go their own way on domestic social services and economic policies, or does competition force convergence? The empirical side of this debate gives rise to research about the actual record of policy and outcomes. It largely finds that considerable differences remain in economic policy (the trade-offs among growth, equality, and stability) and in outcomes.

Trade requires international agreements that set forth the rules by which it will be conducted. The United States influenced those rules in 1945, but it then accounted for 50 percent of world GNP; although it is still the world's most dynamic economy, that figure is now closer to 20 percent. The world is economically multipolar. Can rules be established in the absence of a dominant power, a hegemon? In Europe economic integration has gone remarkably far, encompassing not only the integrated trade market and the concordance of regulatory standards but monetary union as well. In global terms, the shift from the General Agreement on Tariffs and Trade to the World Trade Organization testifies to a desire for stronger dispute resolution mechanisms, and thus for more free trade.

While countries have liberalized trade, disputes remain. Agricultural subsidies in the advanced industrial world harm the developing countries, for whom food exports would be a major instrument for launching a successful export-oriented growth strategy, propounded, indeed, by the very countries urging privatization and market strategies. Nontariff barriers remain potent and the subject of tension among the United States, Japan, and Europe. Regulation extends the debate over "improper" barriers to trade to include many aspects of society traditionally not on the international bargaining table. The United States and European countries accuse Japan of excluding products and investment through these instruments (leading to the "Structural Impediments Initiative"). Japan claims that the *keiretsu* and other forms of organization are simply efficient market instruments which are available to any country, and are therefore not valid elements of international regulation or dispute. Within countries, trade continues to generate political conflict over the degree of economic liberalization and the social support needed to manage the transitions involved. The political economy of trade and international economic relations is a highly developed area of research integrating economics and politics. . . .

Another arena of research explores the causes of efforts to remove central banks from political influence and the consequences of these steps.

c) Equality, social mobility, environment. A third category of policy disputes in political economy concerns the attainment of goals other than growth and efficiency. Arguments are made on behalf of equality of income, opportunity, and participation in public life; over notions of social justice, health, safety, housing, security, a safety "net" for each citizen; over the role of leisure, culture, and individual fulfillment; over gender, ethnicity, race, and other elements of social relationships; over environmental quality and preservation of resources; and finally, over values of national power, domination, attainment, glory, autonomy, and security. All of these goals have an economic component. At a minimum they involve resources and the allocation of resources. They involve the use of politics to interact with the economy in order to attain these goals. The political economy tradition approaches these questions with a set of distinctive tools. It asks cost-benefit questions and considers incentives, markets, and institutions. It proposes solutions that take account of collective action problems, monitoring, "agency," delegation of authority. It examines values, culture, and community in the context of institutions and interests. It is willing to put a price on pollution, for example, or on a type of medical operation, or on disease prevention, and to ask, "How much is saving a life worth?"—an approach which often enrages analysts not trained in this tradition.

The Field Today

Some students of political economy are interested in economics but not politics; as "pure economists" they study the properties of a model. Some are interested in politics but not economics; they study economic reasoning applied to political institutions. Still others explore the elements of interactive systems, as economics and economic reasoning interact with other social systems and influences.

Caveat lector.   Readers can [also] find trends in contemporary writing that evoke something of the historical linkage among morality, politics, economic reality, and economic reasoning with which political economy began more than two centuries ago. . . . In the hands of [the most able theorists,] political economy evokes the power and forcefulness of its ancestors.

3.2

Models of Capitalism in the New World Order

David Coates

How do we identify and distinguish between different models of capitalism? On what grounds should we differentiate national economic models, assess their strengths and weaknesses, and predict the winners and losers in global competitiveness? As David Coates explains in this contribution, these questions have inspired an intense debate in comparative politics. Coates reviews the changing terms of the debate and then provides his own contribution by comparing market-led, state-led, and negotiated models of capitalism. He concludes that an integrated global economy will reduce the space for social democratic models and raises an important note of caution about the social and economic consequences of the unregulated market-driven model. What are the implications of the global financial and economic crisis beginning in 2008 for Coates' account? In particular, to what extent is what Coates calls market-led capitalisms responsible for the crisis? And has the crisis caused a shift in support toward other models? Why or why not?

The Nature of Capitalist Models

There is nothing particularly unusual about academics and political commentators differentiating types of capitalism. On the contrary, there is a long academic tradition of splitting capitalism into different stages. Marxists have been doing it for years: differentiating between "early capitalism" and "late," between "liberal capitalism," "monopoly capitalism" and "state monopoly capitalism" and between "organized" and "disorganized" capitalism. Mainstream scholarship has been equally active, differentiating "stages of economic growth" splitting early capitalism from the later "mixed economy" and even locating stages of competitive development (labelled, by Michael Porter for instance, as respectively "factor-driven," "investment driven," "innovation driven" and "wealth driven").[1]

David Coates, revised excerpt of "Models of Capitalism in the New World Order," *Political Studies* 47, no. 4 (1999): 643–661, Blackwell Publishing. Reprinted by permission of the author and Blackwell Publishing.

In both Marxist and non-Marxist hands, the argument has been much the same: that capitalism as an economic form can be distinguished in different time periods by the qualitatively distinct mixes of technologies, forms of business organisation, characters of labor forces and state functions that come to predominate within it. In arguments of this kind, it is not so much that different models of capitalisms co-exist. They may, but that is not the main point. The main point is that over the lifecycle of capitalism as a whole, different forms of social organization and political structuring emerge as dominant for a period; and capitalism as a whole has, in consequence, to be understood as moving inexorably from one model to another over time. How are these models to be understood?

The key players and terms of debate have evolved over the years. The key players in the debates on models of capitalism today are the "new institutionalists": those economists, political scientists and comparative sociologists who are committed to the notion of the necessary social embeddedness of all economic institutions, and to the resulting path-dependent and socially specific nature of resulting economic trajectories. The new institutionalists have been very productive of late, generating a literature bedecked with an initially bewildering variety of different typologies, labels, and number of cases. So we have "the Scandinavian model," "Asian capitalism," "German social market capitalism," "American liberal capitalism," even Russian "mafia capitalism"; and we have typologies of welfare systems, of cultural networks, of forms of corporate organization, of systems of investment provision, of modes of labor market regulation, and of state-economy relations. We have "liberal," "corporatist" and "social democratic" welfare regimes; "individualistic" or "communitarian" value systems, among others. It is hardly surprising then, that the literature on models gives us not one, but several, listings of capitalist types, with a seemingly endless number of categories inside the various typologies. Capitalism comes in two forms for some writers, in three for some, in four for others, or in a infinite variety of internally differentiated national types for the really committed new institutionalists. But what it does not do is come in one form alone. On that much the new institutionalist scholarship is quite clear.

Putting order on all that complexity is difficult; but it is worth noting how—beneath all the differentiation—clear polar types of capitalist models regularly reappear. For this is a literature concerned with competitiveness; and competition is uniquely a practice that produces winners and losers. So literatures concerned with competitiveness tend ultimately to bifurcate or at most to map out only limited numbers of likely scenarios. For example, Lester Thurow played with a single distinction between Anglo-American and Japanese-German capitalisms, before eventually setting up his head-to-head as a three-way fight between the United States, Japan and Europe:

> America and Britain trumpet individualistic values: the brilliant entrepreneur, Nobel Prize winners, large wage differentials, individual responsibility for skills, easy to fire and easy to quit, profit maximisation, and hostile mergers and takeovers—their hero is the Lone Ranger. In contrast, Germany and Japan trumpet communitarian values: business groups,

social responsibility for skills, teamwork, firm loyalty, industry strategies, and active industrial policies that promote growth. Anglo-Saxon firms are profit maximisers; Japanese business firms play a game that might better be known as "strategic conquest." Americans believe in "consumer economics"; Japanese believe in "producer economics."[2]

In fact, there are real dangers in setting up any simple two-case model of capitalist types. Certainly the great weakness of any modelling that collapses Japan and Germany into a similarly "communitarian" or "trust" based model (to be set against an Anglo-American individualistic one) is its failure to spot the very different role of labor movements in the Japanese and German cases, and therefore to see the very different sources of what, through liberal individualistic eyes, may initially seem to be a similar set of communitarian cultures. In Japan, the labor movement has historically been weak, and the main sources of cultural specificity have been broadly right-wing (conservative, religious and nationalist). In the European welfare capitalisms (especially post-war Sweden, but also to a lesser degree Germany) labor movements have been historically strong, and the sources of market-regulating cultures have been predominantly center-left, social democratic. The result has been that Japanese capital has had to deal with a very different set of welfare, worker, and trade union rights than has Western European capital; and has consolidated a very different set of institutional props for what are—on the surface—quite similar patterns of wage differentials, job security, labor turnover and training in the two systems. Those props in Europe have been largely public (state) props. In Japan, of course, they have been largely private (and corporate).

Moreover, any simple "U.S. versus the rest" tendency in the models literature can only obscure a much more variegated range of differences in who really are the key players (or stakeholders) in each particular capitalist model. Again, the Anglo-Saxon version of stakeholding is reasonably straightforward. The shareholders are the key stakeholders in those capitalisms in which large corporations raise the bulk of their external capital in open financial markets, and where the level of short-term profit yield, executive salaries, and dividend distribution drive the whole system. And such a narrow base of stakeholding clearly differs from more bank-based systems of industrial finance, and from systems where interlocking sets of corporations sustain each other in long-term strategies of market capture and profit consolidation. Industrial companies, financial institutions, and public agencies, that is, interact differently in a variety of national contexts; and any modelling of capitalist types has to make space for that national differentiation.

This is why Thurow's differentiation of three geographical areas of future capitalist competition is probably a better guide to the basic choices here than any simple polarity would be. For the choices do seem to triangulate around a capital-labor-state set of overlapping polarities, a set which then allows a range of positioning within the parameters of the triangle as a whole. The three-way nature of the basic choices before us here can be isolated schematically in diagrammatic form. (See Figure 3.1.)

The diagram graphically depicts the recognition that the core institutional settlement that capitalism has taken (both temporally and spatially) varies

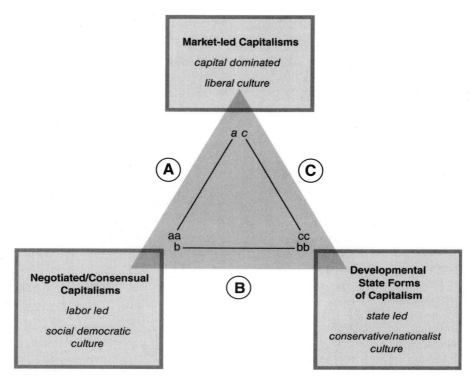

Figure 3.1 Models of Capitalism.

around the central question of who/what decides how capital accumulation will be organized; and that that response can best be measured around two intersecting axes: one charting the degree of state regulation over private capital; the other recording the strength of labor rights in the face of the private ownership ·of the means of production. Is capital accumulation the private concern of individual entrepreneurs and firms—which it is in forms of capitalism that are predominantly market-led? Or is that accumulation a matter settled in some relationship between private firms and the state; or is it negotiated within industrial and political systems in which organized labor also has a voice?

The answers to these questions are invariably matters of degree, which is why a triangular representation of ideal types (allowing for a scaling of position along each dimension of the triangle) seems to work better than a simple set of boxes. Alongside dimension "A" in Figure 3.1, for example, particular models can be distinguished by the set of labor rights within which private capital is obliged to operate: very few such rights at point "a," very many at point "aa." Along dimension "B" in Figure 3.1, models can be differentiated by the political strength of labor movements (and by the associated provision of welfare rights and government policy on full employment): with labor movements strong at point "b," weak at point "bb." Along dimension "C" in Figure 3.1, models can be differentiated by the degree of autonomy of private firms from state regulation, direction, and control: with high levels of autonomy at point "c," and with high levels of state regulation at point "cc." Moreover, each of the defining points of the triangle tends to be associated with a particular cultural mix, and each face of the triangle tends to be associated with a particular distribution of power and rewards. So, as we rotate the triangle, different political ideologies and associated value systems come into view: (liberal political ideologies and values when we get to market-led capitalism, social democratic ideologies and values when we get to negotiated/consensual forms of capitalism, and conservative or nationalist ideologies and values when we reach state-led capitalisms). As we drop down the triangle from top to bottom, the number of stakeholders tends to widen and income inequalities tend to diminish; and as we move across the triangle from right to left, the distribution of social power tends to even out. And so on.

The diagram suggests the following ideal-typical form:

♦ In *market-led* capitalisms, accumulation decisions lie overwhelmingly with private companies, who are left free to pursue their own short-term profit motives and to raise their capital in open financial markets. In such capitalisms, workers enjoy only limited statutory industrial and social rights, and earn only what they can extract from their employers in largely unregulated labor markets. State involvement in economic management is limited largely to market-creating and protecting measures; and the dominant understandings of politics and morality in the society as a whole are individualistic and liberal in form.

♦ In *state-led* capitalisms by contrast, accumulation decisions are again primarily seen as the right and responsibility of private companies, but those decisions are invariably taken only after close liaison with public agencies, and are often indirectly determined through administrative guidance and bank leadership. In such capitalisms, labor movements tend still to lack strong political and social rights; but there is space for forms of labor relation which tie some workers to private corporations through company-based welfare provision. The dominant cultural forms in such capitalisms are likely to be conservative-nationalist in content.

♦ In *negotiated or consensual social* capitalisms the degree of direct state regulation of capital accumulation may still be small; but the political system entrenches a set of strong worker rights and welfare provision which gives organised labor a powerful market presence and the ability to participate directly in industrial decision-making. The dominant cultural networks in these capitalisms are invariably social democratic ones.

The triangle serves as a useful guide to the positioning of whole national economies. It does not seem unreasonable, as a first approximation, to position the United States towards the market-led end of the triangle, Japan nearer the state-led end, and Sweden and Germany along the axis linking market and social capitalism together.

The Viability of Capitalist Models

Recent center-left intellectual commentaries on capitalist models have developed a powerful critique of market-led capitalism and an associated defense of more consensual or negotiated forms of managed capitalism. That critique has been built around a number of linked themes.

One is that economies pursuing more negotiated/consensual forms of capitalist management achieve growth rates and levels of international competitiveness that are at least as good as those achieved by more market-led forms of capitalism; while at the same time attaining social targets (on welfare rights, job security, and income equality) that are distinctly superior. In their defense of organized labor as a key "social partner" in the regulation of economies dominated by privately owned companies, the advocates of Swedish corporatism and German social-market capitalism regularly cite the "beneficial constraints" imposed on capital accumulation by strong worker and trade union rights. By blocking off low wage sweat-shop routes to short-term profitability, such constraints are said to oblige local capitalists to prosper by investment and innovation; and by generating a strong sense of job security and corporate identification in the workforce, they are also said to enable organized labor to cooperate fully in the job changes and re-skilling processes necessarily associated with such high value-added production processes.

A parallel, though normally differently focused, argument from center-left intellectuals emphasizes the superiority of the "developmental state" model over the Anglo-Saxon one; and stresses in particular the superiority of the modes of industrial, social, and political organisation underpinning Japanese post-war economic success. In much of the center-left's comparative writings on Japan, emphasis is placed on the long-term nature of Japanese industrial planning (at both corporate and state levels), a long-termism that is supposedly rooted in the close (non–market-mediated) relationships that exist in Japan between financial and industrial capital, and between private firms and the state. This apparent Japanese propensity for "voice" rather than "exit" strategies in the management of economic life is also often related to the job security afforded to core workers by Japanese life-time employment policies; and to the nonconfrontational industrial relations that Confucian value systems are said to consolidate. Against market-led forms of capitalism, center-left enthusiasts for Asian models emphasize the competitive advantages of "trust-based" systems of economic regulation: and use the argument that "trust" is the missing ingredient in market-led capitalisms to link their enthusiasm for Japanese capitalism to that for the very different systems of European welfare-capitalism.

Both sets of arguments about the superiority of non–market-led models of capitalism share a common critique of neo-liberal economics, and a common reading of the economic weakness of the United Kingdom under Thatcher and Major and of the United States under Reagan and Bush. According to Will Hutton, for example, liberal economics is flawed in three ways: by its narrow view of economic rationality (and associated faith in the capacity of the price mechanism to trigger self-correcting market responses), its commitment to the law of diminishing returns and its belief in unregulated markets mechanisms as self-regulating optimizers.[3] In consequence, they are able to treat Anglo-Saxon ways of running capitalism as inherently outmoded and inappropriate to a modern world in which production has been transformed by more collaborative forms of labor, a tendency toward strategic alliances among firms, and a premium on quality-competitive rather than cost-competitive commodities. The cumulative impact of this embedded liberalism within Anglo-Saxon economies is—on this argument—a long-term loss of international competitiveness: a loss variously related by center-left intellectuals to the short-termism (and high dividend requirements) of stockmarket-led capital provision, and to the adversarial nature of industrial relations triggered by market-led personnel strategies.

According to center-left critics of market-led capitalisms, the absence of trust relationships along dimension "C" of Figure 3.1 leaves U.S. and U.K.-based private firms vulnerable to competition from East Asian and German multinationals who enjoy long-term relationships with their local banking systems and (in the Japanese case) with the planning agencies of the state; a weakness then compounded by the associated absence of trust relationships along dimension A of Figure 3.1, by what William Lazonick has called "the Achilles heel of US manufacturing. . . . [its] organisation of work on the shop-floor . . . and [its] dramatic weakening of the labour movement at precisely the time when unions needed to be brought into the investment decision-making process in both the private and the public sectors."[4]

Of late, such advocates of non–market-led capitalisms have been put on the defensive by the difficulties of first the European and then the East Asian economies. What looked in happier times like long-term relationships of trust between the suppliers and deployers of capital now stand condemned as inadequate financial regulation and systematically induced corruption; and the "beneficial constraints" are widely condemned as machines for the destruction of employment. In truth, center-left defenses of humane capitalism were always heavily challenged from both their left and their right. They were (and continue to be) challenged by a tradition of Marxist scholarship unimpressed by capitalist models of any kind: one concerned in particular with the degree of labor exploitation hidden behind the facade of capitalist trust-relationships, and with the fragility of class compacts and national corporatism in an age of expanding proletarianization and intensified global competition. And they were (and continue to be) challenged by a tradition of liberal scholarship committed to the very market forces that the center-left historically sought to control.

In fact the under-performance of certain capitalist models (the United Kingdom before 1979, European welfare capitalism since) has long been explained by liberal economists in exactly the reverse terms to those deployed by intellectuals of the center-left: as under-performance triggered by the *blunting* of market forces by political interference and labor-market regulation. Liberal scholarship on specific economies has long argued that innovation and change are made more difficult by strong trade unions, high welfare and tax regimes, and over-active governments; and that flexibility (particularly in labor markets) alone holds the key to competitiveness. Such arguments, as we know, held center-stage in the United Kingdom for two decades after 1979, where they shaped economic policy under the Conservatives and inspired the Labour Party to abandon its original commitments to public ownership, Keynesianism and full employment. They also were the standard intellectual tools of a whole series of international regulatory agencies throughout the same twenty-year period; and are now enshrined in the convergence criteria and the subsequent growth and stability pact of the Maastricht treaty on European monetary union (in effect suspended in November 2003 because France and Germany could not conform to the budgetary constraints). And, of course, current understandings (in both policy-making and academic circles) of the economic imperatives associated with intensified global competition are predominantly liberal in kind. Statism is out. Keynesianism is out. Welfare provision and trade union rights are heavily under siege. The current policy consensus in the corridors of power in advanced capitalism is steadily shifting back towards market-led solutions to rising unemployment and slow rates of economic growth.

Where the Marxist and neo-liberal critics of the new institutionalism converge is in their common recognition that this policy shift is not accidental. Where they differ is in their assessment of the likely viability of the convergence now under way. For certainly on a Marxist reading of the logics of contemporary capitalism, changes in the global economy are now squeezing the space for certain kinds of capitalist models. It is not just, as Zysman has it, that "national models of growth in the advanced countries are not collapsing, but are rather undergoing a common transition along distinct trajectories."[5] It is rather that the extensive industrialization of East Asia (and the associated proletarianization of the Asian rural poor) is qualitatively altering the balance of class forces on a world scale; and if that is not requiring a straightforward convergence in the relationships within capitalist classes (and between capital and the state), it *is* squeezing the space within which different relationships between capital and labor can be easily sustained. Globalization, understood in this sense of renewed industrialization on a global scale, has qualitatively altered the class parameters from those within which negotiated/consensual models of capitalism were initially created and sustained in Western Europe in what—for the western European labor movements—now does look as though it was capitalism's "golden age."

There may still be a space for the protection of existing (and construction of new) developmental state forms of capitalism; but those were never in the past (and will not be in the future) necessarily superior to Anglo-Saxon forms of capitalism as far as labor was concerned. But what is now becoming clear is that an increasingly integrated global economy will allow fewer and fewer spaces for social democratic models of capitalism.

If the future is Anglo-Saxon, what comfort are we to take from the progressive collapse of western European welfare capitalism as a viable capitalist model? Right-wing political forces might enjoy that victory, but left-wing ones should not. For if market-led capitalism is all that is left in its place, then the weaknesses of that model—as both a developmental engine and as a guarantor of minimum standards of welfare provision and worker rights, of the kind laid out by its critics in easier times—will simply become generalized through the world economy, and intensified there by the spread of world competition. Unregulated markets in an environment of extensive proletarianization and global capital mobility will generate an upward and permanent momentum in economic activity only if the central contradictions of a capitalist mode of production are suddenly and miraculously a thing of the past. But if they are not, we all face a long period of "ratcheting down" (of wages, job rights, employment, and welfare) and "ratcheting up" (of longer hours, intensified work routines, greater income inequality, and generalized economic insecurity). For, as Marx put it long before it became fashionable to talk of globalization and the convergence of capitalist models, we seem now at last to be approaching that point at which "the bourgeoisie . . . through its exploitation of the world market . . . compels all nations, on pain of extinction, to adopt the bourgeois mode of production. In one word, it creates a world after its own image": that point, moreover, where perhaps "man is at last compelled to face with sober senses his real conditions of life, and his relations with his kind."[6] It is 150 years since Marx wrote *The Communist Manifesto*. Contemporary developments suggest that, though its production was maybe a little premature, its central message has now at last found its time.

Notes

1. Michael Porter, *The Competitive Advantage of Nations* (New York: Free Press, 1990), pp. 545–560.
2. Lester Thurow, *Head to Head: The Coming Economic Battle among Japan, Europe, and America* (New York: William Morrow, 1992), p. 32.
3. Will Hutton, *The State We're In* (London: Cape, 1992), p. 236.
4. William Lazonick, *Business Organization and the Myth of the Market Economy* (Cambridge: Cambridge University Press, 1991), pp. 188, 189.
5. John Zysman, "The myth of the global economy: enduring national foundations and emerging regional realities," *New Political Economy*, 1(2) (July 1996): 159.
6. Karl Marx, *The Communist Manifesto*, reprinted in *Marx-Engels: Selected Works* (London: Lawrence and Wishart, 1968), pp. 38–39.

An Introduction to Varieties of Capitalism

Peter A. Hall and David Soskice

Peter A. Hall and David Soskice highlight the importance of what they term varieties of capitalism among the large countries that belong to the Organization for Economic Cooperation and Development (OECD), that is, affluent countries with capitalist economies. They suggest that these countries can be divided into two clusters that exhibit significant contrasts on measures involving the organization of the economy and economic policy. They designate the two as liberal market economies and coordinated market economies.

According to Hall and Soskice, a basic difference concerns how firms within these economies coordinate their activities. On the one hand, firms in the liberal market economies coordinate via the mechanism of the market, in their words, by "the arm's-length exchange of goods or services in a context of competition and formal contracting." In brief, firms buy and sell what they need from other firms; the market coordinates exchanges among firms. In coordinated market economies, by contrast, "firms depend more heavily on *non-market* [our italics] relationships to coordinate their endeavors." What are these non-market relationships that coordinate their activities? Their answer: institutions that exist outside markets and regulate and coordinate firm activity. These institutions provide *information* to firms, *monitor* their activities to ensure that they are complying with agreements reached, and *sanction* or punish firms that violate cooperative agreements. Examples of non-market-based agreements and institutions include vocational training programs run by employers and unions and durable interrelationships (such as interlocking directorships) between banks and industrial firms to provide firms with adequate finance. In liberal market economies, by contrast, firms raise capital on the stock market by issuing stock purchased by investors with short-term time horizons.

Hall and Soskice claim that the two varieties of capitalist political economies exhibit very different public policy orientations. Can you give some examples? How are they linked to the issue of market-based versus non-market-based coordination? Can you suggest an explanation for the differences? What are the pros and cons of the two varieties of capitalism? And how might the economic crisis beginning in 2008 affect Hall and Soskice's analysis?

Peter A. Hall and David Soskice, "An Introduction to Varieties of Capitalism," in *Varieties of Capitalism: The Institutional Foundations of Comparative Advantage,* ed. Peter A. Hall and David Soskice (New York: Oxford University Press, 2001), pp. 8–17, 19–21.

Liberal Market Economies and Coordinated Market Economies

. . . The core distinction we draw is between two types of political economies, liberal market economies and coordinated market economies, which constitute ideal types at the poles of a spectrum along which many nations can be arrayed.

In *liberal market economies*, firms coordinate their activities primarily via hierarchies and competitive market arrangements. These forms of coordination are well described by a classic literature (Williamson 1985). Market relationships are characterized by the arm's-length exchange of goods or services in a context of competition and formal contracting. In response to the price signals generated by such markets, the actors adjust their willingness to supply and demand goods or services, often on the basis of the marginal calculations stressed by neoclassical economics.[1] In many respects, market institutions provide a highly effective means for coordinating the endeavors of economic actors.

In *coordinated market economies*, firms depend more heavily on non-market relationships to coordinate their endeavors with other actors and to construct their core competencies. These non-market modes of coordination generally entail more extensive relational or incomplete contracting, network monitoring based on the exchange of private information inside networks, and more reliance on collaborative, as opposed to competitive, relationships to build the competencies of the firm. In contrast to liberal market economies (LMEs), where the equilibrium outcomes of firm behavior are usually given by demand and supply conditions in competitive markets, the equilibria on which firms coordinate in coordinated market economies (CMEs) are more often the result of strategic interaction among firms and other actors.

Market relations and hierarchies are important to firms in all capitalist economies, of course, and, even in liberal market economies, firms enter into some relationships that are not fully mediated by market forces.[2] But this typology is based on the contention that the incidence of different types of firm relationships varies systematically across nations. In some nations, for instance, firms rely primarily on formal contracts and highly competitive markets to organize relationships with their employees and suppliers of finance, while, in others, firms coordinate these endeavors differently. In any national economy, firms will gravitate toward the mode of coordination for which there is institutional support.

---

[1]Although we do not emphasize it here, this is not meant to deny the observation of Granovetter (1985) and others that market relations are usually underpinned by personal relationships of familiarity and trust.

[2] This point applies with particular force to market relationships in which one or more of the participants has substantially more market power than the others, as in cases of oligopoly, oligopsony, and the relations found in some supplier chains. We are not arguing that all markets in LMEs are perfectly competitive.

The Role of Institutions and Organizations

Institutions, organizations, and culture enter this analysis because of the support they provide for the relationships firms develop to resolve coordination problems. Following North (1990: 3), we define institutions as a set of rules, formal or informal, that actors generally follow, whether for normative, cognitive, or material reasons, and organizations as durable entities with formally recognized members, whose rules also contribute to the institutions of the political economy.

From this perspective, markets are institutions that support relationships of particular types, marked by arm's-length relations and high levels of competition. Their concomitant is a legal system that supports formal contracting and encourages relatively complete contracts. . . . All capitalist economies also contain the hierarchies that firms construct to resolve the problems that cannot be addressed by markets (Williamson 1985). In liberal market economies, these are the principal institutions on which firms rely to coordinate their endeavors.

Although markets and hierarchies are also important elements of coordinated market economies, firms in this type of economy draw on a further set of organizations and institutions for support in coordinating their endeavors. What types of organizations and institutions support the distinctive strategies of economic actors in such economies? Because the latter rely more heavily on forms of coordination secured through strategic interaction to resolve the problems they face, the relevant institutions will be those that allow them to coordinate on equilibrium strategies that offer higher returns to all concerned. In general, these will be institutions that reduce the uncertainty actors have about the behavior of others and allow them to make credible commitments to each other. A standard literature suggests that these are institutions providing capacities for (i) the *exchange of information* among the actors, (ii) the *monitoring* of behavior, and (iii) the *sanctioning* of defection from cooperative endeavor (see Ostrom 1990). Typically, these institutions include powerful business or employer associations, strong trade unions, extensive networks of cross-shareholding, and legal or regulatory systems designed to facilitate information-sharing and collaboration. Where these are present, firms can coordinate on strategies to which they would not have been led by market relations alone.

The problem of operating collaborative vocational training schemes provides a classic example. Here, the willingness of firms to participate depends on the security of their beliefs that workers will learn useful skills and that firms not investing in training will not poach extensively from those who do, while the participation of workers depends on assurances that training will lead to remunerative employment. It is easier for actors to secure these assurances where there are institutions providing reliable flows of information about appropriate skill levels, the incidence of training, and the employment prospects of apprentices (Finegold and Soskice 1988; Culpepper and Finegold 1999).

Similarly, the terms on which finance is provided to firms will depend on the monitoring capacities present in the economy. Where potential investors have little access to inside information about the progress of the firms they fund, access to capital is likely to depend on highly public criteria about the assets of a firm of the sort commonly found on balance sheets. Where investors are linked to the firms they fund through networks that allow for the development of reputations based on extensive access to information about the internal operations of the firm, however, investors will be more willing to supply capital to firms on terms that do not depend entirely on their balance sheets. The presence of institutions providing network reputational monitoring can have substantial effects on the terms on which firms can secure finance.

In short, this approach to comparative capitalism emphasizes the presence of institutions providing capacities for the exchange of information, monitoring, and the sanctioning of defections relevant to cooperative behavior among firms and other actors; and it is for the presence of such institutions that we look when comparing nations.

In addition, examination of coordinated market economies leads us to emphasize the importance of another kind of institution that is not normally on the list of those crucial to the formation of credible commitments, namely institutions that provide actors potentially able to cooperate with one another with a capacity for *deliberation*. By this, we simply mean institutions that encourage the relevant actors to engage in collective discussion and to reach agreements with each other.[3] Deliberative institutions are important for several reasons.

Deliberative proceedings in which the participants engage in extensive sharing of information about their interests and beliefs can improve the confidence of each in the strategies likely to be taken by the others. Many game-theoretic analyses assume a level of common knowledge that is relatively thin, barely stretching past a shared language and familiarity with the relevant payoffs. When multiple equilibria are available, however, coordination on one (especially one that exchanges higher payoffs for higher risks) can be greatly facilitated by the presence of a thicker common knowledge, one that extends beyond the basic situation to a knowledge of the other players sufficiently intimate to provide confidence that each will coordinate on a specific equilibrium (Eichengreen 1997). Deliberation can substantially thicken the common knowledge of the group.

Although many think only of a 'prisoner's dilemma' game when they consider problems of cooperation, in the political economy many such problems take quite different forms, including 'battle of the sexes' games in which joint gains are available from more than one strategy but are distributed differently depending on the equilibrium chosen. Distributive dilemmas of this sort are endemic to political economies, and agreement on the distribution of the relevant

[3] One political economist who has consistently drawn attention to the importance of deliberation is Sabel (1992, 1994) and the issue is now the subject of a growing game-theoretic literature (see Elster 1998).

gains is often the prerequisite to effective cooperation (Knight 1992). In some cases, such as those of collaborative research and development, the problem is not simply to distribute the gains but also the risks attendant on the enterprise. Deliberation provides the actors with an opportunity to establish the risks and gains attendant on cooperation and to resolve the distributive issues associated with them. In some cases, the actors may simply be negotiating from positions of relative power, but extensive deliberation over time may build up specific conceptions of distributive justice that can be used to facilitate agreement in subsequent exchanges.

Finally, deliberative institutions can enhance the capacity of actors in the political economy for strategic action when faced with new or unfamiliar challenges. This is far from irrelevant since economies are frequently subject to exogenous shocks that force the actors within them to respond to situations to which they are unaccustomed. The history of wage negotiations in Europe is replete with examples. In such instances, developments may outrun common knowledge, and deliberation can be instrumental to devising an effective and coordinated response, allowing the actors to develop a common diagnosis of the situation and an agreed response.

In short, deliberative institutions can provide the actors in a political economy with strategic capacities they would not otherwise enjoy; and we think cross-national comparison should be attentive to the presence of facilities for deliberation as well as institutions that provide for the exchange of information in other forms, monitoring, and the enforcement of agreements.

The Role of Culture, Informal Rules, and History

Our approach departs from previous works on comparative capitalism in another respect.[4] Many analyses take the view that the relevant outcomes in economic performance or policy follow more or less directly from differences in the formal organization of the political economy. Particular types of wage settlements or rates of inflation and unemployment are often said to follow, for instance, from the organizational structure of the union movement. Because we believe such outcomes are the products of efforts to coordinate in contexts of strategic interaction, however, we reject the contention that they follow from the presence of a particular set of institutions alone, at least if the latter are defined entirely in terms of formal rules or organizations.

As we have noted, the presence of a set of formal institutions is often a necessary precondition for attaining the relevant equilibrium in contexts of coordination. But formal institutions are rarely sufficient to guarantee that equilibrium.

---

[4] Here we depart from some of our own previous formulations as well (cf. Hall 1986; Soskice 1990).

In multi-player games with multiple iterations of the sort that characterize most of the cases in which we are interested, it is well known that there exist multiple equilibria, any one of which could be chosen by the actors even in the presence of institutions conducive to the formation of credible commitments (Fudenberg and Maskin 1986). Something else is needed to lead the actors to coordinate on a specific equilibrium and, notably, on equilibria offering high returns in a non-cooperative context.[5] In many instances, what leads the actors to a specific equilibrium is a set of shared understandings about what other actors are likely to do, often rooted in a sense of what it is appropriate to do in such circumstances (March and Olsen 1989).

Accordingly, taking a step beyond many accounts, we emphasize the importance of informal rules and understandings to securing the equilibria in the many strategic interactions of the political economy. These shared understandings are important elements of the 'common knowledge' that lead participants to coordinate on one outcome, rather than another, when both are feasible in the presence of a specific set of formal institutions. By considering them a component of the institutions making up the political economy, we expand the concept of institutions beyond the purely formal connotations given to it in some analyses.

This is an entry point in the analysis for history and culture. Many actors learn to follow a set of informal rules by virtue of experience with a familiar set of actors and the shared understandings that accumulate from this experience constitute something like a common culture. This concept of culture as a set of shared understandings or available 'strategies for action' developed from experience of operating in a particular environment is analogous to those developed in the 'cognitive turn' taken by sociology (Swidler 1986; DiMaggio and Powell 1991). Our view of the role that culture can play in the strategic interactions of the political economy is similar to the one Kreps (1990) accords it in organizations faced with problems of incomplete contracting.

The implication is that the institutions of a nation's political economy are inextricably bound up with its history in two respects. On the one hand, they are created by actions, statutory or otherwise, that establish formal institutions and their operating procedures. On the other, repeated historical experience builds up a set of common expectations that allows the actors to coordinate effectively with each other. Among other things, this implies that the institutions central to the operation of the political economy should not be seen as entities that are created at one point in time and can then be assumed to operate effectively afterwards.

To remain viable, the shared understandings associated with them must be reaffirmed periodically by appropriate historical experience. As Thelen emphasizes in this volume, the operative force of many institutions cannot be taken for granted but must be reinforced by the active endeavors of the participants.

---

[5] Culpepper documents this problem and explores some solutions to it in Culpepper (1998).

Institutional Infrastructure and Corporate Strategy

This varieties of capitalism approach draws its basic conceptions of how institutions operate from the new economics of organization. We apply a set of concepts commonly used to explain behavior at the micro level of the economy to problems of understanding the macroeconomy (Milgrom and Roberts 1992). One of the advantages is an analysis with robust and consistent postulates about what kind of institutions matter and how they affect behavior. Another is the capacity of the approach to integrate analysis of firm behavior with analysis of the political economy as a whole.

However, there are at least two respects in which our account deviates from mainstream views in the new economics of organization. First, although we make use of the influential dichotomy between 'markets' and 'hierarchies' that Williamson (1975) has impressed on the field, we do not think this exhausts the relevant variation. Markets and hierarchies are features of LMEs and CMEs but we stress the systematic variation found in the character of corporate structure (or hierarchies) across different types of economies and the presence of coordination problems even within hierarchical settings (Milgrom and Roberts 1992). Even more important, we do not see these two institutional forms as the only ones firms can employ to resolve the challenges they confront. In coordinated market economies in particular, many firms develop relationships with other firms, outside actors, and their employees that are not well described as either market-based or hierarchical relations but better seen as efforts to secure cooperative outcomes among the actors using a range of institutional devices that underpin credible commitments. Variation in the incidence and character of this 'third' type of relationship is central to the distinctions we draw between various types of political economies.

Second, it is conventional in much of the new economics of organization to assume that the core institutional structures of the economy, whether markets, hierarchies, or networks, are erected by firms seeking the most efficient institutions for performing certain tasks. The postulate is that (institutional) structure follows (firm) strategy (cf. Chandler 1974; Williamson 1975, 1985; Chandler and Daems 1980). In a restricted sense, this is certainly true: firms can choose whether to contract out an endeavor or perform it in-house, for instance, and they enjoy some control over their own corporate form.

However, we think it unrealistic to regard the overarching institutional structures of the political economy, and especially those coordinating the endeavors of many actors (such as markets, institutional networks, and the organizations supporting collaborative endeavor), as constructs created or controlled by a particular firm. Because they are collective institutions, a single firm cannot create them; and, because they have multifarious effects, it may be difficult for a group of firms to agree on them. Instead, as Calvert (1995) observes, the construction of coordinating institutions should be seen as a second-order coordination problem of considerable magnitude. Even when firms can agree, the project may entail regulatory action by the government and the formation of coalitions among political parties and labor organizations motivated by considerations going well beyond efficiency (Swenson 1991, 1997).

As a result, the firms located within any political economy face a set of coordinating institutions whose character is not fully under their control. These institutions offer firms a particular set of opportunities; and companies can be expected to gravitate toward strategies that take advantage of these opportunities. In short, there are important respects in which strategy follows structure. For this reason, our approach predicts systematic differences in corporate strategy across nations, and differences that parallel the overarching institutional structures of the political economy. This is one of the most important implications of the analysis.

Let us stress that we refer here to broad differences. Of course, there will be additional variation in corporate strategies inside all economies in keeping with differences in the resource endowments and market settings of individual firms. The capabilities of management also matter, since firms are actors with considerable autonomy. Our point is that (institutional) structure conditions (corporate) strategy, not that it fully determines it. We also agree that differences in corporate strategy can be conditioned by the institutional support available to firms at the regional or sectoral levels (Campbell et al. 1991; Hollingsworth et al. 1994; Herrigel 1996). Many of the works making this point are congruent with our own in that they stress the importance of the institutional environment to firm strategy, even though there has been fruitful disagreement about which features of that environment matter most (cf. Streeck 1992).

However, we emphasize variations in corporate strategy evident at the national level. We think this justified by the fact that so many of the institutional factors conditioning the behavior of firms remain nation-specific. There are good reasons why that should be the case. Some of the relevant institutions were deeply conditioned by nationally specific processes of development, as are most trade unions and employers' associations. In others, the relevant institutions depend heavily on statutes or regulations promulgated by national states, as do many institutions in the financial arena and labor market, not to mention the sphere of contract law.

In sum, we contend that differences in the institutional framework of the political economy generate systematic differences in corporate strategy across LMEs and CMEs. There is already some evidence for this. For instance, the data that Knetter (1989) has gathered are especially interesting. He finds that the firms of Britain, a typical LME, and those of Germany, a CME, respond very differently to a similar shock, in this case an appreciation of the exchange rate that renders the nation's goods more expensive in foreign markets. British firms tend to pass the price increase along to customers in order to maintain their profitability, while German firms maintain their prices and accept lower returns in order to preserve market share.

Our approach predicts differences of precisely this sort. We would argue that British firms must sustain their profitability because the structure of financial markets in a liberal market economy links the firm's access to capital and ability to resist takeover to its current profitability; and they can sustain the loss of market share because fluid labor markets allow them to lay off workers readily. By contrast, German firms can sustain a decline in returns because the financial system of a coordinated market economy provides firms with access to capital independent of current profitability; and they attempt to retain market share because the labor institutions in such an economy militate in favor of long-term employment strategies and render layoffs difficult.

These are only some of the ways in which the institutional arrangements of a nation's political economy tend to push its firms toward particular kinds of corporate strategies. We explore more of these below with special emphasis on innovation.

To put the point in the most general terms, however, firms and other actors in coordinated market economies should be more willing to invest in *specific* and *co-specific assets* (i.e. assets that cannot readily be turned to another purpose and assets whose returns depend heavily on the active cooperation of others), while those in liberal market economies should invest more extensively in *switchable assets* (i.e. assets whose value can be realized if diverted to other purposes). This follows from the fact that CMEs provide more institutional support for the strategic interactions required to realize the value of co-specific assets, whether in the form of industry-specific training, collaborative research and development, or the like, while the more fluid markets of LMEs provide economic actors with greater opportunities to move their resources around in search of higher returns, encouraging them to acquire switchable assets, such as general skills or multi-purpose technologies. . . .

Among the large OECD nations, six can be classified as liberal market economies (the USA, Britain, Australia, Canada, New Zealand, Ireland) and another ten as coordinated market economies (Germany, Japan, Switzerland, the Netherlands, Belgium, Sweden, Norway, Denmark, Finland, and Austria) leaving six in more ambiguous positions (France, Italy, Spain, Portugal, Greece, and Turkey).[6] However, the latter show some signs of institutional clustering as well, indicating that they may constitute another type of capitalism, sometimes described as 'Mediterranean', marked by a large agrarian sector and recent histories of extensive state intervention that have left them with specific kinds of capacities for non-market coordination in the sphere of corporate finance but more liberal arrangements in the sphere of labor relations (see Rhodes 1997).

Although each type of capitalism has its partisans, we are not arguing here that one is superior to another. Despite some variation over specific periods, both liberal and coordinated market economies seem capable of providing satisfactory levels of long-run economic performance, as the major indicators of national well-being displayed in Table 1.1 indicate. Where there is systematic variation

---

[6] Luxembourg and Iceland have been omitted from this list because of their small size and Mexico because it is still a developing nation.

Table 3.1
The economic performance of liberal and coordinated market economies

Liberal market economies

	Growth rate of GDP			GDP per capita		Unemployment rate		
	61–73	74–84	85–98	74–84	85–97	60–73	74–84	85–98
Australia	5.2	2.8	3.3	7932	16701	1.9	6.2	8.5
Canada	5.3	3.0	2.3	9160	18835	5.1	8.4	9.5
Ireland	4.4	3.9	6.5	4751	12830	5.0	9.1	14.1
New Zealand	4.0	1.8	1.7	7378	14172	0.2	2.2	6.9
UK	3.1	1.3	2.4	7359	15942	2.0	6.7	8.7
United States	4.0	2.2	2.9	11055	22862	4.9	7.5	6.0
LME average	4.3	2.5	3.2	7939	16890	3.2	6.7	8.9

Coordinated market economies

	Growth rate of GDP			GDP per capita		Unemployment rate		
	61–73	74–84	85–98	74–84	85–97	60–73	74–84	85–98
Austria[a]	4.9	2.3	2.5	7852	17414	1.6	2.2	5.3
Belgium	4.9	2.0	2.2	8007	17576	2.2	8.2	11.3
Denmark	4.4	1.8	2.2	8354	18618	1.4	7.1	9.3
Finland	5.0	2.7	2.2	7219	15619	2.0	4.8	9.4
Iceland	5.7	4.1	2.7	8319	18285	0.6	0.6	2.5
Germany	4.3	1.8	2.2	7542	16933	0.8	4.6	8.5
Japan	9.7	3.3	2.6	7437	18475	1.3	2.1	2.8
Netherlands[b]	4.9	1.9	2.8	7872	16579	1.5	5.6	6.8
Norway	4.3	4.0	2.9	8181	19325	1.6	2.1	4.3
Sweden	4.2	1.8	1.5	8450	16710	1.9	2.3	4.8
Switzerland	4.4	0.58	1.3	10680	21398	0.01	0.4	2.5
CME average	5.1	2.4	2.3	8174	17902	1.3	3.6	6.1

Notes: Growth rate of GDP: average annual growth in GDP, averaged for the time-periods indicated. GDP per capita: per capita GDP at purchasing power parity, averaged for the time-periods indicated. Unemployment rate: annual unemployment rate.

[a] Unemployment series begins in 1964.
[b] Unemployment series begins in 1969.

Sources: Growth rate of GDP: World Bank, *World Development Indicators* CD-ROM (2000); except for Germany, for which data were taken from OECD, *Historical Statistics* (1997), for 1960–91, and *WDI* for years thereafter. GDP per capita: OECD, *OECD Statistical Compendium* CD-ROM (2000). Unemployment rate: OECD, *OECD Statistical Compendium* CD-ROM (2000).

between these types of political economies, it is on other dimensions of performance. The two types of economies have quite different capacities for innovation. In addition, they tend to distribute income and employment differently. In liberal market economies, the adult population tends to be engaged more extensively in paid employment and levels of income inequality are high. In coordinated market economies, working hours tend to be shorter for more of the population and incomes more equal. With regard to the distribution of well-being, of course, these differences are important.

Bibliography

Calvert, R. 1995. 'The Rational Choice Theory of Social Institutions: Cooperation, Coordination, and Communication.' In *Modern Political Economy*, ed. J. Banks and E. Hanushek. New York: Cambridge University Press: 216–67.

Campbell, John L., Rogers Hollingsworth, and Leon Lindberg. 1991. *Governance of the American Economy*. New York: Cambridge University Press.

Chandler, Alfred. 1974. *The Visible Hand*. Cambridge, Mass.: Harvard University Press.

—— and Harold Daems, eds. 1980. *Managerial Hierarchies: Comparative Perspectives on the Rise of the Modern Corporation*. Cambridge, Mass: Harvard University Press.

Culpepper, Pepper D. 1998. 'Rethinking Reform: The Politics of Decentralized Cooperation in France and Germany.' Ph.D. dissertation, Harvard University.

Culpepper, Pepper D., and David Finegold. 1999. "Individual Choice, Collective Action, and the Problem of Training Reform." In *The German Skills Machine*, ed. Pepper D. Culpepper and David Finegold. Oxford: Berghahn: 269–325.

DiMaggio, Paul, and Walter Powell. 1991. 'Introduction.' In *The New Institutionalism in Organizational Analysis*. Chicago: University of Chicago Press: 1–40.

Eichengreen, Barry. 1997. 'Institutions and Economic Growth after World War II.' In *Economic Growth in Europe since 1945*, ed. Nicholas Crafts and Gianni Toniolo. Cambridge: Cambridge University Press: 38–72.

Elster, Jon, ed. 1998. *Deliberative Democracy*. New York: Cambridge University Press.

Finegold, David, and David Soskice. 1988. 'The Failure of Training in Britain: Analysis and Prescription.' *Oxford Review of Economic Policy* 4 (3): 21–53.

Fudenberg, Drew, and Eric Maskin. 1986. 'The Folk Theorem in Repeated Games with Discounting and Incomplete Information.' *Econometrica* 54 (May): 533–54.

Granovetter, Mark. 1985. 'Economic Action and Social Structures: The Problem of Embeddedness.' *American Journal of Sociology* 91 (3): 481–510.

Hall, Peter A. 1986. *Governing the Economy: The Politics of State Intervention in Britain and France*. New York: Oxford University Press.

Herrigel, Gary. 1996. *Industrial Constructions: The Sources of German Industrial Power*. Cambridge: Cambridge University Press.

Hollingsworth, J. Rogers, Philippe C. Schmitter, and Wolfgang Streeck, eds. 1994. *Governing Capitalist Economies*. New York: Oxford University Press.

Knetter, M. 1989. 'Price Discrimination by US and German Exporters.' *American Economic Review* 79 (1): 198–210

Knight, Jack. 1992. *Institutions and Social Conflict*. New York: Cambridge University Press.

Kreps, David. 1990. 'Corporate Culture and Economic Theory.' In *Perspectives on Positive Political Economy*, ed. James E. Alt and Kenneth A. Shepsle. New York: Cambridge University Press: 90–143.

March, James G., and Johan P. Olsen. 1989. *Rediscovering Institutions: The Organizational Basis of Politics*. New York: Free Press.

Milgrom, Paul, and John Roberts. 1992. *Economics, Organization and Management*. Englewood Cliffs, NJ: Prentice Hall.

North, Douglass C. 1990. *Institutions, Institutional Change and Economic Performance*. New York: Cambridge University Press.

Ostrom, Elinor. 1990. *Governing the Commons: The Evolution of Institutions for Collective Action*. New York: Cambridge University Press.

Rhodes, Martin. 1997. 'Globalisation, Labour Markets and Welfare States: A Future of "Competitive Corporatism"?' In *The Future of European Welfare*, ed. Martin Rhodes and Yves Meny. London: Macmillan.

Sabel, Charles F. 1992. 'Studied Trust: Building New Forms of Cooperation in a Volatile Economy.' In *Industrial Districts and Local Economic Reorganization*, ed. Frank Pyke and Werner Sengenberger. Geneva: International Institute for Labor Studies: 215–50.

—— 1994. 'Learning by Monitoring: The Institutions of Economic Development.' In *The Handbook of Economic Sociology*, ed. Neil Smelser and Richard Swedberg. Princeton: Princeton University Press: 137–65.

Soskice, David. 1990. 'Reinterpreting Corporatism and Explaining Unemployment: Coordinated and Non-coordinated Market Economies.' In *Labour Relations and Economic Performance,* ed. Renato Brunetta and Carlo Dell'Aringa. Proceedings of a conference held by the International Economics Association in Venice, Italy. Vol. 95. London: Macmillan: 170–214.

Streeck, Wolfgang. 1992. *Social Institutions and Economic Performance: Studies on Industrial Relations in Advanced European Capitalist Countries*. London: Sage.

Swenson, Peter. 1991. 'Bringing Capital Back in, or Social Democracy Reconsidered: Employer Power, Cross-class Alliances and Centralization of Industrial Relations in Denmark and Sweden.' *World Politics* 43 (July): 513–44.

—— 1997. 'Arranged Alliance: Business Interests in the New Deal.' *Politics and Society* 25 (March): 66–116.

Swidler, Ann. 1986. 'Culture in Action: Symbols and Strategies.' *American Sociological Review* 51 (2): 273–86.

Williamson, Oliver. 1975. *Markets and Hierarchies*. New York: Free Press.

—— 1985. *The Economic Institutions of Capitalism: Firms, Markets, Relational Contracting*. New York: Free Press.

Systemic Vulnerability and the Origins of Developmental States: Northeast and Southeast Asia in Comparative Perspective

Richard F. Doner, Bryan K. Ritchie, and Dan Slater

Prior to China's and India's economic surge, the world's most notable recent "miracles" were the Northeast Asian states (South Korea, Taiwan, and Singapore), sometimes designated as Newly Industrializing Countries (NICs). They achieved extraordinary economic success in the 1980s and 1990s, going from among the poorer countries in the world to among the most prosperous. How did they achieve these enviable results? Richard Doner and his coauthors seek an answer by comparing the NICs with four high-growth nations in Southeast Asia— Malaysia, Thailand, the Philippines, and Indonesia. (They belong to the Association of Southeast Asian Nations [ASEAN].) Although the ASEAN states achieved respectable rates of economic growth, compared to the NICs they grew less rapidly and, more important, failed to transform their economies through industrialization. Thus, they did not lay the groundwork for sustained economic growth.

Doner and colleagues claim that the NICs shared a configuration of three factors. Although one or two factors were found in the ASEAN states, it was the combination of the three that explained the NICs' amazing record. In their view, one factor in particular was important, and it is opposite to what is often cited as responsible for these countries' success. Many accounts point to the authoritarian character of the NICs' states, notably, their one-party systems and heavy-handed treatment of labor. Although Doner and coauthors partially agree with this description, they claim that the reality was more complex. Because these countries faced an acute security dilemma (all three feared the People's Republic of China), their leaders were forced to redistribute resources broadly to maintain popular support rather than simply to squeeze popular sectors. However, because these countries had few natural resources or other material advantages, it was no easy matter to muster resources to distribute. The solution, fashioned as much through necessity as choice, was to sponsor rapid economic growth and industrial transformation. By contrast, because the ASEAN states were located far from China and in a relatively peaceful region, they did not confront comparably acute

Richard F. Doner, Bryan K. Ritchie, and Dan Slater, "Systemic Vulnerability and the Origins of Developmental States: Northeast and Southeast Asia in Comparative Perspective," *International Organization* 59, no. 2 (Spring 2005): 327–331, 333–336, 338–341, 355–356.

dilemmas. Thus, their leaders were less pressured to fashion dramatic new policies to achieve rapid economic growth.

The solution to the puzzle that Doner and his coauthors identify is historically specific. It represents an elegant example of a middle-range theory. It is not intended to explain all economically successful states. What are the pros and cons of trying to develop more general theories of developmental states as opposed to focusing on particular case of success and failure?

Scholars of economic development have become increasingly avid students of economic institutions. Studies abound on the norms, rules, and organizations that regulate and, to varying degrees, coordinate a society's productive activities. Few would now question Rodrik's conclusion that "the quality of institutions is key" for economic growth.[1]

Yet our growing understanding of the economic impacts of these institutions has not been matched by our understanding of their political origins.[2] In this article, we aim to narrow this gap by providing a political account of the emergence of a particular type of institutional arrangement: "developmental states." We define developmental states as organizational complexes in which expert and coherent bureaucratic agencies collaborate with organized private sectors to spur national economic transformation. As many scholars have argued, in the small number of countries where they emerged, these institutional features were key to an unparalleled capacity for the promotion of economic development.[3]

But why do these institutional arrangements emerge? In contrast to scholars who portray developmental states as highly autonomous entities, unconstrained by coalitional demands, we contend that developmental states will only emerge when political leaders confront extraordinarily constrained political environments. Specifically, we argue that political elites will only build such institutional arrangements when simultaneously staring down the barrels of three different guns: (1) the credible threat that any deterioration in the living standards of popular sectors could trigger unmanageable mass unrest; (2) the heightened need for foreign exchange and war matériel induced by national insecurity; and (3) the hard budget constraints imposed by a scarcity of easy revenue sources. We call this interactive condition "systemic vulnerability."

Developmental states are significant but rare. In the newly industrializing countries (NICs) of South Korea, Taiwan, and Singapore, these institutional

---

[1] Rodrik 2003, 10. For general reviews of the vast literature on institutions and growth, see, for example, Aron 2000. On institutions as organizations, see, for example, World Bank 2003; and Hall and Soskice 2001.

[2] Bates 1995.

[3] Foundational studies include Johnson 1982; Amsden 1989; Wade 1990; and Haggard 1990. Subsequent work includes Noble 1998; Woo-Cumings 1991; Evans 1995; Kuo 1995; and McNamara 1999.

apparatuses have enhanced information flows both within and between the public and private sector, giving bureaucrats the wherewithal to help firms compete with global rivals in more challenging economic activities. Just as critically, these institutional arrangements have given bureaucrats the political clout to make credible but conditional commitments and thus to withdraw support from firms that under-perform in spite of state assistance. Solving information and commitment problems has helped these states coordinate multiple actors and pursue long-term economic objectives. The result has been an impressive level of "upgrading": shifts, based on growth in local innovation capacities, from lower-value to higher-value economic activities within global commodity chains. In other words, these countries combined export promotion with industrial deepening. This distinguishes the NICs from the four high-growth members of the Association of Southeast Asian Nations (henceforth ASEAN-4)—Malaysia, Thailand, the Philippines, and Indonesia—where "intermediate" state institutions have been associated with impressive growth and economic diversification, but little upgrading. . . .[4]

Any explanation for the scarcity of developmental states must be a political one. Economic institutions ultimately arise from the rough-and-tumble of elite politics, not from choices by private parties to enhance mutual welfare.[5] But politicians are primarily motivated by concerns with securing their power. This typically leads them to de-emphasize the provision of broad collective goods and to fashion institutions as vehicles for channeling largesse to key constituencies—typically economic elites interested in easy profits through speculation and rent seeking—rather than serving any of the more virtuous economic functions noted above.[6]

Political incentives typically lead neither to shared goals of national economic transformation, nor to the creation of monitoring devices and incentive structures through which political leaders (principals) control the bureaucrats (agents) who implement such goals.[7] We thus cannot explain developmental states as a result of either benign motivations or "state autonomy." Rather, to avoid the "thin politics" that has characterized most work on developmental states, we must specify the constraints that make it difficult for politicians to preserve power through clientelist connections to the private sector alone, as well as the incentives that encourage them to build new institutions for economic transformation.[8]

---

[4] In this article, the causal relationship between developmental states and economic performance is presumed, not proven. For arguments that institutions are key for upgrading, see Evans 1995; Wade 1990; Amsden 2001; and Waldner 1999. On the important distinction between upgrading and diversification (or structural change), see Gereffi forthcoming; Waldner 1999; and Weiss 1998. For empirical studies of economic performance differences between the NICs and the ASEAN-4, see Amsden 2001; Wong and Ng 2001; Booth 1999; and Rasiah 2003.

[5] See Bates 1995; and Knight 1992.

[6] Geddes 1994.

[7] Moe 1984.

[8] On "thin politics," see Wade 1992; Moon and Prasad 1998; and Haggard 2004.

In this article, we argue that the political origins of developmental states can be located in conditions of "systemic vulnerability," or the simultaneous interplay of three separate constraints: (1) broad coalitional commitments, (2) scarce resource endowments, and (3) severe security threats. Any subset of these constraints might make it somewhat more difficult for rulers to stay in power without improving institutional performance. Even mild constraints might inspire politicians to forego their individual interest in maximizing patronage resources, and press them to convert the bureaucracy into "more of an instrument, less of an arena."[9] But there is a cavernous gap between the political will necessary to build such "intermediate" states and that which is required to construct a developmental state.[10] Unless political leaders are confronted by all three of these constraints at the same time, we argue, they will find less challenging ways of staying in power (Figure 3.2). In sum, leaders such as South Korea's Park Chung Hee, Singapore's Lee Kuan Yew, and Taiwan's Chiang Kai-Shek only took the lead in building developmental states because they were more tightly bound, not more brilliant or benign, than their counterparts throughout the developing world. . . .

Our causal logic works as follows.[11] Leaders' political survival requires coalitions, which leaders generally try to keep as narrow as possible.[12] But ruling elites can be pressured to enlarge coalitions beyond their initial "minimum winning" size by intense elite or social conflict, or by the credible threat of disruptive mass mobilization. Broad coalitions are best constructed and sustained with side payments to popular sectors; but the provision of such payments is rendered difficult by security threats, which siphon revenues into the defense sector, and by resource limitations, which impose hard budget constraints. Systemic vulnerability thus makes the reconciliation of coalitional, geopolitical, and fiscal constraints a matter of ruling elites' political survival.

How can politicians build and hold together a broad coalition when revenues are desperately needed for national defense, and when there is precious little revenue to go around? Only by continuously expanding the national pie through sustained growth, yet without pursuing a cheap-labor, "race to the bottom" strategy that could alienate coalition members. We thus anticipate that systemic vulnerability will press elites to abandon low-wage-based export growth for a higher-skill, quality-based export trajectory. Elites must thus design side payments without draining the national treasury or raising exporters' costs. In other

---

[9] Emmerson 1978, 105.

[10] See Evans 1995, 60, for the distinction between "intermediate" and developmental states.

[11] By "ruling elites," we refer to the political leaders atop the incumbent regime. By "broad coalitions," we mean those in which ruling elites provide tangible benefits to popular sectors in exchange for political support or acquiescence. By "severe external threat," we mean situations in which outsiders credibly threaten not merely to initiate a military dispute or seize valued territory, but to terminate the target state as a sovereign political unit. By "resource constraints," we refer to a condition in which states enjoy access to neither credible long-term commitments of foreign assistance nor easily exploited commodity resources.

[12] Riker 1962.

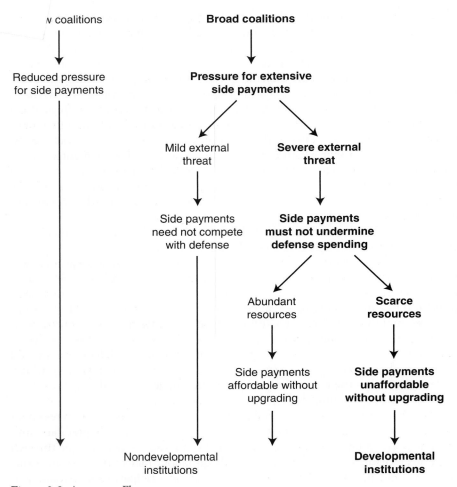

Figure 3.2 Argument Flow.

words, sustaining broad coalitions over the long run requires the ability to export high value-added goods, namely to upgrade. States exhibiting weak or even "intermediate" institutions lack the capacity to overcome these political-economic challenges.

Our suggestion that developmental states partly reflect elite responses to popular pressures might seem counterintuitive, given both the undeniably authoritarian nature of these regimes when these institutions were built, as well as recent work highlighting the contribution of democratic regimes to the provision of public goods.[13] But while popular sectors have been politically subordinated and even brutally repressed in the NICs, they have rarely been economically

---

[13] Baum and Lake 2003.

ignored. The key to the NICs' robust economic institutions lies in how popular sectors have been compensated for their political marginalization. . . .

The Institutional Features of Developmental States

What specific features give institutions the capacity to solve the information, commitment, and coordination problems that plague economic development? Accounting for the origins of developmental states requires that we identify such features, independently from the national economic performance with which they are associated. In this section, we identify these features in the NICs (South Korea, Taiwan, and Singapore), and contrast them with those of the "intermediate" states of the ASEAN-4 (Indonesia, Malaysia, the Philippines, and Thailand).

Institutional Features

Developmental states are complexes of particular types of bureaucratic agencies and public-private–sector linkages. The bureaucracies in question are Weberian in nature: recruitment is by competitive exam; promotion is by merit; remuneration is competitive with rates in the private sector; tenure in office is long; sanctions for corruption are clear and effective; and leadership occurs through a "pilot" agency that "stands outside and astride" individual ministries.[14] Incentives in these bureaucracies encourage the development of independent organizational perspectives and the alignment of broader organizational goals with individual incentives.[15]

But developmental state bureaucracies go beyond the Weberian ideal by promoting linkages with private actors, particularly business and, ideally, labor as well. These public-private institutions can range from formal "deliberation councils" and joint statutory boards to more ad hoc advisory councils. At least three features distinguish these institutions from the broad spectrum of "clientelist" government-business relations that characterize most political systems, especially (but not exclusively) in the developing world. They operate on functional or industry-wide criteria; their private-sector participants tend to be "encompassing," often in the form of official, sectoral, or peak associations; and their operations tend to be transparent, at least to government and business, and to proceed according to explicit and consistent rules and norms.[16]

Institutional Variation

. . . Despite some cross-national differences in institutional design (for example, degrees of centralization, roles of large versus small firms), South Korea, Taiwan, and

---

[14] Weiss 1998, 52.

[15] Haggard 2004.

[16] See Schneider and Maxfield 1997; and Kuo 1995.

Singapore largely conform to the aforementioned characteristics.[17] These countries combine meritocratic promotion and competitive selection. Each has powerful lead development agencies. Each exhibits relatively low levels of corruption and/or has effectively hived off such corruption from leading economic sectors.[18] Each also exhibits high levels of linkages, or "embeddedness," with organized private actors.

These features contrast with those of the "intermediate" states of Indonesia, Malaysia, the Philippines, and Thailand. Bureaucratic coherence in the ASEAN-4 is uneven at best, and public-private linkages exhibit significant degrees of clientelism and private-sector factionalism.[19] Although one finds "pockets of bureaucratic efficiency" and functional public-private–sector linkages, these either serve noneconomic ends, such as managing communal politics in Malaysia, or govern economic domains that are necessary but far from sufficient for upgrading, such as macroeconomics in Thailand.

What accounts for this striking intra-Asian variation in institutional features?

The Argument

. . . Three factors identified in the broader state-building literature and explored in the Northeast Asian context prove more useful. But the utility of each of these variables is limited when considered in isolation.

Broad Coalitions
Despite their well-known preference for "minimum winning coalitions," politicians can be induced to broaden coalitions under specific conditions.[20] Whenever elite or social conflict are perceived by political elites as intense or imminent during the early stages of state formation, coalitions tend to be broadened; where such conflicts are muted or absent, coalitions tend to remain comparatively narrow.[21] Sustaining a broad coalition is not costless: it typically requires that elites provide side payments—goods and services "that can conceivably have value" for coalition partners.[22] For our purposes, the key point is that these side payments have important institutional impacts.

Waldner argues that side payments to popular sectors inexorably increase producers' costs and swamp institutions with particularistic demands. Waldner thus concludes that narrow rather than broad coalitions were a necessary condition for the emergence of developmental states in South Korea and Taiwan.[23] Yet he

---

[17] On inter-NIC differences, see Wong and Ng 2001.

[18] On corruption in Korea and Taiwan, see Kang 2002; and Fields 1997.

[19] Evans 1995, chap. 3.

[20] Riker 1962, 88–89.

[21] See Waldner 1999, 29; Hechter and Brustein 1980; and Crone 1988 for an application to Southeast Asia.

[22] Riker 1962, 105.

[23] Waldner 1999.

does not posit any causal mechanism linking narrow coalitions to developmental states, leaving the reader to wonder why ruling elites facing mild coalitional constraints would seek to strengthen the state rather than simply stealing it. Furthermore, while rightly highlighting the dangers of populist subsidies and unconditional protection, Waldner unnecessarily precludes the possibility that ruling elites might deliver side payments with more salutary effects. There is in fact theoretical and empirical support for the view that the pursuit of selective benefits and rents may result in the "joint production" of both private and public goods. Although such arguments commonly refer to benefits accruing to business, they might also involve broad benefits to popular sectors, such as education and rural infrastructure, that can encourage productivity rather than profligacy.[24]

As we show below, certain types of side payments actually lower factor costs rather than raising them, enhancing rather than undermining a country's export competitiveness. Certain types of side payments also are essentially undeliverable unless state agencies develop enough institutional capacity to distribute them effectively. Indeed, we see side payments as the causal mechanism through which broad coalitions produce stronger institutions. Initial support for this view comes from Campos and Root, who argue that broad rather than narrow coalitions were the basis of institutional development and economic growth in both Northeast and Southeast Asia.[25]

Yet Campos and Root's blanket endorsement of broad coalitions is as problematic as Waldner's unconditional support for narrow ones. Waldner rightly insists on the potentially deleterious economic and institutional consequences of cross-class side payments. Ruling elites typically do meet broad coalitional pressures with ill-conceived subsidies that breed clientelism. The critical question is: Why do some ruling elites sustain broad coalitions with side payments that break the bank and explode factor costs, while others secure support with side payments that increase cost-competitiveness and "call forth" expanded institutional capacities?

External Threat

We find useful guidance in unraveling this puzzle from the literature on state formation in early modern Europe. This literature broadly agrees that strong states arise in response to security threats, as asserted in Tilly's famous dictum: "War made the state, and the state made war."[26] Variants of this argument have been usefully applied to Japan and the Northeast Asian NICs: Woo-Cumings has argued that "economic growth . . . (was) . . . indispensable for military security" and regime survival in South Korea and Taiwan; and Campos and Root contend that an atmosphere of "political contestability," based in large part on external

---

[24] See Bueno de Mesquita et al. 2003, 22–23; Acemoglu et al. 2003; and Knight 1992.
[25] Campos and Root 1996.
[26] Tilly 1975, 42.

threats, compelled leaders to create strong institutions to promote growth and implement wealth-sharing mechanisms for popular sectors.[27]

But research on state formation in the Middle East and Latin America shows that external threats, even in conjunction with mass coalitional pressures, are not always associated with growing institutional capacity.[28] The weakness of any such account is reflected in Campos and Root's inability to provide a systematic explanation for the much weaker commitments to education and training and more sporadic and superficial consultative mechanisms in the ASEAN-4 than in the NICs.[29] We argue that the critical factor explaining this variation is whether, in Centeno's apt phrase, threatened states will be "forced to turn inward to meet the financial challenges of war."[30] How war makes states ultimately depends on how war makes states generate revenue.

Resource Constraints
Research suggests that a state's ease of access to revenue influences institutional development. For example, "rentier state" theorists have argued that resource abundance encourages the creation of distributive rather than extractive state institutions, and Ross has proposed that this "resource curse" encourages politicians to dismantle state institutions in order to "seize" rents.[31] These arguments help to account for variation in institutional capacity between resource-rich and resource-poor economies. Indeed, Rasiah argues that natural-resource exports reduced fiscal pressure on the ASEAN-4 to promote the kinds of "complementary institutional and linkage development" that occurred in the NICs.[32]

But such arguments cannot account for institutional differences between countries with relatively similar resource endowments. Examples include the stark variation in institutional capacity between the Northeast Asian NICs and the resource-poor countries of sub-Saharan Africa, as well as differences between resource-rich countries such as Malaysia and Venezuela, or between Botswana, a country with both diamonds and strong institutions, and its resource-rich but often predatory African neighbors.[33] Underlying all of these weaknesses is a failure to provide a full theory of elite preferences and constraints. As Ross rightly notes, this literature mistakenly assumes that states are invariably revenue satisficers, not revenue maximizers.[34] Whether states satisfice

---

[27] Woo-Cumings 1998, 322; Campos and Root 1996.

[28] On Latin America, see Centeno 1997, 1569. On the Middle East, see Barnett 1992.

[29] Campos and Root 1996, 58–59.

[30] Centeno 1997, 1569.

[31] See Beblawi and Luciani 1987; Ross 2001; and Shafer 1994. On resources and growth, see Auty 1994; and Sachs and Warner 1995.

[32] Rasiah 2003, 66. Similarly, Booth 1999, 311, stresses the negative impacts of "easy to tax" sectors in the ASEAN-4.

[33] See Rodrik 2003.

[34] Ross 1999, 313.

or maximize revenue, we argue, depends fundamentally on the coalitional and geopolitical context in which they are forced to operate.

Systemic Vulnerability

Broad coalitions and external security needs constitute two critical claims on scarce resources that press ruling elites to become revenue maximizers. Under such vulnerable conditions, "easy" development strategies become difficult: shortages of foreign exchange to import inputs for domestic producers means simply subsidizing unprofitable local firms is unsustainable; coalitional obstacles to squeezing wages weaken the long-term feasibility of labor-intensive industrialization; and the lack of foreign exchange makes it difficult to grow simply by buying costly foreign technology. When elites face high levels of systemic vulnerability, they necessarily confront the challenge of simultaneously improving living standards and promoting growth by continuously upgrading local resources.[35]

Reconciling these competing political pressures requires strong institutions. Elites confronting systemic vulnerability must go beyond ensuring property rights, establishing macroeconomic stability, and socializing the risks of new investments. They are also pressed to redistribute assets, such as land, identify areas for new investments with real market potential, establish education and training programs that upgrade skills valued by the market, and set up manufacturing and agricultural extension programs that improve the competitiveness of firms.

Implementing policies in these areas poses particular challenges: they require the active "buy-in" of numerous parties. They have important distributional implications, with benefits often taking longer to appear than costs. They require considerable information, often of a specialized nature. They also lack clear "templates." In these situations, "Policy makers are dealing in much more complex political environments and often walking blind as to what needs to be done to resolve issues of public importance."[36]

Policy implementation under these conditions thus requires institutions able to formulate broad developmental objectives; to facilitate information flows within state agencies and between officials and private actors regarding market requirements; to monitor firms' performance; and to be credible in terms of both commitment to economic policies and willingness to exact reciprocity. Such capacities require Weberian bureaucracies led by pilot agencies "embedded" in organized sets of private interests. Even the smartest policies cannot implement themselves. . . .

---

[35] This argument holds whether one emphasizes upgrading as simply the result of increased factor inputs or improvements in total factor productivity. On this debate, see, for example, Haggard 2004.

[36] Grindle 2001, 373. See also Noble 1998; and Waldner 1999.

Conclusion

As an exercise in empirical analysis, this article has aimed to unravel the political origins of developmental and nondevelopmental states in Northeast and Southeast Asia. We have argued that ruling elites in the NICs constructed coherent bureaucracies and public-private consultative mechanisms in response to a similar set of political-economic constraints: all were pressed to build and maintain broad coalitions and to address security threats without easy access to revenues. In contrast, ruling elites in the ASEAN-4 never confronted such a threatening mix of geopolitical, coalitional, and fiscal constraints. "Intermediate states" thus provided these countries' ruling groups with ample institutional capacity to sustain coalitions and preserve national sovereignty.

Our empirical analysis has also helped us identify a somewhat surprising causal mechanism through which systemic vulnerability actually produces developmental states. Contrary to common views that developmental states were built by utterly unconstrained and ungenerous ruling elites, we have found that the side payments these elites delivered to popular sectors "called forth" impressive new institutional capacities in South Korea, Singapore, and Taiwan. This was an incremental process. Without building new institutions, policies designed to secure mass acquiescence such as land reform, advanced technical training, and subsidized public housing could never have been effectively implemented. Given the fiscal constraints imposed by revenue paucity and daunting defense commitments, ruling elites did not enjoy the luxury of co-opting a restive mass public with more expensive but less institutionally unchallenging types of side payments. Nor was it politically feasible to pursue a low-wage export strategy based on squeezing labor. Over time, then, upholding broad coalitions amid severe fiscal constraints came to require the pursuit of both export promotion and increased domestic inputs, all without sacrificing wage buoyancy. This strategy entailed extensive institutional capacity.

Accounting for these Asian outliers allows us to address broader debates as to the conditions under which political self-interest drives ruling elites to provide growth-promoting public goods and, by implication, to construct better institutions for governance. Implicitly challenging the benefits of "state autonomy," recent scholarship stresses the contribution of democracy to the provision of public goods, such as education.[37] Drawing on market models, this view argues that democracy's competitive pressures limit states' ability to garner and distribute monopoly rents to themselves and a narrow band of supporters. But while democracy is a valuable end in itself, it does not always yield either more capable or more generous states. Democratic competition might inspire improved institutional performance and increased public provision when it helps induce elite vulnerability, as seen in contemporary Thailand. But where ruling elites develop such a stronghold on power resources that they can preserve power without

---

[37] See Lake and Baum 2001; and Baum and Lake 2003.

delivering significant side payments, as we see in the Philippines, the "invisible hand of democracy" fails to deliver the goods.

Nor should we assume that constraints on elite actions are confined to democracies. The primary lesson of state-building in Northeast and Southeast Asia has been that systemic vulnerability, far more than electoral vulnerability, has driven ruling elites to improve institutional performance. At first, this argument might seem crudely functionalist. But it is perfectly consistent with conventional, rationalist premises regarding elite preferences. Developmental states have not arisen from political leaders' selfless love of nation and accompanying recognition that new institutions could help maximize national wealth. Rather, developmental states have arisen from political leaders' recognition that—under conditions of systemic vulnerability—only coherent bureaucracies and broad public-private linkages could produce the resources necessary to sustain coalitions, secure state survival, and thereby maximize their time in office.

We have tested the generalizability of this argument outside Northeast Asia, where our and others' hypotheses regarding the origins of developmental states have been generated. Because Southeast Asia exhibits significant variation on both our key independent variables and on the dependent variable of institutional capacity, it has provided a useful venue for testing our hypotheses. We also believe that our argument is consistent with research outside the Asian theater, such as scholarship on the origins of "nonliberal capitalisms" in the industrialized world and on institutional variation in Africa.[38] Our hope is that the hypotheses generated and tested here inspire assessments of our arguments on a broader scale.

References

Acemoglu, Daron, Simon Johnson, and James A. Robinson. 2003. An African Success Story: Botswana. In *In Search of Prosperity: Analytic Narratives on Economic Growth*, edited by Dani Rodrik, 80–122. Princeton, N.J.: Princeton University Press.

Amsden, Alice. 1989. *Asia's Next Giant: South Korea and Late Industrialization*. New York: Oxford University Press.

———. 1994. Why Isn't the Whole World Experimenting with the East Asian Model to Develop? *World Development* 22 (4):627–33.

Aron, Janine. 2000. Growth and Institutions: A Review of the Evidence. *World Bank Research Observer* 15 (1):99–135.

Auty, Richard M. 1994. *Sustaining Development in Mineral Economies: The Resource Curse Thesis*. London: Routledge.

Barnett, Michael N. 1992. *Confronting the Costs of War: Military Power, State, and Society in Egypt and Israel*. Princeton, N.J.: Princeton University Press.

Bates, Robert H. 1995. Social Dilemmas and Rational Individuals: An Assessment of the New Institutionalism. In *The New Institutional Economics and Third World Development*, edited by John Harriss, Janet Hunter, and Colin Lewis, 27–48. New York: Routledge.

---

[38] See Streeck 2001; Katzenstein 1985; Rodrik 2003; and Acemoglu, Johnson, and Robinson 2003.

Baum, Matthew A., and David A. Lake. 2003. The Political Economy of Growth: Democracy and Human Capital. *American Journal of Political Science* 47 (2):333–47.

Beblawi, Hazem, and Giacomo Luciani. 1987. *The Rentier State.* London: Croom Helm.

Booth, Anne. 1999. Initial Conditions and Miraculous Growth: Why Is South East Asia Different from Taiwan and South Korea? *World Development* 27 (2):301–21.

Bueno de Mesquita, Bruce, Alastair Smith, Randolph M. Siverson, and James D. Morrow. 2003. *The Logic of Political Survival.* Cambridge, Mass: MIT Press.

Campos, José Edgardo, and Hilton L. Root. 1996. *The Key to the Asian Miracle: Making Shared Growth Credible.* Washington, D.C.: Brookings Institution.

Centeno, Miguel Angel. 1997. Blood and Debt: War and Taxation in Nineteenth-Century Latin America. *American Journal of Sociology* 102 (6):1565–605.

Crone, Donald K. 1988. State, Social Elites, and Government Capacity in Southeast Asia. *World Politics* 40 (2):252–68.

Emmerson, Donald K. 1978. The Bureaucracy in Political Context: Weakness in Strength. In *Political Power and Communications in Indonesia,* edited by Karl Jackson and Lucian Pye, 82–136. Berkeley: University of California Press.

Evans, Peter. 1995. *Embedded Autonomy: States and Industrial Transformation.* Princeton, N.J.: Princeton University Press.

Fields, Karl. 1997. Strong States and Business Organization in Korea and Taiwan. In *Business and the State in Developing Countries*, edited by Ben Schneider and Sylvia Maxfield, 122–51. Ithaca, N.Y.: Cornell University Press.

Geddes, Barbara. 1994. *Politicians' Dilemma: Building State Capacity in Latin America.* Berkeley: University of California Press.

Gereffi, Gary. Forthcoming. The Global Economy: Organization, Governance and Development. *Handbook of Economic Sociology.* 2d ed. Edited by Neil J. Smelser and Richard Swedberg, 160–82. Princeton, N.J.: Princeton University Press.

Grindle, Merilee. 2001. In Quest of the Political: The Political Economy of Development Policy-making. In *Frontiers of Development Economics,* edited by Gerald Meier and Joseph Stiglitz, 344–75. New York: Oxford University Press.

Haggard, Stephan, 1990. *Pathways from the Periphery: The Politics of Growth in the Newly Industrializing Countries,* Ithaca, N.Y.: Cornell University Press.

——. 2004. Institutions and Growth in East Asia. *Studies in Comparative and International Development* 38 (4):53–82.

Hall, Peter, and David Soskice 2001. *Varieties of Capitalism: The Institutional Foundations of Comparative Advantage.* New York: Oxford University Press.

Hechter, Michael, and William Brustein. 1980. Regional Modes of Production and Patterns of State Formation in Western Europe. *American Journal of Sociology* 85 (5):1061–94.

Kang, David C. 2002. Bad Loans to Good Friends: Money Politics and the Developmental State in South Korea. *International Organization* 56 (1):177–207.

Katzenstein, Peter J. 1985. *Small States in World Markets: Industrial Policy in Europe.* Ithaca: Cornell University Press.

Knight, Jack. 1992. *Institutions and Social Conflict.* New York: Cambridge University Press.

Kuo, Cheng-Tian. 1995. *Global Competitiveness and Industrial Growth in Taiwan and the Philippines,* Pittsburgh, Penn.: University of Pittsburgh Press.

Lake, David and Matthew Baum. 2001. The Invisible Hand of Democracy: Political Control and the Provision of Public Services. *Comparative Political Studies* 34 (6):587–621.

McNamara, Dennis L. 1999. "From Patron to Partner: Korean State Role in the Textile Transition." In *Corporatism and Korean Capitalism*, edited by Dennis McNamara, 95–109. New York: Routledge.

Moe, Terry. 1984. The New Economics of Organization. *American Journal of Political Science* 28 (4):739–77.

Moon, Chung-in, and Rashemi Prasad. 1998. Networks, Politics and Institutions. In *Beyond the Developmental State: East Asia's Political Economies Reconsidered,* edited by Steve Chan, Cal Clark, and Danny Lam, 9–24. New York: St. Martin's Press.

Noble, Gregory. 1998. *Collective Action in East Asia: How Ruling Parties Shape Industrial Policy.* Ithaca, N.Y.: Cornell University Press.

Rasiah, Rajah. 2003. Manufacturing Export Growth in Indonesia, Malaysia and Thailand. In *Southeast Asian Paper Tigers? From Miracle to Debacle and Beyond*, edited by K. S. Jomo, 19–80. London: Routledge Curzon.

Riker, William H. 1962. *The Theory of Political Coalitions.* New Haven, Conn.: Yale University Press.

Rodrik, Dani. 2003. Introduction. In *In Search of Prosperity: Analytic Narratives on Economic Growth*, edited by Dani Rodrik, 1–22. Princeton, N.J.: Princeton University Press.

Ross, Michael. 2001. *Timber Booms and Institutional Breakdown in Southeast Asia.* New York: Cambridge University Press.

Sachs, Jeffrey D., and Andrew M. Warner. 1995. Natural Resource Abundance and Economic Growth. Development Discussion Paper 517a. Cambridge, Mass.: Institute for International Development, Harvard University.

Schneider, Ben Ross, and Sylvia Maxfield. 1997. Business, the State, and Economic Performance in Developing Countries. In *Business and the State in Developing Countries*, edited by Maxfield and Schneider, 3–35. Ithaca, N.Y.: Cornell University Press.

Shafer, D. Michael. 1994. Winners and Losers: How Sectors Shape the Developmental Prospects of States. Ithaca, N.Y.: Cornell University Press.

Streeck, Wolfgang. 2001. Introduction: Explorations into the Origins of Nonliberal Capitalism in Germany and Japan. In *The Origins of Nonliberal Capitalism: Germany and Japan in Comparison*, edited by Wolfgang Streeck and Kozo Yamamura, 1–38. Ithaca, N.Y.: Cornell University Press.

Tilly, Charles. 1975. Reflections on the History of European State-Making. In *The Formation of National States in Western Europe*, edited by Charles Tilly, 3–83. Princeton, N.J.: Princeton University Press.

Wade, Robert. 1990. *Governing the Market: Economic Theory and the Role of Government in East Asian Industrialization.* Princeton, N.J.: Princeton University Press.

———. 1992. East Asia's Economic Success: Conflicting Paradigms, Partial Insights, Shaky Evidence. *World Politics* 44 (2):270–320.

Waldner, David. 1999. *State Building and Late Development.* Ithaca, N.Y.: Cornell University Press.

Weiss, Linda. 1998. *The Myth of the Powerless State.* Ithaca, N.Y.: Cornell University Press.

Woo-Cummings, Meredith Jung-en. 1991. *Race to the Swift: State and Finance in Korean Industrialization.* New York: Columbia University Press.

———. 1998. National Security and the Rise of the Developmental State in South Korea and Taiwan. In *Behind East Asian Growth,* edited by Henry Rowen, 319–40. New York: Routledge.

Wong Poh-kam, and Chee-Yuen Ng. 2001. Rethinking the Development Paradigm: Lessons from Japan and the Four Asian NIEs. In *Industrial Policy, Innovation and Economic Growth*, edited by Poh-kam Wong and Chee-Yuen Ng, 1–55. Singapore: Singapore University Press.

World Bank. 2003. *Thai Economic Monitor*, June.

From North-South to South-South

Robert J. S. Ross and Anita Chan

Many analyses of the global economy highlight inequalities between the affluent countries of the North and the developing countries of the South. (See Stiglitz [3.7] and McKibben [7.6].) Robert Ross and Anita Chan identify another important issue in contemporary political economy: competition among countries in the South to attract foreign investment. They argue that, in the absence of international treaties to protect labor standards (what is often called the social clause), such competition harms workers in these countries by lowering wages and promoting unsafe working conditions. Can you think of a reply to their argument? Which position is more valid in your opinion (for or against international regulation of labor standards), and why?

A s protesters battled the police in the streets of Seattle in 1999, calling on the World Trade Organization to include environmental and labor issues in its trade negotiations, government representatives in conference rooms were carrying on a battle of another sort. Many developing nations, particularly the Asian countries, were strongly resisting a U.S.-led proposal by developed countries to link trade to environmental and labor standards through a new "social clause" in WTO agreements. The clause, its opponents argued, was a protectionist ploy that rich nations would use to shelter their own workers' jobs from the competition in developing countries. This stance reflected a commonly held perception that the main competition in the production of goods is between the North and the South. But in truth, this competition—particularly in labor-intensive commodities—is not so much North versus South but South versus South. The absence of a mechanism establishing international labor standards is propelling the economies of the South in a race to the bottom in wages and labor conditions.

The social clause, in brief, refers to the proposed insertion of five core labor standards into trade agreements: freedom of association, freedom to organize and to bargain collectively, and freedom from forced labor, child labor, and job

Robert J.S. Ross and Anita Chan, "From North-South to South-South," *Foreign Affairs* 81, no. 5 (September/October 2002): 8–13. Reprinted by permission of *Foreign Affairs,* 81, no. 5, September–October 2002. Copyright 2002 by the Council on Foreign Relations, Inc.

discrimination. Many poorer countries either lack the laws to protect these rights, which are enshrined in the conventions of the International Labor Organization (ILO), or they simply do not bother to enforce those laws in their export industries.

Trade Unions Divided

Governments do not necessarily reflect the interests of their country's workers, but labor unions are supposed to. So how do unions line up on the social-clause question? Although the issue at Seattle had united the government leaders of the South in opposition, the international trade-union movement holds diverse views. The International Confederation of Free Trade Unions, composed of 221 affiliated unions that represent 150 million workers in 148 countries, supports the social clause. But African backing for the clause has not always been uniform: trade unions in some countries, such as South Africa, are in favor, whereas those in others, such as Zimbabwe and Zambia, are opposed.

In Latin America, unions are more amenable to linking trade and labor rights, thanks in part to their strong relationships with their North American counterparts. Struggling unions in Guatemala, Honduras, El Salvador, and Nicaragua have strategically used the U.S. threat of trade sanctions (specifically, in response to violations of labor rights) to secure their own rights to organize. For example, Guatemalan workers formed an unrecognized union at a factory owned by the U.S. clothing giant Phillips–Van Heusen in the early 1990s. In a long and bitter campaign, their North American allies—including UNITE, the U.S. apparel-workers union—filed a lawsuit in the United States at their behest, alleging that Guatemala was ineligible for trade concessions because it denied workers the right to organize. This pressure finally led the firm and the Guatemalan government to recognize the union.

Other Latin American confederations of unions—for example, those in Argentina and Chile—support a social clause, too. The trade unions of several middle-income countries in Asia also approve. The Korean Confederation of Trade Unions believes the "social clause can be a significant and effective instrument to protect and achieve social rights and the basic trade union rights." Likewise, the Malaysian Trade Union Congress supports a linkage between labor standards and trade and exports—out of fear that its members' rights could be undermined by competition from the large number of Asian migrant workers working without labor protection in Malaysia's export zones.

But India's trade unions and China's quasi-governmental trade union federation take a different approach. The governments and trade unions of the two most populous countries in the world are determinedly against a social clause. And because of their dominant weight in the world's cheap-labor market, their positions have enormous repercussions on the wages of unskilled laborers throughout the underdeveloped world. This dominance may also explain the perception that the South is staunchly opposed to the social clause—even though the truth is more variegated.

Neck and Neck

In rejecting a regulated international labor regime, countries of the South lower their own labor standards to remain competitive and provide a "good" investment climate. This imperative gives businesses an excellent opportunity to exploit their work forces to the fullest; examples include the South Korean, Taiwanese, and Hong Kong firms that subcontract from brand-name corporations to do labor-intensive manufacturing in poor countries. The apparel industry aptly illustrates this type of globalized production. The work is highly labor intensive, and the industry continues to use a vast amount of unskilled labor supplied by the South, despite technological upgrading. This sector is also among the most footloose: production facilities can be moved easily from city to city or country to country. Apparel manufacturing employs a large number of workers in the South, mostly young women; in turn, this high volume of jobs affects the overall wage levels and labor standards of these countries.

Over the past four decades, the U.S. apparel industry has been overwhelmed by this global low-wage competition. Apparel imports rose from about 2 percent of U.S. domestic consumption in the early 1960s to more than 60 percent in the 1990s. In the largest categories of clothing imports—men's and women's tops—the $26 billion of imports furnishes more than 70 percent of the market by value and about 90 percent by quantity. Since 1980, imports have cut U.S. apparel-industry employment by half, a loss of more than 600,000 jobs. Many of the workers who remain in the U.S. garment industry, toiling as sweatshop workers or as underpaid home workers, suffer declining wages that today are often below the legal minimum. Even so, the North-South competition is basically over in this industry. The enormous difference in North-South wage levels ensures that those jobs lost will not return to the United States.

A Tale of Two Countries

In recent years, China and Mexico have become the lions of the U.S. clothing market, obtaining an equal market share since the 1993 signing of the North American Free Trade Agreement (NAFTA). By 2000, Mexico and China each supplied around 15 percent of all apparel imports to the United States. (The Chinese total includes Hong Kong's apparel manufacturing, which has relocated almost entirely to the mainland.) But Mexico enjoys two substantial advantages over China: close geography (hence a faster filling of orders) and the absence of quota restrictions, thanks to NAFTA. As a result, Asian investors—particularly

South Koreans and Taiwanese—became increasingly active there in the 1990s, even moving apparel production out of Asia into Mexico.

The dramatic growth of apparel exports from Mexico and China to North America has created a surge of new jobs. In both countries, the export-oriented factories employ migrant workers from poor, rural areas. In China, the growth first began in the mid-1980s in Guangdong province (which neighbors Hong Kong) and picked up speed in the early 1990s. The entire Pearl River Delta in Guangdong, which 20 years ago was largely agricultural, is now a manufacturing powerhouse that churns out labor-intensive goods for the world market. Today, some 12 million migrant workers from poor parts of China's countryside staff these factories' production lines. A similar phenomenon emerged in Mexico in the 1990s. Along the U.S.-Mexican border, new investment created boomtowns where *maquiladoras* (assembly plants) have mushroomed. By 2000, these factories employed about one million workers—an increase of 150 percent since 1990—and production was spreading to other parts of the country.

Contrary to general wisdom, however, more jobs have not meant higher wages or rising labor standards for migrant workers, whether in Mexico or in China. On the contrary, wages have fallen as a result of intensified competition to attract factories that sell to the North's markets. This drop is reflected in both the low legal minimum wages set by the two countries and the real purchasing power of workers.

In China, the setting of a minimum wage is extremely decentralized. Any city, or even a city district, can set its own minimum wage based on a formula provided by Beijing. This formula takes into account such factors as the local cost of living, the prevailing wage, and the rate of inflation, and it is adjusted each year. In 2001, for example, the city of Shenzhen (just north of Hong Kong) had two standards. Inner Shenzhen, the city's commercialized sector, had the highest minimum wage in China at the equivalent of $72 per month, but the outer industrialized sector's minimum wage was only $55 per month. Elsewhere in China, legal minimum wages have been set even lower. Although these local governments comply on paper with Beijing's decrees on minimum wages, they attempt to attract investors by allowing them to pay workers below those rates. The legal minimum wage is set by the month and does not take into account that many migrant workers labor illegally for longer hours. (For example, our survey of China's footwear industry shows that the average number of hours worked each day is 11, and laborers often have no days off.) Furthermore, official statistics do not take into consideration the staggering amount of unpaid back wages. Some 40 percent of the 20,000 workers' complaints lodged with the Shenzhen authorities over nine months in 2001 were related to owed wages. Such abuse has become normal in southern China.

Official minimum wages also obscure other critical facts. They do not show the violence and physical abuses that have become pervasive in the factories in China owned by Taiwanese, Korean, and Hong Kong intermediaries; nor do they take into account the acute and chronic occupational health and safety hazards. These factories record a startlingly high incidence of severed limbs and fingers; Shenzhen alone certified more than 10,000 such accidents in 1999 among a migrant population of 4 million. In short, despite China's dramatic export growth, the benefits have not trickled down to the assembly-line workers who make the exported goods. Indeed, their situation has gotten even worse since the Asian financial crisis of 1997–98; the downturn intensified competition with Southeast Asian labor, which had become much cheaper in the wake of local currency devaluations. (Provincial surveys in China show that a downturn in migrant workers' pay started at that time.)

China's main challenge in apparel and other sectors, however, comes from Mexico. There, workers' conditions in the *maquiladoras* are also grim. But unlike in China, wage levels in Mexico are more regulated. Only three minimum-wage levels exist for the entire country, including one for the U.S.-Mexico border region (equivalent to $93 to $108 per month). These minimum wages, although low, are almost double those of Shenzhen, which are the highest in China. But Mexico's legal minimum wages fell by almost half during the 1990s, due in part to the peso's collapse in 1996. In addition, competition with countries such as China created a downward pressure on average real wages in Mexico. In the manufacturing sector, wages dropped in real purchasing power terms by 20 percent over the same period. And in the booming apparel sector, ILO data show that their wages shed 14 percent of their purchasing power from 1990 to 2000. Since 2000, wages have gained slightly, but that increase is threatened by the prospect of capital flight to regions with even lower labor costs.

In short, export workers in China and Mexico have not benefited from the economic boom. More workers are being employed, but over the course of the 1990s working conditions and wages deteriorated. These assembly workers are caught in an internationally competitive race to the bottom.

Intensifying Competition

In 2005, trade barriers on apparel are due to end under the 1975 Multi-Fiber Agreement (and its 1994 successor). Assuming that its wages remain low, China will then be poised to make more inroads into rich-country apparel markets, offsetting Mexico's advantage of proximity to the U.S. market. In other industries, the WTO's lowering of trade barriers will also tip the scales away from Mexico and toward China. Fearing this, Mexico sought to delay China's entry into the WTO; in fact, it was the last WTO member to sign last year the necessary bilateral agreement with China that paved the way for WTO accession.

Mexico is already feeling the increased competitive heat. Knowing that trade barriers will soon fall, intermediate firms have begun shifting their Mexican assembly lines back to Asia, particularly China. The number of *maquiladoras* swelled from 120 in the 1970s to 3,700 in 2000 but has dropped by 500 since then. Pressures are increasing on other Mexican factories to compete with China's long working hours and bargain-basement wages. These pressures may also threaten the incremental growth of an autonomous Mexican trade-union movement—a result of years of painstaking political and social change, supported by a solidarity movement in the United States and Canada. Employers who resist relocating to China or to other low-wage countries will be tempted to lower standards in Mexico by resisting the fledgling union movement.

Mexican President Vicente Fox has proposed the "Puebla to Panama Plan," which would build an investment corridor for more *maquiladoras* from southern Mexico through Central America—at wages even lower than those at the U.S.-Mexican border. In China, meanwhile, the government is encouraging foreign investors to go north and inland in pursuit of lower costs than can be found in southern China.

The examples of China and Mexico show just how much the international competition among nations of the South influences their workers' well-being. And this race to the bottom affects people elsewhere in the developing world who hold jobs in those sectors. Without regulations to protect labor, akin to rules that protect investors, poor-country workers will not share in the benefits of a growth in world trade. For that reason, labor standards ought to be as much a South-South issue as a North-South one.

Making Standards Stick

The debate over a WTO social clause has reached an impasse. Accordingly, there is no internationally binding enforcement mechanism to protect workers' rights in the South. Even the ILO, charged with this responsibility, has no means to enforce compliance with its conventions. It is doubtful that the Global Compact initiated in 1999 by UN Secretary-General Kofi Annan, which draws up guidelines for good corporate practices in the areas of human rights, labor rights, and the environment, will be useful, because it too lacks an enforcement mechanism. No competent global forum can enforce a verdict when a nation or its enterprises contravene fundamental labor rights.

Governments and trade unions of the South must confront this challenge. Their campaign against the North's protectionism has done little to improve the lot of their own work forces in export industries. They have to face the fact that they are competing among themselves—and that they themselves are partially responsible for the decline in wages and labor standards. The growing crisis in back wages (and wages simply never paid) owed to Chinese migrant workers shows that the bottom is continuing to fall. China is a key player in the South-South competition, and unless other countries can convince China to form or join a Southern consensus to put an international floor beneath wages, the scenario will only worsen. Only through enforceable minimum-wage standards can these countries prevent Northern corporations and intermediate suppliers from playing them off against each other. The possibility of WTO trade sanctions would deter abuses and give incentives to national labor-law enforcement. It would give all nations the right to complain about violations in an international forum. Picking up where President Bill Clinton and other developed-country leaders left off in Seattle, the WTO should devise a regulatory regime in line with a labor "social clause," so that violators, both governments and corporations, can be sanctioned if they contravene it. This scheme or something similar to it will be necessary before labor standards can be expected to improve—or even just stabilize. The globalization of capital has made the world smaller and safer for investors; now the question before the world community is whether it can do the same for workers.

 3.6

Globalism's Discontents

Joseph E. Stiglitz

In this selection, Joseph Stiglitz, who has served as chair of the Council of Economic Advisers and chief economist of the World Bank and who is a Nobel Prize winner in economics, claims that economic globalization can produce great benefits. However, for this to occur, states must provide their citizens with adequate social safety nets, such as social assistance for those dislocated by economic change. States must also impose capital controls, that is, regulate the flow of foreign capital, to reduce the risk of instability, and economic and financial crisis. Unfortunately, Stiglitz warns, these measures run counter to prevailing economic theory and the policies of many states and the International Monetary Fund (IMF), a powerful international financial institution. Stiglitz does not analyze in this excerpt the opposition to these policies that has developed around the world. Do you think they have been influential?

Few subjects have polarized people throughout the world as much as globalization. Some see it as the way of the future, bringing unprecedented prosperity to everyone, everywhere. Others, symbolized by the Seattle protestors of December 1999, fault globalization as the source of untold problems, from the destruction of native cultures to increasing poverty and immiseration. In this

---

article, I want to sort out the different meanings of globalization. In many countries, globalization has brought huge benefits to a few with few benefits to the many. But in the case of a few countries, it has brought enormous benefit to the many. Why have there been these huge differences in experiences? The answer is that globalization has meant different things in different places.

The countries that have managed globalization on their own, such as those in East Asia, have, by and large, ensured that they reaped huge benefits and that those benefits were equitably shared; they were able substantially to control the terms on which they engaged with the global economy. By contrast, the countries that have, by and large, had globalization managed for them by the International Monetary Fund and other international economic institutions have not done so well. The problem is thus not with globalization but with how it has been managed.

The international financial institutions have pushed a particular ideology—market fundamentalism—that is both bad economics and bad politics; it is based on premises concerning how markets work that do not hold even for developed countries, much less for developing countries. The IMF has pushed these economics policies without a broader vision of society or the role of economics within society. And it has pushed these policies in ways that have undermined emerging democracies.

More generally, globalization itself has been governed in ways that are undemocratic and have been disadvantageous to developing countries, especially the poor within those countries. The Seattle protestors pointed to the absence of democracy and of transparency, the governance of the international economic institutions by and for special corporate and financial interests, and the absence of countervailing democratic checks to ensure that these informal and public institutions serve a general interest. In these complaints, there is more than a grain of truth.

Beneficial Globalization

Of the countries of the world, those in East Asia have grown the fastest and done most to reduce poverty. And they have done so, emphatically, via "globalization." Their growth has been based on exports—by taking advantage of the global market for exports and by closing the technology gap. It was not just gaps in capital and other resources that separated the developed from the less-developed countries, but differences in knowledge. East Asian countries took advantage of the "globalization of knowledge" to reduce these disparities. But while some of the countries in the region grew by opening themselves up to multinational companies, others, such as Korea and Taiwan, grew by creating their own enterprises. Here is the key distinction: Each of the most successful globalizing countries determined its own pace of change; each made sure as it grew that the benefits were shared equitably; each rejected the basic tenets of the "Washington Consensus," which argued for a minimalist role for government and rapid privatization and liberalization.

In East Asia, government took an active role in managing the economy. The steel industry that the Korean government created was among the most efficient in the world—performing far better than its private-sector rivals in the United States (which, though private, are constantly turning to the government for protection and for subsidies). Financial markets were highly regulated. My research shows that those regulations promoted growth. It was only when these countries stripped away the regulations, under pressure from the U.S. Treasury and the IMF, that they encountered problems.

During the 1960s, 1970s, and 1980s, the East Asian economies not only grew rapidly but were remarkably stable. Two of the countries most touched by the 1997–1998 economic crisis had had in the preceding three decades not a single year of negative growth; two had only one year—a better performance than the United States or the other wealthy nations that make up the Organization for Economic Cooperation and Development (OECD). The single most important factor leading to the troubles that several of the East Asian countries encountered in the late 1990s—the East Asian crisis—was the rapid liberalization of financial and capital markets. In short, the countries of East Asia benefited from globalization because they made globalization work for them; it was when they succumbed to the pressures from the outside that they ran into problems that were beyond their own capacity to manage well.

Globalization can yield immense benefits. Elsewhere in the developing world, globalization of knowledge has brought improved health, with life spans increasing at a rapid pace. How can one put a price on these benefits of globalization? Globalization has brought still other benefits: Today there is the beginning of a globalized civil society that has begun to succeed with such reforms as the Mine Ban Treaty and debt forgiveness for the poorest highly indebted countries (the Jubilee movement). The globalization protest movement itself would not have been possible without globalization.

The Darker Side of Globalization

How then could a trend with the power to have so many benefits have produced such opposition? Simply because it has not only failed to live up to its potential but frequently has had very adverse effects. But this forces us to ask, why has it had such adverse effects? The answer can be seen by looking at each of the economic elements of globalization as pursued by the international financial institutions and especially by the IMF.

The most adverse effects have arisen from the liberalization of financial and capital markets—which has posed risks to developing countries without commensurate rewards. The liberalization has left them prey to hot money pouring into the country, an influx that has fueled speculative real-estate booms; just as suddenly, as investor sentiment changes, the money is pulled out, leaving in its wake economic devastation. Early on, the IMF said that these countries were being rightly punished for pursuing bad economic policies. But as the crisis spread from country to country, even those that the IMF had given high marks found themselves ravaged.

The IMF often speaks about the importance of the discipline provided by capital markets. In doing so, it exhibits a certain paternalism, a new form of the old colonial mentality: "We in the establishment, we in the North who run our capital markets, know best. Do what we tell you to do, and you will prosper." The arrogance is offensive, but the objection is more than just to style. The position is highly undemocratic: There is an implied assumption that democracy by itself does not provide sufficient discipline. But if one is to have an external disciplinarian, one should choose a good disciplinarian who knows what is good for growth, who shares one's values. One doesn't want an arbitrary and capricious taskmaster who one moment praises you for your virtues and the next screams at you for being rotten to the core. But capital markets are just such a fickle taskmaster; even ardent advocates talk about their bouts of irrational exuberance followed by equally irrational pessimism.

Lessons of Crisis

Nowhere was the fickleness more evident than in the last global financial crisis. Historically, most of the disturbances in capital flows into and out of a country are not the result of factors inside the country. Major disturbances arise, rather, from influences outside the country. When Argentina suddenly faced high interest rates in 1998, it wasn't because of what Argentina did but because of what happened in Russia. Argentina cannot be blamed for Russia's crisis.

Small developing countries find it virtually impossible to withstand this volatility. I have described capital-market liberalization with a simple metaphor: Small countries are like small boats. Liberalizing capital markets is like setting them loose on a rough sea. Even if the boats are well captained, even if the boats are sound, they are likely to be hit broadside by a big wave and capsize. But the IMF pushed for the boats to set forth into the roughest parts of the sea before they were seaworthy, with untrained captains and crews, and without life vests. No wonder matters turned out so badly!

To see why it is important to choose a disciplinarian who shares one's values, consider a world in which there were free mobility of skilled labor. Skilled labor would then provide discipline. Today, a country that does not treat capital well will find capital quickly withdrawing; in a world of free labor mobility if a country did not treat skilled labor well, it too would withdraw. Workers would worry about the quality of their children's education and their family's health care, the quality of their environment and of their own wages and working conditions. They would say to the government: If you fail to provide these essentials, we will move elsewhere. That is a far cry from the kind of discipline that free-flowing capital provides.

The liberalization of capital markets has not brought growth: How can one build factories or create jobs with money that can come in and out of a country overnight? And it gets worse: Prudential behavior requires countries to set aside reserves equal to the amount of short-term lending; so if a firm in a poor country borrows $100 million at, say, 20 percent interest rates short-term from a bank in the United States, the government must set aside a corresponding amount. The reserves are typically held in U.S. Treasury bills—a safe, liquid asset. In effect, the country is borrowing $100 million from the United States and lending $100 million to the United States. But when it borrows, it pays a high interest rate, 20 percent; when it lends, it receives a low interest rate, around 4 percent. This may be great for the United States, but it can hardly help the growth of the poor country. There is also a high opportunity cost of the reserves; the money could have been much better spent on building rural roads or constructing schools or health clinics. But instead, the country is, in effect, forced to lend money to the United States.

Thailand illustrates the true ironies of such policies: There, the free market led to investments in empty office buildings, starving other sectors—such as education and transportation—of badly needed resources. Until the IMF and the U.S. Treasury came along, Thailand had restricted bank lending for speculative real estate. The Thais had seen the record: Such lending is an essential part of the boom-bust cycle that has characterized capitalism for 200 years. It wanted to be sure that the scarce capital went to create jobs. But the IMF nixed this intervention in the free market. If the free market said, "Build empty office buildings," so be it! The market knew better than any government bureaucrat who mistakenly might have thought it wiser to build schools or factories.

The Costs of Volatility

Capital-market liberalization is inevitably accompanied by huge volatility, and this volatility impedes growth and increases poverty. It increases the risks of investing in the country, and thus investors demand a risk premium in the form of higher-than-normal profits. Not only is growth not enhanced but poverty is increased through several channels. The high volatility increases the likelihood of recessions—and the poor always bear the brunt of such downturns. Even in developed countries, safety nets are weak or nonexistent among the self-employed and in the rural sector. But these are the dominant sectors in developing countries. Without adequate safety nets, the recessions that follow from capital-market liberalization lead to impoverishment. In the name of imposing budget discipline and reassuring investors, the IMF invariably demands expenditure reductions, which almost inevitably result in cuts in outlays for safety nets that are already threadbare. Matters are even worse—for under the doctrines of the "discipline of the capital markets," if countries try to tax capital, capital flees. Thus, the IMF doctrines inevitably lead to an increase in tax burdens on the poor and the middle classes. Thus, while IMF bailouts enable the rich to take their money out of the country at more favorable terms (at the overvalued exchange rates), the burden of repaying the loans lies with the workers who remain behind.

The reason that I emphasize capital-market liberalization is that the case against it—and against the IMF's stance in pushing it—is so compelling. It illustrates what can go wrong with globalization. Even economists like Jagdish Bhagwati, strong advocates of free trade, see the folly in liberalizing capital markets. Belatedly, so too has the IMF—at least in its official rhetoric, though less so in its policy stances—but too late for all those countries that have suffered so much from following the IMF's prescriptions.

But while the case for trade liberalization—when properly done—is quite compelling, the way it has been pushed by the IMF has been far more problematic. The basic logic is simple: Trade liberalization is supposed to result in resources moving from inefficient protected sectors to more efficient export sectors. The problem is not only that job destruction comes before the job creation—so that unemployment and poverty result—but that the IMF's "structural adjustment programs" (designed in ways that allegedly would reassure global investors) make job creation almost impossible. For these programs are often accompanied by high interest rates that are often justified by a single-minded focus on inflation. Sometimes that concern is deserved; often, though, it is carried to an extreme. In the United States, we worry that small increases in the interest rate will discourage investment. The IMF has pushed for far higher interest rates in countries with a far less hospitable investment environment. The high interest rates mean that new jobs and enterprises are not created. What happens is that trade liberalization, rather than moving workers from low-productivity jobs to high-productivity ones, moves them from low-productivity jobs to unemployment. Rather than enhanced growth, the effect is increased poverty. To make matters even worse, the unfair trade-liberalization agenda forces poor countries to compete with highly subsidized American and European agriculture.

The Governance of Globalization

As the market economy has matured within countries, there has been increasing recognition of the importance of having rules to govern it. One hundred fifty years ago, in many parts of the world, there was a domestic process that was in some ways analogous to globalization. In the United States, government promoted the formation of the national economy, the building of the railroads, and the development of the telegraph—all of which reduced transportation and communication costs within the United States. As that process occurred, the democratically elected national government provided oversight: supervising and regulating, balancing interests, tempering crises, and limiting adverse consequences of this very large change in economic structure. So, for instance, in

1863 the U.S. government established the first financial banking regulatory authority—the Office of the Comptroller of Currency—because it was important to have strong national banks, and that requires strong regulation.

The United States, among the least statist of the industrial democracies, adopted other policies. Agriculture, the central industry of the United States in the mid-nineteenth century, was supported by the 1862 Morrill Act, which established research, extension, and teaching programs. That system worked extremely well and is widely credited with playing a central role in the enormous increases in agricultural productivity over the last century and a half. We established an industrial policy for other fledgling industries, including radio and civil aviation. The beginning of the telecommunications industry, with the first telegraph line between Baltimore and Washington, D.C., was funded by the federal government. And it is a tradition that has continued, with the U.S. government's founding of the Internet.

By contrast, in the current process of globalization we have a system of what I call global governance without global government. International institutions like the World Trade Organization, the IMF, the World Bank, and others provide an ad hoc system of global governance, but it is a far cry from global government and lacks democratic accountability. Although it is perhaps better than not having any system of global governance, the system is structured not to serve general interests or assure equitable results. This not only raises issues of whether broader values are given short shrift; it does not even promote growth as much as an alternative might.

Governance Through Ideology

Consider the contrast between how economic decisions are made inside the United States and how they are made in the international economic institutions. In this country, economic decisions within the administration are undertaken largely by the National Economic Council, which includes the secretary of labor, the secretary of commerce, the chairman of the Council of Economic Advisers, the treasury secretary, the assistant attorney general for antitrust, and the U.S. trade representative. The Treasury is only one vote and often gets voted down. All of these officials, of course, are part of an administration that must face Congress and the democratic electorate. But in the international arena, only the voices of the financial community are heard. The IMF reports to the ministers of finance and the governors of the central banks, and one of the important items on its agenda is to make these central banks more independent—and less democratically accountable. It might make little difference if the IMF dealt only with matters of concern to the financial community, such as the clearance of checks; but in fact, its policies affect every aspect of life. It forces countries to have tight monetary and fiscal policies: It evaluates the trade-off between inflation and unemployment, and in that trade-off it always puts far more weight on inflation than on jobs.

The problem with having the rules of the game dictated by the IMF—and thus by the financial community—is not just a question of values (though that is important) but also a question of ideology. The financial community's view of the world predominates—even when there is little evidence in its support. Indeed, beliefs on key issues are held so strongly that theoretical and empirical support of the positions is viewed as hardly necessary.

Recall again the IMF's position on liberalizing capital markets. As noted, the IMF pushed a set of policies that exposed countries to serious risk. One might have thought, given the evidence of the costs, that the IMF could offer plenty of evidence that the policies also did some good. In fact, there was no such evidence; the evidence that was available suggested that there was little if any positive effect on growth. Ideology enabled IMF officials not only to ignore the absence of benefits but also to overlook the evidence of the huge costs imposed on countries.

An Unfair Trade Agenda

The trade-liberalization agenda has been set by the North, or more accurately, by special interests in the North. Consequently, a disproportionate part of the gains has accrued to the advanced industrial countries, and in some cases the less-developed countries have actually been worse off. After the last round of trade negotiations, the Uruguay Round that ended in 1994, the World Bank calculated the gains and losses to each of the regions of the world. The United States and Europe gained enormously. But sub-Saharan Africa, the poorest region of the world, lost by about 2 percent because of terms-of-trade effects: The trade negotiations opened their markets to manufactured goods produced by the industrialized countries but did not open up the markets of Europe and the United States to the agricultural goods in which poor countries often have a comparative advantage. Nor did the trade agreements eliminate the subsidies to agriculture that make it so hard for the developing countries to compete.

The U.S. negotiations with China over its membership in the WTO displayed a double standard bordering on the surreal. The U.S. trade representative, the chief negotiator for the United States, began by insisting that China was a developed country. Under WTO rules, developing countries are allowed longer transition periods in which state subsidies and other departures from the WTO strictures are permitted. China certainly wishes it were a developed country, with Western-style per capita incomes. And since China has a lot of "capitas," it's possible to multiply a huge number of people by very small average incomes and conclude that the People's Republic is a big economy. But China is not only a developing economy; it is a low-income developing country. Yet the United States insisted that China be treated like a developed country! China went along with the fiction; the negotiations dragged on so long that China got some extra time to adjust. But the true hypocrisy was shown when U.S.

negotiators asked, in effect, for developing-country status for the United States to get extra time to shelter the American textile industry.

Trade negotiations in the service industries also illustrate the unlevel nature of the playing field. Which service industries did the United States say were very important? Financial services—industries in which Wall Street has a comparative advantage. Construction industries and maritime services were not on the agenda, because the developing countries would have a comparative advantage in these sectors.

Consider also intellectual-property rights, which are important if innovators are to have incentives to innovate (though many of the corporate advocates of intellectual property exaggerate its importance and fail to note that much of the most important research, as in basic science and mathematics, is not patentable). Intellectual-property rights, such as patents and trademarks, need to balance the interests of producers with those of users—not only users in developing countries, but researchers in developed countries. If we underprice the profitability of innovation to the inventor, we deter invention. If we overprice its cost to the research community and the end user, we retard its diffusion and beneficial effects on living standards.

In the final stages of the Uruguay negotiations, both the White House Office of Science and Technology Policy and the Council of Economic Advisers worried that we had not got the balance right—that the agreement put producers' interests over users'. We worried that, with this imbalance, the rate of progress and innovation might actually be impeded. After all, knowledge is the most important input into research, and overly strong intellectual-property rights can, in effect, increase the price of this input. We were also concerned about the consequences of denying lifesaving medicines to the poor. This issue subsequently gained international attention in the context of the provision of AIDS medicines in South Africa. The international outrage forced the drug companies to back down—and it appears that, going forward, the most adverse consequences will be circumscribed. But it is worth noting that initially, even the Democratic U.S. administration supported the pharmaceutical companies.

What we were not fully aware of was another danger—what has come to be called "biopiracy," which involves international drug companies patenting traditional medicines. Not only do they seek to make money from "resources" and knowledge that rightfully belong to the developing countries, but in doing so they squelch domestic firms who long provided these traditional medicines. While it is not clear whether these patents would hold up in court if they were effectively challenged, it is clear that the less-developed countries may not have the legal and financial resources required to mount such a challenge. The issue has become the source of enormous emotional, and potentially economic, concern throughout the developing world. This fall, while I was in Ecuador visiting a village in the high Andes, the Indian mayor railed against how globalization had led to biopiracy.

Globalization and September 11

September 11 brought home a still darker side of globalization—it provided a global arena for terrorists. But the ensuing events and discussions highlighted broader aspects of the globalization debate. It made clear how untenable American unilateralist positions were. President Bush, who had unilaterally rejected the international agreement to address one of the long-term global risks perceived by countries around the world—global warming, in which the United States is the largest culprit—called for a global alliance against terrorism. The administration realized that success would require concerted action by all.

One of the ways to fight terrorists, Washington soon discovered, was to cut off their sources of funding. Ever since the East Asian crisis, global attention had focused on the secretive offshore banking centers. Discussions following that crisis focused on the importance of good information—transparency, or openness—but this was intended for the developing countries. As international discussions turned to the lack of transparency shown by IMF and the offshore banking centers, the U.S. Treasury changed its tune. It is not because these secretive banking havens provide better services than those provided by banks in New York or London that billions have been put there; the secrecy serves a variety of nefarious purposes—including avoiding taxation and money laundering. These institutions could be shut down overnight—or forced to comply with international norms—if the United States and the other leading countries wanted. They continue to exist because they serve the interests of the financial community and the wealthy. Their continuing existence is no accident. Indeed, the OECD drafted an agreement to limit their scope—and before September 11, the Bush administration unilaterally walked away from this agreement too. How foolish this looks now in retrospect! Had it been embraced, we would have been further along the road to controlling the flow of money into the hands of the terrorists.

There is one more aspect to the aftermath of September 11 worth noting here. The United States was already in recession, but the attack made matters worse. It used to be said that when the United States sneezed, Mexico caught a cold. With globalization, when the United States sneezes, much of the rest of the world risks catching pneumonia. And the United States now has a bad case of the flu. With globalization, mismanaged macroeconomic policy in the United States—the failure to design an effective stimulus package—has global consequences. But around the world, anger at the traditional IMF policies is growing. The developing countries are saying to the industrialized nations: "When you face a slowdown, you follow the precepts that we are all taught in our economic courses: You adopt expansionary monetary and fiscal policies. But when we face a slowdown, you insist on contractionary policies. For you, deficits are okay; for us, they are impermissible—even if we can raise the funds through 'selling forward,' say, some natural resources." A heightened sense of inequity prevails, partly because the consequences of maintaining contractionary policies are so great.

Global Social Justice

Today, in much of the developing world, globalization is being questioned. For instance, in Latin America, after a short burst of growth in the early 1990s, stagnation and recession have set in. The growth was not sustained—some might say, was not sustainable. Indeed, at this juncture, the growth record of the so-called post-reform era looks no better, and in some countries much worse, than in the widely criticized import-substitution period of the 1950s and 1960s when Latin countries tried to industrialize by discouraging imports. Indeed, reform critics point out that the burst of growth in the early 1990s was little more than a "catch-up" that did not even make up for the lost decade of the 1980s.

Throughout the region, people are asking: "Has reform failed or has globalization failed?" The distinction is perhaps artificial, for globalization was at the center of the reforms. Even in those countries that have managed to grow, such as Mexico, the benefits have accrued largely to the upper 30 percent and have been even more concentrated in the top 10 percent. Those at the bottom have gained little; many are even worse off. The reforms have exposed countries to greater risk, and the risks have been borne disproportionately by those least able to cope with them. Just as in many countries where the pacing and sequencing of reforms has resulted in job destruction outmatching job creation, so too has the exposure to risk outmatched the ability to create institutions for coping with risk, including effective safety nets.

In this bleak landscape, there are some positive signs. Those in the North have become more aware of the inequities of the global economic architecture. The agreement at Doha to hold a new round of trade negotiations—the "Development Round"—promises to rectify some of the imbalances of the past. There has been a marked change in the rhetoric of the international economic institutions—at least they talk about poverty. At the World Bank, there have been some real reforms; there has been some progress in translating the rhetoric into reality—in ensuring that the voices of the poor are heard and the concerns of the developing countries are listened to. But elsewhere, there is often a gap between the rhetoric and the reality. Serious reforms in governance, in who makes decisions and how they are made, are not on the table. If one of the problems at the IMF has been that the ideology, interests, and perspectives of the financial community in the advanced industrialized countries have been given disproportionate weight (in matters whose effects go well beyond finance), then the prospects for success in the current discussions of reform, in which the same parties continue to predominate, are bleak. They are more likely to result in slight changes in the shape of the table, not changes in who is at the table or what is on the agenda.

September 11 has resulted in a global alliance against terrorism. What we now need is not just an alliance against evil, but an alliance for something positive—a global alliance for reducing poverty and for creating a better environment, an alliance for creating a global society with more social justice.

Discussion Questions

1. Suggest criteria for judging effective or desirable state interventions in the economy.
2. How far have cross-border economic transactions, multinational corporations, and the institutions of global economic governance (such as the World Trade Organization and the International Monetary Fund) overtaken states as the key players that shape political-economic outcomes? Provide one piece of evidence on each side of the debate and develop your own position in the debate.
3. Does the state govern the economy? Or does the economy govern the state? Or does it depend on which state or which period you are studying? Drawing on selections in this chapter, provide one piece of evidence that could be offered in defense of the first position, one piece of evidence in defense of the second, and one in defense of the third. Which of the three alternatives do you find most persuasive and why?

Chapter 4

THE CHALLENGE OF DEMOCRACY

Few concepts in comparative politics have provoked as much scholarly research and debate as democracy. The concept taps into intense emotions, in which the empirical (what is) and the normative (what ought to be) are often closely linked. The fact that democracy is universally popular—it ranks with parenthood and apple pie!—explains why virtually all political leaders claim that their regimes are democratic. (Sen [4.1] claims that democracy is a universal value, whose core elements are the same across all cultures.) But what standards must be met for a regime to qualify as democratic? Many answers have been given to this apparently simple question. An influential book, for example, describes six models of democracy![1]

One way to begin is by identifying two influential approaches. The first emphasizes the importance of *procedures*. It defines democratic regimes as those in which all citizens have an equal right to participate in the selection of governmental leaders. (The selections by Dahl [4.2] and Schmitter and Karl [4.3] suggest that, for a regime to qualify as democratic, other procedures must be present in addition to free and fair elections.) The second approach emphasizes the importance of *outcomes,* that is, the distribution of benefits. It defines democratic regimes as those that distribute power, material benefits, and other important resources relatively equally among all citizens.

The procedural understanding of democracy has been dominant in the current era. The selections by Dahl, and Schmitter and Karl, describe major elements of this approach. Linz and Stepan (4.4) describe further conditions that, in their view, must develop for authoritarian regimes that have undergone democratic reforms to become consolidated or stable democracies. But just how do undemocratic, that is, authoritarian regimes, become democratic? The selections by Bunce (4.5), O'Donnell (4.6), and Carothers (4.7) summarize and criticize an influential approach that analyzed transitions to democracy in the 1970s and 1980s. These are the democracies that constitute the third (democratic) wave analyzed by Huntington (1.2). Bunce describes why she believes that the model, developed on the basis of transitions in southern Europe and Latin America,

---

[1] David Held, *Models of Democracy*, 2nd ed. (Cambridge: Polity Press, 1996). Also see David Collier and Steven Levitsky, "Democracy with Adjectives: Conceptual Innovation in Comparative Research," *World Politics* 49, no. 3 (1997): 430–451.

failed to explain the experience of states that abandoned communism in the former Soviet Union and east-central Europe in the late 1980s and 1990s. The selection by O'Donnell analyzes how, in many recently established regimes that claim to be democratic, there is a wide gulf between the appearance and reality of democracy. (Also see Levitsky and Way [2.4].) Describing these regimes as democratic therefore may give more credit than is due.

Carothers goes even further than O'Donnell. He suggests that "the political trajectories of most third-wave countries call into serious doubt the transition paradigm." For Carothers, the term *transition* mistakenly implies that there is a kind of up escalator propelling post-transition democracies toward consolidation.

Returning to O'Donnell, his critique can be extended beyond the cases of newly established democracies. Even the most durable democracies exhibit immense (and, in the case of the United States, growing) inequalities of wealth and private power. In George Orwell's satirical novel *Animal Farm,* although everyone is equal, some are more equal than others! In the United States, for example, the combined incomes of the wealthiest 300,000 Americans—0.1 percent of the population; that's about 1 in 1,000 Americans—have incomes equal to the combined incomes of the 150,000,000 less affluent Americans—the lower 50 percent of all Americans![2] This situation sharply increases the probability that government policy will represent the interests of the wealthy.

Readings in this chapter explore variations in the character, desirability, and durability of democracy. Other selections in RCP explore additional issues relating to democracy. For example, selections in Chapter 1 analyze democratic trends, Levitsky and Way (2.4) analyze authoritarian elements in some new democracies, Linz (6.1) compares the virtues of parliamentary and presidential institutional forms, Mansfield and Snyder (6.2) and McFaul (6.3) question how war prone newly established democracies are, Przeworski and Wallerstein (7.1) analyze the relationship of democracy and capitalism, and Zakaria (7.5) warns that democratic regimes can be disrespectful of individual and minority rights. The issue of democracy is too large, complex, and important to be confined to a single chapter of RCP!

The readings in this and other chapters provide rich testimony to the fact that democracy remains a terrain of vigorous contestation. They are fine examples of how to pursue a rigorous study of democracy, engage in normative analysis of its character, and integrate the two concerns.

---

[2] David Cay Johnston, *Free Lunch* (New York: Penguin Books, 2007), p. 11, Johnson analyzes the ways that government policies contribute to economic inequality.

Democracy as a Universal Value

Amartya Sen

Nobel Prize winner Amartya Sen challenges the argument, put forward by some scholars and political leaders, that democracy is appropriate only for Western societies. Instead, he claims that democracy reflects universally shared values and that it provides a variety of benefits to people of all cultures and regions.

If democracy is a universal value, why are not all regimes democratic? Who might oppose democracy, and why are opponents more successful in some cases than others?

In the summer of 1997, I was asked by a leading Japanese newspaper what I thought was the most important thing that had happened in the twentieth century. I found this to be an unusually thought-provoking question, since so many things of gravity have happened over the last hundred years. The European empires, especially the British and French ones that had so dominated the nineteenth century, came to an end. We witnessed two world wars. We saw the rise and fall of fascism and Nazism. The century witnessed the rise of communism, and its fall (as in the former Soviet bloc) or radical transformation (as in China). We also saw a shift from the economic dominance of the West to a new economic balance much more dominated by Japan and East and Southeast Asia. Even though that region is going through some financial and economic problems right now, this is not going to nullify the shift in the balance of the world economy that has occurred over many decades (in the case of Japan, through nearly the entire century). The past hundred years are not lacking in important events.

Nevertheless, among the great variety of developments that have occurred in the twentieth century, I did not, ultimately, have any difficulty in choosing one as the preeminent development of the period: the rise of democracy. This is not to deny that other occurrences have also been important, but I would argue that in the distant future, when people look back at what happened in this century,

Amartya Sen, "Democracy as a Universal Value," *Journal of Democracy* 10, no. 3 (July 1999): 3–17. © National Endowment for Democracy and The Johns Hopkins University Press. Reprinted with permission of The Johns Hopkins University Press.

they will find it difficult not to accord primacy to the emergence of democracy as the preeminently acceptable form of governance.

The idea of democracy originated, of course, in ancient Greece, more than two millennia ago. Piecemeal efforts at democratization were attempted elsewhere as well, including in India.[1] But it is really in ancient Greece that the idea of democracy took shape and was seriously put into practice (albeit on a limited scale), before it collapsed and was replaced by more authoritarian and asymmetric forms of government. There were no other kinds anywhere else.

Thereafter, democracy as we know it took a long time to emerge. Its gradual—and ultimately triumphant—emergence as a working system of governance was bolstered by many developments, from the signing of the Magna Carta in 1215, to the French and the American Revolutions in the eighteenth century, to the widening of the franchise in Europe and North America in the nineteenth century. It was in the twentieth century, however, that the idea of democracy became established as the "normal" form of government to which any nation is entitled—whether in Europe, America, Asia, or Africa. . . .

I do not deny that there are challenges to democracy's claim to universality. These challenges come in many shapes and forms—and from different directions. Indeed, that is part of the subject of this essay. I have to examine the claim of democracy as a universal value and the disputes that surround that claim. Before I begin that exercise, however, it is necessary to grasp clearly the sense in which democracy has become a dominant belief in the contemporary world.

In any age and social climate, there are some sweeping beliefs that seem to command respect as a kind of general rule—like a "default" setting in a computer program; they are considered right *unless* their claim is somehow precisely negated. While democracy is not yet universally practiced, nor indeed uniformly accepted, in the general climate of world opinion, democratic governance has now achieved the status of being taken to be generally right. The ball is very much in the court of those who want to rubbish democracy to provide justification for that rejection.

This is a historic change from not very long ago, when the advocates of democracy for Asia or Africa had to argue for democracy with their backs to the wall. While we still have reason enough to dispute those who, implicitly or explicitly, reject the need for democracy, we must also note clearly how the general climate of opinion has shifted from what it was in previous centuries. We do not have to establish afresh, each time, whether such and such a country (South Africa, or Cambodia, or Chile) is "fit for democracy" (a question that was prominent in the discourse of the nineteenth century); we now take that for granted. This recognition of democracy as a universally relevant system, which moves in the direction of its acceptance as a universal value, is a major revolution in thinking, and one of the main contributions of the twentieth century. It is in this context that we have to examine the question of democracy as a universal value. . . .

Democracy and Economic Development

. . . There is, in fact, no convincing general evidence that authoritarian governance and the suppression of political and civil rights are really beneficial to
economic development. Indeed, the general statistical picture does not permit
any such induction. Systematic empirical studies . . . give no real support to the
claim that there is a general conflict between political rights and economic
performance. The directional linkage seems to depend on many other circumstances, and while some statistical investigations note a weakly negative
relation, others find a strongly positive one. If all the comparative studies are
viewed together, the hypothesis that there is no clear relation between economic growth and democracy in *either* direction remains extremely plausible.
Since democracy and political liberty have importance in themselves, the case
for them therefore remains untarnished.[2]

The question also involves a fundamental issue of methods of economic research. We must not only look at statistical connections, but also examine and
scrutinize the *causal* processes that are involved in economic growth and development. The economic policies and circumstances that led to the economic
success of countries in East Asia are by now reasonably well understood. While
different empirical studies have varied in emphasis, there is by now broad consensus on a list of "helpful policies" that includes openness to competition, the
use of international markets, public provision of incentives for investment and
export, a high level of literacy and schooling, successful land reforms, and other
social opportunities that widen participation in the process of economic expansion. There is no reason at all to assume that any of these policies is inconsistent
with greater democracy and had to be forcibly sustained by the elements of
authoritarianism that happened to be present in South Korea or Singapore or
China. Indeed, there is overwhelming evidence to show that what is needed for
generating faster economic growth is a friendlier economic climate rather than
a harsher political system.

To complete this examination, we must go beyond the narrow confines of economic growth and scrutinize the broader demands of economic development,
including the need for economic and social security. In that context, we have to
look at the connection between political and civil rights, on the one hand, and
the prevention of major economic disasters, on the other. Political and civil
rights give people the opportunity to draw attention forcefully to general needs
and to demand appropriate public action. The response of a government to the
acute suffering of its people often depends on the pressure that is put on it. The
exercise of political rights (such as voting, criticizing, protesting, and the like)
can make a real difference to the political incentives that operate on a
government. . . .

There is, I believe, an important lesson here. Many economic technocrats recommend the use of economic incentives (which the market system provides)
while ignoring political incentives (which democratic systems could guarantee).

This is to opt for a deeply unbalanced set of ground rules. The protective power of democracy may not be missed much when a country is lucky enough to be facing no serious calamity, when everything is going quite smoothly. Yet the danger of insecurity, arising from changed economic or other circumstances, or from uncorrected mistakes of policy, can lurk behind what looks like a healthy state. . . .

The Functions of Democracy

I have so far allowed the agenda of this essay to be determined by the critics of democracy, especially the economic critics. I shall return to criticisms again, taking up the arguments of the cultural critics in particular, but the time has come for me to pursue further the positive analysis of what democracy does and what may lie at the base of its claim to be a universal value.

What exactly is democracy? We must not identify democracy with majority rule. Democracy has complex demands, which certainly include voting and respect for election results, but it also requires the protection of liberties and freedoms, respect for legal entitlements, and the guaranteeing of free discussion and uncensored distribution of news and fair comment. Even elections can be deeply defective if they occur without the different sides getting an adequate opportunity to present their respective cases, or without the electorate enjoying the freedom to obtain news and to consider the views of the competing protagonists. Democracy is a demanding system, and not just a mechanical condition (like majority rule) taken in isolation.

Viewed in this light, the merits of democracy and its claim as a universal value can be related to certain distinct virtues that go with its unfettered practice. Indeed, we can distinguish three different ways in which democracy enriches the lives of the citizens. First, political freedom is a part of human freedom in general, and exercising civil and political rights is a crucial part of good lives of individuals as social beings. Political and social participation has *intrinsic value* for human life and well-being. To be prevented from participation in the political life of the community is a major deprivation.

Second, as I have just discussed (in disputing the claim that democracy is in tension with economic development), democracy has an important *instrumental value* in enhancing the hearing that people get in expressing and supporting their claims to political attention (including claims of economic needs). Third—and this is a point to be explored further—the practice of democracy gives citizens an opportunity to learn from one another, and helps society to form its values and priorities. Even the idea of "needs," including the understanding of "economic needs," requires public discussion and exchange of information, views, and analyses. In this sense, democracy has *constructive* importance, in addition to its intrinsic value for the lives of the citizens and its instrumental importance in political decisions. The claims of democracy as a universal value have to take note of this diversity of considerations.

The conceptualization—even comprehension—of what are to count as "needs," including "economic needs," may itself require the exercise of political and civil rights. A proper understanding of what economic needs are—their content and their force—may require discussion and exchange. Political and civil rights, especially those related to the guaranteeing of open discussion, debate, criticism, and dissent, are central to the process of generating informed and considered choices. These processes are crucial to the formation of values and priorities, and we cannot, in general, take preferences as given independently of public discussion, that is, irrespective of whether open interchange and debate are permitted or not.

In fact, the reach and effectiveness of open dialogue are often underestimated in assessing social and political problems. For example, public discussion has an important role to play in reducing the high rates of fertility that characterize many developing countries. There is substantial evidence that the sharp decline in fertility rates in India's more literate states has been much influenced by public discussion of the bad effects of high fertility rates on the community at large, and especially on the lives of young women. If the view has emerged in, say, the Indian state of Kerala or of Tamil Nadu that a happy family in the modern age is a small family, much discussion and debate have gone into the formation of these perspectives. Kerala now has a fertility rate of 1.7 (similar to that of Britain and France, and well below China's 1.9), and this has been achieved with no coercion, but mainly through the emergence of new values—a process in which political and social dialogue has played a major part. Kerala's high literacy rate (it ranks higher in literacy than any province in China), especially among women, has greatly contributed to making such social and political dialogue possible.

Miseries and deprivations can be of various kinds, some more amenable to social remedies than others. The totality of the human predicament would be a gross basis for identifying our "needs." For example, there are many things that we might have good reason to value and thus could be taken as "needs" if they were feasible. We could even want immortality, as Maitreyee, that remarkable inquiring mind in the *Upanishads*, famously did in her 3000-year old conversation with Yajnvalkya. But we do not see immortality as a "need" because it is clearly unfeasible. Our conception of needs relates to our ideas of the preventable nature of some deprivations and to our understanding of what can be done about them. In the formation of understandings and beliefs about feasibility (particularly, *social* feasibility), public discussions play a crucial role. Political rights, including freedom of expression and discussion, are not only pivotal in inducing social responses to economic needs, they are also central to the conceptualization of economic needs themselves.

Universality of Values

If the above analysis is correct, then democracy's claim to be valuable does not rest on just one particular merit. There is a plurality of virtues here, including, first, the *intrinsic* importance of political participation and freedom in human life; second, the *instrumental* importance of political incentives in keeping governments responsible and accountable; and third, the *constructive* role of democracy in the formation of values and in the understanding of needs, rights, and duties. In the light of this diagnosis, we may now address the motivating question of this essay, namely the case for seeing democracy as a universal value.

In disputing this claim, it is sometimes argued that not everyone agrees on the decisive importance of democracy, particularly when it competes with other desirable things for our attention and loyalty. This is indeed so, and there is no unanimity here. This lack of unanimity is seen by some as sufficient evidence that democracy is not a universal value.

Clearly, we must begin by dealing with a methodological question: What is a universal value? For a value to be considered universal, must it have the consent of everyone? If that were indeed necessary, then the category of universal values might well be empty. I know of no value—not even motherhood (I think of *Mommie Dearest*)—to which no one has ever objected. I would argue that universal consent is not required for something to be a universal value. Rather, the claim of a universal value is that people anywhere may have reason to see it as valuable.

When Mahatma Gandhi argued for the universal value of non-violence, he was not arguing that people everywhere already acted according to this value, but rather that they had good reason to see it as valuable. Similarly, when Rabindranath Tagore argued for "the freedom of the mind" as a universal value, he was not saying that this claim is accepted by all, but that all do have reason enough to accept it—a reason that he did much to explore, present, and propagate.[3] Understood in this way, any claim that something is a universal value involves some counterfactual analysis—in particular, whether people might see some value in a claim that they have not yet considered adequately. All claims to universal value—not just that of democracy—have this implicit presumption.

I would argue that it is with regard to this often *implicit* presumption that the biggest attitudinal shift toward democracy has occurred in the twentieth century. In considering democracy for a country that does not have it and where many people may not yet have had the opportunity to consider it for actual practice, it is now presumed that the people involved would approve of it once it becomes a reality in their lives. In the nineteenth century this assumption typically would have not been made, but the presumption that is taken to be natural (what I earlier called the "default" position) has changed radically during the twentieth century.

It must also be noted that this change is, to a great extent, based on observing the history of the twentieth century. As democracy has spread, its adherents have grown, not shrunk. Starting off from Europe and America, democracy as a system has reached very many distant shores, where it has been met with willing participation and acceptance. Moreover, when an existing democracy has been overthrown, there have been widespread protests, even though these protests have often been brutally suppressed. Many people have been willing to risk their lives in the fight to bring back democracy.

Some who dispute the status of democracy as a universal value base their argument not on the absence of unanimity, but on the presence of regional contrasts. These alleged contrasts are sometimes related to the poverty of some nations. According to this argument, poor people are interested, and have reason to be interested, in bread, not in democracy. This oft-repeated argument is fallacious at two different levels.

First, as discussed above, the protective role of democracy may be particularly important for the poor. This obviously applies to potential famine victims who face starvation. It also applies to the destitute thrown off the economic ladder in a financial crisis. People in economic need also need a political voice. Democracy is not a luxury that can await the arrival of general prosperity.

Second, there is very little evidence that poor people, given the choice, prefer to reject democracy. It is thus of some interest to note that when an erstwhile Indian government in the mid-1970s tried out a similar argument to justify the alleged "emergency" (and the suppression of various political and civil rights) that it had declared, an election was called that divided the voters precisely on this issue. In that fateful election, fought largely on this one overriding theme, the suppression of basic political and civil rights was firmly rejected, and the Indian electorate—one of the poorest in the world—showed itself to be no less keen on protesting against the denial of basic liberties and rights than on complaining about economic deprivation.

To the extent that there has been any testing of the proposition that the poor do not care about civil and political rights, the evidence is entirely against that claim. Similar points can be made by observing the struggle for democratic freedoms in South Korea, Thailand, Bangladesh, Pakistan, Burma, Indonesia, and elsewhere in Asia. Similarly, while political freedom is widely denied in Africa, there have been movements and protests against such repression whenever circumstances have permitted them.

The Argument from Cultural Differences

There is also another argument in defense of an allegedly fundamental regional contrast, one related not to economic circumstances but to cultural differences. Perhaps the most famous of these claims relates to what have been called "Asian values." It has been claimed that Asians traditionally value discipline, not political freedom, and thus the attitude to democracy must inevitably be much more skeptical in these countries. . . .

It is very hard to find any real basis for this intellectual claim in the history of Asian cultures, especially if we look at the classical traditions of India, the Middle East, Iran, and other parts of Asia. For example, one of the earliest and most emphatic statements advocating the tolerance of pluralism and the duty of the state to protect minorities can be found in the inscriptions of the Indian emperor Ashoka in the third century B.C.

Asia is, of course, a very large area, containing 60 percent of the world's population, and generalizations about such a vast set of peoples is not easy. Sometimes the advocates of "Asian values" have tended to look primarily at East Asia as the region of particular applicability. The general thesis of a contrast between the West and Asia often concentrates on the lands to the east of Thailand, even though there is also a more ambitious claim that the rest of Asia is rather "similar." . . .

Even East Asia itself, however, is remarkably diverse, with many variations to be found not only among Japan, China, Korea, and other countries of the region, but also *within* each country. Confucius is the standard author quoted in interpreting Asian values, but he is not the only intellectual influence in these countries (in Japan, China, and Korea for example, there are very old and very widespread Buddhist traditions, powerful for over a millennium and a half, and there are also other influences, including a considerable Christian presence). There is no homogeneous worship of order over freedom in any of these cultures.

Furthermore, Confucius himself did not recommend blind allegiance to the state. When Zilu asks him "how to serve a prince," Confucius replies (in a statement that the censors of authoritarian regimes may want to ponder), "Tell him the truth even if it offends him."[4] Confucius is not averse to practical caution and tact, but does not forgo the recommendation to oppose a bad government (tactfully, if necessary): "When the [good] way prevails in the state, speak boldly and act boldly. When the state has lost the way, act boldly and speak softly."[5]

Indeed, Confucius provides a clear pointer to the fact that the two pillars of the imagined edifice of Asian values, loyalty to family and obedience to the state, can be in severe conflict with each other. Many advocates of the power of "Asian values" see the role of the state as an extension of the role of the family, but as Confucius noted, there can be tension between the two. The Governor of She told Confucius, "Among my people, there is a man of unbending integrity: when his father stole a sheep, he denounced him." To this Confucius replied, "Among my people, men of integrity do things differently: a father covers up for his son, a son covers up for his father—and there is integrity in what they do."[6]

The monolithic interpretation of Asian values as hostile to democracy and political rights does not bear critical scrutiny. I should not, I suppose, be too critical of the lack of scholarship supporting these beliefs, since those who have made these claims are not scholars but political leaders, often official or unofficial spokesmen for authoritarian governments. It is, however, interesting to see that while we academics can be impractical about practical politics, practical politicians can, in turn, be rather impractical about scholarship.

It is not hard, of course, to find authoritarian writings within the Asian traditions. But neither is it hard to find them in Western classics: One has only to reflect on the writings of Plato or Aquinas to see that devotion to discipline is not a special Asian taste. To dismiss the plausibility of democracy as a universal value because of the presence of some Asian writings on discipline and order would be similar to rejecting the plausibility of democracy as a natural form of government in Europe or America today on the basis of the writings of Plato or Aquinas (not to mention the substantial medieval literature in support of the Inquisitions).

Due to the experience of contemporary political battles, especially in the Middle East, Islam is often portrayed as fundamentally intolerant of and hostile to individual freedom. But the presence of diversity and variety *within* a tradition applies very much to Islam as well. In India, Akbar and most of the other Moghul emperors (with the notable exception of Aurangzeb) provide good examples of both the theory and practice of political and religious tolerance. The Turkish emperors were often more tolerant than their European contemporaries. Abundant examples can also be found among rulers in Cairo and Baghdad. Indeed, in the twelfth century, the great Jewish scholar Maimonides had to run away from an intolerant Europe (where he was born), and from its persecution of Jews, to the security of a tolerant and urbane Cairo and the patronage of Sultan Saladin.

Diversity is a feature of most cultures in the world. Western civilization is no exception. The practice of democracy that has won out in the *modern* West is largely a result of a consensus that has emerged since the Enlightenment and the Industrial Revolution, and particularly in the last century or so. To read in this a historical commitment of the West—over the millennia—to democracy, and then to contrast it with non-Western traditions (treating each as monolithic) would be a great mistake. This tendency toward oversimplification can be seen not only in the writings of some governmental spokesmen in Asia, but also in the theories of some of the finest Western scholars themselves.

As an example from the writings of a major scholar whose works, in many other ways, have been totally impressive, let me cite Samuel Huntington's thesis on the clash of civilizations, where the heterogeneities *within* each culture get quite inadequate recognition. His study comes to the clear conclusion that "a sense of individualism and a tradition of rights and liberties" can be found in the West that are "unique among civilized societies."[7] Huntington also argues that "the central characteristics of the West, those which distinguish it from other civilizations, antedate the modernization of the West." In his view, "The West was West long before it was modern."[8] It is this thesis that—I have argued—does not survive historical scrutiny.

For every attempt by an Asian government spokesman to contrast alleged "Asian values" with alleged Western ones, there is, it seems, an attempt by a Western intellectual to make a similar contrast from the other side. But even though every Asian pull may be matched by a Western push, the two together do not really manage to dent democracy's claim to be a universal value.

Where the Debate Belongs

I have tried to cover a number of issues related to the claim that democracy is a universal value. The value of democracy includes its *intrinsic importance* in human life, its *instrumental role* in generating political incentives, and its *constructive function* in the formation of values (and in understanding the force and feasibility of claims of needs, rights, and duties). These merits are not regional in character. Nor is the advocacy of discipline or order. Heterogeneity of values seems to characterize most, perhaps all, major cultures. The cultural argument does not foreclose, nor indeed deeply constrain, the choices we can make today.

Those choices have to be made here and now, taking note of the functional roles of democracy, on which the case for democracy in the contemporary world depends. I have argued that this case is indeed strong and not regionally contingent. The force of the claim that democracy is a universal value lies, ultimately, in that strength. That is where the debate belongs. It cannot be disposed of by imagined cultural taboos or assumed civilizational predispositions imposed by our various pasts.

Notes

1. In Aldous Huxley's novel *Point Counter Point*, this was enough to give an adequate excuse to a cheating husband, who tells his wife that he must go to London to study democracy in ancient India in the library of the British Museum, while in reality he goes to see his mistress.
2. I have examined the empirical evidence and causal connections in some detail in my book *Development as Freedom*, forthcoming from Knopf in 1999.
3. See my "Tagore and His India," *New York Review of Books,* 26 June 1997.
4. *The Analects of Confucius*, Simon Leys, trans. (New York: Norton, 1997), 14.22, 70.
5. *The Analects of Confucius*, 14.3, 66.
6. *The Analects of Confucius*, 13.18, 63.
7. Samuel P. Huntington, *The Clash of Civilizations and the Remaking of World Order* (New York: Simon and Schuster, 1996), 71.
8. Huntington, *The Clash of Civilizations*, 69.

Polyarchy: Participation and Opposition

Robert Dahl

In this classic text, political scientist Robert Dahl identifies seven criteria that he considers essential for a regime to be considered democratic. He further suggests that no regime qualifies as fully democratic, judged by this standard. Dahl proposes that the less demanding term *polyarchy* be used to describe regimes that are moderately successful in meeting the standards of democracy.

Four decades after it was published, Dahl's account remains highly influential. Many scholarly studies, including several selections in this chapter, refer to it. Dahl's argument has generated extensive discussion. Some critics claim that he set the bar too low for a regime to qualify as democratic. By suggesting the term *polyarchy,* they suggest, he was letting many regimes off too easy. Better to maintain the more demanding standard, even if this means that few regimes qualify as democratic. Do you agree with Dahl or his critics on this question, and why?

Given a regime in which the opponents of the government cannot openly and legally organize into political parties in order to oppose the government in free and fair elections, what conditions favor or impede a transformation into a regime in which they can? That is the question with which this [discussion] is concerned.

Concepts

Since the development of a political system that allows for opposition, rivalry, or competition between a government and its opponents is an important aspect of democratization, this [discussion] is necessarily about one aspect of democratization. But the two processes—democratization and the development of public opposition—are not, in my view, identical. A full description of the differences could lead us into a tedious exploration of a semantic bog. To avoid this detour, I hope I may be allowed to indicate rather summarily some of my assumptions without much in the way of defense or elaboration.

I assume that a key characteristic of a democracy is the continuing responsiveness of the government to the preferences of its citizens, considered as
political equals. What other characteristics might be required for a system to
be strictly democratic, I do not intend to consider here. In this [discussion] I
should like to reserve the term "democracy" for a political system one of the
characteristics of which is the quality of being completely or almost completely responsive to all its citizens. Whether such a system actually exists, has
existed, or can exist need not concern us for the moment. Surely one can conceive a hypothetical system of this kind; such a conception has served as an
ideal, or part of an ideal, for many people. As a hypothetical system, one end
of a scale, or a limiting state of affairs, it can (like a perfect vacuum) serve as
a basis for estimating the degree to which various systems approach this theoretical limit.

I assume further that in order for a government to continue over a period of
time to be responsive to the preferences of its citizens, considered as political
equals, all full citizens must have unimpaired opportunities:

1. To formulate their preferences
2. To signify their preferences to their fellow citizens and the government by
   individual and collective action
3. To have their preferences weighed equally in the conduct of the government,
   that is, weighted with no discrimination because of the content or source of
   the preference

These, then, appear to me to be three necessary conditions for a democracy,
though they are probably not sufficient. Next, I assume that for these three opportunities to exist among a large number of people, such as the number of people who comprise most nation-states at the present time, the institutions of the
society must provide at least eight guarantees. These are indicated in Table 1.

I am going to make the further assumption that the connections between the
guarantees and the three fundamental opportunities are sufficiently evident to
need no further elaboration here.[1]

Now from examination of the list of eight institutional guarantees, it appears
that they might provide us with a theoretical scale along which it would be
possible to order different political systems. Upon closer examination, however,
it appears that the eight guarantees might be fruitfully interpreted as constituting two somewhat different theoretical dimensions of democratization.

1. Both historically and at the present time, regimes vary enormously in the extent to which the eight institutional conditions are openly available, publicly
   employed, and fully guaranteed to at least some members of the political system who wish to contest the conduct of the government. Thus a scale reflecting these eight conditions would enable us to compare different regimes
   according to the extent of permissible opposition, public contestation, or
   political competition.[2] However, since a regime might permit opposition to a

Table 4.1

Some Requirements for a Democracy Among a Large Number of People

For the opportunity to:	The following institutional guarantees are required:
I. Formulate preferences	1. Freedom to form and join organizations 2. Freedom of expression 3. Right to vote 4. Right of political leaders to compete for support 5. Alternative sources of information
II. Signify preferences	1. Freedom to form and join organizations 2. Freedom of expression 3. Right to vote 4. Eligibility for public office 5. Right of political leaders to compete for support 6. Alternative sources of information 7. Free and fair elections
III. Have preferences weighted equally in conduct of government	1. Freedom to form and join organizations 2. Freedom of expression 3. Right to vote 4. Eligibility for public office 5. Right of political leaders to compete for support 5a. Right of political leaders to compete for votes 6. Alternative sources of information 7. Free and fair elections 8. Institutions for making government policies depend on votes and other expressions of preference

very small or a very large proportion of the population, clearly we need a second dimension.

2. Both historically and contemporaneously, regimes also vary in the proportion of the population entitled to participate on a more or less equal plane in controlling and contesting the conduct of the government: to participate, so to speak, in the system of public contestation. A scale reflecting the breadth of the right to participate in public contestation would enable us to compare different regimes according to their inclusiveness.

The right to vote in free and fair elections, for example, partakes of both dimensions. When a regime grants this right to some of its citizens, it moves toward greater public contestation. But the larger the proportion of citizens who enjoy the right, the more inclusive the regime.

Public contestation and inclusiveness vary somewhat independently. Britain had a highly developed system of public contestation by the end of the eighteenth century, but only a miniscule fraction of the population was fully included in it until after the expansion of the suffrage in 1867 and 1884.

Switzerland has one of the most fully developed systems of public contestation in the world. Probably few people would challenge the view that the Swiss regime is highly "democratic." Yet the feminine half of the Swiss population is still excluded from national elections. By contrast, the USSR still has almost no system of public contestation, though it does have universal suffrage. In fact one of the most striking changes during this century has been the virtual disappearance of an outright denial of the legitimacy of popular participation in government. Only a handful of countries have failed to grant at least a ritualistic vote to their citizens and to hold at least nominal elections; even the most repressive dictators usually pay some lip service today to the legitimate right of the people to participate in the government, that is, to participate in "governing" though not in public contestation.

Needless to say, in the absence of the right to oppose the right to "participate" is stripped of a very large part of the significance it has in a country where public contestation exists. A country with universal suffrage and a completely repressive government would provide fewer opportunities for oppositions, surely, than a country with a narrow suffrage but a highly tolerant government. Consequently, when countries are ranked solely according to their inclusiveness, not taking into account the surrounding circumstances, the results are anomalous. Nonetheless, as long as we keep clearly in mind the fact that the extent of the "suffrage" or, more generally, the right to participate indicates only *one* characteristic of systems, a characteristic that cannot be interpreted except in the context of other characteristics, it is useful to distinguish between regimes according to their inclusiveness.

Suppose, then, that we think of democratization as made up of at least two dimensions: public contestation and the right to participate (Figure 4.1). Doubtless most readers believe that democratization involves more than these two dimensions; in a moment I shall discuss a third dimension. But I propose to limit the discussion here to these two. For the point has already emerged, I think: developing a system of public contestation is not necessarily equivalent to full democratization.

To display the relationship between public contestation and democratization more clearly, let us now lay out the two dimensions as in Figure 4.2. Since a regime may be located, theoretically, anywhere in the space bounded by the two dimensions, it is at once obvious that our terminology for regimes is almost hopelessly inadequate, for it is a terminology invariably based upon classifying rather than ranking. The space enclosed by our two dimensions could of course be cut up into any number of cells, each of which might be given a name. But the purposes of this [discussion] make an elaborate typology redundant. Let me instead provide a small vocabulary—a reasonable one, I hope—that will enable me to speak precisely enough about the kinds of changes in regimes that I want to discuss.

Let me call a regime near the lower left corner of Figure 4.2 a closed hegemony. If a hegemonic regime shifts upward, as along path I, then it is moving toward greater public contestation. Without stretching language too far, one

Figure 4.1 Two Theoretical Dimensions of Democratization.

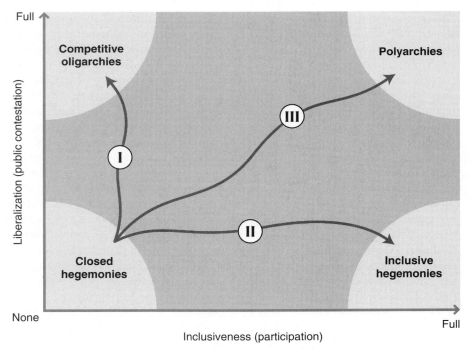

Figure 4.2 Liberalization, Inclusiveness, and Democratization.

could say that a change in this direction involves the liberalization of a regime; alternatively one might say that the regime becomes more competitive. If a regime changes to provide greater participation, as along path II, it might be said to change toward greater popularization, or that it is becoming inclusive. A regime might change along one dimension and not the other. If we call a regime near the upper left corner a competitive oligarchy, then path I represents a change from a closed hegemony to a competitive oligarchy. But a closed hegemony might also become more inclusive without liberalizing, i.e., without increasing the opportunities for public contestation, as along path II. In this case the regime changes from a closed to an inclusive hegemony.

Democracy might be conceived of as lying at the upper right corner. But since democracy may involve more dimensions than the two in Figure 4.2, and since (in my view) no large system in the real world is fully democratized, I prefer to call real world systems that are closest to the upper right corner polyarchies. Any change in a regime that moves it upward and to the right, for example along path III, may be said to represent some degree of democratization. Polyarchies, then, may be thought of as relatively (but incompletely) democratized regimes, or, to put it in another way, polyarchies are regimes that have been substantially popularized and liberalized, that is, highly inclusive and extensively open to public contestation.

You will notice that although I have given names to regimes lying near the four corners, the large space in the middle of the figure is not named, nor is it subdivided. The absence of names partly reflects the historic tendency to classify regimes in terms of extreme types; it also reflects my own desire to avoid redundant terminology. The lack of nomenclature does not mean a lack of regimes; in fact, perhaps the preponderant number of national regimes in the world today would fall into the mid-area. Many significant changes in regimes, then, involve shifts within, into, or out of this important central area, as these regimes become more (or less) inclusive and increase (or reduce) opportunities for public contestation. In order to refer to regimes in this large middle area, I shall sometimes resort to the terms near or nearly: a nearly hegemonic regime has somewhat more opportunities for public contestation than a hegemonic regime; a near-polyarchy could be quite inclusive but would have more severe restrictions on public contestation than a full polyarchy, or it might provide opportunities for public contestation comparable to those of a full polyarchy and yet be somewhat less inclusive.[3]

Notes

1. Some of the relationships are discussed in my *A Preface to Democratic Theory* (Chicago: University of Chicago Press, 1956), pp. 63–81, and in Robert A. Dahl and Charles E. Lindblom, *Politics, Economics and Welfare* (New York: Harper, 1953), chaps. 10 and 11.
2. Throughout this [discussion] the terms liberalization, political competition, competitive politics, public contestation, and public opposition are used interchangeably to refer to this dimension, and regimes relatively high on this dimension are frequently referred to as competitive regimes.

3. The problem of terminology is formidable, since it seems impossible to find terms already in use that do not carry with them a large freight of ambiguity and surplus meaning. The reader should remind himself that the terms used here are employed throughout [this discussion], to the best of my ability, only with the meanings indicated in the preceding paragraphs. Some readers will doubtless resist the term polyarchy as an alternative to the word democracy, but it is important to maintain the distinction between democracy as an ideal system and the institutional arrangements that have come to be regarded as a kind of imperfect approximation of an ideal, and experience shows, I believe, that when the same term is used for both, needless confusion and essentially irrelevant semantic arguments get in the way of the analysis. At the opposite corner, hegemony is not altogether satisfactory; yet given the meaning I have indicated, the term hegemonic seems to me more appropriate than hierarchical, monocratic, absolutist, autocratic, despotic, authoritarian, totalitarian, etc. My use of the term "contestation" in "public contestation" is well within normal (if infrequent) English usage; in English contestation means to contest, which means to make something the subject of dispute, contention, or litigation, and its most immediate synonyms are to dispute, challenge, or vie. The utility of the term was, however, first suggested to me by Bertrand de Jouvenel's "The Means of Contestation," *Government and Opposition* 1 (January 1966): 155–74. Jouvenel's usage is similar to my own, as is the identical French term he used in the original, meaning: *débat, objection, conflit, opposition.* In the same issue of this journal, however, Ghita Ionescu ("Control and Contestation in Some One-Party States" pp. 240–50) uses the term in its narrower but currently quite common meaning as "the anti-system, basic and permanent postulates of any opposition on the grounds of fundamental, dichotomic differences of opinion and ideologies" (p. 241). Clearly this is a more restricted definition of the concept than the one I use here and that, I believe, Jouvenel uses in his essay.

▓ 4.3

What Democracy Is . . . and Is Not

Philippe C. Schmitter and Terry Lynn Karl

Philippe Schmitter and Terry Karl believe that the seven criteria that Robert Dahl provides for defining democracy or polyarchy (see 4.2) are a good start in defining democracy but that they are insufficient. In order for polyarchy to exist, they assert, political institutions must be autonomous; that is, they must not be controlled by extraconstitutional or foreign forces. Schmitter and Karl thus propose setting the bar higher than Dahl specified. On the other hand, Schmitter and Karl caution that one should not expect too much of democracy. Even when it functions effectively, democracy does not necessarily produce ideal policies.

What ways can you suggest to improve the quality of democratic institutions and policies?

For some time, the word democracy has been circulating as a debased currency in the political marketplace. Politicians with a wide range of convictions and practices strove to appropriate the label and attach it to their actions. Scholars, conversely, hesitated to use it—without adding qualifying adjectives—because of the ambiguity that surrounds it. The distinguished American political theorist Robert Dahl even tried to introduce a new term, "polyarchy," in its stead in the (vain) hope of gaining a greater measure of conceptual precision. But for better or worse, we are "stuck" with democracy as the catchword of contemporary political discourse. It is the word that resonates in people's minds and springs from their lips as they struggle for freedom and a better way of life; it is the word whose meaning we must discern if it is to be of any use in guiding political analysis and practice.

The wave of transitions away from autocratic rule that began with Portugal's "Revolution of the Carnations" in 1974 and seems to have crested with the collapse of communist regimes across Eastern Europe in 1989 has produced a welcome convergence towards a common definition of democracy.[1] Everywhere there

---

Philippe C. Schmitter and Terry Lynn Karl, "What Democracy Is . . . and Is Not," *Journal of Democracy* 2 (Summer 1991): 75–87; reprinted in *The Global Resurgence of Democracy*, 2nd ed., ed. Larry Diamond and Marc F. Plattner (Baltimore, MD: The Johns Hopkins University Press, 1996): 49–62. © National Endowment for Democracy and The Johns Hopkins University Press. Reprinted with permission of The Johns Hopkins University Press.

has been a silent abandonment of dubious adjectives like "popular," "guided," "bourgeois," and "formal" to modify "democracy." At the same time, a remarkable consensus has emerged concerning the minimal conditions that polities must meet in order to merit the prestigious appellation of "democratic." Moreover, a number of international organizations now monitor how well these standards are met; indeed, some countries even consider them when formulating foreign policy.[2]

What Democracy Is

Let us begin by broadly defining democracy and the generic *concepts* that distinguish it as a unique system for organizing relations between rulers and the ruled. We will then briefly review *procedures,* the rules and arrangements that are needed if democracy is to endure. Finally, we will discuss two operative *principles* that make democracy work. They are not expressly included among the generic concepts or formal procedures, but the prospect for democracy is grim if their underlying conditioning effects are not present.

One of the major themes of this essay is that democracy does not consist of a single unique set of institutions. There are many types of democracy, and their diverse practices produce a similarly varied set of effects. The specific form democracy takes is contingent upon a country's socioeconomic conditions as well as its entrenched state structures and policy practices.

Modern political democracy is a system of governance in which rulers are held accountable for their actions in the public realm by citizens, acting indirectly through the competition and cooperation of their elected representatives.[3]

A *regime or system of governance* is an ensemble of patterns that determines the methods of access to the principal public offices; the characteristics of the actors admitted to or excluded from such access; the strategies that actors may use to gain access; and the rules that are followed in the making of publicly binding decisions. To work properly, the ensemble must be institutionalized—that is to say, the various patterns must be habitually known, practiced, and accepted by most, if not all, actors. Increasingly, the preferred mechanism of institutionalization is a written body of laws undergirded by a written constitution, though many enduring political norms can have an informal, prudential, or traditional basis.[4]

For the sake of economy and comparison, these forms, characteristics, and rules are usually bundled together and given a generic label. Democratic is one; others are autocratic, authoritarian, despotic, dictatorial, tyrannical, totalitarian, absolutist, traditional, monarchic, oligarchic, plutocratic, aristocratic, and sultanistic.[5] Each of these regime forms may in turn be broken down into subtypes.

Like all regimes, democracies depend upon the presence of *rulers,* persons who occupy specialized authority roles and can give legitimate commands to others. What distinguishes democratic rulers from nondemocratic ones are the norms that condition how the former come to power and the practices that hold them accountable for their actions.

Both democracies

(liberal democratic

The *public realm* encompasses the making of collective norms and choices that are binding on the society and backed by state coercion. Its content can vary a great deal across democracies, depending upon preexisting distinctions between the public and the private, state and society, legitimate coercion and voluntary exchange, and collective needs and individual preferences. The liberal conception of democracy advocates circumscribing the public realm as narrowly as possible, while the socialist or social-democratic approach would extend that realm through regulation, subsidization, and, in some cases, collective ownership of property. Neither is intrinsically more democratic than the other—just *differently* democratic. This implies that measures aimed at "developing the private sector" are no more democratic than those aimed at "developing the public sector." Both, if carried to extremes, could undermine the practice of democracy, the former by destroying the basis for satisfying collective needs and exercising legitimate authority; the latter by destroying the basis for satisfying individual preferences and controlling illegitimate government actions. Differences of opinion over the optimal mix of the two provide much of the substantive content of political conflict within established democracies.

Citizens are the most distinctive element in democracies. All regimes have rulers and a public realm, but only to the extent that they are democratic do they have citizens. Historically, severe restrictions on citizenship were imposed in most emerging or partial democracies according to criteria of age, gender, class, race, literacy, property ownership, tax-paying status, and so on. Only a small part of the total population was eligible to vote or run for office. Only restricted social categories were allowed to form, join, or support political associations. After protracted struggle—in some cases involving violent domestic upheaval or international war—most of these restrictions were lifted. Today, the criteria for inclusion are fairly standard. All native-born adults are eligible, although somewhat higher age limits may still be imposed upon candidates for certain offices. Unlike the early American and European democracies of the nineteenth century, none of the recent democracies in southern Europe, Latin America, Asia, or Eastern Europe has even attempted to impose formal restrictions on the franchise or eligibility to office. When it comes to informal restrictions on the effective exercise of citizenship rights, however, the story can be quite different. This explains the central importance (discussed below) of procedures.

Competition has not always been considered an essential defining condition of democracy. "Classic" democracies presumed decision making based on direct participation leading to consensus. The assembled citizenry was expected to agree on a common course of action after listening to the alternatives and weighing their respective merits and demerits. A tradition of hostility to "faction," and "particular interests" persists in democratic thought, but at least since *The Federalist Papers* it has become widely accepted that competition among factions is a necessary evil in democracies that operate on a more-than-local scale. Since, as James Madison argued, "the latent causes of faction are sown in the nature of man," and the possible remedies for "the mischief of faction" are worse than the disease, the best course is to recognize them and to attempt to control their effects.[6] Yet while democrats may agree on the inevitability of factions, they tend to disagree about the best forms and rules for governing factional competition. Indeed, differences over the preferred modes and boundaries of competition contribute most to distinguishing one subtype of democracy from another.

The most popular definition of democracy equates it with regular *elections*, fairly conducted and honestly counted. Some even consider the mere fact of elections—even ones from which specific parties or candidates are excluded, or in which substantial portions of the population cannot freely participate—as a sufficient condition for the existence of democracy. This fallacy has been called "electoralism" or "the faith that merely holding elections will channel political action into peaceful contests among elites and accord public legitimacy to the winners"—no matter how they are conducted or what else constrains those who win them.[7] However central to democracy, elections occur intermittently and only allow citizens to choose between the highly aggregated alternatives offered by political parties, which can, especially in the early stages of a democratic transition, proliferate in a bewildering variety. During the intervals between elections, citizens can seek to influence public policy through a wide variety of other intermediaries: interest associations, social movements, locality groupings, clientelistic arrangements, and so forth. *Modern democracy, in other words, offers a variety of competitive processes and channels for the expression of interests and values—associational as well as partisan, functional as well as territorial, collective as well as individual. All are integral to its practice.*

Another commonly accepted image of democracy identifies it with *majority rule*. Any governing body that makes decisions by combining the votes of more than half of those eligible and present is said to be democratic, whether that majority emerges within an electorate, a parliament, a committee, a city council, or a party caucus. For exceptional purposes (e.g., amending the constitution or expelling a member), "qualified majorities" of more than 50 percent may be required, but few would deny that democracy must involve some means of aggregating the equal preferences of individuals.

A problem arises, however, when *numbers* meet *intensities*. What happens when a properly assembled majority (especially a stable, self-perpetuating one) regularly makes decisions that harm some minority (especially a threatened cultural or ethnic group)? In these circumstances, successful democracies tend to qualify the central principle of majority rule in order to protect minority rights. Such qualifications can take the form of constitutional provisions that place certain matters beyond the reach of majorities (bills of rights); requirements for concurrent majorities in several different constituencies (confederalism); guarantees securing the autonomy of local or regional governments against the demands of the central authority (federalism); grand coalition governments that incorporate all parties (consociationalism); or the negotiation of social pacts between major social groups like business and labor (neocorporatism). The most common and effective way of protecting minorities, however, lies in the everyday operation of interest associations and social movements. These reflect (some would say, amplify) the different intensities of preference that exist in the population and bring them to bear on democratically elected decision makers. Another way of putting this intrinsic tension between numbers and intensities would be to say that "in modern democracies, votes may be counted, but influences alone are weighted."

Cooperation has always been a central feature of democracy. Actors must voluntarily make collective decisions binding on the polity as a whole. They must cooperate in order to compete. They must be capable of acting collectively through parties, associations, and movements in order to select candidates, articulate preferences, petition authorities, and influence policies.

But democracy's freedoms should also encourage citizens to deliberate among themselves, to discover their common needs, and to resolve their differences without relying on some supreme central authority. Classical democracy emphasized these qualities, and they are by no means extinct, despite repeated efforts by contemporary theorists to stress the analogy with behavior in the economic marketplace and to reduce all of democracy's operations to competitive interest maximization. Alexis de Tocqueville best described the importance of independent groups for democracy in his *Democracy in America*, a work which remains a major source of inspiration for all those who persist in viewing democracy as something more than a struggle for election and re-election among competing candidates.[8]

In contemporary political discourse, this phenomenon of cooperation and deliberation via autonomous group activity goes under the rubric of "civil society." The diverse units of social identity and interest, by remaining independent of the state (and perhaps even of parties), not only can restrain the arbitrary actions of rulers, but can also contribute to forming better citizens who are more aware of the preferences of others, more self-confident in their actions, and more civic-minded in their willingness to sacrifice for the common good. At its best, civil society provides an intermediate layer of governance between the individual and the state that is capable of resolving conflicts and controlling the behavior of members without public coercion. Rather than overloading decision makers with increased demands and making the system ungovernable,[9] a viable civil society can mitigate conflicts and improve the quality of citizenship—without relying exclusively on the privatism of the marketplace.

Representatives—whether directly or indirectly elected—do most of the real work in modern democracies. Most are professional politicians who orient their careers around the desire to fill key offices. It is doubtful that any democracy could survive without such people. The central question, therefore, is not whether or not there will be a political elite or even a professional political class, but how these representatives are chosen and then held accountable for their actions.

As noted above, there are many channels of representation in modern democracy. The electoral one, based on territorial constituencies, is the most visible and public. It culminates in a parliament or a presidency that is periodically accountable to the citizenry as a whole. Yet the sheer growth of government (in large part as a byproduct of popular demand) has increased the number, variety, and power of agencies charged with making public decisions and not subject to elections. Around these agencies there has developed a vast apparatus of specialized representation based largely on functional interests, not territorial constituencies. These interest associations, and not political parties, have become the primary expression of civil society in most stable democracies, supplemented by the more sporadic interventions of social movements.

The new and fragile democracies that have sprung up since 1974 must live in "compressed time." They will not resemble the European democracies of the nineteenth and early twentieth centuries, and they cannot expect to acquire the multiple channels of representation in gradual historical progression as did most of their predecessors. A bewildering array of parties, interests, and movements will all simultaneously seek political influence in them, creating challenges to the polity that did not exist in earlier processes of democratization.

Procedures That Make Democracy Possible

The defining components of democracy are necessarily abstract, and may give rise to a considerable variety of institutions and subtypes of democracy. For democracy to thrive, however, specific procedural norms must be followed and civic rights must be respected. Any polity that fails to impose such restrictions upon itself, that fails to follow the "rule of law" with regard to its own procedures, should not be considered democratic. These procedures alone do not define democracy, but their presence is indispensable to its persistence. In essence, they are necessary but not sufficient conditions for its existence.

Robert Dahl has offered the most generally accepted listing of what he terms the "procedural minimal" conditions that must be present for modern political democracy (or as he puts it, "polyarchy") to exist:

1. Control over government decisions about policy is constitutionally vested in elected officials.
2. Elected officials are chosen in frequent and fairly conducted elections in which coercion is comparatively uncommon.
3. Practically all adults have the right to vote in the election of officials.
4. Practically all adults have the right to run for elective offices in the government. . . .
5. Citizens have a right to express themselves without the danger of severe punishment on political matters broadly defined. . . .
6. Citizens have a right to seek out alternative sources of information. Moreover, alternative sources of information exist and are protected by law.
7. . . . Citizens also have the right to form relatively independent associations or organizations, including independent political parties and interest groups.[10]

These seven conditions seem to capture the essence of procedural democracy for many theorists, but we propose to add two others. The first might be thought of as a further refinement of item 1, while the second might be called an implicit prior condition to all seven of the above.

8. Popularly elected officials must be able to exercise their constitutional powers without being subjected to overriding (albeit informal) opposition from unelected officials. Democracy is in jeopardy if military officers, entrenched civil servants, or state managers retain the capacity to act independently of elected civilians or even veto decisions made by the people's representatives. Without this additional caveat, the militarized polities of contemporary Central America, where civilian control over the military does not exist, might be classified by many scholars as democracies, just as they have been (with the exception of Sandinista Nicaragua) by U.S. policy makers. The caveat thus guards against what we earlier called "electoralism"—the tendency to focus on the holding of elections while ignoring other political realities.

9. The polity must be self-governing; it must be able to act independently of constraints imposed by some other overarching political system. Dahl and other contemporary democratic theorists probably took this condition for granted since they referred to formally sovereign nation-states. However, with the development of blocs, alliances, spheres of influence, and a variety of "neocolonial" arrangements, the question of autonomy has been a salient one. Is a system really democratic if its elected officials are unable to make binding decisions without the approval of actors outside their territorial domain? This is significant even if the outsiders are themselves democratically constituted and if the insiders are relatively free to alter or even end the encompassing arrangement (as in Puerto Rico), but it becomes especially critical if neither condition obtains (as in the Baltic states).

Principles That Make Democracy Feasible

Lists of component processes and procedural norms help us to specify what democracy is, but they do not tell us much about how it actually functions. The simplest answer is "by the consent of the people"; the more complex one is "by the contingent consent of politicians acting under conditions of bounded uncertainty."

In a democracy, representatives must at least informally agree that those who win greater electoral support or influence over policy will not use their temporary superiority to bar the losers from taking office or exerting influence in the future, and that in exchange for this opportunity to keep competing for power and place, momentary losers will respect the winners' right to make binding decisions. Citizens are expected to obey the decisions ensuing from such a process of competition, provided its outcome remains contingent upon their collective preferences as expressed through fair and regular elections or open and repeated negotiations.

The challenge is not so much to find a set of goals that command widespread consensus as to find a set of rules that embody contingent consent. The precise shape of this "democratic bargain," to use Dahl's expression,[11] can vary a good deal from society to society. It depends on social cleavages and such subjective factors as mutual trust, the standard of fairness, and the willingness to compromise. It may even be compatible with a great deal of dissensus on substantive policy issues.

All democracies involve a degree of uncertainty about who will be elected and what policies they will pursue. Even in those polities where one party persists in winning elections or one policy is consistently implemented, the possibility of change through independent collective action still exists, as in Italy, Japan, and the Scandinavian social democracies. If it does not, the system is not democratic, as in Mexico, Senegal, or Indonesia.

But the uncertainty embedded in the core of all democracies is bounded. Not just any actor can get into the competition and raise any issue he or she pleases—there are previously established rules that must be respected. Not just any policy can be adopted—there are conditions that must be met. Democracy institutionalizes "normal," limited political uncertainty. These boundaries vary from country to country. Constitutional guarantees of property, privacy, expression, and other rights are a part of this, but the most effective boundaries are generated by competition among interest groups and cooperation within civil society. Whatever the rhetoric (and some polities appear to offer their citizens more dramatic alternatives than others), once the rules of contingent consent have been agreed upon, the actual variation is likely to stay within a predictable and generally accepted range.

This emphasis on operative guidelines contrasts with a highly persistent, but misleading theme in recent literature on democracy—namely, the emphasis upon "civic culture." The principles we have suggested here rest on rules of prudence, not on deeply ingrained habits of tolerance, moderation, mutual respect, fair play, readiness to compromise, or trust in public authorities. Waiting for such habits to sink deep and lasting roots implies a very slow process of regime consolidation—one that takes generations—and it would probably condemn most contemporary experiences *ex hypothesi* to failure. Our assertion is that contingent consent and bounded uncertainty can emerge from the interaction between antagonistic and mutually suspicious actors and that the far more benevolent and ingrained norms of a civic culture are better thought of as a *product* and not a producer of democracy. . . .

What Democracy Is Not

We have attempted to convey the general meaning of modern democracy without identifying it with some particular set of rules and institutions or restricting it to some specific culture or level of development. We have also argued that it cannot be reduced to the regular holding of elections or equated with a particular notion of the role of the state, but we have not said much more about what democracy is not or about what democracy may not be capable of producing.

There is an understandable temptation to load too many expectations on this concept and to imagine that by attaining democracy, a society will have resolved all of its political, social, economic, administrative, and cultural problems. Unfortunately, "all good things do not necessarily go together."

First, democracies are not necessarily more efficient economically than other forms of government. Their rates of aggregate growth, savings, and investment may be no better than those of nondemocracies. This is especially likely during the transition, when propertied groups and administrative elites may respond to real or imagined threats to the "rights" they enjoyed under authoritarian rule by initiating capital flight, disinvestment, or sabotage. In time, depending upon the type of democracy, benevolent long-term effects upon income distribution, aggregate demand, education, productivity, and creativity may eventually combine to improve economic and social performance, but it is certainly too much to expect that these improvements will occur immediately—much less that they will be defining characteristics of democratization.

Second, democracies are not necessarily more efficient administratively. Their capacity to make decisions may even be slower than that of the regimes they replace, if only because more actors must be consulted. The costs of getting things done may be higher, if only because "payoffs" have to be made to a wider and more resourceful set of clients (although one should never underestimate the degree of corruption to be found within autocracies). Popular satisfaction with the new democratic government's performance may not even seem greater, if only because necessary compromises often please no one completely, and because the losers are free to complain.

Third, democracies are not likely to appear more orderly, consensual, stable, or governable than the autocracies they replace. This is partly a byproduct of democratic freedom of expression, but it is also a reflection of the likelihood of continuing disagreement over new rules and institutions. These products of imposition or compromise are often initially quite ambiguous in nature and uncertain in effect until actors have learned how to use them. What is more, they come in the aftermath of serious struggles motivated by high ideals. Groups and individuals with recently acquired autonomy will test certain rules, protest against the actions of certain institutions, and insist on renegotiating their part of the bargain. Thus the presence of antisystem parties should be neither surprising nor seen as a failure of democratic consolidation. What counts is whether such parties are willing, however reluctantly, to play by the general rules of bounded uncertainty and contingent consent.

Governability is a challenge for all regimes, not just democratic ones. Given the political exhaustion and loss of legitimacy that have befallen autocracies from sultanistic Paraguay to totalitarian Albania, it may seem that only democracies can now be expected to govern effectively and legitimately. Experience has shown, however, that democracies too can lose the ability to govern. Mass publics can become disenchanted with their performance. Even more threatening is the temptation for leaders to fiddle with procedures and ultimately undermine the principles of contingent consent and bounded uncertainty. Perhaps the most critical moment comes once the politicians begin to settle into the more predictable roles and relations of a consolidated democracy. Many will find their expectations frustrated; some will discover that the new rules of competition put them at a disadvantage; a few may even feel that their vital interests are threatened by popular majorities.

Finally, democracies will have more open societies and polities than the autocracies they replace, but not necessarily more open economies. Many of today's most successful and well-established democracies have historically resorted to protectionism and closed borders, and have relied extensively upon public institutions to promote economic development. While the long-term compatibility between democracy and capitalism does not seem to be in doubt, despite their continuous tension, it is not clear whether the promotion of such liberal economic goals as the right of individuals to own property and retain profits, the clearing function of markets, the private settlement of disputes, the freedom to produce without government regulation, or the privatization of state-owned enterprises necessarily furthers the consolidation of democracy. After all, democracies do need to levy taxes and regulate certain transactions, especially where private monopolies and oligopolies exist. Citizens or their representatives may decide that it is desirable to protect the rights of collectivities from encroachment by individuals, especially propertied ones, and they may choose to set aside certain forms of property for public or cooperative ownership. In short, notions of economic liberty that are currently put forward in neoliberal economic models are not synonymous with political freedom—and may even impede it.

Democratization will not necessarily bring in its wake economic growth, social peace, administrative efficiency, political harmony, free markets, or "the end of ideology." Least of all will it bring about "the end of history." No doubt some of these qualities could make the consolidation of democracy easier, but they are neither prerequisites for it nor immediate products of it. Instead, what we should be hoping for is the emergence of political institutions that can peacefully compete to form governments and influence public policy, that can channel social and economic conflicts through regular procedures, and that have sufficient linkages to civil society to represent their constituencies and commit them to collective courses of action. Some types of democracies, especially in developing countries, have been unable to fulfill this promise, perhaps due to the circumstances of their transition from authoritarian rule.[12] The democratic wager is that such a regime, once established, will not only persist by reproducing itself within its initial confining conditions, but will eventually expand beyond them.[13] Unlike authoritarian regimes, democracies have the capacity to modify their rules and institutions consensually in response to changing circumstances. They may not immediately produce all the goods mentioned above, but they stand a better chance of eventually doing so than do autocracies.

Notes

1. For a comparative analysis of the recent regime changes in southern Europe and Latin America, see Guillermo O'Donnell, Philippe C. Schmitter, and Laurence Whitehead, eds., *Transitions from Authoritarian Rule*, 4 vols. (Baltimore: Johns Hopkins University Press, 1986). For another compilation that adopts a more structural approach see Larry Diamond, Juan Linz, and Seymour Martin Lipset, eds., *Democracy in Developing Countries*, vols. 2, 3, and 4 (Boulder, Colo.: Lynne Rienner, 1989).

2. Numerous attempts have been made to codify and quantify the existence of democracy across political systems. The best known is probably Freedom House's *Freedom in the World: Political Rights and Civil Liberties*, published since 1973 by Greenwood Press and since 1988 by University Press of America. Also see Charles Humana, *World Human Rights Guide* (New York: Facts on File, 1986).

3. The definition most commonly used by American social scientists is that of Joseph Schumpeter: "that institutional arrangement for arriving at political decisions in which individuals acquire the power to decide by means of a competitive struggle for the people's vote." *Capitalism, Socialism and Democracy* (London: George Allen and Unwin, 1943), 269. We accept certain aspects of the classical procedural approach to modern democracy, but differ primarily in our emphasis on the accountability of rulers to citizens and the relevance of mechanisms of competition other than elections.

4. Not only do some countries practice a stable form of democracy without a formal constitution (e.g., Great Britain and Israel), but even more countries have constitutions and legal codes that offer no guarantee of reliable practice. On paper, Stalin's 1936 constitution for the USSR was a virtual model of democratic rights and entitlements.

5. For the most valiant attempt to make some sense out of this thicket of distinctions, see Juan Linz, "Totalitarian and Authoritarian Regimes" in *Handbook of Political Science*, eds. Fred I. Greenstein and Nelson W. Polsby (Reading, Mass.: Addison-Wesley, 1975), 175–411.

6. "Publius" (Alexander Hamilton, John Jay, and James Madison), *The Federalist Papers* (New York: Anchor Books, 1961). The quote is from Number 10.

7. See Terry Karl, "Imposing Consent? Electoralism versus Democratization in El Salvador," in *Elections and Democratization in Latin America, 1980–1985*, eds. Paul Drake and Eduardo Silva (San Diego: Center for Iberian and Latin American Studies, Center for US/Mexican Studies, University of California, San Diego, 1986), 9–36.

8. Alexis de Tocqueville, *Democracy in America*, 2 vols. (New York: Vintage Books, 1945).

9. This fear of overloaded government and the imminent collapse of democracy is well reflected in the work of Samuel P. Huntington during the 1970s. See especially Michel Crozier, Samuel P. Huntington, and Joji Watanuki, *The Crisis of Democracy* (New York: New York University Press, 1975). For Huntington's (revised) thoughts about the prospects for democracy, see his "Will More Countries Become Democratic?," *Political Science Quarterly* 99 (Summer 1984): 193–218.

10. Robert Dahl, *Dilemmas of Pluralist Democracy* (New Haven: Yale University Press, 1982), 11.

11. Robert Dahl, *After the Revolution: Authority in a Good Society* (New Haven: Yale University Press, 1970).

12. Terry Lynn Karl, "Dilemmas of Democratization in Latin America," *Comparative Politics* 23 (October 1990): 1–23.

13. Otto Kirchheimer, "Confining Conditions and Revolutionary Breakthroughs," *American Political Science Review* 59 (1965): 964–974.

Toward Consolidated Democracies

Juan J. Linz and Alfred Stepan

Juan Linz and Alfred Stepan assert that for an authoritarian regime to become a
stable democracy, it is not sufficient to eliminate autocratic rulers and install democratic institutions. They distinguish between democratic *transition* and democratic
consolidation. Transition involves toppling an authoritarian regime; consolidation
involves the development of a durable democratic regime. Linz and Stepan identify
additional changes that they consider necessary for a transition to democracy to
become consolidated.

Linz and Stepan do not claim that these additional changes will inevitably
occur. Can you think of why they might or might not? What affects the prospects
that a regime that has experienced a democratic transition will be consolidated?

I n most cases after a democratic transition is completed, there are still many
tasks that need to be accomplished, conditions that must be established,
and attitudes and habits that must be cultivated before democracy can be
regarded as consolidated. What, then, are the characteristics of a consolidated
democracy? Many scholars, in advancing definitions of consolidated democracy,
enumerate all the regime characteristics that would improve the overall quality
of democracy. We favor, instead, a narrower definition of democratic consolidation, but one that nonetheless combines behavioral, attitudinal, and constitutional dimensions. Essentially, by a "consolidated democracy" we mean a
political regime in which democracy as a complex system of institutions, rules,
and patterned incentives and disincentives has become, in a phrase, "the only
game in town."[1]

Behaviorally, democracy becomes the only game in town when no significant
political group seriously attempts to overthrow the democratic regime or to promote domestic or international violence in order to secede from the state. When
this situation obtains, the behavior of the newly elected government that has

emerged from the democratic transition is no longer dominated by the problem of how to avoid democratic breakdown. (Exceptionally, the democratic process can be used to achieve secession, creating separate states that can be democracies.) Attitudinally, democracy becomes the only game in town when, even in the face of severe political and economic crises, the overwhelming majority of the people believe that any further political change must emerge from within the parameters of democratic procedures. Constitutionally, democracy becomes the only game in town when all of the actors in the polity become habituated to the fact that political conflict within the state will be resolved according to established norms, and that violations of these norms are likely to be both ineffective and costly. In short, with consolidation, democracy becomes routinized and deeply internalized in social, institutional, and even psychological life, as well as in political calculations for achieving success.

Our working definition of a consolidated democracy is then as follows: *Behaviorally,* a democratic regime in a territory is consolidated when no significant national, social, economic, political, or institutional actors spend significant resources attempting to achieve their objectives by creating a nondemocratic regime or by seceding from the state. *Attitudinally,* a democratic regime is consolidated when a strong majority of public opinion, even in the midst of major economic problems and deep dissatisfaction with incumbents, holds the belief that democratic procedures and institutions are the most appropriate way to govern collective life, and when support for antisystem alternatives is quite small or is more-or-less isolated from prodemocratic forces. *Constitutionally,* a democratic regime is consolidated when governmental and nongovernmental forces alike become subject to, as well as habituated to, the resolution of conflict within the bounds of the specific laws, procedures, and institutions that are sanctioned by the new democratic process.

We must add two important caveats. First, when we say a regime is a consolidated democracy, we do not preclude the possibility that at some future time it could break down. Such a breakdown, however, would be related not to weaknesses or problems specific to the historic process of democratic consolidation, but to a new dynamic in which the democratic regime cannot solve a set of problems, a nondemocratic alternative gains significant supporters, and former democratic regime loyalists begin to behave in a constitutionally disloyal or semiloyal manner.[2]

Our second caveat is that we do not want to imply that there is only one type of consolidated democracy. An exciting new area of research is concerned with precisely this issue—the varieties of consolidated democracies. We also do not want to imply that consolidated democracies could not continue to improve their quality by raising the minimal economic plateau upon which all citizens stand, and by deepening popular participation in the political and social life of the country. Within the category of consolidated democracies, there is a continuum from low-quality to high-quality democracies. Improving the quality of consolidated democracies is an urgent political and intellectual task, but our goal in this essay, though related, is a different one. As we are living in a period in which an unprecedented number of countries have completed democratic transitions and are attempting to consolidate democracies, it is both politically and conceptually important that we understand the specific tasks in "crafting" democratic consolidation. Unfortunately, too much of the discussion of the current "wave" of democratization focuses almost solely on elections or on the presumed democratizing potential of market mechanisms. Democratic consolidation, however, requires much more than elections and markets.

Crafting and Conditions

In addition to a functioning state, five other interconnected and mutually reinforcing conditions must be present, or be crafted, in order for a democracy to be consolidated. First, the conditions must exist for the development of a free and lively *civil society*. Second, there must be a relatively autonomous *political society*. Third, throughout the territory of the state all major political actors, especially the government and the state apparatus, must be effectively subjected to a *rule of law* that protects individual freedoms and associational life. Fourth, there must be a *state bureaucracy* that is usable by the new democratic government. Fifth, there must be an institutionalized *economic society*. Let us explain what is involved in crafting this interrelated set of conditions.

By "civil society," we refer to that arena of the polity where self-organizing and relatively autonomous groups, movements, and individuals attempt to articulate values, to create associations and solidarities, and to advance their interests. Civil society can include manifold social movements (e.g., women's groups, neighborhood associations, religious groupings, and intellectual organizations), as well as associations from all social strata (such as trade unions, entrepreneurial groups, and professional associations).

By "political society," we mean that arena in which political actors compete for the legitimate right to exercise control over public power and the state apparatus. Civil society by itself can destroy a nondemocratic regime, but democratic consolidation (or even a full democratic transition) must involve political society. Democratic consolidation requires that citizens develop an appreciation for the core institutions of a democratic political society—political parties, legislatures, elections, electoral rules, political leadership, and interparty alliances.

It is important to stress not only the difference between civil society and political society, but also their complementarity, which is not always recognized. One of these two arenas is frequently neglected in favor of the other. Worse, within the democratic community, champions of either civil society or political society all too often adopt a discourse and a set of practices that are implicitly inimical to the normal development of the other.

In the recent struggles against the nondemocratic regimes of Eastern Europe and Latin America, a discourse was constructed that emphasized "civil society versus the state"—a dichotomy that has a long philosophical genealogy. More importantly for our purposes, it was also politically useful to those democratic movements emerging in states where explicitly political organizations were forbidden or extremely weak. In many countries, civil society was rightly considered to be the hero of democratic resistance and transition.

The problem arises at the moment of democratic transition. Democratic leaders of political society quite often argue that civil society, having played its historic role, should be demobilized so as to allow for the development of normal democratic politics. Such an argument is not only bad democratic theory, it is also bad democratic politics. A robust civil society, with the capacity to generate political alternatives and to monitor government and state, can help start transitions, help resist reversals, help push transitions to their completion, and help consolidate and deepen democracy. At all stages of the democratization process, therefore, a lively and independent civil society is invaluable.

But we should also consider how to recognize (and thus help overcome) the false opposition sometimes drawn between civil society and political society. The danger posed for the development of political society by civil society is that normative preferences and styles of organization perfectly appropriate to civil society might be taken to be the desirable—or indeed the only legitimate—style of organization for political society. For example, many civil society leaders view "internal conflict" and "division" within the democratic forces with moral antipathy. "Institutional routinization," "intermediaries," and "compromise" within politics are often spoken of pejoratively. But each of the above terms refers to an indispensable practice of political society in a consolidated democracy. Democratic consolidation requires political parties, one of whose primary tasks is precisely to aggregate and represent differences between democrats. Consolidation requires that habituation to the norms and procedures of democratic conflict-regulation be developed. A high degree of institutional routinization is a key part of such a process. Intermediation between the state and civil society, and the structuring of compromise, are likewise legitimate and necessary tasks of political society. In short, political society—informed, pressured, and periodically renewed by civil society—must somehow achieve a workable agreement on the myriad ways in which democratic power will be crafted and exercised.

The Need for a *Rechtsstaat*

To achieve a consolidated democracy, the necessary degree of autonomy of civil and political society must be embedded in, and supported by, our third arena, the rule of law. All significant actors—especially the democratic government and the state apparatus—must be held accountable to, and become habituated to, the rule of law. For the types of civil society and political society we have just described, a rule of law animated by a spirit of constitutionalism is an indispensable condition. Constitutionalism, which should not be confused with majoritarianism, entails a relatively strong consensus regarding the constitution, and especially a commitment to "self-binding" procedures of governance that can be altered only by exceptional majorities. It also requires a clear hierarchy of laws, interpreted by an independent judicial system and supported by a strong legal culture in civil society.[3]

The emergence of a *Rechtsstaat*—a state of law, or perhaps more accurately a state subject to law—was one of the major accomplishments of nineteenth-century liberalism (long before full democratization) in continental Europe and to some extent in Japan. A *Rechtsstaat* meant that the government and the state apparatus would be subject to the law, that areas of discretionary power would be defined and increasingly limited, and that citizens could turn to courts to defend themselves against the state and its officials. The modern *Rechtsstaat* is fundamental in making democratization possible, since without it citizens would not be able to exercise their political rights with full freedom and independence.

A state of law is particularly crucial for the consolidation of democracy. It is the most important continuous and routine way in which the elected government and the state administration are subjected to a network of laws, courts, semiautonomous review and control agencies, and civil-society norms that not only check the state's illegal tendencies but also embed it in an interconnecting web of mechanisms requiring transparency and accountability. Freely elected governments can, but do not necessarily, create such a state of law. The consolidation of democracy, however, requires such a law-bound, constraint-embedded state. Indeed, the more that all the institutions of the state function according to the principle of the state of law, the higher the quality of democracy and the better the society.

Constitutionalism and the rule of law must determine the offices to be filled by election, the procedures to elect those officeholders, and the definition of and limits to their power in order for people to be willing to participate in, and to accept the outcomes of, the democratic game. This may pose a problem if the rules, even if enacted by a majority, are so unfair or poorly crafted and so difficult to change democratically that they are unacceptable to a large number of citizens. For example, an electoral law that gives 80 percent of the seats in parliament to a party that wins less than 50 percent of the vote, or an ideologically loaded constitution that is extremely difficult to amend, is not likely to be conducive to democratic consolidation.

Finally, a democracy in which a single leader enjoys, or thinks he or she enjoys, a "democratic" legitimacy that allows him or her to ignore, dismiss, or alter other institutions—the legislature, the courts, the constitutional limits of power—does not fit our conception of rule of law in a democratic regime. The formal or informal institutionalization of such a system is not likely to result in a consolidated democracy unless such discretion is checked.

Some presidential democracies—with their tendency toward populist, plebiscitarian, "delegative" characteristics, together with a fixed term of office and a "no-reelection" rule that excludes accountability before the electorate—encourage nonconstitutional or anticonstitutional behavior that threatens the rule of law, often democracy itself, and certainly democratic consolidation. A prime minister who develops similar tendencies toward abuse of power is more likely than a president to be checked by other institutions: votes of no confidence by the opposition, or the loss of support by members of his own party. Early elections are a legal vehicle available in parliamentarianism—but unavailable in presidentialism—to help solve crises generated by such abusive leadership.

A Usable Bureaucracy

These three conditions—a lively and independent civil society, a political society with sufficient autonomy and a working consensus about procedures of governance, and constitutionalism and a rule of law—are virtually definitional prerequisites of a consolidated democracy. However, these conditions are much more likely to be satisfied where there are also found a bureaucracy usable by democratic leaders and an institutionalized economic society.

Democracy is a form of governance in which the rights of citizens are guaranteed and protected. To protect the rights of its citizens and to deliver other basic services that citizens demand, a democratic government needs to be able to exercise effectively its claim to a monopoly of the legitimate use of force in its territory. Even if the state had no other functions than these, it would have to tax compulsorily in order to pay for police officers, judges, and basic services. A modern democracy, therefore, needs the effective capacity to command, to regulate, and to extract tax revenues. For this, it needs a functioning state with a bureaucracy considered usable by the new democratic government.

In many territories of the world today—especially in parts of the former Soviet Union—no adequately functioning state exists. Insufficient taxing capacity on the part of the state or a weak normative and bureaucratic "presence" in much of its territory, such that citizens cannot effectively demand that their rights be respected or receive any basic entitlements, is also a great problem in many countries in Latin America, including Brazil. The question of the usability of the state bureaucracy by the new democratic regime also emerges in countries such as Chile, where the outgoing nondemocratic regime was able to give tenure to many key members of the state bureaucracy in politically sensitive areas such as justice and education. Important questions about the usability of the state bureaucracy by new democrats inevitably emerge in cases where the distinction between the communist party and the state had been virtually obliterated (as in much of postcommunist Europe), and the party is now out of power.

Economic Society

The final supportive condition for a consolidated democracy concerns the economy, an arena that we believe should be called "economic society." We use this phrase to call attention to two claims that we believe are theoretically and empirically sound. First, there has never been, and there cannot be, a consolidated democracy that has a command economy (except perhaps in wartime). Second, there has never been, and almost certainly will never be, a modern consolidated democracy with a pure market economy. Modern consolidated democracies require a set of sociopolitically crafted and accepted norms, institutions, and regulations—what we call "economic society"—that mediate between the state and the market.

No empirical evidence has ever been adduced to indicate that a polity meeting our definition of a consolidated democracy has ever existed with a command economy. Is there a theoretical reason to explain such a universal empirical outcome? We think so. On theoretical grounds, our assumption is that at least a nontrivial degree of market autonomy and of ownership diversity in the economy is necessary to produce the independence and liveliness of civil society that allow it to make its contribution to a democracy. Similarly, if all property is in the hands of the state, along with all decisions about pricing, labor, supply, and distribution, the relative autonomy of political society required for a consolidated democracy could not exist.[4]

But why are completely free markets unable to coexist with modern consolidated democracies? Empirically, serious studies of modern polities repeatedly verify the existence of significant degrees of market intervention and state ownership in all consolidated democracies.[5] Theoretically, there are at least three reasons why this should be so. First, notwithstanding certain ideologically extreme but surprisingly prevalent neoliberal claims about the self-sufficiency of the market, pure market economies could neither come into being nor be maintained without a degree of state regulation. Markets require legally enforced contracts, the issuance of money, regulated standards for weights and measures, and the protection of property, both public and private. These requirements dictate a role for the state in the economy. Second, even the best of markets experience "market failures" that must be corrected if the market is to function well.[6] No less an advocate of the "invisible hand" of the market than Adam Smith acknowledged that the state is necessary to perform certain functions. In a crucial but neglected passage in the *Wealth of Nations*, Adam Smith identified three important tasks of the state:

> First, the duty of protecting the society from the violence and invasion of other independent societies; secondly, the duty of protecting, as far as possible, every member of the society from the injustice or oppression of every other member of it, or the duty of establishing an exact administration of justice; and, thirdly, the duty of erecting and maintaining certain public works and certain public institutions which it can never be for the interest of any individual, or small number of individuals, to erect and maintain; because the profit could never repay the expense to any individual or small number of individuals, though it may frequently do much more than repay it to a great society.[7]

Finally, and most importantly, democracy entails free public contestation concerning governmental priorities and policies. If a democracy never produced policies that generated government-mandated public goods in the areas of education, health, and transportation, and never provided some economic safety net for its citizens and some alleviation of gross economic inequality, democracy would not be sustainable. Theoretically, of course, it would be antidemocratic to take such public policies off the agenda of legitimate public contestation. Thus, even in the extreme hypothetical case of a democracy that began with a pure market economy, the very working of a modern democracy (and a modern advanced capitalist economy) would lead to the transformation of that pure market economy into a mixed economy, or that set of norms, regulations, policies, and institutions which we call "economic society."[8]

Any way we analyze the problem, democratic consolidation requires the institutionalization of a politically regulated market. This requires an economic society, which in turn requires an effective state. Even a goal such as narrowing the scope of public ownership (i.e., privatization) in an orderly and legal way is almost certainly carried out more effectively by a stronger state than by a weaker one. Economic deterioration due to the state's inability to carry out needed regulatory functions greatly compounds the problems of economic reform and democratization.[9]

In summary, a modern consolidated democracy can be conceived of as comprising five major interrelated arenas, each of which, to function properly, must have its own primary organizing principle. Rightly understood, democracy is more than a regime; it is an interacting system. No single arena in such a system can function properly without some support from another arena, or often from all of the remaining arenas. For example, civil society in a democracy needs the support of a rule of law that guarantees to people their right of association, and needs the support of a state apparatus that will effectively impose legal sanctions on those who would illegally attempt to deny others that right. Furthermore, each arena in the democratic system has an impact on other arenas. For example, political society manages the governmental bureaucracy and produces the overall regulatory framework that guides and contains economic society. In a consolidated democracy, therefore, there are constant mediations among the five principal arenas, each of which is influenced by the others. . . .

Democracy and the Quality of Life

While we believe that it is a good thing for democracies to be consolidated, we should make it clear that consolidation does not necessarily entail either a high-quality democracy or a high-quality society. Democratic institutions—however important—are only one set of public institutions affecting citizens' lives. The courts, the central bank, the police, the armed forces, certain independent regulatory agencies, public-service agencies, and public hospitals are not governed democratically, and their officials are not elected by the citizens. Even in established democracies, not all of these institutions are controlled by elected officials, although many are overseen by them. These institutions operate, however, in a legal framework created by elected bodies and thereby derive their authority from them.

In view of all this, the quality of public life is in great measure a reflection not simply of the democratic or nondemocratic character of the regime, but of the quality of those other institutions.

Policy decisions by democratic governments and legislators certainly affect the quality of life, particularly in the long run, but no democracy can assure the presence of reputable bankers, entrepreneurs with initiative, physicians devoted to their patients, competent professors, creative scholars and artists, or even honest judges. The overall quality of a society is only in small part a function of democracy (or, for that matter, a function of nondemocratic regimes). Yet all of those dimensions of society affect the satisfaction of its citizens, including their satisfaction with the government and even with democracy itself. The feeling that democracy is to blame for all sorts of other problems is likely to be particularly acute in societies in which the distinctive contributions of democracy to the quality of life are not well understood and perhaps not highly valued. The more that democrats suggest that the achievement of democratic politics will bring the attainment of all those other goods, the greater will be the eventual disenchantment.

There are problems specific to the functioning of the state, and particularly to democratic institutions and political processes, that allow us to speak of the quality of democracy separately from the quality of society. Our assumption is that the quality of democracy can contribute positively or negatively to the quality of society, but that the two should not be confused. We as scholars should, in our research, explore both dimensions of the overall quality of life.

Notes

This essay is largely drawn from our book *Problems of Democratic Transition and Consolidation: Southern Europe, South America, and Post-Communist Europe* (Baltimore: Johns Hopkins University Press, 1996). Interested readers can find more detailed documentation, analysis, and references there. We thank the Ford Foundation and the Carnegie Corporation of New York for help in our research.

1. For other discussions about the concept of democratic consolidation, see Scott Mainwaring, Guillermo O'Donnell, and J. Samuel Valenzuela, eds., *Issues in Democratic Consolidation: The New South American Democracies in Comparative Perspective* (Notre Dame, Ind.: University of Notre Dame Press, 1992).

2. In essence, this means that the literature on democratic breakdown, such as that found in Juan J. Linz and Alfred Stepan, eds., *The Breakdown of Democratic Regimes* (Baltimore: Johns Hopkins University Press, 1978), would be much more directly relevant to analyzing such a phenomenon than this essay or related books on democratic transition and consolidation. This is not a criticism of the transition literature; rather, our point is that the democratic-transition and democratic-breakdown literatures need to be integrated into the overall literature on modern democratic theory. From the perspective of such an integrated theory, the "breakdown of a consolidated democracy" is not an oxymoron.

3. On the relationships between constitutionalism, democracy, legal culture, and "self-bindingness," see Jon Elster and Rune Slagstad, eds., *Constitutionalism and Democracy* (Cambridge: Cambridge University Press, 1988), 1–18.

4. Robert A. Dahl, in a similar argument, talks about two arrows of causation that produce this result; see his "Why All Democratic Countries Have Mixed Economies," in John Chapman and Ian Shapiro, eds., *Democratic Community, Nomos XXXV* (New York: New York University Press, 1993), 259–82.

5. See, for example, John R. Freeman, *Democracies and Market: The Politics of Mixed Economies* (Ithaca, N.Y.: Cornell University Press, 1989).

6. For an excellent analysis of inevitable market failures, see Peter Murrell, "Can Neoclassical Economics Underpin the Reform of Centrally Planned Economies?" *Journal of Economic Perspectives* 5 (1991): 59–76.

7. Adam Smith, *The Wealth of Nations*, 2 vols. (London: J.M. Dent and Sons, Everyman's Library, 1910), 2:180–81.

8. Robert A. Dahl's line of reasoning follows a similar development. See his "Why All Democratic Countries Have Mixed Economies," 259–82.

9. In postcommunist Europe, the Czech Republic and Hungary are well on the way to becoming institutionalized economic societies. In sharp contrast, in Ukraine and Russia the writ of the state does not extend far enough for us to speak of an economic society. The consequences of the lack of an economic society are manifest everywhere. For example, Russia, with a population 15 times larger than Hungary's and with vastly more raw materials, received only 3.6 billion dollars of direct foreign investment in 1992–93, whereas Hungary received 9 billion dollars of direct foreign investment in the same two years.

Rethinking Democratization: Lessons from the Postcommunist Experience

Valerie Bunce

Most theorizing about how countries became democratic in the 1970s and 1980s was based on countries in Latin America and southern Europe. Valerie Bunce suggests that the process by which democracy developed out of communist regimes in the former Soviet Union and east-central Europe was very different. In particular, she claims, popular or mass mobilization played a much more important role in toppling communist regimes. She warns against generalizing beyond the cases on which a theory (in this case, a theory of democratic transition) is originally based.

More generally, Bunce's article invites us to think about the respective role of grassroots pressure versus the strategies of political leaders in understanding why large-scale change occurs. Does her analysis illuminate why regime change occurs in other settings than formerly communist regimes in east-central Europe?

Comparing New Democracies

This article aims to use the postcommunist experience in East-Central Europe and the former Soviet Union—twenty-seven cases in all—to rethink our understanding of recent democratization. It does so by conducting a conversation between two bodies of research: (1) studies of Latin America and southern Europe, which collectively have constituted the reigning wisdom in the field, and (2) research on postcommunist politics. The discussion will focus on two relationships central to discussions in the field—between transitional politics and subsequent regime trajectories and between the consolidation and the sustainability of democracy. We will see that the postcommunist experience challenges the way both issues have been understood.

Valerie Bunce, "Rethinking Democratization: Lessons from the Postcommunist Experience," *World Politics* 55, no. 2 (January 2003): 170–189. © The Johns Hopkins University Press. Reprinted with permission of The Johns Hopkins University Press.

In particular, I argue the following. First, the degree of uncertainty in democratic transitions varies considerably. This in turn affects the strategies of transition and their payoffs. Second, mass mobilization can contribute to both the founding and the consolidation of democracy. Third, under certain conditions the democratic project is furthered by transitions that involve both nationalist protest and changes in state boundaries. Fourth, while rapid progress in democratic consolidation improves the prospects for democratic survival in the future, it does not follow that unconsolidated democracies are necessarily less sustainable. Indeed, compromising democracy (and the state) may *contribute* to democratic survival. Finally, while comparisons among new democracies can identify the optimal *conditions* for democratization, they may have less to say about optimal *strategies* for democratization.

Transitions to Democracy: Assumptions and Arguments

The analysis of recent democratization has been premised on some core assumptions about transitions from dictatorship to democracy—with the transitional period understood as beginning with an evident weakening of authoritarian rule and ending with the first competitive elections. These assumptions include the following: (1) that immediate influences are more important than historical considerations in shaping transitional dynamics; (2) that transitions are inherently quite uncertain; (3) that the central dynamic in a transition is bargaining between authoritarian leaders and leaders of the democratic opposition, with outcomes a function of their relative power; and (4) that the key issues on the table during the transition are breaking with authoritarian rule, building democratic institutions, and eliciting the cooperation of authoritarians.[1]

These assumptions, coupled with comparative studies of Latin America and southern Europe, have produced several generalizations about what constitutes the ideal approach to transition. First, as Dankwart Rustow argued more than thirty years ago, successful democratization seems to require at the very least a prior settlement of the national and state questions.[2] Second, bargaining about the rules of the transition and the new political order should be limited to a small group of authoritarian elites and representatives of the democratic opposition. Finally, given the uncertainty of transitions, it is useful to forge compromises that promote political stability during the construction of a democratic order. In practice, this means pacting; reducing the range of issues on the bargaining table (for example, avoiding reforms of the state and, if possible, major and inherently destabilizing economic reforms); demobilizing publics (which also limits the issues on the table, while depriving the authoritarians of a rationale for sabotaging democratization); forming interim governments with leaders agreeable to both sides; giving the military some room for political maneuver in the constitution; and holding a competitive election that produces a government broadly representative of both authoritarians and democrats.[3]

Mass Mobilization

The postcommunist experience seems to challenge many of these assumptions about transitional strategies. Let us begin by addressing the role of mass publics in the transition. It is widely agreed among specialists and confirmed by the rankings over time by Freedom House that the most successful transitions to democracy in the postcommunist region have been in the Czech Republic, Estonia, Hungary, Latvia, Lithuania, Poland, and Slovenia. The transition to democracy in every one of these cases, except Hungary, began with mass protests.[4] Moreover, if we restrict our focus to those countries that show significant improvement in their democratic performance over time, or Bulgaria and Romania, we see the same pattern: mass mobilization at the beginning of the transition.

Why was mass mobilization so often helpful to the democratic transition in the postcommunist context? The answer is that political protests performed a number of valuable functions. They signaled the breakdown of the authoritarian order; created a widespread sense that there were alternatives to that order; pushed authoritarian leaders (and sometimes even leaders of the opposition, as with Walesa in Poland) to the bargaining table; created (and sometimes restored) a large opposition united by its rejection of the incumbent regime; and gave opposition leaders a resource advantage when bargaining with authoritarian elites. Finally, mass mobilization created a mandate for radical change that subsequently translated into a large victory for the democratic forces in the first competitive elections and, following that, led to the introduction of far-reaching economic and political reforms.

Uncertainty

If we accept that mass mobilization during the transition can further the democratic project, then we necessarily confront additional challenges to the received wisdom about recent democratization. First, it can be argued that in many cases such mobilization in the postcommunist region reduced the uncertainty of the transition—by providing a clear reading of mass sentiments, by strengthening the bargaining power of opposition leaders, and by forcing the communists to give up their defense of the old order, either stepping aside quickly (as in Czechoslovakia) or, when thinking prospectively, joining the movement for democracy (as in Poland, Slovenia, and the Baltic states).[5] At the same time, mass mobilization promised—and delivered—a popular mandate for democracy in the first competitive elections.

Most of the transitions to democracy in the postcommunist world were, of course, highly uncertain. This is evidenced by the fact that the first competitive election in most of the countries in the region led to a communist victory. Indeed, the larger the victory, the more likely that authoritarian rule continued.

Moreover, even ten years after the transition began, only one-third of the post-communist regimes were ranked fully free. Although this is the highest number since state socialism fell, it is a percentage much lower than what one finds at a comparable point in the Latin American and southern European transitions. When combined with the earlier observations, these patterns suggest that the uncertainty surrounding postcommunist political trajectories varied significantly.[6] In some cases, a democratic outcome was relatively predictable; in most others, the political options after communism were far more open-ended.

Strategic Implications of Uncertainty

The existence of a more certain political environment in some countries calls into question both the necessity and the logic, outlined earlier, of safeguarding the new democracy by forging compromises between authoritarians and democrats. It is precisely the absence of pressure to do so in the Polish, the Czech, and the other highly successful transitions that explains another contrast between the "East" and the "South." It is true that many of the most successful transitions in the postcommunist area included pacting (though rarely as elaborate as the Spanish experience) and that some also evidenced for a brief time broadly representative interim governments.[7] It is also true, however, that the transitions in the postcommunist region that combined pacting with demobilized publics—or what has been asserted to be the preferred approach in the South—were precisely the transitions that were most likely to continue authoritarian rule in the postcommunist region.[8] Moreover, the other compromises that were deemed so beneficial for the southern European and Latin American transitions were rejected by opposition leaders in Poland, Hungary, Slovenia, and the like. Instead, they were strongly positioned to favor an immediate and sharp break with the authoritarian past. Thus, in every highly successful case of democratization in the region, the military was excluded from political influence from the start; the first elections involved a radical break with the political leadership of the past; and major changes in the economy were introduced quickly. Just as important was the commitment in each of these cases to reforming the state, including in most of them its very boundaries. For the Czech Republic, Hungary, Poland, Slovenia, and the Baltic states, then, the agenda of transition was unusually ambitious.

Postcommunist transition dynamics therefore ask us to amend the familiar formulation drawn from the South. It was precisely because mass mobilization was so threatening to authoritarians that leaders of the opposition in some of these countries were free to carry out radical political and economic reforms. Put differently: because of popular mobilization or, in the Hungarian case, reform communism and collaboration between democrats and authoritarians, opposition leaders in what became the most sustainable and full-scale democracies in the East could proceed quickly in breaking with authoritarian rule and building democratic (and, for that matter, capitalist) institutions without worrying as much as their counterparts elsewhere about appeasing authoritarian interests.

This, in turn, altered the strategies of transition and their payoffs. While bridging between the old and the new order constituted by all accounts the most successful approach to democratization in Latin America and southern Europe, the most successful strategy in the postcommunist region was the opposite—severing ties.

The Role of the Military

Also contributing to these interregional contrasts in the optimal strategies of transition was the very different role of the military in Latin America and southern Europe, on the one hand, and in the communist area, on the other hand. Specialists in the South have argued with essentially one voice that the biggest threat to democracy today, as in the past, is the military. One has only to recall, for example, the long history of military interventions in Latin American politics, most of which terminated democracy (though some of them oversaw a return to democratic governance, as also occurred in unusually circuitous fashion, in the Portuguese transition). There is, in addition, the attempted military coup d'état in Spain in 1982. Indeed, precisely because of its long importance in politics, the military has been awarded remarkable powers in many Latin American constitutions, their democratic claims notwithstanding.[9] When combined, these examples carry an obvious message: the military in these contexts can make or break regimes. It is precisely this capacity that contributed to the uncertainty of the transitions in the South and that necessitated compromises with authoritarian forces.

In much of the postcommunist world, by contrast, there is a long tradition of civilian control over the military—a tradition that goes far back in Russian history and that, following the Bolshevik Revolution and the demilitarization after the Civil War, was maintained at home and then after World War II was projected outward to the members of the Soviet bloc.[10] Civil-military relations, in short, constituted one area where the authoritarian past proved to be beneficial, rather than a burden, for democratization after state socialism.[11]

With the military less threatening in the postcommunist context and with mass publics in some cases mobilized in support of democracy, authoritarian elites in the postcommunist region were indeed under siege. This was particularly the case in East-Central Europe, where domestic control over the military (and the secret police)—except in Yugoslavia, Romania, and Albania—had been ceded to the Soviet Union after 1968. All this left the opposition in what came to be the most successful democracies in the region with unusual freedom of maneuver—a freedom enhanced by public support in the streets. As a result, both the effects of mass mobilization *and* the most successful strategies of transition were different in the postcommunist context from what they had been in Latin America and southern Europe.

Nationalist Mobilization

The analysis thus far has sidestepped an issue of considerable importance in the transitions from state socialism: the distinction between protests against the regime and protests against the state. Here, the postcommunist region exhibits another surprising pattern. While popular protest in both the Czech lands and Poland targeted the regime, the Baltic and Slovene demonstrations are better understood as both liberal and nationalist. In the latter cases, then, nationalism supported democratic governance, even when nationalist concerns grew out of and were in part responsible for the disintegration of a state.

There also seems to be another positive linkage between nationalist mobilization and successful, sustained democratization. The republics that made up the Soviet Union, Yugoslavia, and Czechoslovakia varied considerably from each other with respect to whether publics protested, whether the opposition was strong and united, and whether publics, the opposition, and, indeed, even the communists were committed to democratization. With the breakup of these three ethnofederal states along republican lines, those republics with the best conditions for democratic governance were liberated from a political and economic context that made such an outcome unlikely, if not impossible. Thus, not just Slovenia and the Baltic republics, but also Macedonia, Moldova, Russia, and Ukraine were better positioned to pursue a democratic course following state disintegration.[12]

How can we reconcile these observations with the familiar argument that nationalist mobilization poses a threat to democracy on the grounds that the logics of state building and democratization are contradictory? This argument, moreover, has empirical support in the postcommunist world, given the deleterious effects of nationalism on political developments after state socialism in Bosnia, Croatia, Georgia, Serbia and Montenegro (and Kosovo), and Slovakia. In each of these cases the nationalist movement excluded minorities residing within the republic; transformed some communists into nationalists, who then used nationalism to maintain authoritarian control; and constructed illiberal successor regimes while deconstructing successor states.[13] What explains these divergent consequences of nationalism?

When nationalism enters the discussion, parsimonious arguments often give way to thick explanations. In this instance, however, there seems to be a relatively simple distinction: *when* nationalist demonstrations began in the republics. Late nationalist mobilization—or nationalist demonstrations that first appeared when the communist regime and state were disintegrating—is associated in virtually every instance with a rapid transition to democracy and progress since that time in building a stable—or at least increasingly stable—democratic order. This describes, in particular, not just the cases of Estonia, Latvia, Lithuania, and Slovenia, but also the far more flawed, but nonetheless durable democracies of Moldova, Russia, and Ukraine.

By contrast, nationalist demonstrations that first occurred before the regime and state began to unravel are associated with very different political pathways after state socialism—either democratic breakdown or a delayed transition to democracy. There were five republics and one autonomous province that experienced such demonstrations by their titular nation during the 1970s or at the beginning of the 1980s: Armenia, Croatia, Georgia, Kosovo, Slovakia, and, to a more limited extent, Serbia.[14] In every one of these cases the subsequent transition to democracy was undermined, as was the successor state in most cases.

Why is timing so important? The key seems to be differences in regime context. In the "early" cases, nationalist mobilization arose in response to two conditions: a strong sense of identity on the part of members and especially the self-appointed leaders of the republic's titular nation (reflecting earlier developments, such as the experience of statehood prior to communist party rule) coupled with republican political dynamics that featured domination by the titular nation along with significant autonomy from the center. Once demonstrations began, three developments followed: minorities within these republics (except homogeneous Armenia) defended themselves from titular domination by building countermovements while allying with the center; the center, fearing that nationalist protests would spread and thereby challenge both the regime and the state, suppressed the titular national protesters, purged the republican party, and empowered minorities as a counterweight to the titular nation; and the republican party fissured in the face of irreconcilable demands from local nationalists versus central communists.

As a result, by the time state socialism began to dissolve, the stage was already set for an unusually problematic transition to both democratic rule and independent statehood. Two insurmountable divides were in place. The first was between nationalists, who dominated the political scene, and liberals, who had been demobilized. The second was between leaders of the majority nation and leaders of minority communities. The national identities of these groups were well defined and exclusivist, and their competing identities were joined with competing interests, political alliances, and preferences for the future. Moreover, the communist leaders of these republics, facing the loss of both their institutional and their ideological bases for ruling, did not have the option their Slovenian counterparts had, of defecting to an opposition that embraced both independent statehood and liberal democracy. Instead, they could either become nationalists or, if adopting a liberal position, face political marginalization.

By contrast, when nationalist mobilization began only later, in response to the weakening of the regime and the state, all these conditions were absent—or at least less well defined. This meant that the majority and the minorities were free to coalesce around the issues of republican sovereignty and liberal democracy. Thus, in these contexts a liberal agenda combined with a nationalist agenda; and not only opposition forces but even many communists embraced that agenda.

We can now conclude our discussion of transitions in the South versus the East. The experiences of the latter region suggest the following, all running counter to the received wisdom about Latin America and southern Europe. First, historical factors are critical in shaping the resources and especially the preferences of elites during the transition, as well as, more generally, transition trajectories. Second, one proximate and positive influence, lying outside the high politics of the transition, is mass mobilization. Third, transitions seem to vary in their degree of uncertainty, and this affects what constitutes the most successful path. In the postcommunist world, where some transitions were less uncertain, the most successful approach was one that moved quickly on both political and economic fronts. Fourth, democratization can be successful when it is combined with nationalist mobilization and the founding of a new state. This is particularly so when such mobilization first begins with the weakening of the state and the regime. . . .

Conclusions

Research on democratization, particularly the founding and performance of new democracies, is largely a literature about the choices political leaders have made and the consequences of those choices. It is also largely a literature based on the return to democracy in Latin America and southern Europe. The purpose of this article has been both to question and to complicate the focus on elites and the generalizations that have been made about transitions to democracy, democratic consolidation, and democratic sustainability. I have done so by adding an additional region to the empirical equation—the twenty-seven countries that make up the Eurasian postcommunist region.

Several conclusions emerged. First, transitions to democracy seem to vary considerably with respect to the uncertainty surrounding the process. This variance in turn affects the strategies of transition and their payoffs. In the postcommunist region it was widely assumed that the uncertainty surrounding these transitions was unusually high, given, for example, the absence in most cases of a democratic past together, the extraordinary economic and political penetration of state socialism, and the seeming tensions among democratization, state building, the construction of a capitalist economy, and the radically changed relationship of the state to the international system. It turns out, however, that for a number of countries in the region the transition to democracy was in fact not so uncertain, for two reasons. First, the military was eliminated from the transition. Second, there was present a powerful opposition that gained strength from popular mobilization against the regime (often also against the state) (as with the Baltic, Slovenian, Czech, and Polish cases) and/or reform communists who collaborated with an opposition committed to democracy (as with the Baltic countries, Slovenia, Poland, and Hungary).

Because uncertainty was lower, moreover, the transition in all of these cases produced a sharp break with the state socialist past—for example, through founding elections that gave the opposition a large mandate, rapid progress in constructing democratic institutions, quick introduction of far-reaching economic reforms, and, in most of the cases, the construction of a new state.

By contrast, transition was far more uncertain where the military was engaged in the transition, where mass mobilization focused on leaving the state but not building democracy, and/or where the communists were able to command considerable support in the first election. As a result, the break with the authoritarian past was less definitive—in terms of both political leadership and public policy.

These contrasts have several implications. One is that, while the most successful transitions in the South involved bridging, the most successful transitions in the East involved breakage. Indeed, it is precisely the bridging approach in the East that produced the most fragile democracies. The other is that the contrast between bridging and breakage—and the costs and benefits of each approach—in large measure reflected differences in uncertainty.

Another conclusion is that mass mobilization can play a very positive role in the transition, as it did, for example, in the Baltic, Polish, Czech, and Slovenian cases and, most recently, in Serbia and Montenegro. This is largely because mass mobilization can reduce uncertainty, thereby influencing the preferences of the communists, as well as the division of power between them and the opposition.

Nationalist mobilization and the disintegration of the state can also influence the democratic project. Whether this occurs seems to reflect a key distinction: whether such protests first arose when the regime and state were unraveling or whether the demonstrations at that time were the culmination of a longer history of such protests. In the first case, which describes Slovenia, the Baltic countries, Russia, Ukraine, and Moldova, the transition produced sustainable democratic orders, albeit of varying quality. By contrast, in every transition where nationalist protest had a longer lineage, both the old and the new state, as well as the democratic project, experienced continuing contestation.

Notes

1. Guillermo O'Donnell, Philippe C. Schmitter, and Laurence Whitehead, *Transitions from Authoritarian Rule*, vols. 1–4 (Baltimore: Johns Hopkins University Press, 1986); Terry Lynn Karl, "Dilemmas of Democratization in Latin America," *Comparative Politics* 23 (Spring 1990); Guiseppe Di Palma, *To Craft Democracy* (Berkeley: University of California Press, 1990).
2. Dankwart Rustow, "Transitions to Democracy: Toward a Dynamic Model," *Comparative Politics* 2 (April 1970).
3. O'Donnell, Schmitter, and Whitehead; Richard Gunther, "Spain: The Very Model of a Modern Elite Settlement," in John Higley and Richard Gunther, eds., *Elites and Democratic Consolidation in Latin America and Southern Europe* (Baltimore: Johns Hopkins University Press, 1992); Robert M. Fishman, "Rethinking State and Regime: Southern Europe's Transition to Democracy," *World Politics* 42 (April 1990); Stephen Haggard and Robert Kaufman, *The Political Economy of Democratic Transitions* (Princeton: Princeton University Press, 1995); Jose Maria Maravall, "Politics and Policy: Economic Reforms in Southern Europe," in Luiz Carlos Bresser Pereira, Jose Maria Maravall, and Adam Przeworski, eds., *Economic Reforms in New Democracies: A Social Democratic Approach* (Cambridge: Cambridge University Press, 1993). Moderate policies, however, do not imply the absence of political conflict. See Nancy Bermeo, "Myths of Moderation," *Comparative Politics* 29 (April 1997).

4. In Hungary mass mobilization was understood to be politically risky (and turned out ultimately to be unnecessary), given the brutal suppression of the Hungarian Revolution in 1956, on the one hand, and the willingness of the reform communists, even before the roundtable, to jump on the democratic bandwagon, on the other hand. See Patrick H. O'Neil, "Revolution from Within: Institutional Analysis, Transitions from Authoritarianism, and the Case of Hungary," *World Politics* 48 (July 1996).

5. See Anna M. Grzymala-Busse, *Redeeming the Communist Past: The Regeneration of Communist Parties in East-Central Europe* (Cambridge: Cambridge University Press, 2002).

6. Because Poland was the first country in the region to break with communist party rule, its transition was somewhat more uncertain. Given the character of the Soviet bloc, however, developments in Poland during the first half of 1989 lowered the risks of transition for other members of the bloc.

7. Jon Elster, ed., *The Roundtable Talks and the Breakdown of Communism* (Chicago: University of Chicago Press, 1996).

8. Pauline Jones Luong, *Institutional Change and Political Continuity in Post-Soviet Central Asia: Power, Perceptions and Pacts* (Cambridge: Cambridge University Press, 2002).

9. Brian Loveman, "Protected Democracies and Military Guardianship: Political Transitions in Latin America, 1978–1993," *Journal of Inter-American Studies and World Affairs* 36 (Summer 1994).

10. The key phrase is "members of the Soviet bloc." For those communist regimes outside the bloc or mavericks within the bloc (Albania, Romania, and Yugoslavia), party control over the military was compromised. It was precisely in these cases that the exit from state socialism was violent. Variations in civil-military relations also account in part for the violent disintegration of the Yugoslav state, in contrast to the peaceful dissolution of both the Soviet Union and Czechoslovakia.

11. See Bela Greskovits, "Rival Views of Postcommunist Market Society: The Path Dependence of Transitology," in Michel Dobry, ed., *Democratic and Capitalist Transitions in Eastern Europe: Lessons for the Social Sciences* (Dordrecht: Kluwer Academic Publishers, 2000).

12. For a parallel situation, see Michael Bernhard, "Democratization in Germany: A Reappraisal," *Comparative Politics* 33, no. 4 (2001).

13. See Zsuzsa Czergo, "Language and Democracy: A Comparative Study of Contestations over Language Use in Romania and Slovakia" (Ph.D. diss., George Washington University, 2000); Georgi Derluguian, "The Tale of Two Resorts: Abkhazia and Adjaria before and since the Soviet Collapse," in Beverly Crawford and Ronnie D. Lipschutz, eds., *The "Myth" of Ethnic Conflict: Politics, Economics and Cultural Violence*, Research Monograph, no. 98. (Berkeley: University of California International and Area Studies, 1998); Ronald Suny, *The Making of the Georgian Nation*, 2d ed. (Bloomington: Indiana University Press, 1994); Valerie Bunce and Stephen Watts, "Managing Diversity and Sustaining Democracy: Ethnofederal versus Unitary States in the Postsocialist World" (Paper presented at the workshop on Power-Sharing and Peace-Making, San Diego, December 10–11, 2001).

14. See . . . Besnik Pula, "Contested Sovereignty and State Disintegration: The Rise of the Albanian Secessionist Movement in Kosovo" (Master's Thesis, Georgetown University, 2001). On the Serbian case, see Valere P. Gagnon, "Liberalism and Minorities: Serbs as Agents and Victims of Liberal Conceptions of Space" (Paper presented at the workshop on Citizenship in Multicultural States: Comparing the Former Yugoslavia and Israel, Austrian Institute of International Affairs, Vienna, April 20–21, 2001).

4.6

Illusions About Consolidation

Guillermo O'Donnell

Guillermo O'Donnell claims that the transition paradigm may create illusions about the character of democracy and many self-proclaimed democracies that have replaced authoritarian regimes. Basing his argument on an analysis of Latin American and other newly democratic regimes, he claims that although regimes may exhibit the formal characteristics of a democracy or polyarchy (see Dahl [4.2] and Schmitter and Karl [4.3]), this appearance can be deceptive. O'Donnell claims that informal practices, what he terms particularism, often undermine democratic institutions. Examples of particularism include nepotism, where public officials give family members jobs and other favors, and outright corruption, where public officials accept bribes in exchange for illegal actions. (Beyond a certain point, as Levitsky and Way [2.4] argue, such regimes can more accurately be described as authoritarian.)

O'Donnell's article focuses on young democracies. How applicable is it to long-established democracies?

Democracies used to be few in number, and most were located in the northwestern quarter of the world. Over the last two decades, however, many countries have rid themselves of authoritarian regimes. There are many variations among these countries. Some of them have reverted to new brands of authoritarianism (even if from time to time they hold elections), while others have clearly embraced democracy. Still others seem to inhabit a gray area; they bear a family resemblance to the old established democracies, but either lack or only precariously possess some of their key attributes. The bulk of the contemporary scholarly literature tells us that these "incomplete" democracies are failing to become consolidated, or institutionalized.

This poses two tasks. One is to establish a cutoff point that separates all democracies from all nondemocracies. This point's location depends on the questions we ask, and so is always arbitrary. Many different definitions of democracy have been offered.[1] The one that I find particularly useful is Robert Dahl's

Guillermo O'Donnell, "Illusions About Consolidation," *Journal of Democracy* 7, no. 2 (April 1996): 34–51. © National Endowment for Democracy and The Johns Hopkins University Press. Reprinted with permission of The Johns Hopkins University Press.

concept of "polyarchy." Once a reasonably well delimited set of democracies is obtained, the second task is to examine the criteria that a given stream of the literature uses for comparing cases within this set. If the criteria are found wanting, the next step is to propose alternative concepts for these comparisons. This is what I attempt in this essay, albeit in preliminary and schematic fashion.

Contemporary Latin America is my empirical referent, although my discussion probably also applies to various newly democratized countries in other parts of the world. The main argument is that, contrary to what most current scholarship holds, the problem with many new polyarchies is not that they lack institutionalization. Rather, the way in which political scientists usually conceptualize some institutions prevents us from recognizing that these polyarchies actually have two extremely important institutions. One is highly formalized, but intermittent: elections. The other is informal, permanent, and pervasive: particularism (or clientelism, broadly defined). An important fact is that, in contrast to previous periods of authoritarian rule, particularism now exists in uneasy tension with the formal rules and institutions of what I call the "full institutional package" of polyarchy. These arguments open up a series of issues that in future publications I will analyze with the detail and nuance they deserve. My purpose at present is to furnish some elements of what I believe are needed revisions in the conceptual and comparative agenda for the study of all existing polyarchies, especially those that are *informally institutionalized.*[2]

Polyarchy, as defined by Dahl, has seven attributes: 1) elected officials; 2) free and fair elections; 3) inclusive suffrage; 4) the right to run for office; 5) freedom of expression; 6) alternative information; and 7) associational autonomy.[3] Attributes 1 to 4 tell us that a basic aspect of polyarchy is that elections are inclusive, fair, and competitive. Attributes 5 to 7 refer to political and social freedoms that are minimally necessary not only during but also between elections as a condition for elections to be fair and competitive. According to these criteria, some countries of Latin America currently are not polyarchies: the Dominican Republic, Haiti, and Mexico have recently held elections, but these were marred by serious irregularities before, during, and after the voting.

Other attributes need to be added to Dahl's list. One is that elected (and some appointed) officials should not be arbitrarily terminated before the end of their constitutionally mandated terms (Peru's Alberto Fujimori and Russia's Boris Yeltsin may have been elected in fair elections, but they abolished polyarchy when they forcefully closed their countries' congresses and fired their supreme courts). A second addition is that the elected authorities should not be subject to severe constraints, vetoes, or exclusion from certain policy domains by other, nonelected actors, especially the armed forces.[4] In this sense, Guatemala and Paraguay, as well as probably El Salvador and Honduras, do not qualify as polyarchies.[5] Chile is an odd case, where restrictions of this sort are part of a constitution inherited from the authoritarian regime. But Chile clearly meets Dahl's seven criteria of polyarchy. Peru is another doubtful case, since the 1995 presidential elections were not untarnished, and the armed forces retain tutelary powers over various policy areas.

Third, there should be an uncontested national territory that clearly defines the voting population.[6] Finally, an appropriate definition of polyarchy should also include an intertemporal dimension: the generalized expectation that a fair electoral process and its surrounding freedoms will continue into an indefinite future.

These criteria leave us with the three polyarchies—Colombia, Costa Rica, and Venezuela—whose origins date from before the wave of democratization that began in the mid-1970s, and with nine others that resulted from this wave: Argentina, Bolivia, Brazil, Ecuador, Nicaragua, Panama, Uruguay and, with the caveats noted, Chile and Peru. Only in the oldest Latin American polyarchy (Costa Rica) and in two cases of redemocratization (Chile and Uruguay) do the executive branch, congress, parties, and the judiciary function in a manner that is reasonably close to their formal institutional rules, making them effective institutional knots in the flow of political power and policy. Colombia and Venezuela used to function like this, but do so no longer. These two countries, jointly with Argentina, Bolivia, Brazil, Ecuador, Nicaragua, Panama, and Peru— a set that includes a large majority of the Latin American population and GNP— function in ways that current democratic theory has ill prepared us to understand.

We must go back to the definition of polyarchy. This definition, precise in regard to elections (attributes 1 to 4) and rather generic about contextual freedoms (attributes 5 to 7), is mute with respect to institutional features such as parliamentarism or presidentialism, centralism or federalism, majoritarianism or consensualism, and the presence or absence of a written constitution and judicial review. Also, the definition of polyarchy is silent about important but elusive themes such as if, how, and to what degree governments are responsive or accountable to citizens between elections, and the degree to which the rule of law extends over the country's geographic and social terrain.[7] These silences are appropriate: the definition of polyarchy, let us recall, establishes a crucial cutoff point—one that separates cases where there exist inclusive, fair, and competitive elections and basic accompanying freedoms from all others, including not only unabashed authoritarian regimes but also countries that hold elections but lack some of the characteristics that jointly define polyarchy.

Among polyarchies, however, there are many variations. These differences are empirical, but they can also be normatively evaluated, and their likely effect on the survival prospects of each polyarchy may eventually be assessed. These are important issues that merit some conceptual clarification.

By definition, all the Latin American cases that I have labeled polyarchies·are such because of a simple but crucial fact: elections are institutionalized. By an institution I mean a regularized pattern of interaction that is known, practiced, and accepted (if not necessarily approved) by actors who expect to continue interacting under the rules sanctioned and backed by that pattern.[8] Institutions are typically taken for granted, in their existence and continuity, by the actors who interact with and through them. Institutions are "there," usually unquestioned regulators of expectations and behavior. Sometimes, institutions become complex organizations: they are supposed to operate under highly formalized and explicit rules, and materialize in buildings, rituals, and officials. These are the institutions on which both "prebehavioral" and most of contemporary neo-institutionalist political science focus. An unusual characteristic of elections *qua* institutions is that they are highly formalized by detailed and explicit rules, but function intermittently and do not always have a permanent organizational embodiment.

In all polyarchies, old and new, elections are institutionalized, both in themselves and in the reasonable[9] effectiveness of the surrounding conditions of freedom of expression, access to alternative information, and associational autonomy. Leaders and voters take for granted that in the future inclusive, fair, and competitive elections will take place as legally scheduled, voters will be properly registered and free from physical coercion, and their votes will be counted fairly. It is also taken for granted that the winners will take office, and will not have their terms arbitrarily terminated. Furthermore, for this electoral process to exist, freedom of opinion and of association (including the freedom to form political parties) and an uncensored media must also exist. Countries where elections do not have these characteristics do not qualify as polyarchies.[10]

Most students of democratization agree that many of the new polyarchies are at best poorly institutionalized. Few seem to have institutionalized anything but elections, at least in terms of what one would expect from looking at older polyarchies. But appearances can be misleading, since other institutions may exist, even though they may not be the ones that most of us would prefer or easily recognize.

Theories of "Consolidation"

When elections and their surrounding freedoms are institutionalized, it might be said that polyarchy (or political democracy) is "consolidated," that is, likely to endure. This, jointly with the proviso of absence of veto powers over elected authorities, is the influential definition of "democratic consolidation" offered by Juan J. Linz, who calls it a state of affairs "in which none of the major political actors, parties, or organized interests, forces, or institutions consider that there is any alternative to democratic processes to gain power, and . . . no political institution or group has a claim to veto the action of democratically elected decision makers. . . . To put it simply, democracy must be seen as the 'only game in town.'"[11] This minimalist definition has important advantages. Still, I see little analytical gain in attaching the term "consolidated" to something that will probably though not certainly endure—"democracy" and "consolidation" are terms too polysemic to make a good pair.

Other authors offer more expanded definitions of democratic consolidation, many of them centered on the achievement of a high degree of "institutionalization."[12] Usually these definitions do not see elections as an institution.[13] They focus on complex organizations, basically the executive, parties, congress, and sometimes the judiciary. Many valuable studies have been conducted from this point of view. By the very logic of their assessment of many new polyarchies as noninstitutionalized, however, these studies presuppose, as their comparative yardstick, a generic and somewhat idealized view of the old polyarchies. The meaning of such a yardstick perplexes me: often it is unclear whether it is something like an average of characteristics observed within the set of old polyarchies, or an ideal type generated from some of these characteristics, or a generalization to the whole set of the characteristics of some of its members, or a normative statement of preferred traits. Furthermore, this mode of reasoning carries a strong teleological flavor. Cases that have not "arrived" at full institutionalization, or that do not seem to be moving in this direction, are seen as stunted, frozen, protractedly unconsolidated, and the like. Such a view presupposes that there are, or should be, factors working in favor of increased consolidation or institutionalization, but that countervailing "obstacles" stymie a process of change that otherwise would operate unfettered.[14] That some of these polyarchies have been in a state of "protracted unconsolidation"[15] for some 20 years suggests that there is something extremely odd about this kind of thinking. . . .

One way or the other polyarchies that are seen as unconsolidated, noninstitutionalized, or poorly institutionalized are defined negatively, for what they lack: the type and degree of institutionalization presumably achieved by old polyarchies. Yet negative definitions shift attention away from building typologies of polyarchies on the basis of the specific, positively described traits of each type.[16] Such typologies are needed, among other purposes, for assessing each type's likelihood of endurance, for exploring its patterns of change, and for clarifying the various dimensions on which issues of quality and performance of polyarchy may be discussed and researched.

There is no theory that would tell us why and how the new polyarchies that have institutionalized elections will "complete" their institutional set, or otherwise become "consolidated." All we can say at present is that, as long as elections are institutionalized, polyarchies are likely to endure. We can add the hypothesis that this likelihood is greater for polyarchies that are formally institutionalized. But this proposition is not terribly interesting unless we take into account other factors that most likely have strong independent effects on the survival chances of polyarchies.[17] Consequently, calling some polyarchies "consolidated" or "highly institutionalized" may be no more than saying that they are institutionalized in ways that one expects and of which one approves. Without a theory of how and why this may happen, it is at best premature to expect that newer polyarchies will or should become "consolidated" or "highly institutionalized." In any event, such a theory can only be elaborated on the basis of a positive description of the main traits of the pertinent cases.

The Importance of Informal Rules

Polyarchy is the happy result of centuries-long processes, mostly in countries in the global Northwest. In spite of many variations among these countries, polyarchy is embodied in an institutional package: a set of rules and institutions (many of them complex organizations) that is explicitly formalized in constitutions and auxiliary legislation. Rules are supposed to guide how individuals in institutions, and individuals interacting with institutions, behave. The extent to which behavior and expectations hew to or deviate from formal rules is difficult to gauge empirically. But when the fit is reasonably close, formal rules simplify our task; they are good predictors of behavior and expectations. In this case, one may conclude that all or most of the formal rules and institutions of polyarchy are fully, or close to fully, institutionalized.[18] When the fit is loose or practically nonexistent, we are confronted with the double task of describing actual behavior and discovering the (usually informal) rules that behavior and expectations do follow. Actors are as rational in these settings as in highly formalized ones, but the contours of their rationality cannot be traced without knowing the actual rules, and the common knowledge of these rules, that they follow. One may define this situation negatively, emphasizing the lack of fit between formal rules and observed behavior. As anthropologists have long known, however, this is no substitute for studying the actual rules that are being followed; nor does it authorize the assumption that somehow there is a tendency toward increasing compliance with formal rules. This is especially true when informal rules are widely shared and deeply rooted; in this case, it may be said that these rules (rather than the formal ones) are highly institutionalized.[19]

To some extent this also happens in the old polyarchies. The various laments, from all parts of the ideological spectrum, about the decay of democracy in these countries are largely a consequence of the visible and apparently increasing gap between formal rules and the behavior of all sorts of political actors. But the gap is even larger in many new polyarchies, where the formal rules about how political institutions are supposed to work are often poor guides to what actually happens.

Many new polyarchies do not lack institutionalization, but a fixation on highly formalized and complex organizations prevents us from seeing an extremely influential, informal, and sometimes concealed institution: clientelism and, more generally, particularism. For brevity's sake, I will put details and nuances aside[20] and use these terms to refer broadly to various sorts of nonuniversalistic relationships, ranging from hierarchical particularistic exchanges, patronage, nepotism, and favors to actions that, under the formal rules of the institutional package of polyarchy, would be considered corrupt.[21]

Particularism—like its counterparts, neopatrimonial[22] and delegative conceptions and practices of rule—is antagonistic to one of the main aspects of the full institutional package of polyarchy: the behavioral, legal, and normative distinction between a public and a private sphere. This distinction is an important aspect of the formal institutionalization of polyarchy. Individuals performing roles in political and state institutions are supposed to be guided not by particularistic motives but by universalistic orientations to some version of the public good. The boundaries between the public and the private are often blurred in the old polyarchies, but the very notion of the boundary is broadly accepted and, often, vigorously asserted when it seems breached by public officials acting from particularistic motives. Where particularism is pervasive, this notion is weaker, less widely held, and seldom enforced.

But polyarchy matters, even in the institutional spheres that, against their formal rules, are dominated by particularism. In congress, the judiciary, and some actions of the executive, rituals and discourses are performed as if the formal rules were the main guides of behavior. The consequences are twofold. On one side, by paying tribute to the formal rules, these rituals and discourses encourage demands that these rules be truly followed and that public-oriented governmental behavior prevail. On the other side, the blatant hypocrisy of many of these rituals and discourses breeds cynicism about the institutions of polyarchy, their incumbents, and "politicians" in general. As long as this second consequence is highly visible, particularism is taken for granted, and practiced as the main way of gaining and wielding political power. In such polyarchies, particularism is an important part of the regime.[23] Polyarchies are regimes, but not all polyarchies are the same kind of regime.

Here we see the ambiguity of the assertion made by Juan J. Linz, Adam Przeworski,[24] and others who argue that consolidation occurs when democracy becomes "the only game in town." It is clear that these authors are referring to the formal rules of polyarchy. More generally, even though they may not refer to "institutionalization," authors who limit themselves to the term "consolidation" also assert, more or less implicitly, the same close fit between formal rules and actual behavior.[25] For example, Przeworski argues that democratic consolidation occurs "when no one can imagine acting outside the democratic institutions." But this does not preclude the possibility that the games played "inside" the democratic institutions are different from the ones dictated by their formal rules. Przeworski also states: "To put it somewhat more technically, democracy is consolidated when compliance—acting within the institutional framework—constitutes the equilibrium of the decentralized strategies of all the relevant forces."[26] Clearly, Przeworski is assuming that there is only one equilibrium, the one generated by a close fit between formal rules and behavior. Yet however inferior they may be in terms of performances and outcomes that we value, the situations that I am describing may constitute an equilibrium, too.[27]

A Theoretical Limbo

If the main criterion for democratic consolidation or institutionalization is more or less explicitly a reasonably close fit between formal rules and actual behavior, then what of countries such as Italy, Japan, and India? These are long-enduring polyarchies where, by all indications, various forms of particularism are rampant. Yet these cases do not appear problematic in the literature I am discussing. That they are listed as "consolidated" (or, at least, not listed as "unconsolidated") suggests the strength—and the inconsistency—of this view. It attaches the label "consolidated" to cases that clearly do not fit its arguments but that have endured for a significantly longer period than the new polyarchies have so far. This is a typical paradigmatic anomaly. It deals with these cases by relegating them to a theoretical limbo,[28] as if, because they are somehow considered to be "consolidated," the big gaps between their formal rules and behavior were irrelevant. This is a pity, because variations that are theoretically and empirically important for the study of the whole set of existing polyarchies are thereby obscured.

Another confusing issue is raised by the requirement of "legitimacy" that some definitions of consolidation add. Who must accept formal democratic rules, and how deep must this acceptance run? Here, the literature oscillates between holding that only certain leaders need adhere to democratic principles and arguing that most of the country's people should be democrats, and between requiring normative acceptance of these principles and resting content with a mere perception that there is no feasible alternative to democracy. The scope of this adherence is also problematic: Is it enough that it refers to the formal institutions of the regime, or should it extend to other areas, such as a broadly shared democratic political culture?

Given these conceptual quandaries, it is not surprising that it is impossible clearly to specify when a democracy has become "consolidated." To illustrate this point, consider the "tests" of democratic consolidation that Gunther, Diamandouros, and Puhle propose. These tests supposedly help them to differentiate the consolidated Southern European cases from the unconsolidated Latin American, as well as East European and Asian, ones. The indicators that "may constitute evidence that a regime is consolidated" are: 1) "alternation in power between former rivals";[29] 2) "continued widespread support and stability during times of extreme economic hardship"; 3) "successful defeat and punishment of a handful of strategically placed rebels"; 4) "regime stability in the face of a radical restructuring of the party system"; and 5) "the absence of a politically significant antisystem party or social movement."

With respect to Latin America, it bears commenting in relation to each of these points that: 1) alternations in government through peaceful electoral processes have occurred in Latin America as frequently as in Southern Europe; 2) in the former, support for regime stability has persisted—in Argentina, Brazil, and Bolivia, among other countries—even in the face of far more acute recessions than Southern Europe has seen, and in the midst of quadruple-digit inflation; 3) the record of punishment is poor, albeit with important exceptions in both regions; 4) even when thinking about Italy today, it is hard to imagine party-system restructurings more radical than the ones that occurred in Bolivia, Brazil, and Ecuador; and 5) "antisystem" political parties are as absent from the Latin American as from the Southern European polyarchies. The indicators of democratic consolidation invoked by these authors (and shared by many others) suffer from extreme ambiguity.[30] Finally, one might note that their argument points toward a *reductio ad absurdum*, for one could in following its logic argue that Latin America's polyarchies are actually "more consolidated" because they have endured more "severe tests" than their Southern European counterparts.

Polyarchies, Particularism, and Accountability

It almost goes without saying that all actual cases exhibit various combinations of universalism and particularism across various relevant dimensions. This observation, however, should not lead to the Procrustean solution of lumping all cases together; differences in the degree to which each case approximates either pole may justify their separate classification and analysis. Of course, one may for various reasons prefer a political process that adheres quite closely to the formal rules of the full institutional package of polyarchy. Yet there exist polyarchies—some of them as old as Italy, India, and Japan, or in Latin America, Colombia, and Venezuela—that endure even though they do not function as their formal rules dictate. To understand these cases we need to know what games are really being played, and under what rules.

In many countries of the global East and South, there is an old and deep split between the *pays réel* and the *pays légal*. Today, with many of these countries claiming to be democracies and adopting a constitutional framework, the persistence and high visibility of this split may not threaten the survival of their polyarchies—but neither does it facilitate overcoming the split. Institutions are resilient, especially when they have deep historical roots; particularism is no exception. Particularism is a permanent feature of human society; only recently, and only in some places and institutional sites, has it been tempered by universalistic norms and rules. In many new polyarchies, particularism vigorously inhabits most formal political institutions, yet the incumbency of top government posts is decided by the universalistic process of fairly counting each vote as one. This may sound paradoxical but it is not; it means that these are polyarchies, but they are neither the ones that the theory of democracy had in mind as it grew out of reflection on the political regimes of the global Northwest, nor what many studies of democratization assume that a democracy should be or become.

That some polyarchies are informally institutionalized has important consequences. Here I want to stress one that is closely related to the blurring of the boundary between the private and the public spheres: accountability, a crucial aspect of formally institutionalized polyarchy, is seriously hindered. To be sure, the institutionalization of elections means that retrospective electoral accountability exists, and a reasonably free press and various active segments of society see to it that some egregiously unlawful acts of government are exposed (if seldom punished). Polyarchy, even if not formally institutionalized, marks a huge improvement over authoritarian regimes of all kinds. What is largely lacking, however, is another dimension of accountability, which I call "horizontal." By this I mean the controls that state agencies are supposed to exercise over other state agencies. All formally institutionalized polyarchies include various agencies endowed with legally defined authority to sanction unlawful or otherwise inappropriate actions by other state agents. This is an often-overlooked expression of the rule of law in one of the areas where it is hardest to implant, that is, over state agents, especially high-ranking officials. The basic idea is that formal institutions have well-defined, legally established boundaries that delimit the proper exercise of their authority, and that there are state agencies empowered to control and redress trespasses of these boundaries by any official or agency. These boundaries are closely related to the private-public boundary, in that those who perform public roles are supposed to follow universalistic and public-oriented rules, rather than their own particular interests. Even though its actual functioning is far from perfect, this network of boundaries and accountabilities is an important part of the formal institutionalization of the full package of polyarchy.[31]

By contrast, little horizontal accountability exists in most new polyarchies. Furthermore, in many of them the executive makes strenuous, and often successful, efforts to erode whatever horizontal accountability does exist. The combination of institutionalized elections, particularism as a dominant political institution, and a big gap between the formal rules and the way most political institutions actually work makes for a strong affinity with delegative, not representative, notions of political authority. By this I mean a caesaristic, plebiscitarian executive that once elected sees itself as empowered to govern the country as it deems fit. Reinforced by the urgencies of severe socioeconomic crises and consonant with old *volkisch*, nonindividualistic conceptions of politics, delegative practices strive headlong against formal political institutionalization; congress, the judiciary, and various state agencies of control are seen as hindrances placed in the way of the proper discharge of the tasks that the voters have delegated to the executive. The executive's efforts to weaken these institutions, invade their legal authority, and lower their prestige are a logical corollary of this view.[32] On the other hand, as Max Weber warned, institutions deprived of real power and responsibility tend to act in ways that seem to confirm the reasons adduced for this deprivation. In the cases that concern us here, particularism becomes even more rampant in congress and parties, courts ostensively fail to administer justice, and agencies of control are eliminated or reduced to passivity. This context encourages the further erosion of legally established authority, renders the boundary between public and private even more tenuous, and creates enormous temptations for corruption.

In this sea of particularism and blurred boundaries, why does the universalistic process of fair and competitive elections survive? Governments willing to tamper with laws are hardly solid guarantors of the integrity of electoral processes. Part of the answer, at least with respect to elections to top national positions, is close international attention and wide reporting abroad of electoral irregularities. Fair elections are the main, if not the only, characteristic that certifies countries as democratic before other governments and international opinion. Nowadays this certification has important advantages for countries and for those who govern them. Within the country, elections are a moment when something similar to horizontal accountability operates: parties other than the one in government are present at the polling places, sharing an interest in preventing fraud. Elections create a sharp focus on political matters and on the symbols and rituals that surround the act of voting. At this moment, the citizens' sense of basic fairness manifests itself with special intensity. Violations are likely to be immediately reported. Faced with the protests that might ensue and their repercussions in the international media, and considering the further damage that would come from trying to impose obviously tainted results, most governments are willing to run the risks inherent in fair and competitive elections.

Pervasive particularism, delegative rule, and weak horizontal accountability have at least two serious drawbacks. The first is that the generalized lack of control enables old authoritarian practices to reassert themselves.[33] The second is that, in countries that inaugurated polyarchy under conditions of sharp and increasing inequality, the making and implementation of policy becomes further biased in favor of highly organized and economically powerful interests.

In the countries that occupy us here, the more properly political, *democratic* freedoms are effective: uncoerced voting; freedom of opinion, movement, and association; and others already listed. But for large sections of the population, basic *liberal* freedoms are denied or recurrently trampled. The rights of battered women to sue their husbands and of peasants to obtain a fair trial against their landlords, the inviolability of domiciles in poor neighborhoods, and in general the right of the poor and various minorities to decent treatment and fair access to public agencies and courts are often denied. The effectiveness of the whole ensemble of rights, democratic and liberal, makes for full civil and political citizenship. In many of the new polyarchies, individuals are citizens only in relation to the one institution that functions in a manner close to what its formal rules prescribe—elections. As for full citizenship, only the members of a privileged minority enjoy it.[34] Formally institutionalized polyarchies exhibit various mixes of democracy, liberalism, and republicanism (understood as a view that concurs with liberalism in tracing a clear public-private distinction, but that adds an ennobling and personally demanding conception of participation in the public sphere). Informally institutionalized polyarchies are democratic, in the sense just defined; when they add, as they often do, the plebiscitarian component of delegative rule, they are also strongly majoritarian. But their liberal and republican components are extremely weak.

Notes

For their comments on an earlier version of this text, I am grateful to Michael Coppedge, Gabriela Ippolito-O'Donnell, Scott Mainwaring, Sebastián Mazzuca, Peter Moody, Gerardo Munck, and Adam Przeworski.

1. Reflecting the lack of clearly established criteria in the literature, David Collier and Steven Levitsky have inventoried and interestingly discussed the more than one hundred qualifiers that have been attached to the term "democracy." Many such qualifiers are intended to indicate that the respective cases are in some sense lacking the full attributes of democracy as defined by each author. See Collier and Levitsky, "Democracy 'With Adjectives': Finding Conceptual Order in Recent Comparative Research" (unpubl. ms., University of California–Berkeley, Political Science Department, 1995).

2. I have tried unsuccessfully to find terms appropriate to what the literature refers to as highly institutionalized versus noninstitutionalized (or poorly institutionalized), or as consolidated versus unconsolidated democracies, with most of the old polyarchies belonging to the first terms of these pairs, and

most of the new ones to the second. For reasons that will be clear below, I have opted for labeling the first group "formally institutionalized" and the second "informally institutionalized," but not without misgivings: in the first set of countries, many things happen outside formally prescribed institutional rules, while the second set includes one highly formalized institution, elections.

3. This list is from Robert Dahl, *Democracy and Its Critics* (New Haven: Yale University Press, 1989), 221; the reader may want to examine further details of these attributes, discussed by Dahl in this book.

4. See especially J. Samuel Valenzuela, "Democratic Consolidation in Post-Transitional Settings: Notion, Process, and Facilitating Conditions," in Scott Mainwaring, Guillermo O'Donnell, and J. Samuel Valenzuela, eds., *Issues in Democratic Consolidation: The New South American Democracies in Comparative Perspective* (Notre Dame, Ind.: University of Notre Dame Press, 1992), 57–104; and Philippe C. Schmitter and Terry Lynn Karl, "What Democracy Is . . . and Is Not," *Journal of Democracy* 2 (Summer 1991): 75–88.

5. See Terry Lynn Karl, "The Hybrid Regimes of Central America," *Journal of Democracy* 6 (July 1995): 73–86; and "Imposing Consent? Electoralism vs. Democratization in El Salvador," in Paul Drake and Eduardo Silva, eds., *Elections and Democratization in Latin America, 1980–85* (San Diego: Center for Iberian and Latin American Studies, 1986), 9–36.

6. See especially Juan J. Linz and Alfred Stepan, *Problems of Democratic Transition and Consolidation: Southern Europe, South America, and Post-Communist Europe* (Baltimore: Johns Hopkins University Press, 1996); and Philippe Schmitter, "Dangers and Dilemmas of Democracy," *Journal of Democracy* 5 (April 1994): 57–74.

7. For a useful listing of these institutional variations, see Schmitter and Karl, "What Democracy Is . . . and Is Not."

8. For a more detailed discussion of institutions, see my "Delegative Democracy," *Journal of Democracy* 5 (January 1994): 56–69.

9. The term "reasonable" is admittedly ambiguous. Nowhere are these freedoms completely uncurtailed, if by nothing else than the political consequences of social inequality. By "reasonable" I mean that there are neither de jure prohibitions on these freedoms nor systematic and usually successful efforts by the government or private actors to annul them.

10. On the other hand, elections can be made more authentically competitive by, say, measures that diminish the advantages of incumbents or of economically powerful parties. These are, of course, important issues. But the point I want to make at the moment is that these differences obtain among countries that already qualify as polyarchies.

11. Juan J. Linz, "Transitions to Democracy," *Washington Quarterly* 13 (1990): 156. The assertion about "the only game in town" entails some ambiguities that I discuss below.

12. Even though most definitions of democratic consolidation are centered around "institutionalization" (whether explicitly or implicitly, by asserting acceptance or approval of democratic institutions and their formal rules), they offer a wide variety of additional criteria. My own count in a recent review of the literature is twelve; see Doh Chull Shin, "On the Third Wave of Democratization: A Synthesis and Evaluation of Recent Theory and Research," *World Politics* 47 (October 1994): 135–70.

13. Even though he does not use this language, an exception is the definition of democratic consolidation offered by J. Samuel Valenzuela, which is centered in what I call here the institutionalization of elections and the absence of veto powers; see his "Democratic Consolidation in Post-Transitional Settings," 69.

14. It is high time for self-criticism. The term "stunted" I used jointly with Scott Mainwaring and J. Samuel Valenzuela in the introduction to our *Issues in Democratic Consolidation*, 11. Furthermore, in my chapter in the same volume (pp. 17–56), I offer a nonminimalist definition of democratic consolidation, and propose the concept of a "second transition," from a democratically elected government to a consolidated democratic regime. These concepts partake of the teleology I criticize here. This teleological view is homologous to the one used by many modernization studies in the 1950s and 1960s; it was abundantly, but evidently not decisively, criticized at the time. For a critique of the concept of "democratic consolidation" that is convergent with mine, see Ben Ross Schneider, "Democratic Consolidations: Some Broad Comparisons and Sweeping Arguments," *Latin American*

Research Review 30 (1995): 215–34; Schneider concludes by warning against "the fallacy of excessive universalism" (p. 231).

15. Philippe C. Schmitter with Terry Lynn Karl, "The Conceptual Travels of Transitologists and Consolidologists: How Far to the East Should They Attempt to Go?" *Slavic Review* 63 (Spring 1994): 173–85.

16. We should remember that several typologies have been proposed for formally institutionalized polyarchies; see especially Arend Lijphart, *Democracies: Patterns of Majoritarian and Consensus Government in Twenty-one Countries* (New Haven: Yale University Press, 1984). This work has been extremely useful in advancing knowledge about these polyarchies, which underscores the need for similar efforts on the now greatly expanded whole set of polyarchies. For an attempt in this direction see Carlos Acuña and William Smith, "Future Politico-Economic Scenarios for Latin America," in William Smith, Carlos Acuña, and Eduardo Gamarra, eds., *Democracy, Markets, and Structural Reform in Latin America* (New Brunswick, N.J.: Transaction, 1993), 1–28.

17. Adam Przeworski and his collaborators found that higher economic development and a parliamentary regime increase the average survival rate of polyarchies. These are important findings, but the authors have not tested the impacts of socioeconomic inequality and of the kind of informal institutionalization that I discuss below. Pending further research, it is impossible to assess the causal direction and weight of all these variables. I suspect that high socioeconomic inequality has a close relationship with informal institutionalization. But we do not know if either or both, directly or indirectly, affect the chances of survival of polyarchy, or if they might cancel the effect of economic development that Przeworski et al. found. See Adam Przeworski and Fernando Limongi, "Modernization: Theories and Facts" (Working Paper No. 4, Chicago Center for Democracy, University of Chicago, November 1994).

18. A topic that does not concern me here is the extent to which formal rules are institutionalized across various old polyarchies and, within them, across various issue areas, though the variations seem quite important on both counts.

19. The lore of many countries is filled with jokes about the naive foreigner or the native "sucker" who gets into trouble by following the formal rules of a given situation. I have explored some of these issues with reference to Brazil and Argentina in "Democracia en la Argentina: Micro y macro" (Working Paper No. 2, Helen Kellogg Institute for International Studies, Notre Dame, Ind., 1983); "Y a mí qué me importa? Notas sobre sociabilidad y política en Argentina y Brasil" (Working Paper No. 9, Helen Kellogg Institute for International Studies, Notre Dame, Ind., 1984); and "Microescenas de la privatización de lo público en Brasil" (Working Paper No. 21, with commentaries by Roberto DaMatta and J. Samuel Valenzuela, Helen Kellogg Institute for International Studies, Notre Dame, Ind., 1989).

20. For the purposes of the generic argument presented in this essay, and not without hesitation because of its vagueness, from now on I will use the term "particularism" to refer to these phenomena. On the contemporary relevance of clientelism, see Luis Roniger and Ayse Gunes-Ayata, eds., *Democracy, Clientelism, and Civil Society* (Boulder, Colo.: Lynne Rienner, 1994). For studies focused on Latin America that are germane to my argument, see especially Roberto DaMatta, *A Case e a rua: Espaco, cidadania, mulher e morte no Brasil* (São Paulo: Editora Brasiliense, 1985); Jonathan Fox, "The Difficult Transition from Clientelism to Citizenship," *World Politics* 46 (January 1994): 151–84; Francis Hagopian, "The Compromised Transition: The Political Class in the Brazilian Transition," in Mainwaring et al., *Issues in Democratic Consolidation*, 243–93; and Scott Mainwaring, "Brazilian Party Underdevelopment in Comparative Perspective," *Political Science Quarterly* 107 (Winter 1992–93): 677–707. These and other studies show that particularism and its concomitants are not ignored by good field researchers. But, attesting to the paradigmatic force of the prevalent views on democratization, in this literature the rich data and findings emerging from such case studies are not conceptually processed as an intrinsic part of the *problématique* of democratization, or are seen as just "obstacles" interposed in the way of its presumed direction of change.

21. Particularistic relationships can be found in formally institutionalized polyarchies, of course. I am pointing here to differences of degree that seem large enough to require conceptual recognition. One important indication of these differences is the extraordinary leniency with which, in informally

institutionalized polyarchies, political leaders, most of public opinion, and even courts treat situations that in the other polyarchies would be considered as entailing very severe conflicts of interest.

22. For a discussion of neopatrimonialism, see my "Transitions, Continuities, and Paradoxes," in Mainwaring et al., *Issues in Democratic Consolidation,* 17–56. An interesting recent discussion of neopatrimonialism is Jonathan Hartlyn's "Crisis-Ridden Elections (Again) in the Dominican Republic: Neopatrimonialism, Presidentialism, and Weak Electoral Oversight," *Journal of Interamerican and World Affairs* 34 (Winter 1994): 91–144.

23. By "regime" I mean "the set of effectively prevailing patterns (not necessarily legally formalized) that establish the modalities of recruitment and access to governmental roles, and the permissible resources that form the basis for expectations of access to such roles," as defined in my *Bureaucratic Authoritarianism: Argentina, 1966–1973, in Comparative Perspective* (Berkeley: University of California Press, 1988), 6.

24. Adam Przeworski, *Democracy and the Market: Political and Economic Reforms in Eastern Europe and Latin America* (Cambridge: Cambridge University Press, 1991).

25. See, among many others that could be cited (some transcribed in Shin, "On the Third Wave of Democratization"), the definition of democratic consolidation proposed by Richard Gunther, P. Nikiforos Diamandouros, and Hans-Jürgen Puhle, eds., *The Politics of Democratic Consolidation: Southern Europe in Comparative Perspective* (Baltimore: Johns Hopkins University Press, 1995), 3: "the achievement of substantial attitudinal support for and behavioral compliance with the new democratic institutions and the rules which they establish." A broader but equivalent definition is offered four pages later.

26. Przeworski, *Democracy and the Market,* 26.

27. In another influential discussion, Philippe C. Schmitter, although he does not use this language, expresses a similar view of democratic consolidation; see his "Dangers and Dilemmas of Democracy," *Journal of Democracy* 5 (April 1994): 56–74. Schmitter begins by asserting, "In South America, Eastern Europe, and Asia the specter haunting the transition is . . . nonconsolidation. . . . These countries are 'doomed' to remain democratic almost by default." He acknowledges that the attributes of polyarchy may hold in these countries—but then "patterns never quite crystallize" (pp. 60–61). To say that democracy exists "almost by default" (i.e., is negatively defined) and is not "crystallized" (i.e., not formally institutionalized) is another way of stating the generalized view that I am discussing.

28. An exception is Gunther et al., *Politics of Democratic Consolidation,* where Italy is one of the four cases studied. But the way they deal with recent events in Italy is exemplary of the conceptual problems I am discussing. They assert that in Italy "several important partial regimes . . . were challenged, became deconsolidated, and entered into a significant process of restructuring beginning in 1991" (p. 19). On the same page, the reader learns that these partial regimes include nothing less than "the electoral system, the party system, and the structure of the state itself." (Added to this list later on is "the basic nature of executive-legislative relations" [p. 394].) Yet the "Italian democracy remains strong and resilient"—after practically every important aspect of its regime, and even of the state, became "deconsolidated" (p. 412). If the authors mean that, in spite of a severe crisis, the Italian polyarchy is likely to endure, I agree.

29. Actually, the authors are ambiguous about this first "test." Just before articulating their list of tests with this one at its head, they assert that they "reject [peaceful alternation in government between parties that were once bitterly opposed] as a *prerequisite* for regarding a regime as consolidated" (emphasis added). See Gunther et al., *Politics of Democratic Consolidation,* 12.

30. In the text on which I am commenting, the problem is further compounded by the use of categories such as "partial consolidation" and "sufficient consolidation" (which the authors say preceded "full consolidation" in some Southern European cases). They even speak of a stage of "democratic persistence" that is supposed to follow the achievement of "full [democratic] consolidation."

31. I may have sounded naive in my earlier comments about how individuals performing public roles are supposed to be guided by universalistic orientations to some version of the public good. Now I can add that, as the authors of the *Federalist Papers* knew, this is not only, or even mostly, a matter of the subjective intentions of these individuals. It is to a large extent contingent on institutional arrangements

of control and accountability, and on expectations built around these arrangements, that furnish incentives (including the threats of severe sanctions and public discredit) for that kind of behavior. That these incentives are often insufficient should not be allowed to blur the difference with cases where the institutional arrangements are nonexistent or ineffective; these situations freely invite the enormous temptations that always come with holding political power. I wish to thank Adam Przeworski and Michael Coppedge for raising this point in private communications.

32. The reader has surely noticed that I am referring to countries that have presidentialist regimes and that, consequently, I am glossing over the arguments, initiated by Juan J. Linz and followed up by a number of other scholars, about the advantages of parliamentarism over the presidentialist regimes that characterize Latin America. Although these arguments convince me in the abstract, because of the very characteristics I am depicting I am skeptical about the practical consequences of attempting to implant parliamentarism in these countries.

33. For analyses of some of these situations, see Paulo Sérgio Pinheiro, "The Legacy of Authoritarianism in Democratic Brazil," in Stuart S. Nagel, ed., *Latin American Development and Public Policy* (New York: St. Martin's, 1995), 237–53; and Martha K. Huggins, ed., *Vigilantism and the State in Modern Latin America: Essays on Extralegal Violence* (New York: Praeger, 1991). See also the worrisome analysis, based on Freedom House data, that Larry Diamond presents in his "Democracy in Latin America: Degrees, Illusions, and Directions for Consolidation," in Tom Farer, ed., *Beyond Sovereignty: Collectively Defending Democracy in the Americas* (Baltimore: Johns Hopkins University Press, 1996). In recent years, the Freedom House indices reveal, more Latin American countries have regressed rather than advanced. For a discussion of various aspects of the resulting obliteration of the rule of law and weakening of citizenship, see Guillermo O'Donnell, "On the State, Democratization, and Some Conceptual Problems: A Latin American View with Glances at Some Post-Communist Countries," *World Development* 21 (1993): 1355–69.

34. There is a huge adjacent theme that I will not discuss here: the linkage of these problems with widespread poverty and, even more, with deep inequalities of various sorts.

4.7

The End of the Transition Paradigm

Thomas Carothers

In the 1970s and 1980s, it was widely believed that more and more regimes around the world were becoming democratic. (For influential claims along these lines, see Fukuyama [1.1] and Huntington [1.2].) Carothers summarizes and critiques elements of this approach, what he dubs the transition paradigm, which sought to understand the process by which authoritarian regimes were overthrown and replaced by democratic institutions. He goes beyond many scholars that have expressed doubts about this trend and the applicability of the transition model. (See Gat [1.3], Levitsky and Way [2.4], Rapley [2.6], O'Donnell [4.6], and Bunce [4.7].) In the present selection, Carothers proposes abandoning the claim that democracy will be the wave of the future.

What do you consider Carothers's two most important criticisms? How valid are they? Can you identify systematic trends toward or away from democracy? Which ones and why? Or does regime change occur in more random fashion?

I n the last quarter of the twentieth century, trends in seven different regions converged to change the political landscape of the world: 1) the fall of right-wing authoritarian regimes in Southern Europe in the mid-1970s; 2) the replacement of military dictatorships by elected civilian governments across Latin America from the late 1970s through the late 1980s; 3) the decline of authoritarian rule in parts of East and South Asia starting in the mid-1980s; 4) the collapse of communist regimes in Eastern Europe at the end of the 1980s; 5) the breakup of the Soviet Union and the establishment of 15 post-Soviet republics in 1991; 6) the decline of one-party regimes in many parts of sub-Saharan Africa in the first half of the 1990s; and 7) a weak but recognizable liberalizing trend in some Middle Eastern countries in the 1990s.

The causes, shape, and pace of these different trends varied considerably. But they shared a dominant characteristic—simultaneous movement in at least several countries in each region away from dictatorial rule toward more liberal and often more democratic governance. And though differing in many ways,

Thomas Carothers, "The End of the Transition Paradigm," *Journal of Democracy* 13, no. 1 (January 2002): 5–12, 13–18. © National Endowment for Democracy and The Johns Hopkins University Press. Reprinted with permission of The Johns Hopkins University Press.

these trends influenced and to some extent built on one another. As a result, they were considered by many observers, especially in the West, as component parts of a larger whole, a global democratic trend that thanks to Samuel Huntington has widely come to be known as the "third wave" of democracy.[1]

This striking tide of political change was seized upon with enthusiasm by the U.S. government and the broader U.S. foreign policy community. As early as the mid-1980s, President Ronald Reagan, Secretary of State George Shultz, and other high-level U.S. officials were referring regularly to "the worldwide democratic revolution." During the 1980s, an active array of governmental, quasi-governmental, and nongovernmental organizations devoted to promoting democracy abroad sprang into being. This new democracy-promotion community had a pressing need for an analytic framework to conceptualize and respond to the ongoing political events. Confronted with the initial parts of the third wave—democratization in Southern Europe, Latin America, and a few countries in Asia (especially the Philippines)—the U.S. democracy community rapidly embraced an analytic model of democratic transition. It was derived principally from their own interpretation of the patterns of democratic change taking place, but also to a lesser extent from the early works of the emergent academic field of "transitology," above all the seminal work of Guillermo O'Donnell and Philippe Schmitter.[2]

As the third wave spread to Eastern Europe, the Soviet Union, sub-Saharan Africa, and elsewhere in the 1990s, democracy promoters extended this model as a universal paradigm for understanding democratization. It became ubiquitous in U.S. policy circles as a way of talking about, thinking about, and designing interventions in processes of political change around the world. And it stayed remarkably constant despite many variations in those patterns of political change and a stream of increasingly diverse scholarly views about the course and nature of democratic transitions.[3]

The transition paradigm has been somewhat useful during a time of momentous and often surprising political upheaval in the world. But it is increasingly clear that reality is no longer conforming to the model. Many countries that policy makers and aid practitioners persist in calling "transitional" are not in transition to democracy, and of the democratic transitions that are under way, more than a few are not following the model. Sticking with the paradigm beyond its useful life is retarding evolution in the field of democratic assistance and is leading policy makers astray in other ways. It is time to recognize that the transition paradigm has outlived its usefulness and to look for a better lens.

Core Assumptions

Five core assumptions define the transition paradigm. The first, which is an umbrella for all the others, is that any country moving *away* from dictatorial rule can be considered a country in transition *toward* democracy. Especially in the first half of the 1990s, when political change accelerated in many regions, numerous policy makers and aid practitioners reflexively labeled any formerly authoritarian country that was attempting some political liberalization as a "transitional country." The set of "transitional countries" swelled dramatically, and nearly 100 countries (approximately 20 in Latin America, 25 in Eastern Europe and the former Soviet Union, 30 in sub-Saharan Africa, 10 in Asia, and 5 in the Middle East) were thrown into the conceptual pot of the transition paradigm. Once so labeled, their political life was automatically analyzed in terms of their movement toward or away from democracy, and they were held up to the implicit expectations of the paradigm, as detailed below. . . .

The second assumption is that democratization tends to unfold in a set sequence of stages. First there occurs the *opening*, a period of democratic ferment and political liberalization in which cracks appear in the ruling dictatorial regime, with the most prominent fault line being that between hardliners and softliners. There follows the *breakthrough*—the collapse of the regime and the rapid emergence of a new, democratic system, with the coming to power of a new government through national elections and the establishment of a democratic institutional structure, often through the promulgation of a new constitution. After the transition comes *consolidation*, a slow but purposeful process in which democratic forms are transformed into democratic substance through the reform of state institutions, the regularization of elections, the strengthening of civil society, and the overall habituation of the society to the new democratic "rules of the game."

Democracy activists admit that it is not inevitable that transitional countries will move steadily on this assumed path from opening and breakthrough to consolidation. Transitional countries, they say, can and do go backward or stagnate as well as move forward along the path. Yet even the deviations from the assumed sequence that they are willing to acknowledge are defined in terms of the path itself. The options are all cast in terms of the speed and direction with which countries move on the path, not in terms of movement that does not conform with the path at all. And at least in the peak years of the third wave, many democracy enthusiasts clearly believed that, while the success of the dozens of new transitions was not assured, democratization was in some important sense a natural process, one that was likely to flourish once the initial breakthrough occurred. . . .

Related to the idea of a core sequence of democratization is the third assumption—the belief in the determinative importance of elections. Democracy promoters have not been guilty—as critics often charge—of believing that elections equal democracy. For years they have advocated and pursued a much broader range of assistance programs than just elections-focused efforts. Nevertheless, they have tended to hold very high expectations for what the establishment of regular, genuine elections will do for democratization. Not only will elections give new postdictatorial governments democratic legitimacy, they believe, but the elections will serve to broaden and deepen political participation and the democratic accountability of the state to its citizens. In other words, it has been assumed that in attempted transitions to democracy, elections will be not just a foundation stone but a key generator over time of further democratic reforms.

A fourth assumption is that the underlying conditions in transitional countries—their economic level, political history, institutional legacies, ethnic make-up, sociocultural traditions, or other "structural" features—will not be major factors in either the onset or the outcome of the transition process. A remarkable characteristic of the early period of the third wave was that democracy seemed to be breaking out in the most unlikely and unexpected places, whether Mongolia, Albania, or Mauritania. All that seemed to be necessary for democratization was a decision by a country's political elites to move toward democracy and an ability on the part of those elites to fend off the contrary actions of remaining antidemocratic forces. . . .

Fifth, the transition paradigm rests on the assumption that the democratic transitions making up the third wave are being built on coherent, functioning states. The process of democratization is assumed to include some redesign of state institutions—such as the creation of new electoral institutions, parliamentary reform, and judicial reform—but as a modification of already functioning states. As they arrived at their frameworks for understanding democratization, democracy aid practitioners did not give significant attention to the challenge of a society trying to democratize while it is grappling with the reality of building a state from scratch or coping with an existent but largely nonfunctional state. This did not appear to be an issue in Southern Europe or Latin America, the two regions that served as the experiential basis for the formation of the transition paradigm. To the extent that democracy promoters did consider the possibility of state-building as part of the transition process, they assumed that democracy-building and state-building would be mutually reinforcing endeavors or even two sides of the same coin.

Into the Gray Zone

We turn then from the underlying assumptions of the paradigm to the record of experience. . . .

Of the nearly 100 countries considered as "transitional" in recent years, only a relatively small number—probably fewer than 20—are clearly en route to becoming successful, well-functioning democracies or at least have made some democratic progress and still enjoy a positive dynamic of democratization.[4] The leaders of the group are found primarily in Central Europe and the Baltic region—Poland, Hungary, the Czech Republic, Estonia, and Slovenia—though there are a few in South America and East Asia, notably Chile, Uruguay, and Taiwan. Those that have made somewhat less progress but appear to be still advancing include Slovakia, Romania, Bulgaria, Mexico, Brazil, Ghana, the Philippines, and South Korea.

By far the majority of third-wave countries have not achieved relatively well-functioning democracy or do not seem to be deepening or advancing whatever democratic progress they have made. In a small number of countries, initial political openings have clearly failed and authoritarian regimes have resolidified, as in Uzbekistan, Turkmenistan, Belarus, and Togo. Most of the "transitional countries," however, are neither dictatorial nor clearly headed toward democracy. They have entered a political gray zone.[5] They have some attributes of democratic political life, including at least limited political space for opposition parties and independent civil society, as well as regular elections and democratic constitutions. Yet they suffer from serious democratic deficits, often including poor representation of citizens' interests, low levels of political participation beyond voting, frequent abuse of the law by government officials, elections of uncertain legitimacy, very low levels of public confidence in state institutions, and persistently poor institutional performance by the state.

As the number of countries falling in between outright dictatorship and well-established liberal democracy has swollen, political analysts have proffered an array of "qualified democracy" terms to characterize them, including semi-democracy, formal democracy, electoral democracy, façade democracy, pseudo-democracy, weak democracy, partial democracy, illiberal democracy, and virtual democracy.[6] Some of these terms, such as "façade democracy" and "pseudo-democracy," apply only to a fairly specific subset of gray-zone cases. Other terms, such as "weak democracy" and "partial democracy," are intended to have much broader applicability. Useful though these terms can be, especially when rooted in probing analysis such as O'Donnell's work on "delegative democracy," they share a significant liability: By describing countries in the gray zone as types of democracies, analysts are in effect trying to apply the transition paradigm to the very countries whose political evolution is calling that paradigm into question.[7] Most of the "qualified democracy" terms are used to characterize countries as being stuck somewhere on the assumed democratization sequence, usually at the start of the consolidation phase. . . .

The Crash of Assumptions

Taken together, the political trajectories of most third-wave countries call into serious doubt the transition paradigm. This is apparent if we revisit the major assumptions underlying the paradigm in light of the above analysis.

First, the almost automatic assumption of democracy promoters during the peak years of the third wave that any country moving away from dictatorship was "in transition to democracy" has often been inaccurate and misleading. Some of those countries have hardly democratized at all. Many have taken on a

smattering of democratic features but show few signs of democratizing much further and are certainly not following any predictable democratization script. The most common political patterns to date among the "transitional countries"—feckless pluralism and dominant-power politics—include elements of democracy but should be understood as alternative directions, not way stations to liberal democracy. The persistence in official U.S. democracy-promotion circles of using transitional language to characterize countries that in no way conform to any democratization paradigm borders in some case on the surreal—including not just the case of Congo cited above but many others, such as Moldova ("Moldova's democratic transition continues to progress steadily"), Zambia ("Zambia is . . . moving steadily toward . . . the creation of a viable multiparty democracy"), Cambodia ("policy successes in Cambodia towards democracy and improved governance within the past 18 months are numerous"), and Guinea ("Guinea has made significant strides toward building a democratic society").[8]
The continued use of the transition paradigm constitutes a dangerous habit of trying to impose a simplistic and often incorrect conceptual order on an empirical tableau of considerable complexity.

Second, not only is the general label and concept of "transitional country" unhelpful, but the assumed sequence of stages of democratization is defied by the record of experience. Some of the most encouraging cases of democratization in recent years—such as Taiwan, South Korea, and Mexico—did not go through the paradigmatic process of democratic breakthrough followed rapidly by national elections and a new democratic institutional framework. Their political evolutions were defined by an almost opposite phenomenon—extremely gradual, incremental processes of liberalization with an organized political opposition (not softliners in the regime) pushing for change across successive elections and finally winning. And in many of the countries that did go through some version of what appeared to be a democratic breakthrough, the assumed sequence of changes—first settling constitutive issues then working through second-order reforms—has not held. Constitutive issues have reemerged at unpredictable times, upending what are supposed to be later stages of transition, as in the recent political crises in Ecuador, the Central African Republic, and Chad.

Moreover, the various assumed component processes of consolidation—political party development, civil society strengthening, judicial reform, and media development—almost never conform to the technocratic ideal of rational sequences on which the indicator frameworks and strategic objectives of democracy promoters are built. Instead they are chaotic processes of change that go backwards and sideways as much as forward, and do not do so in any regular manner.

The third assumption of the transition paradigm—the notion that achieving regular, genuine elections will not only confer democratic legitimacy on new governments but continuously deepen political participation and democratic accountability—has often come up short. In many "transitional countries," reasonably regular, genuine elections are held but political participation beyond voting remains shallow and governmental accountability is weak. The wide gulf between political elites and citizens in many of these countries turns out to be rooted in structural conditions, such as the concentration of wealth or certain sociocultural traditions, that elections themselves do not overcome. It is also striking how often electoral competition does little to stimulate the renovation or development of political parties in many gray-zone countries. Such profound pathologies as highly personalistic parties, transient and shifting parties, or stagnant patronage-based politics appear to be able to coexist for sustained periods with at least somewhat legitimate processes of political pluralism and competition. . . .

Fourth, ever since "preconditions for democracy" were enthusiastically banished in the heady early days of the third wave, a contrary reality—the fact that various structural conditions clearly weigh heavily in shaping political outcomes—has been working its way back in. Looking at the more successful recent cases of democratization, for example, which tend to be found in Central Europe, the Southern Cone, or East Asia, it is clear that relative economic wealth, as well as past experience with political pluralism, contributes to the chances for democratic success. And looking comparatively within regions, whether in the former communist world or sub-Saharan Africa, it is evident that the specific institutional legacies from predecessor regimes strongly affect the outcomes of attempted transitions. . . .

Fifth, state-building has been a much larger and more problematic issue than originally envisaged in the transition paradigm. Contrary to the early assumptions of democracy-aid practitioners, many third-wave countries have faced fundamental state-building challenges. Approximately 20 countries in the former Soviet Union and former Yugoslavia have had to build national state institutions where none existed before. Throughout much of sub-Saharan Africa, the liberalizing political wave of the 1990s ran squarely into the sobering reality of devastatingly weak states. In many parts of Latin America, the Middle East, and Asia, political change was carried out in the context of stable state structures, but the erratic performance of those states complicated every step.

Where state-building from scratch had to be carried out, the core impulses and interests of powerholders—such as locking in access to power and resources as quickly as possible—ran directly contrary to what democracy-building would have required. In countries with existing but extremely weak states, the democracy-building efforts funded by donors usually neglected the issue of state-building. With their frequent emphasis on diffusing power and weakening the relative power of the executive branch—by strengthening the legislative and judicial branches of government, encouraging decentralization, and building civil society—they were more about the redistribution of state power than about state-building. The programs that democracy promoters have directed at governance have tended to be minor technocratic efforts, such as training ministerial staff or aiding cabinet offices, rather than major efforts at bolstering state capacity.

Letting Go

It is time for the democracy-promotion community to discard the transition paradigm. Analyzing the record of experience in the many countries that democracy activists have been labeling "transitional countries," it is evident that it is no longer appropriate to assume:

◆ that most of these countries are actually in a transition to democracy;
◆ that countries moving away from authoritarianism tend to follow a three-part process of democratization consisting of opening, breakthrough, and consolidation;
◆ that the establishment of regular, genuine elections will not only give new governments democratic legitimacy but foster a longer term deepening of democratic participation and accountability;
◆ that a country's chances for successfully democratizing depend primarily on the political intentions and actions of its political elites without significant influence from underlying economic, social, and institutional conditions and legacies;
◆ that state-building is a secondary challenge to democracy-building and largely compatible with it.

It is hard to let go of the transitional paradigm, both for the conceptual order and for the hopeful vision it provides. Giving it up constitutes a major break, but not a total one. It does not mean denying that important democratic reforms have occurred in many countries in the past two decades. It does not mean that countries in the gray zone are doomed never to achieve well-functioning liberal democracy. It does not mean that free and fair elections in "transitional countries" are futile or not worth supporting. It does not mean that the United States and other international actors should abandon efforts to promote democracy in the world (if anything, it implies that, given how difficult democratization is, efforts to promote it should be redoubled).

It does mean, however, that democracy promoters should approach their work with some very different assumptions. They should start by assuming that what is often thought of as an uneasy, precarious middle ground between full-fledged democracy and outright dictatorship is actually the most common political condition today of countries in the developing world and the postcommunist world. It is not an exceptional category to be defined only in terms of its not being one thing or the other; it is a state of normality for many societies, for better or worse. The seemingly continual surprise and disappointment that Western political analysts express over the very frequent falling short of democracy in "transitional countries" should be replaced with realistic expectations about the likely patterns of political life in these countries.

Aid practitioners and policy makers looking at politics in a country that has recently moved away from authoritarianism should not start by asking,

"How is its democratic transition going?" They should instead formulate a more open-ended query, "What is happening politically?" Insisting on the former approach leads to optimistic assumptions that often shunt the analysis down a blind alley. . . .

A whole generation of democracy aid is based on the transition paradigm, above all the typical emphasis on an institutional "checklist" as a basis for creating programs, and the creation of nearly standard portfolios of aid projects consisting of the same diffuse set of efforts all over—some judicial reform, parliamentary strengthening, civil society assistance, media work, political party development, civic education, and electoral programs. Much of the democracy aid based on this paradigm is exhausted. Where the paradigm fits well—in the small number of clearly successful transitions—the aid is not much needed. Where democracy aid is needed most, in many of the gray-zone countries, the paradigm fits poorly.

Notes

The author would like to thank Jeffrey Krutz for his research assistance relating to this article and Daniel Brumberg, Charles King, Michael McFaul, Marina Ottaway, Chris Sabatini, and Michael Shifter for their comments on the first draft.

1. Samuel P. Huntington, *The Third Wave: Democratization in the Late Twentieth Century* (Norman: University of Oklahoma Press, 1991).

2. Guillermo O'Donnell and Philippe C. Schmitter, *Transitions from Authoritarian Rule: Tentative Conclusions About Uncertain Democracies* (Baltimore: Johns Hopkins University Press, 1986).

3. Ruth Collier argues that a similar transition paradigm has prevailed in the scholarly writing on democratization. "The 'transitions literature,' as this current work has come to be known, has as its best representative the founding essay by O'Donnell and Schmitter (1986), which established a framework that is implicitly or explicitly followed in most other contributions." Ruth Berins Collier, *Paths Toward Democracy: The Working Class and Elites in Western Europe and South America* (Cambridge: Cambridge University Press, 1999), 5.

4. An insightful account of the state of the third wave is found in Larry Diamond, "Is the Third Wave Over?" *Journal of Democracy* 7 (July 1996): 20–37.

5. Larry Diamond uses the term "twilight zone" to refer to a sizeable but smaller set of countries—electoral democracies that are in a zone of "persistence without legitimation or institutionalization," in *Developing Democracy: Toward Consolidation* (Baltimore: Johns Hopkins University Press, 1999), 22.

6. David Collier and Steven Levitsky, "Democracy with Adjectives: Conceptual Innovation in Comparative Research," *World Politics* 49 (April 1997): 430–51.

7. Guillermo O'Donnell, "Delegative Democracy," *Journal of Democracy* 5 (January 1994): 55–69.

8. These quotes are all taken from the country descriptions in the democracy-building section of the USAID website, *www.usaid.gov/democracy.html*.

Discussion Questions

1. What are the pros and cons of the two approaches to democracy—procedural and substantive—identified in the introduction to this chapter? Which selections in this chapter are most helpful in analyzing this issue, and why?
2. Discuss the utility of the concepts of democratic transition and democratic consolidation. Do you agree with Carothers that the transitional paradigm should be eliminated? Why?
3. Are democratic institutions better equipped to produce wise policies? Why or why not?

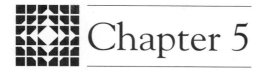 Chapter 5

COLLECTIVE IDENTITIES

How do individuals understand who they are in political terms; in other words, how do they view their collective political identities? And what induces them to come together and mobilize to advance common political interests and aspirations? Comparativists once thought that social class—solidarities based on the shared experience of work and similar economic position—was the most important source of collective identity. We now know that the formation of group attachments and the interplay of politically relevant collective identities are far more complex and uncertain. Politics is shaped in significant ways by a range of group attachments, such as those associated with class, race, ethnicity, nationality, religion, and gender.

The issue of collective identities has become even more complicated given the movement of peoples across borders and between continents, searching for jobs and better lives, fleeing war or repressive regimes, or migrating in cross-generational cycles of colonial and postcolonial encounters. Migration affects politics in profound ways. Today, it is difficult to find any pure case of a culturally, linguistically, and ethnically homogeneous population (the nation) corresponding exactly to the territorial-juridical limits of sovereign control (the state). Instead, virtually all countries encompass multinational, multiethnic societies.

Can liberal democracy, with its emphasis on individual rights, representative assemblies, and the principle of a limited state, be reconciled with the demands by identity groups for rights, the political recognition of their needs and distinctive contributions, and the allocation of scarce resources to meet those needs? How do the requirements of multiethnic, multicultural societies—as well as concerns that women achieve full equality—shape our understandings of citizenship, representation, political rights, and community? Can the increasingly urgent and often violent conflict between religious and secular worldviews be contained—or resolved? Nearly every country faces the challenge of reconciling cultural differences among diverse groups within its borders and national unity. The politics of collective identities is one of the most challenging aspects of governance today and an increasingly significant dimension of the study of comparative politics.

Cultural Obstacles to Equal Representation

Pippa Norris and Ronald Inglehart

In explaining gender inequality in political representation, how important are structural factors, such as levels of socioeconomic development or the percentage of women in professional and managerial positions? How significant are political factors, such as the nature of electoral systems? How important are cultural factors such as traditional attitudes about gender roles? In this contribution, Pippa Norris and Ronald Inglehart examine the worldwide phenomenon of the underrepresentation of women in political leadership. The authors note that both political and institutional arguments produce important insights, yet they do not satisfactorily explain the patterns of cross-national variation in women's leadership. Norris and Inglehart conclude that historical legacies continue to influence cultural attitudes. Further, egalitarian attitudes toward women leaders correlate strongly with the presence of more women in national parliaments.

Can you suggest a research design to measure the relative impact of political, institutional, and cultural factors on women's political representation?

A fundamental problem facing the worldwide process of democratization is the continued lack of gender equality in political leadership. The basic facts are not in dispute: Today women represent only one in seven parliamentarians, one in ten cabinet ministers, and, at the apex of power, one in 20 heads of state or government. Multiple factors have contributed to this situation, including structural and institutional barriers. But what is the influence of political culture? Are attitudes toward women as political leaders a significant barrier to their empowerment? In particular, how important is culture as compared with structural and institutional factors? These are the questions that our study seeks to address.

Despite moves toward gender equality in many spheres, barriers to the entry of women into elected office persist. . . .

. . . Despite the success of some redoubtable and well-known figures, such as Margaret Thatcher, Gro Harlem Bruntland, and Golda Meir, only 39 states have

Pippa Norris and Ronald Inglehart, "Cultural Obstacles to Equal Representation," *Journal of Democracy* 12, no. 3 (July 2001): 126–140. © National Endowment for Democracy and The Johns Hopkins University Press. Reprinted with permission of The Johns Hopkins University Press.

ever elected a woman president or prime minister. According to [a] UN report [*The World's Women 2000: Trends and Statistics*] women today comprise less than one-tenth of the world's cabinet ministers and one-fifth of all subministerial positions. The Inter-Parliamentary Union (IPU) estimates that worldwide there were about 5,400 women in parliaments in Spring 2001, representing 13.8 percent of all members, up from 9 percent in 1987. If growth at this level is maintained (0.36 percent per year), a simple linear projection predicts that women parliamentarians will not achieve parity with men until the beginning of the twenty-second century.

Although worldwide progress has been slow, the proportion of women elected to the legislative branch is much greater in some regions than in others. Women have not achieved equal representation with men in any country. The most gender-balanced parliaments are in the Nordic nations, where on average 38.8 percent of lower-house members are women. Sweden leads the world: Women comprise half of the ministers in Prime Minister Goran Persson's cabinet and 43 percent of the Riksdag, up from 10 percent in 1950. The proportion of women members of parliament is much lower in other regions, including the Americas (15.7 percent), Asia (14.3 percent), non-Nordic Europe (14.0 percent), sub-Saharan Africa (12.5 percent), and the Pacific (11.8 percent). The worst record for women's representation is the Arab countries, where women constitute less than 5 percent of elected representatives and continue to be barred by law from standing for parliament in Kuwait, Qatar, Saudi Arabia, Oman, and the United Arab Emirates. Despite official declarations by many countries of the intent to establish conditions of gender equality in the public sphere, in practice major barriers continue to restrict women's advancement in public life.

Several explanations have been offered to account for the continuing dearth of women in political leadership: *structural factors*, including levels of socioeconomic development and the proportion of women in professional and managerial occupations; the impact of *political institutions*, such as electoral systems based on proportional-representation; and *cultural factors*, like the predominance of traditional attitudes toward gender roles.

Social Structures and Political Institutions

Early sociological accounts commonly assigned a critical role in determining the eligibility pool for elected office to a country's social system, including the occupational, educational, and socioeconomic status of women. In developing societies, women may find it difficult to break into electoral office because they are generally disadvantaged by poor childcare, low literacy, inadequate health care, and poverty. A country's level of socioeconomic development is significantly related to its proportion of women parliamentarians. Comparative studies of established democracies have long emphasized the importance of the pool of women in the professional, administrative, and managerial occupations that typically lead to political careers. Jobs in such fields as law and journalism commonly provide the flexibility, financial resources, experience, and social networks that facilitate running for elected office. In recent decades, women in many postindustrial societies have forged ahead in the private and public sectors and greatly increased their enrollment in higher education.

This study suggests that modernization creates systematic, predictable changes in gender roles, observable in two phases. First, industrialization brings women into the paid workforce and dramatically reduces fertility rates. During this stage, women make substantial gains in educational opportunities and literacy. Women are enfranchised and begin to participate in representative government, but they still have far less power than men. The second, postindustrial phase brings a shift toward greater gender equality, as women move into higher-status economic roles and gain greater political influence within elected and appointed bodies. Over half the world has not yet begun this process, however, and even the most advanced industrial societies are still undergoing it.

Yet in many ways structural explanations fail to account for the barriers facing women who seek elected office. These accounts cannot explain major disparities between relatively similar societies in the proportion of women in national parliaments, such as the contrasts between Canada (where 20 percent of parliamentarians are women) and the United States (13 percent), between the Netherlands (36 percent) and Italy (11 percent), or between South Africa (30 percent) and Niger (1 percent). A worldwide comparison of the proportion of women elected to lower houses of the legislature confirms that a high level of socioeconomic development is not a necessary condition for the success of women. For example, female representation is far greater today in some poorer societies—like Mozambique (ranking 9th in the world), South Africa (10th), and Venezuela (11th)—than in some of the most affluent, including the United States (50th), France (59th), and Japan (94th).

In many postindustrial societies, despite the transformations of women's and men's lifestyles, electoral success has continued to elude women. This pattern is exemplified by the United States: Although almost one-third of all U.S. lawyers are now female and law remains the most common training ground for legislative office in America, only 11 out of 100 U.S. senators are women. This suggests that while improvements in women's educational and professional status serve as *facilitating* conditions for women's empowerment, structural changes by themselves may be insufficient for women to achieve greater success in winning elected office. Indeed, something more than the size of the eligibility pool is at work.

One alternative explanation is provided by *institutional* accounts, which emphasize the type of political system and some of its specific features, like proportional representation in elections and gender quotas in party recruitment processes. This increasingly popular approach is probably the mainstream perspective among scholars today. Institutional accounts suggest that the political rules of the game are the primary explanation for systematic differences in women's representation among relatively similar societies, and that changing those rules is the most effective way to promote women's political leadership.

Among institutional factors, the *level of democratization* has the broadest effects. In general, the transition and consolidation of democratic societies can be expected to promote widespread political and civil liberties, including the right of women to vote and to stand for elected office. Yet the role of democracy in promoting women's role in public life remains in dispute: Andrew Reynolds finds no significant relationship between the level of democratization and that of women's parliamentary representation.[1] . . .

Since the 1955 publication of Maurice Duverger's seminal *The Political Role of Women*, the type of *electoral system* has been regarded as an important factor affecting women's political presence. Many studies have demonstrated that far more women are elected under proportional party-list systems than under majoritarian single-member-district systems. The level of *party competition*, in terms of the number of parties and their degree of ideological polarization, is another factor that may influence women's opportunities for candidacy. Greater party competition may increase the access points for female candidacies, although this in itself does not necessarily lead to more women being elected.

The fact that we can test these propositions—whether the proportion of women in parliaments is significantly related to the level of democratization, the type of electoral system, and the level of party competition—enables institutional accounts to provide many important insights into why women politicians have advanced further and faster in some countries than in others. Yet several puzzles remain. Why do apparently similar institutional reforms turn out to have diverse and often unanticipated consequences, even among relatively similar political and social systems? Why should national-list proportional representation have a very different impact on women's electoral fortunes in Israel than in the Netherlands? Why should the use of gender quotas for candidacies seem to work better in Argentina than in Ecuador? As the failure of Westminster-style parliaments in many African states in the 1960s demonstrated, transplanted institutions do not necessarily flourish in alien environments.

Cultural Barriers

Structural and institutional explanations need to be supplemented by accounts emphasizing the importance of political culture. It has long been assumed that traditional anti-egalitarian attitudes toward gender slow down the political advancement of women, though little systematic crossnational evidence has been available to verify this proposition. Theories of socialization have long emphasized the importance of gender roles—especially the predominance of either egalitarian or traditional attitudes toward women in the private and public spheres. Studies of political recruitment processes in established democracies like Britain, Finland, and the Netherlands have found that these attitudes influence both whether women are prepared to come forward as candidates for office (the supply side of the equation) and the criteria that are used by political gatekeepers when evaluating candidates (the demand side). In cultures with traditional attitudes toward the role of women in the home and family, many women may be reluctant to run and, if they seek office, may fail to attract sufficient support to win. A recent study by the [Inter-Parliamentary Union (IPU)] found that female politicians in many countries cited hostile attitudes toward political participation by women as one of the most important barriers to running for parliament.[2]

Cultural explanations provide a plausible reason why women have made much greater advances in parliaments within the Nordic region than in socially and institutionally comparable European societies like Switzerland, Italy, or Belgium. In Scandinavia, a long tradition of government intervention to promote social equality may have made the public more receptive to the idea of positive actions (such as gender quotas) designed to achieve equality for women in public life. Culture also appears to be an important reason why many nations with strict Islamic traditions have often ranked at the bottom of the list in terms of women in parliament, despite a few notable women in top leadership positions.

In spite of these apparent effects of culture, little systematic crossnational evidence has been available on the subject, and most comparative studies have been forced to adopt proxy indicators of culture, such as religion. An early comparison found that there was less political activism among women in West European Catholic countries than in Protestant ones and suggested that this was because the Catholic Church was associated with a more hierarchical and authoritarian culture. A more recent worldwide comparison of women in politics in 180 countries reveals that the greatest contrasts are between predominantly Christian countries (both Protestant and Catholic) and countries of other religions, including Islam, Buddhism, Judaism, Confucianism, and Hinduism, all of which had lower proportions of women in legislatures and in cabinet offices.[3] An alternative approach has compared attitudes within Western Europe toward the women's movement, feminism, and equality in the home and workplace; while this provides insights into support for feminism within that region, it does not necessarily reveal attitudes toward women in political leadership positions, and there are no comparable results for societies in other regions.

Our own study uses survey and aggregate evidence to compare how political culture is systematically related to the advancement of women in elected office in a wide range of countries with varying political systems and levels of economic development.[4] We focus on four related propositions: 1) There are substantial differences in attitudes toward women's leadership in postindustrial, postcommunist, and developing societies; 2) traditional attitudes are a major barrier to the election of women to parliament; 3) culture continues to be a significant influence on the proportion of women parliamentarians, even with the introduction of prior structural and institutional controls; and 4) as a result of the process of modernization and value change, these cultural barriers have been fading most rapidly among younger generations in postindustrial societies.

Attitudes Toward Women's Political Leadership

First, how does the public regard women as political leaders and how do these attitudes vary systematically between postindustrial, postcommunist, and developing societies? The World Values Survey measures support for gender equality in political leadership with a question asking respondents how far they agreed or disagreed (on a 4-point scale) with the following statement: "On the whole, men make better political leaders than women do." A comparison of responses shows that there are substantial crossnational differences. The countries that are most positive toward women's leadership include the Nordic nations and other postindustrial societies such as New Zealand, Australia, the United States, and Spain; the countries that are most traditional include many of the poorer developing societies, including Egypt, Jordan, Iran, and Nigeria.

Regression analysis, without any prior controls, demonstrates a striking link between socioeconomic development and support for egalitarian gender roles in politics. The simple correlation between these factors is strong and significant (r = .456; sig. = .01);[5] more affluent nations are by far the most egalitarian. Nonetheless, despite the role of socioeconomic development, diverse historical legacies in different world regions continue to affect cultural attitudes. A few postindustrial societies like Norway, West Germany, and Finland express higher than expected support for women's political leadership, while Spain, Australia, and (to a lesser extent) the United States are close behind. Among richer nations, the Asian societies of Japan, Taiwan, and South Korea show lower support for women in politics than would be predicted by their levels of socioeconomic development alone. Middle-income countries in Latin America tend to have the moderately egalitarian attitudes that might be expected. Many postcommunist societies display more traditional attitudes favoring male leadership (with the important exception of East Germany, which is close to West Germany). Finally, Nigeria, Iran, Jordan, and Egypt, all poorer countries with sizeable Muslim populations, evince very traditional attitudes. Therefore, socioeconomic development does appear to be significantly related to the global distribution of egalitarian attitudes toward women's political leadership. Yet the dramatic contrasts between developing nations with similar levels of GNP (India and China are surprisingly egalitarian, while Nigeria and Egypt are quite traditional) indicate that much more is at work than simply differences between rich and poor societies.

To explore the extent to which attitudes toward women as political leaders tap into and reflect deeper cultural values, these responses have been compared with a 24-item scale reflecting a much broader range of traditional versus "rational" values.[6] This scale includes items reflecting belief in the importance of religion and in adherence to traditional moral standards on issues like divorce, euthanasia, and the family. Correlation analysis shows that Scandinavian and West European societies are consistently the most rational in their moral and ethical values, as well as the most favorable toward gender equality in politics. In contrast, Nigeria, Jordan, and Egypt emerge as the most traditional on

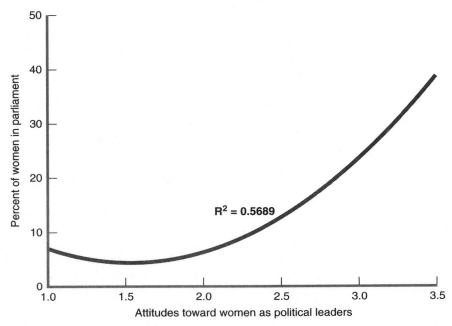

Figure 5.1 Attitudes and Representation.

Sources: For women's representation, see Inter-Parliamentary Union, "Women in National Parliaments," *www.ipu.org/wmn-e/classif.htm*; for attitudes, responses to: "On the whole, men make better political leaders than women do," on a 4-point scale (1 = strongly disagree; 2 = disagree; 3 = agree; 4 = strongly agree) in the World Values Survey conducted in 1995–99; see *http://wvs.isr.umich.edu*.

both dimensions, along with Iran and Azerbaijan. Attitudes toward women and men as political leaders therefore do appear to be related to broader ideological values on a wide range of ethical and moral issues.

Women in Parliaments

Now that we have established the existence of cultural patterns in attitudes toward women's political leadership, we must ask: Do they matter in practice? In particular, do more egalitarian attitudes toward women leaders influence the proportion of women actually elected to office? There is striking evidence that they do (see Figure 5.1 above). Egalitarian attitudes toward women leaders are strongly related to the proportion of women elected to the lower houses of national parliaments (r = .57; sig. = .01). Simply put, countries with a more egalitarian culture have more women in power. The Scandinavian countries are at the forefront of both indicators, while Jordan, Egypt, Pakistan, and many of the Central Asian postcommunist states are low on both scales.

Yet there are some striking outliers to this general pattern that deserve attention. Some established democracies—including Australia, Spain, and the United States—display more egalitarian attitudes than might be expected given the proportion of women elected to their parliaments. In these countries, public opinion may have run ahead of the opportunities that women actually have for pursuing public office. On the other hand, Bosnia-Herzegovina, South Africa, and China all have more women parliamentarians than would be expected from their cultural attitudes alone, suggesting that proactive strategies adopted to boost women's leadership, like the use of gender quotas in South Africa and China, may be ahead of public opinion.

Of course, a pattern of causation cannot be determined from any simple correlation, and we cannot rule out an interaction effect. It could well be that the experience of having many women involved in political life shifts public opinion in a more egalitarian direction, dispelling traditional views that men make better political leaders than women. Nevertheless, it seems equally plausible to assume that the causal direction flows primarily from political culture to the success of women in elected office, since increasingly egalitarian attitudes could persuade more women to seek elected office and could simultaneously influence the political gatekeepers' evaluations of suitable candidates.

One way that this can be tested further is by examining the relationship between the proportion of women in parliament and the broader scale of traditional versus rational values. The results show that there is a strong and significant correlation between these factors ($r = .408$; sig. $= .004$). Since these broader moral values should not be greatly affected by an increase of women in leadership, this strongly suggests that culture drives the success of women in elected office, rather than vice versa.

So far we have demonstrated that culture matters, but not *how much* it matters relative to other factors associated with gender equality in politics. The relationship could, after all, prove spurious if some social or institutional dynamic is simultaneously promoting both egalitarian attitudes and the political success of women. Multivariate analysis is required to test whether the relationship remains significant even with controls. Accordingly, regression models were run to estimate the relative impacts of cultural, structural, and institutional factors on women's representation in parliaments worldwide. Ultimately, the relationship between political culture and women's empowerment survives unscathed our best attempts to explain it away with prior controls.

Generational Shifts

Finally, given the importance of culture, is there evidence that views about women's suitability for political office are changing? The measure of attitudes toward women's political leadership was only included in the third wave of the World Values Survey, so we are unable to compare directly trends over time. But by using cohort analysis, which groups the population by date of birth, we can analyze the distribution of attitudes among generations within each type of society. Many theories of socialization suggest that people's attitudes are shaped by formative experiences in their early years and that their basic values are largely fixed by adulthood. In postindustrial societies, the formative experiences of younger generations of women and men have differed significantly from those of older generations. In the twentieth century, gender roles were affected by a long series of developments, including the extension of suffrage and full citizenship rights to women; the entry of more women into higher education and the paid labor force; the rise of the Second Wave women's movement and radical shifts in sexual mores and lifestyles in the mid-1960s; dramatic changes in the family, marriage, and the division of labor within the home; and the experience of seeing more women as leaders in public life. All these factors can be expected to have altered norms regarding the appropriate role of women in the public sphere and the suitability of women for elected office.

Outside the postindustrial societies, social change has followed different paths. In the postcommunist countries, the experience of women in the workforce, the widespread use of quotas in parliaments under communism and their subsequent abandonment, and the role of the organized women's movement in Central and Eastern Europe have all affected the development of gender-related norms. As a result, we would expect that, while some generational shifts in attitudes will be evident, the pace of change will be slower in these countries.

The evidence confirms these expectations. The traditional belief that men make better leaders than women shows a substantial generational decline in postindustrial societies, with younger postwar generations far more egalitarian than their parents or grandparents. Yet in postcommunist and developing societies, attitudes among younger and older generations are almost identical, with at most a modest shift toward less traditional views among the young. Moreover, when we disaggregate the cohort analysis for women and men in all types of society, the most striking pattern is the substantial widening of a "gender gap" on this issue among younger generations. In prewar generations, there is no difference by sex: Women are as traditional in their attitudes as men, or even slightly more so. Yet with each successive cohort, the gap widens between women's increasingly egalitarian attitudes and men's more traditional ones, until by the youngest generation the disparity has become considerable (see Figure 5.2).

This analysis suggests that, through the gradual process of demographic turnover, attitudes toward women in public leadership roles are likely to become more egalitarian, especially among women themselves. The effects of modernization will proceed in the broader political culture, even if no proactive strategies or institutional reforms are adopted to hasten the election of more women to public office. Nevertheless, there is little evidence that a similar process has yet begun to transform public opinion in postcommunist and developing countries, where traditional values are prevalent among younger as well as older citizens.

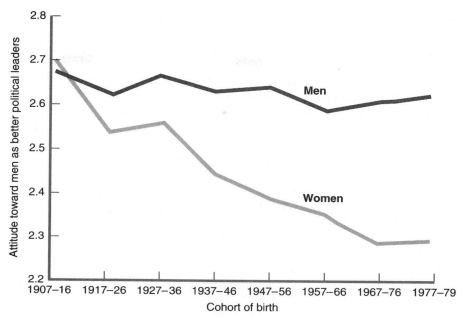

Figure 5.2 The Global Gender Gap in Attitudes Toward Women's Political Leadership.
Source: Responses to: "On the whole, men make better political leaders than women do," on a 4-point scale (1 = strongly disagree; 2 = disagree; 3 = agree; 4 = strongly agree), in the World Values Survey conducted in 1995–99; see *http://wvs.isr.umich.edu.*

The Implications for Change

The idea that the values prevailing in the broader political culture affect the success of women in gaining elected office has always been assumed but rarely, if ever, proved in a convincing fashion using systematic comparative evidence. We have long suspected that culture is the unknown factor that accounts for the striking political achievements of women in Scandinavia as compared to their counterparts in Mediterranean Europe, let alone Latin America, Asia, sub-Saharan Africa, and the Arab states. Yet that factor has proved difficult to capture on the basis of existing aggregate data.

This study demonstrates that egalitarian attitudes toward women in office are more widespread in postindustrial societies, reflecting broad patterns of socioeconomic development and cultural modernization. Such attitudes are not simply interesting for their own sake but are significantly associated with the political success of women. In short, culture matters. Moreover, the more egalitarian attitudes evident among younger generations in postindustrial societies, especially among younger women, suggest that we can expect to see continued progress in female representation in these societies. Yet the empowerment of women remains a complex process. As the cases of Australia, the United States, and Spain demonstrate, favorable attitudes toward women's leadership are not sufficient by themselves to produce breakthroughs, since some social structures and institutions continue to act as barriers. Nor can we expect the overnight transformation of the deep-rooted traditional beliefs about gender roles prevalent in many developing and postcommunist societies. . . .

Trying to alter deep-seated attitudes toward gender roles in public life may prove to be a frustrating exercise in the short term, even with extensive educational and public-awareness campaigns. In the longer term, however, the secular trends in value change associated with modernization, especially among younger generations, are likely to facilitate the process of getting more women into power. Indeed, the combination of cultural shifts in attitudes and institutional reforms of recruitment processes offers considerable promise that women may achieve political parity well before the dawn of the twenty-second century.

Notes

1. Andrew Reynolds, "Women in the Legislatures and Executives of the World: Knocking at the Highest Glass Ceiling," *World Politics* 51 (July 1999): 547–72.
2. Inter-Parliamentary Union, *Politics: Women's Insight*, IPU Reports and Documents No. 36 (Geneva: IPU, 2000).
3. Andrew Reynolds, "Women in the Legislatures and Executives of the World."
4. Data are drawn from the third wave of the World Values Survey, conducted in 1995–99 and covering 55 societies worldwide, including 11 postindustrial, 23 postcommunist, and 21 developing societies. Full information about the nations, fieldwork, methodology, and questionnaire for the survey is available online at *http://wvs.isr.umich.edu*.
5. Socioeconomic development is measured here by logged per-capita income in terms of purchasing power parity. R can vary from − 1 (a perfect inverse association) to 0 (no relationship at all) to 1, meaning a perfect association between the two variables. A significance level of .01 means that the statistical finding would happen by chance only one time in a hundred.
6. Ronald Inglehart and Wayne E. Baker, "Modernization, Cultural Change and the Persistence of Traditional Values," *American Sociological Review* 65 (February 2000): 19–51.

The Claims of Culture

Seyla Benhabib

In December 2003, France inspired a passionate and often anguished debate across Europe about ethnic identity and inclusion when President Jacques Chirac endorsed the proposal from a presidential commission that would ban the wearing of "conspicuously religious" symbols in public schools. Although written to apply equally to diverse religious and ethnic traditions, the recommendation was primarily designed to prohibit Muslim girls from wearing headscarves to school. The proposal, and draft law that followed, reignited the long-standing dispute. Seyla Benhabib's contribution traces the history and explains the importance of this controversy in France. The selection also examines the famous case of Shah Bano in India that raised similar issues about the role of women in society and the challenges of religious tolerance and coexistence in countries where national unity is a highly prized and rather elusive goal. Benhabib argues that there is no simple recipe for accommodating difference and protecting the rights of individuals within a minority group, especially when it comes to the treatment of women. Can you suggest criteria that could help a country strike a desirable balance between promoting and protecting diverse cultural communities while protecting individuals within a community, such as women, who might be harmed by accepted beliefs and practices within the community?

For as long as human societies and cultures have interacted and compared themselves with another, the status of women and children and the rituals of sex, marriage, and death have occupied a special place in intercultural understandings. . . .

In his comprehensive treatment of the puzzles of multicultural coexistence, Bhikhu Parekh lists twelve practices that most frequently lead to clashes of intercultural evaluation: female circumcision; polygamy; Muslim and Jewish methods of animal slaughter; arranged marriages; marriages within prohibited degrees of relationships; scarring children's cheeks or other parts of the body; Muslim withdrawal of girls from coeducational practices such as sports and

Seyla Benhabib, *The Claims of Culture* (Princeton, NJ: Princeton University Press, 2002).

swimming lessons; Muslim insistence that girls wear the *hijab,* or headscarf; Sikh insistence on wearing or taking off the traditional turbans; Gypsy and Amish refusal to send their children to public schools either altogether or after a certain age; Hindu requests to be allowed to cremate their deceased; the subordinate status of women and all that entails (2000, 264–65). Of the twelve practices listed by Parekh, seven concern the status of women in distinct cultural communities; two bear on dress codes pertaining to both sexes (the wearing of the turban and the *hijab*); two are about the lines separating private from public jurisdictional authority in the education of children; and one each concerns dietary codes and funeral rites. How can we account for the preponderance of cultural practices concerning the status of women, girls, marriage, and sexuality that lead to intercultural conflict? . . .

These interconnections between psychic identity, the practices of the private sphere, and cultural difference assume a new configuration in modern liberal democracies. These societies demarcate the private from the public along the following lines: the political sphere, together with the economy and certain domains of civil society, is considered "public" in multiple senses: accessible to all; shared by all; and in the interests of all. The household is considered private, in the sense that it strictly regulates access through kinship and marriage, and does not concern itself with the interest of all. In liberal societies, institutional patterns of regulating the private and the public spheres are undergirded by other assumptions as well. Liberalism is based on the conviction that privacy extends to those most deeply held beliefs pertaining to religion, culture, aesthetics, and lifestyle. Liberalism not only respects "the privacy" of the familial-domestic sphere; it also requires that the state not regulate matters of religious, cultural, and aesthetic belief. . . . Of course, matters are never that simple, and the line between the public and the private is always contested. From the standpoint of the liberal state, the family is a public institution in which practices governing marriage and divorce are defined and regulated by political as well as legal norms. The state confers fiscal and economic status upon the family in that it defines the tax status of those who are considered family members; in not recognizing same-sex unions as marriages, the state also upholds a specific conception of the family. Viewed as an institution within the modern state, then, the family has nothing "private" about it. Likewise, the lines separating religion from the state, aesthetics from politics, are always hotly contested.

In this [discussion] I focus on a number of highly publicized multicultural disputes regarding . . . family law, in the course of which traditional distinctions between the public and the private were contested and resignified. I then revisit the debate in feminist theory initiated by Susan Moller Okin's provocative question, "Is multiculturalism bad for women?" (1999). I argue that this manner of posing the question has led to an unnecessary impasse and polarization, because both opponents and proponents of multiculturalism, despite disclaimers to the contrary, continue to defend a faulty understanding of cultures as unified, holistic, and self-consistent wholes. Therefore cultural processes of resignification and reinterpretation, which women in minority ethnic communities engaged in, are ignored. A deliberative democratic multicultural politics does not confine women and children to their communities of origin against their will, but encourages them to develop their autonomous agency vis-à-vis their ascribed identities. . . .

Multiculturalism and Personal and Family Law

A divorced Muslim woman, Shah Bano Begum, filed an application for maintenance under section 125 of the Indian Code of Criminal Procedure against her husband, the advocate Mohammad Ahmad Khan. Married to Ahmad Khan in 1932, Shah Bano was driven out of the matrimonial home in 1975. In April 1978, she filed an application against her husband in the court of the judicial magistrate, Indore, asking for maintenance at the rate of 500 rupees. On November 6, 1978 the apellant (Khan) divorced the respondent (Shah Bano) by an irrevocable *talaq* (divorce), permitted under Muslim personal law. Mohammad Ahmad Khan filed a criminal appeal against Shah Bano Begum and others in the Supreme Court of India in 1985. His claim was that Shah Bano had ceased to be his wife after his second marriage, and that in accordance with Muslim law, he had paid a maintenance allowance for two years prior to the date at which Shah Bano filed her claim, as well as depositing 3,000 rupees by way of a dower. The principal legal dispute centered on whether section 125 of the Code of Criminal Procedure was applicable to Muslims in India.

The judgment of the Indian Supreme Court, which decided that the Code of Criminal Procedure was indeed applicable to Muslims, ordered the appellant to raise his maintenance to Shah Bano from 70 to 130 rupees. But the court's decision went much further than this. Chief Justice Chandrachud commented on the injustice done to women of all religions, on the desirability of evolving a common civil code as envisaged by paragraph 44 of the Indian Federal Constitution, and on the provisions in the Shariat (Muslim religious law) regarding the obligation of a husband to his divorced wife. According to most interpreters, the Supreme Court of India thus opened the floodgates to a series of debates between the Muslim and Indian communities, and within the Muslim community itself—between "progressives" and "fundamentalists," between women's groups and Muslim leaders, and so forth. The political debates, pressures, and counterpressures led to the passage of the Muslim Women (Protection of Rights and Divorce) Bill of 1986. Clearly, the Shah Bano controversy raised issues that went far beyond the case at hand, into the very heart of the practice of legal pluralism, of religious coexistence and tolerance, and of the meaning of Indian national unity and identity. . . .

The Muslim community was forced to rework distinctions and modalities of coexistence in view of growing demands for the recognition of women's equality on the one hand and changing family lives and economic patterns on the other. A movement for the passing of the Muslim Women's Bill developed. As passed in 1986, this bill stipulated that a divorced woman was to be supported by relatives,

such as brothers and sons, who were in the category of heirs, and when such relatives were unable to support the woman, then it was the responsibility of the
community to support her through its *waqf* (obligatory charitable organizations)
boards. Clearly, the purpose of even this supposed reform bill was to anchor the
dependency of women upon a male-dominated, hierarchical structure, either the
natal family or the community board. The possibility of assuring the divorced
woman's independence through integrating her into a larger civil society and
making her to some extent financially autonomous was totally blocked. . . .
Under pressure from the Muslim community, Shah Bano eventually withdrew
her claim and accepted the earlier alimony settlement. Multiculturalist juggling,
in this case as well, produced the defeat of women. . . .

Multiculturalism, Laicité, and the Scarf Affair in France

Consider now what has been referred to as *l'affaire foulard*—the scarf affair—in
France. Whereas in the cases of "cultural defense" and Shah Bano, we have encountered the liberal-democratic state and its institutions reinscribing women's
identities within their natal communities of faith and culture, in the foulard
affair we encounter public officials and institutions that supposedly champion
women's emancipation from these communities by suppressing the practice of
veiling. The state here acts as the champion of women's emancipation from
their communities of birth. Yet, as we shall see, some women resisted the state
not to affirm their religious and sexual subordination as much as to assert a
quasi-personal identity independent of the dominant French culture.

The practice of veiling among Muslim women is a complex institution that exhibits great variety across many Muslim countries. The terms *chador, hijab, niqab*,
and *foulard* refer to distinct items of clothing worn by women from different Muslim communities: for example, the chador is essentially Iranian and refers to the
long black robe and head scarf worn in a rectangular manner around the face;
the niqab is a veil that covers the eyes and the mouth and leaves only the nose
exposed; it may or may not be worn in conjunction with the chador. Most
Muslim women from Turkey are likely to wear either long overcoats and a
foulard (a head scarf) or a *carsaf* (a black garment that most resembles the
chador). These items of clothing have a symbolic function within the Muslim
community itself: women from different countries signal to one another their
ethnic and national origins through their clothing, as well as their distance or
proximity to tradition. The brighter the colors of their overcoats and scarves—
bright blue, green, beige, lilac, as opposed to brown, gray, navy, and, of course,
black—and the more fashionable their cuts and material by Western standards,
the more we can assume the distance from Islamic orthodoxy of the women who
wear them. Seen from the outside, however, this complex semiotic of dress codes
is reduced to one or two items of clothing that then assume the function of
crucial symbols of complex negotiations between Muslim religious and cultural
identities and Western cultures.

L'affaire foulard refers to a long and drawn-out set of public confrontations that began in France in 1989 with the expulsions from their school in Creil (Oise) of three scarf-wearing Muslim girls and continued to the mass exclusion of twenty-three Muslim girls from their schools in November 1996 upon the decision of the Conseil d'Etat. The affair, referred to as a "national drama" or even a "national trauma," occurred in the wake of France's celebration of the second centennial of the French Revolution and seemed to question the foundations of the French educational system and its philosophical principle, *laicité*. This concept is difficult to translate in terms like the "separation of Church and State" or even secularization: at its best, it can be understood as the public and manifest neutrality of the state toward all kinds of religious practices, institutionalized through a vigilant removal of sectarian religious symbols, signs, icons, and items of clothing from official public spheres. Yet within the French Republic the balance between respecting the individual's right to freedom of conscience and religion, on the one hand, and maintaining a public sphere devoid of all religious symbolisms, on the other, was so fragile that it took only the actions of a handful of teenagers to expose this fragility. The ensuing debate went far beyond the original dispute and touched upon the self-understanding of French republicanism for the left as well as the right, on the meaning of social and sexual equality, and liberalism versus republicanism versus multiculturalism in French life.

The affair began when on October 19, 1989, Ernest Chenière, headmaster of the college Gabriel-Havez of Creil, forbade three girls—Fatima, Leila, and Samira—to attend classes with their heads covered. Each had appeared in class that morning wearing her scarf, despite a compromise reached between their headmasters and their parents encouraging them to go unscarfed. The three girls had apparently decided to wear the scarf once more upon the advice of Daniel Youssouf Leclerq, the head of an organization called Integrité and the former president of the National Federation of Muslims in France (FNMF). Although hardly noted in the press, the fact that the girls had been in touch with Leclerq indicates that wearing the scarf was a conscious political gesture on their part, a complex act of identification and defiance. In doing so, Fatima, Leila, and Samira on the one hand claimed to exercise their freedom of religion as French citizens; on the other hand they exhibited their Muslim and North African origins in a context that sought to envelop them, as students of the nation, within an egalitarian, secularist ideal of republican citizenship. In the years to come, their followers and supporters forced what the French state wanted to view as a private symbol—an individual item of clothing—into the shared public sphere, thus challenging the boundaries between the public and the private. Ironically, they used the freedom given to them by French society and French political traditions, not the least of which is the availability of free and compulsory public education for all children on French soil, to juxtapose an aspect of their private identity onto the public sphere. In doing so, they problematized the school as well as the home: they no longer treated the school as a neutral space of French acculturation, but openly manifested their cultural and religious differences. They used the symbol of the home in the public sphere, retaining the modesty required of them by Islam in covering their heads; yet at the same time, they left the home to become public actors in a civil public space, in which they defied the state. Those who saw in the girls' actions simply an indication of their oppression were just as blind to the symbolic meaning of their deeds as were those who defended their rights simply on the basis of freedom of religion. . . .

The complexity of the social and cultural negotiations hidden behind the simple act of veiling elicited an equally ambigious and complex decision by the French Conseil d'Etat. On November 4, 1989, the French minister of education, Lionel Jospin, took the matter to the Conseil d'Etat (the French Supreme Court). The Conseil rendered a notoriously ambiguous decision. The minister of education asked three questions, two of which were related to the administrative handling of the answer, which would result from an answer to the first question: "If, in view of the principles of the Constitution and the laws of the Republic and with respect to the totality of rules pertaining to the organization and functioning of the public school, the wearing of signs of belonging to a religious community is or is not compatible with the principle of laïcité" (cited in Brun-Rovet 2000, 28). The court responded by citing France's adherence to constitutional and legislative texts and to international conventions, and invoked from the outset the necessity of doing justice to two principles: that the laïcité and neutrality of the state be retained in the rendering of public services and that the liberty of conscience of the students be respected. All discrimination based upon the religious convictions or beliefs of the students would be inadmissable. . . .

. . . Yet instead of articulating some clear guidelines, the court left the proper interpretation of the meaning of these signs to the judgment of the school authorities. The decisive factors in curtailing the students' freedom of religion was not the individual students' beliefs about what a religious scarf (or for that matter yarmulke) meant to them, but how the school authorities interpreted the scarf's meaning, and whether or not it could be seen as a means of provocation, confrontation, or remonstration. It is not difficult to see why this judgment encouraged both sides to the conflict to pursue their goals further and led to additional repression through the promulgation on September 10, 1994, of the Bayrou Guidelines, issued by Minister of Education François Bayrou. Lamenting the ambiguities of the judgment of the court for conveying an impression of "weaknesses" vis-à-vis Islamicist movements, the minister declared that students had the right to wear discrete religious symbols, but that the veil was not among them.

The Bayrou declaration further hardened the fronts of various political actors: intellectuals, teachers' unions, various Islamic organizations, antiimmigrant groups, and the like. The French population was already highly polarized on the issues of Islam, immigration, and national security. In the summer of 1994, a bomb planted by Muslim fundamentalist groups exploded in the metro in Paris; thus it seemed that France, despite herself, was sucked into the vortex of violence coming from fundamentalist Islamic groups, and that its traditions of tolerance and pluralism were misused by these groups to further their own sectarian political goals.

The evolution of SOS-Racisme's attitudes in view of these developments is quite telling. During the Creil episode in 1989, SOS-Racisme—one of the most militant antiracist groups, drawing its membership particularly from among the young—led large sections of the French left into defending laïcité and protesting the exclusion of the Muslim girls. But by 1994, the new president of the association called for a ban on all religious symbols; many had now come to see the recurrence of the wearing of the scarfs not as isolated incidents, but as a provocation on the part of an organized Islam that had to be confronted clearly and unequivocally (Brun-Rovet 2000). L'affair foulard eventually came to stand for all dilemmas of French national identity in the age of globalization and multiculturalism: how to retain French traditions of laïcité, republican equality, and democratic citizenship in view of France's integration into the European Union, on the one hand, and the pressures of multiculturalism generated through the presence of second- and third-generation immigrants from Muslim countries on French soil, on the other hand. Would the practices and institutions of French citizenship be flexible and generous enough to encompass multicultural differences within an ideal of republican equality? Clearly, this affair is by no means over. As European integration and multiculturalist pressures continue, France, just like India and the United States, will have to discover new models of legal, pedagogical, social, and cultural institutions to deal with the dual imperatives of liberal democracies to preserve freedom of religious expression and the principles of secularism.

Is Multiculturalism Bad for Women?

These [two] cases suggest that multicultural institutional arrangements and legal compromises very often work to the detriment of women. Either they imprison them in arcane arrangements of dependency upon their husbands and male relatives—as was the case with Shah Bano—. . . or they make women and girls objects of state regulation and punishment in order to teach the nation a lesson, as in the case of the scarf affair in France. . . .

Yet the standpoint of the feminist critic, in this respect, is not all that different from the standpoint of the legislator. . . . The Indian courts are obliged to accept the jurisdictional division of labor between a unified criminal code and separate private and family law for India's Muslim and Hindu communities. The French Conseil d'Etat tries to do justice to the principles of laïcité as well as the freedom of conscience and religion, but delivers the girls with the head scarves to the intensified scrutiny and authority of their school supervisors and disregards the students' own understanding of their actions.

The cases discussed in this [contribution] illustrate what Ayelet Shachar has named "the paradox of multicultural vulnerability" (2000, 386). "Well-meaning accommodation policies by the state, aimed at leveling the playing field between minority communities and the wider society," argues Shachar, "may unwittingly allow systematic maltreatment of individuals within the accommodated minority group—an impact, in certain cases, so severe that it nullifies these individuals' rights as citizens" (386). The tension and, in many cases, the moral dilemma between accommodating difference and doing justice to all members of a minority group propels contemporary discussions of multiculturalism into a new phase.

References

Brun-Rovet, Marianne. 2000. "A Perspective on the Multiculturalism Debate: 'L'affaire foulard' and *laicité* in France, 1989–1999." Seminar paper submitted to Professor Benhabib's class "Nations, States, and Citizens," Harvard University, Department of Government. On file with the author.

Okin, Susan Moller. 1999. "Is Multiculturalism Bad for Women?" In *Is Multiculturalism Bad for Women?* by Susan Moller Okin, edited by Joshua Cohen, Matthew Howard, and Martha C. Nussbaum. Princeton: Princeton University Press.

Parekh, Bhikhu. 2000. *Rethinking Multiculturalism: Cultural Diversity and Political Theory.* Cambridge: Harvard University Press.

Shachar, Ayelet. 2000. "The Puzzle of Interlocking Power Hierarchies: Sharing the Pieces of Jurisdictional Authority." *Harvard Civil Rights—Civil Liberties Law Review* 35, no. 2 (Summer 2000): 387–426.

 5.3

Race in the Twenty-First Century

Howard Winant

In this selection, Howard Winant brings a historical and comparative perspective to the theme of racial politics. At the start of the twenty-first century, Winant argues, racial politics has been reinvented along seemingly nonracist lines, yet racial inequality and injustice persist as defining features of the contemporary global order. Drawing on the national cases of the United States, South Africa, and Brazil, as well as the regional experience of the European Union countries, Winant concludes that racism remains a crucial component of contemporary social and political life. More optimistically, he suggests that the world still has a chance not to move beyond race but rather to break the association between racial politics and injustice.

In what ways does Winant's analysis help us understand Barack Obama's election as president in 2008?

Howard Winant, "Race in the Twenty-First Century," *Tikkun* [Bimonthly Interfaith Critique of Politics, Culture and Society] (January/February 2002).

As the world lurches forward into the twenty-first century, there is widespread confusion and anxiety about the political significance, and even the meaning, of race. The future of democracy itself depends on the outcomes of racial politics and policies, as they develop both in various national societies and in the world at large. This means that the future of democracy also depends on the concept of race, the meaning that is attached to race. Contemporary threats to human rights and social well-being—including the resurgent dangers of fascism, increasing impoverishment, and massive social polarization—cannot be managed or even understood without paying new and better attention to issues of race. We need a set of conceptual tools that can facilitate this task.

The present moment is unique in the history of race. Starting during World War II and culminating in the 1960s, there was a global shift, a "break," in the worldwide racial system that had endured for centuries. The shift occurred because many challenges to the old forms of racial hierarchy converged after the war: anti-colonialism, anti-apartheid, worldwide revulsion at fascism, and perhaps most important, the U.S. civil rights movement and U.S.–USSR competition in the world's South. All called white supremacy into question to an extent unparalleled in modern history. These events and conflicts linked anti-racism to democratic political development more strongly than ever before. As a result, for the first time in modern history, there is widespread, indeed worldwide, support for what had until recently been a "dream," Dr. King's dream let us say, of racial equality.

Yet white supremacy is hardly dead. It has proven itself capable of absorbing and adapting much of the "dream," repackaging itself as "colorblind," nonracialist, and meritocratic. In our post-imperial, post–Cold War world, a new racial politics is developing, one which has tried to reinvent itself along overtly nonracist lines. In fact, its capacity to present itself as "beyond race" is in many ways the crucial index of its stability. Paradoxically, however, in this reformed version racial inequality can live on, still battening on all sorts of stereotypes and fears, still resorting to exclusionism and scapegoating when politically necessary, still invoking the supposed superiority of "mainstream" (a.k.a. white) values, and cheerfully maintaining that equality has been largely achieved. Despite all the political reforms, despite the real amelioration of the most degrading features of the old-world racial system, the centuries-old and deeply entrenched system of racial inequality and injustice has hardly been eliminated. Rather, this new "colorblind" racial system may be more effective in containing the challenges posed over the past few decades by movements for racial justice than any intransigent, overtly racist "backlash" could possibly have been.

Although the reformed and officially nonracial version of white supremacy has succeeded in curtailing progress toward the "dream" in many dubious battles—over immigration and citizenship, income redistribution and poverty, and above all in respect to the compensatory programs commonly called "affirmative action"—the new racial politics has hardly won the day. It has certainly not eliminated the movement for racial justice that spawned it. Rather, the racial politics that results from this synthesis of challenge and incorporation, racial conflict and racial reform, has proved neither stable nor certain. It is a strange brew, often appearing more inclusive, more pluralistic than ever before, yet also filled with threats: of "ethnic cleansing," resurgent neofascism, and perhaps equally insidious, a renewed racial complacency.

No longer unabashedly white supremacist, the new racial politics is, so to speak, abashedly white supremacist.

The Modern World Racial System

Popular culture tends to represent racism as an archaic phenomenon, an outgrowth of pre-modern slave-based societies. But modernity has to be acknowledged as a racial phenomenon in its own right. The Enlightenment's recognition of a unified, intelligible world, the construction of an international economy, the rise of democracy and popular sovereignty, and the emergence of a global culture were all deeply racialized processes. To understand how race was fundamental to the construction of modernity is of more than historical interest: it also explains much about the present. Notably, it demolishes the commonly-held belief that racism is largely a thing of the past, the idea that after the bad old days of white supremacism and colonial rule, there has occurred in our own time a belated resolution to the "race problem."

The tension between slavery on the one hand, and nascent democracy on the other, structured the lengthy transition to the modern world. Resistance against slavery contributed crucially to the broader redefinition of political rights for which early advocates of democracy yearned and fought. Indeed, the violence and genocide of earlier racial phenomena prefigured contemporary atrocities like the Holocaust, "ethnic cleansing," and totalitarianism.

The abolition of African slavery was the great rehearsal for the "break" with white supremacy that took place in our own time. Abolition was not completed with the triumph of the Union in the American Civil War and the passage of the Reconstruction amendments to the Constitution. Only when Brazil, the last country to free its slaves, did so in 1888, did the first crucial battle in the centuries-long war against white supremacy draw to a close. Abolition, that is, was not the result of one war in one country, but was made possible by three momentous social changes: the triumph of industrial capitalism, the upsurge of democratic movements, and the mobilization of slaves themselves in search of freedom.

But abolition left many emancipatory tasks unfinished. New forms of racial inequality succeeded slavery. Even after slavery had been ended, democracy was still partial. Racialization—for example the U.S. laws and social practices known as "Jim Crow"—continued to define the mechanisms of authoritarian rule and to distribute resources, not only in the U.S. but on a global scale. Racial thought and practices continued to associate subordinated status almost irrevocably with distinct types of human bodies, thus enabling and justifying world systemic rule. Generalized processes of racial stratification continued to support enormous and oppressive systems of commercial agriculture and mining. Through the mid-twentieth century, the unfulfilled dreams of human rights and equality were still tied up with the logic of race.

Although there was always resistance to racist rule, it was only in the period after World War II that opposition to racial stratification and racial exclusion once again turned into major political conflicts. Civil rights and anti-racist movements, as well as nationalist and indigenous ones, fiercely contested the racial limitations on democracy. These movements challenged the conditions under which racialized labor was available for exploitation in the former colonies as well as the metropoles. Picking up the anti-fascist legacy of World War II, they also took advantage of the geopolitical conflicts of the Cold War. They rendered old forms of political exclusion problematic, and revealed the inherent racist bias in many mainstream cultural icons—artistic, linguistic, scientific, and of course political—that had long been considered unproblematic. To cite some U.S. examples: many of the "founding fathers," for example, were newly recognized as committed slaveholders; corporate complicity with slavery and imperialism was rediscovered. Familiar writers such as Hemingway were reread with racial issues in mind. And popular culture, the "material culture" with its Aunt Jemima pancakes and Cream of Wheat cereal boxes, suddenly appeared surprising (to whites at least).

Drawing on the experience of millions who had undergone military mobilization followed by an embittering return to a segregated or colonized homeland, the anti-racist movements were able to recognize anew their international character, as massive postwar labor demand sparked international migration from the world's South to its North, from areas of peasant agriculture to industrial areas. These enormous transformations manifested themselves in a vast demand to complete the work begun a century before with slavery's abolition. They sparked the worldwide "break" with the tradition of white supremacy.

As the tumultuous 1960s drew to a close, the descendants of slaves and ex-colonials had forced at least the partial dismantling of most official forms of discrimination and empire. But with these developments—the enactment of a new series of civil rights laws, decolonization, and the adoption of cultural policies of a universalistic character—the global racial system entered a new period of instability and tension. The immediate result of the "break" was an uneven series of racial reforms that had the general effect of ameliorating racial injustice and inequality, but also worked to contain social protest. Thus the widespread demands of the racially subordinated and their supporters were at best answered in a limited fashion; in this way a new period of racial instability and uncertainty was inaugurated.

Some National Cases

The "break" was a worldwide phenomenon, but it obviously took very different forms in particular national settings. Racial conditions are generally understood to vary dramatically in distinct political, economic, and cultural contexts. Here I'd like to focus, however briefly, on four national case studies: the United States, South Africa, Brazil, and the European Union (considered as a whole). I chose these four cases, because they are crucial variants, important laboratories in which new racial dynamics are being developed.

These comparative case studies demonstrate that the post–World War II "break" is a global backdrop, an economic, political, and cultural context in which national racial conflicts are being worked out. They give us a context for understanding the developing nature of the new racial politics.

The United States

How permanent is the "color line"? The activities of the civil rights movement and related anti-racist initiatives achieved substantial, if partial, democratic reforms in earlier postwar decades. These innovations continue to coexist, however, with a weighty legacy of white supremacy whose origins lie in the colonial and slavery era. How do these two currents combine and conflict today?

Massive migration, both internal and international, has reshaped the U.S. population, both numerically and geographically. A multipolar racial pattern has largely supplanted the old racial system, which was often (and somewhat erroneously) viewed as a bipolar white-black hierarchy. In the contemporary United States, new varieties of inter-minority competition, as well as new awareness of the international "embeddedness" of racial identity, have greater prominence. Racial stratification varies substantially by class, region, and indeed among groups, although comprehensive racial inequality certainly endures. Racial reform policies are under attack in many spheres of social policy and law, where the claim is forcefully made that the demands of the civil rights movement have largely been met, and that the United States has entered a "post-racial" stage of its history.

The racial "break" in the United States was a partial democratization, produced by the moderate coalition that dominated the political landscape in the post–World War II years. The partial victory of the civil rights movement was achieved by a synthesis of mass mobilization on the one hand, and a tactical alliance with U.S. national interests on the other. This alliance was brokered by racial "moderates": political centrists largely affiliated with the Democratic Party, who perceived the need to ameliorate racial conflict and end outright racial dictatorship, but who also understood and feared the radical potential of the black movement.

There was a price to be paid for civil rights reform. It could take place only in a suitably deradicalized fashion, only if its key provisions were articulated (legislatively, juridicially) in terms compatible with the core values of U.S. politics and culture: individualism, equality, competition, opportunity, and the accessibility of "the American dream," etc. This price was to be paid by the movement's radicals: revolutionaries, socialists, and political nationalists—black, brown, red, yellow, and white—who were required to forego their vision of major social transformation or to face marginalization, repression, or death if they would not.

The radical vision was an alternative "dream," Dr. King's dream let us call it, a dream in which racial justice played the central part. To be "free at last" meant something deeper than symbolic reforms and palliation of the worst excesses of white supremacy. It meant substantive social reorganization that would be manifested in egalitarian economic and democratizing political consequences. It meant something like social democracy, human rights, and social citizenship for blacks and other "minorities."

But it was precisely here that the "moderate" custodians of racial reform drew their boundary line, both in practical terms and in theoretical ones. To strike down officially sanctioned racial inequality was permissible; to create racial equality through positive state action was not. The danger of redistribution—of acceding to demands to make substantive redress for the unjustified expropriation and restriction of black economic and political resources, both historically and in the present—was to be avoided at all costs.

Civil rights reform thus became the agenda of the political center, which moved "from domination to hegemony." The key component of modern political rule, of "hegemony" as theorized by Gramsci most profoundly, is the capacity to *incorporate opposition*. By adopting many of the movement's demands, by developing a comprehensive and coherent program of "racial democracy" that hewed to a centrist political logic and reinforced key dimensions of U.S. nationalist ideology, racial "moderates" were able to define a new racial "common sense." Thus they divided the movement, reasserted a certain stability, and defused a great deal of political opposition. This was accomplished not all at once, but over a prolonged period from about the mid-1960s to the mid-1980s.

This partial reconfiguration of the U.S. racial order was based on real concessions but left major issues unresolved, notably the endurance of significant patterns of inequality and discrimination. Still, the reform that did occur was sufficient to reduce the political challenge posed by antiracist movements. Certainly it has been more successful than the intransigent strategy of diehard segregationists—based in the slogan of "massive resistance" to even minimal integration—would have been.

Yet the fundamental problems of racial injustice and inequality, of white supremacy, of course remain: moderated perhaps, but hardly resolved.

So in the U.S. context, race not only retains its significance as a social structural phenomenon, but also continues to define North American identities and life chances, well after the supposed triumph of the "civil rights revolution." Indeed "the American dilemma" may be more problematic than ever as the twenty-first century commences. For achieving a "moderate" race policy agenda has required that the civil rights vision be drawn and quartered, beginning in the late 1960s and with ever-greater success in the following two decades.

The tugging and hauling, the escalating contestation over the meaning of race, has resulted in ever more disrupted and contradictory notions of racial

identity. The significance of race ("declining" or increasing?), the interpretation of racial equality ("colorblind" or color-conscious?), the institutionalization of racial justice ("reverse discrimination" or affirmative action?),
and the very categories—black, white, Latino/Hispanic, Asian American, and
Native American—employed to classify racial groups . . . all these were called
into question as they emerged from the civil rights "victory" of the mid-1960s.

Despite this continuous degradation of the dream of equality, the view that
racial injustice has largely been surpassed in a post–civil rights era has become
the new national "common sense." This view has acquired not only elite and
academic spokespeople, but also widespread mass adherence, especially among
whites. As a result, the already limited racial reform policies ("affirmative
action") and the relatively powerless state agencies charged with enforcing civil
rights laws (Equal Employment Opportunity Commission) developed in the
1960s are undergoing new and severe attack.

The argument is now made that the demands of the civil rights movement
have largely been met, and that the United States has entered a "post-racial"
stage of its history. Advocates of such positions—usually classified as "neocon-
servative" (but sometimes also found on the left)—ceaselessly instruct racially-
defined minorities to "pull themselves up by their own bootstraps," and, in
callous distortion of Martin Luther King Jr.'s message, exhort them to accept the
"content of their character" (rather than "the color of their skin") as the basic
social value of the country. . . .

After the dust had settled from the titanic confrontation between the movement's radical propensities and the "establishment's" tremendous capacity for
incorporative "moderate" reform, a great deal remained unresolved. The
ambiguous and contradictory racial conditions in the United States today result
from decades-long attempts to simultaneously ameliorate racial opposition and
to placate the *ancien regime raciale*. The unending reiteration of these opposite
gestures, these contradictory practices, itself testifies to the limitations of
democracy and the continuing significance of race in the United States.

South Africa

In the mid-1990s, South Africa—the most explicitly racialized society in
the late twentieth century—entered a difficult but promising transition. The
apartheid state had of course been committed to a racialized framework of citizenship, civic inclusion, and law in general; the post-apartheid constitution
incorporates the principles of nonracialism originally articulated in the ANC-
based Freedom Charter of 1955. Yet the country still bears the terrible burden of
apartheid's sequelae: persistent racial inequality across every level of society.
The legacies of segregated residential areas, combined with a highly racialized
distribution of resources of every sort, combine to urge moderation on political
leadership. White fears must be placated in order to sustain the country's

economic base and to minimize capital flight. Whites continue to hold controlling positions throughout the economy; the handful of blacks who have made their way into the corporate and state elites understand very well the price the country would pay for a radical turn in policy.

Yet this is a state committed to racial equality, and to promoting black advancement, individually and collectively. Can the post-apartheid state stabilize the process of political, social, and economic integration of the black majority? Can it maintain an official nonracialism in the face of such comprehensive racial inequality? How can the vast majority of citizens—excluded until so recently from access to land, education, clean water, and decent shelter; debarred from Africa's wealthiest economy; and denied the most elementary civic and political rights—garner the economic access they so desperately need, without reinforcing white paranoia and fear? How can the post-apartheid state facilitate the reform of racial attitudes and practices, challenging inequality, white supremacism, and the legacy of racial separatism, without engendering white flight and subversion?

Both the anti-apartheid movement and the new government's policies were shaped by global concerns as well as by local ones. Internal political debates reflect changing global discussions around race and politics. Just as the South African Black Consciousness Movement drew on the speeches of Malcolm X and Aimé Cesaire in its understanding of racial oppression, just as the anti-apartheid movement used international anti-racist sentiment to build momentum for sanctions on the old regime, so too the current government is both guided and constrained by international pressures and issues.

Moreover, internal politics bring international resources to bear: through the post-war era, the anti-apartheid movement drew much of its resources and ideas from an international anti-racist movement, largely linked to an international trend to support decolonization. Since the 1994 election, however, international constraints have limited the sphere of action of the new democratic government. Critics of affirmative action policies, for example, emphasize the danger of undermining efficiency in the name of redistribution, much as critics of redistributive policies deploy neoliberal economic arguments to reject nationalization. In each case, they invoke international discourses that are nonracial in form, yet have racial implications in practice. The South African state continues to face considerable challenges from both left and right: will it be possible to reconstruct South Africa by building not only a democracy but a greater degree of consensus, of citizenship and belonging? To what degree can a policy of "class compromise" forestall the dangers of social upheaval and capital flight?

Understanding these processes requires viewing South African racial debates in global perspective, and exploring the ways in which local actors seek to change the rules of engagement as they restructure national politics. The 1994 elections changed the racial character of the state, although many white civil servants remain in place; affirmative action policies, to which the ANC-led government is committed, could reorganize racial distribution of incomes, if not wealth. Yet in the context of a global debate over affirmative action, and in the face of the threat of the flight of white capital and skills, the process of reform has been far slower than many South Africans, white and black, expected. This dilemma remains unresolved: how can democratic nonracial institutions be constructed in a society where most attributes of socioeconomic position and identity remain highly racialized?

Brazil

Brazil presents significant parallels, both historical and contemporary, to other American nations, including the United States. These similarities include Brazil's history of slavery and black inequality, its displacement and neglect of a large indigenous population, its intermittent and ambiguous commitment to immigration, its incomplete democracy, and its vast, increasingly urban, and disproportionately black underclass. Brazilian racial dynamics have traditionally received little attention, either from scholars or policy makers, despite the fact that the country has the second largest black population in the world (after Nigeria). Its post-emancipation adoption of a policy of "whitening," which was to be achieved by concerted recruitment of European immigrants, owed much to the U.S. example, and also drew on nineteenth century French racial theorizing.

Amazingly, the "myth of racial democracy" still flourishes in Brazil, even though it has been amply demonstrated to be little more than a fig leaf covering widespread racial inequality, injustice, and prejudice. The Brazilian racial system, with its "color continuum" (as opposed to the more familiar "color line" of North America), tends to dilute democratic demands. Indeed, Brazilian racial dynamics have made it difficult to promote policies that might address racial inequality. Public discourse resolutely discourages any attempt to define inequality along racial lines; the [former] President, Fernando Henrique Cardoso, [was] the first even to broach the subject seriously, although vociferous denials both official and informal persist. If politicians do point out racial inequalities, they challenge the myth of racial democracy, and are subject to charges that they are themselves provoking racial discrimination by stressing difference. . . .

The emergence of the *Movimento Negro Unificado* as a force to be reckoned with—though by no means as strong as the 1960s U.S. civil rights movement—represents a new development. The MNU used the 1988 centennial of the abolition of Brazilian slavery, as well as the 1990–91 census, to dramatize persistent racial inequalities. As in South Africa, this phase of the black movement takes its reference points partly from international anti-racist struggles, often drawing on examples, symbols, and images from the civil rights and anti-apartheid movements.

In the 1990s, a range of racial reforms were proposed in Brazil—largely in response to the increasingly visible *Movimento Negro*. To enact these reforms, to prompt the state to adopt anti-racist policies, however, will require far greater support for change than presently exists. The political dilemma is familiar. Blacks need organized allies: in the party system, among other impoverished and disenfranchised groups, and on the international scene. Yet in order to mobilize, they must also begin to assert a racialized political identity, or there will be little collective support for racial reforms. How can blacks address this dualistic, if not contradictory, situation? How can Afro-Brazilians assert claims on the basis of group solidarity, without simultaneously undermining the fragile democratic consensus that has begun to emerge across many constituencies? How can democratic institutions be built alongside policies designed to address racial inequalities, without undermining a vision of common citizenship and equality?

The European Union

The last few decades have established that, indeed, "the empire strikes back." Racially plural societies are in place throughout Europe, especially in former imperial powers like the United Kingdom, the Netherlands, France, and Spain, but also in Germany, Italy, the Scandinavian countries, and to some extent in the East. The influx of substantial numbers of nonwhites during the post-colonial period has deeply altered a dynamic in which the racial system and the imperial order had been one, and in which the "other" was by and large kept outside the walls of the "mother country." As a stroll around London, Frankfurt, Paris, or Madrid quickly reveals, those days are now gone forever. Yet the re-sponse to the new situation too often takes repressive and anti-democratic forms, focusing attention on the "immigrant problem" (or the "Islamic problem"), seeking not only to shut the gates to Maghrebines or sub-Saharan Africans, Turks, or Slavs (including Balkan refugees), but often also to define those "others" who are already present as enemies of the national culture and threats to the "ordinary German" (or English, or French, etc.) way of life. This ratio-nale for racial exclusion and restriction in Europe has been analyzed as "differ-entialist": its distinction from the meritocratic logic of discrimination in the United States has been linked to a generally lower European interest in issues of individual equality, and a relatively greater concern with the integrity of national cultures.

Thus the particular racial issue that must be confronted in Europe is the newly heterogeneous situation, the multiplication of group identities. Currently, anti-democratic tendencies are widely visible: new right-wing and neofascist groups are widespread. At both the state and regional levels the agenda of restriction is gaining adherence, jeopardizing mobility of employment or residence, and sometimes stigmatizing religious or other cultural practices. Conflicts over im-migration and citizenship have taken on new intensity, with crucial implications for the character of democracy.

The dynamics of integration raise a wide range of questions about future European racial logics. Conflicting principles of citizenship should it be based on principles of descent or on those of territory, *jus sanguinis* or *jus soli?*—are deeply imbedded in the distinct European national makeups, and their resolu-tion in a common cultural/political framework will not come easily. Relations with ex-colonies vary, raising serious questions not only of immigrant access and economic ties between the old empires and the new Europe, but also giving rise to serious anxieties about "security" and "terrorism." Popular anti-racist sentiments stimulated the formation of many multiculturalist and pluralist organizations, particularly in the early 1980s. But over the past decade they have largely ceased to function as mass mobilization initiatives in support of democracy. So, while the slogan *"Touche pas mon pôte"* ("Hands off my buddy") no longer summons tens of thousands into the street in defense of the democratic rights of racially-defined minorities, the transition to racial pluralism is still very much underway.

Toward New Racial Dynamics

To understand the changing significance of race in the aftermath of the twentieth century—the century whose central malady was diagnosed by W. E. B. Du Bois as "the problem of the color-line"—we must reconsider where the racialized world came from, and where it is going. In the settings I've discussed, the "break" that began with movement activity after World War II, and that was contained from the late 1960s onward by political reforms, has not been consolidated. At the end of the century the world as a whole, and our national cases as well, are far from overcoming the tenacious legacies of colonial rule, apartheid, and segregation. All still experience continuing confusion, anxiety, and contention about race. Yet the legacies of epochal struggles for freedom, democracy, and human rights persist as well. To evaluate the transition to a new world racial system in comparative and historical perspective requires keeping in view the continuing tension that characterizes the present.

It is impossible to address worldwide dilemmas of race and racism by ignoring or "transcending" this situation, for example by adopting so-called "colorblind" policies. In the past, the centrality of race deeply determined the economic, political, and cultural configuration of the modern world; although recent decades have seen a tremendous efflorescence of movements for racial equality and justice, the legacies of centuries of racial oppression have not been overcome. Nor is a vision of racial justice fully worked out. Certainly the idea that such justice has already been largely achieved—as seen in the "colorblind" paradigm in the United States, the "nonracialist" rhetoric of the South African Freedom Charter, the Brazilian rhetoric of "racial democracy," the emerging "racial differentialism" of the European Union—remains problematic.

What would a more credible vision entail? The pressing task today is not to jettison the concept of race, but instead to come to terms with it as a form of flexible human variety.

What does this mean in respect to racism? Racism has been a crucial component of modernity, a key pillar of the global capitalist system, for 500 years. So it remains today. Yet it has been changed, damaged, and forced to reorganize by the massive social movements which have taken place in recent decades. In the past these movements were international in scope and influence. They were deeply linked to democratizing and egalitarian trends, such as labor politics and feminism. They were able both to mobilize around the injustices and exclusion experienced by racially subordinated groups, and simultaneously to sustain alliances across racial lines. This is background; such experiences cannot simply recur.

Still, the massive mobilizations which created the global "break" that followed World War II have certainly reshaped our world. Were these movements fated to be the last popular upsurges, the last egalitarian challenges to elite supremacy, to racial hierarchy? Surely not. In the countries I have discussed, and in transnational anti-racist networks as well, these earlier precedents still wield their influence. They still spark new attempts to challenge racism.

Will race ever be "transcended"? Will the world ever "get beyond" race? Probably not. But the entire world still has a chance of overcoming the stratification, the hierarchy, the taken-for-granted injustice and inhumanity that so often accompanies the "race concept." Like religion or language, race can be accepted as part of the spectrum of the human condition, while it is simultaneously and categorically resisted as a means of stratifying national or global societies. Nothing is more essential in the effort to reinforce democratic commitments, not to mention global survival and prosperity, as we enter a new millennium.

Migration and Politics: Explaining Variation Among Rich Democracies in Recent Nativist Protest

Harold L. Wilensky[1]

In this selection, Harold Wilensky argues that rich democracies display significant convergence in their cultural and social diversity as well as in their experiences of immigration. Although there are variations over time and place, the economic impact of immigrants tends to be positive. In the United States, for example, immigrants contribute more to tax revenues than they receive in welfare state benefits. What then explains anti-immigrant violence and the popular support for anti-immigrant (nativist) movements and parties? In a wide-ranging comparative analysis, Wilensky asserts that public policies toward immigration shape both voting and violence, and offers the intriguing suggestion that these two expressions of anti-immigrant sentiment may be inversely correlated.

Rich democracies evidence convergent trends in immigration experience (cf. Gary P. Freeman, 1994, pp. 17–30; Collinson, 1993, pp. 57–59; and Hollifield, 1992, pp. 32–33, 84–85, 204–213):

- Increasing effort and capacity to regulate migration flows, especially absolute numbers.
- The increased moral resonance of family unification as a major criterion for admission, accounting for an increasing percentage of total immigration and decreasing state control of the social characteristics (education, skills) of the immigrants.
- An hour-glass shape of the education and skills of the recent immigration population. Although there are some national differences here, the central tendency is toward some overrepresentation of college graduates and a very big overrepresentation of the least educated and least skilled. [It is estimated] that American immigrants are 30 percent highly skilled, 20 percent in the middle, and 50 percent unskilled.

Harold L. Wilensky, "Migration and Politics: Explaining variation among rich democracies in recent nativist protest," paper presented at the 14th World Conference of Sociology, Montreal, Canada, July 26–August 1, 1998. Institute of Industrial Relations Working Paper Series (University of California, Berkeley). Copyright 1998 by Harold L. Wilensky. Reprinted by permission of the author.

- The transformation of temporary work programs into permanent immigration. (Like The Man Who Came to Dinner and stayed for several months, the guest workers of Europe increasingly settled down in the host countries for long periods, even their whole working lives.) Movements for expanding immigrant rights were a natural outcome.
- The uneven spread of migrants in Western Europe 1950–93. The explanation: variation in (1) the demand for and recruitment of "temporary" labor; (2) the openness to the rising tide of political refugees, East to West and increasingly South to North.[2]
- As legal entry routes are restricted in response to xenophobic political pressure, illegal entrants and visa overstayers have increased, although nations vary in their capacity to police their borders and control illegal immigration.[3]

Economic Effects of Immigration

The economic impact of immigration, considering all costs and benefits over the long run, is very likely positive. This reality, however, is not what plays out in politics, where immigrants are used as scapegoats for a wide range of troubles. Complicating any assessment, the real economic effects vary over time and place.

Studies of the U.S. using data from before 1980 show that ". . . immigrants have been absorbed into the American labor market with little adverse effect on natives." In fact, in areas of greatest immigrant concentration—e.g. Miami, Los Angeles, New York, San Francisco—employment of natives increased with rising immigration, except for New York. The reasons: immigrants purchase goods and services where they work, thereby raising demand for labor; immigrant skills complement the skills of many native workers, raising demand for them; even with their concentration in gateway cities, if immigrants had not taken the low-skilled jobs there, similarly young, uneducated Americans would have filled the gap via migration from other areas; and natives attenuate the negative earnings effects of recent immigration by moving to other localities while at least 20 to 30 percent of the foreign born in the U.S., probably the least self-supporting, return to their birthplace or migrate elsewhere within a decade or two, thereby relieving pressure on the labor market.

But as the percentage of uneducated, unskilled immigrant labor rose in the 1980s when the U.S. job market for the least educated was deteriorating, studies of that decade concluded that immigration was depressing the earnings of natives, especially the relative earnings of high-school dropouts, including young Blacks and earlier-arriving Hispanics. An oversupply of cheap immigrant labor was competing with an oversupply of cheap native labor.

It is a popular idea that immigrants are a disproportionate burden on the welfare state. This is largely a myth. In the United States, immigrants are probably ripped off by American taxpayers. The reasons: First, they are overwhelmingly young workers who pay Social Security and Medicare taxes (not the native aged who use most of the expensive pension, disability, and health-care services)

whose fertility rates are as low as the comparable young natives (no disproportionate use of schools). The very youth of the immigrant population is a boon
for the U.S.; the immigrants will help pay for the babyboomers' retirement and
medical care, partially offsetting the looming mismatch of pensioners and workers. Second, they pay state sales taxes, local property taxes, and gasoline taxes;
their employers pay unemployment insurance and worker's compensation
taxes. Third, if they are legal, their use of social welfare benefits in earlier
decades was less than that of natives. Although such use is now slightly above
the natives' (because of higher unemployment rates of the young and because
the aged among them use means-tested SSI), these are the smallest parts of welfare-state burdens and have deteriorated in real value. Finally, if they are illegals
they are by law denied almost all welfare benefits and are afraid to use *any* services for fear of being deported. . . .

National experiences differ depending on institutions and policies. In
Germany, for instance, although foreigners are increasingly overrepresented
among the recipients of social assistance (which is only 5 percent of the Federal
Republic's social expenditures), the aggregate impact of foreigners on the entire
German system of taxes and transfers is positive—e.g. a fiscal gain of about
14 billion DM in 1991. A similar finding of net gain is reported from studies of
France. Regarding the labor market, both Australia and Germany evidence
much less negative earnings impact than the U.S. because their occupational
wage differentials are smaller than those of the U.S. and their unionization rates
are much higher. Germany also invests more in training, job creation, and job
placement. And Australia from the 1970s through the early 1980s used education and skills as criteria for admission so the differences between natives and
immigrants did not grow so much. On the other hand, countries that match
Sweden's generosity in social programs for immigrants may find that the costs
exceed the benefits even in the long run.

Whatever the European political economies do about the welfare state, labor-
market and social policies, and whatever the real economic effects of immigration,
I suspect that they will all experience a moderate increase in ethnic-racial-religious
conflict, hardly unknown to the Continent in the past, only this time without
major war.

Explaining Variation in Nativist Protest

Insofar as rich democracies converge in the number of immigrants as a fraction
of the labor force, they are likely to experience cycles of nativist, xenophobic
protest, some of it parliamentary, some violent, as in the history of the older
immigrant nations, the U.S., Australia, and Canada. The cycles of protest
are driven by the convergence of economic downturns (unemployment, downward mobility, declines in income), immigrant population numbers and
concentration, and the social distance between immigrants and natives. How

anti-immigrant sentiments are channeled, however, is another matter.[4] National and local mobilizing structures—political parties, legislatures, prime ministers, interest groups—can either legitimize or oppose xenophobic expression, exploit mass fears and prejudices in a search for scapegoats or try to contain them.

We can see the interaction of strong economic deprivation, much immigrant concentration, big social distance, and nativist political mobilization at work in the U.S. and Germany in the early 1990s. In the Los Angeles riots of 1992 much of the violence of blacks was targeted at Koreans and Chinese; the locations were areas of high unemployment of young males. In the 1994 election in California and in most closely-contested Congressional districts in many states the Republicans used the problems of crime, welfare mothers, and illegal Mexican or Caribbean immigrants as negative symbols in a successful campaign to direct a frenzy of anger at their Democratic opponents. Media "talk-shows" poured oil on that fire. White men of the middle mass (high school or part-college educated) from the West and South who said that their family's economic situation had worsened in the last four years were especially attracted to those appeals (based on exit polls, *New York Times* 2002, pp. 46–47, 375–378 on the revolt of the middle mass).

Anti-immigrant violence and voting in Germany has similar roots. Since 1961 the percentage of foreigners in the German population rose from 1.2 percent to over 8 percent—about the same as the 8.7 percent of the United States in 1994. As Alber shows bursts of nativist violence (acts/1000 asylum seekers) occurred in 1983–84, a time of accelerating unemployment, and 1991–1993 (combining recession, the economic strain of reunification, and rising immigration). He reports an average of nearly 6 violent acts per 1000 asylum seekers every day, including several arson fires during 1991–1993. Regarding social distance, although Germany's proportion of resident foreigners is not as large as Belgium's, its percentage of immigrants from non-European countries (6%) puts it first among countries of the European Union. Regarding mobilization, in the 1990 election male East German voters below the age of 25, whose unemployment was greatest, gave the extreme right nativist Republican Party its best election result of 7 percent. The party broke through first in Bremen, a port city with a declining industrial center, a high rate of unemployment and a heavy concentration of Turks, Poles and other immigrants. The combination of youth unemployment and social distance is also captured in Solingen, where the killers of a Turkish girl in May 1993 were members of a youth gang who had been kicked out of a Turkish restaurant; five other Turkish females, long-term residents, were killed in a single gruesome arson fire in the same city that month.

That public policies toward immigration shape the intensity of anti-immigrant violence and voting is suggested by a comparison of two countries with substantial recent immigration, generous social policies, and low rates of poverty and inequality, but contrasting immigration policies: Germany, where the principle of *jus sanguinis* is dominant and nationality is conferred mainly by blood ties, and Sweden, where the principle of *jus soli* is dominant and nationality is conferred mainly by place of birth. In 1992 Germany accepted 5.3 times as many asylum seekers as Sweden but experienced 29 times as many acts of anti-foreign arson or bombing attacks. In a rough comparison of nativist violence in the early 1990s in five European countries (France, Britain, Switzerland, Sweden, and Germany), Alber suggests that while Britain, Switzerland, Sweden, and Germany all experienced an increase in violent incidents, the number and intensity of anti-foreign violence is highest in Germany. An explanation of Sweden's much lower rate of violence is its policy of assimilating immigrants by aggressive education, training, and integrative social programs and by giving immigrants the right to vote and run for office in community and regional elections after three years of residence. Sweden is also first among 12 European countries in its naturalization rate.[5]

Voting vs. Violence

Comparing Germany and France yields a hint of an inverse relationship between anti-immigration voting and anti-immigrant violence.[6] It also validates the idea that integration policies reduce the rate of violence even where perceived economic deprivation and social distance are similar.

First, the similarities. The supporters of anti-immigrant, populist-right groups and parties in both countries are concentrated in areas of exceptional immigrant concentration and economic instability or at least perceived instability. These groups draw support from both the losers and winners of structural readjustment. It is not only economic deterioration alone that provokes protest; it is any major economic change, up or down, that heightens the sense of insecurity. For instance, among the German winners are Baden-Württemberg and Bavaria; among the French winners are Paris and the Ile-de-France and Alsace. German losers include Schleswig-Holstein and Bremen; French losers include Marseilles and Bouche du Rhône. All of these areas are either strongholds of protest voting or evidence above-average support for anti-immigrant politicians.

The core supporters of Le Pen in France and the Republikaner in Germany are not especially marginal. They are citizens of the middle mass (lower white collar, upper working class, self-employed). In both countries, most are males with vocational training or high school but no higher education. Whether they are employed or not they have a strong sense of insecurity—economic and physical—that is much more intense and widespread than among voters for other more established parties. They rank insecurity, law-and-order and crime at the top of their concerns. Even the lawless skinheads in Germany identify their biggest worry as Zukunftssicherheit or "future security." Responding to political demagogues, they blame their job insecurities and other troubles on immigrants.

In both countries the targets of protest voters and violent gangs are distant in language and appearance; they are typically Islamic—e.g. "guestworker" Turks and Balkan refugees in Germany, Arabs from North Africa and the Sub-Sahara in France. In both countries ethnic segregation in substandard housing and poor neighborhoods is common. Both include immigrants in universal welfare-state benefits, whose alleged drain on the taxpayer-citizen is a centerpiece of political propaganda. All this should sound familiar to television viewers in the United States who were exposed to saturation advertising on crime, immigrants and welfare during the poisonous Congressional campaign of 1994.

With all these French-German similarities it is striking that Germany has much more anti-immigrant violence than France while France has much higher populist right anti-immigrant voting than Germany. For instance, per capita acts of extreme right xenophobic violence in Germany after 1990 were at least 2.5 times higher than in France. But electoral support shows the reverse pattern: Le Pen's *Front National* received between 26 and 28 percent of the vote in 1988 Presidential elections in areas of high immigrant concentration in Southwest France—Marseilles, Toulon, and Nice; in February 1997, the *Front National* won its first absolute majority of the vote in a municipal election in the Marseilles suburb of Vitrolles. In contrast, from 1973 to 1989 German support for similar extreme right-wing parties at its peak in the 1989 Euro-elections was only 7.1 percent (excluding Bavaria and Baden-Württemberg the other Länder ranged between 4 and 6 percent of the vote going to the REPs). At its peak in national elections since unification that vote was less than 5 percent. In fact, in the 1994 national election the Republikaner got only 1.9 percent of the vote.

Contrasts in public policy and politics as well as rates of immigration provide a reasonable explanation. The German policy of ethnic exclusion based on descent and combined with wide open access to refugees up to 1993 (perhaps driven by historical guilt) makes the cultural and social integration of minorities difficult, no matter how long they stay (some of the Turks are third-generation workers).[7] Sheer numbers add to nativist resentment and violence.[8] In contrast, French policy, while not as assimilative as that of the U.S. or Canada, is inclusive. French official administrative classifications from the first have been socio-professional or "national"; from the Third Republic on, the French forbade all Census questions about ethnic, religious, and linguistic origins. The French version of the melting pot myth is that the fusion of peoples came to an end with the Revolution and no redefinition of "French" can come from subsequent waves of immigration. French universalism has had a paradoxical result: it exaggerates the social distance between nation-conscious Frenchmen and foreigners; at the same time it shapes the law of immigration in more liberal directions. Encouragement of assimilation may reduce violence but still permit political expression of nativist sentiments. As an added explanation of Le Pen's strength, France has run a much higher rate of unemployment than Germany for many years. Vitrolles, where LePen's party reached its first majority, has not only a large concentration of North African immigrants; it also has an abundance of alienated French workers hard hit by 19 percent unemployment.

A final piece of this puzzle is the role of electoral laws as they shape protest voting. Both France and Germany have mixed proportional-plurality electoral systems with two-stage voting. But the two ballots in the French case are cast a week or two apart; only the second is decisive. The two ballots of the Germans—one for the candidate, one for the party—are simultaneous and both ballots shape the final political composition of the government. French voters can therefore indulge their xenophobic sentiments in a first-ballot protest against the political establishment with little consequence in most cases; German voters are denied any second thoughts. In short, the German combination of much higher numbers of socially-distant strangers, an exclusionary naturalization policy, and an electoral system that discourages pure protest voting (and incidentally makes neo-Nazi parties illegal) encourages violence; the French combination of lower numbers of immigrants, universalistic ideology and assimilative policies, greater unemployment but electoral laws and traditions favorable to protest voting minimizes violence and provides xenophobic movements with an abundance of voters.

Nativism and Tax-Welfare Backlash Go Together[9]

[W]e also analyzed tax-welfare backlash in 19 rich democracies—the universe of democracies in the upper one-sixth of GNP per capita with a million or more population. By tax-welfare backlash I mean strong social-political movements and/or parties that emphasize anti-tax, anti-social spending, anti-bureaucratic ideological themes and achieve electoral success for substantial periods. . . .

What is most interesting for our understanding of nativism is that when we analyzed tax-welfare backlash, it proved impossible to separate anti-tax, anti-social spending, anti-bureaucratic protest movements and parties from nativist, xenophobic or racist protests; these two themes appear together in all the high-scoring countries except Denmark in the 1970s. (Even in Denmark the Progress Party began to complain about immigrants in the 1980s.) When Hollywood-actor Ronald Reagan swept California in the 1966 gubernatorial election he sounded not only the familiar anti-tax, anti-social spending, anti-bureaucratic themes but at the same time baited welfare mothers. He brought the house down when he asserted that welfare recipients (code words for black welfare poor) are on a "prepaid lifetime vacation plan." In 1970, after four years in office, with taxes rising, welfare costs soaring, and campus disruption recurring (all of which he vowed to stop), Governor Reagan ran and won on the same slogans: "We are fighting the big-spending politicians who advocate a welfare state, the welfare bureaucrats whose jobs depend on expanding the welfare system, and the cadres of professional poor who have adopted welfare as a way of life." That movement culminated in eight years of the Reagan Presidency, and ultimately a Republican takeover of Congress in 1994 with identical campaign themes—anti-tax, anti-spend, anti-bureaucracy combined with the complaint that immigrants and other poor racial and linguistic minorities were creating immense burdens of welfare and crime. For backlash politicians the slogan "no welfare for immigrants" is a "two-fer": it encapsulates two unpopular targets, recipients of social assistance (the undeserving poor) and despised minority groups. As President, Reagan repeatedly referred to mythical "welfare queens" as symbols of welfare fraud and abuse.[10]

Similarly, in the U.K. in the early 1970s, Conservative Enoch Powell, the Cambridge-educated establishment version of George Wallace or Ronald Reagan, became the charismatic hero of the middle mass. He not only targeted social spending and taxing as a drag on the British economy; he also railed against the hordes of West Indian blacks and other immigrants who were un-English and would undermine the British way of life. Although Powell failed to become top man of the Tories—they were embarrassed by his racism—Margaret Thatcher managed to become their top person articulating all of Powell's arguments except the overt complaints about racial minorities. Switzerland, too, has blended tax-welfare backlash with nativism. James Schwarzenbach in 1970 reached his peak of 46 percent of the total vote in a national referendum which proposed to limit the admission of foreign workers, a measure that his party claimed essential not only to preserve the Swiss way of life but to avoid an ultimately staggering burden of social services. In the late 1970s, a Schwarzenbach-type movement was still operating—various right-wing populist parties rose in votes in the late 1970s and early 1980s and remained strong in the 1991 election. They include the Swiss Democrats, especially strong in Berne, Zurich and Graubünden; the Lega Ticinese (anti-tax, anti-spend, anti-bureaucratic, anti-corruption) in Italian-speaking Ticino; and more recently the Motorist Party ("Parti des Automobilistes") who favor privatization of transportation, denial of social benefits to foreign workers, and are generally anti-government and anti-Green. In the 1990s, the populist, charismatic leader of the right, Christopher Blocher of Zurich, was orchestrating the themes of these disparate parties and groups. Although small right-wing parties lost votes in the 1995 election, Blocher's People's Party was a winner (up 3 percent); the total backlash vote remained steady. Finally, Canada, with an above-average backlash score based largely on the populist tax revolts confined to Alberta and British Columbia, evidences the same merging of anti-tax, anti-social spending, anti-bureaucratic sentiments with a rising Western resentment of the Francophones of Quebec and the politicians in Ottawa who coddle them. (The Social Credit Party, in office in Alberta from 1935 to 1971, also appealed to anti-Semites.) More recently, the Reform Party, emerging in Alberta, then BC, rose to third in popular vote nationally in 1993; it even more clearly combined tax-welfare backlash with hostility to Francophones and all foreigners.[11] And in June 1997 it became the official opposition to the ruling Liberals in Parliament.

In short, while nativism is widespread among all rich democracies, only a few rank high on tax-welfare backlash; these few cases almost always combine hostility to taxing, spending, and government bureaucracy with hostility to socially-distant minority groups. Facilitating the merger of tax-welfare backlash and nativism is the social locus of both in the middle mass. Politicians mobilizing lower-middle class and upper working-class people who feel economically-squeezed between the privileged top and the competing bottom can easily add racial-ethnic resentments prevalent in the same population.

Summary and Conclusion

Migration from poor areas to rich is new neither in its rate nor in its consequences. Rich democracies are now converging in their cultural and social diversity and in their conflict focused on immigration. They differ, however, in their openness to political and economic refugees, their policies toward immigrant integration, and the intensity of anti-immigrant mobilization. Anti-immigrant sentiments are most intense where the number and concentration of immigrants are heavy, the social distance between natives and strangers (in education, religion, language, ethnicity, and race) is great, and the economic instability of industrial readjustment is most widely experienced. Most important, industrial democracies differ in their ways of channeling mass prejudices and populist-right movements. A country that makes a serious effort to minimize illegal immigration, and to assimilate immigrants via inclusionary naturalization policies, job creation, training, and placement, and language and citizenship education will minimize nativist violence. It may ultimately reduce the electoral appeal of political demagogues who intensify mass fears and hatreds to achieve power.

Finally, I doubt that European democracies and Japan, as they experience increased immigration, must necessarily produce an alienated underclass, the target of a middle-mass revolt, American style. Only if they abandon the public policies that encouraged labor peace and kept their poverty rates low—family policies, an active labor-market policy, an accommodative framework for industrial relations, a universalistic welfare state—will they drift into the Anglo-American pattern. Some may choose that road; but the choice is there.

There is no tidal wave of immigrants to the affluent democracies. In relation to world population international migration is a rare event. In general, the negative economic effects of increased migration are exaggerated and the political effects can be contained.

Notes

1. Paper is based on Harold L. Wilensky, *Rich Democracies: Political Economy, Public Policy, and Performance* (Berkeley: University of California Press, 2002), chaps. 1, 5, 10, and 18 (parts of); and Harold L. Wilensky (1993). I am grateful to Karen Adelberger and Fred Schaffer for research assistance and to the Institute of Governmental Studies, the Center for German and European Studies, and the Institute of Industrial Relations for support.

2. According to Heinz Fassman and Rainer Münz (1994), of an estimated 14,160,000 migrants from East to West (including those from the GDR, ex-Yugoslavia, Poland, Soviet Union and the Balkans) from 1950 to 1993, 68.1 percent landed in Germany, 8.1 percent in Israel, 6.6 percent in

Turkey, 4.8 percent in the U.S. and 12.8 percent in other countries (Austria, Scandinavia, France, U.K., Canada, etc.) Of these 14 million about three in four can be classified as "ethnic" migrants, often the product of bilateral agreements between sender and receiver. Less than 15 percent can be classified as regular or irregular labor migrants or as dependent family of labor migrants. For much of the postwar period, the political and economic split of East and West prevented much movement of labor (or capital), except for more than half a million Yugoslavs. About ten percent can be classified as political refugees and asylum seekers escaping persecution (Hungarians 1956–57, Czechoslovaks 1968–69, Poles 1980–81, Albanians 1990–91, former Yugoslavs 1991–93). Fassman and Muenz's category of "ethnic" migrants doubtless includes some political and economic migrants.

3. Employer sanctions, used by almost all our 19 countries (Britain is an exception) vary in their effectiveness: Vital to their success are adequate resources for enforcement, a secure identification system, links to broader strategies for controlling illegal migration and enforcing labor standards, and steps to prevent employer discrimination. The U.S. fails on all counts. Several European countries—Germany, France, Switzerland—approximate them. (M. J. Miller 1987.)

   Openness to refugees also varies. In 1992 Germany took in two-thirds of the 572,000 asylum-seekers entering Europe as it struggled to get other countries to share the burden. On July 1, 1993 it changed its open asylum policy to accept refugees only from regimes that were persecuting them. It made it difficult for persons who passed through "presumably safe countries"—including Romania, Bulgaria, Gambia, Ghana, and Poland—to apply for asylum. Germany worked out arrangements with each adjacent country to help police its borders, giving money to Czechoslovakia and Poland for that purpose. All this sharply cut the number of applicants. The German Bundestag later approved an expansion of the number and power of the border police and raised penalties on illegal alien smugglers. Again, it is far from impossible to regulate immigration. (*Migration News*, vol. 1, #7). Of course it is a beggar-thy-neighbor policy—one country's successful border control is often another country's headache, a powerful reason for international agreements on burden-sharing.

4. These three forces that encourage nativist protest action—economic deprivation, large numbers and concentration of immigrants, and great social distance between immigrants and natives (Wilensky, 1975, pp. 57–59)—are the same as the forces that foster prejudice and the perception of group threat. See Lincoln Quillian (1995), an analysis of Eurobarometer Survey #30 results on attitudes toward immigrants and racial minorities in 12 EEC countries, Fall 1988. Individual characteristics had little impact on prejudice and explained none of the country differences. Economic conditions of the country, the size of the minority group and its social composition (e.g. non-EEC immigration) are the important variables shaping both levels of prejudice and the militancy of protest movements discussed below.

5. In the most recent year available (circa 1991) naturalizations as a percentage of the stock of foreign population in the year before was 5.4 percent in Sweden, 2.7 percent in Germany (Guimezanes, 1994, p. 25).

6. The next six paragraphs draw on data developed in a 1993 paper by my assistant, Karen Adelberger, from French and German surveys and recent literature. See also Wilensky (1975, p. 57–59 and 1976, pp. 12–34).

7. For an account of recent German immigration debates, policies, and administrative practices, see Halfmann, 1995. Brubaker (1992) describes the evolution of French and German citizenship policies.

8. Alber (1994), using Eurobarometer surveys and data from Wiegand and Fuchs, Gerhards and Roller, devises an index of "rejection of foreigners" (respondents who say that there are too many foreigners in their country, that the presence of foreigners is disturbing, that the rights of foreigners should be restricted, and that asylum seekers should no longer be accepted). For 11 EC countries this index of xenophobia correlates .82 with the percentage of foreigners from non-EC countries in each nation, underscoring the importance of numbers.

9. This section is based on chapter 10, "Tax-Welfare Backlash: How to Tax, Spend, and Yet Keep Cool" of my *Rich Democracies: Political Economy, Public Policy, and Performance* (2002) and Wilensky (1976).

10. Chapter 8 of Wilensky's *Rich Democracies* discusses why "welfare"—means-tested public assistance, a small fraction of public expenditures—became a political obsession in the United States.

11. A careful analysis of the 1993 election showed that the defectors from the Progressive Conservatives who went in droves to the Reform Party, while they shared the Reform Party's protest against taxing and spending, were virulently anti-immigrant and anti-Quebec—more xenophobic than other Tory voters (Nevitte et al., 1995). With the victory of the Conservative party of Ontario in June 1995, a third provincial backlash movement with explicit inspiration from the campaigns of Ronald Reagan and Margaret Thatcher, came to power (*Wall Street Journal*, June 12, 1995 and October 3, 1995). Thus, developments in the 1990s might justify a score for Canada of 3.5 rather than 3, which would strengthen the results reported in my earlier analysis (1976). (Interviews with politicians and journalists confirm this.) In my update I note that recent developments in Norway and Finland would move their above-average scores of 3 toward Sweden's 2, strengthening the idea that corporatist consensus insulates a democracy against backlash. Similarly, a study of 16 of the most threatening ethno-regional parties in five West European democracies (Britain, Italy, Spain, Belgium, Finland) shows that their electoral success from 1980 to 1992 is related to the degree of centralized corporatist bargaining. These parties had less success in corporatist Belgium and Finland, more where such structures are non-existent (Britain) or weak (Italy) (Müller-Rommel, 1994, p. 194 and Table 2.) Müller-Rommel (1994) confines analysis to ethno-regional parties that contested at least two national and regional elections from 1980 to 1992, polled at least 3 percent of the regional vote, and actually gained seats in the national parliament—a fair test of serious challenges to established parties. In the United Kingdom these include separatists such as the Ulster Unionists and Loyalists and United Ireland/Sinn Fein, as well as the left-libertarian federalists, the Scottish National Party and the Social Democratic Labour Party. In Belgium, it includes parties that demand autonomy and language rights within the nation-state—the Christeijk Vlaame Volksunie and the Front Démocratique des Bruxellois Francophoners. In Finland, it includes the Svenska Folkpartiet, which aims to defend the interests of a linguistic community without secession or a major restructuring of the state. In Italy, the Union Valdotaine fought for linguistic rights and regional decentralization; today the Northern League advocates federalism, threatens secession, and expresses great hostility to the backward, corrupt South as well as all immigrants (see chapter 8). The secessionist Parti Québécois in Canada, like the Basques in Spain, would fit the more-militant secessionists in the Müller-Rommel study.

Finally, a study of the radical right in Europe similarly concludes that its greatest electoral successes occur when it couples a fierce commitment to free markets with equally-fierce xenophobia or racism (Kitschelt, 1995).

References

Abowd, John M. and Richard B. Freeman. "Introduction and Summary." In *Immigration, Trade and the Labor Market*, ed. John M. Abowd and Richard B. Freeman. 1–25. Chicago: University of Chicago Press, 1991.

Abowd, John M. and Richard J. Freeman, ed. *Immigration, Trade and the Labor Market*. Chicago: University of Chicago Press, 1991.

Alber, Jens. "Towards Explaining Anti-Foreign Violence in Germany." Unpublished lecture at the Center for European Studies, Harvard University, March 17, 1994.

Borjas, George J. *Friends of Strangers: The Impact of Immigrants on the U.S. Economy*. New York: Basic Books, 1990.

Borjas, George J., Richard B. Freeman, and Kevin Lang. "Undocumented Mexican-born Workers in the United States: How Many, How Permanent?" In *Immigration, Trade and the Labor Market*, ed. John M. Abowd and Richard B. Freeman. 77–100. Chicago: University of Chicago Press, 1991.

Borjas, George J., Richard B. Freeman, and Lawrence F. Katz. "On the Labor Market Effects of Immigration and Trade." In *Immigration and the Work Force: Economic Consequences for the United States and Souce Areas*, ed. George J. Borjas and Richard B. Freeman. 213–244. Chicago: University of Chicago Press, 1992.

Borjas, George J. and Richard B. Freeman. "Introduction and Summary." In *Immigration and the Work Force: Economic Consequences for the United States and the Source Areas*, ed. Geroge J. Borjas and Richard B. Freeman. 1–15. Chicago: University of Chicago Press, 1992.

Borjas, George J. "National Origin and Skills of Immigrants in the Postwar Period." In *Immigration and the Work Force: Economic Consequences for the United States and Source Areas*, ed. George J. Borjas and Richard B. Freeman. 17–47. Chicago: University of Chicago Press, 1992.

Brubaker, Rogers. *Citizenship and Nationhood in France and Germany*. Cambridge, Mass.: Harvard University Press, 1992.

Clark, Rebecca L. and Jeffrey S. Passel. *How Much Do Immigrants Pay in Taxes? Evidence from Los Angeles County*. Program for Research on Immigration Policy, Washington, D.C.: The Urban Institute, 1993.

Esman, Milton J. "The Political Fallout of International Migration." *Diaspora* 2 (1 1992): 3–41.

Fassmann, Heinz and Rainer Münz, "European East-West Migration 1945–1992." *International Migration Review* 28 (1994): 520–538.

Fix, Michael and Jeffrey S. Passel. *Immigration and Immigrants: Setting the Record Straight*. Washington, D.C.: The Urban Institute, 1994.

Freeman, Gary P. "Can Liberal States Control Unwanted Migration?" *Annals of the American Academy of Political and Social Science* 534 (1994): 17–30.

Guimezanes, Nicole. "What Laws for Naturalization?" *OECD Observer* 188 (1994): 24–26.

Halfmann, Jost. "Two Discourses of Citizenship in Germany: The Difference Between Public Debate and Administrative Practice." In *The Postwar Transformation of Germany: Democracy, Prosperity and Nationhood*. Center for German and European Studies, University of California, Berkeley, Berkeley CA, 1995.

Hollifield, James F. *Immigrants, Markets, and States: The Political Economy of Postwar Europe*. Cambridge, MA: Harvard University Press, 1992.

Huddle, Donald. *The Costs of Immigration: Executive Summary*. Carrying Capacity Network, 1993.

Kitschelt, Herbert, in collaboration with Anthony J. McGann. *The Radical Right in Western Europe: A Comparative Analysis*. Ann Arbor: University of Michigan Press, 1995.

Nee, Victor, Jimy M. Sanders, and Scott Sernau. "Job Transitions in an Immigrant Metropolis: Ethnic Boundaries and the Mixed Economy." *American Sociological Review* 59 (1994): 849–872.

Noiriel, Gérard. "Difficulties in French Historical Research on Immigration." In *Immigrants in Two Democracies: French and American Experience*, ed. Donald L. Horowitz and Gérard Noiriel. New York: New York University Press, 1992.

Passel, Jeffrey S. *Immigrants and Taxes: A Reappraisal of Huddle's "The Cost of Immigrants."* Program for Research on Immigration Policy, Washington, D.C.: The Urban Institute, 1994.

Quillian, Lincoln. "Prejudice as a Response to Perceived Group Threat: Population Composition and Anti-Immigrant and Racial Prejudice in Europe." *American Sociological Review* 60 (1995): 586–611.

Wilensky, Harold L. *The Welfare State and Equality: Structural and Ideological Roots of Public Expenditures*. Berkeley, CA: University of California Press, 1975.

Wilensky, Harold L. *The 'New Corporatism,' Centralization and the Welfare State*. London and Beverly Hills: Sage Publications, 1976.

Wilensky, Harold L. "The Nation-State, Social Policy, and Economic Performance." In *Globalizzazione e sistemi di welfare*, ed. M. Ferrara. 41–63. Torino, Italy: Edzioni della Fondazione G. Agnelli, 1993.

Wilensky, Harold L. *Rich Democracies: Political Economy, Public Policy, and Performance*. Berkeley: University of California Press, 2002.

A Nation Is a Nation, Is a State, Is an Ethnic Group, Is a . . .

Walker Connor

Why is the key institution of global governance and international diplomacy called the United Nations when membership is based on statehood? As Walker Connor explains in this selection, although the terms *nation* and *state* are often used almost interchangeably, there are important differences between the two concepts. In fact, the term *nation-state* (what in common usage is called a country) can be highly misleading, for it implies that citizens share a sense of common national identity. A one-to-one correspondence between a nation or people and the exclusive political organization of a given territory by a state is usually considered the best way to divide the world into stable units. Yet Connor observes that nation-states (where there is a one-to-one correspondence of the two) are very much the exception. Forty years ago, scholars thought that no more than 10 percent of states could properly be called nation-states. Today, in this era of immigration and cultural diffusion, even that figure is probably on the high side. It is difficult to think of any pure cases of a culturally, ethnically, and linguistically homogeneous people (the nation) corresponding perfectly to the sovereign territory of political control (the state).

One of the most common manifestations of terminological license is the interutilization of the words *state* and *nation*. This tendency is perplexing because at one level of consciousness most scholars are clearly well aware of the vital distinctions between the two concepts. The state is the major political subdivision of the globe. As such, it is readily defined and, what is of greater moment to the present discussion, is easily conceptualized in quantitative terms. Peru, for illustration, can be defined in an easily conceptualized manner as the territorial–political unit consisting of the sixteen million inhabitants of the 514,060 square miles located on the west coast of South America between 69° and 80° West, and 2° and 18°, 21° South.

Defining and conceptualizing the nation is much more difficult because the essence of a nation is intangible. This essence is a psychological bond that joins

Walker Connor, "A Nation Is a Nation, Is a State, Is an Ethnic Group, Is a . . .," *Ethnic and Racial Studies* 1, no. 4 (1978): 379–388. Reprinted by permission of Taylor & Francis Ltd. http://www.tandf.co.uk/journals.

a people and differentiates it, in the subconscious conviction of its members, from all other people in a most vital way. The nature of that bond and its well-spring remain shadowy and elusive, and the consequent difficulty of defining the nation is usually acknowledged by those who attempt this task. Thus, a popular dictionary of International Relations defines a nation as follows:

> A social group which shares a common ideology, common institutions and customs, and a *sense* of homogenetry. "Nation" is difficult to define so precisely as to differentiate the term from such other groups as religious sects, which exhibit some of the same characteristics. In the nation, however, there is also present a strong group *sense* of belonging associated with a particular territory considered to be peculiarly its own.

Whereas the key word in this particular definition is *sense,* other authorities may substitute *feeling* or *intuition,* but proper appreciation of the abstract essence of the nation is customary *in definitions.* But after focusing attention upon that essential psychological bond, little probing of its nature follows. Indeed, having defined the nation as an essentially psychological phenomenon, authorities [. . .] then regularly proceed to treat it as fully synonymous with the very different and totally tangible concept of the state.

Even when one restricts *nation* to its proper, non-political meaning of a human collectivity, the ambiguity surrounding its nature is not thereby evaporated. How does one differentiate the nation from other human collectivities? The above cited definition spoke of "a sense of homogeneity." Others speak of a feeling of sameness, of oneness, of belonging, or of consciousness of kind. But all such definitions appear a bit timid, and thereby fail to distinguish the nation from numerous other types of groups. Thus, one can conceive of the Amish, Appalachian hill people, or "down Mainers" as all fitting rather neatly within any of the preceding standards.

With but very few exceptions, authorities have shied away from describing the nation as a kinship group and have usually explicitly denied that the notion of shared blood is a factor. Such denials are supported by data illustrating that most groups claiming nationhood do in fact incorporate several genetic strains. But such an approach ignores the wisdom of the old saw that when analysing sociopolitical situations, what ultimately matters is not *what is* but *what people believe is.* And a subconscious belief in the group's separate origin and evolution is an important ingredient of national psychology. When one avers that he is Chinese, he is identifying himself not just with the Chinese people and culture of today, but with the Chinese people and their activities throughout time. The Chinese Communist Party was appealing to just such a sense of separate origin and evolution in 1937:

> [W]e know that in order to transform the glorious future into a new China, independent, free, and happy, all our fellow countrymen, every single, zealous descendant of Huang-ti [the legendary first emperor of China] must determinedly and relentlessly participate in the concerted struggle.
>   . . . Our great Chinese nation, with its long history is inconquerable.

Bismarck's famous exhortation to the German people, over the heads of their particular political leaders, to "think with your blood" was a similar attempt to activate a mass psychological vibration predicated upon an intuitive sense of consanguinity. An unstated presumption of a Chinese (or German) nation is that there existed in some hazy, prerecorded era a Chinese (or German) Adam and Eve, and that the couple's progeny has evolved in essentially unadulterated form down to the present. It was recognition of this dimension of the nation that caused numerous writers of the nineteenth and early twentieth centuries to employ *race* as a synonym for *nation*, references to a German race or to the English race being quite common.

Since the nation is a self-defined rather than an other-defined grouping, the broadly held conviction concerning the group's singular origin need not and seldom will accord with factual data. Thus, the anthropologist may prove to his own satisfaction that there are several genetic strains within the Pushtun people who populate the Afghani-Pakistani border-region and conclude therefrom that the group represents the variegated offspring of several peoples who have moved through the region. The important fact, however, is that the Pushtuns themselves are convinced that all Pushtuns are evolved from a single source and have remained essentially unadulterated. This is a matter which is *known* intuitively and unquestionably, a matter of attitude and not of fact. It is a matter, the underlying conviction of which is not apt to be disturbed substantially even by the rational acceptance of anthropological or other evidence to the contrary. Depending upon the sophistication of the treatise, this type of sensory knowledge may be described as "a priori," "an emotional rather than a rational conviction," "primordial," "thinking with the heart (or with the blood) rather than with the mind," or "a 'gut' or 'knee-jerk' response." Regardless of the nomenclature, it is an extremely important adjunct of the national idea. It is the intuitive conviction which can give to nations a psychological dimension approximating that of the extended family, i.e. a feeling of common blood lineage.

The word *nation* comes from the Latin and, when first coined, clearly conveyed the idea of common blood ties. It was derived from the past participle of the verb *nasci*, meaning to be born. And hence the Latin noun, *nationem*, connoting *breed* or *race*. Unfortunately, terms used to describe human collectivities (terms such as race and class) invite an unusual degree of literary license, and *nation* certainly proved to be no exception. Thus, at some medieval universities, a student's *nationem* designated the sector of the country from whence he came. But when introduced into the English language in the late thirteenth century, it was with its primary connotation of a blood related group. One etymologist notes, however, that by the early seventeenth century, *nation* was also being used to describe the inhabitants of a country, regardless of that population's ethnonational composition, thereby becoming a substitute for less specific human categories such as *the people* or *the citizenry*. This infelicitous practice continues to the present day, and accounts for often encountered references to the American citizenry as the American nation. Whatever the American people are (and they may well be *sui generis*), they are not a nation in the pristine sense of the word. However, the unfortunate habit of calling them a nation, and thus verbally equating American with German, Chinese, English, and the like, has seduced scholars into erroneous analogies. Indeed, while proud of being "a nation of immigrants" with a "melting pot" tradition, the absence of a common origin may well make it more difficult, and conceivably impossible, for the American to appreciate instinctively the idea of the nation in the same dimension and with the same poignant clarity as do the Japanese, the Bengali, or the Kikuyu. It is difficult for an American to appreciate what it means for a German to be German or for a Frenchman to be French, because the psychological effect of being American is not precisely equatable. Some of the associations are missing and others may be quite different.

Far more detrimental to the study of nationalism, however, has been the propensity to employ the term nation as a substitute for that territorial juridical unit, the state. How this practice developed is unclear, though it seems to have become a relatively common practice in the late seventeenth century. Two possible explanations for this development present themselves. One involves the rapid spread of the doctrine of popular sovereignty that was precipitated about this time by the writings of men such as Locke. In identifying *the people* as the font of all political power, this revolutionary doctrine made the people and the state almost synonymous. *L'état c'est moi* became *l'état c'est le peuple*. And therefore the nation and the state had become near synonyms, for we have already noted the tendency to equate nation with the entire people or citizenry. Thus, the French *Declaration of Rights of Man and Citizen* would proclaim that "the source of all sovereignty resides essentially in the nation; no group, no individual may exercise authority not emanating expressly therefrom." Though the drafters of the Declaration may not have been aware, "the nation" to which they referred contained Alsatians, Basques, Bretons, Catalans, Corsicans, Flemings, and Occitanians, as well as Frenchmen.

It is also probable that the habit of interutilizing *nation* and *state* developed as alternative abbreviations for the expression *nation-state*. The very coining of this hyphenate illustrated an appreciation of the vital differences between *nation* and *state*. It was designed to describe a territorial–political unit (a state) whose borders coincided or nearly coincided with the territorial distribution of a national group. More concisely, it described a situation in which a nation had its own state. Unfortunately, however, *nation-state* has come to be applied indiscriminately to all states. Thus one authority has stated that "a prime fact about the world is that it is largely composed of nation-states." The statement should read that "a prime fact about the world is that it is *not* largely composed of nation-states." A survey of the 132 entities generally considered to be states as of 1971, produced the following breakdown:

1. Only 12 states (9.1%) can justifiably be described as nation-states.
2. Twenty-five (18.9%) contain a nation or potential nation accounting for more than 90% of the state's total population but also contain an important minority.

3. Another 25 (18.9%) contain a nation or potential nation accounting for between 75% and 89% of the population.
4. In 31 (23.5%), the largest ethnic element accounts for 50% to 74% of the population.
5. In 39 (29.5%), the largest nation or potential nation accounts for less than half of the population.

Were all states nation-states, no great harm would result from referring to them as nations, and people who insisted that the distinction between *nation* and *state* be maintained could be dismissed as linguistic purists or semantic nitpickers. Where *nation* and *state* essentially coincide, their verbal interutilization is inconsequential because the two are indistinguishably merged in popular perception. The state is perceived as the political extension of the nation, and appeals to one trigger the identical, positive psychological responses as appeals to the other. To ask a Japanese *kamikaze* pilot or a banzai-charge participant whether he was about to die for *Nippon* or for the Nipponese people would be an incomprehensible query since the two blurred into an inseparable whole. Hitler could variously make his appeals to the German people in the name of state (Deutsches Reich), nation (Volksdeutsch), or homeland (Deutschland), because all triggered the same emotional associations. Similar responses can be elicited from members of a nation that is clearly predominant within a state. But the invoking of such symbols has quite a different impact upon minorities. Thus, "Mother Russia" evokes one type of response from a Russian and something quite different from a Ukrainian. De Gaulle's emotional evocations of *La France* met quite different audiences within the Île de France and within Brittany or Corsica.

Whatever the original reason for the interutilization of *nation* and *state*, even the briefest reflection suffices to establish the all-pervasive effect that this careless use of terminology has had upon the intellectual–cultural milieu within which the study of nationalism is perforce conducted. The League of Nations and the United Nations are obvious misnomers. The discipline called International Relations should be designated *Interstate* Relations. One listing of contemporary organizations contains sixty-six entries beginning with the word *International* (e.g. the International Court of Justice and the International Monetary Fund), none of which, either in its membership or in its function, reflects any relationship to nations. International Law and International Organization are still other significant illustrations of the common but improper tendency to equate state and nation. National income, national wealth, national interest, and the like, refer in fact to statal concerns. A recently coined malapropism, *transnational* (and even *transnationalism*) is used to describe interstate, extragovernmental relations. *Nationalization* is still another of the numerous misnomers that muddy understanding of the national phenomenon.

With the concepts of the nation and the state thus hopelessly confused, it is perhaps not too surprising that *nationalism* should come to mean identification with the state rather than loyalty to the nation. Even the same International

Relations Dictionary whose definition of the *nation* we cited for its proper appreciation of the psychological essence of the nation, makes this error. After carefully noting that "a nation may comprise part of a state, or extend beyond the borders of a single state," it elsewhere says of *nationalism* that "it makes the state the ultimate focus of the individual's loyalty." It also says of nationalism that "as a mass emotion it is the most powerful political force operative in the world." Few would disagree with this assessment of the power of nationalism, *and this is precisely the problem. Impressed with the force of nationalism, and assuming it to be in the service of the state, the scholar of political development has been pre-programmed to assume that the new states of Africa and Asia would naturally become the foci of their inhabitants' loyalties.* Nationalism, here as elsewhere, would prove irresistible, and alternative foci of loyalty would therefore lose the competition to that political structure alternately called the nation, the state, or the nation-state. This syndrome of assumptions and terminological confusion which has generally characterized the political development school is reflected in the early self-description of its endeavors as "nation-building." Contrary to its nomenclature, the "nation-building" school has in fact been dedicated to building viable states. And with a very few exceptions, the greatest barrier to state unity has been the fact that the states each contain more than one nation, and sometimes hundreds. Yet, a review of the literature will uncover little reflection on how the psychological bonds that presently tie segments of the state's population are to be destroyed. One searches the literature in vain for techniques by which group-ties predicated upon such things as a sense of separate origin, development, and destiny are to be supplanted by loyalty to a state-structure, whose population has never shared such common feelings. The nature and power of those abstract ties that identify the true nation remain almost unmentioned, to say nothing of unprobed. The assumption that the powerful force called nationalism is in the service of the state makes the difficult investigation of such abstractions unnecessary.

As in the case of substituting the word *nation* for *state*, it is difficult to pinpoint the origin of the tendency to equate nationalism with loyalty to the state. It is unquestionably a very recent development, for the word *nationalism* is itself of very recent creation. G. de Bertier de Sauvigny believes it first appeared in literature in 1798 and did not reappear until 1830. Moreover, its absence from lexicographies until the late nineteenth and early twentieth centuries suggests that its use was not extensive until much more recently. Furthermore, all of the examples of its early use convey the idea of identification *not* with the state, but with the nation as properly understood. While unable to pinpoint nationalism's subsequent association with the state, it indubitably followed and flowed from the tendency to equate state and nation. It also unquestionably received a strong impetus from the great body of literature occasioned by the growth of militant nationalism in Germany and Japan during the 1930s and early 1940s.

As outstanding illustrations of the fanatical responses that nationalism can engender, German and Japanese nationalism of this period have come to occupy an important place in all subsequent scholarship on nationalism. And, unfortunately, these manifestations of extreme nationalism have been firmly identified with the loyalty to the state. The most common word applied to them has been *fascism*, a doctrine postulating unswerving obedience to an organic, corporate state. The most popular alternative descriptive phrase, *totalitarianism*, perhaps even more strongly conveys the idea of the complete (total) identification of the individual with the state.

The linking of the state to these examples *par excellence* of extreme nationalism suggests the likelihood that other states will also become the object of mass devotion. If some states could elicit such fanatical devotion, why not others? Granted, few would wish to see such extreme and perverted dedication to the state arise elsewhere. But if the concept of a Japanese state could, during World War II, motivate "banzai charges," kamikaze missions, and numerous decisions of suicide rather than surrender (as well as the many post-war illustrations of people enduring for years an animal-like existence in caves on Pacific islands) because of a loyalty to the Japanese state that was so unassailable as to place that state's defeat beyond comprehension, then surely the states of the Third World should at least be able to evoke a sufficiently strong loyalty from their inhabitants so as to prevail against any competing group-allegiances. If a loyalty to a German state could motivate Germans to carry on a war long after it became evident that the cause was hopeless and that perseverance could only entail more deprivation, destruction, and death, then surely other states could at least elicit a sense of common cause and identity from their populations that would prove more powerful than any counter-tendencies to draw distinctions among segments of the populace. If the German and Japanese experiences were pertinent elsewhere, then optimism concerning the stability of present state structures would be justified.

But what has been too readily ignored is the fact that Germany and Japan were among the handful of states that clearly qualify as nation-states. As earlier noted, in such cases the state and the nation are indistinguishably linked in popular perception. Japan to the Japanese, just as Germany to the Germans, was something far more personal and profound than a territorial–political structure termed a state; it was an embodiment of the nation-idea and therefore an extension of self. As postulated by fascist doctrine, these states were indeed popularly conceived as corporate organisms, for they were equated with the Japanese and German nations. As Hitler wrote in *Mein Kampf*: "We as Aryans, are therefore able to imagine a State only to be the living organism of a nationality which not only safeguards the preservation of that nationality, but which, by further training of its spiritual and ideal abilities, leads it to its highest freedom."

But could such an emotion-laden conception of the state take root where the nation and the state were not popularly equated? The single rubric of fascism was applied to Hitler's Germany, Tojo's Japan, Mussolini's Italy, Franco's Spain, and Peron's Argentina. It is evident, however, that appeals in the name of Spain have not elicited any great emotion from the Basques, Catalans, and

Galicians. In polygenetic Argentina, Peron's message was not a unifying appeal to all Argentinians, but was in fact a divisive call in the name of socioeconomic class. Within Italy, a sense of loyalty to the state proved woefully and surprisingly inadequate in the face of its first major test, the invasion by Allied forces. The reason appears to be that the concept of a single people (national awareness) has not yet permeated the subconsciousness of the Italians to the same measure as a similar concept had permeated the German and Japanese people. In equating nationalism with loyalty to the state, scholars had failed to inquire how many cases there have been where fanatical devotion to a state has arisen in the absence of a popular conception of the state as the state of one's particular nation. Rather than suggesting certain victory on the part of new states in the competition for loyalty, the experiences of Germany and Japan exemplify the potential strength of those emotional ties to one's nation with which the multiethnic state must contend. German and Japanese nationalism were more prophetic auguries of the growth of concepts such as, *inter alia,* Ibo, Bengali, Kikuyu, Naga, Karen, Lao, Bahutu, Kurd, and Baganda, than they were auguries of the growth of concepts such as Nigeria, Pakistan, Kenya, India, Burma, Thailand, Rwanda, Iraq and Uganda.

Mistakenly equating nationalism with loyalty to the state has further contributed to terminological confusion by leading to the introduction of still other confusing terms. With nationalism preempted, authorities have had difficulty agreeing on a term to describe the loyalty of segments of a state's population to their particular nation. Ethnicity, primordialism, pluralism, tribalism, regionalism, communalism, and parochialism are among the most commonly encountered. This varied vocabulary further impedes an understanding of nationalism by creating the impression that each is describing a separate phenomenon. Moreover, reserving nationalism to convey loyalty to the state (or, more commonly, to the word *nation* when the latter is improperly substituted for state), while using words with different roots and fundamentally different connotations to refer to loyalty to the nation, adds immeasurably to the confusion. Each of the above terms has exercised its own particular negative impact upon the study of nationalism.

Ethnicity

Ethnicity (identity with one's ethnic group) is, if anything, more definitionally chameleonic than *nation*. It is derived from *Ethnos*, the Greek word for *nation* in the latter's pristine sense of a group characterized by common descent. Consonant with this derivation, there developed a general agreement that an ethnic group referred to a basic human category (i.e. not a subgroup). Unfortunately, however, American sociologists came to employ *ethnic group* to refer to "a group with a common cultural tradition and a sense of identity which exists as a subgroup of a larger society." This definition makes ethnic group synonymous with minority, and, indeed, with regard to group relations within the United States, it has been used in reference to nearly any discernible minority, religious, linguistic, or otherwise.

The definition of ethnic group by American sociologists violates its original meaning with regard to at least two important particulars. In the traditional sense of an ancestrally related unit, it is evident that an ethnic group need not be a subordinate part of a larger political society but may be the dominant element within a state (the Chinese, English, or French, for example) or may extend across several states, as do the Arabs. Secondly, the indiscriminate application of ethnic group to numerous types of groups, obscures vital distinctions between various forms of identity. In a stimulating and often cited introduction to a volume entitled *Ethnicity*, Nathan Glazer and Daniel Patrick Moynihan, while rejecting the notion that ethnicity refers only to minorities, defended the incorporation of several forms of identity under this single rubric.

> Thus, there is some legitimacy to finding that forms of identification based on social realities as different as religion, language, and national origin all have something in common, such that a new term is coined to refer to all of them: "ethnicity." What they have in common is that they have all become effective foci for group mobilization for concrete political ends . . .

However, despite the usefulness that such a categorization possesses for the study of the politics of special interest groups, there is little question but that it has exerted a damaging influence upon the study of nationalism. One result is that the researcher, when struggling through thousands of entries in union catalogs, indices to periodicals, and the like cannot be sure whether a so-called ethnic study will prove germane to the study of nationalism. Sometimes the unit under examination does constitute a national or potential national group. Other times it is a transnational (inter- or intrastate) group such as the Amerindians. And, in most instances, it is a group related only marginally, if at all, to the nation, as properly understood (e.g. the Catholic community within the Netherlands). Moreover, a review of the indices and bibliographies found in those ethnic studies that do deal with a national or potential national group, illustrate all too often that the author is unaware of the relationship of his work to nationalism. The student of nationalism and the student of ethnicity seldom cross-fertilize. The American journal, *Ethnicity*, and the *Canadian Review of Studies in Nationalism*, for example, are remarkably free of overlap with regard to (1) the academic background of their contributors and (2) footnoted materials.

Even if the author uses the term *ethnicity* solely in relation to national groups, his equating of nationalism with loyalty to the state will predispose him to underestimate the comparative magnetism of the former. But the much more common practice of employing ethnicity as a cloak for several different types of identity exerts a more baneful effect. Such a single grouping presumes that all of the identities are of the same order. We shall reserve further comment on the adverse consequences of this presumption to a later discussion of *primordialism* and *pluralism*, noting here only that this presumption circumvents raising the key question as to which of a person's several identities is apt to win out in a test of loyalties.

Anthropologists, ethnologists, and scholars concerned with global comparisons have been more prone to use *ethnicity* and *ethnic group* in their pristine sense of involving a sense of common ancestry. Max Weber, for example, noted:

> We shall call "ethnic groups" those human groups that entertain a subjective belief in their common descent . . . , this belief must be important for the propagation of group formation; conversely, it does not matter whether or not an objective blood relationship exists. Ethnic membership (*Gemeinsamkeit*) differs from the kinship group precisely by being a presumed identity . . .

This definition would appear to equate *ethnic group* and *nation* and [. . .] Weber did indeed link the two notions. However, elsewhere Weber made an important and useful distinction between the two:

> [T]he idea of the nation is apt to include the notions of common descent and of an essential though frequently indefinite homogeneity. The "nation" has these notions in common with the sentiment of solidarity of ethnic communities, which is also nourished from various sources, as we have seen before. *But the sentiment of ethnic solidarity does not by itself make a "nation."* Undoubtedly, even the White Russians in the face of the Great Russians have always had a sentiment of ethnic solidarity, yet even at the present time they would hardly claim to qualify as a separate "nation." The Poles of Upper Silesia, until recently, had hardly any feeling of solidarity with the "Polish nation." They felt themselves to be a separate ethnic group in the face of the Germans, but for the rest they were Prussian subjects and nothing else.

Weber is here clearly speaking of pre-national peoples or [. . .] potential nations. His illustrations are of peoples not yet cognizant of belonging to a larger ethnic element. The group consciousness to which he refers—that rather low level of ethnic solidarity that a segment of the ethnic element feels when confronted with a foreign element—need not be very important politically and comes closer to xenophobia than to nationalism. To the degree that it represents a step in the process of nation-formation, it testifies that a group of people must know ethnically what they *are not* before they know what they *are*. Thus, to Weber's illustrations, we can add the Slovaks, Croats, and Slovenes who, under the Habsburg Empire, were aware that they were neither German nor Magyar, long before they possessed positive opinions concerning their ethnic or national identity. In such cases, meaningful identity of a positive nature remains limited to locale, region, clan, or tribe. Thus, members need not be conscious of belonging to the ethnic group. Ernest Barker made this same point with regard to all peoples prior to the nineteenth century:

> The self-consciousness of nations is a product of the nineteenth century. This is a matter of the first importance. Nations were already there; they had indeed been there for centuries. But it is not the things which are simply "there" that matter in human life. What really and finally matters is the thing which is apprehended as an idea, and, as an

idea, is vested with emotion until it becomes a cause and a spring of action. In the world of action apprehended ideas are alone electrical; and a nation must be an idea as well as a fact before it can become a dynamic force.

To refine Barker's wording only slightly, and his meaning not at all, a nation is a self-aware ethnic group. An ethnic group may be readily discerned by an anthropologist or other outside observer, but until the members are themselves aware of the group's uniqueness, it is merely an ethnic group and not a nation. While an ethnic group *may*, therefore, be other-defined, the nation *must* be self-defined. Employing ethnic group or ethnicity in relationship to several types of identities therefore beclouds the relationship between the *ethnic group* and the *nation* and also deprives scholarship of an excellent term for referring to both nations and potential nations.

 5.6

Lessons from the Muslim World

Vali Nasr

In recent decades, fundamentalism in all its varieties—Christian, Islamic, Hindu, and Jewish among others—has inspired profound challenges to secular societies in both the developed and the developing world. Particularly since 9/11, the violent and destabilizing role of fundamentalism in the Muslim world has attracted tremendous interest. In this contribution, Vali Nasr explains that the raging conflict between religious and secular worldviews may lead to a distinctive homegrown model of government in the Muslim world. What are the prospects that a moderate fundamentalism open to compromise can ally with secular forces to help advance development and modernization in Muslim states?

Secularism has come under assault over the course of the last two decades, in developing as well as industrialized societies, in democracies as well as dictatorships. Christian, Hindu, Islamic, and Jewish fundamentalisms,

Vali Nasr, "Lessons from the Muslim World," *Daedalus* 132, no. 3 (Summer 2003): 67–72. © 2003 by the American Academy of Arts and Sciences. Reprinted by permission of MIT Press Journals.

with different political aspirations representing diverse constituencies, have spearheaded the resurgence of religious values, institutions, and organizations. On a global scale, the fundamentalist juggernaut has eroded the place of secularism in politics, policy-making, law, and social relations, and has posed a profound challenge to old ways of thinking about modernity, its prerequisites, directives, and institutions. . . .

. . . To understand the shape of things to come we have to take stock of the changes that have taken place over the past few decades and also look closely at changes that are currently unfolding. This we should do not through the lens of old paradigms, but with a view to identifying emerging trends.

Nowhere is the scope of change produced by fundamentalism more evident than in the Muslim world. It was here that fundamentalism found its most vociferous and disruptive expression and mounted its most direct and poignant challenge to secularism and its institutions. It is also here that the intensity of the struggle between religion and secularism is producing new paradigms and institutions that will shape our world for years to come.

In the Muslim Middle East and Asia, secularism was not a product of socio-economic, technological, or cultural change—it was not associated with any internal social dynamic. In fact, it was not even an indigenous force. Secularism was first and foremost a project of the state—first the colonial state, and later the postcolonial state. It was a Western import, meant to support the state's aim of long-run development. As a result, from the outset a religious-secular divide came to reflect the increasingly contentious relations between the society and the colonial state.

The postcolonial state in the Muslim world reproduced these tensions in a voluntary effort to emulate the Western state, which it understood to be inherently secular. The Turkish Republic established after World War I serves as the most lucid example here. It was militantly secular and adopted nationalism in lieu of religion to forge a modern nation. The Turkish state soon became a model for state formation in much of the Muslim world; Iran during the Pahlavi period, Arab nationalist regimes, Indonesia, Pakistan—all to varying degrees emulated the Turkish model.

In the Muslim world, the postcolonial state thus sought to drive religion out of politics and public life—just as Atatürk had done in Turkey. Attempting to use nationalism or socialism or both to mold citizens into a secular whole, the state showed a great concern for regulating the daily lives and cultural outlook of its subjects. Social engineering went hand in hand with the conscious secularization of the judiciary and the educational system, and with the nationalization of religious endowments, thus truncating the sociopolitical role of religion.

Still, the process of secularization was problematic in the Muslim world, insofar as it did not seek to separate religion from politics, but rather to subjugate religion to political control. This had the effect of politicizing religion as Muslim institutions struggled with the state, often in an effort to loosen the state's control over society. Though forcibly marginalized, religion thus remained relevant: in the struggle between state and society, religion in some cases became a focus for resisting authoritarian forms of secularism. In Egypt for instance, Gamal Abd al-Nasser's imposition of reforms on the al-Azhar Islamic educational institution to bring its values into alignment with the goals of the state had the effect of imparting political attitudes on religious leaders and institutions, which eventually culminated in the growing influence of fundamentalism and parties dedicated to a "re-Islamization" of Egyptian society after 1980.

Secularism in the Muslim world never overcame its colonial origins and never lost its association with the postcolonial state's continuous struggle to dominate society. Its fortunes became tied to those of the state: the more the state's ideology came into question, and the more its actions alienated social forces, the more secularism was rejected in favor of indigenous worldviews and social institutions—which were for the most part tied to Islam. As such, the decline of secularism was a reflection of the decline of the postcolonial state in the Muslim world.

The crisis facing states from Malaysia to Morocco in the latter part of the twentieth century fostered an Islamic challenge to secularism and the postcolonial state. The emerging trend became most spectacularly evident with the Iranian revolution of 1979. The revolution was the first instance of a fundamentalist movement replacing a secular state, and it inspired similar challenges to state authority and its secular underpinnings across the Muslim world.

Since 1979, revolutionary movements in Algeria, Lebanon, Egypt, Palestine, Afghanistan, Pakistan, and Indonesia, as well as international umbrella groups such as Al Qaeda, have harkened to the Iranian model. But in Iran itself fundamentalism is no longer the revolutionary force that it once was; the Islamic Republic of Iran has failed to produce a viable model for Islamic government and is today facing a crisis that will likely end the political dominance of religion there. Equally important, elsewhere in the Muslim world fundamentalism has proved to be neither as successful nor as intractable and uncompromising as the example of revolutionary Iran suggests. It has interacted with secularism and the state to produce new approaches to modern society and politics and the role of religion therein.

In the process, fundamentalism has by and large matured. Although it still inspires extremism, that tendency is no longer the dominant force in many Muslim societies. Indeed, fundamentalism has developed new perspectives on society and politics, compromised on its narrow ideals, and become an ingredient in the broader movement toward the modernization and development of Muslim states. And what comes out of this process will inevitably determine the relation between religion and secularism in the Muslim world and beyond.

Islamic fundamentalism was not successful in its assault on secularism and the state in the wake of the Iranian revolution—but it was able to institutionalize a role for Islam in society and politics. In so doing, it both gave impetus to a greater popular role for Islam in the public sphere and made Islam a legitimate—and in many cases attractive—tool with which to achieve political goals, thus encouraging many more social and political actors to use Islam in a largely secular public arena. Though unable to achieve its own avowed goal of replacing the postcolonial state, fundamentalism was able to make Islam a critical force in society and politics.

The advocates of a return to Islam have been able to make religious values, however rigid, seem relevant to modern society. They have been able to bridge traditional and modern segments of society. At the same time, fundamentalists have done much to politicize Islamic symbols and to formulate new Islamic concepts of relevance to politics—such as "Islamic economics," "Islamic education," "Islamization of knowledge," and the "Islamic state." They have both articulated the manner in which these symbols should serve political ends and convinced large numbers of citizens that "Islamization" is a necessary and beneficial process. Despite their opposition to secularism, many fundamentalists have supported extensive state intervention in the economy and society, and, in some countries, have given fresh legitimacy to the idea of a domineering state.

As a result, fundamentalists have been able to redefine the concept of politics in much of the Muslim world, shaping how politicians, state institutions, dissident groups, even how educated youth and segments of the intelligentsia define their goals.

Islamic fundamentalism became ensconced in the politics of Muslim societies at a time when the secular conception of the state and its nationalist underpinning were losing legitimacy and, hence, political efficacy. Still, because fundamentalism was not able to completely replace existing political and social structures, it has set the stage for an ongoing and intense struggle over the proper balance between religion and secularism in Muslim societies.

Many secular states have responded to the fundamentalist challenge by appropriating aspects of its discourse, to bolster their legitimacy and thus augment their power. Malaysia and Pakistan exemplify this trend. In both countries, the leadership has successfully confounded its fundamentalist opposition while reaping the fruits of its propaganda. By introducing "fundamentalism from above," they have been able to exploit the fundamentalist challenge from below, while strengthening their control over politics and society.

Faced with the staying power of the secular state, still other fundamentalist forces in other countries have opted to change. By compromising, they have been able to gain a foothold in the political process. Here it is Islamic forces rather than the state that have been at the forefront of political change, defining the ways in which Islam and secular politics could blend to produce new models for state and society to follow.

Turkey is perhaps the best example in this regard. Faced with the uncompromising secularism of the state, Turkish Islamic forces have abandoned their narrow fundamentalist views in favor of an inclusive and pragmatic approach to the role of religion in politics: they have dropped their demands for strict adherence to Islamic law, they support Turkey's relations with the West, and they even accept the need to maintain relations with Israel. The pragmatism of Turkey's Islamic forces has produced a model for the rest of the Muslim world to follow, one in which modern state and social institutions that are secular in nature also reflect Islamic values.

Iran—a secular state that fell to an Islamic revolution that now faces a secular backlash—represents a very different model of what the future may hold. Through the crucible of revolution, and the rise and fall of popular support for creating an Islamic republic, Iran has been experimenting with a unique combination of religion and secularism. There the state is now the repository of Islam and the society is pushing for secularization—the obverse of what is happening in the rest of the Muslim world.

Iran's Islamic Republic enjoyed only temporary success in implementing its vision. Its theocratic ideal quickly became a facade behind which religious and political authorities stood increasingly apart from one another. The state was never able to completely control its sizable secular social stratum, which has become a primary source of secular resistance to the Islamic Republic. So in time the Republic had to bow to other pressures that, for one, have necessitated the use of elections to settle struggles for power. And the practice of voting has, in turn, inadvertently produced a certain degree of pluralism and also a distinct political momentum for institutionalizing more democratic practices and modes of political behavior.

This dialectic—a growing secularism in society reinforced by a gradual opening of the Islamic state—is peculiar to Iran. It represents a unique model in which secularism and the sociopolitical institutions associated with it are not merely imported ideals imposed from above, but homegrown trends that have emerged to curtail the power of the Islamic state. As a result, Iran promises to produce a religio-secular model whose point of origin is Islamic rather than secular—and quite different from what one finds elsewhere in the Muslim Middle East and Asia.

As the example of Iran suggests, the Muslim world is in the midst of a process of change, experimenting with models that, by balancing the competing demands of religion and secularism, can create viable ways for these societies to modernize. What is likely to emerge at the end is nation-states that strike a very different balance between religion and secularism from that drawn in the West. These states will call upon the cultural resources of religion to address their social and economic needs—but not necessarily in the manner that European history suggests.

Discussion Questions

1. Suggest two policies or institutions that can help reconcile cultural diversity and national unity.
2. In what ways does Huntington's "Clash of Civilizations?" (1.4) help or hinder understanding of any one selection in this chapter?
3. Why does the topic of immigration often provoke intense political controversy?

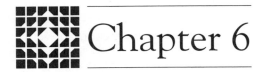 Chapter 6

POLITICAL INSTITUTIONS

An important topic of research in comparative politics these days involves the study of political institutions. Why? Because political institutions have a critical impact on citizens' lives and political and social life, often in ways that are subtle and possibly unintended. When it comes to political institutions and public policies, the devil is often in the details. That is, a small difference in the way that an institution is organized can make a big difference in its impact.

What, then, are institutions? One of the most frequently used definitions has been suggested by political scientist Peter A. Hall: "The concept of institutions . . . refer[s] to the formal rules, compliance procedures, and standard operating practices that structure the relationship between individuals in various units of the polity and economy."[1] Note that Hall defines institutions both as formal rules and procedures—what are commonly described as organizations—and as standard operating procedures—informal understandings. Formal rules and procedures are enumerated in constitutions and law books. Although it is more difficult to define and identify informal institutions, they may be extremely influential. For example, no law dictates that U.S. senators from a given state who share the president's party affiliation should possess a veto over the president's nominees for the position of federal judge from that state. But this time-honored custom has such force that it can be considered an institution.

Comparativists engage in extensive research to understand how institutions originate, how they change, and what impact they have. The selections in this chapter provide some fine examples of institutional analysis. Linz [6.1] claims that presidential systems are more likely than parliamentary regimes to promote political instability. Mansfield and Snyder [6.2] assert that political leaders in newly established democracies are tempted to play the "war card" in order to build support when political institutions do not provide them with adequate power. McFaul [6.3] questions Mansfield and Snyder's interpretations of their statistical findings. He claims that new democracies are less war prone than Mansfield and Snyder suggest. Hale [6.4] suggests that federal institutions can have divergent effects on ethnic conflict depending on how territorial boundaries are drawn. Reilly [6.5] suggests that electoral procedures have an important impact on the

---

[1] Peter A. Hall, *Governing the Economy: The Politics of State Intervention in Britain and France* (New York: Oxford University Press, 1986), p. 19.

extent of conflict among ethnic groups. And Weldon [6.6] reports that low rates of violence against women are more likely in those countries that have both ministries of women's affairs and strong grassroots women's movements.

The design of political institutions heavily influences the distribution of costs and benefits among groups in a society. It also reflects values or preferences. For this reason, institutions rarely command unanimity. When we study this topic, therefore, we are studying not only what is but what should be. Most of the articles in this chapter are rich with policy implications. Thus, the design of political institutions involves the most fundamental issues in the study of politics: representation, distribution, order, and conflict.

6.1

The Perils of Presidentialism

Juan Linz

If asked whether the presidential or parliamentary system is the most common form of democratic regime, most Americans would choose the presidential system. In fact, the parliamentary form is the correct answer by a long shot. Juan Linz suggests that this is for good reason: Parliamentary regimes are far more likely to be stable democracies. This article, later expanded into the opening essay of a book examining the question in Latin America, seeks to explain why.

Linz claims that the root cause of problems in a presidential regime is the separation of powers, that is, that the legislature and executive are elected separately and have independent powers. Each branch of government can thus claim to possess democratic legitimacy. The problem is compounded by the fact that there is no easy way to resolve conflict between the two branches when it arises. And, since both branches have fixed terms in office, conflict or stalemate can persist until at least the next election.

Adding to the constitutional problem of presidential systems is a host of informal problems. The winner-take-all aspect of a presidential system (one country, one presidential election, one president) often produces a tendency toward polarization and the escalation of conflict. For example, because the president is directly elected by the entire country, presidents are tempted to claim that they are the only legitimate voice of the entire nation. This situation contains the seeds of Bonapartism, named for Napoléon Bonaparte of France, the revolutionary leader who sponsored a referendum on his leadership and used it to name himself emperor. Linz observes that, because of a relatively long history, Americans have learned to deal with the problems just identified. But that is no reason to prefer presidential systems for young regimes that lack the experience to overcome the perils of presidentialism.

By contrast, although Linz does not give equal attention to parliamentary systems, he elsewhere praises them for promoting compromise rather than polarization. First, they avoid the problem of competing legitimacy, since they involve a fusion rather than separation of powers. Further, the legislature in these systems is generally elected according to proportional representation. By allotting seats on the basis of the proportion of the popular votes that parties receive,

Juan Linz, "The Perils of Presidentialism," *Journal of Democracy* 1, no. 1 (January 1990): 51–57, 60–65, 68–69.

proportional representation tends to promote multiparty systems. Because in most cases no single party gains a majority, the common situation is that parties must compromise their differences in order to form a coalition government.

Linz's article and the book that he co-edited several years later have generated extensive discussion. For a challenge to his position and a defense of presidentialism, see José Antonio Cheibub, *Presidentialism, Parliamentarism, and Democracy* (New York: Cambridge University Press, 2007).

Can you think of desirable features of presidential systems that Linz does not identify? On balance, which system do you think is preferable and why?

As more of the world's nations turn to democracy, interest in alternative constitutional forms and arrangements has expanded well beyond academic circles. In countries as dissimilar as Chile, South Korea, Brazil, Turkey, and Argentina, policymakers and constitutional experts have vigorously debated the relative merits of different types of democratic regimes. Some countries, like Sri Lanka, have switched from parliamentary to presidential constitutions. On the other hand, Latin Americans in particular have found themselves greatly impressed by the successful transition from authoritarianism to democracy that occurred in the 1970s in Spain, a transition to which the parliamentary form of government chosen by that country greatly contributed.

Nor is the Spanish case the only one in which parliamentarism has given evidence of its worth. Indeed, the vast majority of the stable democracies in the world today are parliamentary regimes, where executive power is generated by legislative majorities and depends on such majorities for survival.

By contrast, the only presidential democracy with a long history of constitutional continuity is the United States. The constitutions of Finland and France are hybrids rather than true presidential systems, and in the case of the French Fifth Republic, the jury is still out. Aside from the United States, only Chile has managed a century and a half of relatively undisturbed constitutional continuity under presidential government—but Chilean democracy broke down in the 1970s.

Parliamentary regimes, of course, can also be unstable, especially under conditions of bitter ethnic conflict, as recent African history attests. Yet the experiences of India and of some English-speaking countries in the Caribbean show that even in greatly divided societies, periodic parliamentary crises need not turn into full-blown regime crises and that the ousting of a prime minister and cabinet need not spell the end of democracy itself.

The burden of this essay is that the superior historical performance of parliamentary democracies is no accident. A careful comparison of parliamentarism as such with presidentialism as such leads to the conclusion that, on balance, the former is more conducive to stable democracy than the latter. This conclusion applies especially to nations with deep political cleavages and numerous political parties; for such countries, parliamentarism generally offers a better hope of preserving democracy.

Parliamentary vs. Presidential Systems

A parliamentary regime in the strict sense is one in which the only democratically legitimate institution is parliament; in such a regime, the government's authority is completely dependent upon parliamentary confidence. Although the growing personalization of party leadership in some parliamentary regimes has made prime ministers seem more and more like presidents, it remains true that barring dissolution of parliament and a call for new elections, premiers cannot appeal directly to the people over the heads of their representatives. Parliamentary systems may include presidents who are elected by direct popular vote, but they usually lack the ability to compete seriously for power with the prime minister.

In presidential systems an executive with considerable constitutional powers—generally including full control of the composition of the cabinet and administration—is directly elected by the people for a fixed term and is independent of parliamentary votes of confidence. He is not only the holder of executive power but also the symbolic head of state and can be removed between elections only by the drastic step of impeachment. In practice, as the history of the United States shows, presidential systems may be more or less dependent on the cooperation of the legislature; the balance between executive and legislative power in such systems can thus vary considerably.

Two things about presidential government stand out. The first is the president's strong claim to democratic, even plebiscitarian, legitimacy; the second is his fixed term in office. . . . Following British political thinker Walter Bagehot, we might say that a presidential system endows the incumbent with both the "ceremonial" functions of a head of state and the "effective" functions of a chief executive, thus creating an aura, a self-image, and a set of popular expectations which are all quite different from those associated with a prime minister, no matter how popular he may be.

But what is most striking is that in a presidential system, the legislators, especially when they represent cohesive, disciplined parties that offer clear ideological and political alternatives, can also claim democratic legitimacy. This claim is thrown into high relief when a majority of the legislature represents a political option opposed to the one the president represents. Under such circumstances, who has the stronger claim to speak on behalf of the people: the president or the legislative majority that opposes his policies? Since both derive their power from the votes of the people in a free competition among well-defined alternatives, a conflict is always possible and at times may erupt dramatically. There is no democratic principle on the basis of which it can be resolved, and the mechanisms the constitution might provide are likely to prove too complicated and aridly legalistic to be of much force in the eyes of the electorate. It is therefore no accident that in some such situations in the past, the armed forces were often tempted to intervene as a mediating power. One might argue that the United States has successfully rendered such conflicts "normal" and thus defused them. To explain how American political institutions and practices have achieved this result would exceed the scope of this essay, but it is worth noting that the uniquely diffuse character of American political parties—which, ironically, exasperates many American political scientists and leads them to call for responsible, ideologically disciplined parties—has something to do with it. Unfortunately, the American case seems to be an exception; the development of modern political parties, particularly in socially and ideologically polarized countries, generally exacerbates, rather than moderates, conflicts between the legislative and the executive.

The second outstanding feature of presidential systems—the president's relatively fixed term in office—is also not without drawbacks. It breaks the political process into discontinuous, rigidly demarcated periods, leaving no room for the continuous readjustments that events may demand. The duration of the president's mandate becomes a crucial factor in the calculations of all political actors, a fact which (as we shall see) is fraught with important consequences. Consider, for instance, the provisions for succession in case of the president's death or incapacity: in some cases, the automatic successor may have been elected separately and may represent a political orientation different from the president's; in other cases, he may have been imposed by the president as his running mate without any consideration of his ability to exercise executive power or maintain popular support. . . .

Zero-Sum Elections

The preceding discussion has focused principally on the institutional dimensions of the problem; the consideration of constitutional provisions—some written, some unwritten—has dominated the analysis. In addition, however, one must attend to the ways in which political competition is structured in systems of direct presidential elections; the styles of leadership in such systems; the relations between the president, the political elites, and society at large; and the ways in which power is exercised and conflicts are resolved. It is a fair assumption that institutional arrangements both directly and indirectly shape the entire political process, or "way of ruling." Once we have described the differences between parliamentary and presidential forms of government that result from their differing institutional arrangements, we shall be ready to ask which of the two forms offers the best prospect for creating, consolidating, and maintaining democracy.

Presidentialism is ineluctably problematic because it operates according to the rule of "winner-take-all"—an arrangement that tends to make democratic politics a zero-sum game, with all the potential for conflict such games portend. Although parliamentary elections can produce an absolute majority for a single party, they more often give representation to a number of parties. Power-sharing and coalition-forming are fairly common, and incumbents are accordingly attentive to the demands and interests of even the smaller parties. These parties in turn retain expectations of sharing in power and, therefore, of having a stake in the system as a whole. By contrast, the conviction that he possesses independent authority and a popular mandate is likely to imbue a president with a sense of power and mission, even if the plurality that elected him is a slender one. Given such assumptions about his standing and role, he will find the inevitable opposition to his policies far more irksome and demoralizing than would a prime minister, who knows himself to be but the spokesman for a temporary governing coalition rather than the voice of the nation or the tribune of the people. . . .

The danger that zero-sum presidential elections pose is compounded by the rigidity of the president's fixed term in office. Winners and losers are sharply defined for the entire period of the presidential mandate. There is no hope for shifts in alliances, expansion of the government's base of support through national-unity or emergency grand coalitions, new elections in response to major new events, and so on. Instead, the losers must wait at least four or five years without any access to executive power and patronage. The zero-sum game in presidential regimes raises the stakes of presidential elections and inevitably exacerbates their attendant tension and polarization.

On the other hand, presidential elections do offer the indisputable advantage of allowing the people to choose their chief executive openly, directly, and for a predictable span rather than leaving that decision to the backstage maneuvering of the politicians. But this advantage can only be present if a clear mandate results. If there is no required minimum plurality and several candidates compete in a single round, the margin between the victor and the runner-up may be too thin to support any claim that a decisive plebiscite has taken place. To preclude this, electoral laws sometimes place a lower limit on the size of the winning plurality or create some mechanism for choosing among the candidates if none attains the minimum number of votes needed to win; such procedures need not necessarily award the office to the candidate with the most votes. More common are run-off provisions that set up a confrontation between the two major candidates, with possibilities for polarization that have already been mentioned. One of the possible consequences of two-candidate races in multiparty systems is that broad coalitions are likely to be formed (whether in run-offs or in preelection maneuvering) in which extremist parties gain undue influence. If significant numbers of voters identify strongly with such parties, one or more of them can plausibly claim to represent the decisive electoral bloc in a close contest and may make demands accordingly. Unless a strong candidate of the center rallies widespread support against the extremes, a presidential election can fragment and polarize the electorate. . . .

Let me now add a moderating note of my own. I am *not* suggesting that the polarization which often springs from presidential elections is an inevitable concomitant of presidential government. If the public consensus hovers reliably around the middle of the political spectrum and if the limited weight of the fringe parties is in evidence, no candidate will have any incentive to coalesce with the extremists. They may run for office, but they will do so in isolation and largely as a rhetorical exercise. Under these conditions of moderation and pre-existing consensus, presidential campaigns are unlikely to prove dangerously divisive. The problem is that in countries caught up in the arduous experience of establishing and consolidating democracy, such happy circumstances are seldom present. They certainly do not exist when there is a polarized multiparty system including extremist parties.

The Style of Presidential Politics

Since we have thus far focused mostly on the implications of presidentialism for the electoral process, one might reasonably observe that while the election is one thing, the victor's term in office is another: once he has won, can he not set himself to healing the wounds inflicted during the campaign and restoring the unity of the nation? Can he not offer to his defeated opponents—but not to the extremist elements of his own coalition—a role in his administration and thus make himself president of all the people? Such policies are of course possible, but must depend on the personality and political style of the new president and, to a lesser extent, his major antagonists. Before the election no one can be sure that the new incumbent will make conciliatory moves; certainly the process of political mobilization in a plebiscitarian campaign is not conducive to such a turn of events. The new president must consider whether gestures designed to conciliate his recent opponents might weaken him unduly, especially if he risks provoking his more extreme allies into abandoning him completely. There is also the possibility that the opposition could refuse to reciprocate his magnanimity, thus causing the whole strategy to backfire. The public rejection of an olive branch publicly proffered could harden positions on both sides and lead to more, rather than less, antagonism and polarization.

Some of presidentialism's most notable effects on the style of politics result from the characteristics of the presidential office itself. Among these characteristics are not only the great powers associated with the presidency but also the limits imposed on it—particularly those requiring cooperation with the legislative branch, a requirement that becomes especially salient when that branch is dominated by opponents of the president's party. Above all, however, there are the time constraints that a fixed term or number of possible terms imposes on the incumbent. The office of president is by nature two-dimensional and, in a sense, ambiguous: on the one hand, the president is the head of state and the representative of the entire nation; on the other hand, he stands for a clearly partisan political option. If he stands at the head of a multiparty coalition, he may even represent an option within an option as he deals with other members of the winning electoral alliance.

The president may find it difficult to combine his role as the head of what Bagehot called the "deferential" or symbolic aspect of the polity (a role that Bagehot thought the British monarch played perfectly and which, in republican parliamentary constitutions, has been successfully filled by presidents such as Sandro Pertini of Italy and Theodor Heuss of West Germany) with his role as an effective chief executive and partisan leader fighting to promote his party and its program. It is not always easy to be simultaneously the president, say, of all Chileans and of the workers; it is hard to be both the elegant and courtly master of La Moneda (the Chilean president's official residence) and the demagogic orator of the mass rallies at the soccer stadium. Many voters and key elites are likely to think that playing the second role means betraying the first—for should not the president as head of state stand at least somewhat above party in order to be a symbol of the nation and the stability of its government? A presidential system, as opposed to a constitutional monarchy or a republic with both a premier and a head of state, does not allow such a neat differentiation of roles.

Perhaps the most important consequences of the direct relationship that exists between a president and the electorate are the sense the president may have of being the only elected representative of the whole people and the accompanying risk that he will tend to conflate his supporters with "the people" as a whole. The plebiscitarian component implicit in the president's authority is likely to make the obstacles and opposition he encounters seem particularly annoying. In his frustration he may be tempted to define his policies as reflections of the popular will and those of his opponents as the selfish designs of narrow interests. This identification of leader with people fosters a certain populism that may be a source of strength. It may also, however, bring on a refusal to acknowledge the limits of the mandate that even a majority—to say nothing of a mere plurality—can claim as democratic justification for the enactment of its agenda. The doleful potential for displays of cold indifference, disrespect, or even downright hostility toward the opposition is not to be scanted.

Unlike the rather Olympian president, the prime minister is normally a member of parliament who, even as he sits on the government bench, remains part of the larger body. He must at some point meet his fellow legislators upon terms of rough equality, as the British prime minister regularly does during the traditional question time in the House of Commons. If he heads a coalition or minority government or if his party commands only a slim majority of seats, then he can afford precious little in the way of detachment from parliamentary opinion. A president, by contrast, heads an independent branch of government and meets with members of the legislature on his own terms. Especially uncertain in presidential regimes is the place of opposition leaders, who may not even hold public office and in any case have nothing like the quasi-official status that the leaders of the opposition enjoy in Britain, for example.

The absence in presidential regimes of a monarch or a "president of the republic" who can act symbolically as a moderating power deprives the system of flexibility and of a means of restraining power. A generally neutral figure can provide moral ballast in a crisis or act as a moderator between the premier and his opponents—who may include not only his parliamentary foes but military leaders as well. A parliamentary regime has a speaker or presiding member of parliament who can exert some restraining influence over the parliamentary antagonists, including the prime minister himself, who is after all a member of the chamber over which the speaker presides.

The Problem of Dual Legitimacy

Given his unavoidable institutional situation, a president bids fair to become the focus for whatever exaggerated expectations his supporters may harbor. They are prone to think that he has more power than he really has or should have and may sometimes be politically mobilized against any adversaries who bar his way. The interaction between a popular president and the crowd acclaiming him can generate fear among his opponents and a tense political climate. Something similar might be said about a president with a military background or close military ties—which are facilitated by the absence of the prominent defense minister one usually finds under cabinet government.

Ministers in parliamentary systems are situated quite differently from cabinet officers in presidential regimes. Especially in cases of coalition or minority governments, prime ministers are much closer to being on an equal footing with their fellow ministers than presidents will ever be with their cabinet appointees. . . .

A presidential cabinet is less likely than its parliamentary counterpart to contain strong and independent-minded members. The officers of a president's cabinet hold their posts purely at the sufferance of their chief; if dismissed, they are out of public life altogether. A premier's ministers, by contrast, are not his creatures but normally his parliamentary colleagues; they may go from the cabinet back to their seats in parliament and question the prime minister in party caucuses or during the ordinary course of parliamentary business just as freely as other members can. A president, moreover, can shield his cabinet members from criticism much more effectively than can a prime minister, whose cabinet members are regularly hauled before parliament to answer queries or even, in extreme cases, to face censure.

One need not delve into all the complexities of the relations between the executive and the legislature in various presidential regimes to see that all such systems are based on dual democratic legitimacy: no democratic principle exists to resolve disputes between the executive and the legislature about which of the two actually represents the will of the people. In practice, particularly in those developing countries where there are great regional inequalities in modernization, it is likely that the political and social outlook of the legislature will differ from that held by the president and his supporters. The territorial principle of representation, often reinforced by malapportionment or federal institutions like a nonproportional upper legislative chamber, tends to give greater legislative weight to small towns and rural areas. Circumstances like these can give the president grounds to question the democratic credentials of his legislative opponents. He may even charge that they represent nothing but local oligarchies and narrow, selfish clienteles. This may or may not be true, and it may or may not be worse to cast one's ballot under the tutelage of local nota-bles, tribal chieftains, landowners, priests, or even bosses than under that of trade unions, neighborhood associations, or party machines. Whatever the case may be, modern urban elites will remain inclined to skepticism about the de-mocratic bona fides of legislators from rural or provincial districts. In such a context, a president frustrated by legislative recalcitrance will be tempted to mobilize the people against the putative oligarchs and special interests, to claim for himself alone true democratic legitimacy as the tribune of the people, and to urge on his supporters in mass demonstrations against the opposition. It is also conceivable that in some countries the president might represent the more tra-ditional or provincial electorates and could use their support against the more urban and modern sectors of society.

Even more ominously, in the absence of any principled method of distin-guishing the true bearer of democratic legitimacy, the president may use ideo-logical formulations to discredit his foes; institutional rivalry may thus assume the character of potentially explosive social and political strife. Institutional tensions that in some societies can be peacefully settled through negotiation or legal means may in other, less happy lands seek their resolution in the streets.

The Issue of Stability

Among the oft-cited advantages of presidentialism is its provision for the stabil-ity of the executive. This feature is said to furnish a welcome contrast to the ten-uousness of many parliamentary governments, with their frequent cabinet crises and changes of prime minister, especially in the multiparty democracies of West-ern Europe. Certainly the spectacle of political instability presented by the Third and Fourth French Republics and, more recently, by Italy and Portugal has contributed to the low esteem in which many scholars—especially in Latin America—hold parliamentarism and their consequent preference for presiden-tial government. But such invidious comparisons overlook the large degree of stability that actually characterizes parliamentary governments. The superficial volatility they sometimes exhibit obscures the continuity of parties in power, the enduring character of coalitions, and the way that party leaders and key minis-ters have of weathering cabinet crises without relinquishing their posts. In addi-tion, the instability of presidential cabinets has been ignored by students of governmental stability. It is also insufficiently noted that parliamentary systems, precisely by virtue of their surface instability, often avoid deeper crises. A prime minister who becomes embroiled in scandal or loses the allegiance of his party or majority coalition and whose continuance in office might provoke grave turmoil can be much more easily removed than a corrupt or highly unpopular president. Unless partisan alignments make the formation of a democratically legitimate cabinet impossible, parliament should eventually be able to select a new prime minister who can form a new government. In some more serious cases, new elections may be called, although they often do not resolve the problem and can even, as in the case of Weimar Germany in the 1930s, compound it.

The government crises and ministerial changes of parliamentary regimes are of course excluded by the fixed term a president enjoys, but this great stability is bought at the price of similarly great rigidity. Flexibility in the face of constantly changing situations is not presidentialism's strong suit. Replacing a president who has lost the confidence of his party or the people is an extremely difficult proposition. Even when polarization has intensified to the point of violence and illegality, a stubborn incumbent may remain in office. By the time the cumbersome mechanisms provided to dislodge him in favor of a more able and conciliatory successor have done their work, it may be too late. Impeachment is a very uncertain and time-consuming process, especially compared with the simple parliamentary vote of no confidence. An embattled president can use his powers in such a way that his opponents might not be willing to wait until the end of his term to oust him, but there are no constitutional ways—save impeachment or resignation under pressure—to replace him. There are, moreover, risks attached even to these entirely legal methods; the incumbent's supporters may feel cheated by them and rally behind him, thus exacerbating the crisis. It is hard to imagine how the issue could be resolved purely by the political leaders, with no recourse or threat of recourse to the people or to nondemocratic institutions like the courts or—in the worst case—the military. The intense antagonisms underlying such crises cannot remain even partially concealed in the corridors and cloakrooms of the legislature. What in a parliamentary system would be a government crisis can become a full-blown regime crisis in a presidential system. . . .

Parliamentarism and Political Stability

This analysis of presidentialism's unpromising implications for democracy is not meant to imply that no presidential democracy can be stable; on the contrary, the world's most stable democracy—the United States of America—has a presidential constitution. Nevertheless, one cannot help tentatively concluding that in many other societies the odds that presidentialism will help preserve democracy are far less favorable.

While it is true that parliamentarism provides a more flexible and adaptable institutional context for the establishment and consolidation of democracy, it does not follow that just any sort of parliamentary regime will do. Indeed, to complete the analysis one would need to reflect upon the best type of parliamentary constitution and its specific institutional features. Among these would be a prime-ministerial office combining power with responsibility, which would in turn require strong, well-disciplined political parties. Such features—there are of course many others we lack the space to discuss—would help foster responsible decision making and stable governments and would encourage genuine party competition without causing undue political fragmentation. In addition, every country has unique aspects that one must take into account—traditions of federalism, ethnic or cultural heterogeneity, and so on. Finally, it almost goes without saying that our analysis establishes only probabilities and tendencies, not determinisms. No one can guarantee that parliamentary systems will never experience grave crisis or even breakdown.

In the final analysis, all regimes, however wisely designed, must depend for their preservation upon the support of society at large—its major forces, groups, and institutions. They rely, therefore, on a public consensus which recognizes as legitimate authority only that power which is acquired through lawful and democratic means. They depend also on the ability of their leaders to govern, to inspire trust, to respect the limits of their power, and to reach an adequate degree of consensus. Although these qualities are most needed in a presidential system, it is precisely there that they are most difficult to achieve. Heavy reliance on the personal qualities of a political leader—on the virtue of a statesman, if you will—is a risky course, for one never knows if such a man can be found to fill the presidential office. But while no presidential constitution can guarantee a Washington, a Juárez, or a Lincoln, no parliamentary regime can guarantee an Adenauer or a Churchill either. Given such unavoidable uncertainty, the aim of this essay has been merely to help recover a debate on the role of alternative democratic institutions in building stable democratic polities.

Democratic Transitions, Institutional Strength, and War

Edward D. Mansfield and Jack Snyder

Edward Mansfield and Jack Snyder reported in previous research that regimes that had recently become democratic were especially likely to engage in foreign war. In the present selection, they analyze which features of the institutional design of new democracies increase the chances of initiating war. They find that political institutions that fragment and reduce the power of rulers, such as federalism, may tempt rulers to initiate war to increase their power. (They have more fully developed their argument in *Electing to Fight: Why Emerging Democracies Go to War* [Cambridge, MA: MIT Press, 2005].)

Mansfield and Snyder don't consider the possibility that federalism may have other advantages. For example, some scholars have suggested that it provides ethnic minorities with a share of power that they would not have in more centralized systems. (See Hale [6.4] for a discussion of conditions under which federalism may promote or de-escalate ethnic conflict.) What might Mansfield and Snyder reply?

The centerpiece of U.S. foreign policy in the 1990s was the claim that promoting democracy would foster peace. Noting that no two democracies have ever fought a war against each other, President Bill Clinton argued that support for democratization would be an antidote to international war and civil strife.[1] Yet the 1990s turned out to be a decade of both democratization and chronic nationalist conflict, both within and between some transitional states.

While the world would probably be more peaceful if all states were mature democracies, Clinton's conventional wisdom failed to anticipate the dangers of getting from here to there. Prominent critics have pointed out that newly democratizing states are often neither liberal nor peaceful.[2] Since the French

---

Edward D. Mansfield and Jack Snyder, "Democratic Transitions, Institutional Strength, and War," *International Organization* 56, no. 2 (Spring 2002): 297–304. © 2002 by the IO Foundation and the Massachusetts Institute of Technology.

Revolution, the earliest phases of democratization have triggered some of the world's bloodiest nationalist struggles. Similarly, during the 1990s, intense armed violence broke out in a number of regions that had just begun to experiment with electoral democracy and more pluralist public discourse. In some cases, such as the former Yugoslavia, the Caucasus, and Indonesia, transitions from dictatorship to more pluralistic political systems coincided with the rise of national independence movements, spurring separatist warfare that often spilled across international borders.[3] In other cases, transitional regimes clashed in interstate warfare. Ethiopia and Eritrea, both moving toward more pluralistic forms of government in the 1990s, fought a bloody border war from 1998 to 2000.[4] The elected regimes of India and Pakistan battled during 1999 in the mountainous borderlands of Kashmir. Peru and Ecuador, democratizing in fits and starts during the 1980s and 1990s, culminated a series of armed clashes with a small war in the upper Amazon in 1995.[5]

In previous research, we reported that states undergoing democratic transitions were substantially more likely to participate in external wars than were states whose regimes remained unchanged or changed in an autocratic direction.[6] We argued that elites in newly democratizing states often use nationalist appeals to attract mass support without submitting to full democratic accountability and that the institutional weakness of transitional states creates the opportunity for such war-causing strategies to succeed. However, these earlier studies did not fully address the circumstances under which transitions are most likely to precipitate war, and they did not take into account various important causes of war. Equally, some critics worried that the time periods over which we measured the effects of democratization were sometimes so long that events occurring at the beginning of a period would be unlikely to influence foreign policy at its end.[7]

Employing a more refined research design than in our prior work, we aim here to identify more precisely the conditions under which democratization stimulates hostilities. We find that the heightened danger of war grows primarily out of the transition from an autocratic regime to one that is partly democratic. The specter of war during this phase of democratization looms especially large when governmental institutions, including those regulating political participation, are especially weak. Under these conditions, elites commonly employ nationalist rhetoric to mobilize mass support but then become drawn into the belligerent foreign policies unleashed by this process. We find, in contrast, that transitions that quickly culminate in a fully coherent democracy are much less perilous.[8] Further, our results refute the view that transitional democracies are simply inviting targets of attack because of their temporary weakness. In fact, they tend to be the initiators of war. We also refute the view that any regime change is likely to precipitate the outbreak of war. We find that transitions toward democracy are significantly more likely to generate hostilities than transitions toward autocracy.

Weak Institutions, Incomplete Democratic Transitions, and War

The early stages of democratization unleash intense competition among myriad social groups and interests. Many transitional democracies lack state institutions that are sufficiently strong and coherent to effectively regulate this mass political competition. To use Samuel Huntington's terminology, such countries frequently suffer from a gap between high levels of political participation and weak political institutions.[9] The weaker these institutions, the greater the likelihood that war-provoking nationalism will emerge in democratizing countries.[10]

Belligerent nationalism is likely to arise in this setting for two related reasons. The first and more general reason is that political leaders try to use nationalism as an ideological motivator of national collective action in the absence of effective political institutions. Leaders of various stripes find that appeals to national sentiment are essential for mobilizing popular support when more routine instruments of legitimacy and governance—parties, legislatures, courts, and independent news media—are in their infancy. Both old and new elites share this incentive to play the nationalist card. Often such appeals depend for their success on exaggerating foreign threats. Allegations that internal foes have treasonous ties to these external enemies of the nation help the regime hold on to power despite the weakness of governmental institutions. At the outset of the French Revolution, for example, mass nationalism was weak, but soon the leaders of various republican factions found that the rhetoric of war and treason was indispensable to their political survival in the revolutionary institutional wasteland.[11] Newspapers tied to political factions inflamed public opinion with the paired themes of war and treason.

A second reason democratization often fosters belligerent nationalism is that the breakup of authoritarian regimes threatens powerful interests, including military bureaucracies and economic actors that derive a parochial benefit from war and empire. To salvage their position, threatened interests frequently try to recruit mass support, typically by resorting to nationalist appeals that allow them to claim to rule in the name of the people, but without instituting full democratic accountability to the average voter. Exploiting what remains of their governmental, economic, and media power, these elites may succeed in establishing terms of inclusion in politics that force opposition groups to accept nationalism as the common currency of public discourse. For example, Bismarck and his successors in Prussia and Germany used nationalist, military, and colonial issues to rally middle class and rural voters against the working classes while perpetuating a system of rule that kept the power to name government ministers in the hands of the hereditary Kaiser rather than the elected legislature.[12]

Competition to rally popular support around elite interests has different consequences when democratic institutions are weak and highly imperfect than when they are better developed. In mature democracies, the average voter who would suffer from reckless, nationalist policies has more chance to obtain accurate information about those risks and punish reckless politicians through the ballot box. This greater accountability and better information helps to explain not only the absence of war between mature democracies but also their more prudent policies toward states of any regime type. Although democracies are about as likely as nondemocratic regimes to become embroiled in wars,[13] democracies choose their wars more wisely,[14] tend to win them and suffer fewer casualties,[15] are less likely to initiate crises,[16] rarely fight preventive wars,[17] and are more adept at signaling the credibility of their commitments.[18] Moreover, democratic great powers pull back more astutely from imperial overstretch than their nondemocratic counterparts.[19] . . .

The happy outcomes of the democratic peace, however, emerge only after a transition to democracy is well consolidated. Establishing effective democratic institutions takes time. Where powerful groups feel threatened by democracy, they seek to keep its institutions weak and malleable. Thus the practices of many newly democratizing states are only loose approximations of those that characterize mature democracies. Limited suffrage, unfair constraints on electoral competition, disorganized political parties, corrupt bureaucracies, or partial media monopolies may skew political outcomes in newly democratizing states away from the patterns that coherent democracies generally produce. Although elites in newly democratizing states need to solicit mass support, the weakness of democratic institutions allows them to avoid full public accountability. Nationalist ideas help perpetuate this semidemocratic condition by justifying the exclusion of opponents from political participation on the grounds that they are enemies of the nation. Such claims are harder to refute in newly democratizing states, where partial media monopolies prevent a complete airing of evidence and argument. In Weimar Germany, for example, the monopoly wire-service feeding nationalist-slanted news to most smaller cities and towns was owned by a former director of Krupp Steel who was the head of the largest nationalist party. These readers became a central part of the constituency that voted for Hitler.[20]

Moreover, while federalism may generate certain benefits for mature democracies, the decentralization and fragmentation of power in newly democratizing regimes is likely to exacerbate the problems attendant to democratic transitions. As the bloody breakups of Yugoslavia and the Soviet Union show, divisive nationalism is especially likely when the state's power is dispersed among ethnically defined federal regions. Hence, none of the mechanisms that produce the democratic peace among mature democracies operate in the same fashion in newly democratizing states. Indeed, in their imperfect condition, these mechanisms have the opposite effect.

In short, newly democratizing countries often experience a weakening of central state institutions because their old institutions have eroded and their new ones are only partially developed. Autocratic power is in decline vis-à-vis both elite interest groups and mass groups, and democratic institutions lack the strength to integrate these contending interests and views. Not all newly democratizing states suffer from institutional weakness, but for those that do the resulting political dynamic creates conditions that encourage hostilities. In the face of this institutional deficit, political leaders rely on expedient strategies to cope with the political impasse of democratization. Such tactics, which often include the appeasement of nationalist veto groups or competition among factions in nationalist bidding wars (or both), can breed reckless foreign policies and the resort to war.

Nationalist Veto Groups and Logrolling

The power of central authorities is typically reduced in newly democratizing states. The old authoritarian state has broken up, leaving behind the vestiges of its ruling class as still-powerful interest groups. Some of these groups, including the military bureaucracy and dominant economic interests, may have self-serving reasons to lobby for military expansion or the exclusion of foreign economic competition, policies that could cause tensions with other states. At the same time, dissatisfied ethnic elites or rising proponents of commercial expansion may press their demands on the weakened state. These elite groups and the political parties aligned with them may become even further committed to nationalism, foreign expansion, or economic protectionism as a result of their rhetorical appeals for popular support. Consequently, political coalitions in newly democratizing states are especially likely to be beholden to veto groups, at least some of which have a stake in assertive foreign policies and nationalist political rhetoric.

One form that such veto-group politics may take is "logrolling," that is, mutual back-scratching among narrowly self-serving interests. In forging a logrolled bargain, each group in the coalition agrees to support the others on the issue that each cares about most. For example, the ruling coalition in Germany before World War I was the nationalist "marriage of iron and rye," in which aristocratic landowners supported a fleet-building program that industrial interests desired; in exchange, big business supported high agricultural tariffs.[21]

To some degree, logrolling and other forms of veto-group politics occur in all political systems; but they tend to be especially pervasive in partially democratized states, such as pre-1914 Germany. Since mature democracies have strong mechanisms of accountability to the average voter, logrolls that impose huge costs and risks on the citizenry are likely to provoke strong and effective opposition. Democracy, when it works correctly, confers power on the taxpayers, consumers, and military conscripts who would have to pay the diffuse costs that are side effects of the logroll. In newly democratizing states, however, the power of elite groups is likely to be strengthened vis-à-vis the weakened autocratic center, though the power of mass groups is not yet institutionalized in the manner of a mature democracy. Thus democratizing states are especially at risk for unchecked logrolling among elite interest groups, and this can fuel violent nationalist conflicts.

Furthermore, partially democratizing countries with weak political institutions often lack the governmental coherence and predictability to send clear and credible signals of commitment to allies and enemies alike. With multiple centers of authority and uncertain tenure of office, leaders in transitional states may have difficulty making credible deterrent commitments or believable promises to refrain from attacking in the future. One faction may signal willingness to compromise, whereas another may signal an inclination for preventive war. As the puzzled Austrian chief of staff asked about strategic authority in semidemocratic Germany in July 1914, "Who rules in Berlin, [Chancellor] Bethmann or [Chief of Staff] Moltke?"[22] Whereas the superior signaling and bargaining ability of mature democracies may be a factor underpinning the democratic peace,[23] the signaling handicaps of newly democratizing states may hinder their ability to negotiate the settlement of disputes.

Popular Nationalist Bidding Wars

Even if elite coalitions worry that the costs and risks of their belligerent foreign policies are beginning to get out of hand, they can find themselves locked into these policies by the tactics they have used to recruit mass support. To survive in an era of democratization, these elite interests must attract a degree of popular support, often through the use of nationalist rhetoric. Elite control over a dependent, unprofessional news media may provide a ready vehicle for this campaign of persuasion. However, rising alternative elites may seize on this rhetoric and try to turn it against the old elites, triggering a nationalist bidding war. Prior to World War I, for instance, German middle-class nationalist groups such as the Navy League argued that if Germany was really encircled by national enemies, as the ruling elites claimed, then the government's ineffectual policies were endangering the nation. The old elite should step aside, they argued, and let the more vigorous middle classes reform Germany's army, toughen its foreign policy, and use coercion to break up the encircling alliance of France, Russia, and England. The "iron and rye" government felt compelled to outbid these nationalist critics. In an attempt to gain nationalist prestige in the eyes of the domestic audience, the German government trumped up a series of international crises, such as the showdowns with France over control of Morocco in 1905 and 1911. This reckless and counterproductive strategy served only to tighten the noose around the neck of the German elites and pushed them toward a decision to launch a preventive war in 1914.[24]

This argument has some points in common with so-called diversionary theories of war, which contend that regimes sometimes attempt to use rivalry abroad to strengthen their shaky position at home. Such theories invoke two rather different causal mechanisms. The first asserts a psychological propensity for out-group conflict to increase in-group cohesion. If such a mechanism exists, however, research shows that it is likely to come into play only if the group demonstrates considerable cohesion before the conflict breaks out, the external threat is seen as endangering the in-group as a whole, and the instigators of the conflict are seen to be the outsiders rather than the leadership of the in-group.[25] Our argument suggests how these conditions might be created in newly democratizing states through the development of a nationalist ideology, which constitutes a set of ideas for interpreting conflict with outgroups. . . .

A second set of causal mechanisms is rationalistic. Alastair Smith speculates that international assertiveness helps domestically hard-pressed regimes to demonstrate their competence by achieving foreign policy successes.[26] Unlike mature democracies, however, newly democratizing states are not particularly good at choosing wars that are easy to win and cheap to fight. A more plausible rationalistic argument for their wars is that elites in transitional states are "gambling for resurrection," that is, taking a risk at long odds that foreign policy confrontations will help them avoid losing power. Deductive arguments of this type propose that elites' informational advantages relative to their mass audience help them carry out such gambles.[27] Empirical research suggests that the strength of the incentive for downwardly mobile elites to gamble depends on the regime type and on the elites' ability to use their influence over the media to make the reckless strategy seem plausible to their constituents.[28] Our argument explains why the motive and opportunity to use this strategy are especially likely to be present when incomplete transitions to democracy occur in states with weak institutions.

In short, elites in newly democratizing states typically face the difficult political task of cobbling together a heterogeneous coalition of elite and popular supporters in a context of weakly developed democratic institutions. Many of the expedients that they adopt, such as logrolled overcommitments and nationalist outbidding strategies, heighten the risk of external conflict. These outcomes are most likely when threatened elites' interests cannot be easily adapted to a fully democratic setting and when mass political participation increases before the basic foundation for democratic institutions is firmly in place. Under such conditions, political entrepreneurs have both the incentive and the opportunity to promote conflict-causing nationalist myths.

Notes

1. See transcript of Clinton's 1994 State of the Union address, *New York Times*, 26 January 1994, A17.
2. Zakaria 1997.
3. Snyder 2000.
4. Gurr codes Ethiopia as making a transition to a regime with both democratic and autocratic characteristics in 1994. Gurr 2000, 293. Eritrea adopted a democratic constitution in 1997 in a process involving nationwide grassroots meetings, but the war precluded holding elections. Tronvoll argues that the war reflected the Eritrean regime's need to use a violent policy of border demarcation to solidify its territorial form of popular nationalism in a multiethnic state. See Iyob 1997; and Tronvoll 1999.

5. Mares 2001.
6. Mansfield and Snyder 1995a,b.
7. On the latter point, see Maoz 1998.
8. Similarly, Gurr finds that since the late 1980s, the likelihood of ethnic conflict has increased in the initial phase of transitions to democracy, especially in new states, but that democratic consolidation reduced this likelihood. Gurr 2000, 153–54.
9. Huntington 1968.
10. We define nationalism as the doctrine that a people who see themselves as distinctive in their culture, history, institutions, or principles should rule themselves in a political system that expresses and protects those distinctive characteristics.
11. Furet 1981.
12. See Fairbairn 1997; and Wehler 1985.
13. Russett and Oneal 2001, 47–50. However, some observers challenge this claim and argue that, in monadic terms, democracies are less prone to conflict than nondemocracies. See, for example, Ray 2000.
14. Reiter and Stam 1998.
15. See Bennett and Stam 1998; Lake 1992; and Siverson 1995.
16. Rousseau et al. 1996.
17. Schweller 1992.
18. Fearon 1994.
19. Snyder 1991.
20. Eksteins 1975, 78–81.
21. Snyder 1991.
22. Quoted in Ritter 1969, 257–63. See also Davis 2000.
23. Schultz 1998.
24. See Eley 1980; and Retallack 1993.
25. See Levy 1989; and Stein 1976.
26. Smith 1996.
27. See Downs and Rocke 1993; and Smith 1996.
28. See Goemans 2000; Levy 1989, 277–79; Levy and Vakili 1992; and Snyder 2000.

References

Bennett, D. Scott, and Allan C. Stam. 1998. The Declining Advantages of Democracy: A Combined Model of War Outcomes and Duration. *Journal of Conflict Resolution* 42 (3):344–66.

Davis, James W., Jr. 2000. *Threats and Promises: The Pursuit of International Influence*. Baltimore, Md.: Johns Hopkins University Press.

Downs, George W., and David M. Rocke. 1993. Conflict, Agency, and Gambling for Resurrection: The Principal-Agent Problem Goes to War. *American Journal of Political Science* 38 (2):362–80.

Eksteins, Modris. 1975. *The Limits of Reason: The German Democratic Press and the Collapse of Weimar Democracy*. London: Oxford University Press.

Eley, Geoff. 1980. *Reshaping the German Right*. New Haven, Conn.: Yale University Press.

Enterline, Andrew. 1996. Driving While Democratizing. *International Security* 20 (4):183–96.

Fairbain, Brett. 1997. *Democracy in the Undemocratic State: The German Reichstag Elections of 1898 and 1903*. Toronto: University of Toronto Press.

Fearon, James. 1994. Domestic Political Audiences and the Escalation of International Disputes. *American Political Science Review* 88 (3):577–92.

Furet, François. 1981. *Interpreting the French Revolution*. Cambridge: Cambridge University Press.

Gurr, Ted Robert. 2000. *Peoples Versus States*. Washington, D.C.: United States Institute of Peace.

Huntington, Samuel P. 1968. *Political Order in Changing Societies*. New Haven, Conn.: Yale University Press.

Iyob, Ruth. 1997. The Eritrean Experiment: A Cautious Pragmatism? *Journal of Modern African Studies* 35 (4):647–73.

Lake, David A. 1992. Powerful Pacifists: Democratic States and War. *American Political Science Review* 86 (1):24–37.

Levy, Jack S. 1989. The Causes of War: A Review of Theories and Evidence. In *Behavior, Society, and Nuclear War*. Vol. 1, edited by Philip E. Tetlock, Jo L. Husbands, Robert Jervis, Paul C. Stern, and Charles Tilly, 209–313. New York: Oxford University Press.

Levy, Jack S., and Lily Vakili. 1992. Diversionary Action by Authoritarian Regimes. In *The Internationalization of Communal Strife*, edited by Manus Midlarsky, 118–46. London: Routledge.

Mansfield, Edward D., and Jack Snyder. 1995a. Democratization and the Danger of War. *International Security* 20 (1):5–38.

———. 1995b. Democratization and War. *Foreign Affairs* 74 (3):79–97.

———. Forthcoming. *Democratization and War*. Cambridge, Mass.: MIT Press.

Maoz, Zeev. 1998. Realist and Cultural Critiques of the Democratic Peace: A Theoretical and Empirical Re-assessment. *International Interactions* 24 (1):3–89.

Mares, David R. 2001. *Violent Peace: Militarized Interstate Bargaining in Latin America*. New York: Columbia University Press.

Ray, James Lee. 2000. Democracy: On the Level(s), Does Democracy Correlate with Peace? In *What Do We Know About War?*, edited by John A. Vasquez, 299–316. Lanham, Md.: Rowman and Littlefield.

Reiter, Dan, and Allan C. Stam. 1998. Democracy, War Initiation, and Victory. *American Political Science Review* 92 (2):377–90.

Retallack, James. 1993. The Road to Philippi: The Conservative Party and Bethmann Hollweg's "Politics of the Diagonal," 1909–1914. In *Between Reform, Reaction, and Resistance: Studies in the History of German Conservatism from 1789 to 1945*, edited by Larry Eugene Jones and James Retallack, 261–98. Providence, R.I.: Berg.

Ritter, Gerhard. 1969. *The Sword and the Sceptre: The Problem of Militarism in Germany*, Vol. 2. Coral Gables, Fla.: University of Miami Press.

Russett, Bruce, and John R. Oneal. 2001. *Triangulating Peace: Democracy, Interdependence, and International Organizations*. New York: Norton.

Sater, William F. 1986. *Chile and the War of the Pacific*. Lincoln: University of Nebraska Press.

Schultz, Kenneth. 1998. Domestic Opposition and Signaling in International Crises. *American Political Science Review* 92 (4):829–44.

Schweller, Randall. 1992. Domestic Structure and Preventive War: Are Democracies More Pacific? *World Politics* 44 (2):235–69.

Siverson, Randolph M. 1995. Democracies and War Participation: In Defense of the Institutional Constraints Argument. *European Journal of International Relations* 1 (4):481–89.

Smith, Alastair. 1996. Diversionary Foreign Policy in Democratic Systems. *International Studies Quarterly* 40 (1):133–53.

Snyder, Jack. 1991. *Myths of Empire: Domestic Politics and International Ambition*. Ithaca, N.Y.: Cornell University Press.

———. 2000. *From Voting to Violence: Democratization and Nationalist Conflict*. New York: Norton.

Stein, Arthur A. 1976. Conflict and Cohesion: A Review of the Literature. *Journal of Conflict Resolution* 20 (1):143–72.

Tronvoll, Kjetil. 1999. Borders of Violence—Boundaries of Identity: Demarcating the Eritrean Nation-State. *Ethnic and Racial Studies* 22 (6):1037–60.

Wehler, Hans-Ulrich. 1985. *The German Empire: 1871–1918*. Dover, N.H.: Berg.

Zakaria, Fareed. 1997. The Rise of Illiberal Democracy. *Foreign Affairs* 76 (6):22–43.

6.3

Are New Democracies War-Prone?

Michael McFaul

This selection is a review article analyzing Mansfield and Snyder's *Electing to Fight*. Since the book elaborates the argument that Mansfield and Snyder develop in selection 6.2, McFaul's critique also applies to that article. McFaul questions Mansfield and Snyder's claim that states that have recently undergone democratic transitions are especially prone to initiate war. He emphasizes a point that they acknowledge: This situation is relatively unusual. Moreover, McFaul claims, a fuller examination reveals that dictatorships, not democracies (old or new), are more likely to be war-prone. He further asserts that Mansfield and Snyder's argument does not apply to all new democracies but to a small subset: those cases where there are stalled democratic transitions (that is, where democratic transitions are not followed by fuller democratic consolidation; see Linz and Stepan [4.4]). And one can narrow the list even further since Mansfield and Snyder specify that, among these cases, the war-prone culprits are states where political institutions, especially those promoting responsible political participation, are weak.

Critically analyze and evaluate McFaul's critique. Do Mansfield and Snyder misinterpret their findings? How well does their basic argument hold up in light of McFaul's criticisms?

Electing to Fight: Why Emerging Democracies Go to War. By Edward D. Mansfield and Jack Snyder. MIT Press, 2005. 300 pp.

Electing to Fight seeks to explain an alleged paradox: Democracies do not fight each other, but "the beginning stages of transitions to democracy often give rise to war rather than peace. Since the end of the Cold War, this causal connection between democratization and war has been especially striking" (p. 2). Why are democratizing states so belligerent? Mansfield and Snyder offer a parsimonious answer—unleashed nationalism: "In democratizing states, nationalism is an ideology with tremendous appeal for elites whose privileges are threatened. It

Michael McFaul, "Are New Democracies War-Prone?" *Journal of Democracy* 18, no. 2 (April 2007): 161–167.

can be used to convince newly empowered constituencies that the cleavage between the privileged and the masses is unimportant compared to the cleavages that divide nations, ethic groups, or races" (p. 2).

The intuition guiding this study—that shifts within states lead to conflicts between them—is powerful and familiar. Scholars of revolution have made a similar claim about how internal change within a state triggers aggressive external behavior; modernization theorists have long argued that states experiencing rapid economic growth often expand beyond their borders; and observers have noted that state collapse invites conflict, as neighbors prey upon a target of opportunity.

The twist in *Electing to Fight* is its argument that one particular kind of internal change—democratization—is especially likely to lead to interstate conflict. Through an impressive compilation of cross-national regressions and a handful of case studies, Mansfield and Snyder claim to show that democratization is the most dangerous form of regime change, and that countries in transition to democracy are much more dangerous than stable autocracies, stable democracies, or countries transitioning to autocracy. The policy implications of the analysis are clear: Promoting democracy can trigger war.

Before discussing the *actual* theory presented in the book, it is important to clarify what it does *not* claim. First, it concedes that countries making successful transitions to democracy rarely go to war: "[T]here is only scattered evidence that transitions culminating in a coherent democracy influence war" (p. 101). Second, it acknowledges that democratizing states rarely initiate war; the authors report that only "ten case studies . . . comprise all of the democratizing states in our data set that initiated interstate wars." Yet Table 4.1 (p. 81) reports that the book covers a time period (1816 to 1992) in which there were 90 incomplete democratic transitions in 64 countries and 50 complete transitions in 35 countries. Given this observation, one must wonder about the book's subtitle. *Electing to Fight* is not about "why emerging democracies go to war," but rather about why *failed* democratic transitions under *very special* circumstances lead to war *some* of the time.

The results would be even more meager if the analysis focused on the latest wave of democratization. In the "third wave" of democratization, from 1973 to 2004, there were 179 instances of democratization, defined as countries moving from either Not Free to Free (25 cases) or Not Free to Partly Free (154 cases), as determined by Freedom House rankings. (This set of cases includes countries that experienced democratization more than once, after regressing from democracy earlier during this period.) Between 1973 and 2004, there were only 30 instances of a democratizing state experiencing political violence—civil war or interstate war—within five years after democratization. (The data set for political violence I use here comes from the Center for Systemic Peace, *http://members.aol.com/ cspmgm/warlist.htm.*) In other words, during the third wave conflict occurred after democratization only 16 percent of the time, and most of these conflicts were internal rather than interstate wars. During the third wave, emerging democracies have rarely gone to war.

But then Mansfield and Snyder never claim the contrary. Instead, their argument is that democratizing states are *more likely* to go to war than either stable democratic or authoritarian regimes (p. 29). Even this narrower claim seems counterintuitive to the casual student of twentieth-century history. In recalling the millions slaughtered in the twentieth century, we think of ruthless dictators such as Stalin, Mao, Hitler, Pol Pot, Idi Amin, and Saddam Hussein, not leaders of democratizing states such as Adolfo Suarez in Spain, Lech Wałęsa in Poland, or Nelson Mandela in South Africa. But the reader of *Electing to Fight* has to read more carefully to grasp that the universe of belligerent democratizing states in question in this book is much smaller than all cases of democratization.

The authors add two crucial qualifiers. First, Mansfield and Snyder are concerned not with democratizing countries in general, but rather with a subset that they call "stalled transitions" or cases of "incomplete democratization." In their view, these are cases that move away from autocracy but fail to consolidate democracy. In the numerical language of Polity III, which is the coding system used in this book, these are countries stuck between a score of 6 and –6, while regimes with scores greater than 6 are coded as coherent democracies and regimes with scores less than –6 are coded as coherent autocracies. Remember, successful cases of democratization are not war-prone.

Yet the universe of belligerent democratizers is actually smaller still, since Mansfield and Snyder tag on a second important qualifier to every statement about the relationship between democratization and war. Stalled transitions lead to war *only* in countries that have weak political institutions. Without the presence of this variable, there is no bivariate relationship between democratization and war.

What are weak institutions? Mansfield and Snyder give a conventional description, writing that "the chance of war arises mainly in those transitional states that lack the strong political institutions needed to make democracy work (such as an effective state, the rule of law, organized political parties that compete in fair elections, and professional news media)" (p. 2). Note that the first two institutions in this list (an effective state, the rule of law) can be present in both autocracies and democracies, while the remaining two are specifically associated with liberal democracies.

Later in the book, Mansfield and Snyder admit that measures for such institutions "are scarce" (p. 87), compelling them to use a proxy from the Polity III data set called "domestic concentration"—that is, "the degree to which domestic authority is concentrated in a state i's central government in year t-1." For students of democratization, this seems an odd way to measure the strength of political institutions, since most analysts tend to equate concentration of power with democratic erosion and dispersion of power with democratic consolidation. Checks and balances or veto players are often good for effective government. Moreover, there are plenty of regimes today with highly concentrated levels of decision making but very ineffective states, such as Angola. Given how much of the authors' argument rests on a measure of institutional strength, the conflation of state-power measures with regime attributes is confusing.

Indeed, Mansfield and Snyder at times use the terms "state" and "regime" interchangeably. It would have been easier to follow their argument if they had adopted the more standard practice (for students of democratization) of treating regime type and "stateness" as two separate categories, since some autocratic regimes can have little state capacity (think of Angola) while others have strong states (think of China), and some democratic regimes have weak states (think of the Philippines) while others have strong state capacity (think of the United States). Given how much of Mansfield and Snyder's argument rests on assessments of weak or strong institutions, it would have been useful to help the reader understand when they are talking about the type of institutions (democratic or autocratic) as opposed to the capacity of those institutions (strong or weak).

Moreover, the qualitative discussion of their case studies would have been a good place to describe a correlation between the Polity variable—domestic concentration—and the more recognizable features of weak or strong institutions. But in their case studies, qualitative descriptions of the level of "rule of law," "professional news media," or "organized political parties" are disappointingly thin.

Once the importance of "stalled transitions" and "weak institutions" to the authors' causal argument becomes clear, the reader begins to question why Mansfield and Snyder continue to label the independent variable "democratization." The book really describes why *failed* state-building and *failed* democratization lead to war. As Thomas Carothers has forcefully explained in the pages of this journal ("The End of the Transition Paradigm," January 2002), a stalled transition is *not* democratization—the latter connotes motion, the former the absence of motion. Moreover, in Mansfield and Snyder's discussion of their case studies, the weakening of states—not regime type—does most of the explanatory work. With reference to their entire data set, the authors report that "states with weak institutions are not especially war-prone unless they are at the same time undergoing incomplete democratic transitions" (p. 33). This claim would have been strengthened if the alternative hypothesis—that weakening institutions increase the probability of war—had been tested independently and the results reported.

The authors' restricted set of cases of democratization is also a small fraction of the total set of cases of war. Between 1816 and 1992, there were 79 interstate wars and 108 "extra-systemic" wars (that is, colonial conflicts against nonstate actors). In these conflicts, 47 allegedly democratizing states were involved in war. But as Mansfield and Snyder state explicitly, "we survey ten case studies that comprise *all of the democratizing states* in our data set that *initiated* interstate wars" (p. 169, emphasis added). Even if democratizing regimes are war-prone, they did *not* cause the vast majority of wars over this 178-year period. Moreover, when the scale of various wars is taken into account, the asymmetries between wars started by autocrats and wars started by democrats are even greater. The Second World War and the 1879 War of the Pacific (a brief conflict involving Chile, Bolivia, and Peru) should never be treated in any data survey simply as "two observations."

With regard to their case studies, the authors report that "of the ten cases reviewed in this chapter, seven—France [1849–70], Prussia/Germany [1848–70 and after], Chile [1879], Serbia [1877, 1885, 1912, 1913, and 1914], Iraq in 1948, Argentina [1982], and Turkey [1974]—provide clear support for our theory," but "two cases (the United States in the Mexican War and Thailand in the Franco-Thai War) neither clearly support nor refute our theory," and "four wars with ostensibly democratizing initiators are false positives: Guatemala's two wars, the Franco-Spanish War of 1823, and the Iran-Iraq War" (p. 225). This result is hardly robust.

The results are even less compelling when one looks more closely at the cases allegedly confirming the theory. Most of them are not cases of "democratizing" states, but instead cases of regime collapse or a return to autocracy. Long ago, theorists of democratization and revolution counseled against conflating the analysis of regime failure with what comes later. Greater clarity in classifying regimes is essential if the kind of regime is to be assigned so much causal power in the theory.

Space does not permit a full reassessment of the coding of all ten cases. For several, though, one can use the language provided by Mansfield and Snyder themselves to ask why democratization is getting blamed for war. For instance, in the discussion of belligerent France in the nineteenth century, Mansfield and Snyder report that Polity III codes the Orléans constitutional monarchy (1830–48) as a democratizing regime which "completed its democratic transition in 1848" (p. 187). Yet their own narrative undermines this claim of completeness, since they report that *Emperor* Napoleon III seized power in a coup d'état in 1851. Comparativists usually code coups as a return to autocracy. Therefore when France goes to war with Russia in 1854, it is odd to call Napoleon III's Second Empire a "democratizing participant" (p. 187).

The same "concept-stretching" must be deployed to label Prussia and then Germany as democratizing states in the various wars fought between 1864 and 1945. Mansfield and Snyder report that Otto von Bismarck became minister-president of "autocratic" Prussia in 1862 (p. 194); two years later, however, Prussia gets recoded as a democratizing state. Then, according to the authors, "Prussia/Germany shows up as a war initiator undergoing incomplete democratization only for the wars of 1864 and 1866, but the causal processes set in motion by Germany's pattern of incomplete democratization left their mark on all of the wars between 1848 and 1945" (p. 196). Again, leaving aside the coding of Bismarck's Prussia as a democratizing state, it is hard to defend the claim that Germany's "tortured path *toward* democracy created the impetus toward its five aggressive wars between 1864 and 1939" (p. 6, emphasis added)—in other words, Hitler was the ruler of an "emerging democracy" (remember the subtitle of the book). Most scholars (see, for instance, Nancy Bermeo's *Ordinary People in Extraordinary Times*, 2003, p. 23) mark January 1933 as the initiation of autocracy in Germany, so surely it was a dictatorship that started the Second World War, not an emerging democracy. It was democratization in West Germany after 1945—when political institutions were weak, not strong as during the Nazi period—that made this country a more peaceful neighbor. (Of course, U.S. military power also helped to keep the peace, but occupation, as we know from Iraq today, is not a sufficient condition for peace.)

The same concept-stretching is on display when the authors categorize as *democratizing* regimes the Ottoman *Empire* in 1911, 1912, and 1913 (the Young Turks became increasingly authoritarian after 1908, the parliament was shut down in 1912, and a coup occurred in 1913), or the *military junta* in power in Argentina during the Falklands War, or the Iraqi *monarchy* in 1948. If one does a library search for books on democratization with respect to these cases, nothing comes up; specialists on these countries and historical periods simply do not use the label "emerging democracy" to describe the kind of political change that was taking place.

In Mansfield and Snyder's data set of democratizing countries, there are also some very strange "false positives" (cases where they acknowledge that their theory's causal mechanisms do not apply)—the Soviet Union in 1956, Cambodia in 1975, and Iran in 1980 (p. 285)—but these thankfully get left out of the case-study discussion. Their appearance in the data set, however, should have given the authors pause concerning both their data and their model.

The objection to calling regimes led by juntas, emperors, and fascist dictators "emerging democracies" is not just a matter of proper labels or normative claims. Rather, it is crucial to understanding the central causal claim of the book about the pernicious effects of elected leaders using nationalist rhetoric to mobilize voters. After a coup or a suspension of elections, why should the voters be blamed for what belligerent leaders do? More generally, for a book called *Electing to Fight*, there is very little discussion about voter preferences for war. In all the case-study discussions, elites are seen capturing institutions and manipulating coalitions to go to war; voters are not "electing to fight."

The same problem of miscoding taints the ad hoc discussion of democratizing states initiating war in the 1990s, the final empirical chapter of the book. Again, due to space limitations, I can consider only a few examples. Before discussing them, however, let us again be clear: Despite Mansfield and Snyder's assertion that the causal connection between democratization and war is especially striking since the end of the Cold War, most countries that democratized in the 1990s did not go to war. Even amid the tumultuous transitions in the communist world after the collapse of the Soviet empire, the overwhelming majority of new states in the region avoided interstate war.

Nagorno-Karabakh is the first war discussed in this chapter, but its timing undermines the book's argument. This conflict began in February 1988, two years before the first multiparty elections in either Armenia or Azerbaijan, and well before either republic had become an independent state. The obvious cause of this conflict was Soviet imperial breakdown. The kind of regime in place in either country (or republic, before independence) is inconsequential for explaining the conflict.

Another case, the Russian war against Chechnya in the years 1994–96, is intriguing, but also revealing for what the authors leave out. Incomplete democratization contributed to the beginning of this war, although again, the real driver was state collapse, not regime type. Yet what the authors do not discuss is that democratic institutions also helped to end this war. Independent media coverage, most notably by NTV television, undermined popular support for the war in Russia. Yeltsin and his campaign team then responded to these electoral preferences by ending the war in April 1996, three months before the presidential election. The faction that had originally pressed for intervention, the so-called "party of war," was dismissed from government in 1996. It is the absence of these democratic institutions in autocratic Russia today that has prolonged the second Chechen war, now in its eighth year. Independent opinion polls show that strong majorities in Russia no longer support the war, but Putin's regime does not provide a mechanism for these preferences to shape policy. More democratization in Russia would lead to more peace, the opposite of the claim made in *Electing to Fight*.

The Kosovo War demonstrates the same pattern. By the time that Slobodan Milošević launched his project of ethnic cleansing in Kosovo in 1999, few analysts considered the Serbian regime "democratic." Milošević was a dictator, albeit a weak one, who was then overthrown in the first "color" revolution in October 2000. This democratic breakthrough made the regime more democratic, albeit still not a consolidated democracy. Nonetheless, since October 2000 Serbia has not initiated any wars. Democratization has made Serbia more peaceful—again, the exact opposite of what *Electing to Fight* claims or predicts.

Finally, the policy suggestions following from the analysis in *Electing to Fight*—which, it is only fair to note, are often made by others invoking the book and not by the authors themselves—are misleading and impractical. Even without invoking the violence, repression, and disorder involved in producing strong state institutions in Europe in the eighteenth and nineteenth centuries or South Africa in the twentieth century, there is simply no just or practical way to ask citizens to accept disenfranchisement until their elites build strong institutions, especially when today's autocracies have such a poor record of actually building them. Moreover, as confirmed by Michael Bratton and Eric Chang's recent article, "State Building and Democratization in Sub-Saharan Africa: Forwards, Backwards, or Together?" (*Comparative Political Studies*, November 2006), successful democratic transitions help to strengthen state institutions (think of Poland in 1989, South Africa in 1994, or Ukraine in 2004). And while gradualism can sometimes be useful for producing democracy and strong states, it is not a necessary condition for producing either (think of the Czech Republic, Romania, or Mongolia).

The historical evidence provided in this book fails to support the notion that voters in new democracies are the cause of war. Therefore, to reduce our support for democracy out of fear that electorates will be war-prone is not only questionable from a normative perspective; it is also unjustified empirically.

Divided We Stand: Institutional Sources of Ethnofederal State Survival and Collapse

Henry E. Hale

Comparativists have engaged in extensive research on what affects ethnic conflict (see selections 1.5, 1.6, 5.5, and 6.5). One candidate is political institutions. Do institutions have an independent impact on encouraging conflict or cooperation among ethnic groups? If so, which ones?

The role of federalism—an institutional design whereby subnational territorial governments are guaranteed autonomy and other resources—has been of particular interest in this respect. But what is its impact? Two opposite alternatives seem plausible. On one hand, federalism might reduce ethnic conflict. Since ethnic groups can gain partial autonomy by controlling subnational governments, this might induce them to moderate their demands and compromise. On the other hand, federalism might encourage the escalation of ethnic demands, consistent with the adage: Give an inch, demand a mile. And federalism may further promote conflict by alienating ethnic minorities, in those cases where an ethnic group that gains control of a subnational government abuses its authority, for example, by channeling resources to its ethnic supporters at the expense of ethnic minorities in the territory.

Henry Hale claims that federalism does not always have the same impact on in all settings. Whether it moderates or enflames ethnic conflict depends on how territorial boundaries are drawn. If a country contains what he calls a core ethnic region—a subnational unit that is significantly larger than the others—and it is controlled by a core ethnic group—a numerically dominant ethnic group—this is a recipe for disaster. Hale suggests that in such a situation, the core ethnic region is tempted to escalate demands. On the contrary, if there is no core ethnic group or a core ethnic group is not concentrated within a core ethnic region but is divided among a number of regions, these factors reduce the likelihood of ethnic conflict.

Hale's argument is persuasive. However, designing political institutions in a way that will minimize the possibility of violent conflict may require a philosopher king—the rational, wise, disinterested ruler described by Plato in the *Republic*. It follows from Hale's analysis that the way regional boundaries are drawn will affect the impact of federal institutions. Any recommendations on how to proceed?

Henry E. Hale, "Divided We Stand: Institutional Sources of Ethnofederal State Survival and Collapse," *World Politics* 56 (January 2004): 165–178, 192.

D oes ethnofederalism, a federal political system in which component territorial governance units are intentionally associated with specific ethnic
categories, tend to promote state survival or collapse? This question is
critical, since many of the world's largest and most important states—including
India, China, Russia, and Canada—have at least nascent ethnofederal structures. Moreover, ethnofederalism is frequently recommended for countries torn
by ethnic conflict and, indeed, has been proposed as the foundation for efforts to
rebuild both post-Taliban Afghanistan and post-Saddam Iraq.[1]

Recent scholarship tends to point in contradictory directions. Many researchers have attributed the dramatic collapses of the USSR, Yugoslavia, and
Czechoslovakia at least in part to ethnofederalism.[2] Others have argued that
ethnofederal arrangements generally do not work well in Africa while "segmen-
tal federalism" has been blamed for Canada's flirtation with breakup.[3] This
institutional arrangement, they concur, has had the effect of strengthening
ethnic difference and providing resources for political entrepreneurs to play the
"nationality card," thereby promoting secessionist activity.[4] Others, typically
citing cases like India and Switzerland, have argued that ethnofederalism can
help preserve ethnically divided states by satisfying demands for autonomy on
key issues, localizing potential conflicts, promoting unifying identities, and
reducing opportunities for the central government to exploit minority regions.[5]
While some theorists have ventured hypotheses to explain part of this variation, these remain tentative first steps.[6] Even William Riker's seminal work on
federalism docs not take a stand on this question despite noting some of the
issues involved.[7]

This article brings these studies together by elaborating an institutional logic
that underpins the findings they identify Specifically, ethnofederal states are
more likely to collapse when they contain a *core ethnic region*—a single ethnic
federal region that enjoys dramatic superiority in population. Such regions tend
(1) to promote the rise of "dual power" situations that are frequently at the heart
of state breakdown and revolution; (2) to reduce the capacity of central governments to credibly commit to the security of ethnic minority regions, and; (3) to
facilitate the collective imagining of a core-group nation-state separate from the
union state. Conversely, in ethnofederal countries where one group dominates
in population but where that group is divided up into a number of distinct federal regions rather than united in one core ethnic region, the dominant group
faces major obstacles to collective action that inhibit it from creating the most
serious dual-power situations, that reduce the threats perceived by minority ethnic regions, and that hinder the efforts of political entrepreneurs to promote the
collective imagining of an independent core nation-state. So long, therefore, as
ethnofederalism is instituted without a core ethnic region, it presents a viable alternative to partition as a way of avoiding the most deadly forms of conflict in
ethnically divided countries.

This article begins by defining key concepts and proceeds to elaborate the
theoretical logic. It breaks down the notion of state collapse into two categories,

state breakup and large-scale civil war, and distinguishes these from individual secessions and other smaller-scale problems facing states. The theory is then tested in two ways. The article first examines broad patterns evident in all of the world's major ethno-federal states that have existed since World War II. Strikingly, it is found that *all* ethnofederations that have collapsed have possessed core ethnic regions, whereas no ethnofederation lacking a core ethnic region has collapsed. Second, the article turns to a more detailed examination of two key cases, Nigeria and the USSR/Russia, each of which experienced ethnofederalism both with and without core ethnic regions. These case studies demonstrate that the institutional logic of core ethnic regions was in fact the key causal factor distinguishing the instances of state collapse and state survival in these countries. Thus, the theory accounts not only for broad patterns but also for how the patterns obtained in individual states.

Key Concepts

Ethnofederalsim
An ethnofederal state is a federal state in which at least one constituent territorial governance unit is intentionally associated with a specific ethnic category.[8] A federal state is any state with both of the following two elements. First, it must have a federal constitution, as specified by Riker to be "federal if (1) two levels of government rule the same land and people; (2) each level has at least one area of action in which it is autonomous; and (3) there is some guarantee (even though merely a statement in the constitution) of the autonomy of each government in its own sphere."[9] *And* second, it must have at least the minimum level of democracy needed, such that the concept of regional autonomy has some meaning, including some land of direct popular election to state organs of the highest level of territorial governance unit underneath nationwide state organs. This definition, therefore, clearly includes cases like India and Canada and excludes countries like Australia (a federation that is not based on ethnic divides) and Romania (a multiethnic but unitary state). It also excludes cases like Uganda, in which a decentralizing reform did not institute direct elections for its forty-five districts but instead chose to directly elect village committees, which then were to elect parish committees, which then were to elect subcounty committees, and so on through the county and ultimately district levels.[10]

Operationally, countries are considered to possess the necessary "minimum level of democracy" if they hold direct regional elections and if Freedom House rates these countries as either "free" or "partially free."[11] This clearly disqualifies countries such as China, whose constitution nominally grants autonomy to certain regions designated for particular ethnic minorities (such as the Uighurs in Xinjiang) but which has no significant electoral democracy at the level of these ethnic regions. . . .

Core Ethnic Region
An ethnofederal region is a core ethnic region if it contains either an outright majority of the population or makes up at least 20 percent more of the whole country's population than does the second largest region. While the number of 20 percent is, of course, somewhat arbitrary, it is a good indicator of a point beyond which one group is likely to be considered "clearly" dominant in terms relevant to the logic of the theory and thus suffices for the purposes of operationalizing the theory.[12] This relative (population) size requirement applies to the territorial administrative unit (that is, the region) rather than to the ethnic group. This is because, as the theory conceives it, the destabilizing dynamics primarily have to do with the institution rather than the group, as will become clear below. The category of core ethnic region thus fits, for example, the following cases: the USSR's giant Russian Republic (RSFSR), which contained a majority of the Soviet population and whose dominant nationality (Russian) was also the majority group in the country; the Nigerian First Republic's Northern region, which included a majority of the country's population and was dominated by the Hausa-Fulani group even though this group was not an actual majority nationwide (though it did constitute a plurality); and the former Yugoslavia's Serb Republic, which constituted 42 percent of the country's population as against the 20 percent of the population made up by Croatia, the second-largest republic.[13]

Ethnofederal State Collapse
Many problems can befall states but not all of these problems constitute state collapse. In using the term state collapse, one hopes to capture the occurrence of extreme events, specifically those instances when central state institutions effectively lose their ability to provide even the most modest degree of order over the bulk of their territory. More specifically, in talking about the actual collapse of ethnofederations, we have in mind two such extreme events.

First is the notion of state *breakup:* an ethnofederal state "collapses" when it fragments along more than half of its ethnofederal lines. We can operationalize this by noting whether the central government of a given country loses control of over half of its constituent ethnic minority units for a period of a year or more. Collapse is thus something more momentous than simple secession, which can happen in isolated instances without threatening central government control over the rest of its territory. The successful secession of a single ethnic region does not constitute ethnofederal state *collapse* unless it is part of a wave of multiple successful secessions from the same country or unless it is the only ethnic minority region in that country. Thus, we typically say that the USSR collapsed because the Gorbachev government faced multiple secessions that effectively undermined its authority across the rest of the country. We did not say, however, that "Russia collapsed" when Chechnya successfully defended its de facto independence in a war with Russia during 1994–96.

A second extreme event falling under the category of state collapse is *large-scale civil war*. Here we have in mind the kind of systematic and sustained domestic violence that results in the effective suspension or elimination of regular government institutions throughout the whole country (typically involving the institution of dictatorship), regardless of who wins. Operationally, to qualify as state collapse, we require that such a civil war (1) involve the suspension of regular government institutions and (2) endure for at least one year. Both of these things are empirically identifiable and clearly distinguish polities that have effectively lost control of their countries (the cases of greatest interest to us in this article) from those that might face isolated or tightly geographically contained emergencies that the state is equipped to manage. Thus, for example, looking at sustained but contained rebel activity in Assam or periodic communal violence in Gujarat, we do not say that India has collapsed. This is because neither set of violent episodes, despite spanning more than a year, has involved the effective suspension of regular Indian government institutions across the entire country. One can say, however, that Nigeria (its First Republic) collapsed for the period of the Biafran civil war and that Pakistan collapsed during 1971–72, when a newly ethnofederal regime was abandoned and the ensuing civil war killed hundreds of thousands.[14] A peaceful decision to turn an ethnofederal state into a unitary one is also not "state collapse" unless this decision is somehow forced on the central government through civil war. Thus, unlike 1971–72, Pakistan did not "collapse" in 1999, when Musharraf suspended democratic government.

In seeking to explain why some ethnofederal states have collapsed but others have not, this article attempts to account for why some countries have suffered the most extreme forms of breakdown with the greatest consequences both for their own citizens and for the international community.[15] We thus leave for future work the determinants of very important but smaller-scale conflicts that federations face. As Watts observes: "Federal systems that have persisted do so not because they have eliminated conflict, but because they have managed it."[16] We seek to distinguish between those that have managed and those that have not.

The Core-Led Collapse of Ethnofederal States

Virtually all explanations of the collapse of ethnofederations argue that ethnofederal systems reinforce minority ethnocentric, demands and give minority politicians greater resources to push for their eventual realization. Nevertheless, one of the least disputed conclusions in the literature on secessionism is that separatist movements rarely actually *succeed* of their own accord. For one thing, governments are rarely disposed to part with territory voluntarily and are usually in a strong position to suppress such revolts; for another, the international community also tends to reinforce the status quo.[17] In order to understand the sources of ethnofederal state collapse, it would therefore seem prudent to focus not only on sources of separatism but also on factors that make ethnofederal *regimes* more or less *able* to overcome serious secessionist threats when they do arise. If the factors influencing regime capacity are also found to play a role in provoking or amplifying separatism in the first place, then we will be in possession of an even more powerful theory.

The present article focuses on one particular institutional feature that can greatly weaken an ethnofederal regime's capacity to cope with separatism while at the same time promoting separatism. This factor is not always present among ethnofederal systems. It is the existence of a single, demographically dominant core ethnic region. Core ethnic regions can bring down their "own" ethnofederal states, often unwittingly, for the following three reasons.

How Core Ethnic Regions Promote Ethnofederal State Collapse

Dual Power

Theorists of revolution have long noted that successful revolutions are almost always accompanied by a situation of dual power (or multiple sovereignty), in which a rival source of authority comes to compete with the state for control over state territory.[18] The presence of a single federal territorial-administrative structure that contains far more citizens than other regions, in other words a core ethnic region, is almost ready-made for a dual-power situation, posing an inherent challenge to the union state. To see how this is the case, it is helpful to start with a paraphrase of four conditions that Charles Tilly argues are associated with revolutions:

—the appearance of contenders with rival claims to control of the government
—a "commitment to those claims by a significant segment of the subject population"
—the forging of coalitions between incumbent government members and the contenders
—the incapacity (or unwillingness) of government agents to suppress the contenders[19]

Addressing each of these conditions in turn, we can see, first, that core ethnic regions are in fact institutional networks of people and resources that can potentially organize a rival claim to sovereignty and are of sufficient scope to make any such challenge meaningful. Furthermore, leaders of core-region institutions are likely to have interests regarding resource distribution that differ from those of central state leaders, with the former being bound more tightly to narrow core-group interests and the latter having a greater interest in concessions to minority regions that might be necessary to win the consent of these minority regions to stay in the union. Core-region leaders also tend to have electoral incentives to highlight these differences and to challenge central authorities on these matters.

Turning to Tilly's second condition, core ethnic regions are also well positioned to win the backing of a significant segment of the union's population in any struggle with the union state. Indeed, because of the nature of federalism, the core regions government is already recognized as representative of the will of its own constituents, who by the above definition of "core ethnic region" constitute a large share of the state's citizens. This makes it feasible to argue that under certain circumstances this "core" representative institution is actually a truer representative of *its* people than is the central government, whose claim can thereby be delegitimated. Especially when the core ethnic region represents an ethnic group that has historically been politically dominant in the region, as is often the case, it is not hard for core-region politicians to justify a claim to be the leading voice of the entire federation.

Third, the resources and claims to loyalty that core regions possess can also be used to co-opt members of the central government in the course of any conflict between the core region and the central government. This potential, too, makes a core ethnic region a formidable rival to any federal government whose country contains one.

Fourth and finally, central leaders will likely find it very costly to suppress core ethnic regions that do all of the above and directly challenge central authority. Such a situation makes a federal crackdown less likely to succeed. If the union faces separatist pressures from minority regions, it may also be unable to make the kind of concessions demanded by the core region in return for peacefully relinquishing its challenge to central sovereignty.

Ironically, therefore, even when a core ethnic region intends to save the larger union or to improve its own group's position in it, it threatens to undermine the union. This is because its very existence as a core ethnic region creates the potential for the rise of the type of dual-power situation that historically has proved as deadly to multiethnic states as have the processes of ethnic minority nationalist "outbidding" or separatist "bandwagoning" that are often considered the main danger. Crane Brinton writes of a typical rival power center in a dual-sovereignty situation:

> [N]ot all of its leaders and followers are from the beginning consciously aiming to supplant the legal government. Very often they think of themselves as merely supplementing it, perhaps also as preserving it in a revolutionary course. Yet a rival government they are, and no mere critics or opponents. At a given revolutionary crisis they step naturally and easily into the place of the defeated government.[20]

Security Threats

The existence of a single core ethnic region can also be particularly threatening to minority republics, thereby sowing distrust, undermining cooperative arrangements, and potentially provoking conflict. For one thing, the existence of a core region—the institutions of which may cover a large share of the country's territory and resources—is often seen as strengthening the bargaining position of the core group (a disproportionately populous group potentially or actually constituting a core ethnic region) in negotiations over ethnofederal arrangements: other regions fear that they will permanently get the short end of the federal stick in resource allocations and federal policy-making more generally.[21] That the core ethnic region may represent an alternative institutional base for core-ethnic-group members disaffected from the central government creates additional possibilities for core-group "defection" from loyalty to the federal government. The result can pose a potential threat to the very existence of the central government and can foster fears in other regions that the central government, in an effort to avert defection of this most critical group, will be more responsive to core-region demands than to those of other regions. A central government will typically try to reassure minority regions that it has their best interests at heart, of course. But the fact remains that the core ethnic region may possess the capacity to force the central government to renege, either by refusing to implement concessions to minority regions that come at a core group's expense or by forcing the central government to take more aggressive actions against minorities. Central efforts at trust building and bargaining, widely held to be key to the capacity of federal systems to hold together and avoid conflict, are thus likely to be seen as less credible when a core ethnic region is present.

Community Imagining
The existence of a core ethnic region renders more conceivable the idea that the core ethnic group can exist apart politically from other sections of the country designated for other minorities. Political entrepreneurs can point to a premade, "embryonic" core nation, complete with borders and state institutions, that can be said not to need the minority regions or that can be said even to be better off without them.[22] As such, its institutions can serve as focal points around which to promote powerful new identifications.[23] The presence of a core institutional structure also lowers the expected costs involved in creating a new core-group state separate from the other ethnic regions.

How the Absence of a Core Ethnic Region Promotes Ethnofederal State Survival

There are two ways in which a core ethnic region can be absent. The first is important and needs little elaboration. If no ethnic region is large enough to be considered dominant by the criteria given earlier, no region is likely by itself to become a source of dual power or to pose extraordinary difficulties for the central government in making credible commitments to the security of other ethnic regions. This is so even when all such ethnic regions represent "fully imagined" communities. This, then, addresses two of the three key union-destabilizing dynamics just discussed and renders the third less threatening.

   A second way in which a core ethnic region can be absent involves a situation where a core ethnic group is divided up into a number of regions with or without official ethnic status. This recalls Donald Horowitz's well-known argument that subdividing regions generally tends to facilitate ethnofederal stability.[24] When a core ethnic region is carved up, the core group faces high hurdles to collective action. . . . This has the following implications.

Dual Power

The concept of dual power directly assumes collective action on the part of the challenging authority. Certainly, a charismatic core-nationalist leader may organize a power structure to rival that of the official government solely on the basis of ideology or his own personal authority But this task is made that much easier to the extent that there is a ready-made set of representative institutions and integrated resources that already claim to be the democratic voice of the core group in the state. Creating numerous smaller institutional structures representing different segments of the core group makes dual power much less likely to arise, since it produces many rival claims to the same voice and opens up many possibilities for central governments to divide and conquer. This point is supported by Horowitz's important insight that dividing up massive federal regions can refocus much political, conflict away from competition for control of the central state and toward competition for control of the smaller federal units.[25]

Security Threats

The division of the core group into more than one territorial unit can also reduce the perception of threat that minority regions feel coming from the core group. Nationalist rhetoric and signs of chauvinistic intent are more threatening when they are articulated by core-region leaders who look to be capable of one day carrying out related actions either through their own or through federal institutions. Furthermore, such threatening symbolics are more likely to come from a core region s leadership than from a central government because the central government has more of a direct interest in avoiding alienating minority regions, since its future depends more immediately upon keeping them in the union. The presence of multiple, smaller core-group regions can also help make cooperative agreements reached with ethnic minority regions sturdier and more attractive. In this kind of union, the central government can play one core-group region off the other in order to extract concessions from the core group as a whole and thereby co-opt or appease minority regions. Likewise, any deals struck are likely to be more credible since none of the many core-group regions (at whose expense concessions might be made) is likely alone to be capable of reneging on commitments made.

Community Imagining

Finally, breaking up core groups into multiple regions without a broader core federal territorial unit makes it more costly for political entrepreneurs to advance the idea of a core-group state independent of ethnic minority regions. Because such political actors are less likely to have institutional resources that stretch (or are fully mobile) across the span of "core-group territory," it is more difficult to mobilize people around a specific identification with the territory defined by these particular borders. Any attempt to build an independent core-group country would likewise face enormous costs of institution building that weaves together many separate regional administrative structures. Identity, as a result, will instead tend to be politicized more intensely at other levels—not just around the union as a whole but also at the level of subgroups, as Horowitz argues, as well as around individual core-group regions. . . .[26]

Conclusion

While most works on ethnofederalism and state collapse have focused on the impact of these institutions on ethnic *minority* separatism, this institutionalist study has argued that dealing with *core* ethnic groups is even more important in terms of ethnofederalism's impact both on the intensity of minority secessionism and, critically, on the capacity of central governments to deal with such demands. Ethnofederal states are much more likely to avoid the most extreme problems when any dominant ethnic group is institutionally divided or when no group's region clearly dominates. If the dominant group is so divided, it faces a greater number of hurdles to engaging in core-group-oriented collective action. This, in turn, reduces the likelihood that the central government will face a core-group challenge and also gives the central government opportunities to exploit divisions within the core group. Central governments without core ethnic regions, therefore, are freer to pursue strategies of state preservation that combine bargaining, trust building, and/or coercion. Accordingly, a survey of global patterns has found that all instances of ethnofederal state collapse since World War II have occurred in countries with core ethnic regions and that no state without one has experienced such an extreme event, be it state breakup or large-scale civil war. Paradoxically, therefore, the institutional *disunity* of dominant groups promotes the *unity* of the ethnofederations they dominate.

Of course, this study has also found that core ethnic regions are only part of the story. The cases of Tanzania and Belgium, for example, indicate that complex ethnic power-sharing arrangements might be able to overcome many of the most dangerous patterns associated with core ethnic regions. Conversely, . . . ethnofederalism, even in the absence of a core ethnic region, cannot be expected to eliminate all violence. Since this theory predicts only that states without core ethnic regions are less *likely* to collapse, we also cannot rule out the collapse of such a state in the future. Accordingly, we should certainly guard against overconfidence in prescribing non-core- ethnic-region ethnofederalism alone as a solution for conflict-ridden societies; and when we do recommend it, we should be sure to combine it with other compatible measures of conflict resolution and prevention.

Notes

1. Kanan Makiya, presentation at the American Enterprise Institute, reported in *Washington File*, October 8, 2002 (http://usinfo.state.gov/products/washfile); Michael Rubin, "What Do Iraqis Think about Life after Hussein?" *New York Times*, August 11, 2002; Nazif Shahrani, "Afghanistan Can Learn from Its Past," *New York Times*, October 14, 2001, sec. 4, 13; Peter Slevin, "Undefined U.S. Plans for Post-Hussein Iraq Stir Questions," *Washington Post*, October 10, 2002, A18.

2. Rogers Brubaker, *Nationalism Reframed* (New York: Cambridge University Press, 1996); Valerie Bunce, *Subversive Institutions* (New York: Cambridge University Press, 1999); Beverly Crawford, "Explaining Cultural Conflict in Ex-Yugoslavia," in Crawford and Ronnie D. Lipschutz, eds., *The Myth of Ethnic Conflict*, International and Area Studies Research Series, no. 98 (Berkeley: University of California, Berkeley, 1998); Gail W. Lapidus, "From Democratization to Disintegration," in Lapidus and Victor Zaslavsky, with Philip Goldman, eds., *From Union to Commonwealth* (New York: Cambridge University Press, 1992); Carol Skalnik Leff, "Democratization and Disintegration in Multinational States: The Breakup of the Communist Federations," *World Politics* 51 (January 1999); Philip G. Roeder, "Soviet Federalism and Ethnic Mobilization," *World Politics* 43 (January 1991); idem, "Peoples and States after 1989," *Slavic Review* 58 (Winter 1999); Yuri Slezkine, "How a Socialist State Promoted Ethnic Particularism," *Slavic Review* 53 (Summer 1994); Anthony D. Smith, "Ethnic Identity and Territorial Nationalism in Comparative Perspective," in Alexander J. Motyl, ed., *Thinking Theoretically about Soviet Nationalities* (New York: Columbia, 1992); Ronald Grigor Suny, *The Revenge of the Past* (Stanford, Calif.: Stanford University Press, 1993).

3. On Africa, see Shaheen Mozaffar and James R. Scarritt, "Why Territorial Autonomy Is Not a Viable Option for Managing Ethnic Conflict in African Plural Societies," *Nationalism and Ethnic Politics* 5 (Autumn-Winter 1999); and Augustine Wamala, "Federalism for Africa," in Bertus De Villiers, ed., *Evaluating Federal Systems* (Boston: Martinus Nijhoff, 1994). On Canada, see Hudson Meadwell, "Breaking the Mould?" in Sukumar Periwal, ed., *Notions of Nationalism* (Budapest: Central European University Press, 1995).

4. Jack Snyder, *From Voting to Violence* (New York: W. W. Norton, 2000).

5. Nancy Bermeo, "The Import of Institutions," *Journal of Democracy* 13 (April 2002), 96–110; Paul R. Brass, "Language and National Identity in the Soviet Union and India," in Motyl (fn. 2); Ted Robert Gurr, *Minorities at Risk* (Washington, D.C.: U.S. Institute of Peace, 1993), 300–301; Atul Kohli, "Can Democracies Accommodate Ethnic *Nationalism?*" *Journal of Asian Studies* 56 (May 1997); Arend Lijphart, *Democracy in Plural Societies* (New Haven: Yale University Press, 1977); Graham Smith, ed., *Federalism: The Multiethnic Challenge* (New York: Longman, 1995), 3.

6. Bunce (fn. 2); Michael Hechter, *Containing Nationalism* (New York: Oxford University Press, 2000), 140,149–58; Donald L. Horowitz, *Ethnic Groups in Conflict* (Berkeley: University of California Press, 1985), 601–28; Rita Jalali and Seymour Martin Lipset, "Racial and Ethnic Conflicts," *Political Science Quarterly* 107 (Winter 1992–93), 601; Kohli. (fn. 5); Leff (fn. 2); Juan J. Linz and Alfred Stepan, "Political Identities and Electoral Sequences," *Daedalus* 121 (Spring 1992); Alfred Stepan, "Federalism and Democracy: Beyond the U.S. Model," *Journal of Democracy* 10 (October 1999), 19–34; Ronald L. Watts, "Contemporary Views on Federalism," in De Villiers (fn. 3), 10–12.

7. Riker, *Federalism: Origin, Operation, Significance* (Boston: Little, Brown, 1964).

8. Roeder (fn. 2, 1991). in what follows, the terms "ethnofederalism" and "ethnofederal system" refer to the set of institutions that make a state an ethnofederal state and the term "ethnofederation" denotes an ethnofederal state. "Ethnofederal regime" refers to the central government of an ethnofederal state.

9. Riker(fn. 7), 11.

10. Nelson Kasfir, "Uganda," *Microsoft Encarta Online Encyclopedia 2002* (http://encarta.msn.com).

11. These ratings (available at www.freedomhouse.org) cover 1972–2003. For cases not covered by Freedom House ratings, judgment was based on expert accounts (in such instances, judgments about temporary shifts away from democracy are not reported in Figure 1, for simplicity's sake, as these do not matter for the overall findings). Since the general conclusions of this study are confirmed regardless of whether any borderline-democracy cases are excluded or included, the presumption is to

include them so readers can see for themselves that their inclusion or exclusion makes no difference to the overall empirical findings and argument.

12. In general, while we cannot assume a perfectly linear relationship, one should expect to see the dynamics of the present theory at work more clearly the greater the gap between the largest and second-largest regions.

13. Dennison Rusinow, "Yugoslavia," *Microsoft Encarta Online Encyclopedia 2002* (http://encarta.msn.com).

14. India ultimately intervened after the bloody civil war had ground on for close to nine months, producing a quick surrender by the unionist Pakistani army and securing independence for Bangladesh. Violence related to this war, mostly involving unionist groups that had fought with the Pakistani army in Bangladesh, continued sporadically for over three more months after the formal Pakistani surrender in Bangladesh; see reports by Sydney Schanberg, *New York Times,* March 17, 1972, 1–2, and March 23, 1972, 12. If, for coding purposes, we treat the formal Pakistani army surrender to India in December 1971 as the end of the civil war, then Pakistan simply becomes an especially bloody case of "state survival"; this does not have any impact on the overall assessment of patterns in the evidence and still reflects badly on core-ethnic-region ethnofederalism, as will be clear below.

15. The notion of state collapse, therefore, is only one form (but an extremely important form) of "state failure" as defined by Gary King and Langche Zeng, "Improving Forecasts of State Failure," *World Politics* 53 (July 2001). For them, state failure includes not only state collapse as defined here but also such phenomena as state sponsorship of terrorism, which can certainly be conducted by very strong states that in no way can be said to have collapsed.

16. Watts (fn. 6).

17. Horowitz (fn. 6); Hechtcr (fn. 6), 83.

18. Crane Brinton, *The Anatomy of Revolution* (New York: Vintage Books, 1965); Charles Tilly, "Revolutions and Collective Violence," in Fred I. Greenstein and Nelson W. Polsby, eds., *Handbook of Political Science,* vol. 3 (Reading, Mass.: Addison-Wesley, 1975).

19. Tilly (fn. 18), 521. Of course, dual-power situations can occur within isolated regions of a country, as when the. Chechen leadership challenges Moscow's authority locally. What makes a core ethnic region particularly important is that it spawns challenges that threaten the authority of the central government across the country's whole territory.

20. Brinton (fn. 18), 133–34.

21. Others, from John Stuart Mill in *Representative Government* to Jonathan Lemco, stress a closely related form of tension in federations more generally, noting that it often comes to a head when deciding how many seats to allocate to each region in federal parliaments; see Lemco, *Political Stability in Federal Government* (New York: Praeger, 1991).

22. See sources in fn. 2. On community imagining, see Benedict Anderson, *Imagined Communities* (New York: Verso, 1991),

23. Henry E. Hale, "Explaining Ethnicity," *Comparative Political Studies* 37 (May 2004); Thomas C. Schclling, *The Strategy of Conflict* (Cambridge: Harvard University Press, 1980).

24. Horowitz (fn. 6).

25. Horowitz (fn. 6).

26. Horowitz (fn. 6); Hale (fn. 23).

6.5

Electoral Systems for Divided Societies

Benjamin Reilly

As other selections in RCP have demonstrated (see Marx [2.1], Connor [5.5], and Mansfield and Snyder [6.2]), ethnic differences are an important political cleavage in many countries. At the extreme, ethnic conflicts have involved violence and even genocide (for example, in Rwanda, Sudan, and the former Yugoslavia). Benjamin Reilly suggests that the choice of electoral procedures for choosing legislators may affect the extent of ethnic conflicts. He finds that the voting procedure known as preferential voting, which he defines in the article, reduces the likelihood of ethnic separatism. In his view, preferential voting encourages political leaders to cooperate across the ethnic divide.

What kinds of electoral systems can help democracy survive in countries split by deep cleavages of race, religion, language, or ethnicity? As is well-known, politicians in such "divided societies" often have strong incentives to "play the ethnic card" at election time, using communal appeals to mobilize voters. "Outbidding"—increasingly extreme rhetoric and demands—can offer rewards greater than those of moderation. In such circumstances, politics can quickly turn centrifugal, as the center is pulled apart by extremist forces and "winner-take-all" rules the day. The failure of democracy is often the result.[1]

Any strategy for building sustainable democracy in divided societies must place a premium on avoiding this depressingly familiar pattern and must instead find ways to promote interethnic accommodation, multiethnic political parties, and moderate, centrist politics. Because elections help shape broader norms of political behavior, scholars and practitioners alike agree that electoral systems can play a powerful role in promoting both democracy and successful conflict management. For example, by changing the incentives and payoffs available to political actors in their search for electoral victory, astutely crafted electoral rules can make some types of behavior more politically rewarding than others. Over the past two decades, such "electoral engineering" has become increasingly attractive for those attempting to build democracy in divided societies.[2]

Benjamin Reilly, "Electoral Systems for Divided Societies," *Journal of Democracy* 13, no. 2 (April 2002): 155–159, 161–162. © National Endowment for Democracy and The Johns Hopkins University Press. Reprinted with permission of The Johns Hopkins University Press.

While political scientists agree broadly that electoral systems do much to shape the wider political arena, they disagree deeply about which electoral systems are most appropriate for divided societies.

Two schools of thought predominate. The scholarly orthodoxy has long argued that some form of proportional representation (PR) is needed in cases of deep-rooted ethnic divisions. PR is a key element of *consociational* approaches, which emphasize the need to develop mechanisms for elite power-sharing if democracy is to survive ethnic or other conflicts. Arend Lijphart, the scholar most associated with the consociational model, developed this prescription from a detailed examination of the features of power-sharing democracy in some continental European countries (the Netherlands, Belgium, and Switzerland), and there is disagreement over how well these measures can work (if at all) when applied to ethnic conflict in developing countries.[3] Yet there is little doubt that among scholars consociationalism represents the dominant model of democracy for divided societies. In terms of electoral systems, consociationalists argue that party-list PR is the best choice, as it enables all significant ethnic groups, including minorities, to "define themselves" into ethnically based parties and thereby gain representation in the parliament in proportion to their numbers in the community as a whole.[4]

The "Preferential" Option

In contrast to this orthodoxy, some critics argue that the best way to mitigate the destructive patterns of divided societies is not to encourage the formation of ethnic parties, thereby replicating existing ethnic divisions in the legislature, but rather to utilize electoral systems that encourage cooperation and accommodation among rival groups, and therefore work to reduce the salience of ethnicity. One core strategy, advocated by Donald Horowitz, is to design electoral rules that promote reciprocal vote-pooling, bargaining, and accommodation across group lines.[5] Presidential elections in Nigeria, for example, require the winning candidate to gain support from different regions, thus helping to diminish claims of narrow parochialism or regionalism. Lebanon's electoral system attempts to defuse the importance of ethnicity by pre-assigning ethnic proportions in each constituency, thus requiring parties to present ethnically mixed slates of candidates for election and making voters base their choices on issues other than ethnicity.

Yet the most powerful electoral systems for encouraging accommodation are those that make politicians reciprocally dependent on votes from groups other than their own. This essay examines the empirical record of one such electoral innovation as a tool of conflict management: the use of "preferential" electoral systems that enable voters to rank-order their choices among different parties or candidates on the ballot paper. All preferential electoral systems share a common, distinguishing feature: They enable electors to indicate how they would vote if their favored candidate was defeated and they had to choose among those remaining. Such systems include the "alternative vote" (AV) and the "single transferable vote" (STV).

AV is a majoritarian system used in single-member electoral districts that requires the winning candidate to gain not just a plurality but an absolute majority of votes. If no candidate has an absolute majority of first preferences, the candidate with the lowest number of first-preference votes is eliminated and his or her ballots are redistributed to the remaining candidates according to the lower preferences marked. This process of sequential elimination and transfer of votes continues until a majority winner emerges.

STV, by contrast, is a proportional system based around multimember districts that, depending on the number of members elected in each district, can allow even small minorities access to representation. Voters rank candidates in order of preference on the ballot in the same manner as AV. The count begins by determining the "quota" of votes required to elect a single candidate.[6] Any candidate who has more first preferences than the quota is immediately elected. If no one has achieved the quota, the candidate with the lowest number of first preferences is eliminated, and his or her second and later preferences are redistributed to the candidates left in the race. At the same time, the "surplus" votes of elected candidates (that is, their votes above the quota) are redistributed at a reduced value according to the lower preferences on the ballots, until all seats for the constituency are filled.

Because they enable electors to rank candidates in their order of preference, such systems can encourage politicians in divided societies to campaign not just for first-preference votes from their own community, but for "second-choice" votes from other groups as well—thus providing parties and candidates with an incentive to "pool votes" across ethnic lines. To attract second-level support, candidates may need to make crossethnic appeals and demonstrate their capacity to represent groups other than their own. Alternately, where a moderate or nonethnic "middle" part of the electorate exists, candidates may need to move to the center on policy issues to attract these voters.

Either way, negotiations between rival candidates and their supporters for reciprocal vote transfers can greatly increase the chances that votes will shift from ethnic parties to nonethnic ones—thus encouraging, even in deeply divided societies, the formation and strengthening of a core of "moderate middle" sentiment within the electorate as a whole. Such negotiations can also stimulate the development of alliances between parties and aid the development of multiethnic parties or coalitions of parties. Scholars have increasingly found that aggregative party systems can help new or transitional democracies achieve stability.

This broad approach to conflict management has been dubbed "centripetalism" because "the explicit aim is to engineer a centripetal spin to the political system— to pull the parties toward moderate, compromising policies and to discover and reinforce the center of a deeply divided political spectrum."[7] A centripetal political system or strategy is designed to focus competition at the moderate center rather than the extremes by making politicians do more than just shop for votes in their own community.

Accordingly, I use the term centripetalism as a shorthand for three related but distinct phenomena: 1) the provision of *electoral incentives* for campaigning politicians to reach out to and attract votes from ethnic groups other than their own, thus encouraging candidates to moderate their political rhetoric on potentially divisive issues and forcing them to broaden their policy positions; 2) the presence of an *arena of bargaining*, in which political actors from different groups have an incentive to come together and cut deals on reciprocal electoral support, and hence perhaps on other more substantial issues as well; and 3) the development of *centrist, aggregative, and multiethnic political parties* or coalitions of parties that are capable of making crossethnic appeals and presenting a complex and diverse range of policy options to the electorate. . . .

Evaluating the Evidence

All of these cases provide important empirical evidence for evaluating claims that preferential electoral systems can, under certain circumstances, promote cooperation among competing groups in divided societies. This in itself is an important conclusion, as a recurring criticism of centripetal theories in general, and of the case for preferential voting in particular, has been a perceived lack of real-world examples. Apparently similar institutional designs, however, also appear to have had markedly different impacts in different countries. In Northern Ireland, for example, it is clear that vote transfers assisted the process of moderation in the breakthrough 1998 election. But the evidence from elections held under similar rules in 1973 or 1982—or, for that matter, from Estonia's 1990 election—is much more ambiguous. Similarly, Papua New Guinea's experience with AV in the 1960s and 1970s was markedly more successful than that of its Pacific neighbor, Fiji, more recently. Why?

A key facilitating condition appears to be the presence of a core group of *moderates*, both among the political leadership and in the electorate at large. Centripetal strategies for conflict management assume that there is sufficient moderate sentiment within a community for crossethnic voting to be possible. In some circumstances, the presence of vote-pooling institutions may even encourage the development of this type of moderate core, via repeated interelite interaction within bargaining arenas. But it cannot invent moderation where none exists. It is likely that a major factor in the success or failure of centripetalism in Northern Ireland was the lack of a moderate core in earlier elections and its clear presence in 1998. This is reflected in part by the fact that, in the 1998 election, far more votes were transferred from sectarian to nonsectarian "middle" parties than across the ethnic divide per se.[8]

The argument that preferential election rules induce moderation rests on the assumption that politicians are rational actors who will do what needs to be done to gain election. Under different types of preferential voting rules, however, "what needs to be done" varies considerably, depending on the electoral formula in place and the social makeup of the electorate. For example, if candidates are confident of achieving an absolute majority or winning the required quota of first preferences, they need only focus on maximizing votes from their own supporters in order to win the seat. In cases where no candidate has outright majority support, however, the role of second and later preferences becomes crucial to gaining an overall majority. Thus some scholars such as Horowitz favor majoritarian forms of preferential voting like AV over the proportional variant of STV, since the former's threshold for immediate victory is higher. In addition, Horowitz's case for "vote pooling" is based on the purported possibility of cross-ethnic voting—that is, the assumption that even in deeply divided societies some electors will be prepared to give some votes, even if only lower-order ones, to members of another ethnic group. In Northern Ireland, however, while vote transfers played an important role in promoting accommodation, these ran predominantly from anti-agreement to pro-agreement parties on the same side of the sectarian divide, or from sectarian to nonsectarian "middle" parties, rather than across the communal cleavage between unionists and nationalists.

Second, *continuity of experience* appears to be a critical variable. The evidence suggests that successive elections held under the same rules encourage a gradual process of political learning. Structural incentives need to be kept constant over several elections before the effects of any electoral package can be judged—particularly with preferential systems, where the routines of deal-making and preference-swapping by politicians, and the understanding of these devices by voters, take time to emerge. In the world's two longest-running cases of preferential voting—Australia and Ireland—it took many years for the full strategic potential of vote-transfers to became clear to politicians and voters alike (in fact, rates of preference-swapping in Australian elections have increased steadily over recent decades), while Estonia's preferential system may have been so short-lived that voters and politicians never became adjusted to it.

Third, the *social context* in which elections are held appears all-important. Countries like Northern Ireland and Estonia feature "bipolar" splits between two large and relatively cohesive ethnic groups, both of which were effectively guaranteed representation under STV's proportional election rules. But in 1998, Northern Ireland also had a third group: the middle, nonsectarian parties that were not clearly bound to either community. By advantaging the representation of this group, STV promoted outcomes that would not have been likely under AV or other majority systems, or under party-list PR. In other cases, however, where there is greater ethnic heterogeneity or a much smaller nonethnic center, STV may not work so well—indeed, it did not work well in Northern Ireland's previous elections. All this suggests that a key element of any electoral-engineering prescription must be a careful understanding of the prevailing social and demographic conditions—particularly the size, number, and dispersion of ethnic groups.

The importance of ethnic demography is highlighted by the cases of Fiji and Papua New Guinea. In Fiji, most open electoral districts—which are supposed to encapsulate a "good proportion" of members of both major communities—are drawn in such a way as to become the exclusive preserve of one ethnic group or the other. Thus genuine opportunities for interethnic cooperation at the constituency level are rare, and most contests provide no opportunity at all for crossethnic campaigns, appeals, or outcomes. Indeed, only six seats were genuinely competitive between ethnic groups in the 1999 election, while in the rest clear Indian or Fijian majorities prevailed.[9]

Contrast this with the situation in Papua New Guinea, where the extreme fragmentation of traditional society means that most districts feature dozens of small tribal ethnopolities. To be elected under a preferential majority system like AV, candidates had no option but to amass votes from a range of groups beyond their own. Under such conditions, candidates had a strong incentive to behave accommodatingly toward rival groups. Not surprisingly, electoral violence was much rarer under the AV system than under the more recent plurality rules, which lacks such incentives.

Such cases remind us that divided societies, like Tolstoy's unhappy families, tend to be divided in different ways. Yet it is surprising how many "one-size-fits-all" conflict-management packages have been recommended for divided societies without sufficient understanding of the structure of the society itself. Differences in ethnic demography need to be matched by differences in constitutional designs across different regions. African minorities, for example, have been found to be more highly concentrated in contiguous geographical areas than minorities in other regions, making it difficult to create ethnically heterogenous electorates.[10] Contrast this with the highly intermixed patterns of ethnic settlement found in many parts of Europe (the Baltics), Asia (India, Singapore, Malaysia), and the Caribbean (Guyana, Suriname, Trinidad and Tobago), in which members of various ethnic groups tend to have more day-to-day contact with one another. In such contexts, electoral districts are likely to be ethnically heterogeneous, and ethnic identities will often be mitigated by other crosscutting cleavages, so that centripetal designs which encourage parties to seek the support of various ethnic groups may very well break down interethnic antagonisms and promote the development of broad, multiethnic parties. Such prosaic details can determine the success of centripetal approaches to the management of ethnic conflict.

Notes

1. For good discussions of the interaction between ethnicity and electoral politics, see Donald L. Horowitz, *Ethnic Groups in Conflict* (Berkeley: University of California Press, 1985); Larry Diamond and Marc F. Plattner, eds., *Nationalism, Ethnic Conflict, and Democracy* (Baltimore: Johns Hopkins University Press, 1994); and Timothy D. Sisk, *Power Sharing and International Mediation in Ethnic Conflicts* (Washington, D.C.: U.S. Institute of Peace Press, 1996).

2. See, for example, Arend Lijphart, *Democracy in Plural Societies: A Comparative Exploration* (New Haven: Yale University Press, 1977); Donald L. Horowitz, *A Democratic South Africa? Constitutional Engineering in a Divided Society* (Berkeley: University of California Press, 1991); Giovanni Sartori, *Comparative Constitutional Engineering: An Inquiry into Structures, Incentives and Outcomes* (London: Macmillan, 1994); and Benjamin Reilly and Andrew Reynolds, *Electoral Systems and Conflict in Divided Societies* (Washington, D.C.: National Research Council, 1999).

3. See Arend Lijphart, *Democracy in Plural Societies;* and Timothy D. Sisk, *Power Sharing and International Mediation in Ethnic Conflicts,* 27–45. See also Donald L. Horowitz, "Making Moderation Pay: The Comparative Politics of Ethnic Conflict Management," in Joseph V. Montville, ed., *Conflict and Peacemaking in Multiethnic Societies* (New York: Lexington Books, 1991), 451–76.

4. Arend Lijphart, "Electoral Systems, Party Systems and Conflict Management in Segmented Societies," in R.A. Schrire, ed., *Critical Choices for South Africa: An Agenda for the 1990s* (Cape Town: Oxford University Press, 1990), 10–13.

5. See Donald L. Horowitz, *Ethnic Groups in Conflict;* and Donald L. Horowitz, "Making Moderation Pay."

6. The formula used divides the total number of votes in the count by one more than the number of seats to be elected, and then adds one to the result. For example, if there are 6,000 votes and five members to be elected, the quota for election is $6,000/(5 + 1) + 1$, or 1,001 votes.

7. Timothy D. Sisk, *Democratization in South Africa: The Elusive Social Contract* (Princeton: Princeton University Press, 1995), 19.

8. See Richard Simmott, "Centrist politics makes modest but significant progress: cross-community transfers were low," *Irish Times* (Dublin), 29 June 1998.

9. See Nigel Roberts, "Living up to Expectations? The New Fijian Electoral System and the 1999 General Election," paper presented to Citizens Constitutional Forum, Suva, Fiji, 18 July 1999.

10. James R. Scarritt, "Communal Conflict and Contention for Power in Africa South of the Sahara," in Ted Robert Gurr, ed., *Minorities at Risk: A Global View of Ethnopolitical Conflicts* (Washington, D.C.: U.S. Institute of Peace Press, 1993).

6.6

Protest, Policy, and the Problem of Violence Against Women: A Cross-National Comparison

S. Laurel Weldon

Laurel Weldon seeks to explain why the extent of violence against women varies considerably among stable democracies. Her answer, based on analyzing a large sample of countries, is that violence against women is significantly lower when there are both powerful grassroots women's movements in society and a powerful government agency specifically charged with promoting women's interests. She finds that either one alone is apparently insufficient; both must be present to deter violence against women.

Weldon does not ask what factors promote the existence of powerful women's movements. Any suggestions?

The Limits of Effective Women's Policy Machineries

When they provide access to activists and have sufficient resources, women's policy agencies can improve government responsiveness to violence against women. But sometimes, it appears, these agencies and offices have little or no effect on government responsiveness. Although eight national governments among the thirty-six stable democracies considered here have a women's policy machinery that meets the criteria for institutional effectiveness, only three of these (Canada, Australia, and Costa Rica) are among the most responsive countries, that is, those addressing five or more areas of policy (see Table 6.1). Moreover, some national governments with effective women's institutions (such as Portugal and Germany) are addressing only two of seven areas of policy. Venezuela had not undertaken any action to address violence against women by 1994.

S. Laurel Weldon, *Protest, Policy, and the Problem of Violence Against Women: A Cross-National Comparison* (Pittsburgh, PA: University of Pittsburgh Press, 2002), 139–143, 163–164. © 2002 by University of Pittsburgh Press. Reprinted by permission of University of Pittsburgh Press.

Table 6.1

Responsiveness of Eight National Governments with Effective Policy Machineries, 1994

Country	Strong, Autonomous Women's Movement	Percent of Women in Cabinet	No. of Policy Areas Addressed
Australia	Yes	12.9	7
Belgium	Yes	11.1	4
Canada	Yes	13.6	7
Costa Rica	Yes (after 1984)	9.5	5
Germany	No	5.2	2
Netherlands	Yes	10.3	3
Portugal	No	5.1	2
Venezuela	No	0.0	0

Source: Data provided by the United Nations.

Venezuela, Germany, and Portugal are also characterized by the absence of a strong, autonomous women's movement. We know that women's movements are important for articulating the issue of violence against women but are, on their own, unlikely to produce a broad, multifaceted government response. We also know that the presence of an effective women's policy machinery is strongly related to the scope of government response. This suggests that the relationship between institutional structure and policy outcome may be an interactive one, that is, it may depend on the *interaction* between women's movements and institutional structure.

The Interaction of Institutions and Women's Movements

Women's movements and effective women's policy machineries interact to improve government responsiveness to violence against women. Understanding the interaction between these elements is key to understanding the effect of each on violence-against-women policy, and to understanding their joint effect.

An effective women's policy machinery can strengthen a women's movement. By providing research support and opportunities for input on policy development, women's policy machineries can greatly increase the effectiveness of women's movement activists. In addition, by giving financial support for organizing and for independent research, women's policy machineries provide additional resources to women's organizations. These agencies also offer continuity over time for women's movement activists—sort of institutional memory. Instead of having to spend their energies reeducating each new policymaker about past efforts, activists can work to improve existing policies.

Duerst-Lahti (1989) has shown that the state commissions on the status of women in the United States played a very important role in the development of the women's movement, providing research, funding, and other organizational resources. The state commissions thereby strengthened the nascent women's movement, and they were especially critical in its transition from a loose collection of dispersed local movements to a national movement.

✗ Conversely, strong, autonomous women's movements improve the institutional capabilities of government to address women's issues. When the women's movement is a significant political force, the women's policy machinery has more leverage over other government departments. Government departments will want to avoid conflict with activists and will want to be able to show that their policies take women's concerns into account; and bureaucrats inside the women's policy machinery can point to demands from the women's movement when asking for increased funding and other resources.

Increased leverage on the part of the women's policy machinery improves the institutional capability to coordinate policy action across departments and to revise departmental agendas to reflect women's priorities. Women's policy machineries can also provide the research support and analytic focus required for sound policy design and evaluation. A strong women's movement therefore improves the capacity of a set of political institutions to respond to women's concerns, when that set includes a women's policy agency.

Thus, strong, autonomous women's movements and effective women's policy agencies reinforce one another. This effect is not purely additive; it is interactive. Each factor magnifies the effect of the other.

Policy Development in the Most Responsive Governments

Does the account developed above seem to explain the process of policy development in the most responsive countries? I focus on the most responsive countries as a form of plausibility probe: if the development of policy in these eight countries cannot be explained by the account I have developed, then it is possible that I am not accurately interpreting the relationships I have discovered, or that they are an artifact of the measurements I am using, or of the year on which I have chosen to focus. After establishing the plausibility of the theoretical account, I examine whether the statistical analysis supports the account.

I consider those governments addressing five or more areas to be the most responsive. There are eight governments in this category: Australia, Canada, the United States, France, Costa Rica, Israel, New Zealand, and Ireland. I focus both on explaining why these countries were more responsive and on accounting for the variation in responsiveness across these eight governments. Why are they more responsive than the other democratic governments identified in this study? Furthermore, why are Canada and Australia even more responsive than the others?

The process of policy development in these eight governments appears to conform to the hypothesized pattern. In every case, it was the women's movement that first articulated the issue of violence against women and pressed for government action. And every country had a strong, autonomous women's movement.

In all eight countries, powerful insiders who took up the demands of the women's movement placed violence against women on the government agenda. Strategically placed allies of the women's movement were also important in retaining the feminist content of legislation despite pressure to the contrary. In Ireland in 1987, for example, a submission by a rape crisis center to a nonpartisan committee of legislators resulted in a public report recommending policy reforms. Feminist bureaucrats inside the Irish government helped ensure that there was such a committee in the first place and that the final policy recommendations reflected the original ones from the rape crisis center (Mahon 1995). Following this report, there was a significant expansion in the Irish government's response to this problem. The government began addressing more areas after the publication of the report (with these new measures taking effect in 1990) and continues to improve its response (Ireland, Office of the Tanaiste, 1997). Similarly, the response by the Costa Rican government appears to be a product of cooperation between feminists in a government agency (the Center for the Development of Women and the Family) and a variety of women's organizations. In the United States, the proposals of organized women's groups were taken up by sympathetic legislators both in the early policy initiatives of the 1970s and in the case of the Violence Against Women Act, passed in 1994. Although male legislators played an important role in the passage of the act, it appears that a feminist in the office of Senator Joseph Biden was key to retaining the feminist content of the bill despite pressure from Senator Orrin Hatch to the contrary. The women's caucus also seems to have played a role (Gelb 1998).

These examples illustrate the general pattern of policy development in this area: independent women's movements partner with feminist insiders to achieve policy change. This explains why some democracies with strong, autonomous women's movements have been able to procure government action on violence while others have not. I stress that it is feminist allies in influential positions, rather than simply women in government, who provide the window of opportunity.

In order to explain policy development in the two most responsive countries, however, we must examine the interaction of the institutional structure—the women's policy machinery—with the women's movement. Why did the government response in Canada and Australia not remain limited to a primarily criminal justice response, as it did in the United States? Why was the response not restricted to a focus on domestic violence, as it was in New Zealand and Ireland? Why did it go beyond the partial response of France and Costa Rica? In Canada and Australia, the relationship between women's movements and their internal allies was particularly effective because of the presence of an effective women's policy machinery. Feminist bureaucrats working inside the government worked with women's movements and with the resources of the women's policy machinery to get violence on the government agenda and to ensure feminist input into the policymaking process.

The national governments of Australia and Canada first began addressing the issue of violence against women in 1975. Since that time, there has been a proliferation of institutions designed to improve the status of women in both countries. This institutionalization has provided a permanent point of contact and an institutional memory that has strengthened both the women's movement and its allies within government. The institutionalization has made the difference between the fleeting window of opportunity provided by the election of legislative allies and the more long-term possibility of the ongoing development of government response with critiques and suggestions from the women's movement. It has also provided the institutional framework needed for a comprehensive, cross-sectoral response to violence against women. . . .

Conclusion

In summary, women's movements are always necessary for the initial articulation of violence against women as an issue. The initiative to address violence against women is always a response on the part of government to a demand that originates outside political institutions. However, women's movements alone almost never put the issue on the government agenda. Hence, a women's movement alone is not sufficient to produce a government response. Allies inside government are critical: when there are policymakers sympathetic to the women's movement, or even part of it, the issue of violence against women is more likely to be adopted as part of the decision agenda. Most policies to address violence against women are thus products of partnerships between women's movements and sympathetic insiders.

Such partnerships are much less effective in the absence of a women's policy machinery. In that case, the insider-outsider partnerships tend to produce partial, fragmented responses. In the presence of an effective women's policy machinery, they are more likely to result in broad, multifaceted policies to address violence against women.

A women's policy machinery, however, is not necessary for putting violence on the public agenda. It should also be noted that a women's policy machinery without a strong, autonomous women's movement will not articulate the issue of violence against women, so it is not sufficient, on its own, to produce a government response. It is only in the context of a strong, autonomous women's movement articulating the issue and pressing for government action that women's policy machineries have such a strong effect.

An effective women's policy machinery can strengthen a women's movement. Conversely, a strong women's movement improves the capacity of a set of political institutions to respond to women's concerns when that set includes a women's policy agency. Thus, strong, autonomous women's movements and effective women's policy agencies reinforce one another. This effect is not purely additive; it is interactive, meaning that each factor magnifies the effect of the other.

This argument also appears to hold for marginalized subgroups of women: policy responsiveness to the distinct needs of minority women is enhanced by independent organization combined with some degree of solidarity from the broader women's movement. When minority women are organized independently of organizations dominated by white women or minority men, the existence of government offices for women seems to improve policy response to minority women as well as to women in general. It also seems that offices for multiculturalism or Aboriginal affairs may increase policy responsiveness to women of color.

These findings have important implications for theories of democratic policy-making, as well as for feminist theory. They also suggest some concrete ways of improving government responsiveness to violence against women and to marginalized groups in general.

References

Duerst-Lahti, Georgia. 1989. "The Government's Role in Building the Women's Movement." *Political Science Quarterly* 104, no. 3:249–68.

Gelb, Joyce. 1998. "Legislating Against Violence: The Violence Against Women Act of 1994." Paper presented at the Annual Meeting of the American Political Science Association, Boston, September 3–6.

Ireland. Office of the Tanaiste. 1997. *Report of the Task Force on Violence Against Women.* Dublin: Government of Ireland.

Mahon, Evelyn. 1995. "Ireland's Policy Machinery: The Ministry of State for Women's Affairs and Joint Oireachtas Committees for Women's Rights." In *Comparative State Feminism,* edited by Dorothy McBride Stetson and Amy G. Mazur. Thousand Oaks, Calif.: Sage.

Discussion Questions

1. It is often claimed that violent political conflicts and other forms of political behavior are based on ancient hatreds, human nature, or other immutable factors. However, the selections in this chapter claim that the design of institutions significantly affects the structure and extent of conflict on such varied issues as the prospects for democratic stability, the likelihood that new democracies will initiate wars, the prospects that federal systems will dissolve, ethnic conflict, and violence against women. How do you explain this puzzle? Can you specify the extent and limits of the impact that institutions can have?

2. Suggest a research design to measure the influence of institutions. *Hint:* Think of two settings that are alike in most respects but differ with respect both to some difference in outcome (the dependent variable) and to the presence of a particular institution (the independent variable). You can then hypothesize that the different outcomes (the dependent variable) are due to the presence or absence of the institution in question (the independent variable).

3. Compare two selections in this chapter. Which one makes a more persuasive case for the importance of institutions? Provide evidence to defend your answer.

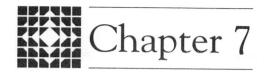 Chapter 7

POLITICAL CHALLENGES
AND CHANGING AGENDAS

We conclude *Readings in Comparative Politics* with a selection of readings that highlight political challenges and proposals for change. In one sense this entire book has focused on political challenges and reform proposals. Even the most stable democratic countries are confronted with challenges from within their borders and external attacks (see the selections by Tarrow [7.2], Putnam [7.3], and Zakaria [7.5]).

The concluding chapter of *Readings in Comparative Politics* focuses on proposals for change. Of course, there is rarely agreement on the character and causes of political, economic, and social problems, much less what should be done about them. Thus, this chapter will highlight diversity and debates. One of the major reasons for concluding RCP in this way is to urge students to apply their best thinking to honing ideas for change.

We have sampled a range of problems and proposals to convey the notion that politics involves choice. Some proposals may strike you as foolish, utopian, and even dangerous or all of these! Others may strike you as overly timid. Fine! We hope that you will provide good reasons why you think so. We recommend that you apply the same standards of rigor to evaluating reform proposals as you do to assessing the validity and value of empirically focused research. But the fact that vigorous debate exists about what should be done is no reason to avoid entering the debate. As Rosa Luxemburg, a revolutionary thinker and activist, warned long ago, the most naive utopianism is the claim that the present can be preserved unchanged.

7.1

Democratic Capitalism at the Crossroads

Adam Przeworski and Michael Wallerstein

In this selection, Adam Przeworski and Michael Wallerstein explore the dilemmas of social democracy (the project of center-left parties, particularly in Europe, to parlay working-class support into electoral victory and the opportunity to implement a set of policies to guarantee employment, improve wages, and deliver robust social protections). The authors claim that social democracy, and democratic capitalism more generally, was made possible by the Keynesian Revolution. They conclude that since the late 1970s the Right has waged a counterrevolution against social democracy with far- reaching consequences for democracy.

Opponents of Keynesianism and social democracy reply that there are excellent reasons to reject social democracy. Drawing on the selections in Chapter 3 describing models of capitalism [3.3] and varieties of capitalism [3.4], suggest some of these reasons and evaluate this debate. During the economic crisis that occurred in 2008, many economists suggested that a Keynesian approach should be revived to deal with the crisis. What are the arguments pro and con on this question?

The Keynesian Revolution as a Compromise

The combination of democracy and capitalism constitutes a compromise: those who do not own instruments of production consent to the institution of the private ownership of capital stock while those who own productive instruments consent to political institutions that permit other groups to effectively press their claims to the allocation of resources and the distribution of output. It may be worth recalling that this compromise was deemed unfeasible by Marx, who claims that the "bourgeois republic" is based on a contradiction that renders it inherently unstable as a form of social organization. A combination of private ownership of the means of production with universal suffrage, Marx argued, must lead either to "social emancipation" of the oppressed classes utilizing their

Adam Przeworski, *Capitalism and Social Democracy* (Cambridge, UK: Cambridge University Press, 1985), chap. 6 (written jointly with Michael Wallerstein), 207–211; 218–221. © Maison des Sciences de l'homme and Cambridge University Press 1985. Reprinted with the permission of Cambridge University Press.

political power or to "political restoration" of the oppressing class utilizing its economic power. Hence, Marx held, capitalist democracy is "only the political form of revolution of bourgeois society and not its conservative form of life," "only a spasmodic, exceptional state of things . . . impossible as the normal form of society."

It was Keynesianism that provided the ideological and political foundations for the compromise of capitalist democracy. Keynesianism held out the prospect that the state could reconcile the private ownership of the means of production with democratic management of the economy. As Keynes himself put it: "It is not the ownership of the instruments of production which it is important for the state to assume. If the state is able to determine the aggregate amount of resources devoted to augmenting the instruments and the basic reward to those who own them, it will have accomplished all that is necessary." Democratic control over the level of unemployment and the distribution of income became the terms of the compromise that made democratic capitalism possible.

The problem of the 1930s was that resources lay fallow: machines stood idle while men were out of work. At no time in history was the irrationality of the capitalist system more blatant. As families starved, food—already produced food—was destroyed. Coffee was burned, pigs were killed, inventories rotted, machines rusted. Unemployment was the central political problem of society.

According to the economic orthodoxy of the time, this state of affairs was simply a given and the only recourse was to cut the costs of production, which meant cutting wages and transfers. Some relief measures to assist the employed were obviously urgently required, but whether such measures were advisable from an economic point of view was at best controversial. In Great Britain the Labour government in fact proposed to reduce unemployment compensations: this was the condition for being bailed out by the I.M.F. of the time, where "M." stood for the Morgan Bank. But in Sweden the Social Democratic Party, having won the election of 1932, broke the shell of the orthodox monetary policy. As unemployment climbed sharply with the onset of the Great Depression, they stumbled upon an idea that was truly new: instead of assisting the unemployed, the Swedish Social Democrats employed them. It was the beginning of the marriage of the Left and Keynesian economics.

Keynesianism provided the foundation for class compromise by supplying those political parties representing workers with a justification for holding office within capitalist societies. And such a justification was desperately needed. Ever since the 1890s, social democrats had thought that their irreversible electoral progress would culminate in an electoral majority that would allow them one day to enter into office and legislate their societies into socialism. They were completely unprepared for what ensued: in several countries social democratic, labor, and socialist parties were invited to form governments by default, without winning the majority that would have been necessary to pursue the program of nationalization, because the bourgeois parties were too divided to continue their traditional coalitions. Indeed, the first elected socialist government in the world was formed by the Swedish Social Democrats in 1920 just as they suffered their first electoral reversal. And once in office, socialists found themselves in the embarrassing situation of not being able to pursue the program of nationalization and not having any other program that would distinguish them from their bourgeois opponents. They could and did pursue ad-hoc measures designed to improve conditions for their electoral constituency: the development of public housing, the institution of unemployment relief, the introduction of minimum wages, income and inheritance taxes, and old age pensions. But such measures did not differ from the tradition of conservative reforms associated with Bismarck, Disraeli, or Giolitti. Socialists behaved like all other parties: with some distributional bias toward their own constituency but full of respect for the golden principles of the balanced budget, deflation, gold standard, etc.

Keynesianism suddenly provided working-class political parties with a reason to be in office. It appeared that there was something to be done, that the economy was not moving according to natural laws, that economic crises could be attenuated and the waste of resources and the suffering alleviated if the state pursued anticyclical policies of demand management. If the economy was producing at a level below its capacity, given the existing stock of capital and labor, a proper government policy could increase output until it approached the economy's full potential. The government had the capacity to close the "full-employment gap," to insure that there would be no unemployment of men and machines. Full employment became a realistic goal that could be pursued at all times.

How was this to be done? Here again Keynesian economics provided a technical justification for class compromise. The answer it provided was to increase consumption. In the Keynesian diagnosis, the cause of unemployment was the insufficiency of demand. Hence any redistribution of income downwards to people who consume most of it and any expansion of government spending will stimulate production and reduce unemployment. Given the existing capital stock, the actual output can always be raised by increasing wages, transfers to the poor, and government spending, or by reducing taxes. Since raising output means augmenting the rate of utilization of resources, the same policies will diminish unemployment. Thus the distributional bias of the Left toward their electoral constituency found a rationalization in a technical economic theory. As Léon Blum put it, "a better distribution . . . would revive production at the same time that it would satisfy justice."

But more was at stake. In the orthodox thinking, any demands by workers or the unemployed for higher consumption appeared as a particularistic interest, inimical to future national development. To increase wages or social services was to raise costs of production and to divert resources from the investment necessary for growth, accumulation of capital, and improved productivity. The welfare of the poor was a matter of private charity, not of economics. But in the Keynesian framework it is consumption that provides the motor force for production, and suddenly workers and the poor turned out to be the representatives of the universal interest. Their particularistic interest in consumption coincided with the general interest in production. The "people" became the hegemonic force in society. . . . The terms of discourse became transformed.

Not all "Keynesian" positions are the same. One policy direction—warmly embraced by the radical Left—focused on the redistribution of income toward wages and transfers. This is what happened in France in 1936. A more cautious and more successful, policy consisted of manipulating government spending, taxation, and the money supply. The Swedish policy of 1932 was exclusively an "employment policy": it consisted of productive public employment financed by deficits and increased taxation. Wage rates did not increase in Sweden until 1938, well after the economy was out of the slump. In fact, the simple formal framework of Keynesian economics, as is found in modern macro-economic textbooks, favors government spending over redistribution of income: the "multiplier" for government spending is greater than unity, while for wages and transfers it is less than unity. Hence, at least in principle, government spending more than pays for itself in increased production, while distribution of income partially hurts other components of demand.

In all of its forms, the Keynesian compromise consisted of a dual program: "full employment and equality," where the first term meant regulation of the level of employment via the management of demand, particularly government spending, and the latter consisted of the net of social services that constituted the "welfare state." The Keynesian compromise, therefore, came to consist of more than an active role for the government in macro-economic management. As the provider of social services and regulator of the market, the state acted in multiple social realms. Governments developed manpower programs, family policies, housing schemes, income assistance nets, health systems, etc. They attempted to regulate the labor force by mixing incentives and deterrents to participation in the labor market. They sought to alter patterns of racial and regional disparities. The result is that social relations are mediated through democratic political institutions rather than remaining private.

At the same time, the Keynesian compromise became increasingly dependent upon economic concessions granted to groups of people organized as non-market actors. Politics turned into an interplay of coalitions among such groups, giving rise to corporatist tendencies of direct negotiation, either between organized groups—particularly labor and capital—under the tutelage of the government or between each group and the government. The allocation of economic resources became increasingly dominated by relations of political forces.

The compromise was tenable as long as it could provide employment and material security. Indeed, by most criteria of economic progress the Keynesian era was a success. Whether or not this was due to the efficacy of Keynesian economic policies or was merely fortuitous is a matter of debate. Nevertheless, output grew, unemployment was low, social services were extended, and social peace reigned. Until the late 1960s, Keynesianism was the established ideology of class compromise, under which different groups could conflict within the confines of a capitalist and democratic system. And, with the possible exception of Karl Rehn's 1951 program in Sweden and the Italian Communist Party's short-lived austerity policy of the mid-1970s, Keynesianism provided the only framework for such a compromise. The crisis of Keynesianism is a crisis of democratic capitalism. . . .

Market Economics as a Political Project

In any society some decisions have a public impact while others have a private, or limited, effect. And in any society some decisions are made by the public while others are restricted to the private realm. Investment decisions—decisions to withhold a part of society's resources from current consumption and to allocate them to replace or augment the instruments of production—have an impact that is both general and long-lasting, that is, public. Yet the very institution of private property implies that they are a private prerogative. Control over investment is the central political issue under capitalism precisely because no other privately made decisions have such a profound public impact.

The program of the Right is to let the type and quantity of investment be determined by the market. The market, after all, is an institution that coordinates private decisions and aggregates preferences. If the market is undistorted by monopolies, externalities, etc., and consumers are sovereign, the market aggregates private decisions in a way that corresponds to preferences of individuals as consumers. The decisions made by profit-maximizing investors will respond to the preference of consumers concerning the atemporal and intertemporal allocation of resources. But the preferences to which the market responds are weighted by the amount of resources each individual controls. That an idealized "perfect" market matches aggregated consumer preferences for private goods efficiently is the first lesson of welfare economics. That aggregated consumer preferences reflect the distribution of income and wealth is an often neglected corollary.

A democratic political system constitutes another mechanism by which individual preferences are aggregated. If political competition is free of coercion and if voters are sovereign, then government policies will reflect the aggregated preferences of individuals as citizens. But as citizens individuals are weighted equally. Hence, the same set of individual preferences, for private as well as public goods, will normally yield a demand for a different allocation of resources when they are aggregated by political institutions rather than by the market.

Further, the market provides no guarantee that those whose consumption is most restrained in the present will reap the rewards of investment in the future. In any society some part of the current output must be withheld from consumption if production is to continue and consumption is to increase. What distinguishes capitalism is that investment is financed mostly out of profits, the part of the product withheld from wage-earners. It is upon profits that the renewal and enlargement of the capital stock depend. Hence, under capitalism, the presence of profits is a necessary condition for the improvement of material conditions of any group within the society. But it is not sufficient. Profits may be hoarded, consumed, exported, or invested badly. Even if capitalists are abstemious, efficient, and prescient, their market relation with workers ends as the cycle of production is completed and the wages are paid, and there is nothing in the structure of the capitalist system of production that would guarantee that wage-earners would be the ones to benefit from the fact that a part of the product is currently withheld from them as profit.

Any class compromise must, therefore, have at least two aspects: one concerning the distribution of income and the second concerning investment. If those who do not own capital are to consent voluntarily to the private property of the instruments of production, they must have a reasonable certainty that their material conditions would improve in the future as the result of current appropriation of profit by capitalists. Until recently, this compromise was rarely stated explicitly, for it is basically institutional: workers consent to the institution of private property of the instruments of production and owners of these instruments consent to political institutions through which other groups can effectively process their demands. Today, as trust in the compromise is eroding, workers are demanding more explicit commitments. . . .

The current period, however, is the first moment since the 1920s in which owners of capital have openly rejected a compromise that involves public influence over investment and the distribution of income. For the first time in several decades, the Right has an historical project of its own: to free accumulation from all the fetters imposed upon it by democracy. For the bourgeoisie never completed its revolution.

Just as it freed accumulation from the restraint of the feudal order, the bourgeoisie was forced to subject it to the constraint of popular control exercised through universal suffrage. The combination of private property of the means of production with universal suffrage is a compromise, and this compromise implies that the logic of accumulation is not exclusively the logic of private actors.

What is involved in the current offensive of the Right is not simply a question of taxes, government spending, or even the distribution of income. The plans for relaxing taxation of profits, abolishing environmental controls, eliminating welfare programs, removing government control over product safety and conditions of work, and weakening the labor unions add up to more than reorientation of the economic policy. They constitute a project for a new society, a bourgeois revolution.

It is thus necessary to consider the following question: what kind of a society would it be in which accumulation would be free from any form of political control, free from constraints of income distribution, from considerations of employment, environment, health of workers, and safety of consumers? Such hypothetical questions have no ready-made answers, but let us speculate.

It would be a society composed of households and firms, related to each other exclusively through the market. Social relations would become coextensive with market relations and the role of the political authority would be reduced to defending the market from attempts by any group organized as nonmarket actors (i.e. other than households and firms) to alter the rationality of market allocations. Since social and political relations would be depoliticized, demands by nonmarket actors would find no audience. The tension between accumulation and legitimation would be overcome: accumulation would be self-legitimizing for those who benefit from it and no other legitimacy would be sought. As it has been said, "the government does not owe anybody anything."

Household income would depend solely upon the market value of the labor performed. Reproduction of the labor force would be reprivatized and the traditional division of labor within the household—between earners and nurturers—would be restored. Persons excluded from participation in gainful activities would have no institutional guarantee of survival. They might be isolated on "reservations," whether inner cities or depressed regions, where they could be forgotten or ignored.

Workers would be disorganized as a class. If wage bargaining is decentralized by law to the level of the firm (as it is now in Chile) and if the process of internationalization of production continues, the monopoly power of unions would be effectively broken. Workers would be controlled by a combination of decentralized co-optation by some firms, by repression oriented against monopoly power, and—most importantly—by the threat of unemployment.

All of these changes would represent a reversal of trends that we are accustomed to see as irreversible. Indeed, the picture we drew can be easily obtained by combining the trends of contemporary capitalism described by, say, E. H. Carr or Jürgen Habermas, and reversing them. Economic relations would be depoliticized. Government economic planning would be abandoned. Legitimation would be left to the market. The "economic whip" would be reinstated as the central mechanism of political control.

Is such a society feasible? . . .

Where electoral participation has traditionally been high, where working-class parties enjoy electoral support, and where access to the electoral system is relatively open—in most Western European countries—the project of the Right seems doomed to failure under democratic conditions. But in the United States, where about 40 percent of adults never vote, where parties of notables have a duopolistic control over the electoral system, and where the barriers to entry are prohibitive, one must be less sanguine about the prospects. For suppose that the project is economically successful, even if for purely fortuitous reasons, and beneficial for a sizeable part of the electorate, that the Right captures both parties, and the offensive enjoys the support of the mass media. . . . Such a prospect is not totally far-fetched.

7.2

A Movement Society?

Sidney Tarrow

In this selection, from the concluding chapter of his path-breaking work on the elusive but often formidable power of social movements, Sidney Tarrow provides a fascinating retrospective on two hundred years of social movements. He argues that in many ways the transnational rebellion of 1989, which marked the unraveling of the communist world, reflected a set of trends in cycles and forms of protest that began with the French Revolution of 1789. At the same time, the movement of 1989 reveals a set of cumulative changes in social movements. Above all, Tarrow suggests that movements today are increasingly transnational, in part because they are able to cross national borders so rapidly. Is the result that we have we entered a state of perpetual disorder and violence? Or have disorder and violence been relatively contained in today's world?

In 1789, as word of France's revolution reached England, abolitionist Thomas Clarkson crossed the Channel to urge his French colleagues to join his country's antislavery agitation. Clarkson took the same route again in 1814, following a second wave of agitation in Britain. But "twice," writes the leading American student of antislavery, "he failed utterly." Although the French abolished slavery in their colonies in 1794, this was no more than "a desperate response to wartime contingencies," writes Drescher (1991: 712), and was reversed when Napoleon came to power. Only when it coincided with greater political earthquakes did antislavery cross the channel (pp. 719–20).

Two hundred years later, diffused by word of mouth, printed page and television, collective action spread rapidly across the internal boundaries of the Soviet bloc. As the French were commemorating—and burying!—the bicentennial of their Revolution,[1] a new wave of revolution swept over the Communist world. Centered on Eastern and Central Europe, enjoying a brief, tragic echo in China, the movement eventually gave way to savage confrontations in Romania, in the Caucasus and ultimately in Yugoslavia. Not only in semi-Stalinized Poland and in the restive Baltic states, but in ironfisted East Germany and subjugated

Sidney Tarrow, *Power in Movement: Social Movements, Collective Action and Politics* (Cambridge, UK: Cambridge University Press, 1994), chap. 11, 187–199. © Cambridge University Press 1994. Reprinted with the permission of Cambridge University Press.

Czechoslovakia, within a year communism was gone. By 1991, even the Soviet Union, heartland of proletarian internationalism, had collapsed, giving way to a galaxy of semi-democratic, semi-market, deeply conflicted societies.

When we compare the rapid diffusion of the movements of 1989 to Clarkson's inability to bring abolitionism across 30 miles of water, we can begin to understand the progress of the social movement over the past two hundred years. For not only did Eastern Europeans rebel *en masse* in 1989: They did so against similar targets, at virtually the same time and in the name of goals that varied only in their details. In 1789 antislavery advocates had difficulty crossing the English Channel. But in 1989 the democracy movement spread from Berlin to Beijing in a matter of weeks.

The significance of this change is still emerging, and its implications for democracy are mixed—to say the least. But its implications for the nature of social movements were profound. For not only did these changes close the door on the most important revolutionary movement of the twentieth century; by the end of 1989, not only in Eastern Europe, but all over the Communist bloc, the movement against state socialism had become general and its modalities modular. Even in Italy, so far from the periphery of world communism that its Communist Party was barely recognizable by 1989, party leaders rejected their historic identity and changed their flag.

But the heart of the movement was in Eastern Europe. There, with little prior organization, people who had never met (or who knew each other in the apolitical networks of what Eastern Europeans were calling "civil society"), were employing similar forms of organization and action, and in the name of similar frames of meaning, rose up against authorities. If the Communist Party elites gave in practically without a fight, it was not only because they had lost heart, but because they could see what forces were arrayed against them and knew what it would take to suppress them. Not only this movement, but *the* social movement triumphed in 1989.

The rapid spread and dramatic success of the movement of 1989 was a reflection of the powers of movement. . . . But it also raises some troubling questions for social movement theory and about the emerging world order; about the increase of violence, the recrudescence of ethnic conflicts, the possible transcendence of the national state and the internationalization of conflict. In this [discussion], I will first [offer some reflections about] the power in movement before turning to the questions raised by the cataclysm of 1989 and its violent aftermath.

Two Hundred Years of Movement

Since collective action is the common denominator of all kinds of social movements, we began with the theory of collective action. Twenty years ago, political scientists and sociologists interested in social movements began to look at their subject not from the standpoint of actions taken, but as a puzzle; based on the assumption that collective action is difficult to bring about. I argue . . . that this puzzle *is* only a puzzle (and not a sociological law), because in so many situations and against so many odds, collective action *does* occur, often instigated by people with few resources and little inherent power.

The "solution" to that puzzle was first sought by collective action theorists building on economist Mancur Olson's theory that "large groups" mobilize members through selective incentives and constraints. While the Olsonian theory worked well for interest groups, it was inadequate for social movements for the simple reason that they are multipolar actors in sustained conflict with opponents and have few incentives or constraints to deploy. Unlike voluntary associations, movements are not organizations, and those who try to lead them have little or no control over those they hope will follow them.

The central task for movement organizers is to resolve what I called the "social transaction costs of collective action"; creating focal points for people who have no sources of compulsory coordination, who often lack direct connections with one another and have few, if any, internal resources. While large firms and interest groups solve their transaction cost problem by internalizing their assets, movements seldom have this option. Indeed, organizers who try to turn their "base" into disciplined cadres squander much of their energy on achieving internal control. How movements become the focal points for collective action and sustain it against opponents and the state [remains] the central question. . . .

I argued, in response to this question, that the main incentives for movement creation and diffusion are found in the structure of political opportunities. Increasing access to power, realignments in the political system, conflicts among elites and the availability of allies give early challengers the incentives to assault the power structure and create opportunities for others. The diffusion of movements takes place by many mechanisms and draws on a variety of resources; but the major incentive for new groups to join a movement are the political opportunities that are exposed by the actions of "early risers" and exploited by others.

In response to political opportunities, movements use different forms of collective action singly and in combination to link people to one another and with opponents, supporters and third parties. They take advantage of both the familiarity of these forms of action . . . innovating around their edges to inspire the imagination of supporters and create fear and uncertainty among opponents. Collective action is best seen not as a simple cost, but as both a cost and a benefit for social movements.

The balance between the costs and benefits helps determine the dynamics of the movement. As the benefits of a particular form of collective action decline, organizers have incentives to develop new actions, increase the numbers of participants or radicalize their interaction with opponents. The conflicts and defections within social movements, as well as their confrontations with the state, are, in part, the result of the attempt to maintain the movement's momentum through the use of new and more daring collective actions.

But in the formation of a social movement, there is more than a "pull" toward particular forms of action; there must also be a "push" from solidarity and collective

identity. Solidarity has much to do with interest, but it produces a sustained movement only when consensus is built around common meanings and values. These
meanings and values are partly inherited and partly constructed in the act of confronting opponents. They are also constituted by the interactions within movements. One of the main factors distinguishing successful movements from failures is
their capacity to link inherited understandings to the imperative for activism.

Collective action is often led by movement organizations, but these are sometimes beneficiaries, sometimes inciters and at other times destroyers of popular
politics. The recurring controversy about whether organizations produce movements or suppress them can be resolved only if we examine the less formal structures that they draw upon—the social networks at the base of society, and the
mobilizing structures that link them to the focal points of conflict. Sustaining
a movement is the result of a delicate balance between suffocating the power in
movement by providing too much organization and leaving it to spin off use-
lessly away through the tyranny of decentralization.

Opportunities, Cycles and the Consumption of Movement

But collective action repertoires, cultural frames and organization are only the
potential sources of power; they can be employed just as easily for social control
as for insurgency. [R]ecurring protest cycles . . . are the products of the diffusion
of political opportunities that transform the potential for mobilization into action.
In these crucibles of conflict and innovation, movements not only take advantage of available opportunities; they create them for others by producing new
forms of action, hammering out new "master frames," activating social networks
and making coalitions that force the state to respond to the disorder around it.

That response is often repressive, but even repression is often mixed with reform. Particularly when counterelites within the system see the opportunity to
aggrandize themselves in alliance with challengers, rulers are placed in a vulnerable position to which reform is a frequent response. As conflict collapses and
militants retire to lick their wounds, many of their advances are reversed, but
they leave behind incremental expansions in participation, changes in popular
culture and residual movement networks. Movement cycles are a season for sowing, but the reaping is often done during the periods of demobilization that
follow, by latecomers to the cause.

If cycles of protest are opened up by expanding opportunities, how do they
decline as they inevitably do? Is it simply because people tire of agitation, because
enervating factional struggles develop within their movements, because organizations become oppressive or because elites repress and placate challengers? All
of these are contributory causes of cyclical decline, but there is a more systemic
cause as well: Since the power in movement depends on the mobilization of
external opportunities, when opportunities expand from challengers to other
groups and shift to elites and authorities, movements lose their primary source of

had done, by a process of imitation, diffusion, reaction and transformation of scattered movements, culminating in elite negotiations and the attempt to build new institutions out of struggle.

But like 1848, as the movement wound through Eastern Europe, the mood shifted from liberalism and representative government to ethnic particularism and national assertiveness. If crowds of Czechs and Slovaks turned out to demonstrate for freedom in Prague and Bratislava in 1989, by 1992 these cities had become the capitals of a country split in two; if thousands of Hungarians demonstrated at the tomb of Imre Najy in 1988, by the early 1990s, the parties that liberated their country from communism were having difficulty attracting a plurality of voters. If West and East Germans joined in an ode to freedom on the Berlin Wall in 1989, by 1991 "Ossies" and "Wessies" were watching each other with suspicion. In Poland, the Solidarity leaders who had started the process a decade earlier split into rival political parties. And in Russia the democratic movement of the late 1980s gave way to a range of semi-parties, some of them holdovers from the recent regime and others reviving forms of xenophobia from the Czarist past.

Immediately after the ebullience of 1989, some observers foresaw old elites being rapidly swept off the public scene, state-run economies rapidly privatized and a new democratic politics emerging in the image of the West. But by the early 1990s, not only were old elites still active in many parts of the former Communist world—some of them transformed from *apparachniks* into *entrepreneurniks*—but the privatization of their economies was making heavy weather. Under the strain, the opportunities and the uncertainties of the post-1989 years provided space for a variety of players, not all of whom had democracy or the market as their goals. Just as the Springtime of Freedom of 1848 was closed by Napoleon's coup of 1851, the Ode to Freedom at the Berlin Wall was the prelude to the ethnic conflicts of the 1990s and the carnage at Sarajevo.

A Movement Society: Transnational and Violent?

How representative was the movement of 1989? It certainly had peculiarities due to the nearly unique nature of the Soviet bloc. For example, it was the first movement in history to destroy a powerful multistate empire in one blow. It was also—at least at first—predominantly handled through peaceful negotiation, with the menace of mass violence held in abeyance in almost every country of the region until state socialism was gone. But despite its particularity, the 1989 cycle can help us to see some of the ways in which the national social movement has changed in its two-hundred-year history. If these changes are substantial and cumulative, then the world may be moving from a logic of alternation between periods of movement and periods of quiescence into a permanent movement society. At this stage, all we can do is guess at the possibilities and speculate about their implications.

Transnational Movements

When we return to the comparison between Clarkson's failure in 1789 and the success of 1989, we see one major difference; that movements spread far more rapidly now than they did in the past—even in the absence of formal organizations. This is, in part, an expression of the universality of the repertoire of collective action, in part, due to the rapidity of global communication, and, in part, because of the appearance of transnational movements. The contrast between antislavery in 1789 and the movements of 1989 will illustrate all three points.

In contrast to Clarkson's inability to bring abolitionism across a mere thirty miles of water in 1789, the knowledge of how to mount a social movement had become so general by 1989 that the liberation from state socialism took remarkably similar form across a continent and a half. For example, the human chain that protestors stretched across the Baltics in 1989 was the same tactic that had been used a few years earlier by the European peace movement. The "round table" that was used to outline the future division of power in Poland was adopted in many other countries of the region. "What is remarkable," write Valerie Bunce and Dennis Chong, "is the speed with which the masses in each country converged on particular strategies, coordinated its actions, and successfully executed its plans" (1990: 3).

Second, the appearance of global television had a great influence in the diffusion of the movement, and this is not limited to Eastern Europe in 1989. In the eighteenth century, movements were still diffused by word of mouth, by print and association or by people like Clarkson who acted as missionaries of movement. But in 1989, the spread of the democratic movement in Eastern Europe—not to mention its tragic echo in China—left little doubt that collective action can spread by global communication. Not only do potential protestors learn about political opportunities through the mass media; when they see people not very different from themselves acting in contentious ways succeeding, it is easy for them to imagine themselves doing the same. And just as they learn *from* television, they have become skilled at using it to project word of their movements to international centers of power.

Third, because of the centrality of the national state, movements like antislavery spread slowly and took different forms in different parts of Europe; so did the democratic movement of the late eighteenth century. In the nineteenth century, both radical democracy and socialism were diffused more quickly, but it still took fifty years for social democracy to reach Russia—and it arrived in very different form than in the West.

The most recent cycles of protest have been inherently—and perhaps increasingly—transnational and thus have diffused more rapidly. The decolonization movements in the former British and French empires; the European and American New Left of the 1960s; the peace movements of the 1980s; global environmental movements like Greenpeace: These are no longer cases of simple imitation and diffusion, but expressions of the same movement acting against similar targets. The movements of 1989 in Eastern Europe were extreme in this respect, but in their interdependence and mutual dependence on international trends, they were not so different than these other recent movements.

The archetypical case of a transnational movement in recent years has been militant, fundamentalist Islam. Its spread from Iran to Afghanistan, to the Bekaa Valley and the Gaza Strip, and more recently to North Africa bridges institutional religion and guerilla warfare. In between these extremes of violence and institutionalization, its organizers have employed an array of similar tactics everywhere: the mobilization of slum dwellers, the intimidation of women, the extortion of funds from small businessmen—even elections, when this has been convenient. One deeply rooted secular movement—the Palestinian Liberation Organization—has been severely challenged by Islamic competition; the Soviet army was forced out of Afghanistan by another; while the Sudanese government was overthrown by a third. The Algerian government was only saved from Islamic domination by a military takeover. And by 1992, even secular Egypt was under attack from internationally supported fundamentalists.

The spread of such transnational movements as militant Islam leads to a larger and more portentous question. Since we seem to be living in an increasingly interdependent world, are we becoming a single movement society? And if we are, will movements lose the cyclical and national rhythms of the past and take on the character of continual turbulence spreading across national boundaries out of the control of national states? A movement society may be an increasingly violent society. What is the evidence for such a claim?

Ex-Prisoners of the State?[2]

In his book *Turbulence in World Politics*, James Rosenau argues that we are becoming a single, more turbulent world. Rosenau sees the entire period since the end of World War II as the beginning of a new era of "global turbulence." Among the factors that convince him that ours is an era of turbulence is "a marked increase in the number of spontaneous collective actions" and their rapid spread around the world (1990: 369). If Rosenau is right, then the implications for the future of civil politics is troubling.

The national social movement grew out of the efforts of states to consolidate power, integrate their peripheries and standardize discourse among groups of citizens and between them and their rulers. Many of the characteristics of the social movements we have seen in this [discussion] grew out of that relationship—including the conventionalization of collective action, the channeling of movements into national opportunity structures and the institution of citizenship itself. If movements are becoming transnational, they may be freeing themselves of state structures and thence of the constraining influence of state-mediated contention.

Three kinds of arguments can be made on behalf of this thesis. First, the dominant economic trends of the late twentieth century have been towards greater international interdependence. "The increasing fluidity of capital, labor, commodities, money, and cultural practices," argues Charles Tilly in a recent paper, "undermines the capacity of any particular state to control events within its boundaries" (1991: 1). One result is that strikes that used to be mounted against domestic capitalists must now be risked against multinational corporations whose capital can be moved elsewhere. The interdependent global economy may be producing transnational collective action.[3]

Second, the economic growth of the 1970s and 1980s increased the imbalance of wealth and poverty between the North and West and the East and South, while bringing their citizens cognitively and physically closer to one another. This is not only the result of faster communication and cheaper transportation, but because, since the end of World War II, Third World countries have attempted to mimic the economic success of the West. . . .

Interdependence and the international gap in income both contribute to a third factor: a continued stream of migration that takes different forms than in the past. In the nineteenth century, much of the international movement of population went from core to periphery, with migrants permanently leaving their homes behind. The current wave of migration overwhelmingly favors the industrial countries of the West and immigrants seldom lose touch with their country of origin. "The Filipino maid in Milan and the Tamil busdriver in Toronto," observes Benedict Anderson, "are only a few sky hours away" from their homeland and seconds away by satellite telephone communication (1992: 8).

While mass population movements have become one of the major sources of domestic conflict in the contemporary world, citizenship—the expected outcome of immigration in the nineteenth century—has become an impossible dream for most immigrants. A major cultural cleavage pits immigrant groups with restricted citizenship rights against increasingly restive indigenous populations in states whose governments, from Paris to California, are under pressure to reduce the rights of resident immigrants and to cut them off from further entry. All over the West, from the eastern border of Germany to the southern border of the United States, doors are being shut to immigrants, and—just as important—earlier arrivals are being sealed off into immigrant ghettos.

One result—the rise of racist movements in Western Europe—we have already seen. But another is the rise of what Anderson calls "long-distance nationalism." For every nineteenth-century Mazzini and Garibaldi who fomented revolution at a great distance from their home country, there are thousands of Palestinians in New York, Punjabis in Toronto, Croats in Australia, Tamils in Britain, Irish in Massachusetts, Algerians in France and Cubans in Miami whose ties to their countries of origin are kept alive through transnational social networks (Anderson 1992: 12).

Most of these meekly accept their subaltern status and hope for an affluent re-turn to their homelands. But others use the ease of international communica-tion and transportation to support movements at home. By more-or-less covert financial contributions, by fax and E-mail, by letter bombs and discrete arms purchases, these long-distance nationalists are disturbing the neat symmetry between national states and national social movements that the world has inherited from the last century.

Not only nationalist migrants, but transnational ecologists, developmentalists and fighters for the rights of minorities increasingly aim their actions at other people's governments. We live in an age when rubber tappers in Brazil can enjoy the assistance of American nongovernmental organizations; when U.N.-supported technical teams teach Indian ecologists to use video cameras that they can employ to mobilize peasants; and when racist propaganda produced in the United States finds its way to the apartments of European skinheads. The modern state, which began its consolidation in opposition to its territorial enemies, is becoming increasingly permeable to nonterritorial movements. As a result, the social movement may be becoming an ex-prisoner of the state.

If this is true, what are the implications for the character of social movements and for social conflict in general? If nothing else, the characteristic pattern whereby political cycles result from the processing of challenges within national states may be extended over time and space by crossnational extension. Funda-mentalist Islam is the most successful example: When the expansion of the Iran-ian revolution failed in the Iran–Iraq war, Afghanistan became the major field of action; when the Red Army left Kabul, fundamentalist militants moved on from Peshawar to Cairo, to Algiers and eventually to New York.[4] Where movements respond to political opportunities across state boundaries, they can escape the mediation and control of any single state.

As long as these expressions of integral religious nationalism were bounded within the Third World, Western governments and their citizens remained rela-tively indifferent. But with the attack by Islamic militants on the World Trade Center in New York in 1993, long-distance nationalism moved to the West. The diffusion of militant fundamentalism to the heart of world capitalism showed that, in the interdependent contemporary world, modernization does not equal secu-larization and that international trends deeply affect the internal order of states.

This leads to an even more worrying concern. Over the past two hundred years, there has been a slow, ragged but inexorable civilizing trend in the nature of collective action and in the state's means of controlling it. . . . [A]s modular repertoires linked social movements to the state, violent and direct forms of attack were increasingly replaced by the power of numbers, by solidarity and an informal dialogue between states and movements. The cycle of the 1960s, with its remarkably low level of violence and employment of nonviolent direct action, was the apotheosis of this trend. But the guerilla wars, the hostage takings and the ethnic conflicts of the past two decades must make us wonder

whether the trend to a peaceful repertoire was no more than a historical paren-
thesis and is now being reversed.

The integralist beliefs—if not the violent methods—of militant Islam bear a
striking resemblance to trends in Western culture: to politicized ministers who
preach intolerance on Sunday morning television; to the "rescuers" of unborn
fetuses who refuse to recognize women's rights to reproductive freedom; to
orthodox attacks on secular values in education and personal life; and to xenophobic political parties that claim their nations' natural superiority. The methods
are different, but how different are the French *Front National* or the Hungarian
Way, from the zealots of Gush Emunim or the fanatics of the Party of God?

Citizens of modern states have lived through such "moments of madness"
before. It is enough to remember that severed heads were paraded around the
streets of Paris on pikes during the great democratic French Revolution, or that
Jews were attacked in France and Germany during the Springtime of Freedom in
1848, to find parallels for the violence and intolerance that have emerged in the
West since the 1980s. The concern raised by these more recent outbreaks is
that—if, in fact a "movement society" *is* developing out of the social, economic
and cultural changes of the late twentieth century—it will have a different
cultural valence than the movements that broke out in Boston in 1765, in Paris
in 1848 and in the nonviolent movements of the 1960s.

Is the New World Order that was supposed to result from the liberation of
1989 turning instead into a permanent state of violence and disorder? Have
the resources for violent collective action become so widely accessible, integralist identities so widespread, and militants so freed of the national state that
a permanent and violent movement society is resulting? Or will the current
plethora of ethnic and religious movements be partially outgrown, partially
domesticated and partially mediated by the political process, as in previous
cycles of protest?

The violence and intolerance of the 1990s constitute a truly alarming trend.
But this is not the first great wave of movement in history, nor will it be the last.
If its dynamic comes to resemble the social movements that we have encountered in this [discussion], then its power will at first be ferocious, uncontrolled
and widely diffused, but later ephemeral. If so, then like previous waves of movement, it will ultimately disperse "like a flood tide which loosens up much of the
soil but leaves alluvial deposits in its wake" (Zolberg 1972: 206).

Notes

1. "No hint of subsequent radicalization, no echo of social conflict, no shadow of the Terror could
   mar this season of commemoration," observed historians Keith Baker and Steven Kaplan of the
   Bicentennial in their preface to Roger Chartier's *The Cultural Origins of the French Revolution*, p. xii.
   Even as they celebrated it, the French in 1989 were interring their Revolution. See Kaplan's *Adieu
   1789*, which reads the Bicentennial as a celebratory rite for the funeral of the Revolution.
2. In a 1991 paper, Charles Tilly provocatively writes, "As Europeans unconsciously subvert the state in
   the very act of affirming its desirability, comparative-historical sociologists are unwittingly peripher-
   alizing the state while declaring its centrality." See his "Prisoners of the State," p. 1.

3. The most articulate advocates of this global view of industrial conflict are Giovanni Arrighi, and Beverly Silver. See the former's "World Income Inequalities and the Future of Socialism," and the latter's "Class Struggle and Kondratieff Waves, 1870 to the Present," as well as her "Labor Unrest and Capital Accumulation on a World Scale."
4. See the account of the links between Afghan-trained Islamic militants and the attackers of the World Trade Center in the *New York Times*, August 11, 1993.

References

Anderson, Benedict (1992). "Long Distance Nationalism. World Capitalism and the Rise of Identity Politics." Center for Identity Studies. Amsterdam, Netherlands.

Baker, Keith Michael (1990). *Inventing the French Revolution. Essays on French Political Culture in the Eighteenth Century.* Cambridge and New York: Cambridge University Press.

Bunce, Valerie, and Dennis Chong (1990). "The Party's Over: Mass Protest and the End of Communist Rule in Eastern Europe," presented to the annual meeting of the American Political Science Association, San Francisco, Calif.

Chartier, Roger (1991). *The Cultural Origins of the French Revolution.* Durham, N.C.: Duke University Press.

Drescher, Seymour (1987). *Capitalism and Antislavery: British Mobilization in Comparative Perspective.* Oxford and New York: Oxford University Press.

———. (1991). "British Way, French Way: Opinion Building and Revolution in the Second French Slave Emancipation," *American Historical Review* 96:709–34.

Rosenau, James (1990). *Turbulence in World Politics: A Theory of Change and Continuity.* Princeton: Princeton University Press.

Tilly, Charles (1991). "Prisoners of the State." Working Paper No. 129, the Center for Studies of Social Change, the New School for Social Research, New York.

Zolberg, Aristide R. (1972). "Moments of Madness," *Politics and Society* 2:183–207.

Bowling Alone: America's Declining Social Capital

Robert D. Putnam

This selection documents what Robert Putnam considers to be a fundamental change that has recently occurred in the United States: that Americans are increasingly less likely to form voluntary associations (what he calls social capital). He uses the decline of bowling leagues as a metaphor for this development. After "Bowling Alone" was published, Putnam became an instant celebrity: He was invited to meet with the president and became a frequent commentator on radio and television. He speculates in an account published elsewhere that the reason was because his research apparently confirmed a widespread concern that the U.S. social fabric was weakening.

Not everyone agreed with Putnam's argument. Some critics asserted that Americans were less likely to form associations because of widening economic inequalities; other critics claimed that Putnam did not consider the role of government policies. (See [7.4] for one such critique.) How well does Putnam's argument withstand these criticisms?

Many students of the new democracies that have emerged over the past decade and a half have emphasized the importance of a strong and active civil society to the consolidation of democracy. Especially with regard to the postcommunist countries, scholars and democratic activists alike have lamented the absence or obliteration of traditions of independent civic engagement and a widespread tendency toward passive reliance on the state. To those concerned with the weakness of civil societies in the developing or postcommunist world, the advanced Western democracies and above all the United States have typically been taken as models to be emulated. There is striking evidence, however, that the vibrancy of American civil society has notably declined over the past several decades.

Ever since the publication of Alexis de Tocqueville's *Democracy in America*, the United States has played a central role in systematic studies of the links between

Robert D. Putnam, "Bowling Alone: America's Declining Social Capital," *Journal of Democracy* 6, no. 1 (Jan. 1995): 65–78. Reprinted by permission of the Sagalyn Agency.

democracy and civil society. Although this is in part because trends in American life are often regarded as harbingers of social modernization, it is also because America has traditionally been considered unusually "civic" (a reputation that, as we shall later see, has not been entirely unjustified).

When Tocqueville visited the United States in the 1830s, it was the Americans' propensity for civic association that most impressed him as the key to their unprecedented ability to make democracy work. "Americans of all ages, all stations in life, and all types of disposition," he observed, "are forever forming associations. There are not only commercial and industrial associations in which all take part, but others of a thousand different types—religious, moral, serious, futile, very general and very limited, immensely large and very minute.... Nothing, in my view, deserves more attention than the intellectual and moral associations in America."[1]

... American social scientists of a neo-Tocquevillean bent have unearthed a wide range of empirical evidence that the quality of public life and the performance of social institutions (and not only in America) are indeed powerfully influenced by norms and networks of civic engagement. Researchers in such fields as education, urban poverty, unemployment, the control of crime and drug abuse, and even health have discovered that successful outcomes are more likely in civically engaged communities. Similarly, research on the varying economic attainments of different ethnic groups in the United States has demonstrated the importance of social bonds within each group. These results are consistent with research in a wide range of settings that demonstrates the vital importance of social networks for job placement and many other economic outcomes.

Meanwhile, a seemingly unrelated body of research on the sociology of economic development has also focused attention on the role of social networks. Some of this work is situated in the developing countries, and some of it elucidates the peculiarly successful "network capitalism" of East Asia.[2] Even in less exotic Western economies, however, researchers have discovered highly efficient, highly flexible "industrial districts" based on networks of collaboration among workers and small entrepreneurs. Far from being paleoindustrial anachronisms, these dense interpersonal and interorganizational networks undergird ultramodern industries, from the high tech of Silicon Valley to the high fashion of Benetton.

The norms and networks of civic engagement also powerfully affect the performance of representative government. That, at least, was the central conclusion of my own 20-year, quasi-experimental study of subnational governments in different regions of Italy.[3] Although all these regional governments seemed identical on paper, their levels of effectiveness varied dramatically. Systematic inquiry showed that the quality of governance was determined by longstanding traditions of civic engagement (or its absence). Voter turnout, newspaper readership, membership in choral societies and football clubs—these were the hallmarks of a successful region. In fact, historical analysis suggested that these networks of organized reciprocity and civic solidarity, far from being an epiphenomenon of socioeconomic modernization, were a precondition for it.

No doubt the mechanisms through which civic engagement and social connectedness produce such results—better schools, faster economic development, lower crime, and more effective government—are multiple and complex. While these briefly recounted findings require further confirmation and perhaps qualification, the parallels across hundreds of empirical studies in a dozen disparate disciplines and subfields are striking. Social scientists in several fields have recently suggested a common framework for understanding these phenomena, a framework that rests on the concept of *social capital*.[4] By analogy with notions of physical capital and human capital—tools and training that enhance individual productivity—"social capital" refers to features of social organization such as networks, norms, and social trust that facilitate coordination and cooperation for mutual benefit.

For a variety of reasons, life is easier in a community blessed with a substantial stock of social capital. In the first place, networks of civic engagement foster sturdy norms of generalized reciprocity and encourage the emergence of social trust. Such networks facilitate coordination and communication, amplify reputations, and thus allow dilemmas of collective action to be resolved. When economic and political negotiation is embedded in dense networks of social interaction, incentives for opportunism are reduced. At the same time, networks of civic engagement embody past success at collaboration, which can serve as a cultural template for future collaboration. Finally, dense networks of interaction probably broaden the participants' sense of self, developing the "I" into the "we," or (in the language of rational-choice theorists) enhancing the participants' "taste" for collective benefits.

I do not intend here to survey (much less contribute to) the development of the theory of social capital. Instead, I use the central premise of that rapidly growing body of work—that social connections and civic engagement pervasively influence our public life, as well as our private prospects—as the starting point for an empirical survey of trends in social capital in contemporary America. I concentrate here entirely on the American case, although the developments I portray may in some measure characterize many contemporary societies.

Whatever Happened to Civic Engagement?

We begin with familiar evidence on changing patterns of political participation, not least because it is immediately relevant to issues of democracy in the narrow sense. Consider the well-known decline in turnout in national elections over the last three decades. From a relative high point in the early 1960s, voter turnout had by 1990 declined by nearly a quarter; tens of millions of Americans had forsaken their parents' habitual readiness to engage in the simplest act of citizenship. Broadly similar trends also characterize participation in state and local elections.

It is not just the voting booth that has been increasingly deserted by Americans. A series of identical questions posed by the Roper Organization to national samples ten times each year over the last two decades reveals that since 1973 the number of Americans who report that "in the past year" they have "attended a public meeting on town or school affairs" has fallen by more than a third (from 22 percent in 1973 to 13 percent in 1993). Similar (or even greater) relative declines are evident in responses to questions about attending a political rally or speech, serving on a committee of some local organization, and working for a political party. By almost every measure, Americans' direct engagement in politics and government has fallen steadily and sharply over the last generation, despite the fact that average levels of education—the best individual-level predictor of political participation—have risen sharply throughout this period. Every year over the last decade or two, millions more have withdrawn from the affairs of their communities.

Not coincidentally, Americans have also disengaged psychologically from politics and government over this era. The proportion of Americans who reply that they "trust the government in Washington" only "some of the time" or "almost never" has risen steadily from 30 percent in 1966 to 75 percent in 1992.

These trends are well known, of course, and taken by themselves would seem amenable to a strictly political explanation. Perhaps the long litany of political tragedies and scandals since the 1960s (assassinations, Vietnam, Watergate, Irangate, and so on) has triggered an understandable disgust for politics and government among Americans, and that in turn has motivated their withdrawal. I do not doubt that this common interpretation has some merit, but its limitations become plain when we examine trends in civic engagement of a wider sort.

Our survey of organizational membership among Americans can usefully begin with a glance at the aggregate results of the General Social Survey, a scientifically conducted, national-sample survey that has been repeated 14 times over the last two decades. Church-related groups constitute the most common type of organization joined by Americans; they are especially popular with women. Other types of organizations frequently joined by women include school-service groups (mostly parent-teacher associations), sports groups, professional societies, and literary societies. Among men, sports clubs, labor unions, professional societies, fraternal groups, veterans' groups, and service clubs are all relatively popular.

Religious affiliation is by far the most common associational membership among Americans. Indeed, by many measures America continues to be (even more than in Tocqueville's time) an astonishingly "churched" society. For example, the United States has more houses of worship per capita than any other nation on Earth. Yet religious sentiment in America seems to be becoming somewhat less tied to institutions and more self-defined.

How have these complex crosscurrents played out over the last three or four decades in terms of Americans' engagement with organized religion? The general pattern is clear: The 1960s witnessed a significant drop in reported weekly churchgoing—from roughly 48 percent in the late 1950s to roughly 41 percent in the early 1970s. Since then, it has stagnated or (according to some surveys) declined still further. Meanwhile, data from the General Social Survey show a modest decline in membership in all "church-related groups" over the last 20 years. It would seem, then, that net participation by Americans, both in religious services and in church-related groups, has declined modestly (by perhaps a sixth) since the 1960s.

For many years, labor unions provided one of the most common organizational affiliations among American workers. Yet union membership has been falling for nearly four decades, with the steepest decline occurring between 1975 and 1985. Since the mid-1950s, when union membership peaked, the unionized portion of the nonagricultural work force in America has dropped by more than half, falling from 32.5 percent in 1953 to 15.8 percent in 1992. By now, virtually all of the explosive growth in union membership that was associated with the New Deal has been erased. The solidarity of union halls is now mostly a fading memory of aging men.[5]

The parent-teacher association (PTA) has been an especially important form of civic engagement in twentieth-century America because parental involvement in the educational process represents a particularly productive form of social capital. It is, therefore, dismaying to discover that participation in parent-teacher organizations has dropped drastically over the last generation, from more than 12 million in 1964 to barely 5 million in 1982 before recovering to approximately 7 million now.

Next, we turn to evidence on membership in (and volunteering for) civic and fraternal organizations. These data show some striking patterns. First, membership in traditional women's groups has declined more or less steadily since the mid-1960s. For example, membership in the national Federation of Women's Clubs is down by more than half (59 percent) since 1964, while membership in the League of Women Voters (LWV) is off 42 percent since 1969.[6]

Similar reductions are apparent in the numbers of volunteers for mainline civic organizations, such as the Boy Scouts (off by 26 percent since 1970) and the Red Cross (off by 61 percent since 1970). But what about the possibility that volunteers have simply switched their loyalties to other organizations? Evidence on "regular" (as opposed to occasional or "drop-by") volunteering is available from the Labor Department's Current Population Surveys of 1974 and 1989. These estimates suggest that serious volunteering declined by roughly one-sixth over these 15 years, from 24 percent of adults in 1974 to 20 percent in 1989. The multitudes of Red Cross aides and Boy Scout troop leaders now missing in action have apparently not been offset by equal numbers of new recruits elsewhere.

Fraternal organizations have also witnessed a substantial drop in membership during the 1980s and 1990s. Membership is down significantly in such groups as the Lions (off 12 percent since 1983), the Elks (off 18 percent since 1979), the Shriners (off 27 percent since 1979), the Jaycees (off 44 percent since 1979), and the Masons (down 39 percent since 1959). In sum, after expanding steadily throughout most of this century, many major civic organizations have experienced a sudden, substantial, and nearly simultaneous decline in membership over the last decade or two.

The most whimsical yet discomfiting bit of evidence of social disengagement in contemporary America that I have discovered is this: more Americans are bowling today than ever before, but bowling in organized leagues has plummeted in the last decade or so. Between 1980 and 1993 the total number of bowlers in America increased by 10 percent, while league bowling decreased by 40 percent. (Lest this be thought a wholly trivial example, I should note that nearly 80 million Americans went bowling at least once during 1993, *nearly a third more than voted in the 1994 congressional elections* and roughly the same number as claim to attend church regularly. Even after the 1980s' plunge in league bowling, nearly 3 percent of American adults regularly bowl in leagues.) The rise of solo bowling threatens the livelihood of bowling-lane proprietors because those who bowl as members of leagues consume three times as much beer and pizza as solo bowlers, and the money in bowling is in the beer and pizza, not the balls and shoes. The broader social significance, however, lies in the social interaction and even occasionally civic conversations over beer and pizza that solo bowlers forgo. Whether or not bowling beats balloting in the eyes of most Americans, bowling teams illustrate yet another vanishing form of social capital. . . .

Good Neighborliness and Social Trust

I noted earlier that most readily available quantitative evidence on trends in social connectedness involves formal settings, such as the voting booth, the union hall, or the PTA. One glaring exception is so widely discussed as to require little comment here: the most fundamental form of social capital is the family, and the massive evidence of the loosening of bonds within the family (both extended and nuclear) is well known. This trend, of course, is quite consistent with—and may help to explain—our theme of social decapitalization.

A second aspect of informal social capital on which we happen to have reasonably reliable time-series data involves neighborliness. In each General Social Survey since 1974 respondents have been asked, "How often do you spend a social evening with a neighbor?" The proportion of Americans who socialize with their neighbors more than once a year has slowly but steadily declined over the last two decades, from 72 percent in 1974 to 61 percent in 1993. (On the other hand, socializing with "friends who do not live in your neighborhood" appears to be on the increase, a trend that may reflect the growth of workplace-based social connections.)

Americans are also less trusting. The proportion of Americans saying that most people can be trusted fell by more than a third between 1960, when 58 percent chose that alternative, and 1993, when only 37 percent did. The same trend is apparent in all educational groups; indeed, because social trust is also correlated with education and because educational levels have risen sharply, the overall decrease in social trust is even more apparent if we control for education.

Our discussion of trends in social connectedness and civic engagement has tacitly assumed that all the forms of social capital that we have discussed are themselves coherently correlated across individuals. This is in fact true. Members of associations are much more likely than nonmembers to participate in politics, to spend time with neighbors, to express social trust, and so on.

The close correlation between social trust and associational membership is true not only across time and across individuals, but also across countries. Evidence from the 1991 World Values Survey demonstrates the following:[7]

1. Across the 35 countries in this survey, social trust and civic engagement are strongly correlated; the greater the density of associational membership in a society, the more trusting its citizens. Trust and engagement are two facets of the same underlying factor—social capital.

2. America still ranks relatively high by cross-national standards on both these dimensions of social capital. Even in the 1990s, after several decades' erosion, Americans are more trusting and more engaged than people in most other countries of the world.

3. The trends of the past quarter-century, however, have apparently moved the United States significantly lower in the international rankings of social capital. The recent deterioration in American social capital has been sufficiently great that (if no other country changed its position in the meantime) another quarter-century of change at the same rate would bring the United States, roughly speaking, to the midpoint among all these countries, roughly equivalent to South Korea, Belgium, or Estonia today. Two generations' decline at the same rate would leave the United States at the level of today's Chile, Portugal, and Slovenia.

Why Is U.S. Social Capital Eroding?

As we have seen, something has happened in America in the last two or three decades to diminish civic engagement and social connectedness. What could that "something" be? Here are several possible explanations, along with some initial evidence on each.

The movement of women into the labor force. Over these same two or three decades, many millions of American women have moved out of the home into paid employment. This is the primary, though not the sole, reason why the weekly working hours of the average American have increased significantly during these years. It seems highly plausible that this social revolution should have reduced the time and energy available for building social capital. For certain organizations, such as the PTA, the League of Women Voters, the Federation of Women's Clubs, and the Red Cross, this is almost certainly an important part of the story. The sharpest decline in women's civic participation seems to have come in the 1970s; membership in such "women's" organizations as these has been virtually halved since the late 1960s. By contrast, most of the decline in participation in men's organizations occurred about ten years later; the total decline to date has been approximately 25 percent for the typical organization. On the other hand, the survey data imply that the aggregate declines for men are virtually as great as those for women. It is logically possible, of course, that the male declines might represent the knock-on effect of women's liberation, as dishwashing crowded out the lodge, but time-budget studies suggest that most husbands of working wives have assumed only a minor part of the housework. In short, something besides the women's revolution seems to lie behind the erosion of social capital.

Mobility: The "re-potting" hypothesis. Numerous studies of organizational involvement have shown that residential stability and such related phenomena as homeownership are clearly associated with greater civic engagement. Mobility, like frequent re-potting of plants, tends to disrupt root systems, and it takes time for an uprooted individual to put down new roots. It seems plausible that the automobile, suburbanization, and the movement to the Sun Belt have reduced the social rootedness of the average American, but one fundamental difficulty with this hypothesis is apparent: the best evidence shows that residential stability and homeownership in America have risen modestly since 1965, and are surely higher now than during the 1950s, when civic engagement and social connectedness by our measures was definitely higher.

Other demographic transformations. A range of additional changes have transformed the American family since the 1960s—fewer marriages, more divorces, fewer children, lower real wages, and so on. Each of these changes might account for some of the slackening of civic engagement, since married, middleclass parents are generally more socially involved than other people. Moreover, the changes in scale that have swept over the American economy in these years—illustrated by the replacement of the corner grocery by the supermarket and now perhaps of the supermarket by electronic shopping at home, or the replacement of community-based enterprises by outposts of distant multinational firms—may perhaps have undermined the material and even physical basis for civic engagement.

The technological transformation of leisure. There is reason to believe that deepseated technological trends are radically "privatizing" or "individualizing" our use of leisure time and thus disrupting many opportunities for social-capital formation. The most obvious and probably the most powerful instrument of this revolution is television. Time-budget studies in the 1960s showed that the growth in time spent watching television dwarfed all other changes in the way Americans passed their days and nights. Television has made our communities (or, rather, what we experience as our communities) wider and shallower. In the language of economics, electronic technology enables individual tastes to be satisfied more fully, but at the cost of the positive social externalities associated with more primitive forms of entertainment. The same logic applies to the replacement of vaudeville by the movies and now of movies by the VCR. The new "virtual reality" helmets that we will soon don to be entertained in total isolation are merely the latest extension of this trend. Is technology thus driving a wedge between our individual interests and our collective interests? It is a question that seems worth exploring more systematically.

What Is to Be Done?

The last refuge of a social-scientific scoundrel is to call for more research. Nevertheless, I cannot forbear from suggesting some further lines of inquiry.

* We must sort out the dimensions of social capital, which clearly is not a unidimensional concept, despite language (even in this essay) that implies the contrary. What types of organizations and networks most effectively embody—or generate—social capital, in the sense of mutual reciprocity, the resolution of dilemmas of collective action, and the broadening of social identities? In this essay I have emphasized the density of associational life. In earlier work I stressed the structure of networks, arguing that "horizontal" ties represented more productive social capital than vertical ties.[8]

* Another set of important issues involves macrosociological crosscurrents that might intersect with the trends described here. What will be the impact, for example, of electronic networks on social capital? My hunch is that meeting in an electronic forum is not the equivalent of meeting in a bowling alley—or even in a saloon—but hard empirical research is needed. What about the development of social capital in the workplace? Is it growing in counterpoint to the decline of civic engagement, reflecting some social analogue of the first law of thermodynamics—social capital is neither created nor destroyed, merely redistributed? Or do the trends described in this essay represent a deadweight loss?

* A rounded assessment of changes in American social capital over the last quarter-century needs to count the costs as well as the benefits of community engagement. We must not romanticize small-town, middle-class civic life in the America of the 1950s. In addition to the deleterious trends emphasized in this essay, recent decades have witnessed a substantial decline in intolerance and probably also in overt discrimination, and those beneficent trends may be related in complex ways to the erosion of traditional social capital. Moreover, a balanced accounting of the social-capital books would need to reconcile the insights of this approach with the undoubted insights offered by Mancur Olson and others who stress that closely knit social, economic, and political organizations are prone to inefficient cartelization and to what political economists term "rent seeking" and ordinary men and women call corruption.[9]

◆ Finally, and perhaps most urgently, we need to explore creatively how public policy impinges on (or might impinge on) social-capital formation. In some well-known instances, public policy has destroyed highly effective social networks and norms. American slum-clearance policy of the 1950s and 1960s, for example, renovated physical capital, but at a very high cost to existing social capital. The consolidation of country post offices and small school districts has promised administrative and financial efficiencies, but full-cost accounting for the effects of these policies on social capital might produce a more negative verdict. On the other hand, such past initiatives as the county agricultural-agent system, community colleges, and tax deductions for charitable contributions illustrate that government can encourage social-capital formation. Even a recent proposal in San Luis Obispo, California, to require that all new houses have front porches illustrates the power of government to influence where and how networks are formed.

The concept of "civil society" has played a central role in the recent global debate about the preconditions for democracy and democratization. In the newer democracies this phrase has properly focused attention on the need to foster a vibrant civic life in soils traditionally inhospitable to self-government. In the established democracies, ironically, growing numbers of citizens are questioning the effectiveness of their public institutions at the very moment when liberal democracy has swept the battlefield, both ideologically and geopolitically. In America, at least, there is reason to suspect that this democratic disarray may be linked to a broad and continuing erosion of civic engagement that began a quarter-century ago. High on our scholarly agenda should be the question of whether a comparable erosion of social capital may be under way in other advanced democracies, perhaps in different institutional and behavioral guises. High on America's agenda should be the question of how to reverse these adverse trends in social connectedness, thus restoring civic engagement and civic trust.

Notes

1. Alexis de Tocqueville, *Democracy in America*, ed. J.P. Maier, trans. George Lawrence (Garden City, N.Y.: Anchor Books, 1969), 513–17.

2. On social networks and economic growth in the developing world, see Milton J. Esman and Norman Uphoff, *Local Organizations: Intermediaries in Rural Development* (Ithaca: Cornell University Press, 1984), esp. 15–42 and 99–180; and Albert O. Hirschman, *Getting Ahead Collectively: Grassroots Experiences in Latin America* (Elmsford, N.Y.: Pergamon Press, 1984), esp. 42–77. On East Asia, see Gustav Papanek, "The New Asian Capitalism: An Economic Portrait," in Peter L. Berger and Hsin-Huang Michael Hsiao, eds., *In Search of an East Asian Development Model* (New Brunswick, N.J.: Transaction, 1987), 27–80; Peter B. Evans, "The State as Problem and Solution: Predation, Embedded Autonomy and Structural Change," in Stephan Haggard and Robert R. Kaufman, eds., *The Politics of Economic Adjustment* (Princeton: Princeton University Press, 1992), 139–81; and Gary G. Hamilton, William Zeile, and Wan-Jin Kim, "Network Structure of East Asian Economies," in Stewart R. Clegg and S. Gordon Redding, eds., *Capitalism in Contrasting Cultures* (Hawthorne, N.Y.: De Gruyter, 1990),

105–29. See also Gary G. Hamilton and Nicole Woolsey Biggart, "Market, Culture, and Authority: A Comparative Analysis of Management and Organization in the Far East," *American Journal of Sociology* (Supplement) 94 (1988): S52–S94; and Susan Greenhalgh, "Families and Networks in Taiwan's Economic Development," in Edwin Winckler and Susan Greenhalgh, eds., *Contending Approaches to the Political Economy of Taiwan* (Armonk, N.Y.: M.E. Sharpe, 1987), 224–45.

3. Robert D. Putnam, *Making Democracy Work: Civic Traditions in Modern Italy* (Princeton: Princeton University Press, 1993).

4. James S. Coleman deserves primary credit for developing the "social capital" theoretical framework. See his "Social Capital in the Creation of Human Capital," *American Journal of Sociology* (Supplement) 94 (1988): S95–S120, as well as his *The Foundations of Social Theory* (Cambridge: Harvard University Press, 1990), 300–21. See also Mark Granovetter, "Economic Action and Social Structure: The Problem of Embeddedness," *American Journal of Sociology* 91 (1985): 481–510; Glenn C. Loury, "Why Should We Care About Group Inequality?" *Social Philosophy and Policy* 5 (1987): 249–71; and Robert D. Putnam, "The Prosperous Community: Social Capital and Public Life," *American Prospect* 13 (1993): 35–42. To my knowledge, the first scholar to use the term "social capital" in its current sense was Jane Jacobs, in *The Death and Life of Great American Cities* (New York: Random House, 1961), 138.

5. Any simplistically political interpretation of the collapse of American unionism would need to confront the fact that the steepest decline began more than six years before the Reagan administration's attack on PATCO. Data from the General Social Survey show a roughly 40-percent decline in reported union membership between 1975 and 1991.

6. Data for the LWV are available over a longer time span and show an interesting pattern: a sharp slump during the Depression, a strong and sustained rise after World War II that more than tripled membership between 1945 and 1969, and then the post-1969 decline, which has already erased virtually all the postwar gains and continues still. This same historical pattern applies to those men's fraternal organizations for which comparable data are available—steady increases for the first seven decades of the century, interrupted only by the Great Depression, followed by a collapse in the 1970s and 1980s that has already wiped out most of the postwar expansion and continues apace.

7. I am grateful to Ronald Inglehart, who directs this unique cross-national project, for sharing these highly useful data with me. See his "The Impact of Culture on Economic Development: Theory, Hypotheses, and Some Empirical Tests" (unpublished manuscript, University of Michigan, 1994).

8. See my *Making Democracy Work*, esp. ch. 6.

9. See Mancur Olson, *The Rise and Decline of Nations: Economic Growth, Stagflation, and Social Rigidities* (New Haven: Yale University Press, 1982), 2.

The State and Social Capital: An Institutional Theory of Generalized Trust

Bo Rothstein and Dietlind Stolle

The selection by Putnam [7.3] analyzes the decline of social capital in the United State, what he describes in that selection as "networks, norms, and social trust that facilitate coordination and cooperation for mutual benefit." Putnam suggests that the decline of social capital is linked to the weakening of major social institutions, including organized religion; labor unions; and civic, fraternal, and other voluntary associations. He claims that the causes are increasing residential mobility, changing family structures, and technological innovations, notably television (he might have added the Internet), that divert people from civic engagement.

Bo Rothstein and Dietlind Stolle highlight the importance of a factor affecting the extent of social capital that Putnam doesn't emphasize: the quality of government institutions. Their analysis suggests that government institutions that administer law and order impartially significantly promote what they call generalized trust in the society.

Rothstein and Stolle recognize that it is difficult to establish the direction of causality between government and generalized trust. That is, while effective government can promote trust, societies in which generalized trust exists are more likely to possess effective government institutions. Can you think of ways to solve this problem?

Rothstein and Stolle conclude that their analysis has important policy implications. Much research studying social capital has claimed that the basic problem is a lack of trust and too little volunteering. However, Rothstein and Stolle contend, if low levels of trust and social capital are caused by biased government institutions, then priority should be put on improving the quality of government institutions. What might this mean? How might it be accomplished? If the goal is to promote a more peaceful, trusting society, should priority be put on improving governmental institutions or promoting social capital directly?

Bo Rothstein and Dietlind Stolle, "The State and Social Capital: An Institutional Theory of Generalized Trust," *Comparative Politics* 40, no. 4 (July 2008): 441–446, 456–458.

The Theory of Social Capital

How is social capital generated? A wealth of empirical research shows that social capital is associated with a number of outcomes that for most people are normatively desirable. Among these outcomes are well-performing democratic institutions,[1] personal happiness,[2] optimism and tolerance,[3] economic growth,[4] and democratic stability.[5] However, in this abundance of positive associations between social capital and various social and political outcomes, the sources of social capital often remain undertheorized and empirically unexplored.

Social capital has been defined as generalized trust, access to and membership in various types of networks, and norms of reciprocity.[6] The attitudinal aspects of the concept such as generalized interpersonal trust, are the most important part of social capital. The reason is that individuals can be members of networks that consist of untrustworthy agents, which play a destructive role for the values listed above. There is thus no logical reason why membership in networks per se should be a desired social value. Attitudes of generalized trust extend beyond the boundaries of face-to-face interaction and incorporate people who are not personally known to each other.[7]

That citizens in some countries, regions, cities, or villages are able to trust each other and thereby solve many of their collective action problems while others are not turns out to be one of the most interesting puzzles in the social sciences.[8] This article addresses this particular issue in more detail and sketches out a theory of the formation of generalized trust that is embedded in the structure and characteristics of political institutions. In fact, many of the effects that social capital has been shown to have on institutions might be caused as much by the effects of institutional differences on social capital. Thus, this article presents a theory in which the causal logic that has been the established wisdom in most studies of social capital is reversed.

The Generation of Social Capital: Society and Institution Centered Models

Studies of social capital are divided on its causes and origins. On the one side are scholars who argue that variations in the amount and type of social capital can be explained primarily by society-centered approaches.[9] In this Tocquevillian approach, the capacity of a society to produce social capital among its citizens is determined by its long-term experience of social organization, anchored in historical and cultural experiences that can be traced back over very long periods. The society-centered approach views regular social interaction, preferably through membership in voluntary associations, as the most important mechanism for the generation of social capital. Following the Tocquevillian tradition, formal and informal associations and networks are seen as creators of social capital because of their socializing effects on democratic and cooperative values and norms.

A number of studies carried out in different democratic countries over the last few years has called into question the effect of participation in many voluntary associations directed at benevolent purposes on social trust and the willingness to cooperate outside of the specific group. While it is true that people who are joiners also generally trust others more, this categorization seems to be an effect of self-selection. People who—for some other reason—score high on the social ability to trust and cooperate with others join voluntary associations disproportionately. However, activity in such organizations does not add much in these desired traits, at least not for adults. Members become purely more trusting of their fellow members and they cooperate more for group purposes only.[10] Thus, the evidence that associational membership of adults creates social capital that can be used in the wider society simply does not hold.[11]

A second issue is that, even if the importance of voluntary engagement is accepted, not all associations serve a normatively desirable purpose. In fact, many associations are established to create distrust. Alan Brinkley refers to parochial communities that do not reach out but instead manifest and nurture an inward-looking and segregating culture.[12] Sheri Berman has argued that the Nazis in Weimar Germany used existing voluntary associations as vehicles for their *Machtübernahme*.[13] Far from such extreme cases, some voluntary associations may use their power, for example as producer organizations, to extract resources from society in a way that comes close to blackmail, giving undue or disproportional advantages to their members to the detriment of the rest of society.[14]

The problem of having good and bad associations is readily admitted in social capital research, and promising new analyses distinguish groups according to the degree of contact members have with individuals unlike themselves. This distinction in social interaction has been labeled as bridging (contact with many people who are dissimilar) versus bonding (contact with people like oneself). Bridging interactions are believed to create more desirable outcomes.[15] In a similar vein, Warren distinguishes between groups oriented toward status, group identity, and material goods, as well as those focused on inclusive social, public, or identity goods.[16] However, both theoretical accounts need to be tested empirically.[17] Generally, the struggle to distinguish between the good, the bad, and the ugly in the world of voluntary associations underlines the lack of theoretical parameters that define a micro-theory of social capital. The use of membership in adult voluntary associations as a measurement of social capital should be handled with great caution, and its use as a producer of social capital is in all likelihood misplaced.

As a response to the society-centered approach, the institution-centered accounts of social capital theory claim that for social capital to flourish it needs to be embedded in and linked to the political context as well as formal political and legal institutions.[18] According to this group of scholars, government institutions and policies create, channel, and influence social capital. However, it is noteworthy that the "new institutionalism" and the social capital research agenda have been mostly disconnected.[19]

Two main types of institutional arguments can be distinguished in relation to social capital: an attitudinal and an institutional-structural approach. In the former, scholars examine the relationship between institutional/political trust and generalized trust. For example, Hall indicates that political trust and generalized trust are correlated in Britain.[20] Kaase discusses the consistently positive but weak correlation between the two types of trust in cross-national survey samples.[21] However, interpretations of this correlation vary. Some recognize the correlation between the two types of trust but see generalized trust mostly as a predictor of political trust. For example, Lipset and Schneider claim that in the United States what they call the "personal characteristic of trust in others" might explain developments in public confidence. "A general feeling of confidence in institutions seems to derive from a personal outlook of optimism, satisfaction and trust."[22] Newton and Norris elaborate this causal flow when they find a strong positive correlation at the aggregate level in the analysis of the World Value surveys in seventeen trilateral democracies. They interpret their findings as evidence that social capital "can help build effective social and political institutions, which can help governments perform effectively, and this in turn encourages confidence in civic institutions."[23] Putnam's argument also follows this logic. It shows that regional governmental performance depends on levels of regional social capital.[24] The problem with these analyses is that it is not clear how the causality operates. For example, using the U.S. General Social Surveys (GSS), Brehm and Rahn found that confidence in institutions has a larger effect on interpersonal trust than the other way around.[25]

There are three main problems with the attitudinal arguments regarding the relationship between institutions and social capital. First, attitudes are not connected to the actual institutional characteristics. It is not known what in the institutional characteristics may generate or destroy generalized trust. Second, since there is a variety of forms of institutional trust that can be identified in the study of advanced industrialized democracies, it is problematic to collapse them all under one label (trust in government). The reason why several studies find weak or no correlations between generalized trust and trust/confidence in political institutions is that they focus on political institutions in general without further specification. Third, the mechanism for both causal claims remains unclear. Given Putnam's logic from generalized trust to institutional performance to confidence in politicians, it is not known how trusting people create better service performance and better, more responsive local politicians.[26] Do more trusting citizens contact governmental officials more frequently to pressure them into good performance? Or do local politicians just reflect the culture of trust or distrust that prevails in their local societies? The reverse logic is just as plausible.

The second institutional approach overcomes some of these problems because it centers on the role of the state as a source of social capital generation.[27] States, for example, enable the establishment of reliable contracts between citizens because they provide information and monitor legislation about contracts and enforce rights and rules that sanction lawbreakers, protect minorities, and actively support the integration and participation of citizens.[28] Certain types of institutions, such as those that deal with lawbreakers, are also emphasized. Still missing is a specification of the causal mechanism between institutional arrangements and generalized trust.

The Role of Political Institutions, but Which Ones?

As stated above, the problem is that many forms of institutional trust and confidence are collapsed under one label as trust in government. No distinction has been made between confidence in the institutions on the representational side of the political system (parties, parliaments, cabinets) and confidence in the institutions on the implementation side of the political system. The theoretical reason why the confidence that people place in these two types of political institutions differ is the following. On the representational side, one of the main roles for political institutions is to be partisan. A political party that holds government power is supposed to try to implement its ideology in a partisan way. Thus, people who support the ideology of the ruling party (or parties) are likely to have confidence in them, while citizens who oppose their ideology are likely to report a lack of confidence. However, it is less likely that this type of partisan trust or distrust should influence one's generalized trust in other people. There is no plausible causal mechanism linking these two phenomena. A strong correlation is thus usually between political leanings and political trust, but a weak correlation is found between confidence in these types of political institutions and social trust.[29] The weak findings of causal relationships between generalized trust and trust in government are mostly due to this failure to distinguish the cause of trust in various kinds of political institutions.

The major source of variations in generalized trust is to be found at the other side of the state machinery, the legal and administrative branches of the state responsible for the implementation of public policies. These branches of government need to be distinguished from the influence of representational institutions such as the legislative and the executive for two main reasons. First, while the basis for trusting (or distrusting) the institutions dominated by politicians is partisanship, the reason for trusting civil servants, judges, the police, and social service institutions is their even-handedness and/or impartiality.[30] Second, compared to other political institutions the courts, the police, and the other legal institutions of the state have a special task: to detect and punish people who, in game theory parlance, use opportunistic strategies (treacherous would be a better term). In other words, these political institutions—the order institutions— are in the business of taking care of people who are better not to be trusted. How do the implementation side of the state in general and the order institutions in particular influence generalized trust?

Institutions, Corruption, and Social Capital:
The Causal Mechanism

Why would unfair, corrupt, inefficient, and biased practices in the administrative machinery of the state influence people's propensity to trust others in their society? The causal link is by no means obvious since there are (at least) two possible answers. First, in societies where people can not trust the police or the judicial system, citizens would compensate by increasing their trust-based networks. In this vein, Michael Woolcook writes that "rampant corruption, frustrating bureaucratic delays, suppressed civil liberties, failure to safeguard property rights and uphold the rule of law, force communities back on themselves, demanding that they supply privately and informally what should be delivered publicly and formally."[31] Della Porta, a leading authority on corruption, claims that in order to make corrupt exchanges one has to trust the others who are involved in corruption.

However, the type of trust that can thrive in such communities would be particularized and not generalized trust. For example, the small, dense niche networks in former East Germany characterized by high levels of in-group trust were so special because they actually were created as a protection against weak ties and other types of broader networks.[32] The high degree of norm conformity within such networks and the resulting trust relations can not be revealed and applied to the outside world.

For attitudes of a generalized nature, such as generalized trust, things work the other way around. A biased, unfair, and corrupt administrative system generally goes hand in hand with low levels of social capital, particularly when measured as generalized trust. Institutions of law and order have one particularly important task, to detect and punish people who break contracts and who therefore should not be trusted. Thus, if citizens think that these order institutions do what they are supposed to do in a fair, reasonably efficient, and unbiased manner, then they also have reason to believe that the chance people will get away with treacherous behavior is relatively small. If so, citizens believe that most people have good reason to refrain from acting in a treacherous manner and thus conclude that most people can be trusted. However, it is not just the efficiency with which treacherous behavior is punished that matters for generalized trust, but also the combination of efficiency and fairness of order institutions. Police officers, social service bureaucrats, and judges are both representatives of the people and exhibitors of institutionalized values. In short, their behaviors function as important signals to citizens about the moral standard of the society in which they live.[33] This theory might work asymmetrically, in the sense that over time the building of fair and efficient institutions might yield slower and less visible success than the decline in institutional quality. This asymmetry is expected as generally trust is more easily destroyed than created.[34]

This theory helps to identify some of the important dimensions of state institutions that are closely related to generalized trust.[35] Four different parts of this causal mechanism between institutional characteristics and generalized trust will be developed. First, various levels of institutional efficiency and fairness influence the individual agent's perception of his/her safety and security. The absence or presence of fear of others will obviously influence the belief that most other people ought or ought not to be trusted. Second, they determine the individual agent's inference from those who are given the responsibility of guarding the public interest to the rest of society. For example, if those in positions of responsibility can not be trusted, then most other people can surely not be trusted. Third, they shape the observance of the behavior of fellow citizens, as institutional fairness sets the tone. The message of corrupt systems is, for example, that in order to get what one needs in life one must be engaged in various forms of corruption. Hence the individual agent will witness the use of corruption among fellow citizens and will feel obliged to engage in corrupt practices in order to get what he or she deems necessary in life. However, there can be no generalized trust in those individuals who just take advantage of others and the system. Fourth, they cause positive or negative experiences with these institutions when in direct contact with them. Corrupt and unfair institutions, for example, might lead to experiences of discrimination and injustice, which negatively influence generalized trust. . . .

Conclusion

The structure and characteristics of contemporary government institutions are both important and often overlooked factors that matter for the generation of generalized trust. The theory presented here explains how the causal flow from impartial institutions to generalized trust might operate. The procedural fairness of these institutions influences citizens' institutional trust and, more specifically, how citizens experience feelings of safety and protection, how they make inferences from the system and public officials to other citizens, how they observe the behavior of fellow citizens, and how they experience discrimination against themselves or those close to them.

Empirical data provide evidence for these causal mechanisms. The empirical analysis especially works at both the micro and the macro levels. Citizens seem to make distinctions between various types of institutions, and trust in order institutions and in other institutions that implement policy is more important for generalized trust than other types of institutional confidence, in most of the models. A key point is the direction of causality. How can it be proven that institutions shape social capital and not the other way around? Clearly, many more tests and analyses have to be performed in order to ensure that this direction of causality holds. However, the first step in this discussion must surely be the development of a causal mechanism based on a strong theoretical account. Taken alone, each of the results is not enough to make the point. Yet the causal mechanism and the multiplicity of results presented throughout this article reveal a great deal about how civic attitudes such as trust are related to and most likely embedded in impartial, fair, and efficient institutions.

Finally, important policy implications may follow from these results. If the society-centered model is correct, governments can claim that the main problems that plague their societies are caused by too little volunteering. To make democracy work and the economy grow, citizens have to get involved. However, if the theory presented here is correct, governments can not blame their citizens for the lack of social capital. Instead, the policy message becomes a very different one: that the lack of social capital is caused by dysfunctional government institutions.

Notes

1. Robert D. Putnam, *Making Democracy Work: Civic Traditions in Modern Italy* (Princeton: Princeton University Press, 1993); Kenneth Newton, "Social Capital and Democracy in Modern Europe," in J. W. van Deth, M. Maraffi, K. Newton, and P. F. Whiteley, eds., *Social Capital and European Democracy* (London: Routledge, 1999); Michael Woolcook, "The Place of Social Capital in Understanding Social and Economic Outcomes," *ISUMA: Canadian Journal of Policy Research*, 2 (2001), 11–16.
2. John F. Helliwell, "How's Life? Combining Individual and National Variables to Explain Subjective Well-Being" (Cambridge, Mass.: National Bureau for Economic Research, 2002).
3. Eric Uslaner, *The Moral Foundation of Trust* (New York: Cambridge University Press, 2002).
4. Steve Knack and Philip Keefer, "Does Social Capital Have an Economic Payoff? A Cross-Country Investigation," *Quarterly Journal of Economics*, 112 (1997), 1251–88; Paul J. Zak and Stephen Knack, "Trust and Growth," *Economic Journal*, 111 (2001), 295–321.
5. Ronald Inglehart, "Trust, Well-being and Democracy," in M. E. Warren, ed., *Democracy and Trust* (New York; Cambridge University Press, 1999), pp. 88–120.
6. James S. Coleman, *Foundations of Social Theory* (Cambridge. Mass.: The Belknap Press of Harvard University Press, 1990); Putnam, *Making Democracy Work*.
7. Dietlind Stolle, "Trusting Strangers: The Concept of Generalized Trust in Perspective," *Österreichische Zeitschrift für Politikwissenschaft*, 31 (2002), 397–412.
8. Elinor Ostrom, *Governing the Commons: The Evolution of Institutions for Collective Action* (New York Cambridge University Press, 1990); Anirudh Krishna, *Active Social Capital: Tracing the Roots of Development and Democracy* (New York: Columbia University Press, 2002).
9. Francis Fukuyama, "Social Capital and Civil Society," paper presented at the Conference on Second Generation Reform, Washington, D.C., November 8–9, 1999; Robert D. Putnam, *Bowling Alone: The Collapse and Revival of American Community* (New York: Simon & Schuster, 2000).
10 Dietlind Stolle, "Clubs and Congregations: The Benefit of Joining Organizations," in K. S. Cook ed., *Trust in Society* (New York: Russell Sage Foundation, 2001), pp. 202–44.
11. Jan Delhey and Kenneth Newton, "Who Trusts? The Origins of Social Trust in Seven Societies," *European Societies*, 5 (2003), 93–137; M. P. Claiborn and P S. Martin, "Trusting and Joining? An Empirical Test of the Reciprocal Nature of Social Capital," *Political Behavior*, 22 (2000), 267–91; Francisco Herreros, *The Problem of Forming Social Capital: Why Trust?* (New York: Palgrave/Macmillan, 2004); Uslaner, *The Moral Foundation of Trust*.
12. Alan Brinkley, "Liberty, Community, and the National Idea," *The American Prospect*, 7 (2002).
13. Sheri Berman, "Civil Society and the Collapse of the Weimar Republic," *World Politics*, 49 (1997), 401–29.
14. Sarah L. Henderson, "Selling Civil Society: Western Aid and the Nongovernmental Organization Sector in Russia," *Comparative Political Studies*, 35 (2002), 139–69.
15. Putnam, *Bowling Alone: The Collapse and Revival of American Community*.
16. Mark Warren, *Democracy and Association* (Princeton: Princeton University Press, 2001).
17. Melissa Marschall and Dietlind Stolle, "Race and the City: Neighborhood Context and the Development of Generalized Trust," *Political Behavior*, 26 (2004), 126–53.
18. Berman, "Civil Society and the Collapse of the Weimar Republic"; Omar G. Encarnación, "Civil Society Reconsidered," *Comparative Politics*, 38 (2006), 357–76; Peter Hall, "Social Capital in Britain,"

British Journal of Political Science, 29 (1999), 417–64; Margaret Levi, "A State of Trust," in V. Braithwaite and M. Levi, eds., *Trust and Governance* (New York: Russell Sage Foundation, 1998); Sidney Tarrow, "Making Social Science Work across Space and Time: A Critical Reflection on Robert Putnam's *Making Democracy Work*," *American Political Science Review*, 90 (1996); Staffan Kumlin and Bo Rothstein, "Making and Breaking Social Capital: The Impact of Welfare State Institutions," *Comparative Political Studies*, 38 (2005), 339–65.

19. Kathleen Thelen, "Historical Institutionalism in Comparative Perspective," *Annual Review of Political Science*, 2 (1999), 369–404.

20. Hall, "Social Capital in Britain."

21. Max Kaase, "Interpersonal Trust, Political Trust and Non-Institutionalized Political Participation in Western Europe," *West European Politics*, 22 (1999), 14.

22. S, M. Lipset and W. Schneider, *The Confidence Gap* (New York: The Free Press, 1983), p. 120.

23. Ken Newton and Pippa Norris, "Confidence in Public Institutions," in S. J. Pharr and R. D. Putnam, eds., *Disaffected Democracies: What's Troubling the Trilateral Countries* (Princeton: Princeton University Press, 2000).

24. Putnam, *Making Democracy Work*.

25. J. Brehm and W. Rahn, "Individual Level Evidence for the Causes and Consequences of Social Capital," *American Journal of Political Science*, 41 (1997), 1014.

26. Putnam, *Making Democracy Work*.

27. Tarrow, p. 395.

28. Levi, p. 85.

29. For the original argument, see Jack Citrin, "The Political Relevance of Trust in Government," *American Political Science Review*, 68 (1974), 973–88; Kenneth Newton, "Social and Political Trust in Established Democracies," in P. Norris, ed., *Critical Citizens: Global Support for Democratic Government* (New York: Oxford University Press, 1999): Newton and Norris, "Confidence in Public Institutions."

30. Bo Rothstein and Jan Teorell, "What Is Quality of Government: A Theory of Impartial Political Institutions," paper presented at the Annual Meeting of the American Political Science Association, Washington, D. C., 2005.

31. Wooicook, p. 16.

32. Beate Völker and Henry Flap, "Weak Ties as a Liability: The Case of East Germany," *Rationality and Society*, 13 (2001), 397–428.

33. Andrew Kydd, "Overcoming Mistrust," *Rationality and Society*, 12 (2000), 397–424; Jan Delhey and Kenneth Newton, "Social Trust. Global Pattern or Nordic Expectionalism?," Discussion Paper 2004, 202, Wissenschaftszentrum Berlin für Sozialforschung,

34. Claus Offe, "How Can we Trust Our Fellow Citizens?," in Warren, ed., *Democracy and Trust*.

35. The argument is certainly not that all forms of "generalized trust" are caused by experiences with and trust in the impartiality and fairness of certain government institutions.

The Future of Freedom: Illiberal Democracy at Home and Abroad

Fareed Zakaria

Fareed Zakaria claims that democratic political institutions can produce out-comes that diminish freedom because majorities may trample on the rights of minorities. The answer, he suggests, is to limit democracy by insulating political institutions, that is, by reducing the influence of elections and other democratic procedures. Zakaria does not consider two opposite dangers: first, that because institutions are insulated and unaccountable, they may abuse their power and limit freedom; second, the price for protecting minority rights can be to thwart the will of the majority. A challenge for scholars and citizens, then, is to devise a way for institutions *both* to safeguard freedom *and* to be accountable and responsive to the majority. Any suggestions?

The twentieth century was marked by two broad trends: the regulation of capitalism and the deregulation of democracy. Both experiments over-reached. They were sensible solutions to the problems of the time, unregulated capitalism and oligarchy. But as Evelyn Waugh pointed out in his comic novel *Scoop*, every good idea is valid "up to a point."

In the early years of the twentieth century, free markets and free trade seemed to be the inevitable way of the future. Countries around the world were trading with one another, opening up their markets, indeed, their entire societies. Markets were on the march. But it turned out that those years before World War I, hyper-inflation, and the Great Depression were a watershed for laissez faire. From then on, whenever a problem developed—economic, social, political—government intervention was the solution. Every crisis brought forth new regulations, and every regulation brought forth a new bureaucracy. As a result, for most of the twentieth century, capitalism was taxed, licensed, controlled, and even national-ized, so much so that by 1945 Britain's preeminent historian, A. J. P. Taylor, could assert, "Nobody believes in the American way of life—that is, private enterprise." In 1961, when Britain's Queen Elizabeth II visited Ghana, she was hailed as "the greatest socialist monarch in the world," which even her Tory government accepted as a compliment. When the conservative Republican Richard Nixon imposed wage and price controls on the U.S. economy in 1971 and announced, "We are all Keynesians now," he was reflecting the widespread view—even in America—that capitalism had to be intrusively managed by the state.

Democracy moved in the opposite direction. "The cure for the ailments of democracy," wrote the influential American philosopher John Dewey in 1927, "is more democracy." He was prescient. Most problems faced by most democracies during the twentieth century were addressed by broadening the franchise, eliminating indirect elections, reducing the strength of elite groups, and empowering more and more people in more and more ways. The results were thrilling. In America that meant blacks and women got the right to vote, senators were directly elected, parties chose their candidates on the basis of popular votes, and clubs changed their character and rules. The political history of the twentieth century is the story of ever-greater and more direct political participation. And success kept expanding democracy's scope. Whatever the ailment, more democracy became the cure.

The regulation of capitalism had gone overboard by the 1970s, resulting in heavy tax rates and Byzantine government controls. Over the last two decades, governments all over the world, from the United States to France to India to Brazil, have been deregulating industries, privatizing companies, and lowering tariffs. As the economic boom of the late 1990s unravels, there will be need for new regulation and a renewed appreciation of the role of government in capitalism. But few countries are likely to return to the bloated practices of a generation ago. The state has retreated from the commanding heights of the economy.

The deregulation of democracy has also gone too far. It has produced an unwieldy system, unable to govern or command the respect of people. Although none would dare speak ill of present-day democracy, most people instinctively sense a problem. Public respect for politics and political systems in every advanced democracy is at an all-time low. More intriguingly, in poll after poll, when Americans are asked what public institutions they most respect, three bodies are always at the top of their list: the Supreme Court, the armed forces, and the Federal Reserve System. All three have one thing in common: they are insulated from public pressures and operate undemocratically. It would seem that Americans admire these institutions precisely because they lead rather than follow. By contrast, Congress, the most representative and reflective of political institutions, scores at the bottom of most surveys. People view the pandering and the resulting paralysis with dismay, even disgust. Of course that does not stop them from celebrating the processes that have made such pandering inevitable.

Delegating Democracy

When the stakes are high we do not entrust day-to-day politics to ourselves. No democracy has ever conducted a war by weekly vote. The struggle against terrorism is, inevitably, being waged by governments that have been given much leeway by their societies. We now face new threats but also new and deep pressures on government. Democracies will have to demonstrate that they can cope with terrorism effectively, or else in many developing countries we will see the rise of a new authoritarianism. Developing countries, particularly in the Islamic world, will need to manage a difficult balancing act. They must remain strong enough to handle the new dangers of terrorism but yet be open and democratic enough that they don't create political opposition that morphs into extremism. In other words, they must be able to kill terrorists without breeding terrorism. When it works right, the state's power, legitimacy, and effectiveness can work together, each reinforcing the other, in a virtuous cycle. When things go awry, however, the virtuous cycle becomes vicious—and violent. Repression produces extremism, which produces more repression. Russia's approach to Chechnya is a sorry illustration of this downward spiral.

Globalization has produced a special set of challenges. The increasingly open world economy has forced governments to adopt disciplined policies that maintain fiscal stability over the long term. When they do not, markets punish countries faster and more severely than ever before, plunging currencies and stock markets into ruin. And yet long-term policies cause short-term pain—to voters. Demographic changes are pressing Western governments to reform their welfare states, in particular their benefits for the elderly. This will prove nearly impossible because senior citizens are politically powerful; they are well organized, contribute money, lobby hard, and vote regularly. Real reform, however, will inevitably mean trimming back their benefits. Governments will have to make hard choices, resist the temptation to pander, and enact policies for the long run. The only possible way that this can be achieved in a modern democracy is by insulating some decision-makers from the intense pressures of interest groups, lobbies, and political campaigns—that is to say, from the intense pressures of democracy.

It is already happening. The rise of independent central banks, like the U.S. Federal Reserve, over the last few decades is the clearest example of this trend. In most advanced democracies, the government's most powerful economic lever is now exercised by an unelected body. And it works. Though they have their flaws, by and large independence of central banks has resulted in more responsible monetary policy. In part because of this discipline, the business cycle, which was once sharp and severe, has increasingly been smoothed out. The bust of 2000–2002, which followed the longest boom in half a century, is still (as of this writing) less extreme than many had feared. . . .

Less Is More

What we need in politics today is not more democracy but less. By this I do not mean we should embrace strongmen and dictators but rather that we should ask why certain institutions within our society—such as the Federal Reserve and the

Supreme Court—function so well and why others—such as legislatures—function poorly. As it happens, Alan Blinder, a Princeton professor, pondered just this question in a fascinating essay in *Foreign Affairs* magazine in 1997.[1] Blinder had completed two stints in government, first at the White House on the Council of Economic Advisers and then at the Federal Reserve, where he served as vice chairman. He noted in his essay that policymaking at the White House was dominated by short-term political and electoral considerations, whereas policy-making at the Federal Reserve was concerned largely with a policy's social, economic, and legal merits. This difference in large part accounted for the con-sistently high quality of decision-making at the Fed.

Blinder argued that Federal Reserve decision-making was insulated from politics for three good reasons. First, interest rates are a technical subject that specialists are better equipped to handle than amateurs. Second, monetary policy takes a long time to work and so requires patience and a steady hand. Finally, the pain of fight-ing inflation (higher unemployment) comes well before the benefits (permanently lower costs of goods, lower interest rates, etc.). As a result, good interest-rate pol-icy cannot be made in an atmosphere dominated by short-term considerations. But then Blinder admitted that "a nasty little thought kept creeping through my head: the argument for the Fed's independence applies just as forcefully to many other areas of government. Many policy decisions require complex technical judgments and have consequences that stretch into the distant future." He cited health care, environmental policy, and tax policy as just such cases.

Consider the U.S. federal income tax. In its first incarnation in 1914, the en-tire tax code was 14 pages long, and individuals' tax returns fit on a single page. Today the tax code runs over 2,000 pages, with 6,000 pages of regulations and tens of thousands of pages of rulings and interpretations. The Internal Revenue Service publishes 480 tax forms and 280 forms to explain them. It is unclear exactly how much it costs Americans to comply with these Byzantine rules; es-timates go as high as $600 billion per year, but most scholars place the number at about $100 billion, or about 15 percent of income-tax revenue (about $375 to $450 per person per year). Dale Jorgenson, chairman of the Economics Depart-ment at Harvard, calculates that moving to a flat-rate tax on consumption would raise as much revenue as the current income-tax system while increasing economic growth by more than $200 billion a year.

The tax code has become time-consuming, complex, and expensive for a sim-ple reason: democratic politics. It presents a golden opportunity for politicians to fund their favorite programs, groups, and companies without attracting much attention. An outright grant would be noticed; a small change in tax law will not. Corporations with very similar balance sheets can pay widely differing taxes, depending on whether they have effective lobbyists who can bully Con-gress into rewriting the code to their benefit. Often a new law is so narrowly written as to be in effect a subsidy to one particular company. Although each tax break might seem small, the overall cost is staggering, totaling more than $550 billion in forgone revenue for the federal government in 2001. Some of these "tax expenditures" are designed to support programs with broad public approval, but others—such as narrowly targeted tax breaks for industry—can only be described as corporate welfare.

Americans of all political stripes agree that the tax code is unwieldy, inefficient, and unfair. Yet no one believes it will ever be reformed, because it is embedded in democratic politics. Blinder points out that the three reasons that the Federal Reserve is independent all apply particularly strongly to tax policy. He proposes the creation of an independent federal tax authority, much like the Federal Reserve. Congress would give it broad directions and guidelines, and on this basis it would prepare tax legislation. Congress would then vote on the bill but no amendments would be allowed. Although hardly flawless, such a system would undoubtedly produce a better tax code than the one we have now.

The United States government already experiments with this kind of delegation in some areas. The president is usually given the authority to negotiate trade agreements, which are then presented to Congress as a complete package. Congress votes on the bill as a whole with no amendments allowed. Congress used a similar procedure in the early 1990s, when it needed to close dozens of military bases as the country demobilized after the Cold War. Faced with a crisis, legislators realized that the only way to arrive at a fair outcome was to take politics out of the process. Otherwise members of Congress would all be strongly in favor of closing bases, just not the ones in their districts. They delegated the task of determining which bases should be closed to a nonpartisan commission. The final list was presented to Congress for a single vote, up or down, with no changes permitted. These processes have all worked well, combining effective government with democratic control.

Delegation is the modern-day equivalent of the strategy that Homer's wandering hero, Ulysses, used as he sailed past the Sirens, whose singing made men cast themselves into the sea. Ulysses had his sailors fill their ears with wax so that they could not hear the Sirens' calls. For his part, he wanted to hear the music, so he had himself bound tightly to the mast of his ship and told his men that no matter what he said, they were not to untie him. As they passed the treacherous waters, Ulysses was seduced by the music and begged to be released. But the system worked. His men held to his initial orders and kept him bound. As a result, the boat and its sailors emerged safely from their trial. Politicians today should bind themselves more often to the ship of state as they pass through turbulent political waters.

The Highest Stakes

In developing countries the need for delegation is even greater because the stakes are often higher. Governments must demonstrate deep commitment and discipline in their policies or else markets quickly lose faith in them. They must focus on the long-term with regard to urban development, education, and health care, or their societies will slowly descend into stagnation or even anarchy. Far-sighted policies pay huge dividends; short-term patronage politics have immense costs.

In general dictators have not done better at these policies than democrats—far from it. Most dictators have ravaged their countries for personal gain. Scholars have asked whether democracy helps or hurts the economic growth of poor countries and, despite many surveys, have come to no conclusive answer.[2] But over the past fifty years almost every success story in the developing world has taken place under a liberal authoritarian regime. Whether in Taiwan, South Korea, Singapore, Chile, Indonesia, or even China, governments that were able to make shrewd choices for the long term were rewarded with strong economic growth and rising levels of literacy, life expectancy, and education. It is difficult to think of a Third World democracy that has achieved sustained growth rates like those of the countries listed above. Those that have gone down the path of reform are quickly stymied by the need to maintain subsidies for politically powerful groups. India has been unable to engage in sustained reform largely because its politicians will not inflict any pain—however temporary—on their constituents. As a result, for all its democratic glories, the country has slipped further and further behind on almost every measure of human development: life expectancy, infant mortality, health, literacy, education. It now ranks a shocking 124 (out of 173) on the United Nations 2002 human development index, behind China, of course, but even behind Guatemala, Bolivia, and Syria, and well behind Cuba. Surely it is time to ask whether democracies such as India, so lauded by Western intellectuals, are working for their people.

The solution is not to scuttle democracy in the Third World. Democracy has immense benefits regardless of its effects on development and growth. It also has real economic virtues. Although it does not achieve the best results, it usually protects against the worst. You may not get a Lee Kuan Yew through elections, but you will not get a Mobutu Sese Seko either. Yet cheerleading about democracy will not solve its problems. There must be a way to make democratic systems work so that they do not perennially produce short-term policies with dismal results. The stakes in poor countries are just too high.

Some form of delegation might be one solution. Central banks should become more powerful, a process that is already under way. Judges should have similar independent standing. In order to strengthen the judiciary and fight corruption, justice ministries and law-enforcement authorities should also be given more independence. Many American institutions, such as the Federal Reserve System, the Securities and Exchange Commission, and the Federal Bureau of Investigation, have their leaders appointed to long terms (7–10 years) that do not coincide with the electoral cycle. This is done deliberately, to give them some distance from politics.

A crucial area in which a creative new arrangement might be possible is in the economic realm. Decision-making in this arena should be distanced from day-to-day politics. The finance minister in a Third World country should have the ability to present his annual budget as a package that cannot be amended, only approved or denied as a whole. (The United Kingdom, because of its parliamentary system and tight party discipline, does this informally, and as a result has a reputation for being able to enact effective fiscal policy.) One might even go further and allow the economics minister to be appointed to a longer term than the norm—as with the head of the Federal Reserve—so that when a political crisis triggers the fall of a government it does not automatically result in the collapse of economic reform. None of these measures will take politics out of the process entirely. Nor should they. Politics is healthy; it is how people assert their power in a democracy. You need political support for any policy, reformist or otherwise. Instead, the goal is simply to weaken the intense pressure of politics on public policy in the stressed circumstances of the Third World, to shift the balance somewhat to make the system work better. It will not always work better. Some ministers and bureaucrats will abuse the greater authority they are given. Others will pursue well-intentioned but foolish policies. But it will probably work better than the system now prevalent in most developing democracies, which has delivered so little to its people.

It is important to emphasize that these changes are utterly compatible with democracy. They delegate authority to institutions, but ultimate power rests with the people through their elected representatives. This check should be strengthened. Two-thirds majorities in legislatures should be able to override most of the special protections outlined above. Parliamentary committees should regularly oversee the work of all unelected bodies. In a sense these new arrangements are simply an extension of the way an administrative department, say the Department of Health and Human Services, works in the United States. It formulates and implements policies based on broad guidelines handed down by Congress. The legislature exercises ultimate control but leaves much of the policy to unelected bureaucrats. If it works for welfare policy, why not for taxes? Most of all politicians should defend these systems to the public, explaining that delegation can produce a reasonable balance between good government and democratic control. Given their appreciation (in the West, at least) of courts and central banks, clearly people understand this argument.

Delegation is not simply a phenomenon that exists in the political realm. In many other areas we face the same choice. Do we want to go down the path of loosening controls, bypassing mediators, and breaking down old standards—in economics and culture, for example—or do we want instead to retain and reshape some of the guides and buffers that have traditionally been part of our society? Technology has combined with ideology to offer the alluring prospect of a world without mediation. You can become your own stockbroker, newspaper editor, lawyer, and doctor. But do you want to? Attitudes on this matter are less giddy than they were during the boom years of the 1990s. People have begun to recognize that perhaps there is a reason that mediators have existed in so many different areas in so many ages. It turns out that most investors would gladly pay slightly higher fees for the proper execution of stock trades, for financial and investment advice, and even for old-fashioned hand-holding. Those with legal complaints and medical problems realized that self-diagnosis—by reading internet sites and participating in chat groups—is only so useful. In the world of journalism, the personal Web site ("blog") was hailed as the killer of the traditional media. In fact it has become something quite different. Far from replacing newspapers and magazines, the best blogs—and the best are very clever—have become guides to them, pointing to unusual sources and commenting on familiar ones. They have become new mediators for the informed public. Although the creators of blogs think of themselves as radical democrats, they are in fact a new Tocquevillean elite. Much of the Web has moved in this direction because the wilder, bigger, and more chaotic it becomes, the more people will need help navigating it.

Onward and Downward

But for all these encouraging signs, the broad trends still move us toward the unceasing democratization of society. Politics becomes more and more permeable, European societies become "Americanized," old institutions open up, professions and guilds die out, and technology continues to threaten most intermediaries. All of which will result in much good, as it has in the past. But it will also destroy parts of the fabric of our culture. The institutions and attitudes that have preserved liberal democratic capitalism in the West were built over centuries. They are being destroyed in decades. Once torn down they will not be so easy to repair. We watch this destruction without really being able to stop it—that would be undemocratic. But it will leave its mark on our politics, economics, and culture, all of which will increasingly be dominated by short-term interests and enthusiasms. Edmund Burke once described society as a partnership between the dead, the living, and the yet unborn. It is difficult to see in the evolving system who will speak for the yet unborn, for the future.

Meanwhile, public dissatisfaction with the effects of all these changes will continue to grow. If these problems build, eventually people will define democracy by what it has become: a system, open and accessible in theory, but ruled in reality by organized or rich or fanatical minorities, protecting themselves for the present and sacrificing the future. This is a very different vision from that of the enthusiasts of direct democracy, who say that the liberating new world we will live in will harken back to the city-states of ancient Greece. I leave it to the reader to judge whether Californian politics today resembles Athenian democracy in its prime. In any event, it is worth remembering that direct democracy was tried only in a few small cities in ancient Greece where a few thousand men were allowed to vote. It is also worth remembering that within a hundred years all those democracies collapsed into tyranny or chaos—frequently both.

Such gloom may seem far-fetched, but if current trends continue, democracy will undoubtedly face a crisis of legitimacy, which could prove crippling. Legitimacy is the elixir of political power. "The strongest is never strong enough to be the master," Jean-Jacques Rousseau observed, "unless he translates strength into right and obedience into duty." Only democracy has that authority in the world today. But it can lose its hold on our loyalties. The greatest danger of unfettered and dysfunctional democracy is that it will discredit democracy itself, casting all popular governance into a shadowy light. This would not be unprecedented. Every wave of democracy has been followed by setbacks in which the system is seen as inadequate and new alternatives have been proposed by ambitious leaders and welcomed by frustrated people. The last such period of disenchantment, in Europe during the interwar years, was seized upon by demagogues, many of whom capitalized on the public's disenchantment with democracy. It is worth remembering that the embrace of communism and fascism in the 1930s did not seem as crazy at the time as it does now. While the democracies were mired in depression and gloom, authoritarian states had mobilized their societies and were on the march.

Modern democracies will face difficult new challenges—fighting terrorism, adjusting to globalization, adapting to an aging society—and they will have to make their system work much better than it currently does. That means making democratic decision-making effective, reintegrating constitutional liberalism into the practice of democracy, rebuilding broken political institutions and civic associations. Perhaps most difficult of all, it requires that those with immense power in our societies embrace their responsibilities, lead, and set standards that are not only legal, but moral. Without this inner stuffing, democracy will become an empty shell, not simply inadequate but potentially dangerous, bringing with it the erosion of liberty, the manipulation of freedom, and the decay of a common life.

This would be a tragedy because democracy, with all its flaws, represents the "last best hope" for people around the world. But it needs to be secured and strengthened for our times. Eighty years ago, Woodrow Wilson took America into the twentieth century with a challenge to make the world safe for democracy. As we enter the twenty-first century, our task is to make democracy safe for the world.

Notes

1. Alan Blinder, "Is Government Too Political," *Foreign Affairs*, November/December, 1997.
2. There is a large and interesting literature on this topic. A good starting point would be the overview in United Nations Development Program, *Human Development Report 2002: Deepening Democracy in a Fragmented World* (New York: Oxford University Press, 2002), 56. All the works it cites are worth reading, but in particular see Adam Przeworski, Michael E. Alvarez, Jose Antonio Cheibub, and Fernando Limongi, *Democracy and Development: Political Institutions and Well-Being in the World, 1950–1990* (New York: Cambridge University Press, 2000).

An Alternative to Progress

Bill McKibben

What does Gorasin, a remote village in Bangladesh, suggest about how to promote economic improvement in developing regions of the world? Bill McKibben claims that Gorasin has lessons aplenty to offer. Villagers in Gorasin have achieved progress by rejecting the advice offered by most economists and technical experts. Rather than shifting to high-value crops for export, involving the use of pesticides and genetically modified seed, they use traditional methods to produce food for local consumption.

Critics might reply that McKibben tends to idealize traditional village life. Farming by age-old methods can involve backbreaking labor and produce meager output. Nor does McKibben explain how villagers who raise subsistence crops (food grown for local consumption) can earn money to purchase necessities (like medicines) that are not produced in the village. Any suggestions about how to resolve this dilemma?

The eastern end of the village of Gorasin, on the edge of the Louhajang River in the district of Taugail, in the nation of Bangladesh, has no store that we would recognize, no car, no electric lines, no television. No telephone. There are just small fields, a cow, some chickens, barefoot children, banana palms swaying in the breeze. The call to prayer from a nearby muezzin drifts over the croplands. It is about as far from the center of the world as you can possibly get. And that may be the point.

Hovering over all the issues about the World Bank and the World Trade Organization and the spread of genetically modified crops, hovering over everything that's happened since the 1999 Battle of Seattle is a big question: Is there really any alternative to the General Course of things? Is there some imaginable future that does not lead through the eternal Westernization, the endless economic expansion, that is the gospel of our time? Is there some alternative to progress?

Gorasin is one of those places that suggests there might be. "Suggests" is about as strong as I'd like to get. Alternatives get quickly overwhelmed in the modern

---

Bill McKibben, "An Alternative to Progress," *Mother Jones* 26, no. 3 (May/June 2001): 78–83.

world, co-opted or submerged beneath the staggering flow of business as usual. But, at least right now, life in Gorasin is worth a look.

If we think about Bangladesh at all, it is as a basket case. A hundred and thirty million people crowded into an area the size of Wisconsin. Constant flooding, with the regular scattering of killer cyclones. A 10-letter word for woe.

If you ask the World Bank what needs to happen in Bangladesh, their answer—detailed in a report called "Bangladesh 2020"—is to turn it into another Thailand or, better yet, another Singapore: to ramp up its growth rate, produce crops like cut flowers for export, "manage" a "transition" to urbanization, and exploit its huge supply of cheap labor to allow a leap up the development ladder. "There is no alternative to accelerated growth." If you ask Monsanto, the key is high-yielding varieties of rice, including new genetically engineered strains: "golden rice," say, designed to eliminate vitamin A deficiency. If you ask international donor agencies, the secret is more microcredit, like the pioneering Grameen Bank projects that have captured worldwide attention in recent years. "If you want to work on misery, Bangladesh is the ultimate misery you can have," says Atiq Rahman, of the Bangladesh Center for Advanced Studies, a local NGO.

Those are the standard views: that Bangladesh lives in a state of backwardness that can be "fixed" through an application of technology, capital, exposure to the discipline of the markets. To quote from the World Bank report, "Backwardness in the form of cheap labor gives Bangladesh a strong competitive potential edge." In other words, an inexhaustible supply of poor people willing to work at low wages is its greatest asset. In the words of Rahman, who co-authored the Bank report, Bangladeshis are now at a "survival" stage and need to make a "quantum leap" to some higher level of development, a leap that inevitably leads to urbanization, an export-oriented economy, more fertilizer, big electric power plants. And when you look at the country's sad statistics for nutrition, for life expectancy, for literacy, then it's easy to defend the conventional wisdom: The average person dies at 60, and the infant mortality rate is 10 times that of the United States.

But there is another way of looking at things, a Gorasin way, one developed closer to home, less despairing and less grandiose at the same time. "People say that it's a miracle Bangladesh can survive its food and energy crises, that it somehow perseveres," Sajed Kamal, a solar energy educator, told me as we walked the town's fields. "The real miracle, though, is that you could contrive a way to have a food crisis. If you stick something in the ground here, it grows." So Bangladesh, it's worth noting, is able to feed itself.

Our guides that day were the people who lived in Gorasin, who lived in small huts, smaller than trailer homes. They were showing us sesame seed plants, loofah sponge gourds, eggplants, sugarcane, bamboo. Onions, pulses, all manner of local leafy greens. All grown without pesticides, without fertilizer, and without seed imported from the laboratories of the West. Gorasin sits in a large self-declared pesticide-free zone, one of several organic oases established around the country by adherents of the Nayakrisbi, or "New Agriculture" movement. The movement arose in response to numerous environmental hazards that the villagers believe were traceable to pesticides.

"When we women went to collect water, we would be affected," one villager was saying. She was twenty something, beautiful, gregarious. "Our skin would absorb the poisons. We would get itchiness, get gastric trouble. Now we've adopted our own solution. The water is pure again."

"The cows used to eat the grass and drop dead," one man added. "And then the villagers would fight each other."

"We grew up with a saying: 'We Bengalis are made of rice and fish,'" said another man. "Then the fish started catching diseases. We are not scientists, but we made the connection between pesticide and fish death. Since we've started organic farming, the fish are now healthier and more plentiful."

"A fertilized plant jumps up fast and falls right over," said a third. "Our plants are strong and healthy. Theirs, you eat it and you get sick. The minute you say 'Nayakrishi' in the market, though, people will pay more, because they know they're saving on health care."

A few miles away, at the Nayakrishi training school for the Tangail district, 25 varieties of papaya are growing. A hundred and twelve varieties of jackfruit, all cataloged by the farmers by taste, size, color, season, habitat. Wicker baskets and clay pots in a darkened shed contain 300 varieties of local rice, 20 kinds of bitter gourd, 84 varieties of local beans.

"Do you know how much it costs to build a gene bank like the ones where botanists store plant varieties?" asks Farhad Mazhar, a founder of the Center for Development Alternatives, known by its Bengali acronym, UBINIG, the Dhaka-based NGO that helped launch the Nayakrishi movement. "No scientist can afford to catalog hundreds of varieties of rice. But farmers are doing it as part of household activity. Our little seed station has more vegetables than the national gene bank, which spends millions. But we can do it for free."

For free, and in the process, they insist, they can rejuvenate village life. Farida Akhter, Mazhar's partner running UBINIG, is one of Bangladesh's leading feminists. She set up the nation's only women's bookstore and led a long fight against contraceptive abuses by international agencies. But if you ask her what single step would do the most to improve the lot of Bengali women, she does not hesitate: "I'd want rural women to have control over seeds again. That's women's power, or was before the multinationals started selling their new varieties in the last few decades. Traditionally, the woman is the one who knows what a good seed is, what will germinate, how to store it. Maybe they like the sound of the seed when they flick it, the weight of it on the winnowers, how it looks. They'll cut a seed with their teeth and listen to the sound it makes. They know how to dry it, how many times to put it under the sun, and whether to use the morning sun or the afternoon sun. Men used to discuss with their wives what kind of crop to raise for next year. But now they listen to the seed seller. The woman has become redundant, a burden."

Farhad Mazhar was in Seattle for the WTO protests. "I strongly believe in globalization," he says. "I'm not a national chauvinist. We need more interaction at the international level. We need cultural exchanges, all that sort of thing. But that's not happening here in Bangladesh, and it's not happening in all the other countries like us. We're just a source of raw materials." Certainly not a source of ideas. Ideas flow the other way.

Bangladesh became a country in 1971, following a brief civil war. "Civil war" is actually a misnomer: Pakistan, backed rhetorically by the United States, carried out what may have been the most efficient genocide of the 20th century, killing as many as 3 million Bengalis in nine months before a resistance army aided by Indian troops drove them out. That carnage was followed in short order by famine and cyclones. Then a military coup shut off the new nation's political life. Since then, Bangladesh has made the world news only sporadically, usually when the waters of the Ganges and the Brahmaputra overflow their banks. (Two or three thousand need to drown before it makes the back pages of American newspapers.) As a relatively calm Muslim country, without geopolitical significance and with a minuscule economy, it would be hard to imagine a less news-worthy place. But 1 human in 50 now lives there, and its grand history stretches back into the mists far enough to qualify it as a cradle of civilization. Still, for the rest of the planet, its only outstanding feature today is poverty.

"Poverty is the most salable commodity we have here," says Khushi Kabir, a longtime grassroots organizer. Experts jet in, stay at the Sheraton in Dhaka, issue reports, and leave. Local academics vie for "consultancies," making bids that sometimes require kickbacks to government officials. And the expert advice has often gone spectacularly wrong. A huge Flood Action Plan, for instance, called for ever-higher embankments to keep the rivers at bay. But Bangladesh is not Holland: The huge silt deposits kept raising riverbeds, and the floodwater that eventually topped the dikes had nowhere to drain. "One area in the southwest was underwater for 10 years," says Kabir.

Later, in an effort to curb diarrheal disease, UNICEF helped drill thousands of deep tube wells around the country and ran advertisements urging people to stop drinking surface water. But they neglected to sample the subsurface geology, and so tens of millions began drinking water contaminated with naturally occurring arsenic. The water has killed some already; others, disfigured by the melanoma lesions that arsenic causes, can no longer be given in marriage. UNICEF's new ads tell people not to drink from the tube wells.

Other international aid has worked better: The country's fertility rate has fallen quickly and the International Center for Diarrheal Disease Research has cut the incidence of cholera, which is endemic in the region. But local activists say the benefits aren't worth the costs: "Absolutely we would be better off if everyone trying to 'help' us just went home," says Mazhar. "If they did, then the people in the country would be able to come up with their own ideas." Those ideas would, necessarily, center on village life. Though Dhaka, a chaotic megacity with a population uncountably north of 10 million, dominates the political life of the nation, 80 percent of Bengalis still live in rural areas. Which is not to say that they live in Iowa, or the Punjab, or any of the other places that the word rural conjures in our minds. In the first place, Bangladesh is almost as much liquid as solid. There is water everywhere you look, and much of the year many villages are accessible mostly by canoe. Land holdings tend to be tiny, many under an acre. And the place feels, to a Westerner, almost unbelievably crowded. The population density dwarfs that of India or China; it approaches the density of Hong Kong. Even in rural farming districts, there is simply no such thing as a lonely road. Rickshaws, bicycles, buses, draft animals, and pedestrians jam every vista. One Bengali said the reason his country did not excel at most international sports was simple: "Where is the room for a soccer pitch?"

That picture of a standingroom-only floodplain sounds pretty desperate to our ears, as if the population of our Eastern seaboard were ordered to somehow make a living in Chesapeake Bay. But at least for the moment this huge population of Bengalis manages to feed itself. Partly that's a result of the "Green Revolution," the rice strains that, whatever their toll in pesticides and fertilizers, have boosted grain yields. But mostly that's a function of the simple biology of a hot delta. Floods regularly renew the soil, the sun shines most of the year, and so fruit trees grow in two years to a girth that would require five decades on a New England hillside. Plants jump from the ground. There's an almost obscene lushness everywhere. And the large population means that there are plenty of people to manage that lushness, to help make the most of it.

Here's what I mean. We were sitting one day on the front porch of a one-acre organic farm about an hour from Dhaka. It was a hobby farm, whose owner was mostly concerned with his rosebushes. Still, without getting up, we could see guava, lemon, pomegranate, coconut, betel nut, mango, jackfruit, apple, lichee, chestnut, date, fig, and bamboo trees, as well as squash, okra, eggplant, zucchini, blackberry, bay leaf, cardamom, cinnamon, and sugarcane plants, not to mention dozens of herbs, far more flowers, and a flock of ducklings. A chicken coop produced not just eggs and meat, but waste that fed a fishpond, which in turn produced thousands of pounds of protein annually, and a healthy crop of water hyacinths that were harvested to feed a small herd of cows, whose dung in turn fired a biogas cooking system. "Food is everywhere, and in 12 hours it will double," Kamal said.

So what do you do with that kind of fertility? The World Bank report recommends that you figure out ways to grow "higher value" crops for export; they cite the Colombian cut-flower industry as an example. It could supply vegetables to other parts of Asia, "graduating from a minor supplier at present to a major player in the long term." That would probably generate the most money, cash that would be plowed into expanding the industries that could take advantage of the country's cheap labor pool.

Or you could follow UBINIG's advice and focus on farms like those of Gorasin. "Any 'development' policy here must give agriculture priority," says

Farhad Mazhar. "Don't destroy it any further, because you've got no way to take care of those people." The choice you make will depend on your sense of the future. The sheer growth in human numbers—Bangladesh's population may double again by 2020—could mean that you have no choice but to make a mad dash for modernization, figuring out every possible way to convert your country's resources to cash. But it will also depend on how you see the people living in Bengali villages. Are they desperately poor? Or is, in Mazhar's words, "the whole Western construction of poverty" suspect? "The real question," he insists, "is, What are the livelihood strategies of the bulk of people, and what kind of development enhances or destroys those strategies?"

That is, do you want a few lightbulbs run off rooftop solar generators, or do you want to run electric lines to the three-quarters of the country that currently lacks them? Do you want more people moving to the cities, or do you want to develop an organic agriculture that can absorb more labor? Those are questions, not answers. Rahman, the development expert, says that rooftop solar is only a beginning: "Once people have the 'little power,' they want 'big power' from electric lines," he says. Even though big power in a poor country can imply expense, pollution, dependence.

Here's another way of asking the same thing: How do you address the problem of vitamin A deficiency? Large numbers of poor people around South Asia suffer from a variety of micronutrient deficiencies—their diets lack sufficient iron or zinc or vitamin A, also known as beta-carotene. If you don't get enough, you can go blind. In 1999, European researchers announced they had managed to genetically modify rice so that it would express vitamin A to anyone who ate a bowlful, as surely as if they had popped a vitamin pill. Within a year the major biotech companies had announced agreements to license the technology free of charge to poor nations. As Time magazine put it last year, "The biotech industry sees golden rice as a powerful ally in its struggle to win public acceptance." An industry group ran a massive ad campaign touting the new technology with a rapid-fire montage of children and farms against a backdrop of swelling music.

But the advertisements look a little different from the organic farms of the Bengali floodplain, where farmers insist they have a different solution to the problem. The Nayakrishi movement held a small seminar for peasant farmers on the new technology at an open-air meeting hall in the Tangail district one day while I was there. A Filipino agriculture expert discussed the plans—that by 2003 the International Rice Research Institute would be producing genetically modified seeds for them to plant. The farmers—illiterate, most of them—kept interrupting with questions and sermonettes. They weren't concerned about frankenfoods. Instead, they instantly realized that the new rice would require fertilizer and pesticide. More to the point, they kept saying, they had no need of golden rice because the leafy vegetables they could grow in their organic fields provided all the nutrition they needed. "When we cook the green vegetables, we are aware not to throw out the water," said one woman. "Yes," said another. "And we don't like to eat rice only. It tastes better with green vegetables."

This is neither simplistic nor sentimental. In fact, there's plenty of evidence to show that as the Green Revolution spread in the last four decades, nutrient deficiency followed close behind. A plant like bathua, a leafy vegetable that provided beta-carotene to Indians for an eternity, becomes such a competitor of wheat once you start using chemical fertilizers that it requires herbicides to destroy it. A steady decline in the consumption per capita of vegetables, fruits, beans, and spices took place in Bangladesh even as the consumption of rice increased. Plants growing wild around the margins of Gorasin's fields provide massive quantities of vitamins A and C, or folic acid, iron, and calcium. But the spread of any high-yielding variety like golden rice tends to reduce that crop diversity. "There may or may not be issues of biosafety," said the Filipino expert. "The real question is, Do we really need this?"

Again, the answer depends on how you see the world. Maybe it's too late for Bangladesh to go back to a balanced diet, particularly in urban areas where bathua and amaranth are hard to come by. There's a kind of inevitability to the argument for a technological, capital-intensive future that comes from a scarcity of successful counterexamples. There aren't many places that have chosen an alternative path. Kerala, perhaps, the state of 30 million people in the south of India that has achieved Western levels of life expectancy, literacy, infant mortality, and fertility on an average income per capita of $300 per year. But the World Bank and Monsanto don't talk about Kerala; they talk about Thailand and Singapore.

"The Nayakrishi fields can be twice as productive as 'modern' agriculture," says Mazhar. "But I can't get anyone from the World Bank to come out and test my claims. We don't fit with the model." The Nayakrishi movement is small, with only tens of thousands of farmers in a nation with tens of millions. And although it is growing, it remains insubstantial against the sheer scale of Bangladesh. But Nayakrishi hints at other ways of addressing other issues, like energy: The Bangladesh Rural Advancement Committee has begun using microcredit programs to help peasants finance solar systems for their rooftops, and biogas generators for their cookstoves. The dung from three cows lets you cook all your meals for a day and frees you from crouching by the fireside to feed rice straw to the flame. That's a kind of progress that doesn't show up easily in anyone's statistics, but you can feel it in the strain on your back at the end of the day. It's a kind of progress that could conceivably mix with newer technologies. In his recent primer, *Food's Frontier: The Next Green Revolution*, Richard Manning notes that Western researchers are just beginning to focus more intensely on how people have grown food for generations.

There are few certainties when talking about the future of places like Bangladesh. Here's one, though: The most important Western export to Bangladesh in the next few decades will almost certainly be the higher sea level caused by global warming. When the Bay of Bengal rises a foot or two, the waters of the Ganges and the Brahmaputra will back up when they flood, unable to flow smoothly into the ocean. The Bay of Bengal rose a few inches higher than normal in 1998, and that year the floodwaters covered vast swaths of the country for as long as three months. Forget the fertility-promoting "normal" floods of the Bengali summer; this was 90 days of wading through thigh-deep water—more or less because Americans can't manage to stop driving Explorers. That near-geological force may be enough to end all these debates, to shut off the experimentation and innovation that offer curious and unexpected twists on what we've taken to calling development. Which would be the biggest shame of all.

The night we left Gorasin, we sat in the courtyard by everyone's small huts. The whole village of 35 or 40 people was on hand. Two babies were using a grapefruit as a ball, which every person in the village would roll back to them with great smiles. It takes a village to raise a child, indeed, and to raise a crop. And to raise a song, as well: One of the men, Akkas Ali, mentioned that he had written a hundred songs praising organic agriculture, tunes he and the other men had sung at local markets in an effort to convert other farmers. We ate fat bananas, and rosy grapefruit, and listened as the sun set.

"Nayakrishi has corrected my mistakes," he sang in a reedy Bengali, as the rest of the village clapped rhythmically.

"Food from Nayakrishi is so much better. No longer do I eat the poisons.

Why should I eat that life-destroying stuff? Bangladesh will come to an end, Unless you turn to Nayakrishi.

If you use organic fertilizer, the Almighty will be behind you,

And you'll be having no more gastric problems."

As I say, the sun was setting over Gorasin. I have no idea if this represents a vision of the future, or a fragment of a fleeting past.

It depends on how you look at it.

Common Wealth: Economics
for a Crowded Planet

Jeffrey D. Sachs

The economist Jeffrey Sachs, director of the Whole Earth Institute at Columbia University, analyzes the importance of the massive production of carbon dioxide emissions in the world, what he describes as "a novel challenge that [we] didn't know existed a generation ago, and for many of us, even a few years ago." What challenge? The near consensus among scientists that, if present levels of carbon emissions continue, the result will be global warming that will likely cause major ecological disasters (some of which we have already experienced), including rising sea levels, droughts that render regions unfit for human settlement, heat waves, and an increase in intense storms.

Sachs suggests that meeting the challenge of reducing our carbon footprint will require a major reordering of public priorities and policies. However, he claims that changing priorities and policies is manageable, since a small number of activities produce the bulk of carbon emissions. What is required to meet the challenge is strong political will and large amounts of money. However, Sachs does not explain in this selection how to muster the will and the resources to meet this challenge. Who is likely to support and who is likely to oppose these changes? What are the resources that the two sides can muster? And how should the costs of meeting the challenge be distributed among groups within and among countries and regions of the world? Can you help Sachs answer these questions?

Carbon Management

. . . The world faces a novel challenge that it didn't know existed a generation ago, and for many of us, even a few years ago. The problem can be called carbon management. The world must manage the global carbon budget so that the atmospheric concentration of carbon dioxide remains at safe levels, especially so that we avoid dangerous thresholds that could have devastating effects on human societies and ecosystems. To manage our carbon budget, we must have a good

Jeffrey D. Sachs, *Common Wealth: Economics for a Crowded Planet* (New York: Penguin Press, 2008), 96–100, 102–103, 105–112.

look at its precise components, and then home in on the areas that are most effectively controlled by human activity.

The bad news about the carbon budget is that every one of us on the: planet participates in the carbon cycle, by driving, using electricity produced by fossil fuels, eating food, using fuel wood, and a thousand and one other actions. It often seems too complicated to get one's arms around, especially if each of us is to adjust our own carbon budget (or carbon footprint, as our carbon-related actions are sometimes called). Yet we can simplify the picture by realizing that the vast bulk of carbon emissions is due to a small number of activities. Table 7.1 provides a useful breakdown.

To manage the carbon budget, we don't need to change everything about our society, but we do need to face head-on six important activities:

- We must slow or stop deforestation.
- We must reduce emissions from electricity production.
- We must reduce emissions from automobiles.
- We must clean up industrial processes in a few major sectors (especially steel, cement, refineries, and petrochemicals).
- We must economize on electricity use through more efficient motors, appliances, lighting, insulation, and other electrical demands.
- We must convert point-source emissions in buildings (such as furnaces) into electricity-based systems powered by low-emission electricity.

These are big challenges to be sure, but they are each manageable. Indeed, with modest economic incentives, big reductions in emissions can be achieved.

Table 7.1
Total Carbon Dioxide Emissions in 2007 (in gigatons and percent of total)

	GT	%
Total	36	100
Fossil fuels	29	81
of which: electricity	11.5	32
industry	8	22
transportation	6.5	18
residential	2	6
commercial	1	3
Deforestation	7	19

Source: Author's estimates based on fossil fuel emission estimates for 2005 from International Energy Agency (2007), extrapolated to 2007 assuming that all categories increase by 2.3 percent par annum during 2005–7. Deforestation is estimated to be 7 GT per year, based on World Resources Institute (2007) for the year 2000. Note that industry includes emissions from cement due to direct materials transformation as well as fossil fuel use.

Let's briefly consider some of the technological options. Deforestation, interestingly, is one of the easiest of all of the processes to slow or stop. Most deforestation that takes place has little economic value. Forest is cleared to make new pastures, say in the Amazon, but these are lands of low agricultural quality and end up being abandoned shortly after clearing. With modest economic incentives, such as a payment to the local community to preserve the forest rather than turn it into pastures, it is possible to overcome the weak economic incentives that now lead to deforestation.

The challenge of reducing emissions from electricity generation is much more complicated, but that, too, is a solvable problem. There are three major avenues to reduced emissions from the power sectors: greater efficiency in the use of electricity (more usable output per kilowatt-hour), a greater proportion: of electricity generation with nonfossil fuel sources of energy (including wind, solar, hydro, geothermal, biofuels, and nuclear), and special engineering processes to capture the carbon dioxide from fossil fuel electricity plants and to safely store it, using a technology known as carbon capture and sequestration (CCS).

The expert assessments of these options agree on several broad conclusions. First, much greater energy efficiency is possible, with more consumer awareness and more government R & D support. Second, energy efficiency will not be sufficient by itself to reduce carbon emissions. The world economy might grow sixfold by 2050. Even if efficiency allows us to keep the rise of electricity usage to half of that, we would still face a tripling of global electricity use by 2050! Third, renewable and other nonfossil fuel energy sources (such as nuclear) can play an important but also limited role in reducing carbon emissions from power generation from now to 2050. Fourth, many kinds of fossil fuels, especially coal, will remain inexpensive, plentiful, and in widespread use. Fifth, the option of carbon capture and sequestration will be very important, assuming that the CCS technologies prove to be as cost-effective as engineers now predict. If CCS proves feasible, this technology will allow the world to continue to use low-cost fossil fuels such as coal in a manner that does not wreck the climate.

If we look to the best engineering predictions, the cost of reducing carbon emissions from electricity production, relative to the current business-as-usual trajectory, is likely to be around $10 to $50 per ton of CO_2, which translates into a modest and manageable 1 cent to 5 cents per kilowatt hour. In places especially favored by wind or solar power or where the geology is favorable for carbon sequestration, the costs will be lower. In some other places, the costs could be higher. The overall cost levels will depend on public investments we make in R & D needed to take these basic technologies from paper to practice. The greater the early investments in R & D are, the lower the eventual costs per ton of avoided carbon dioxide will be. All in all, the costs are likely to be moderate if we think and plan ahead.

With regard to automobile emissions, we have all recently become aware of the potentially enormous increase in miles per gallon from the new hybrid technology that combines the use of gasoline with battery power. That technology is already roughly doubling the miles per gallon of some car models (depending on driving patterns). Another doubling of miles per gallon on top of that is becoming feasible if the hybrid can be plugged into the power grid as well. The idea is that a car would depend mainly on battery power for the first forty or so miles each day and carry a reserve of gasoline for when the battery runs low or when peak power is needed. The car would be recharged in the evening by plugging it into a wall socket at a time of day when the electricity grid is off-peak and therefore available to recharge tens of millions of cars. In this way an automobile could soon reliably get one hundred miles per gallon of gasoline rather than the twenty-five miles per gallon or so it gets today. This kind of plug-in hybrid technology is nearly at hand, and depends mainly on some further improvements in battery technology. Of course, the net benefit of such a move will depend enormously on the mix of technologies used to produce the electricity that recharges the hybrid each night. If we were to merely shift the automobile from gasoline to electricity produced by standard coal-fired power plants, the benefits wouldn't be large. The trick will be to shift from gasoline to electricity produced by renewable sources or by power plants that capture and sequester their carbon emissions.

The plug-in hybrid option will likely be available shortly, and if combined with clean electricity, it will avoid emissions at very low cost. Taking into account all of the changes from conventional engines to plug-in hybrids (for example, the extra costs of batteries, the costs of clean electricity production and transmission, and so on) is not a straightforward calculation, but it is likely that plug-in hybrids would avoid carbon dioxide emissions at a cost below $25 per ton of avoided emissions. In fact, the fuel economies could well pay for themselves if the battery costs are kept low enough. I should also mention that other automobile technologies, such as low-weight construction materials, or the use of biofuels (if produced in an ecologically and economically sound manner), can also significantly improve mileage and thereby reduce carbon dioxide emissions per mile at low cost or net saving. So too can a shift to more convenient public transport and greater reliance on bicycling and walking. There are, in short, many options for large-scale and low-cost solutions to reducing emissions from automobiles.

Industrial solutions also exist. A few industrial sectors—steel, cement, refineries, petrochemicals—produce the preponderance of carbon emissions by industry. These industries have good options for low-cost avoidance of carbon emissions. Like power plants, the bigger factories are likely to be able, at low cost, to capture and sequester their carbon dioxide and connect their own pipelines from the factories to the CO_2 pipelines used by power plants. Many factories can also convert from burning coal and oil on site to using electricity from the grid, which is beneficial as long as the grid electricity is produced in a low-carbon manner. The factories can also convert from fossil fuels to on-site low-carbon alternatives, such as solar power and hydrogen fuel cells (which are beneficial as long as the hydrogen is produced in a low-emission process). The combinations and permutations are endless. The chances for low-cost carbon reduction are therefore plentiful.

Another area ripe for powerful results is green building, that is, designing homes and commercial buildings to reduce the on-site use of fossil fuels and to economize on energy use more generally. Green buildings are designed to tap more effectively into solar radiation (both direct sunlight and solar panels), re-cycle waste and water, use better insulating materials, and harvest rainwater. Furnaces and boilers on the premises can be converted to electricity-driven units connected to the power grid, providing a net carbon reduction if the elec-tricity is produced by a low-carbon method. . . .

Substitutes for Fossil Fuels

We can reasonably expect nonfossil energy sources to provide a meaningful and growing fraction of the world's energy supply. While fossil fuels will likely pre-dominate for some decades more, in the longer term, nonfossil alternatives are likely to come to preeminence. Wind, hydroelectricity, ocean waves, bio-fuels, and geothermal energy will likely be extremely competitive in certain regions, but each of these is limited in some way. They depend on favorable local condi-tions and are generally not applicable as global solutions by themselves. The bulk of the large-scale nonfossil fuel alternatives are likely to come from nuclear power and solar energy. The constraints on nuclear energy will be primarily se-curity related, centering on fears of nuclear proliferation. They will also be envi-ronmental and political because of concerns about nuclear waste disposal. Solar energy, potentially the largest, safest, and longest-lasting energy source, is cur-rently too expensive, but it is reasonable to assume that large-scale R & D over the coming decades will make it a viable and very attractive alternative energy source at the grand scale. Happily, incoming solar radiation represents about ten thousand times our society's use of commercial energy. There is a vast amount of solar energy to harvest, and we've hardly begun heading down that path.

One of the many potential forms of solar power is biofuels, which are produced through photosynthesis. There is currently a boom in enthusiasm for biofuels, most notably for ethanol derived from crops such as sugarcane, as in Brazil, and maize, as in the U.S. Midwest. While there is merit in the cane-to-ethanol pro-duction in Brazil, there is considerably less merit in the maize-to-ethanol boom-let, which is driven more by farm interests than good energy policy. There are two problems. The first is that Midwestern corn is actually extremely energy intensive, indeed fossil-fuel intensive, once the full life cycle of the crop is taken into ac-count, from the needed fertilizer input (produced with natural gas), to the trans-port of the input and output, to the processing into ethanol. In other words, the net carbon reduction involved is slight, or even nonexistent according to some calculations. The second problem is the direct competition of corn-based ethanol and other biofuels with food crops. The amount of farmland that would have to be converted to supply a significant proportion of America's driving needs through ethanol would be huge. As one analyst has summarized: "Anything but a marginal contribution from biofuel would pose a serious threat to both food security and the natural resource base of land, soil, and water." The best hope for more than a marginal contribution would be biofuels derived from inedible grasses (such as switch-grass) and woody plants on lands that are not appropriate for food crops. Such technologies, including so-called cellosic ethanol, may well arrive soon, but they do not yet exist on a commercial basis. . . .

Creating Market Incentives

The climate risks of business as usual are dire. The costs of mitigation—limiting carbon emissions—are manageable. Yet even the lowest-cost steps are unlikely to be taken on their own. Each individual emitter, whether a power plant, industrial facility, homeowner, or car driver, has no incentive to spend the extra sums required to sequester carbon or adopt low-carbon technologies if the new technologies are costlier than high-carbon technologies. Similarly, scientists and engineers have little incentive to undertake the science and engineering of low-carbon energy systems under conditions in which the atmosphere is treated like a global commons, and emissions of carbon dioxide (and other greenhouse gases) are made without market penalty.

We have noted the core areas where public policy is needed to augment market forces. The first is in basic climate science. We must continue, and indeed greatly increase, the public financing of scientific efforts such as the Intergovernmental Panel on Climate Change, which assesses the published scientific research on climate issues for the global public and policy community. Similarly, there is an urgent need to increase funding for climate science in the poorest countries to help those countries understand how to adapt to climate changes already under way and to changes that are likely to occur in the years ahead. Science is also needed to enable those countries to participate effectively in global mitigation efforts, for example, by reducing the rate of deforestation and by adopting low-carbon energy strategies in the course of economic development.

The second area where public policy is needed is in the development of new scalable alternatives to carbon emissions. The most urgent is a global effort to prove, and if successful, to disseminate, CCS technologies. If CCS works, then we can combine continued large-scale fossil fuel use with reduced emissions. Other large-scale scientific and engineering efforts are also needed regarding solar, nuclear, biofuel, geothermal, wind, and other alternative energy sources.

Yet these efforts will lead nowhere in terms of widespread adoption unless additional incentives are put in place. There must be a cost, in one form or another, of choosing a high-carbon technology over a low-carbon technology. We have noted the many ways that such a cost can be imposed. Most directly, the world (or individual nations) might agree to industry standards, for example, that every power plant built after a target date must emit no more than a specified level of CO_2 per KWh of electricity produced. The plant would be free to select a nonfossil fuel energy supply (for example, hydro, wind, solar, or nuclear) or to use a CCS approach. Mileage standards could be imposed on automobiles in the same manner. An alternative would be to tax carbon dioxide emissions and to subsidize any CCS activities. Such a tax could be easily collected by taxing the underlying carbon-based fuel and then offering a subsidy per ton of CO_2 that is sequestered. A certification process would be needed to verify the sequestration. Yet another mechanism, as we've discussed, would be a tradable permit system. This, too, would impose a cost per unit of CO_2 emissions equal to the price of a permit for that amount of emissions. The main problem with such a system is that it is very cumbersome, requires extensive monitoring and auditing, and also requires a system for allocations of the valuable permits, possibly leading to favoritism and even corruption. I believe that after a considerable debate on these alternatives, the world will ultimately agree to phase in a set of industrial standards (for power, automobiles, cement, steel, and other key sectors) augmented by a gradually rising tax on carbon emissions, a subsidy for sequestration, and perhaps some limited use of a tradable permit system.

It is worth noting that revenues from a carbon tax or from auctioning carbon permits could be used to finance public goods or perhaps to offset other distortionary taxes.

Living with Climate Change

Climate change is already upon us, and it will get worse. The planet will continue to warm even without any further emissions, and further emissions are certainly on the way. Many countries have already begun to experience the consequences of climate change: more droughts (as in the U.S. Southwest, the African Sahel, and Australia), heat waves (notably in Europe), rising tropical storm intensity (as with Hurricane Katrina), a widening transmission belt for malaria, and more. Countries need to invest in adaptation to climate change alongside their critical investments in mitigating emissions. Adaptation and mitigation are not alternatives. Both are needed.

Adaptation will be required in several spheres of life. Coastal regions will have to protect themselves against rising sea levels and more intense storms and storm surges. This will involve physical infrastructure and disaster preparedness. Highland tropical regions, which are currently too elevated to experience malaria transmission (because of cooler temperatures), must protect themselves against the epidemics that could arise. Farmers everywhere will require new seeds that are adapted to the changing climate; they must be more heat resistant, for example, or able to withstand torrential rains in the equatorial regions and more droughts and water stress in the semiarid regions. Climate uncertainties will require new forms of insurance, but they will also put strain on traditional insurance contracts that may have been priced according to out-of-date assumptions.

In the worst cases, . . . water stress may render some regions no longer farmable, and perhaps no longer even livable. Environmental refugees could destabilize nations and global politics as desperate people, especially in rural areas, crowd into cities or across national borders. Such problems are bound to arise. They will be vastly more manageable to the extent that we also manage global cooperation on climate mitigation, population policies, and poverty reduction, and to the extent that special international funding is available to poor countries to manage the adaptation process. Moreover, a new science and profession of climate change adaptation must be encouraged, given the scale of the change and dislocation that lie ahead.

A Strategy for Global Climate Cooperation

We have seen that climate change is a truly global problem: Every country shares some responsibility, albeit to a widely varying degree, for the rise in CO_2 emissions, retrospectively (bringing us from the preindustrial 280 ppm to 380 ppm today) as well as prospectively. No part of the world will be spared the consequences of global warming. This truly global problem requires a global action plan. Of course, there is nothing new in this insight. The UN Framework Convention on Climate Change (UNFCCC) was adopted in 1992 by the world's governments for exactly this purpose. President George H. W. Bush adopted the treaty on behalf of the United States, and the U.S. Senate duly ratified it shortly after, in 1994, agreeing to the treaty's objective to stabilize greenhouse gas concentrations to avoid dangerous anthropogenic interference in the climate system.

The problem is not the framework or purpose but the implementation. The UNFCCC needs a protocol for action, and the first of such protocols was the Kyoto Protocol, adopted in 1997 to prevail until 2012. The Kyoto Protocol divided the world between high-income (Annex I) and developing (non-Annex I) signatories of the UN Framework Convention. The rich countries are required by the protocol to reduce their greenhouse gas emissions by at least 5 percent during the commitment period 2008–12, compared with the baseline of 1990. The poor countries are not bound by any obligations, but they have some opportunities under the protocol to receive payments for voluntarily adopted emission-reducing projects.

The Kyoto commitments were very modest (a 5 percent reduction) and short term (till 2012). At best, the treaty formed a very early step to set the world on a carbon management trajectory. Even so, the protocol generated a political firestorm in the United States. The so-called Byrd-Hagel Senate Resolution, passed 95–0 in 1997 in the lead-up to the final round of negotiations on the Kyoto Protocol, held that ". . . the disparity of treatment between Annex I Parties and Developing Countries and the level of required emission reductions, could result in serious harm to the United States economy." The resolution thereby made it the sense of the Senate that the United States should reject any new commitments that did not also limit the developing countries. The resolution exemplifies the declining sense of global responsibility felt by U.S. politicians, because it conveniently and even self-righteously puts aside the small detail that the United States, with just 5 percent of the world's population, accounts for one quarter of the world's emissions! Here is the United States, far and away the biggest contributor to greenhouse gas emissions, indignantly telling poor countries bearing the consequences in famines, droughts, increased malaria transmission, and more that the United States will not even start on emissions control because the developing countries are not yet bound to do so.

In the end, the Kyoto Protocol was adopted by the rest of the world, with the United States refusing to ratify it. President Clinton never sent it to the Senate for ratification (fearing immediate defeat), and President George W. Bush rejected it out of hand at the start of his administration. Strangely, though, President Bush went much further than that, even denying until 2007 the climate science his father had endorsed fifteen years earlier. The prevarication on this issue was reckless. It went far beyond mere dissatisfaction with specific elements of the protocol, and it marked an inexcusable assault on evidence and science itself. The world recoiled at the Bush administration's brazen neglect of the risks of climate change. Most Americans did as well after they experienced the climate disaster of Hurricane Katrina.

We are now in a new era. Climate change is upon us, and the scientific consensus is strong. After heat waves, droughts, powerful hurricanes, and more, the world's public knows all of this too. The world's leading climate scientists, organized under the auspices of the UN's Intergovernmental Panel on Climate Change (IPCC), in their Fourth Assessment Report, have recently brought us up to date on the scientific consensus, and the message is stark: the risks are enormous and time is running out. The Kyoto Protocol has accomplished one major advance: the start of a market price on carbon emissions, in the form of tradable carbon permits, albeit only in Europe. We must now move beyond Kyoto, which, in any event, expires shortly. Even to reach a new global agreement by 2012 will require diplomatic agreement by 2009–10 to give time for countries to ratify a new protocol.

There is a practical way ahead. Since the spring of 2005, The Earth Institute at Columbia University has sponsored the Global Roundtable on Climate Change (GROCC), which brings together leaders from business, government, universities, and international organizations. The GROCC has developed and adopted a concrete plan of action (GROCC Consensus Statement on Climate Change) to address the climate change problem, one that has won assent from leading businesses, scientists, and organizations around the world. The GROCC's starting point is that there is a scientific consensus that global warming is real and that it is caused by greenhouse gas emissions and primarily by our consumption of fossil fuels. The GROCC proposes a three-pronged solution to address global warming: mitigation; adaptation; and research, development, and demonstration (RD & D) of new technologies.

Mitigation

At the core of the GROCC's consensus statement is the importance of setting a global target to stabilize atmospheric concentrations of carbon dioxide over the coming century, including midcentury interim targets for CO_2 concentrations and rates of emission. Unlike Kyoto, which focused only on emissions targets, the new protocol would embrace a limit on overall greenhouse gas concentrations as well. As discussed earlier, mitigation efforts will involve increased energy efficiency, carbon capture and sequestration, development of nonfossil technologies, green buildings, hybrid cars, and other promising technologies. These will be spurred by putting a price on carbon emissions, implemented through a combination of emission taxes and tradable permits as well as by industry standards in key emitting sectors. While the world will have to agree on shared targets and a division of responsibilities among individual countries, it is likely that the countries will keep flexibility in choices over specific policies to achieve targets. Instead of one grand scheme, there will be many variations of policy.

Adaptation

Since global warming is already under way, and will get worse before it is stabilized, we must also prepare for and adapt to the impacts of climate change. Many of the impacts will fall most heavily on the poorest and most vulnerable communities and in developing countries with the least ability to adapt. Technical and financial assistance will be needed by particularly vulnerable, low-income, developing countries to meet their mounting adaptation needs (that is, to protect society and the economy against droughts, floods, extreme weather events, and climate-related disease transmission). Mitigation and adaptation efforts need to be part of a coherent dual strategy. As the GROCC puts it, "Effective climate adaptation will require stronger efforts within international climate agreements as well among development agencies, the private sector, and non-governmental organizations."

RD & D

Governments will need to support, through direct funding or incentives for the private sector, major increases in research, development, and demonstration (RD & D) of advanced noncarbon energy technologies. Funding currently is just a few billion dollars per year. Worldwide RD & D needs are probably closer to $30 billion per year at the minimum (comparable, for example, to what the United States spends on health research in the National Institutes of Health). Targets for increased RD & D should include technologies such as solar photovoltaic cells, solar thermal, geothermal, tidal, wave, and nuclear energy; carbon capture and sequestration; improved land management; and sustainable transportation. Special demonstration programs and other kinds of public policies that support innovation should be adopted so that promising new technologies and practices can reach the market quickly. Such programs will be of special importance in the rapidly industrializing developing countries, where most of the growth in emissions will be coming from. The highest demonstration priority, without question, is a series of CCS projects in the United States, India, China, Russia, and Australia, the world's heavy coal-using economies. If CCS works, we will have much clearer sailing toward global action. If CCS proves highly costly and unreliable, our option will be much worse and we'll have to redouble our efforts and creativity.

Who Will Pay?

Having a global road map for action is the critical first step. The next step is figuring out who will pay for the plan. The issue is especially important when considering the developing countries. Soon the developing world, with roughly five sixths of the world's population, will be emitting more carbon dioxide in total than the industrialized world, though still much less on a per capita basis. The world cannot reach a viable solution for reducing carbon emissions without including the developing countries. Yet because of their limited resources, the developing nations cannot afford to pay for mitigation, adaptation, and RD & D on their own. They will necessarily require support from the developed countries, which will remain the much larger emitters of greenhouse gases per person.

There are many reasons why the developed countries should help finance the developing countries' efforts to limit and adapt to climate change. First, it is in their best interest to do so. A solution that excludes the developing world would be no solution at all. If the developed countries wish to protect themselves from the negative effects of climate change, they had better help the developing countries protect themselves as well. Second, the developed countries are responsible for the preponderance of global carbon dioxide emissions since the start of the industrial era. Most important, however, cost must not be used as an excuse to postpone action. The longer we wait, the more expensive and dire the problem will end up being.

The issue of cost sharing will be highly charged and could cause negotiations to drag on for years. But the costs should not be exaggerated, nor should we wait for a perfect standard of fairness and efficiency, since no such standard exists. It would be one thing if the costs were huge—say, several percent of the GNP in high-emitting countries. But the good news, emphasized earlier, is that the global costs of keeping carbon dioxide concentrations below a long-term doubling of preindustrial CO_2 (or even much less) are likely to be considerably below 1 percent of the world's annual income. Yes, there will be a fight over allocating costs, but it need not be a huge battle.

on Questions

1. In your opinion, which selection in this chapter makes the most important contribution to the study of comparative politics and why? How do you define contribution?
2. Analyze and evaluate Rothstein and Stolle's critique of Putnam's explanation for the decline of social capital in the United States.
3. What difference, if any, does it make for the quality of U.S. democracy that there has been a decline of social capital?
4. Would McKibben's proposal to reduce dependence on commercially produced food (and other goods) solve the problem of carbon dioxide emissions that Sachs identifies? Why or why not? Evaluate the pros and cons of McKibben's proposal, compared to Sachs' recommendations.